VOLUME II: THE RENAISSANCE TO THE PRESENT

The
Western
Humanities

FOURTH EDITION

Roy T. Matthews & F. DeWitt Platt
MICHIGAN STATE UNIVERSITY

MAYFIELD PUBLISHING COMPANY
MOUNTAIN VIEW, CALIFORNIA
LONDON • TORONTO

Library of Congress Cataloging-in-Publication Data
Matthews, Roy T.
    The Western humanities/Roy T. Matthews, F. DeWitt Platt.—4th ed.
        p. cm.
    Includes bibliographical references and index.
    ISBN 1-7674-1595-7
    1. Civilization, Western—History.   I. Platt, F. DeWitt.
    II. Title.
CB245.M375   2000   99-086580
909'.09821—dc21   CIP

International Standard Book Number information:

The Western Humanities, Fourth Edition . . . . ISBN 0-7674-1592-2
The Western Humanities, Fourth Edition, Volume I . . . . ISBN 0-7674-1594-9
The Western Humanities, Fourth Edition, Volume II. . . . . ISBN 0-7674-1595-7
Readings in the Western Humanities, Fourth Edition, Volume I. . . . . ISBN 0-7674-1596-5
Readings in the Western Humanities, Fourth Edition, Volume II . . . . ISBN 0-7674-1597-3

Shrink-wrap titles for significant savings to your students! Additional packages also available: for more information, please call us at (800) 433-1279.
Complete edition with *The Mayfield Quick View Guide to the*
    Internet for Students of the Humanities, Version 2.0 . . . . ISBN 0-7674-2100-0
Complete edition with both readers . . . . ISBN 0-7674-2101-9
Complete edition with the electronic study guide . . . . ISBN 0-7674-2109-4
Complete edition with *Music in the Western Tradition* . . . . ISBN 0-7674-2115-9
Complete edition with reader volume I . . . . ISBN 0-7674-2105-1
Complete edition with reader volume II . . . . ISBN 0-7674-2107-8

The Western Humanities, Volume I, with reader volume I . . . . ISBN 0-7674-2126-4
The Western Humanities, Volume II, with reader volume II . . . . ISBN 0-7674-2133-7

Please call Mayfield Publishing Company at (800) 433-1279 to inquire about additional packaging options.

Manufactured in the United States of America
10   9   8   7   6   5   4   3   2   1

Mayfield Publishing Company
1280 Villa Street
Mountain View, CA 94041

Sponsoring editor, Holly J. Allen; developmental editors, Barbara Armentrout and Kathleen Engelberg; production editor, Julianna Scott Fein; manuscript editor, Joan Pendleton; design manager, Jean Mailander; text designer, Anna George; cover designer, Linda Robertson; cover art, Edgar Degas, *Three Dancers in Peasant Costume*. Pastel. Private Collection/© The Bridgeman Art Library; art manager, Robin Mouat; illustrators, Robin Mouat, Judith Ogus, and Parrott Graphics; photo researcher, Brian Pecko; manufacturing manager, Randy Hurst. The text was set in 9.5/12 Palatino by GTS Graphics, Inc., and printed on acid-free 60# Sterling Web Gloss, by R. R. Donnelley & Sons Company.

To Lee Ann and Dixie

There is nothing nobler or more admirable than when two people who see eye to eye keep house as man and wife, confounding their enemies and delighting their friends, as they themselves know better than anyone.

—HOMER, *Odyssey*

PREFACE

We offer this new edition of *The Western Humanities* with a great sense of satisfaction. From the start of this project we wrote from a particular perspective on the arts and humanities, and we wondered how many others shared our point of view. Today, we are gratified to know that our textbook has helped many students develop an understanding and, we hope, an enthusiasm for the arts and humanities. And now, with this fourth edition, we continue in the same spirit with which we first approached the arts and humanities. In the first edition, we placed Western cultural achievements within their historical context. In the second and especially the third editions, we expanded coverage of the contributions of women and other artists outside the traditional canon. And, in this edition, we are adding a multicultural dimension, with the expectation that students will gain a greater appreciation of world cultures beyond the Western traditions. It is our hope that the fourth edition of *The Western Humanities* will continue to assist instructors in meeting today's teaching challenges as well as help the next generation of students understand and claim their cultural heritage.

AIMS OF *THE WESTERN HUMANITIES*

When we sat down to write the first edition of *The Western Humanities*, we feared that the world of the late twentieth century was in danger of being engulfed by present-minded thinking. Now, we believe this fear is even more real. As historians, we know that history has always had its naysayers, but it seems to us that an ahistorical view is even more prevalent today. For many people, the past is viewed as either a burden to be overcome or simply irrelevant—and thus safely ignored. Students merely mirror the wider society when they show little knowledge of or even concern about the great artistic and literary monuments and movements of the Western tradition or about the political, economic, and social milestones of Western history. What intensifies present-minded thinking among today's students is their close involvement in popular culture, with its obsessive faddishness, and the Internet, which provides information and voluminous data but not knowledge.

In *The Western Humanities*, we address the problem of present-mindedness by discussing not only the works that were produced in successive periods but also the prevailing historical and material conditions that so powerfully influenced their form and content. Our intention is to demystify the cultural record by showing that literature and the arts do not spring forth spontaneously and independently of each other but reflect a set of specific historical circumstances. By providing this substantial context, out of which both ideas and artifacts emerge, we hope to give students a deeper understanding of the meaning of cultural works and a broader basis for appreciating the humanities.

At the same time that we point out the linkages between cultural expression and historical conditions, we also emphasize the universal aspects of creativity and expression. People everywhere have the impulse to seek answers to the mysteries of human existence; to discover or invent order in the universe; to respond creatively to nature, both inner and outer; to delight the senses and the mind with beauty and truth; to communicate their thoughts and share their visions with others. Thus, another of our intentions is to demonstrate that the desire to express oneself and to create lasting monuments has been a compelling drive in human beings since before the dawn of civilized life. We believe that this emphasis will help students see that they, along with their ideas, questions, and aspirations, are not isolated from the past but belong to a tradition that began thousands of years ago.

Our third aim is to help students prepare themselves for the uncertainties of the future. When they examine the past and learn how earlier generations confronted and overcame crises—and managed to leave enduring legacies—students will discover that the human spirit is irrepressible. In the humanities—in philosophy, religion, art, music, literature—human beings have found answers to their deepest needs and most perplexing questions. We hope that students will be encouraged by this record as they begin to shape the world of the twenty-first century.

In its origin *The Western Humanities* was an outgrowth of our careers as university teachers. Instructing thousands of undergraduate students throughout the years had left us dissatisfied with available textbooks. In our eyes, the existing books failed in one of two ways: They either ignored material developments and focused exclusively on cultural artifacts without context or perspective, or they stressed political, social, and economic history with too little or too disjointed a discussion of literature and the arts. Our goal in writing this book was to balance and integrate these two elements—that is, to provide an analysis and an appreciation of cultural expression and artifacts within an interpretive historical framework.

ORGANIZATION AND CONTENT

The Western Humanities is organized chronologically, in twenty-one chapters, around successive historical periods, from prehistory to the present. In our introduction for students we distinguish three sweeping historical periods—ancient, medieval, and modern—although we do not formally divide our study into parts. We explain that the first of these periods extends from about 3000 B.C. to A.D. 500 and includes the civilizations of Mesopotamia, Egypt, Greece, and Rome (covered in Chapters 1–7). The second period extends from about 500 to 1500, when Western civilization became centered in Europe and was largely dominated by the Christian church (Chapters 8–10). The third period, beginning in about 1400 and extending to the present, witnessed the gradual birth of the modern world (Chapters 11–21). Timelines are provided in the introduction to support these distinctions and to give students a basic framework for the study of the humanities.

In the body of the book, the first part of every chapter covers the material conditions of the era—the historical, political, economic, and social developments. From the mass of available historical information we have distilled what we consider the crucial points, always aiming to capture the essence of complex periods and to fashion a coherent narrative framework for the story of Western culture. In this discussion many of the major themes, issues, and problems of the period come into view.

The remaining part of each chapter is devoted to cultural expression, both in the realm of attitude and idea—philosophy, history, religion, science—and in the realm of cultural artifact—art, music, drama, literature, and film. In this part we describe and analyze the significant cultural achievements of the age, focusing on pervasive themes, choices, and elements of style. We examine how intellectuals, artists, writers, and other creative individuals responded to the challenges presented to them by their society and how they chose values and forms by which to live. Included among these individuals are those whom the Western tradition has often neglected or discounted, namely, women and members of racial and ethnic minorities. Their experiences, roles, and rich contributions are given their rightful place alongside those of the more conventionally favored artists, thinkers, and writers.

The Western Humanities strives to balance the historical background with cultural and artistic achievements. We believe that the clearest and most effective way to present this closely woven web of experience and expression is to untangle the various realms and discuss them separately. Thus, our treatment of cultural achievements is broken down into sections on art, architecture, music, literature, and so on. These sections vary in length, order, and focus from chapter to chapter, just as preferred or more developed forms of expression vary from one period to another. This approach gives students an unobstructed view of each form and reveals the continuities—as well as the strains and disruptions—in that form from one period to the next.

At the same time, we work from a unified perspective and stress the integrated nature of the humanities. We emphasize that the creative works of a particular period represent a coherent response to the unique character and deepest urges of that period. By pointing out linkages and reverberations, we show that the various areas of expression are tied together by shared stylistic elements and by the themes and issues that inform and shape the era. Rather than weave our own synthesis so tightly into this discussion that instructors would have to spend their class time sorting out our point of view from the true subject of the book, we prefer to present the material in as direct a way as possible. We believe this approach gives instructors the flexibility to teach from their own strengths and perspectives, and we invite them to do so. We have paid special attention to sorting out and explaining complex ideas and sequences of events carefully and clearly, to make the study of the humanities accessible to a broad range of students.

Each chapter ends with a brief section describing the cultural legacy of that era. Here we show what achievements proved to be of lasting value and endured into succeeding periods, even to the present day. Students will find that some ideas, movements, or artistic methods with which they are familiar have a very long history indeed. They will also discover that the meaning and ascribed value of cultural objects and texts can change from one time and place to another. Our goal here is not only to help students establish a context for their culture but to show that the humanities have developed as a dynamic series of choices made by individuals in one era and transformed by individuals in other eras. We hope to convey both the richness and the energy of the Western tradition, to which so many have contributed and from which so many have drawn.

SPECIAL FEATURES

In addition to the overall distinctive features of *The Western Humanities*—its interpretive context for the humanities, its balanced treatment of history and culture, its focus on the cultural legacy of each period—the book has some special features that we believe contribute to its usefulness and appeal. Chapter 8 includes an extended discussion and analysis of Islamic history and culture, broadening the horizons of the Western tradition to cover this important area. Chapter 15 presents a concise discussion of the seventeenth-century revolutions in science and political philosophy that laid the foundations for what we consider modern thinking. Chapter 21 extends the narrative of Western history and culture to the present day and includes expanded coverage of the global style known as Post-Modernism. Throughout the book, we consider not just art, literature, and music but also less commonly covered topics such as history, theology, and technology.

CHANGES TO THE FOURTH EDITION

The major change to this fourth edition of *The Western Humanities* is the "Windows on the World" feature—timelines that outline the most important events in Africa, the Americas, and Asia. These two-page en-

tries, through text and art illustration, summarize historical developments and highlight cultural contributions of selected societies. Limited by reasons of space, we have focused on regional cultures in Africa; Andean, Mesoamerican, and North American cultures in the Americas; and China, India, and Japan in Asia. This new feature helps to expand students' cultural horizons by giving them the opportunity to see how other societies were developing and to note their contributions to the arts and humanities. The twelve "Windows on the World" timelines complement the major time periods covered in *The Western Humanities*.

Another innovation is "A Humanities Primer: How to Understand the Arts," which has been added to the Introduction. In order to make the West's achievements more familiar to students, this new feature includes a set of general terms and concepts used across the arts and humanities plus some basic terms that apply to the arts, architecture, literature, music, theater, history, philosophy, and religion. We have also outlined the major analytical methods used for understanding cultural works.

We have revised the art program for this edition. More than 50 new artworks are included, either replacing works previously illustrated or adding to the overall art program. Each new artwork is discussed in both a detailed caption and the text. The revised art program includes four new sections: the rise of printmaking in late medieval times; the origin of the Venetian School of Renaissance painting; and, in the Post-Modern period, video art and installation art. The new illustrations come from sculpture, painting, architecture, photography, and other media, including the *Torso of Miletus*, the Dura Europas Synagogue, *Leisure Time at the Bath* from the *Medieval Housebook*, Hans Memling's *Madonna and Child with Angels*, Giovanni Bellini's *St. Francis in Ecstasy*, Rachel Whiteread's *Untitled (Yellow Tub)*, and Nam June Paik's *My Faust—Channel 5—Nationalism*.

We made specific changes to the text to address reviewers' suggestions. In Chapter 13, we rearranged the chronology of the main topics: northern humanism, the religious reformations, the Northern Renaissance, and Late Mannerism. We also expanded it to include the Golden Age of Spanish literature and shifted Hieronymus Bosch from Chapter 10 to Chapter 13. We then added Hans Memling to Chapter 10. We extended Chapter 21 to include developments in the late 1990s.

Finally, we continued with our goal of expanding our discussion of women writers and artists as well as artists from cultures beyond the Western traditions. Some of these new additions include Toni Morrison, Ann Hamilton, Nam June Paik, Rachel Whiteread, Emily Dickinson, and Frederick Douglass. We replaced nine "Personal Perspectives" (a feature added in the last edition to bring history to life for the reader) with new eyewitness accounts from such historical figures as Amenemope, Solon, Henry Knighton, Samuel Pepys, and Charlotte Brontë.

TEACHING RESOURCES

As instructors, we are keenly aware of the problems encountered in teaching the humanities, especially to large, diverse classes. We have therefore created an Instructor's Manual, as well as a comprehensive package of ancillary resource materials, designed to help solve those problems.

The fourth edition of the Instructor's Manual has been revised and expanded. For each chapter this manual includes teaching strategies and suggestions, test items, learning objectives, key cultural terms, film and reading suggestions, and a detailed outline revised to accompany the fourth edition of *The Western Humanities*. Additionally, there is background on the "Personal Perspective" boxes found throughout the book and, new to this edition, there is "Windows on the World Background," which provides additional information on the cultures and artworks described in each Windows feature. Also new to this edition of the manual are suggested Web sites that instructors will find useful for lecture preparation and additional images.

In addition to chapter-by-chapter materials, you'll find the following features in the Instructor's Manual:

- Five basic teaching strategies
- Seven lecture models
- Timeline of developments in non-Western cultures
- Music listening guides
- Comparative questions covering material from more than one chapter (designed to test students on broader patterns and comparisons)

The Mayfield Quick View Guide to the Internet for Students of the Humanities has been thoroughly revised and updated by Jeffrey Hodges of Michigan State University. This guide provides step-by-step instructions on accessing the Internet and finding and using information on the humanities. It also helps students evaluate the credibility of online information sources, use listserves and newsgroups, and even create a Web page. The guide is available to students at no additional cost.

Music in the Western Tradition offers expanded coverage of music concepts and history. This supplemental text is available to students at a minimal cost.

Electronic Ancillaries and Presentation Aids

New to this edition is an interactive Web site, which can be accessed at www.mayfieldpub.com/mp.

Instructor's resources on the site include PowerPoint slides, a custom syllabus generator, and links to recommended Western and global humanities Internet sites. Resources for students include interactive quizzes for each chapter, a tutorial for doing research using the Internet, and links.

The *Electronic Study Guide*, developed by Julius J. Jackson, Jr., San Bernardino Valley College, has been thoroughly revised and updated. This CD-ROM offers students several ways to review and expand their knowledge, with study aids for each chapter that include guided tours to highlight important concepts; pronunciation guides for key terms; flash cards; true-false, multiple-choice, and fill-in-the-blank questions; and mini-lectures that provide an in-depth study of selected concepts. The study guide can be used with either Windows- or Macintosh-based computers.

For use in presentations, particularly in large lecture settings, there are two slide sets available. The art slides present 100 artworks reflecting the range of art and architecture covered in *The Western Humanities*. The 25 map slides reproduce the maps found in the text.

The complete test bank is available in both Windows and Macintosh formats. The MicroTest III testing program allows you to design tests using the questions included with *The Western Humanities*, to edit those questions, and to incorporate your own questions.

Finally, additional multimedia resources, including videotapes and CD-ROMs, are available to qualified adopters.

ACKNOWLEDGMENTS

Preparing the fourth edition of this text has been a rewarding experience for us. The task has been made more enjoyable by the participation and support of many people. We acknowledge and express gratitude for the help of former students over the years. Their questions and insights have affected the way we address certain issues and frame particular arguments.

Beyond the confines of Michigan State University we are grateful for the many comments and suggestions provided to us by the following reviewers: Judith Chambers, Hillsborough Community College; Robert Eisner, San Diego State University; Connie Frankel, Pasco Hernando Community College; Robin Hardee, Brevard Community College; Grant Hardy, University of North Carolina, Asheville; Sara Hollis, Southern University at New Orleans; Kimberley Jones, Seminole Community College; Seth R. Katz, Bradley University; Sandi S. Landis, St. John's River Community College; Michael Phillips, Brigham Young University; Robert Prescott, Bradley University; William Stockton, Johnson County Community College.

We have also benefited from the staff at Mayfield Publishing Company. First and foremost, we wish to thank Holly Allen, the sponsoring editor, who remains patient and supportive all the way. Thanks also to Barbara Armentrout and Kate Engelberg, the developmental editors who helped us especially with the new features in this edition. Susan Shook, developmental editor, helped us pull together all the teaching supplements. Joan Pendleton, the copyeditor, has done an outstanding job, checking our grammar, spelling, and punctuation. She has made it easier for all of us with her fine sense of humor. We also wish to thank the Mayfield production team. Once again, senior production editor Julianna Scott Fein has shepherded the manuscript through the production process with care and grace. Brian Pecko, photo researcher, has done an excellent job ensuring that the art reproductions are of the highest quality. Credit for the beautiful cover goes to the cover designer, Linda Robertson; for the elegant interior design to the designer, Anna George, and to the design manager, Jean Mailander; and for the handsome timelines and maps to the art manager, Robin Mouat. Manufacturing manager Randy Hurst is responsible for the printing and paper that make *The Western Humanities* so attractive. The efforts of Marty Granahan, permissions editor, ensured the integrity of the work. To all we express our thanks.

CONTENTS

13

NORTHERN HUMANISM, NORTHERN RENAISSANCE, RELIGIOUS REFORMATIONS, AND LATE MANNERISM
1500–1603   345

14

THE BAROQUE AGE
Glamour and Grandiosity
1600–1715   373

15

THE BAROQUE AGE II
Revolutions in Scientific
and Political Thought,
1600–1715   403

21
THE AGE OF ANXIETY AND BEYOND 1945–
575

INTRODUCTION
Why Study Cultural History?

To be ignorant of what occurred before you were born is to remain always a child.

—CICERO, FIRST CENTURY B.C.

Anyone who cannot give an account to oneself of the past three thousand years remains in darkness, without experience, living from day to day.

—GOETHE, NINETEENTH CENTURY A.D.

The underlying premise of this book is that some basic knowledge of the Western cultural heritage is necessary for those who want to become educated human beings in charge of their own destinies. If people are not educated into their place in human history—five thousand years of relatively uninterrupted though sometimes topsy-turvy developments—then they are rendered powerless, subject to passing fads and outlandish beliefs. They become vulnerable to the flattery of demagogues who promise heaven on earth, or they fall prey to the misconception that present-day events are unique, without precedent in history, or superior to everything that has gone before.

Perhaps the worst that can happen is to exist in a limbo of ignorance—in Goethe's words, "living from day to day." Without knowledge of the past and the perspective it brings, people may come to believe that their contemporary world will last forever, when in reality much of it is doomed to be forgotten. In contrast to the instant obsolescence of popular culture, the study of Western culture offers an alternative that has passed the unforgiving test of time. Long after today's heroes and celebrities have fallen into oblivion, the achievements of our artistic and literary ancestors—those who have forged the Western tradition—will remain. Their works echo down the ages and seem fresh in every period. The

ancient Roman writer Seneca put it well when he wrote, in the first century A.D., "Life is short but art is long."

When people realize that the rich legacy of Western culture is their own, their view of themselves and the times they live in can expand beyond the present moment. They find that they need not be confined by the limits of today but can draw on the creative insights of people who lived hundreds and even thousands of years ago. They discover that their own culture has a history and a context that give it meaning and shape. Studying and experiencing their cultural legacy can help them understand their place in today's world.

THE BOUNDARIES OF THE WEST

The subject of this text is Western culture, but what exactly do we mean, first, by "culture" and, second, by the "West"? *Culture* is a term with several meanings, but we use it here to mean the artistic and intellectual expressions of a people, their creative achievements. By the *West* we mean that part of the globe that lies west of Asia and Asia Minor and north of Africa, especially Europe—the geographical framework for much of this study.

The Western tradition is not confined exclusively to Europe as defined today, however. The contributions of peoples who lived beyond the boundaries of present-day Europe are also included in Western culture, either because they were forerunners of the West, such as those who created the first civilizations in Mesopotamia and Egypt, or because they were part of the West for periods of time, such as those who lived in the North African and Near Eastern lands bordering the Mediterranean Sea during the Roman and early

Christian eras. Regardless of geography, Western culture draws deeply from ideals forged in these lands.

When areas that had been part of the Western tradition at one time were absorbed into other cultural traditions, as happened in Mesopotamia, Egypt, and North Africa in the seventh century when the people embraced the Muslim faith, then they are generally no longer included in Western cultural history. Because of the enormous influence of Islamic civilization on Western civilization, however, we do include in this volume both an account of Islamic history and a description and appreciation of Islamic culture. Different in many ways from our own, the rich tradition of Islam has an important place in today's world.

After about 1500, with voyages and explorations reaching the farthest parts of the globe, the European focus of Western culture that had held for centuries began to dissolve. Starting from this time, the almost exclusive European mold was broken and Western values and ideals began to be exported throughout the world, largely through the efforts of missionaries, soldiers, colonists, and merchants. Coinciding with this development and further complicating the pattern of change were the actions of those who imported and enslaved countless numbers of black Africans to work on plantations in North and South America. The interplay of Western culture with many previously isolated cultures, whether desired or not, forever changed all who were touched by the process.

The Westernization of the globe that has been going on ever since 1500 is perhaps the dominant theme of the twentieth century. What human greed, missionary zeal, and dreams of empire failed to accomplish before 1900 has been achieved in this century by modern technology, the media, and popular culture. The world today is a global village, much of it dominated by Western values and styles of life. In our time, Westernization has become a two-way interchange. When artists and writers from other cultures adopt Western forms or ideas, they are not only Westernizing their own traditions but also injecting fresh sensibilities and habits of thought into the Western tradition. The globalization of culture means that a South American novel or a Japanese film can be as accessible to Western audiences as a European painting and yet carry with it an intriguingly new vocabulary of cultural symbols and meanings.

HISTORICAL PERIODS AND CULTURAL STYLES

In cultural history the past is often divided into historical periods and cultural styles. A historical period is an interval of time that has a certain unity because it is characterized by the prevalence of a unique culture, ideology, or technology or because it is bounded by defining historical events, such as the death of a military leader like Alexander the Great or a political upheaval like the fall of Rome. A cultural style is a combination of features of artistic or literary expression, execution, or performance that define a particular school or era. A historical period may have the identical time frame as a cultural style, or it may embrace more than one style simultaneously or two styles successively. Each chapter of this survey focuses on a historical period and includes significant aspects of culture—usually the arts, architecture, literature, religion, music, and philosophy—organized around a discussion of the relevant style or styles appropriate to that time.

The survey begins with prehistory, the era before writing was invented, setting forth the emergence of human beings from an obscure past. After the appearance of writing in about 3000 B.C., the Western cultural heritage is divided into three sweeping historical periods: ancient, medieval, and modern.

The ancient period dates from 3000 B.C. to A.D. 500 (Timeline 1). During these thirty-five hundred years the light of Western civilization begins to shine in Mesopotamia and Egypt, shines more brightly still in eighth-century-B.C. Greece and Rome, loses some of its luster when Greece succumbs to Rome in 146 B.C., and finally is snuffed out when the Roman empire collapses in the fifth century A.D. Coinciding with these historical periods are the cultural styles of Mesopotamia; Egypt; Greece, including Archaic, Classical (or Hellenic), and Hellenistic styles; and Rome, including Republican and Imperial styles.

The medieval period, or the Middle Ages, covers events between A.D. 500 and 1500, a one-thousand-year span that is further divided into three subperiods (Timeline 2). The Early Middle Ages (500–1000) is typified by frequent barbarian invasions and political chaos so that civilization itself is threatened and barely survives. No single international style characterizes this turbulent period, though several regional styles flourish. The High Middle Ages (1000–1300) is a period of stability and the zenith of medieval culture. Two successive styles appear, the Romanesque and the Gothic, with the latter dominating culture for the rest of the medieval period. The Late Middle Ages (1300–1500) is a transitional period in which the medieval age is dying and the modern age is struggling to be born.

The modern period begins in about 1400 (there is often overlap between historical periods) and continues today (Timeline 3). With the advent of the modern period a new way of defining historical changes starts to make more sense—the division of history into

Timeline 1   THE ANCIENT WORLD

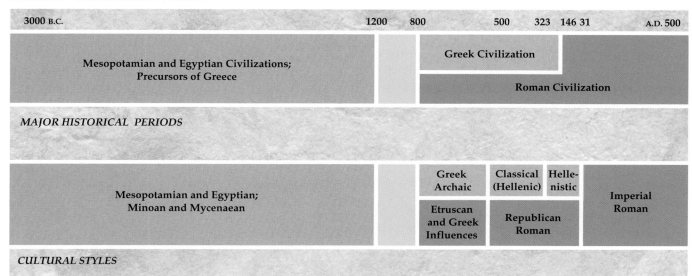

movements, the activities of large groups of people united to achieve a common goal. The modern period consists of waves of movements that aim to change the world in some specific way.

The first modern movement is the Renaissance (1400–1600), or "rebirth," which attempts to revive the cultural values of ancient Greece and Rome. It is accompanied by two successive styles, Renaissance style and Mannerism. The next significant movement is the Reformation (1500–1600), which is dedicated to restoring Christianity to the ideals of the early church set forth in the Bible. Although it does not spawn a specific style, this religious upheaval does have a profound impact on the subjects of the arts and literature and the way they are expressed, especially in the Mannerist style.

The Reformation is followed by the Scientific Revolution (1600–1700), a movement that results in the abandonment of ancient science and the birth of modern science. Radical in its conclusions, the Scientific

Revolution is somewhat out of touch with the style of its age, which is known as the Baroque. This magnificent style is devoted to overwhelming the senses through theatrical and sensuous effects and is associated with the attempts of the Roman Catholic Church to reassert its authority in the world.

The Scientific Revolution gives impetus to the Enlightenment (1700–1800), a movement that pledges to reform politics and society according to the principles of the new science. In stylistic terms the eighteenth century is schizophrenic, dominated first by the Rococo, an extravagant and fanciful style that represents the last phase of the Baroque, and then by the Neoclassical, a style inspired by the works of ancient Greece and Rome and reflective of the principles of the Scientific Revolution. Before the eighteenth century is over, the Enlightenment calls forth its antithesis, Romanticism (1770–1870), a movement centered on feeling, fantasy, and everything that cannot be proven scientifically. The Romantic style, marked by a

Timeline 2   THE MEDIEVAL WORLD

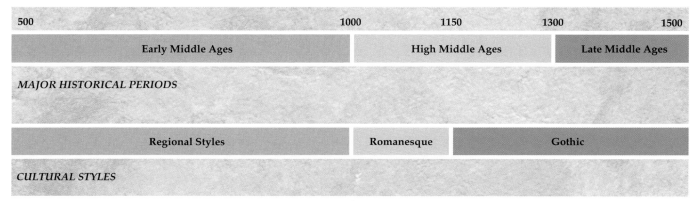

Timeline 3   THE MODERN WORLD

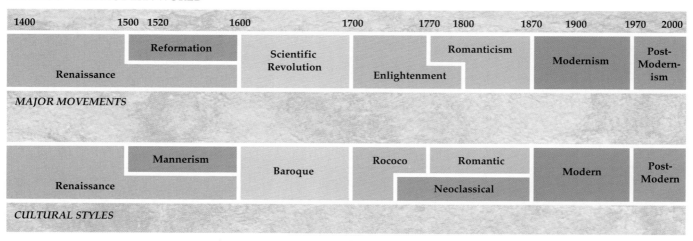

revived taste for the Gothic and a love of nature, is the perfect accompaniment to this movement.

Toward the end of the nineteenth century Modernism (1870–1970) arises, bent on destroying every vestige of both the Greco-Roman tradition and the Christian faith and on fashioning new ways of understanding that are independent of the past. Since 1970 Post-Modernism has emerged, a movement that tries to make peace with the past by embracing old forms of expression while at the same time adopting a global and multivoiced perspective.

Although every cultural period is marked by innovation and creativity, our treatment of them in this book varies somewhat, with more space and greater weight given to the achievements of certain times. We make these adjustments because some periods or styles are more significant than others, especially in the defining influence that their achievements have had on our own era. For example, some styles seem to tower over the rest, such as Classicism in fifth-century-B.C. Greece, the High Renaissance of sixteenth-century Italy, and Modernism in the mid–twentieth century, as compared with other styles, such as that of the Early Middle Ages or the seventeenth-century Baroque.

AN INTEGRATED APPROACH TO CULTURAL HISTORY

Our approach to the Western heritage in this book is to root cultural achievements in their historical settings, showing how the material conditions—the political, social, and economic events of each period—influenced their creation. About one-third of each chapter is devoted to an interpretive discussion of material history, and the remaining two-thirds are devoted to the arts, architecture, philosophy, religion, literature, and music

of the period. These two aspects of history do not occur separately, of course, and one of our aims is to show how they are intertwined.

As just one example of this integrated approach, consider the Gothic cathedral, that lofty, light-filled house of worship marked by pointed arches, towering spires, and radiant stained-glass windows. Gothic cathedrals were erected during the High Middle Ages, following a bleak period when urban life had virtually ceased. Although religion was still the dominant force in European life, trade was starting to flourish once again, town life was reviving, and urban dwellers were beginning to prosper. In part as testimonials to their new wealth, cities and towns commissioned architects and hired workers to erect these soaring churches, which dominated the landscape for miles around and proclaimed the economic well-being of their makers.

We adopt an integrated approach to Western culture not just in considering how the arts are related to material conditions but also in looking for the common themes, aspirations, and ideas that permeate the artistic and literary expressions of every individual era. The creative accomplishments of an age tend to reflect a shared perspective, even when that perspective is not explicitly recognized at the time. Thus, each period possesses a unique outlook that can be analyzed in the cultural record. A good example of this phenomenon is Classical Greece in the fifth century B.C., when the ideal of moderation, or balance in all things, played a major role in sculpture, architecture, philosophy, religion, and tragic drama. The cultural record in other periods is not always as clear as that in ancient Greece, but shared qualities can often be uncovered that distinguish the varied aspects of culture in an era to form a unifying thread.

A corollary of this idea is that creative individuals and their works are very much influenced by the times in which they live. This is not to say that incomparable geniuses—such as Shakespeare in Renaissance England—do not appear and rise above their own ages, speaking directly to the human mind and heart in every age that follows. Yet even Shakespeare reflected the political attitudes and social patterns of his time. Though a man for the ages, he still regarded monarchy as the correct form of government and women as the inferiors of men.

THE SELECTION OF CULTURAL WORKS

The Western cultural heritage is vast, and any selection of works for a survey text reflects choices made by the authors. All the works we chose to include have had a significant impact on Western culture, but for different reasons. We chose some because they blazed a new trail, such as Picasso's *Demoiselles d'Avignon* (see Figure 19.21), which marked the advent of Cubism in painting, or Fielding's *Tom Jones,* one of the earliest novels. Other works were included because they seemed to embody a style to perfection, such as the regal statue called *Poseidon* (or *Zeus*) (see Figure 3.21), executed in the Classical style of fifth-century-B.C. Athens, or Dante's *Divine Comedy,* which epitomized the ideals of the High Middle Ages. On occasion, we chose works on a particular topic, such as the biblical story of David and Goliath, and demonstrated how different sculptors interpreted it, as in sculptures by Donatello (see Figure 11.11), Verrocchio (see Figure 11.12), and Michelangelo (see Figure 12.19). Still other works caught our attention because they served as links between successive styles, as is the case with Giotto's frescoes (see Figure 10.19), or because they represented the end of an age or an artistic style, as in the haunting sculpture called *The Last Pagan* (see Figure 7.15). Finally, we included some works, especially paintings, simply because of their great beauty, such as Ingres's *Madame Jacques Louis Leblanc* (see Figure 17.7).

Through all the ages of Western cultural history, through all the shifting styles and tastes embodied in painting, sculpture, architecture, poetry, and song, there glows a creative spark that can be found in human beings in every period. This diversity is a hallmark of the Western experience, and we celebrate it in this book.

A CHALLENGE TO THE READER

The purpose of all education is and should be self-knowledge. This goal was first established by the ancient Greeks in their injunction to "Know thyself," the inscription carved above the entrance to Apollo's temple at Delphi. Self-knowledge means awareness of oneself and one's place in society and the world. Reaching this goal is not easy, because becoming an educated human being is a lifelong process, requiring time, energy, and commitment. But all journeys begin with a single step, and we intend this volume as a first step toward understanding and defining oneself in terms of one's historical and cultural heritage. Our challenge to the reader is to use this book to begin the long journey to self-knowledge.

A HUMANITIES PRIMER
How to Understand the Arts

INTRODUCTION

We can all appreciate the arts. We can find pleasure or interest in paintings, music, poems, novels, films, and many other art forms, both contemporary and historical. We don't need to know very much about art to know what we like, because we bring ourselves to the work: What we like has as much to do with who we are as with the art itself.

Many of us, for example, will respond positively to a painting like Leonardo da Vinci's *The Virgin of the Rocks*. The faces of the Madonna and angel are lovely; we may have seen images like these on Christmas cards or in other commercial reproductions. We respond with what English poet William Wordsworth calls the "first careless rapture," which activates our imaginations and establishes a connection between us and the work of art. However, if this is all we see, if we never move from a subjective reaction, we can only appreciate the surface, the immediate form, and then, perhaps subconsciously, accept without question the values it implies. We appreciate, but we do not understand.

Sometimes we cannot appreciate because we do not understand. We may reject Picasso's *Les Demoiselles d'Avignon*, for it presents us with images of women that we may not be able to recognize. These women may make us uncomfortable, and the values they imply may frighten us rather than please or reassure us. Rather than rapture, we may experience disgust; but when we realize that this painting is considered a groundbreaking work, we may wonder what we're missing and be willing to look deeper. (*The Virgin of the Rocks* and *Les Demoiselles d'Avignon* are discussed in the text on pages 310–311 and pages 530, 532–533, respectively.)

LEONARDO DA VINCI. *The Virgin of the Rocks.*

To understand a work of art (a building, a poem, a song, a symphony), we need to keep our "rapture" (our emotional response and connection) but make it less "careless," less superficial and subjective, less restricted to that which we recognize. We need to enrich our appreciation by searching for a meaning that goes beyond ourselves. This involves understanding the intent or goal of the artist, the elements of form present in the work, the ways in which those elements contribute to the artist's goal, the context within which the artwork evolved, and the connections of the work to other works. Understanding an artwork requires intellectual involvement as well as an emotional connection. The purpose of this primer is to provide you with some of the tools you will need to understand—as well as appreciate—literature, art, and music.

APPROACHES TO THE ANALYSIS OF LITERATURE, ART, AND MUSIC

When we analyze a work of art, we ask two questions: What is the artist trying to do, and how well is it done? We want to identify the intent of the work, and we want to evaluate its execution. To answer these questions, we can examine the formal elements of the work—an approach known as formalism—and we can explore its context—known as contextualism.

Formalism

A formal analysis is concerned with the aesthetic (artistic) elements of a work separate from context. This type of analysis focuses on medium and technique. The context of the work—where, when, and by whom a work was created—may be interesting but is considered unnecessary to formalist interpretation and understanding. A formal analysis of a painting, sculpture, or architectural structure examines its line, shape, color, texture, and composition, as well as the artist's technical ability within the medium used; it is not concerned with anything extraneous to the work itself. A formal analysis of a literary work, such as a short story or novel, would explore the relationships among theme, plot, characters, and setting, as well as how well the resources of language—word choice, tone, imagery, symbol, and so on—are used to support the other elements. A formal analysis of a film would also explore theme, plot, characters (as developed both verbally and nonverbally), and setting, as well as how the resources of cinematography—camera techniques, lighting, sound, editing, and so on—support the other elements. A formal analysis of *The Virgin of the Rocks* would examine the artist's use of perspective, the arrangement

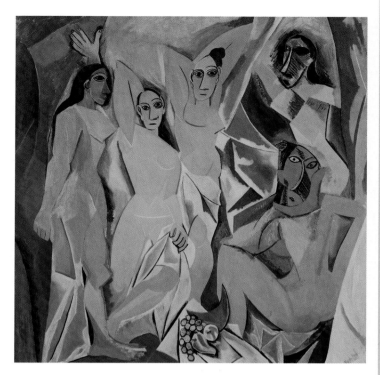

PABLO PICASSO. *Les Desmoiselles d'Avignon.*

of figures as they relate to each other and to the grotto that surrounds them, the technical use of color and line, the dramatic interplay of light and shadow (known as *chiaroscuro*). The same technical considerations would be explored in a formal analysis of *Les Demoiselles d'Avignon*. The fact that the two paintings were completed in 1483 and 1907, respectively, would be important only in terms of the technology and mediums available to the artists. In a formal analysis, time and place exist only within the work.

Contextualism

In contrast, a contextual analysis focuses on factors outside the work: why it was created, in response to what artistic, social, cultural, historical, and political forces, events, and trends; who the artist is, and what his or her intent and motives were in creating the work; how the work fits in with other works of the same genre of the same or different eras; and how the work fits in with the rest of the artist's body of work. Time and place are very important.

A contextual analysis of the da Vinci and Picasso paintings would include information about where and when each painting was completed; the conditions from which it arose; the prevailing artistic styles of the times; the life circumstances of the artists; and so on. The paintings alone do not provide enough information for contextual inquiry. Similarly, contextual analysis of a novel by Dostoevsky would consider both his personal circumstances and the conditions in Russia and Europe when he wrote. A contextual analysis of a chorale and fugue by Bach would include information on Bach's life, his religious beliefs, and the political climate of Germany in the eighteenth century.

An Integrated Approach

In a strictly contextual analysis of an artwork, the work itself can sometimes be lost in the exploration of context. In a strictly formal analysis, important knowledge that can contribute to understanding may remain unknown. The most effective analyses, therefore, combine and integrate the two approaches, examining the formal elements of the work and exploring the context within which it was created. Such an approach is more effective and, in a sense, more honest than either the formal or the contextual approach alone. A work of art, whether a poem or a painting, a cathedral or a cantata, is a complex entity, as are the relationships it fosters between the artist and the art and between the art and its audience. The integrative approach recognizes these relationships and their complexity. This is the approach to artistic and cultural analysis most frequently used in *The Western Humanities*.

A Variety of Perspectives

Many students and critics of culture, while taking an integrative approach, are also especially interested in looking at things from a particular perspective, a set of interests or a way of thinking that informs and influences their investigations and interpretations. Common perspectives are the psychological, the feminist, the religious, the economic, and the historical.

People working from a psychological perspective look for meaning in the psychological features of the work, such as sexual and symbolic associations; they do a kind of retroactive psychological analysis of the artist. They might look for meaning in the facial expressions, gestures, and body positions of Mary and the angel in *The Virgin of the Rocks*. They might be interested in da Vinci's attitudes toward women and his relationships with them, and they might compare this painting with the *Mona Lisa* in a search for clues about who he was.

Someone working from a feminist perspective would examine the art itself and the context in which it arose from a woman's point of view. To take a feminist perspective is to ask how the work depicts women, what it says about women and their relationships in general, and how it may or may not reflect a patriarchal society. Many people have discussed the apparent hatred of women that seems to come through in Picasso's *Les Demoiselles d'Avignon*. At the same time, the work, in its size (8 feet by 7 feet 8 inches) and in the unblinking attitude of its subjects, suggests that these women have a kind of raw power. Feminist critics focus on such considerations.

Analysis from a religious perspective is often appropriate when a work of art originated in a religious context. The soaring spires and cruciform floor plans of medieval cathedrals reveal religious meaning, for example, as do Renaissance paintings depicting biblical characters. Many contemporary works of art and literature also have religious content. Religious analyses look to the use of symbolism, the representation of theological doctrines and beliefs, and intercultural connections and influences for meaning.

Someone approaching a work of art from an economic perspective focuses on its economic content—the roles and relationships associated with wealth. Often drawing upon Marx's contention that class is the defining consideration in all human relationships and endeavors, an economic analysis would examine both purpose and content: Was the work created as a display of power by the rich? How does it depict people of different classes? What is the artist saying about the distribution of wealth?

The historical perspective is perhaps the most encompassing of all perspectives, because it can include explorations of psychological, religious, and economic issues, as well as questions about class and gender in various times and places. Historical analysis requires an understanding of the significant events of the time and how they affect the individual and shape the culture. *The Western Humanities* most often takes a historical perspective in its views of art and culture.

The Vocabulary of Analysis

Certain terms and concepts are fundamental to the analysis of any artwork. We review several such general concepts and terms here, before moving on to a consideration of more specific art forms.

Any artwork requires a relationship between itself and its audience. **Audience** is the group for whom a work of art, architecture, literature, drama, film, or music is intended. The audience may be a single person, such as the Medici ruler to whom Machiavelli dedicated his political treatise *The Prince*. The audience can be a small group of people with access to the work, such as the monks who dined in the room where Leonardo da Vinci painted *The Last Supper* on the wall. The audience can also be a special group of people with common interests or education; for example, films like *I Know What You Did Last Summer* and *Scream* are intended for a youthful audience. Sometimes the audience is limited by its own understanding of the art; we often feel excluded from what we don't understand. Consequently, some art requires an educated audience.

Composition is the arrangement of constituent elements in an individual work. In music, composition also refers to the process of creating the work.

Content is the subject matter of the work; content can be based on mythology, religion, history, current events, personal history, or almost any idea or feeling deemed appropriate by the artist.

Context is the setting in which the art arose, its own time and place. Context includes the political, economic, social, and cultural conditions of the time; it can also include the personal conditions and circumstances that shape the artist's vision.

A **convention** is an agreed-upon practice, device, technique, or form. A sonnet, for example, is a fourteen-line poem with certain specified rhyme schemes. A poem is not a sonnet unless it follows this formal convention. A convention of the theater is the "willing suspension of disbelief": We know that the events taking place before our eyes are not real, but we agree to believe in them for the duration of the play. Often, conventions in the arts are established as much by political powerbrokers as by artists. The Medicis and the Renaissance popes, for example, wanted portraits and paintings that glorified their reigns, and conventions in Renaissance art reflect these demands. Today, museum directors, wealthy individuals, and government funding agencies play a role in influencing the direction of contemporary art by supporting and showing the work of artists whose conventions they agree with or think are important.

Genre is the type or class to which a work of art, literature, drama, or music belongs, depending on its style, form, or content. In literature, for example, the novel is a genre in itself; the short story is another genre. In music, symphonies, operas, and tone poems are all different genres. Beginning in the Renaissance, genres were carefully distinguished from one another, and a definite set of conventions was expected whenever a new work in a particular genre was created.

The **medium** is the material from which an art object is made—marble or bronze, for example, in sculpture, or water colors or oils in painting. (The plural of *medium* in this sense is often *mediums*; when *medium* is used to refer to a means of mass communication, such as radio or television, the plural is *media*.)

Style is the combination of distinctive elements of creative execution and expression, in terms of both form and content. Artists, artistic schools, movements, and periods can be characterized by their style. Styles often evolve out of existing styles, as when High Renaissance style evolved into Mannerism in the sixteenth century, or in reaction to styles that are perceived as worn out or excessive, as when Impressionism arose to challenge Realism in the nineteenth century.

When we talk about **technique,** we are referring to the systematic procedure whereby a particular creative task is performed. If we were discussing a dancer's technique, we might be referring to the way he executes leaps and turns; a painter's technique might be the way she applies paint to a canvas with broad, swirling brushstrokes.

The dominant idea of a work, the message or emotion the artist intends to convey, is known as the **theme.** The theme, then, is the embodiment of the artist's intent. In a novel, for example, the theme is the abstract concept that is made concrete by character, plot, setting, and other linguistic and structural elements of the work. We often evaluate the theme of a work in terms of how well it speaks to the human condition, how accurate its truth is, how valuable its message or observation is. We usually make these judgments by exploring the extent to which the theme confirms or denies our own experience.

In addition to these general concepts and terms, each art form has its own vocabulary. These more specific terms will be introduced in the sections that follow on literary, artistic, and musical analysis, along with brief illustrative analyses in each area. These informal illustrations are meant not as definitive analyses but as examples of the kinds of productive questions you can ask as you approach a creative work. The analyses differ in their depth and level of detail.

LITERARY ANALYSIS

Literary analysis begins with a consideration of various literary genres and forms. A work of literature is written either in **prose,** the ordinary language used in speaking and writing, or in **poetry,** a more imaginative and concentrated form of expression usually marked by meter, rhythm, or rhyme. Part of poetry's effect comes from the sound of words; it can often best be appreciated when spoken or read aloud. Prose is often divided into nonfiction (essays, biography, autobiography) and fiction (short stories, novels).

In literature, *genre* refers both to form—essay, short story, novel, poem, play, film script, television script—and to specific type within a form—tragedy, comedy, epic, lyric, and so on. According to Aristotle, a **tragedy** must have a tragic hero—a person of high stature who is brought down by his own excessive pride *(hubris);* he doesn't necessarily die at the end, but whatever his greatness was based upon is lost. A **comedy** is a story with a complicated and amusing plot; it usually ends with a happy and peaceful resolution of any conflicts. An **epic** poem, novel, or film is a relatively long recounting of the life of a hero or the glorious history of a people. A **lyric** poem is a short, subjective poem usually expressing an intense personal emotion. In a general sense, an epic tells a story and a lyric expresses an idea or feeling. Lyric poetry includes ballads (dramatic verse meant to be sung or recited, often by more than one singer or speaker), elegies (short, serious meditations, usually on death or other significant themes), odes (short lyric poems dealing with a single theme), and sonnets (formal fourteen-line poems identified by the arrangement of lines as either Italian [Petrarchan] or English [Shakespearean]).

In literature, the author's intent—the message or emotion the author wishes to convey—is usually discussed as the theme of the work. In an essay, the theme is articulated as the thesis: the idea or conclusion that the essay will prove or support. In a novel, story, or play, we infer the theme from the content and the development of ideas and imagery.

In fiction, the action of the story, what Aristotle calls "the arrangement of incidents," is the **plot.** There may be a primary plot that becomes the vehicle by which the theme is expressed, with subplots related to secondary (or even tertiary) themes. Plot can be evaluated by how well it supports the theme. Plot can also be evaluated according to criteria established by Aristotle in his *Poetics*. According to these criteria, the action expressed should be whole, with a beginning that does not follow or depend on anything else, a middle that logically follows what went before, and an end, or logical culmination of all prior action. The plot should be unified, so that every action is necessary and interrelated with all other actions. Few works of fiction adhere to these criteria completely; nevertheless, the criteria do provide a way of beginning to think about how a plot works.

Characters are also important both for themselves and for their effect on the plot and support of the theme. **Characters** provide the human focus, the embodiment, of the theme; they act out and are affected by the plot. The protagonist, or primary character, of the work is changed by the dramatic action of the plot and thus is a dynamic character; static characters remain unchanged throughout the story. An antagonist is a character in direct opposition to the protagonist. Some characters are stock characters, representing a type rather than an individual human being: the romantic fool, the nosy neighbor, the wise old woman, the vain beauty, the plain girl or dumb boy with a heart of gold.

Readers need to believe that characters' actions are authentic reactions to various events. The believability of a work of fiction—the writer's ability to express the truth—is called verisimilitude. Even in works of science fiction or fantasy, where events occur that could not occur in reality, readers must believe that what characters say and do makes sense under the conditions described.

The background against which the action takes place is the **setting.** It can include the geographical location, the environment (political, social, economic) in which the characters live, the historical time in which the action takes place, and the culture and customs of the time, place, and people.

The story or poem is told from the point of view of the **narrator.** The narrator is not necessarily identical with the author of the work. The narrator (or **narrative voice**) can be examined and analyzed like any other element of the work. When a narrator seems to know everything and is not limited by time or place, the work has an omniscient point of view. Such a narrator tells us what everyone is thinking, feeling, and doing. When the story is told from the perspective of a single character who can relate only what he or she knows or witnesses, the work has a first-person point of view. Such a narrator is limited in his or her understanding. Thus, we need to consider the narrator in order to judge how accurate or complete the narrative is.

Sometimes a narrator proves to be unreliable, and we have to piece together an account of the story ourselves. Other times an author uses multiple narrators to tell a story from multiple points of view. William Faulkner uses this device in his novel *The Sound and the Fury* to show that a story can be fully told only when several different characters have a chance to speak. Japanese film director Akira Kurosawa uses a similar device in *Rashomon* to show that there are many equally valid—or invalid—versions of the truth.

A literary analysis of a drama, whether a play for the stage or a film script, will consider not only the elements already mentioned—theme, plot, character, setting, language, and so on—but also the technical considerations specific to the form. In theater, these would include the work of the director, who interprets the play and directs the actors, as well as stage design, light and sound design, costumes, makeup, and so on. In film, technical considerations would include direction, editing, cinematography, musical score, special effects, and so on.

Let's turn now to a poem by Shakespeare and see how to approach it to enrich our understanding. Identifying a poem's intent and evaluating its execution is called an *explication,* from the French *explication de texte.* An explication is a detailed analysis of a poem's meaning, focusing on narrative voice, setting, rhyme, meter, words, and images. An explication begins with what is immediately evident about the poem as a whole, followed by a more careful examination of its parts.

William Shakespeare (1564–1616) was not just a great playwright; he was also a great poet. His works portray human emotions, motives, and relationships that we recognize today as well as the conditions and concerns of his time. In this sense, they are an example of aesthetic universality, the enduring connection between a work of art and its audience.

Shakespeare's sonnets are his most personal work. Scholars disagree about whether they are generic love poems or are addressed to a specific person and, if the latter, who that person might be. Formally, an English (or Shakespearean) sonnet is a 14-line poem consisting of three 4-line stanzas, or quatrains, each with its own rhyme scheme, and a concluding 2-line stanza, or couplet, that provides commentary on the preceding stanzas. The rhyme scheme in a Shakespearean sonnet is abab cdcd efef gg; that is, the first and third lines of each quatrain rhyme with each other, as do the second and fourth lines, though the rhymes are different in each quatrain. The last two lines rhyme with each other.

The meter of most Shakespearean sonnets is iambic pentameter; that is, each line has five feet, or units ("pentameter"), and each foot consists of an iamb, an unaccented syllable followed by an accented syllable (as in *alone*). An example of iambic pentameter is, "My mistress' eyes are nothing like the sun"; each foot consists of an unaccented and an accented syllable, and there are five feet. Unrhymed iambic pentameter—the verse of most of Shakespeare's plays—is known as **blank verse.**

Sonnet 130 ("My mistress' eyes are nothing like the sun") is a poem that not only illustrates sonnet form but also showcases Shakespeare's wit and his attitude toward certain conventions of his time. The poem was originally written in Elizabethan English, which looks and sounds quite different from modern English. We reproduce it in modern English, as is customary today for Shakespeare's works.

Sonnet 130

My mistress' eyes are nothing like the sun;
Coral is far more red than her lips' red;
If snow be white, why then her breasts are dun;
If hairs be wires, black wires grow on her head.

I have seen roses damask'd, red and white,
But no such roses see I in her cheeks,
And in some perfumes is there more delight
Than in the breath that from my mistress reeks.

I love to hear her speak, yet well I know
That music hath a far more pleasing sound;
I grant I never saw a goddess go,
My mistress when she walks treads on the ground.

And yet, by heaven, I think my love as rare
As any she belied with false compare.

Because the poet's intent may not be immediately evident, paraphrasing each line or stanza can point the reader to the theme or meaning intended by the poet. Let's begin, then, by paraphrasing the lines:

> My mistress' eyes are nothing like the sun;
> *The speaker's lover's eyes are not bright.*
> Coral is far more red than her lips' red;
> *Her lips are not very red, certainly not as red as coral.*
> If snow be white, why then her breasts are dun;
> *Her breasts are mottled in color, not as white as snow.*
> If hairs be wires, black wires grow on her head.
> *Her hair is black (not blond, as was the conventional beauty standard then, when poets referred to women's hair as "golden wires").*
>
> I have seen roses damask'd, red and white,
> But no such roses see I in her cheeks,
> *Her cheeks are not rosy.*
> And in some perfumes is there more delight
> Than in the breath that from my mistress reeks.
> *Her breath doesn't smell as sweet as perfume.*
>
> I love to hear her speak, yet well I know
> That music hath a far more pleasing sound;
> *Her voice doesn't sound as melodious as music.*
> I grant I never saw a goddess go,
> My mistress when she walks treads on the ground.
> *Although the speaker has never seen a goddess walk, he knows his lover does not float above ground, as goddesses are supposed to do, but walks on the ground, a mortal woman.*
>
> And yet, by heaven, I think my love as rare
> As any she belied with false compare.
> *His lover is as rare and valuable as any idealized woman glorified by false poetic comparisons.*

Remember that to analyze a poem, we ask questions like, What is the theme of the poem, the poet's intent? How does Shakespeare support his point with specific images? From the paraphrased lines it is clear that the narrator is stating that his love is a real woman who walks upon the ground, not an unattainable ideal to be worshiped from afar. Idealized qualities are irrelevant to how he feels about her; the qualities he loves are the ones that make her human.

Closely examining each line of a poem helps to reveal the rhyme scheme (abab cdcd efef gg), the meter (iambic pentameter), and thus the form of the poem (sonnet). Explication of the formal elements of the poem would also include examining the use of language (such as word choice, imagery, comparisons, metaphors), the tone of the narrative voice, and so on.

To understand the context of the poem, we would consider the cultural climate of the time (was "courtly love" a prevalent cultural theme?); common contemporary poetic conventions (were many other poets proclaiming their eternal love for idealized women?); and the political, social, and economic conditions (what roles were open to women in Elizabethan England, and how were they changing? What influence might Queen Elizabeth have had on the poet's point of view? What comments about his society is Shakespeare making?)

Finally, we might consider how honest and accurate we find the emotional content of the poem to be, how relevant its truth. Are Shakespeare's observations germane to today, a time when the mass media present us with a nearly unattainable ideal as the epitome of female beauty?

✺ FINE ARTS ANALYSIS

As with literature, knowledge of a particular vocabulary helps us "speak the language" of art critics. The terms introduced here are in addition to those discussed earlier, such as *medium* and *technique.* They apply to all the visual arts, including drawing and painting, sculpture—the art of shaping material (such as wood, stone, or marble) into three-dimensional works of art—and architecture—the art and science of designing, planning, and building structures, usually for human habitation. In architecture, the critic would also pay attention to the blending of artistry and functionality (how well the structure fulfills its purpose).

Generally, art is more or less representational or more or less abstract. **Representational art** is true to human perception and presents a likeness of the world much as it appears to the naked eye. An important convention of representational art is **perspective,** the appearance of depth and distance on a two-dimensional surface. **Abstract art** presents a subjective view of the world, the artist's emotions or ideas; some abstract art simply presents color, line, or shape for its own sake.

The formal elements of visual art include line, shape, texture, color, composition, and so on. **Line** is the mark made by the artist, whether with pencil, pen, or paintbrush. Lines can be straight or curved, thick or thin, light or dark, spare or plentiful. **Color** is the use in the artwork of hues found in nature; color can enhance the sense of reality presented in a visual image, or it can distort it, depending on how it is used. The primary colors are red, blue, and yellow, and the secondary colors are orange (a combination of red and yellow), green (a combination of yellow and blue), and purple (a combination of blue and red). Blue, green, and purple hues are "cool" colors that appear to recede from the eye; red, yellow, and orange are "warm" colors that appear to move forward. Color has symbolic associations within specific historical and cultural settings. For example, in Western culture, white is a symbol of purity and is worn by brides. In Eastern cultures, white is a symbol of death; Chinese brides wear red to symbolize good luck.

How the artist arranges the work is referred to as the composition. Often the artist controls how the eye

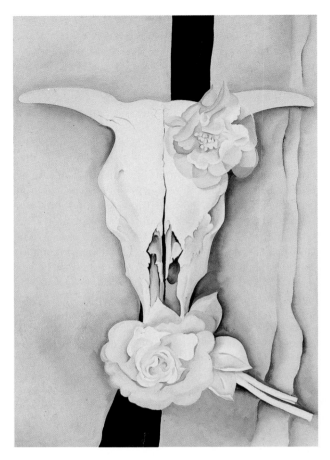

GEORGIA O'KEEFFE. *Cow's Skull with Calico Roses.*

moves from one part to another by means of the composition. Through the composition the artist leads us to see the artwork in a particular way. The setting of an artwork is the time and place depicted in a representational work, as defined by visual cues—the people, how they are dressed, what they are doing, and so on.

With these terms in hand, let's consider *Cow's Skull with Calico Roses* by Georgia O'Keeffe (1887–1986), painted in 1931. What is the artist's intent? How well is that intent executed? Front and center we see the cow's skull, placed so the strong vertical line of the skull, accentuated by the skull's vertical midline crack, aligns with the center of the canvas. A broad band of black extending from the top of the canvas to the bottom behind the skull further reinforces the vertical axis, as do the wavy lines on the right. The skull's horns form a shorter, secondary horizontal line, creating a cross shape. At the bottom of the canvas, the black band seems to open; its expansion to the left is balanced by the rose stem in the lower right and the right-of-center rose at the top. The image overall is balanced and symmetrical, conveying a sense of stillness and repose rather than dynamic action.

The artist has not used broad or bold lines in her painting; rather, the lines of the skull and flowers are drawn delicately against the background; shading suggests contours and subtleties of lighting, and shadows blend softly. The surface is shallow and flat, conveying little sense of depth. The background material is ambiguous; is it cloth, paper, parchment, or some other material? The skull appears to float in front of this background. At the same time, the black band behind the skull seems to open into a mysterious space that recedes from the viewer.

The colors of the painting are muted, subtle, neutral—shades of black, gray, cream, and white. A slightly different color tone comes from the inside of the broken skull, where shades of tan and ochre are revealed. Within this world of muted tones, the white skull stands out rather starkly against the off-white background, and the flowers show up silvery gray against the white, beige, and black. The colors are quiet, almost somber, with a balance between the heavy black band and the other lighter-colored surfaces.

What are we to make of the image itself—a skull dressed up with cloth flowers? The animal almost appears to be eating or nuzzling one flower, and the other adorns its forehead. Many artists have used human skulls to remind us of our mortality, and in this painting suggestions of death and spirituality are reinforced, perhaps to the subconscious mind, by the cross shape that underlies the composition. In this context, the cow skull strikes an odd and discordant note. Cow skulls are often used to suggest the unforgiving nature of the desert, where animals and humans alike perish in a waterless, forbidding landscape. Here, the skull is transformed, first by its placement in an abstract setting and second by its adornment with artificial flowers. Is the image morbid, macabre? Is it humorous, playful, ironic? Or are we meant simply to see the skull in a new way, as a unique and interesting object, apart from the living animal it once was? Aged in the desert, bleached by the sun, the skull, though evocative of death, has its own stark beauty. The flowers too have their beauty; at the same time, the artist makes it clear that they are calico, not real. They are artificial, created by human hands to resemble living flowers

Although the skull and flowers are painted realistically, the ambiguous background suggests that the artist is moving toward abstraction, toward an expression of feeling and mood rather than pure representation. The overall feeling evoked by the painting is one of contemplation, meditation. Faced with the juxtaposition of these incongruous objects, we are reminded of the intimate relationships between life and death, beauty and ugliness, art and nature.

How can we augment our appreciation and understanding of this painting with contextual knowledge?

Georgia O'Keeffe grew up on a farm in Wisconsin, where she reveled in every detail of nature, bringing to it an attention and appreciation that would later be reflected in her paintings. She knew from an early age that she wanted to be an artist, and she studied art in Chicago and New York, developing a highly refined technique that quickly became recognized as uniquely her own. Among important early influences were the paintings and theories of Russian abstract artist Wassily Kandinsky, who believed that art and especially color had powerful spiritual effects. In 1929 O'Keeffe visited Taos, New Mexico, for the first time, where she became enraptured by the desert, the light, the colors of the landscape, the expanse of the sky. She was especially intrigued by bones—their form, shape, color, texture—and she shipped boxes of them back to her studio in New York to paint. Eventually she spent more and more time in the Southwest, developing a style that blends realism and abstraction. Her trademark was the selection and abstraction of an object or a view in nature, which she then transformed in accordance with her inner vision. She became known for her particular way of seeing and for her ability to enable others to see the same way.

When she painted *Cow's Skull with Calico Roses*, O'Keeffe was at a difficult time in her personal life. Perhaps depression led her to paint in subdued colors (rather than the brilliant colors of earlier and later paintings) and to focus on bones and other images of death (rather than the images of flowers for which she was already famous). Some have suggested that the seemingly suspended nature of the skull in this painting was suggestive of her own unsettled frame of mind. Whether or not personal details like these help us appreciate and understand the work, what is clear is that when we contemplate *Cow's Skull with Calico Roses,* we see not just the beauty of natural forms but also the power of nature to transform objects and the power of the artist to transform them once again.

MUSICAL ANALYSIS

Like literature and art, music has its own vocabulary, and we need to be familiar with it in order to analyze a composition. A basic distinction we can apply to music is the one between religious music, or **sacred music**—such as Gregorian chants, Masses, requiems, and hymns—and **secular music**—such as symphonies, songs, and dances. Another distinction we can make is between vocal or choral music, which is sung and generally has lyrics (words), and instrumental music, which is written for and performed on instruments.

In music, composers choose among many different **forms,** or particular structures or arrangements of elements. Symphonies, songs, concertos, string quartets, sonatas, Masses, and operas are some of the many different forms in which composers may write their music. As in literature and the visual arts, various musical forms have been more or less popular according to the styles and fashions of the time. The madrigal, for example, was a popular vocal form of the Renaissance period; the church cantata was a common form in the Baroque period; and the symphony became the most important orchestral form beginning in the eighteenth century.

Music itself is a combination of tone, tempo, and texture. **Tone** is a musical sound of definite pitch (pitch is determined by the frequency of the air waves producing the sound). A set pattern of tones (or notes) arranged from low to high (or high to low) is known as a **scale.** The modern Western scale is the familiar do, re, mi, fa, sol, la, ti, do, with half-steps in between the tones. In other cultures, more or fewer tones may be distinguished in a scale. The term *tone* can also refer to the quality of a sound. **Tempo** is the rate of speed of a musical passage, usually set or suggested by the composer. **Texture** describes the number and the nature of the voices or instruments employed and how the parts are combined. In music a theme is a characteristic musical idea upon which a composition is built or developed.

Melody is a succession of musical tones, usually having a distinctive musical shape, or line, and a definite rhythm (the recurrent alternation of accented and unaccented beats). **Harmony** is the simultaneous combination of two or more tones, producing a chord. More generally, harmony refers to the chordal characteristics of a work and the way in which chords interact with one another.

Music differs from literature and the visual arts in some important ways. First, unlike visual art, which does not change after the artist finishes it, music begins when the composition is complete. Like drama, music is lifeless until it is interpreted and performed. The written music represents the composer's intent, but the actual execution of the work is up to conductors and musicians.

A second difference is the fleeting, temporal nature of music. When we listen to live music, we hear it once and it's gone. We cannot study it like a painting or reread a passage as we can in a novel. Of course, recording devices and musical notation enable us to revisit music again and again, but by its very nature, music exists in time in a way that literature and the visual arts do not. For this reason, it is often particularly difficult to appreciate or understand a piece of music on first hearing; instead, we have to listen to it repeatedly.

Music is also more difficult to describe in words than literature or the visual arts. At best, words can only approximate, suggest, and refer to sounds. Sometimes it's helpful to use imagery from other sense modalities to describe a piece of music. What visual images does the work evoke? What colors? What textures? If you were to choreograph the work, how would the dancers move?

Finally, when we analyze a painting, we can reproduce it for our audience, and when we analyze a poem, we can reprint it. When we analyze music, we often have to hope that members of our audience know the work and can "hear" it in their heads. Alternatively, we can hope to generate enough interest in the work that they will want to make a point of hearing it themselves.

With these few basics in mind, let's consider a well-known musical work, *Rhapsody in Blue,* by George Gershwin (1898–1937). Even if you don't know this piece by name, it's very likely that you've heard it. It's been used in ads and in the sound tracks of numerous movies, including *Fantasia 2000;* it is also a standard accompaniment to images of New York City.

Imagine that you're seated in a concert hall and hearing this piece performed by a symphony orchestra (probably a "pops" orchestra, one that performs more popular classical music). When listening to a new piece of music or one you're not terribly familiar with, it's a good idea to simply try to get a sense of its general mood and character—again, focusing on the creator's intent. What emotions or ideas is the composer trying to convey? What musical elements does the composer use to execute that intent?

You'll notice, first of all, that the work is written for a small orchestra and a solo piano, the same instrumental configuration you would expect for a classical piano concerto (a concerto is a work for one or a few instruments and an orchestra, with much of its interest coming from the contrasts between the solo voice and the ensemble voice). But the opening notes of *Rhapsody in Blue* reveal something other than classical intentions: a solo clarinet begins low and sweeps up the scale in a seemingly endless "smear" of sound, finally reaching a high note, briefly holding it, and then plunging into the playful, zigzag melody that becomes one of the major themes of the work. Within moments, the orchestra enters and repeats the theme in the strings and brass, to be followed by the entry of the solo piano. Throughout the work, piano and orchestra alternate and combine to sing out beautiful melodies and create a varied and colorful texture. Variety also comes from different instrumentation of the themes and tunes, played first by a slinky muted trumpet, then by a sweet solo violin, later by a whole lush string section or a brash horn section.

You'll notice too the constant changes in tempo, now slower, now faster, almost as if the work is being improvised. Complex, syncopated, off-the-beat rhythms give the piece a jazzy feeling, and the combination of tones evokes the blues, a style of music in which certain notes are "bent," or lowered slightly in pitch, creating a particular sound and mood. The general feeling of the piece is upbeat, exciting, energetic, suggestive of a bustling city busy with people on the go. It may also make you think of Fred Astaire and Ginger Rogers movies you've seen on late-night TV—sophisticated, playful, casually elegant—and in fact, Gershwin wrote the music for some of their films.

What can we learn about this work from its title? Musical works often reveal their form in their title ("Fifth Symphony," "Violin Concerto in D," and so on). A rhapsody is a composition of irregular form with an improvisatory character. Although you may have heard themes, repetitions, and echoes in *Rhapsody in Blue,* you probably were not able to discern a regular form such as might be apparent in a classical sonata or symphony. The word *rhapsody* also suggests rapture, elation, bliss, ecstasy—perhaps the feelings conveyed by that soaring first phrase on the clarinet. *Blue,* on the other hand, suggests the melancholy of the blues. The dissonance created by the combination of the two terms—like the combinations and contrasts in the music—creates an energetic tension that arouses our curiosity and heightens our interest.

In making these observations about *Rhapsody in Blue,* we've been noticing many of the formal elements of a musical work and answering questions that can be asked about any composition: What is the form of the work? What kind of instrumentation has the composer chosen? What is the primary melodic theme of the work? What tempos are used? How do the instruments or voices work together to create the texture? What is the overall mood of the piece—joyful, sad, calm, wild, a combination?

Now, at your imaginary concert, there may be notes in the program that will provide you with some context for the work. You'll find that George Gershwin was a gifted and classically trained pianist who quit school at 15 and went to work in Tin Pan Alley, a district in New York City where popular songs were written and published. His goal in writing *Rhapsody in Blue* (1924) was to blend classical and popular music, to put the energy and style of jazz into a symphonic format. Many listeners "see" and "hear" New York City in this piece. Gershwin created his own unique idiom, a fast-paced blend of rhythm, melody, and harmony that followed certain rules of composition but gave the impression of improvisation. He went on to write musicals, more serious compositions like the opera *Porgy and Bess,* and music for Hollywood films, all in his distinctive style. Information like this can help you begin to compare *Rhapsody in Blue* both with other works of the time and with other works by Gershwin. As in any analysis, integrating the formal and the contextual rounds out your interpretation and understanding of the work.

CONCLUSION

These three brief analyses should give you some ideas about how literature, art, and music can be approached in productive ways. By taking the time to look more closely, we gain access to the great works of our culture. This statement leads us to another issue: What makes a work "great"? Why do some works of art have relevance long beyond their time, while others are forgotten soon after their designated "fifteen minutes of fame"? These questions have been debated throughout history. One answer is that great art reflects some truth of human experience that speaks to us across the centuries. The voice of Shakespeare, the paintings of Georgia O'Keeffe, the music of George Gershwin have a universal quality that doesn't depend on the styles of the time. Great art also enriches us and makes us feel that we share a little more of the human experience than we did before.

As both a student of the humanities and an audience member, you have the opportunity to appreciate and understand the arts. Despite the formal nature of academic inquiry, an aesthetic analysis is a personal endeavor. In looking closely at a creative work, seeking the creator's intent and evaluating its execution, you enrich your appreciation of the work with understanding; you bring the emotional reaction you first experienced to its intellectual completion. As twentieth-century composer Arnold Schoenberg once wrote, "You get from a work about as much as you are able to give to it yourself." This primer has been intended to help you learn how to bring more of yourself to works of art, to couple your subjective appreciation with intellectual understanding. With these tools in hand, you won't have to say you don't know much about art but you know what you like; you'll be able to say you know *about* what you like.

11 THE EARLY RENAISSANCE
Return to Classical Roots
1400–1494

Believing they had broken radically with the past, Italian artists and intellectuals in the fifteenth century began to speak of a rebirth of civilization. Since the nineteenth century, the term *Renaissance* (meaning "rebirth") has described the cultural and artistic activities of the fifteenth and sixteenth centuries that began in Italy and spread northward. The Renaissance profoundly altered the course of Western culture, although scholars have differing interpretations of the significance of this first modern period.

THE RENAISSANCE: SCHOOLS OF INTERPRETATION

In the 1860s, Swiss historian Jacob Burckhardt, agreeing with the fifteenth-century Italians, asserted that the Renaissance was a rebirth of ideas after centuries of cultural stagnation. He maintained that a new way of understanding the world had emerged, as the Italians looked back to ancient Greece and Rome for inspiration and declared themselves part of a revitalized civilization that was distinctive and superior to the immediate past.

By the mid–twentieth century, Burckhardt's interpretation began to be viewed as too simplistic. According to some scholars, the Italians, after the fall of Rome, never lost sight of their Classical roots. These historians considered the revival of learning in the fifteenth century to be more of a shift in educational and cultural emphasis than a rediscovery of antiquity. They also noted that the Renaissance had at least two phases, the Early and the High, each with different contributions.

◀ **Detail** FRA ANGELICO. *Annunciation.* 1438–1445. Fresco, 7′6″ × 10′5″. Monastery of San Marco, Florence.

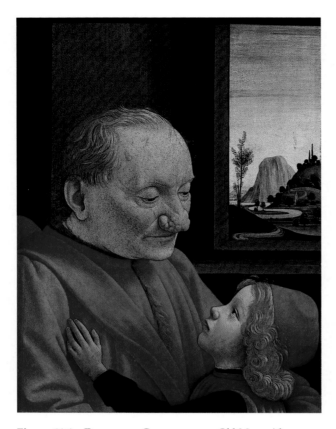

Figure 11.1 DOMENICO GHIRLANDAIO. *Old Man with a Child.* Ca. 1480. Panel, 24½ × 18″. Louvre. *This double portrait by the Florentine artist Ghirlandaio summarizes many of the new secular values of the Early Renaissance, such as its human centeredness and its preference for simple scenes. Further, the work's subject, possibly a man with his grandchild, indicates the important role that the family played in the life of the times. In addition, the age's commitment to direct observation of the physical world is evident in the treatment of the man's diseased nose (acne rosacea) and the landscape glimpsed through the open window. Finally, the painter has made the exterior scene realistic by using linear and atmospheric perspective—two new techniques invented during the period.*

Since the 1960s, a third interpretation has dominated Renaissance studies. In this view, the Renaissance label should be used cautiously and only to describe what was happening in learning and the arts, not in politics and society. The authors of this book tend to agree with this third interpretation. In politics, economics, and society, Italy in the 1400s differed little from Italy in the 1300s; however, the Italians of the 1400s did start down a new *cultural* path (Figure 11.1).

This chapter examines the first phase of this new cultural style, the Early Renaissance (1400–1494); Chapter 12 is devoted to the brief High Renaissance (1494–1520) and to Early Mannerism (1520–1564), an anti-Classical phase of the Renaissance. Chapter 13 considers Northern Humanism, the Northern Renaissance, the early-sixteenth-century religious reformations, and Late Mannerism (1564–1603), when Renaissance style was slowly undermined by new trends (Timeline 11.1).

EARLY RENAISSANCE HISTORY AND INSTITUTIONS

For most of the fifteenth century, the city-states of northern Italy were prosperous and peaceful enough to sustain upper-class artists and writers. This supportive climate encouraged the innovations of Renaissance culture. By the end of the century, however, disputes among Italy's city-states and a shift in maritime trade from the Mediterranean to the Atlantic, coupled with the French invasion of Florence in 1494, had dimmed northern Italy's cultural preeminence.

Italian City-States During the Early Renaissance

The erratic fortunes of Italy's economy were a major factor in the region's politics in this period. The northern Italian city-states had emerged from the High Middle Ages in 1300 as Europe's leading commercial center and manufacturer of finished woolens (see Chapter 9), but by 1500 they had been eclipsed by various European nations to the north. In the 1300s, Italian population, productivity, and prosperity declined because

Timeline 11.1 STAGES OF THE ITALIAN RENAISSANCE

1400		1494	1520	1600
Early Renaissance		High Renaissance	Late Renaissance	

of the Black Death and the birth of the English woolen industry. Although the Italians made a limited economic recovery in the 1400s, history was moving against them. Even their domination of international banking was challenged by German businessmen.

During the Early Renaissance, five Italian states competed for dominance: the Republic of Venice, the Duchy of Milan, the Republic of Florence, the Papal States, and the Kingdom of Naples. Other small states, such as the artistic and intellectual centers of Ferrara and Modena, played minor but crucial roles (Map 11.1). In the first half of the fifteenth century, the Italian states waged incessant wars among themselves, shifting sides when it was to their advantage.

The continuous warfare and the uncertain economy provided the conditions for the emergence of autocratic rulers called *signori,* who were from ruling families or elitist factions. Taking advantage of economic and class tensions, these autocrats pledged to solve local problems, and in so doing they proceeded to accumulate power in their own hands. What influence the guilds, business leaders, and the middle class had

wielded in the fourteenth century gave way to these despots, ending the great medieval legacy of republicanism in Venice, Milan, and Florence.

Under the *signori,* the conduct of warfare also changed. Technological developments changed weaponry, and battles were fought with mercenary troops led by *condottieri,* soldiers of fortune who sold their military expertise to the highest bidder. But the most significant change in Renaissance warfare was the emergence of diplomacy as a peaceful alternative to arms, a practice that gradually spread throughout the continent. The Italian regimes began sending representatives to other states, and it soon became customary for these diplomats to negotiate peace settlements. In turbulent fifteenth-century Italy, these agreements seldom lasted long—with the notable exception of the Peace of Lodi. This defensive pact, signed in 1454 by Milan, Florence, and Venice, established a delicate balance of power and ensured peace in Italy for forty years.

The Peace of Lodi came apart in 1494, when a French army led by Charles VIII entered Italy in the hope of promoting French monarchic ambitions.

Map 11.1   THE STATES OF ITALY DURING THE RENAISSANCE, CA. 1494

Figure 11.2 PEDRO BERRUGUETE (?). *Federico da Montefeltro and His Son Guidobaldo.* Ca. 1476–1477. Oil on panel, 4′5⅛″ × 2′5⅞″. Galleria Nazionale della Marche, Urbino. *Urbino, under the Montefeltro dynasty, was transformed from a sleepy hill town with no cultural history into a major center of Renaissance life. Federico, the founder of the dynasty and one of the greatest* condottieri *of his day, was created duke of Urbino and captain of the papal forces by Pope Sixtus IV in 1474. Federico then devoted his energies to making Urbino a model for Italian Renaissance courts. In this portrait, the seated Federico wears the armor of a papal officer while reading a book—symbols that established him as both a soldier and a scholar, later the ideal of Castiglione's* Courtier. *At the duke's right knee stands his son and heir, Guidobaldo, wearing an elaborate robe and holding a scepter, a symbol of power. Federico's dream ended with his son, the last of the Montefeltro line.*

At the Urbino court, artists combined Flemish and Italian styles, as in this double portrait. The internal lighting, emanating from some unseen source on the left, is adopted from the tradition pioneered by Jan van Eyck; the profile portrait of the duke follows the Italian practice, based on portrait heads rendered on medals. This double portrait was probably painted by Pedro Berruguete, Spain's first great Renaissance artist, who studied painting in Naples and worked briefly in Urbino before returning to his homeland.

Outside Italy, three events further weakened the region's prospects for regaining its position as a major economic power: the fall of Constantinople in 1453, Portugal's opening of the sea route around Africa to India at the end of the century, and Columbus's Spanish-sponsored voyage to the New World.

These three events shifted the focus of international trade from the Mediterranean to the Atlantic. The fall of Constantinople to the Ottoman Turks in 1453 temporarily closed the eastern Mediterranean markets to the Italian city-states. At the same time, by virtue of the wide-ranging global explorations they sponsored, some European powers—most notably Portugal and Spain—were extending their political and economic interests beyond the geographical limits of continental Europe.

Before the Italian city-states were eclipsed by other European powers, however, upper-class families enjoyed unprecedented wealth, which they used to cultivate their tastes in literature and art and thus substantially determine the culture of the Early Renaissance (Figure 11.2). One reason for the importance these families gave to cultural matters is that they put high value on family prestige and on educating their sons for their predestined roles as head of the family business and their daughters as loyal wives and successful household managers. The courts of the local rulers, or *grandi,* became places where educated men—and, on occasion, women—could exchange ideas and discuss philosophical issues.

Although the status of women did not improve appreciably, more were educated than ever before. Many ended up behind the walls of a convent, however, if their parents could not afford the costly dowry expected of an upper-class bride (Figure 11.3). The few upper-class women with an independent role in society were those who had been widowed young. The women at the ducal courts who exercised any political influence did so because of their family alliances. One of the most powerful of these women was Lucrezia Borgia [loo-KRET-syah BOR-juh] (1480–1519), the illegitimate daughter of Pope Alexander VI. Married three times before the age of twenty-one, she held court in Ferrara and was the patron of many writers and artists. Most women who tried to exercise real power, however, found it unattainable.

Florence, the Center of the Renaissance

Amid the artistic and intellectual activity occurring throughout Italy, Florence, the capital of the Tuscan region, was the most prominent of the city-states. After 1300 Florence's political system went through three phases, evolving from republic to oligarchy to family

Figure 11.3 GIOVANNI TOSCANI. *The Palli* Cassone *(Chest)*. Ca. 1430. Bargello, Florence. *Richly decorated cassoni, or wedding chests, which held a prospective bride's clothing and linens, became a popular piece of furniture among wealthy Italian families. The painted panel on this* cassone *illustrates the annual procession of the Feast of John the Baptist and shows Florentine nobles carrying banners, or "palli," emblazoned with coats of arms and guild emblems, toward the Florentine Baptistery (on the left). The chest embodies the Florentine ethos of family, city, and church.*

rule. During these turbulent political times, however, Florentine artists and writers made their city-state the center of the Early Renaissance (Timeline 11.2).

The republic, which began in the fourteenth century with hopes for political equality, fell into the hands of a wealthy oligarchy. This oligarchy, composed of rich bankers, merchants, and successful guildsmen and craftsmen, ruled until the early fifteenth century, when the Medici family gained control. The Medicis dominated Florentine politics and cultural life from 1434 to 1494, sometimes functioning as despots.

The Medicis rose from modest circumstances. Giovanni di Bicci de' Medici [jo-VAHN-nee dee BEET-chee day MED-uh-chee] (1360–1429) amassed the family's first large fortune through banking and close financial ties with the papacy. His son Cosimo (1389–1464) added to the Medicis' wealth and outmaneuvered his political enemies, becoming the unacknowledged ruler of Florence. He spent his money on books, painting, sculptures, and palaces, and, claiming to be the common man's friend, he was eventually awarded the title *Pater patriae*, Father of His Country—a Roman title revived during the Renaissance.

Cosimo's son, Piero, ruled for only a short time and was succeeded by his son Lorenzo (1449–1492), called the Magnificent because of his grand style of living.

Timeline 11.2   THE EARLY RENAISSANCE IN FLORENCE, 1400–1494

1400							1494
			Early Renaissance				
1403–1424 Ghiberti's north doors, Florentine Baptistery	**1425** Invention of linear perspective (Brunelleschi)	**1429–1437** Ghiberti's east doors, Florentine Baptistery	**1438–1445** Fra Angelico's *Annunciation*	**1461** Completion of Pazzi Chapel by Brunelleschi	**1473–1475** Verrocchio's *David*	**1480s** Botticelli's *Primavera* and *The Birth of Venus*	**1483** Leonardo da Vinci's *The Virgin of the Rocks*
	1425–1428 Masaccio's frescoes for Santa Maria Novella	**1430–1432** Donatello's *David*		**1462** Founding of Platonic Academy, Florence			
		1435 Alberti's *On Painting*					

Lorenzo and his brother Giuliano controlled Florence until Giuliano was assassinated in 1478 by the Pazzi family, rivals of the Medicis. Lorenzo brutally executed the conspirators and then governed autocratically for the next fourteen years.

Within two years of Lorenzo's death, the great power and prestige of Florence began to weaken. Two events are symptomatic of this decline in Florentine authority. The first was the invasion by Charles VIII's French army in 1494. The invasion initiated a political and cultural decline that would eventually overtake Italy, whose small city-states could not withstand the incursions of the European monarchies. The French army drove the Medici family from Florence; they remained in exile until 1512.

The second event was the iconoclastic crusade against the city led by the Dominican monk Fra Savonarola [sav-uh-nuh-ROH-luh] (1452–1498). He opposed the Medicis' rule and wanted to restore a republican form of government. In his fire-and-brimstone sermons, he denounced Florence's leaders and the city's infatuation with the arts. He eventually ran afoul of the papacy and was excommunicated and publicly executed, but not before he had had an enormous effect on the citizens—including the painter Botticelli, who is said to have burned some of his paintings while under the sway of Savonarola's reforming zeal.

The Resurgent Papacy, 1450–1500

The Great Schism was ended by the Council of Constance in 1418, and a tattered Christendom reunited under a Roman pope (see Chapter 10). By 1447 the so-called Renaissance popes were back in command and had turned their attention to consolidating the Papal States and pursuing power. Like the secular despots, these popes engaged in war and, when that failed, diplomacy. They brought artistic riches to the church but also lowered its moral tone by accepting bribes for church offices and filling positions with kinsmen. But above all, these popes patronized Renaissance culture.

Three of the most aggressive and successful of these church rulers were Nicholas V (pope 1447–1455), Pius II (pope 1458–1464), and Sixtus IV (pope 1471–1484). Nicholas V, who had been librarian for Cosimo de' Medici, founded the Vatican Library, an institution virtually unrivaled for its holdings of manuscripts and books. He also continued the rebuilding of Rome begun by his predecessors. Pius II, often considered the most representative of the Renaissance popes because of his interest in the Greek and Roman classics and in writing poetry himself, rose rapidly through the ecclesiastical ranks. This clever politician practiced both war and diplomacy with astounding success. As a student of the new learning and as a brilliant writer in Latin, Pius II attracted intellectuals and artists to Rome. His personal recollections, or *Commentaries,* reveal much about him and his turbulent times.

Sixtus IV came from the powerful and scheming della Rovere family, and he increased his personal power through nepotism, the practice of giving offices to relatives. He continued the papal tradition of making Rome the most beautiful city in the world. The construction of the Sistine Chapel, later adorned with paintings by Botticelli and Michelangelo, was his greatest achievement (see Chapter 12).

THE SPIRIT AND STYLE OF THE EARLY RENAISSANCE

Drawing inspiration from ancient Greek and Roman models, the thinkers and the artists of the Early Renaissance explored such perennial questions as, What is human nature? How are human beings related to God? and What is the best way to achieve human happiness? Although they did not reject Christian explanations outright, they were intrigued by the secular and humanistic values of the Greco-Roman tradition and the answers they might provide to these questions. They also rightfully claimed kinship with certain fourteenth-century predecessors such as the writer Petrarch and the artist Giotto (see Chapter 10).

Those artists, scholars, and writers who are identified with the Early Renaissance and who embodied its spirit were linked, through shared tastes and patronage, with the entrepreneurial nobility, the progressive middle class, and the secular clergy. Until about 1450, most artistic works were commissioned by wealthy patrons for family chapels in churches and for public buildings; later, patrons commissioned paintings and sculptures for their private dwellings.

Even though artists, scholars, and writers stamped this age with their fresh perspectives, some of the old cultural traits remained. Unsettling secular values emerged in the midst of long-accepted religious beliefs, creating contradictions and tensions within the society. In other ways, however, the past held firm, and certain values seemed immune to change. For example, Early Renaissance thought made little headway in science, and church patronage still strongly affected the evolution of the arts and architecture, despite the growing impact of the urban class on artistic tastes.

The artists, scholars, and writers who flourished in the Early Renaissance were almost exclusively men, in contrast with the Middle Ages, when women occasionally played cultural roles. Recent scholarship has pointed out that women living in the Italian Renaissance were subjected to new constraints, especially in well-to-do families. For example, the learned Laura Cereta [che-RAY-tah], daughter of a physician in Brescia, was silenced at eighteen years of age for her outspokenness, though not before she had published a defense of herself, asserting the right of women to be educated the same as men.

Humanism, Scholarship, and Schooling

Toward the end of the 1300s, Italy's educated circles became fascinated by ancient Roman civilization. Inspired by Petrarch's interest in Latin literature and language, scholars began to collect and translate Roman manuscripts uncovered in monastic libraries and other out-of-the-way depositories. There was a shift in emphasis from the church Latin of the Middle Ages to the pure Latin style of Cicero, the first-century B.C. Roman writer whose eloquent essays established a high moral and literary standard.

In the 1400s, these scholars spoke of their literary interests and new learning as **studia humanitatis.** They defined this term, which may be translated as humanistic studies, as a set of intellectual pursuits that included moral philosophy, history, grammar, rhetoric, and poetry. At first, the men who studied these disciplines read the appropriate works in Latin, but after the Greek originals began to appear about 1400 and the study of ancient languages spread, they learned from the Greek texts as well.

In response to the demand for humanistic learning, new schools sprang up in most Italian city-states. In these schools was born the Renaissance ideal of an education intended to free or to liberate the mind—a liberal education. To that end, study was based on the recently recovered Latin and Greek works rather than on the more narrowly defined curriculum of scholasticism and Aristotelianism that had been favored in the Middle Ages.

The first Renaissance scholars, who were primarily searching for original Latin manuscripts, were philologists—that is, experts in the study of languages and linguistics. In time, they came to call themselves humanists because of their training in the *studia humanitatis.* These early humanists created a branch of learning, now called textual criticism, that compares various versions of a text to determine which one is most correct or authentic. They recognized that knowledge of the evolution of language was necessary to make a critical judgment on the authenticity of a text. As a result of their studies, they revealed writing errors committed by medieval monks when they copied ancient manuscripts—revelations that, in the case of religious documents, raised grave problems for the church.

The most spectacular application of textual criticism was made by Lorenzo Valla (1406–1457), who exposed the Donation of Constantine as a forgery. Throughout the Middle Ages, this famous document had been cited by the popes as proof of their political authority over Christendom. By the terms of the document, the Roman emperor Constantine gave the popes his western lands and recognized their power to rule in them. But by comparing the Latin of the fourth century, when Constantine reigned, with the Latin of the eighth century, when the document first came to light, Valla concluded that the Donation must have been produced then and not in the fourth century.

Other humanists played an active role in the life of their states, modeling themselves on the heroes of the Roman republic. Outstanding among them is Leonardo Bruni (1374–1444), who typifies the practical, civic humanist. A one-time chancellor, or chief secretary, of Florence's governing body, or *signoria*, Bruni also worked for both the Medicis and the papacy and wrote the *History of the Florentine People.* This work reflected his humanistic values, combining as it did his political experience with his knowledge of ancient history. To Bruni, the study of history illuminated contemporary events. Bruni and the other civic humanists, through their writings and their governmental service, set an example for later generations of Florentines and helped infuse them with love of their city. Moreover, by expanding the concept of humanistic studies, they contributed new insights into the ongoing debate about the role of the individual in history and in the social order.

An important consequence of humanistic studies was the rise of educational reforms. Vittorino da Feltre [veet-toe-REE-no dah FEL-tray] (1378–1446) made the most significant contributions. Vittorino favored a curriculum that exercised the body and the mind—the ideal of the ancient Greek schools. His educational theories were put into practice at the school he founded in Mantua at the ruler's request. At this school, called the Happy House, Vittorino included humanistic studies along with the medieval curriculum. A major innovation was the stress on physical exercise, which arose from his emphasis on moral training. At first, only the sons and daughters of Mantuan nobility attended his school, but gradually the student body became more democratic as young people from all classes were enrolled. Vittorino's reforms were slowly introduced into the new urban schools in northern Europe, and their model—the well-rounded student of sound body, solid learning, and high morals—helped to lay the foundation for future European schools and education.

PERSONAL PERSPECTIVE

Laura Cereta
Defense of the Liberal Instruction of Women

In this letter, dated January 13, 1488, the young Laura Cereta responds fiercely to a critic who admired her writing by wondering how it could possibly be the work of a woman.

My ears are wearied by your carping. You brashly and publicly not merely wonder but indeed lament that I am said to possess as fine a mind as nature ever bestowed upon the most learned man. You seem to think that so learned a woman has scarcely before been seen in the world. You are wrong on both counts. . . .

I would have been silent, believe me, if that savage old enmity of yours had attacked me alone. . . . But I cannot tolerate your having attacked my entire sex. For this reason my thirsty soul seeks revenge, my sleeping pen is aroused to literary struggle, raging anger stirs mental passions long chained by silence. With just cause I am moved to demonstrate how great a reputation for learning and virtue women have won by their inborn excellence, manifested in every age as knowledge. . . .

Only the question of the rarity of outstanding women remains to be addressed. The explanation is clear: women have been able by nature to be exceptional, but have chosen lesser goals. For some women are concerned with parting their hair correctly, adorning themselves with lovely dresses, or decorating their fingers with pearls and other gems. Others delight in mouthing carefully composed phrases, indulging in dancing, or managing spoiled puppies. Still others wish to gaze at lavish banquet tables, to rest in sleep, or, standing at mirrors, to smear their lovely faces. But those in whom a deeper integrity yearns for virtue, restrain from the start their youthful souls, reflect on higher things, harden the body with sobriety and trials, and curb their tongues, open their ears, compose their thoughts in wakeful hours, their minds in contemplation, to letters bonded to righteousness. For knowledge is not given as a gift, but [is gained] with diligence. The free mind, not shirking effort, always soars zealously toward the good, and the desire to know grows ever more wide and deep. It is because of no special holiness, therefore, that we [women] are rewarded by God the Giver with the gift of exceptional talent. Nature has generously lavished its gifts upon all people, opening to all the doors of choice through which reason sends envoys to the will, from which they learn and convey its desires. The will must choose to exercise the gift of reason. . . .

I have been praised too much; showing your contempt for women, you pretend that I alone am admirable because of the good fortune of my intellect. . . . Do you suppose, O most contemptible man on earth, that I think myself sprung [like Athena] from the head of Jove? I am a school girl, possessed of the sleeping embers of an ordinary mind. Indeed I am too hurt, and my mind, offended, too swayed by passions, sighs, tormenting itself, conscious of the obligation to defend my sex. For absolutely everything—that which is within us and that which is without—is made weak by association with my sex.

Thought and Philosophy

The Italian humanists were not satisfied with medieval answers to the perennial inquiries of philosophy because those answers did not go beyond Aristotelian philosophy and Christian dogma. Casting their nets wider, the Renaissance thinkers concluded that the ancients had given worthwhile responses to many of the same issues as Christians and that they should not be dismissed simply because they were non-Christian.

Renaissance scholars came to advocate more tolerance toward unorthodox beliefs and began to focus on the important role played by the individual in society. Individual fulfillment became a leading Renaissance idea and remains a central notion in Western thought today. During the Renaissance, the growing emphasis on the individual resulted in a more optimistic assessment of human nature—a development that in time led to a rejection of Christianity's stress on original sin.

After the fall of Constantinople in 1453 and the flight of Byzantine scholars bearing precious manuscripts, the humanists began to focus increasingly on Greek literature, language, and, in particular, philosophy. The philosophy of Plato found a home in Italy in 1462 when Cosimo de' Medici established the Platonic Academy at one of his villas near Florence. Here, scholars gathered to examine and to discuss the writings of Plato as well as the Neo-Platonists, whose reinterpreted Platonism had influenced early Christian theology. The academy was under the direction of the brilliant humanist Marsilio Ficino [mar-SILL-e-o fe-CHEE-no] (1433–1499), whom Cosimo commissioned to translate Plato's works into Latin.

In two major treatises, Ficino made himself the leading voice of Florentine Neo-Platonism by harmonizing Platonic ideas with Christian teachings. Believing that

Figure 11.4   SANDRO BOTTICELLI. *The Birth of Venus.* 1480s. Tempera on canvas, 5'8" × 9'1". Uffizi Gallery, Florence. *With the paintings of Botticelli, the nude female form reappeared in Western art for the first time since the Greco-Roman period. Botticelli's Venus contains many Classical echoes, such as the goddess's lovely features and her modest pose. But the artist used these pre-Christian images to convey a Christian message and to embody the principles of Ficino's Neo-Platonist philosophy.*

Platonism came from God, Ficino began with the principle that both thought systems rested on divine authority. Like Plato, Ficino believed that the soul was immortal and that complete enjoyment of God would be possible only in the afterlife, when the soul was in the divine realm. Ficino also revived the Platonic notion of free will. In Ficino's hands, free will became the source of human dignity because human beings were able to choose to love God.

Ficino had the most powerful impact on the Early Renaissance when he made Plato's teaching on love central to Neo-Platonism. Following Platonism, he taught that love is a divine gift that binds all human beings together. Love expresses itself in human experience by the desire for and the appreciation of beauty in its myriad forms. Platonic love, like erotic love, is aroused first by the physical appearance of the beloved. But Platonic love, dissatisfied by mere physical enjoyment, cannot rest until it moves upward to the highest spiritual level, where it finally meets its goal of union with the Divine. Under the promptings of Platonism, the human form became a metaphor of the soul's desire for God. Many Renaissance writers and artists came under the influence of Ficino's Neo-Platonism, embracing its principles and embodying them in their works. Sandro Botticelli, for example, created several allegorical paintings in which divine love and beauty were represented by an image from pre-Christian Rome—Venus, goddess of love (Figure 11.4).

Ficino's most prized student, Pico della Mirandola [PEE-koh DAYL-lah me-RAHN-do-lah] (1463–1494), surpassed his master's accomplishments by the breadth of his learning and the virtuosity of his mind. Pico—a wealthy and charming aristocrat—impressed everyone with his command of languages, his range of knowledge, and his spirited arguments. His goal was the synthesis of Platonism and Aristotelianism within a Christian framework that also encompassed Hebraic, Arabic, and Persian ideas. Church authorities and traditional scholars attacked Pico's efforts once they grasped the implication of his ambitious project—that all knowledge shared basic common truths and that Christians could benefit from studying non-Western, non-Christian writings.

Pico's second important contribution—the concept of individual worth—had been foreshadowed by Ficino. Pico's *Oration on the Dignity of Man* gives the highest expression to this idea, which is inherent in the humanist tradition. According to Pico, human beings, endowed with reason and speech, are created as a microcosm of the universe. Set at the midpoint in the scale of God's creatures, they are blessed with free will—the power to make of themselves what they wish—which enables them either to raise themselves to God or to sink lower than the beasts. This liberty to determine private fate makes human beings the masters of their individual destinies and, at the same time, focuses attention on each human being as the measure of all things—a Classical belief now reborn.

Architecture, Sculpture, and Painting

It was in architecture, sculpture, and painting that the Renaissance made its most dramatic break with the medieval past. The **Early Renaissance style** was launched in Florence by artists who wanted to make a complete break with the Late Gothic style (Figure 11.5). Led by the architect Filippo Brunelleschi [bru-nayl-LAYS-kee] (1377–1446), this group studied the ruins of Classical buildings and ancient works of sculpture to unlock the secrets of their harmonious style. They believed that once the Classical ideals were rescued from obscurity, new works could be fashioned that captured the spirit of ancient art and architecture without slavishly copying it.

Artistic Ideals and Innovations   Guided by Brunelleschi's findings, architects, sculptors, and painters made the Classical principles of balance, simplicity, and restraint the central ideals of the Early Renaissance style. The heaviest debt to the past was owed by the architects, for they revived the Classical orders—the Doric, the Ionic, and the Corinthian. The new buildings, though constructed to accommodate modern needs, were symmetrical in plan and relied on simple decorative designs. The theoretician of Early Renaissance style and its other guiding light was Leone Battista Alberti [ahl-BAIR-tee] (1404–1472), who wrote at length on Brunelleschi's innovations and published a highly influential book on the new painting. Alberti believed

Figure 11.5   LEONE BATTISTA ALBERTI. Tempio Malatestiano (Malatesta Temple) (Church of San Francesco). Ca. 1450. Rimini, Italy. *Although unfinished, this church strikingly demonstrates the revolution in architecture represented by Early Renaissance ideals. Nothing could be further from the spires of Late Gothic cathedrals than this simple, symmetrical structure with its plain facade, post-and-lintel entrance, rounded arches, and Classical columns. Designed by the leading theoretician of the new style, the Malatesta Temple served as a model for artists and architects of the later Renaissance.*

that architecture should embody the humanistic qualities of dignity, balance, control, and harmony and that a building's ultimate beauty rested on the mathematical harmony of its separate parts.

Sculpture and painting, freed from their subordination to architecture, regained their ancient status as independent art forms and in time became the most cherished of the visual arts. Renaissance sculptors and painters aspired to greater realism than had been achieved in the Gothic style, seeking to depict human musculature and anatomy with a greater degree of credibility. Sculptors, led by this period's genius Donatello [dah-nah-TEL-lo] (about 1386–1466), revived Classical practices that had not been seen in the West for more than a thousand years: the free-standing figure; the technique of contrapposto, or a figure balanced with most of the weight resting on one leg (see Figure 3.22); the life-size nude statue; and the equestrian statue.

Whereas architecture and sculpture looked back to ancient Greek and Roman traditions, developments in painting grew from late medieval sources. In the early fourteenth century, Giotto had founded a new realistic and expressive style (see Chapter 10), on which Florentine painters began to build at the opening of the fifteenth century. Much of Giotto's genius lay in his ability to show perspective, or the appearance of spatial depth, in his frescoes, an illusion he achieved largely through the placement of the figures (see Figure 10.19). Approximately one hundred years after Giotto, painters learned to enhance the realism of their pictures by the use of linear perspective, the most significant artistic innovation of the age.

The invention of linear perspective was another of Brunelleschi's accomplishments. Using principles of architecture and optics, he conducted experiments in 1425 that provided the mathematical basis for achieving the illusion of depth on a two-dimensional surface (and, coincidentally, contributed to the enhancement of the status of the arts by grounding them in scholarly learning). Brunelleschi's solution to the problem of linear perspective was to organize the picture space around the center point, or **vanishing point.** After determining the painting's vanishing point, he devised a structural grid for placing objects in precise relation to each other within the picture space. He also computed the ratios by which objects diminish in size as they recede from view, so that pictorial reality seems to correspond visually with physical accuracy. He then subjected the design to a mirror test—checking its truthfulness in its reflected image.

When the camera appeared in the nineteenth century, it was discovered that the photographic lens "saw" nature according to Brunelleschi's mathematical rules. After the 1420s, Brunelleschi's studies led to the concept of Renaissance space, the notion that a composition should be viewed from one single position. For four hundred years, or until first challenged by Manet in the nineteenth century, linear perspective and Renaissance space played a leading role in Western painting (see Chapter 18).

A second type of perspective, atmospheric or aerial, was perfected by painters north of the Alps in the first half of the fifteenth century, although the Italian painter Masaccio was the first to revive atmospheric perspective in the 1420s, based on the Roman tradition. Through the use of colors, these artists created an illusion of depth by subtly diminishing the tones as the distance between the eye and the object increased; at the horizon line, the colors become grayish and the objects blurry in appearance. When atmospheric perspective was joined to linear perspective, as happened later in the century, a greater illusion of reality was achieved than was possible with either type used independently.

Again commenting on the innovations of Brunelleschi was Alberti, who published a treatise in 1435 that elaborated on the mathematical aspects of painting and set forth brilliantly the humanistic and secular values of the Early Renaissance. Alberti was an aristocratic humanist with both a deep knowledge of Classicism and a commitment to its ideals. In his treatise, he praised master painters in rousing terms, comparing their creativity to God's—a notion that would have been considered blasphemous by medieval thinkers. He asserted that paintings, in addition to pleasing the eye, should appeal to the mind with optical and mathematical accuracy. But paintings, he went on, should also present a noble subject, such as a Classical hero, and should be characterized by a small number of figures, by carefully observed and varied details, by graceful poses, by harmonious relationships among all elements, and by a judicious use of colors. These Classical ideals were quickly adopted by Florentine artists eager to establish a new aesthetic code.

Architecture   In the High Middle Ages, most architects were stonemasons and were regarded as artisans, like shoemakers or potters. But by the fifteenth century, the status of architects had changed. Because of the newly discovered scientific aspects of their craft, the leading architects were now grouped with those practicing the learned professions of medicine and law. By 1450 Italian architects had freed architecture from Late Gothicism, as well as from the other arts. Unlike Gothic cathedrals adorned with sculptures and paintings, these new buildings drew on the Classical tradition for whatever simple decorative details were needed. This transformation became the most visible symbol of Early Renaissance architecture.

Although Brunelleschi established the new standards in architecture, most of his buildings have been either destroyed or altered considerably by later hands. However, the earliest work to bring him fame still survives in Florence largely as he had planned it— the dome of the city's cathedral (Figure 11.6). Although the rest of the cathedral—nave, transept, and choir— was finished before 1400, no one had been able to devise a method for erecting the projected dome until Brunelleschi received the commission in 1420. Using the learning he had gained from his researches in Rome as well as his knowledge of Gothic building styles, he developed an ingenious plan for raising the dome, which was virtually completed in 1436.

Faced with a domical base of 140 feet, Brunelleschi realized that a hemispheric dome in the Roman manner, like the dome of the Pantheon, would not work (see Figure 5.14). Traditional building techniques could not span the Florentine cathedral's vast domical base, nor could the cathedral's walls be buttressed to support a massive dome. So he turned to Gothic methods, using diagonal ribs based on the pointed arch. This innovative dome had a double shell of two relatively thin walls held together by twenty-four stone ribs, of which only eight are visible. His crowning touch was to add a lantern that sits atop the dome and locks the ribs into place (Figure 11.7). The dome's rounded windows echo the openings in the upper nave walls, thereby ensuring that his addition

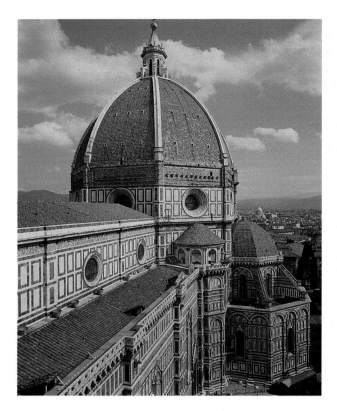

Figure 11.6 FILIPPO BRUNELLESCHI. Cathedral Dome, Florence. 1420–1436. Ht. of dome from floor 367′. *After the dome of the Florence cathedral was erected according to Brunelleschi's plan, another architect was employed to add small galleries in the area above the circular windows. But the Florentine authorities halted his work before the galleries were fully installed, leaving the structure in its present state.*

Figure 11.7 FILIPPO BRUNELLESCHI. Design for Construction of Dome of Florence Cathedral. *Brunelleschi designed the dome of the Florence cathedral with an inner and an outer shell, both of which are attached to the eight ribs of the octagonal-shaped structure. Sixteen smaller ribs, invisible from the outside, were placed between the shells to give added support. What held these elements together and gave them stability was the lantern, based on his design, that was anchored to the dome's top sometime after 1446.*

would harmonize with the existing elements. But the octagonal-shaped dome was Brunelleschi's own creation and expresses a logical, even inevitable, structure. Today, the cathedral still dominates the skyline of Florence, a lasting symbol of Brunelleschi's creative genius.

Brunelleschi's most representative building is the Pazzi Chapel, as the chapter house, or meeting room, of the monks of Santa Croce is called. This small church embodies the harmonious proportions and Classical features that are the hallmark of the Early Renaissance style. In his architectural plan, Brunelleschi centered a dome over an oblong area whose width equals the dome's diameter and whose length is twice its width and then covered each of the chapel's elongated ends with a barrel vault. Double doors opened into the center wall on one long side, and two rounded arch windows flanked this doorway. A loggia, or porch, which Brunelleschi may not have designed, preceded the entrance (Figure 11.8). Inside the chapel, following the Classical rules of measure and proportion, Brunelleschi employed medallions, rosettes, **pilasters** (or applied columns), and square panels. In addition to these Classical details, the rounded arches and the bar-

rel vaults further exemplify the new Renaissance style (Figure 11.9). His Classical theories were shared by Florence's humanist elite, who found religious significance in mathematical harmony. Both they and Brunelleschi believed that a well-ordered building such as the Pazzi Chapel mirrored God's plan of the universe.

The other towering figure in Early Renaissance architecture was Alberti. Despite the influence of his ideas, which dominated architecture until 1600, no completed building based on his design remains. A splendid unfinished effort is the Tempio Malatestiano in Rimini (see Figure 11.5), a structure that replaced the

Figure 11.8 (Inset), FILIPPO BRUNELLESCHI AND OTHERS. Exterior, Pazzi Chapel, Santa Croce Church. 1433–1461. Florence. *The Pazzi Chapel's harmonious facade reflects the Classical principles of the Early Renaissance style: symmetry and simplicity. By breaking the rhythm of the facade with the rounded arch, the architect emphasizes its surface symmetry so that the left side is a mirror image of the right side. Simplicity is achieved in the architectural decorations, which are either Greco-Roman devices or mathematically inspired divisions.*

Figure 11.9 FILIPPO BRUNELLESCHI. Interior. Pazzi Chapel, Santa Croce Church. Ca. 1433–1461. 59′9″ long × 35′8″ wide. Florence. *Decorations on the white walls of the Pazzi Chapel's interior break up its plain surface and draw the viewer's eye to the architectural structure: pilasters, window and panel frames, medallions, capitals, and dome ribs. The only non-architecturally related decorations are the terra-cotta sculptures by Luca della Robbia of the four evangelists and the Pazzi family coat of arms, mounted inside the medallions.*

Figure 11.10 DONATELLO. *The Feast of Herod.* Ca. 1425. Gilt bronze, 23½″ square. Baptismal font, San Giovanni, Siena. *The first low-relief sculpture executed in the Early Renaissance style,* The Feast of Herod *is a stunning example of the power of this new approach to art. Its theatrical force arises from the successful use of linear perspective and the orderly placement of the figures throughout the three rooms.*

existing church of San Francesco. Rimini's despot, Sigismondo Malatesta, planned to have himself, his mistress, and his court buried in the refurbished structure, and he appointed Alberti to supervise the church's reconstruction.

Alberti's monument represents the first modern attempt to give a Classical exterior to a church. Abandoning the Gothic pointed arch, he designed this church's unfinished facade with its three rounded arches after a nearby triumphal arch. He framed the arches with Corinthian columns, one of his favorite decorative devices. Although the architect apparently planned to cover the church's interior with a dome

Figure 11.11 DONATELLO. *David.* Ca. 1430–1432. Bronze, ht. 62¼″. Bargello, Florence. *The David and Goliath story was often allegorized into a prophecy of Christ's triumph over Satan. But Donatello's sculpture undermines such an interpretation, for his* David *is less a heroic figure than a provocative image of refined sensuality, as suggested by the undeveloped but elegant body, the dandified pose, and the incongruous boots and hat. Donatello's* David *is a splendid modern portrayal of youthful male power, self-aware and poised on the brink of manhood.*

comparable to Brunelleschi's on the Florentine cathedral, Malatesta's fortunes failed, and the projected temple had to be abandoned. Nevertheless, Alberti's unfinished church was admired by later builders and helped to point the way to the new Renaissance architecture.

Sculpture   Like architecture, sculpture blossomed in Florence in the early 1400s. Donatello, the leader of the sculptural revival, was imbued with Classical ideals but obsessed with realism. He used a variety of techniques—expressive gestures, direct observation, and mathematical precision—to reproduce what his eyes saw. Donatello accompanied Brunelleschi to Rome to study ancient art, and he adapted linear perspective as early as 1425 into a small **relief** called *The Feast of Herod* (Figure 11.10).

The subject is the tragic end of John the Baptist, Florence's patron saint, as recounted in Mark 6:20–29. In Donatello's square bronze panel, the saint's severed head is being displayed on a dish to King Herod at the left, while the scorned Salome stands near the right end of the table. A puzzled guest leans toward the ruler, who recoils with upraised hands; two children at the left back away from the bloody head; and a diner leans back from the center of the table—all depicted under the rounded arches of the new Brunelleschian architecture. The sculpture's rich details and use of linear perspective point up the horror of the scene and thus achieve the heightened realism that was among the artistic goals of this era. The scene's vanishing point runs through the middle set of arches, so that the leaning motions of the two figures in the foreground not only express their inner turmoil but also cause them to fall away from the viewer's line of sight.

Donatello also revived the free-standing male nude, one of the supreme expressions of ancient art. Donatello's bronze *David*, probably executed for Cosimo de' Medici, portrays David standing with his left foot on the severed head of the Philistine warrior Goliath—a pose based on the biblical story (Figure 11.11). This sculpture had a profound influence on later sculptors, who admired Donatello's creation but produced rival interpretations of David (Figure 11.12). Donatello and his successors used the image of David to pay homage to male power—a major preoccupation of Renaissance artists and intellectuals.

Like other Renaissance masters, Donatello owed debts to Classical artists, but he also challenged them by adapting their principles to his own times. For example, the Roman statue of Marcus Aurelius (see Figure 5.11) inspired Donatello's bronze called the *Gattamelata,* the first successful equestrian sculpture in over twelve hundred years (Figure 11.13). As Donatello's *David* portrays the subtleties of adolescent male beauty, his *Gattamelata* pays homage to mature mas-

Figure 11.12   ANDREA DEL VERROCCHIO. *David.* 1473–1475. Bronze, ht. 4′ 2″. Bargello, Florence. *Verrocchio's* David *inaugurated the tradition in Renaissance Florence of identifying the Jewish giant-killer with the city's freedom-loving spirit. A masterpiece of bravado, Verrocchio's boyish hero stands challengingly over the severed head of Goliath. In its virility, this work surpasses the sculpture that inspired it, Donatello's* David *(see Figure 11.11). Florence's ruling council liked Verrocchio's statue so much that they placed it in the Palazzo Vecchio, the seat of government, where it remained until Michelangelo's* David *(see Figure 12.19) displaced it.*

culine power. This work honored the memory of Erasmo da Narni, a Venetian *condottiere* nicknamed Gattamelata, or "Honey Cat." The warrior's pose resembles the Roman imperial style, but in almost every other way, the sculptor violates the harmonious ideas of ancient art.

Most significant, the rider's face owes its sharp realism—firm jawline, bushy eyebrows, widely set eyes, and close-cropped hair—to fifteenth-century sources, especially to the cult of the ugly, an aesthetic attitude that claimed to find moral strength in coarse features that did not conform to the Classical ideals (Figure

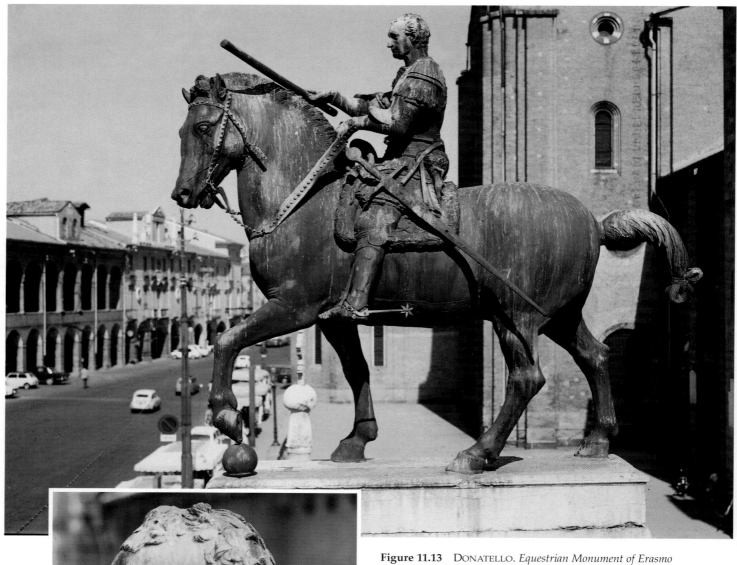

Figure 11.13 DONATELLO. *Equestrian Monument of Erasmo da Narni, Called "Gattamelata."* 1447–1453. Bronze, approx. 11 × 13'. Piazza del Santo, Padua. *This equestrian statue of the* condottiere *was funded by his family but authorized by a grateful Venetian senate in honor of his military exploits. Conceiving of the dead military leader as a "triumphant Caesar," Donatello dressed him in Classical costume and decorated his saddle and armor with many allusions to antique art, such as flying cupids and victory depicted as a goddess.*

Figure 11.14 DONATELLO. Detail of *"Gattamelata."* 1447–1453. Piazza del Santo, Padua. *Donatello deliberately designed the monument's stern, deeply lined, and serious face to conform to the Renaissance ideal of a strong military commander.*

11.14). Since this work was commissioned after the hero's death and since Donatello had no way of knowing how the soldier looked, he sculptured the face to conform to his notion of a strong-minded general. The massive horse, with flaring nostrils, open mouth, and lifted foreleg, seems to be an extension of the soldier's forceful personality.

The only serious rival to Donatello in the Early Renaissance was another Florentine, Lorenzo Ghiberti [gee-BAIR-tee] (about 1381–1455), who slowly adapted to the new style of art. In 1401 he defeated Brunelleschi in a competition to select a sculptor for the north doors

Figure 11.15 LORENZO GHIBERTI. *The Annunciation.* Panel from the north doors of the Baptistery. 1403–1424. Gilt bronze, 20½ × 17¾". Florence. *Ghiberti's rendition of the Annunciation was typical of his panels on the north doors. Mary and the angel are placed in the shallow foreground and are modeled almost completely in the round. The background details, including a sharply foreshortened representation of God on the left, are scarcely raised from the metal. The contrast between these design elements enhances the illusion of depth.*

of Florence's Baptistery. The north doors consist of twenty-eight panels, arranged in four columns of seven panels, each depicting a New Testament scene. These doors, completed between 1403 and 1424, show Ghiberti still under the influence of the International Gothic style that prevailed in about 1400. Illustrative of this tendency is the panel of *The Annunciation* (Luke 1:26–38), which depicts the moment when Mary learns from an angelic messenger that she will become the mother of Christ (Figure 11.15). The Gothic quatrefoil, or four-leafed frame, was standard for these panels, and many of Ghiberti's techniques are typical of the Gothic style—the niche in which the Virgin stands, her swaying body, and the angel depicted in flight. Nevertheless, Ghiberti always exhibited a strong feeling for Classical forms and harmony, as in the angel's well-rounded body and Mary's serene face.

The artistic world of Florence was a rapidly changing one, however, and Ghiberti adapted his art to conform to the emerging Early Renaissance style of Donatello. Between 1425 and 1452, Ghiberti brought his mature

art to its fullest expression in the east doors, the last of the Baptistery's three sculptured portals. These panels, larger than those on the north doors, depict scenes from the Old Testament, such as the story of Cain and Abel from Genesis (Figure 11.16). Most of the Gothic touches are eliminated, including the framing quatrefoils, which are now replaced with rectangular panels. In many other ways, the Cain and Abel panel on the east doors shows Ghiberti's growing dedication to Classical ideals: the graceful contrapposto of the standing figures and their proportional relationships, for example. This work translates Albertian aesthetics into bronze by creating an illusion of depth. But according to Ghiberti's *Commentaries,* the sculptor's purpose was not illusion for its own sake but, rather, a clear presentation of the biblical story. Five incidents from the story of Cain and Abel are illustrated: (1) Cain and Abel as children with their parents, Adam and Eve, at the top left; (2) Cain and Abel making sacrifices before an altar, at the top right; (3) Cain plowing with oxen and Abel watching his sheep, in the middle and foreground, respectively, on the left; (4) Cain slaying Abel with a club, in the right middle; and (5) Cain being questioned by God, in the right foreground. So sublime was Ghiberti's accomplishment that Michelangelo, in the next century, is said to have referred to these doors as "the Gates of Paradise."

Figure 11.16 LORENZO GHIBERTI. *The Story of Cain and Abel.* Detail from the east doors of the Baptistery (the "Gates of Paradise"). 1425–1452. Gilt bronze, 31¼ × 31¼". Florence. *This exquisite panel from the Florence Baptistery's east doors is a testament to Ghiberti's absorption of Early Renaissance taste. He followed Brunelleschi's new rules for linear perspective by placing the vanishing point in the middle of the tree trunks in the center of the panel, and he adhered to Alberti's principle of varied details by adding the oxen, sheep, and altar.*

Figure 11.17 MASACCIO. *The Holy Trinity.* 1427 or 1428. Fresco, 21′10½″ × 10′5″. Santa Maria Novella, Florence. *Masaccio achieved a remarkable illusion of depth in this fresco by using linear and atmospheric perspective. Below the simulated chapel he painted a skeleton in a wall sarcophagus (not visible in this photograph) with a melancholy inscription reading, "I was once that which you are, and what I am you also will be." This* memento mori, *or reminder of death, was probably ordered by the donor, a member of the Lenzi family. His tomb is built into the floor and lies directly in front of the fresco.*

Painting The radical changes taking place in architecture and sculpture were minor compared with the changes in painting. Inspired by Classicism though lacking significant examples from ancient times, painters were relatively free to experiment and to define their own path. As in the other arts of the 1400s, Florentine painters led the way and established the standards for the new style—realism, linear perspective, and psychological truth. This movement climaxed at the end of the century with the early work of Leonardo da Vinci.

After 1450 Florence's dominance was challenged by Venetian painters, who were forging their own artistic tradition. Venice, having won its freedom from the Byzantine Empire only in the High Middle Ages, was still in the thrall of Byzantine culture (see Chapter 8). As a result, Venetian painters and their patrons showed a pronounced taste for the stylized effects and sensual surfaces typical of Byzantine art. However, a distinct school of Venetian painters emerged, which eventually was to have a major impact on the course of painting in the West.

North of the Alps, a third Early Renaissance development was taking place in Burgundy and the Low Countries. There, the painters pursued an art more religious than that of Italy and closer in spirit to the Late Gothic. The northern artists concentrated on minute details and landscapes rather than on the problems of depth and composition that concerned Italy's painters. This survey confines itself to the major figures in the Florentine school, which is divided into two generations, and to the founder of the Venetian school.

The guiding genius of the revolution in painting in the earlier Florentine school was the youthful Masaccio [mah-ZAHT-cho] (1401–1428), whose career was probably cut short by the plague. He adopted mathematical perspective in his works almost simultaneously with its invention by Brunelleschi. In the history of Western painting, Masaccio's *Holy Trinity* fresco, painted in 1425, is the first successful depiction in painting of the new concept of Renaissance space.

Masaccio's design for this fresco in the church of Santa Maria Novella, Florence, shows that he was well aware of the new currents flowing in the art of his day. The painting offers an architectural setting in the style of Brunelleschi, and the solidity and vitality of the figures indicate that Masaccio had also absorbed the values of Donatello's new sculpture. Masaccio's fresco portrays the Holy Trinity—the three divine beings who make up the Christian idea of God—within a simulated chapel (Figure 11.17). Jesus' crucified body appears to be held up by God the Father, who stands on a platform behind the cross; between the heads of God and Jesus is a dove, symbolizing the Holy Spirit and completing the Trinitarian image. Mary and Saint John, both clothed in contemporary dress, flank the holy trio. Mary points dramatically to the Savior. Just outside the chapel's frame, the donors kneel in prayer—the typical way of presenting patrons in Renaissance art.

In the Trinity fresco, Masaccio uses a variety of innovations. He is the first painter to show light falling from a single source, in this instance, from the left, bathing the body of Christ and coinciding with the actual light-

Figure 11.18 MASACCIO. *The Tribute Money.* Ca. 1425. Fresco, 8′2⅜″ × 19′8¼″.
Santa Maria del Carmine, Florence. *This fresco represents the highest expression of the
art of Masaccio, particularly in his realistic portrayal of the tax collector. This official, who
appears twice, first confronting Christ in the center and then receiving money from Peter
on the right, is depicted with coarse features—a typical man of the Florentine streets.
Even his posture, though rendered with Classical contrapposto, suggests a swagger—
a man at home in his body and content with his difficult occupation.*

ing in Santa Maria Novella. This realistic feature adds
to the three-dimensional effect of the well-modeled figures. The use of linear perspective further heightens
the scene's realism. Finally, the perspective, converg-
ing to the midpoint between the kneeling donors, reinforces the hierarchy of beings within the fresco: from
God the Father at the top to the human figures at the
sides. In effect, mathematical tidiness is used to reveal
the divine order—an ideal congenial to Florence's intellectual elite.

A second fresco by Masaccio, *The Tribute Money,*
painted in the Brancacci Chapel of the church of Santa
Maria del Carmine, Florence, is recognized as Masaccio's masterpiece (Figure 11.18). This fresco illustrates
the Gospel account (Matthew 17:24–27) in which Jesus
advises Peter, his chief disciple, to pay the Roman
taxes. Because this painting depicts a biblical subject
virtually unrepresented in Christian art, it was probably commissioned by a donor to justify a new and
heavy Florentine tax. Whether the fresco had any effect
on tax collection is debatable, but other artists were
captivated by Masaccio's stunning technical effects:
the use of perspective and **chiaroscuro,** or the modeling with light and shade.

The Tribute Money fresco follows the continuous narrative form of medieval art. Three separate episodes

are depicted at the same time—in the center, Jesus is
confronted by the tax collector; on the left, Peter, as foretold by Jesus, finds a coin in the mouth of a fish; and,
on the right, Peter pays the coin to the Roman official.
Despite this Gothic effect, the fresco's central section is
able to stand alone because of its spatial integrity and
unified composition. Jesus is partially encircled by his
apostles, and the tax gatherer, viewed from the back,
stands to the right. In this central group, the heads are
all at the same height, for Masaccio aligned them according to Brunelleschi's principles. Fully modeled in
the round, each human form occupies a precise, mathematical space.

Painters like the Dominican friar Fra Angelico
(about 1400–1455) extended Masaccio's innovations.
Fra Angelico's later works, painted for the renovated
monastery of San Marco in Florence and partially
funded by Cosimo de' Medici, show his mature blending of biblical motifs in Renaissance space. *The Annunciation* portrays a reflective Virgin receiving the angel
Gabriel (Figure 11.19). Mary and Gabriel are framed in
niches in the Gothic manner, but the other elements—
the mastery of depth, the simplicity of gestures, the purity of colors, and the integrated scene—are rendered
in the new, simple Renaissance style. The painting's
vanishing point is placed to the right of center in the

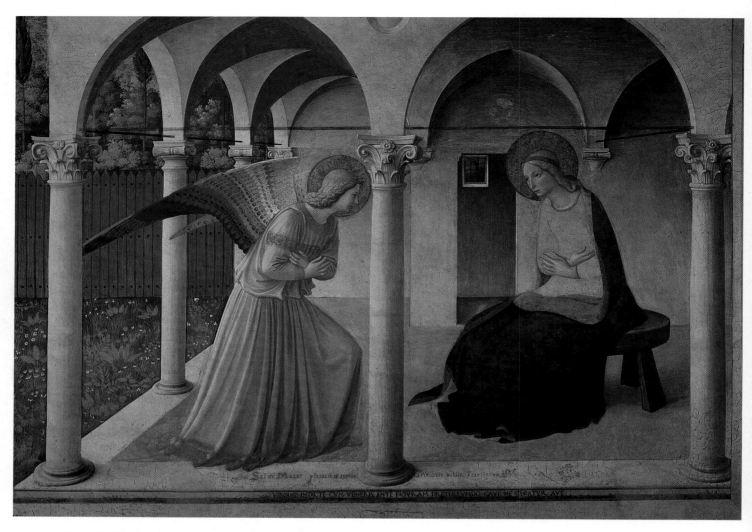

Figure 11.19 FRA ANGELICO. *Annunciation.* 1438–1445. Fresco, 7′ 6″ × 10′ 5″. Monastery of San Marco, Florence. *Fra Angelico's portrayal of the Virgin at the moment when she receives the news that she will bear the baby Jesus is a wonderful illustration of the painter's use of religious symbols. Mary's questioning expression and her arms crossed in a maternal gesture help to establish the painting's subject. Moreover, the physical setting of the scene, bare except for the rough bench on which she sits, suggests an ascetic existence—an appropriate detail for the painting's original setting, a monastery.*

small barred window looking out from the Virgin's bedroom. The loggia, or open porch, in which the scene takes place was based on a new architectural fashion popular among Florence's wealthy elite. Religious images abound in this painting; the enclosed garden symbolizes Mary's virginity, and the barred window attests to the purity of her life. Because of his gracious mastery of form and space, Fra Angelico's influence on later artists was pronounced.

One of those he influenced was Piero della Francesca [PYER-o DAYL-lah frahn-CHAY-skah] (about 1420–1492), a great painter of the second Florentine generation, who grew up in a Tuscan country town near Florence. His panel painting *The Flagellation* shows the powerful though mysterious aesthetic effects of his controversial style (Figure 11.20). The sunlight flooding the scene unites the figures, but the composition places them in two distinct areas. At the extreme left sits Pilate, the judge, on a dais. The painting's subject—the scourging of Christ before his crucifixion—is placed to the left rear. Reinforcing this odd displacement are the figures on the right, who are apparently lost in their own conversation. Aesthetically this strange juxtaposition arises because della Francesca has placed the horizon line around the hips of the figures beating Christ, causing the three men on the right to loom in such high perspective; thus the men in the foreground appear to be indifferent to Christ and unaware of his importance. The effect is distinctly unsettling in a religious scene. The modern world, which loves conundrums, has developed a strong passion for the private vision of della Francesca as represented in his art.

Sandro Botticelli [baht-tuh-CHEL-lee] (1445–1510) is the best representative of a lyrical aspect of this second generation and one of the most admired painters

Figure 11.20 PIERO DELLA FRANCESCA. *The Flagellation.* 1460s. Oil on panel, 23 × 32". Galleria Nazionale della Marche, Palazzo Ducale, Urbino. *A secondary religious message may be found in this work. In 1439 the Orthodox Church discussed union with Rome at the Council of Florence but later repudiated the merger when the Byzantine populace rioted in favor of Turkish rule. The hats on Pilate (seated at the left) and the third man from the right are copies of Greek headdresses that were worn at the council. In effect, these figures suggest that the Greek Church is a persecutor of true Christianity, for the papacy regarded the Greek Orthodox faith as schismatic.*

in the Western tradition. One of the first Florentine artists to master both linear and atmospheric perspective, he was less interested in the technical aspects of painting than he was in depicting languid beauty and poetical truth.

Until the 1480s, Botticelli's art was shaped by the Neo-Platonic philosophy of the Florentine Academy, and thus he often allegorized pagan myths, giving them a Christian slant. Especially prominent in Neo-Platonic thought was the identification of Venus, the Roman goddess of love, with the Christian belief that "God is love." Botticelli, with the support of his patrons, notably the Medici family, made the Roman goddess the subject of two splendid paintings, the *Primavera* and *The Birth of Venus.* In this way, female nudes once again became a proper subject for art, though male nudes had appeared earlier, in Donatello's generation (see Figure 11.11).

Botticelli's *Primavera,* or *Allegory of Spring,* presents Venus as a Christianized deity, dressed in a revealingly transparent gown (Figure 11.21). At first glance, the goddess, standing just slightly to the right of center,

appears lost amid the general agitation, but on closer view she is seen to be presiding over the revels. Venus tilts her head coyly and holds up her right hand, establishing by these commanding gestures that this orange grove is her garden and the other figures are her familiars, or associates, all of them symbolically linked with divine love.

Even though the *Primavera* is one of the most beloved works of Western art, in technical terms the painting shows that Botticelli was out of step with the Early Renaissance. He has placed the scene in the near foreground, stressing this area's extreme shallowness by the entangled backdrop of trees and shrubs. The figures

Figure 11.21 SANDRO BOTTICELLI. *Primavera*. Ca. 1482. Tempera on panel, 6′8″ × 10′4″. Uffizi Gallery, Florence. *Botticelli's lyricism is evident in his refined images of human beauty. His figures' elegant features and gestures, such as the sloping shoulders and the tilted heads, were copied by later artists. The women's blond, ropelike hair and transparent gowns are typical of Botticelli's style.*

are flattened, and the background appears more decorative than real.

An even more famous work by Botticelli, and one of the great landmarks of Western art, is *The Birth of Venus* (see Figure 11.4). Painted in an even more flattened style than the *Primavera,* this masterpiece was probably intended as a visual complement to it. In Neo-Platonic terms, Venus is an image of beauty and love as it is born and grows in the human mind; the birth of Venus corresponds to the baptism of Jesus, because baptism is a symbol of rebirth.

In the 1480s, Florentine art was moving toward its culmination in the early works of Leonardo da Vinci (1452–1519). Leonardo is the quintessential representative of a new breed of artist: the Renaissance man, who takes the universe of learning as his province. Not only did he defy the authority of the church by secretly studying human cadavers, but he also rejected the Classical values that had guided the first generation of the Early Renaissance. He relied solely on empirical

truth and what the human eye could discover. His notebooks, encoded so as to be legible only when read in a mirror, recorded and detailed his lifelong curiosity about both the human and the natural worlds. In his habits of mind, Leonardo joined intellectual curiosity with the skills of sculptor, architect, engineer, scientist, and painter.

Among his few surviving paintings from this period, the first version of *The Virgin of the Rocks* reveals both his scientific eye and his desire to create a haunting image uniquely his own (Figure 11.22). In this scene, set in a grotto or cave, Mary is portrayed with the infant Jesus, as a half-kneeling infant John the Baptist prays and an angel watches. The plants underfoot and the rocks in the background are a treasure of precise documentation. Nevertheless, the setting is Leonardo's own invention—without a scriptural or a traditional basis—and is a testimony to his creative genius.

Leonardo's plan of *The Virgin of the Rocks* shows the rich workings of his mind. Ignoring Brunelleschian

Figure 11.22 Leonardo da Vinci. *The Virgin of the Rocks.* 1483. Oil on panel, approx. 6′3″ × 3′7″. Louvre. *Two slightly different versions of this work exist, this one dating from 1483 and a later one done in 1506 and on view in the National Gallery in London. The Louvre painting, with its carefully observed botanical specimens, is the culmination of the scientific side of the Early Renaissance. The painting's arbitrary features—the grotto setting and the unusual perspective—point ahead to the High Renaissance; the dramatic use of chiaroscuro foreshadows the "night pictures" of the Baroque period (see Figure 14.8).*

perspective, he placed the figures his own way. He also developed a pyramid design for arranging the figures in relation to one another; Mary's head is the pyramid's apex, and her seat and the other three figures anchor its corners. Within this pyramid, Leonardo creates a dynamic tension by using gestures to suggest a circular motion: The angel points to John the Baptist, who in turn directs his praying hands toward Jesus. A second, vertical, line of stress is seen in the gesturing hands of Mary, the angel, and Christ. Later artists so admired this painting that its pyramidal composition became the standard in the High Renaissance.

No prior artist had used chiaroscuro to such advantage as Leonardo does in this work, causing the figures to stand out miraculously from the surrounding gloom. And unlike earlier artists, he colors the atmosphere, softening the edges of surfaces with a fine haze called **sfumato.** As a result, the painting looks more like a vision than a realistic scene. Leonardo's later works are part of the High Renaissance (see Chapter 12), but his early works represent the fullest expression of the scientific spirit of the second generation of Early Renaissance painting.

While the Florentine painters were establishing themselves as the driving force in the Early Renaissance, a rival school was beginning to emerge in Venice. The Venetian school, dedicated to exploring the effects of light and air and re-creating the sensuous effects of textured surfaces, was eventually to play a major role in the history of painting in Italy and the West. Founded by Giovanni Bellini, a member of a dynasty of painters, the Venetian school began its rise to greatness.

Giovanni Bellini (about 1430–1516), who trained in the workshop of his father, the Late Gothic painter Jacopo Bellini (about 1400–about 1470), made Venice a center of Renaissance art comparable to Florence and Rome. Ever experimenting, always striving to keep up with the latest trends, he frequently reinvented himself. Nevertheless, there were constants in his approach to painting. He combined the traditions of the Florentine school (the use of linear perspective and the direct observation of nature) and the Flemish school (the technique of oil painting, the use of landscape as background, and the practice of religious symbolism). Made aware of the importance of atmosphere by the Venetian setting, Bellini also experimented with a range of colors, variations in color intensity, and changes in light. In particular, Bellini perfected the landscape format as a backdrop for foreground figures. A great teacher, Bellini founded a workshop where his methods were taught to young painters, including Giorgione and Titian (see Chapter 12).

An excellent example of Bellini's use of landscape may be seen in *St. Francis in Ecstasy* (Figure 11.23). This work, which depicts an ecstatic St. Francis displaying the stigmata, shows Bellini's typical treatment of landscape. He divides the painting surface into zones, beginning with the area around the saint in the foreground, continuing through a second zone occupied by a donkey and a crane, to a third zone featuring Italian castles nestled into a hillside, and concluding with a fourth zone marked by a fortress and the sky. To heighten the realism, Bellini uses both a rich palette of colors and numerous objects to lead the viewer's eye into the vast distance. He adds to the realism by suffusing the scene

Figure 11.23 GIOVANNI BELLINI. *St. Francis in Ecstasy.* 1470s. Oil in tempera on panel, 49 × 55⅞". Frick Collection, New York. *In the foreground, Bellini renders his vision of the grotto at Alvernia, a mountain retreat near Assisi, where St. Francis went to pray and fast for forty days, in imitation of Christ's forty days in the wilderness. The artist reinforces the scene's religious significance through various symbols, such as the grapevine and the stigmata, alluding to the sacrifice of Christ, and the donkey (in the middle distance), emblematic of Jesus' entry into Jerusalem prior to the Crucifixion.*

with natural light. The landscape, with its vivid rendering of flora and fauna, expresses the Franciscan belief that humankind should live in harmony with the natural world (see Chapter 9).

Music

The changes affecting the cultural life of fifteenth-century Europe naturally also affected the music of the time. The impetus for a new musical direction, however, did not spring from Classical sources, because ancient musical texts had virtually perished. Instead, the new music owed its existence to meetings between English and Continental composers at the church councils that were called to settle the Great Schism (see Chapter 10) and the Continental composers' deep regard for the seductive sound of English music. The English composer John Dunstable [DUHN-stuh-bull] (about 1380–1453) was a central figure in the new musical era that began with the opening of the fifteenth century. Working in England and in France, he wrote mainly religious works—motets for multiple voices and settings for the Mass—that showed his increasingly harmonic approach to polyphony. The special quality of his music is its freedom from the use of mathematical proportion—the source of medieval music's dissonance.

Dunstable's music influenced composers in France, in Burgundy, and in Flanders, known collectively as the Franco-Netherlandish school. This school, which became the dominant force in fifteenth-century music, blended Dunstable's harmonics with northern European and Italian traditions. The principal works of this group were Latin **Masses,** or musical settings of the most sacred Christian rite; motets, or multivoiced songs set to Latin texts; and secular *chansons,* or songs, with French texts, including such types as the French ballade and the Italian madrigal, poems set to music for two and six voices, respectively. Together, these polyphonic compositions established the musical ideal of the Early Renaissance: multiple voices of equal importance singing *a cappella* (without instrumental accompaniment) and stressing the words so they could be understood by listeners.

Between 1430 and 1500, the continent's musical life was guided by composers from the Franco-Netherlandish school, the most important of whom was the Burgundian Josquin des Prez [zho-SKAN day PRAY] (about 1440–1521). Josquin was influential in his day and is now recognized as one of the greatest composers of all time. He was the first important composer to use music expressively so that the sounds matched the words of the text, thereby moving away from the abstract church style of the Middle Ages. One of his motets was described at the time as evoking Christ's suffering in a manner superior to painting. Josquin also began to organize music in the modern way, using major and minor scales with their related harmonies. All in all, he is probably the first Western composer whose music on first hearing appeals to modern ears.

The Legacy of the Early Renaissance

Today, modern times are considered to begin with the Early Renaissance in Italy. This period saw the rebirth of the study and practice of the arts and the humanities and the rise of the idea of the "Renaissance man," the supreme genius who makes all of human knowledge his province. Under the powerful stimulus of humanism, the liberal arts were restored to primacy over religion in the educational curriculum, a place they had not held for a thousand years, or since the triumph of Christianity in the fourth century. With humanism also came a skeptical outlook that expressed itself in a new regard for the direct role of human causality in history and the rise of textual criticism. A new ingredient in Renaissance humanism was the drive to individual fulfillment, perhaps the defining trait of Western civilization from this point onward.

The greatest cultural changes took place in the arts and in architecture, largely under the spell of humanistic learning. Now freed from subordination to architecture, sculpture and painting became independent art forms. Fifteenth-century architects, inspired by the Greco-Roman tradition, adapted Classical forms and ideals to their own needs. For the next four hundred years, until the Gothic revival in the nineteenth century, Classicism was the ruling force in a succession of architectural styles. Sculpture also used its Classical roots to redefine its direction, reviving ancient forms and the practice of depicting male and female nudes. Of all the visual arts, painting was least influenced by the Classical tradition, except for its ideals of simplicity and realism. Perhaps as a consequence of its artistic freedom, painting became the dominant art form of this era and continues to hold first rank today.

KEY CULTURAL TERMS

Renaissance	chiaroscuro
studia humanitatis	*sfumato*
Early Renaissance style	Mass
vanishing point	*chanson*
pilaster	*a cappella*
relief	

SUGGESTIONS FOR FURTHER READING

PRIMARY SOURCES

CASSIRER, E., KRISTELLER, P. O., AND RANDALL, J., eds. *The Renaissance Philosophy of Man.* Chicago: University of Chicago Press, 1948. Selections from Pico, Valla, and other Renaissance scholars accompanied by a useful text.

PICO DELLA MIRANDOLA. *On the Dignity of Man.* Indianapolis: Bobbs-Merrill, 1956. A succinct statement on Renaissance thought by one of its leading scholars.

SUGGESTIONS FOR LISTENING

DUNSTABLE (or DUNSTAPLE), JOHN (about 1380–1453). Dunstable's sweet-sounding harmonies helped inaugurate Early Renaissance music. Predominantly a composer of sacred music, he is best represented by motets, including *Veni Sancte Spiritus—Veni Creator Spiritus* and *Sancta Maria, non est similis.* He also wrote a few secular songs of which the two most familiar are *O Rosa bella* and *Puisque m'amour.*

JOSQUIN DES PREZ (1440–1521). Josquin's Masses, motets, and *chansons* all illustrate his skill at combining popular melodies with intricate counterpoint and his use of harmonies commonly heard today. The motet *Ave Maria*, the *chanson Faulte d'argent*, and the Mass *Malheur me bat* are good examples of his style.

12 THE HIGH RENAISSANCE AND EARLY MANNERISM
1494–1564

Between 1494 and 1564, one of the most brilliantly creative periods in Western history unfolded in Italy. During this span of seventy years, there flourished three artists—Leonardo da Vinci, Raphael, and Michelangelo—and a writer—Machiavelli—whose achievements became legendary. The works of these geniuses, and of other talented but less well known artists and intellectuals, affected the basic Western concept of art and fundamentally influenced how we understand ourselves and the world.

The **High Renaissance,** lasting from 1494 to 1520, was the first phase of this creative period and was a time when the Classical principles of beauty, balance, order, serenity, harmony, and rational design reached a state of near perfection. The center of culture shifted from Florence, the heart of the Early Renaissance, to Rome, where the popes became the leading patrons of the new style in their desire to make Rome the world's most beautiful city. Florence even had to yield the services of Michelangelo, its favorite son, to the wealthy and powerful Roman pontiffs (Figure 12.1).

After 1520, however, the Renaissance veered away from the humanistic values of Classicism toward an antihumanistic vision of the world, labeled **Mannerism** because of the self-conscious, or "mannered," style adopted by its artists and intellectuals. Mannerist art and culture endured from 1520 until the end of the century, when the style was affected by religious controversy. This chapter covers the High Renaissance style and the Mannerist style through the end of its first phase in 1564, with the death of Michelangelo.

◄ **Detail** LEONARDO DA VINCI. *The Last Supper*. 1495–1498. Oil tempera on wall, 13′10″ × 29′7½″. Refectory, Santa Maria delle Grazie, Milan.

THE RISE OF THE MODERN SOVEREIGN STATE

The most important political development in the first half of the sixteenth century was the emergence of powerful sovereign states in the newly unified and stabilized nations of France, England, and Spain. This process was already under way in the late fifteenth century (see Chapter 10), but it now began to influence foreign affairs. The ongoing rivalries of these aggressive national kingdoms led to the concept of balance of power—a principle that still dominates politics today.

From 1494 to 1569, Europe's international political life was controlled, either directly or indirectly, by France and Spain. France's central role resulted from the policies of its strong Valois kings, who had governed France since the early fourteenth century. Spain's fortunes soared during this period, first under the joint rule of Ferdinand V and Isabella and then under Charles I. In 1519 Charles I was also elected Holy Roman Emperor as Charles V (he was of the royal house of Hapsburg), thus joining the interests of Spain and the Holy Roman Empire until his abdication in 1556. England kept aloof from Continental affairs during this time.

After 1591 the French and the Spanish rulers increasingly dispatched their armies and allies into the weaker states, where they fought and claimed new lands. As the sovereign monarchs gained power, the medieval dream of a united Christendom—pursued by Charlemagne, the popes, and the Holy Roman emperors—slowly faded away. These new states were strong because they were united around rulers who exercised increasing central control. Although most kings claimed to rule by divine right, their practical policies were more important in increasing their power. They surrounded themselves with ministers and consultative councils, both dependent on the crown. The ministers were often chosen from the bourgeois class, and they advised the rulers on such weighty matters as religion and war and also ran the developing bureaucracies. The bureaucracies in turn strengthened centralized rule by extending royal jurisdiction into matters formerly administered by the feudal nobility, such as the justice system.

Figure 12.1   MICHELANGELO. *Dying Slave.* 1513–1516. Marble, approx. 7′ 5″. Louvre. *Michelangelo's so-called* Dying Slave *embodies the conflicting artistic tendencies at work between 1494 and 1564. The statue's idealized traits—the perfectly proportioned figure, the restrained facial expression, and the body's gentle* S-curve *shape—are hallmarks of the High Renaissance style. But the figure's overall sleekness and exaggerated arm movements—probably based on one of the figures in the first-century A.D.* Laocoön Group *(see Figure 4.19), which had recently been rediscovered—were portents of Early Mannerism.*

The crown further eroded the status of the feudal nobles by relying on mercenary armies rather than on the warrior class, a shift that began in the Late Middle Ages. To pay these armies, the kings had to consult with representative bodies, such as Parliament in England, and make them a part of their regular administration.

The Struggle for Italy, 1494–1529

Italy's relative tranquility, established by the Peace of Lodi in 1454, was shattered by the French invasion in 1494. For the next thirty-five years, Italy was a battleground where France, Spain, and the Holy Roman Empire fought among themselves, as well as with the papacy and most of the Italian states.

The struggle began when France, eager to reassert a hereditary claim to Naples, agreed to help Milan in a controversy involving Naples, Florence, and the pope. The French king, Charles VIII (r. 1483–1498), took Florence in 1494 and then advanced to Rome and Naples. But the Italians did not relinquish ground easily. Joined by Venice and the pope and supported by the Holy Roman emperor and the Spanish monarch, they drove out the French. In 1499 the French returned to Italy to activate their claim to Milan, and the Spanish and the Germans joined with the Italians to drive them out. Over the next several decades, however, France continued to invade Italy intermittently. In the course of their campaigns, the French rulers, who were enamored of the Italian Renaissance, brought its artistic and intellectual ideals to northern Europe (Figure 12.2).

In 1522 full-scale hostilities broke out between France and the Holy Roman Empire over Italy's future, a struggle that pitted the old Europe against the new. The Holy Roman Empire, ruled by Charles V, was a decentralized relic from the feudal age. France, under the bold and intellectual leadership of Francis I (r. 1515–1547) of the royal house of Valois, was the epitome of the new sovereign state.

The first Hapsburg-Valois war was the only one fought in Italy. In 1527 the troops of Charles V ran riot in Rome, raping, looting, and killing. This notorious sack of Rome had two major consequences. First, it cast doubt on Rome's ability to control Italy—long a goal of the popes—for it showed that the secular leaders no longer respected the temporal power of the papacy. Second, it ended papal patronage of the arts for almost a decade, thus weakening Rome's role as a cultural leader. It also had a chilling effect on artistic ideals and contributed to the rise of Mannerism.

In 1529 the Treaty of Cambrai ended this first phase of the Hapsburg-Valois rivalry. Years of invasions and wars had left most of Italy divided and exhausted. Some cities had suffered nearly irreparable harm. Flor-

Figure 12.2 JEAN CLOUET. *Francis I.* Ca. 1525. Oil on panel, 37¾ × 29⅛". Louvre. *During his thirty-two-year-long reign, Francis I was a major force in sixteenth-century European affairs. He also embarked on an extensive artistic program, inspired by the Italian Renaissance, to make his court the most splendid in Europe. Under his personal direction, Italian artworks and artists, including Leonardo da Vinci, were imported into France. Ironically, this rather stylized portrait by Jean Clouet, Francis's chief court artist, owes more to the conventionalized portraits of the Gothic style than it does to the realistic works of the Italian Renaissance.*

ence, because it had so much to lose, fared the worst. In the 1530s, the Medici rulers resumed ducal power, but they were little more than puppets of the foreigners who controlled much of the peninsula. The only Italian state to keep its political independence was Venice, which became the last haven for artists and intellectuals in Italy for the rest of the sixteenth century.

Charles V and the Hapsburg Empire

By 1530 the struggle between the Valois and the Hapsburgs had shifted to central Europe. The French felt hemmed in by the Spanish in the south, the Germans to the east, and the Dutch to the north—peoples all ruled by the Hapsburg emperor Charles V. In French

Map 12.1 EUROPEAN EMPIRE OF CHARLES V, CA. 1556

Lands inherited by Charles V
Lands gained by Charles V, 1519–1556
Enemies of Charles V
States favorable to Charles V
— Boundary of the Holy Roman Empire

eyes, Charles had an insatiable appetite for power and for control of the Continent. In turn, the Hapsburg ruler considered the French king a land-hungry upstart who stood in the way of a Europe united under a Christian prince—in other words, the dream of Christendom. In 1559, after a number of exhausting wars and a series of French victories, the belligerents signed the Treaty of Cateau-Cambrésis, which ushered in a brief period of peace (Map 12.1).

Charles V, the man at the center of most of these events, lived a life filled with paradoxes (Figure 12.3). Because of the size of his empire, he was in theory one of the most powerful rulers ever to live; but in actual-ity, again because of the vastness of his lands, he never quite succeeded in gaining complete control of his empire. In some ways, he was the last of medieval kings; in other ways, he foreshadowed a new age driven by sovereign kings, standing armies, diplomatic agreements, and strong religious differences.

Charles V's unique position at the center of Europe's political storm was the result of a series of timely deaths and births and politically astute arranged marriages. These circumstances had permitted the Hapsburg rulers to accumulate vast power, wealth, and land. Charles was born in 1500 to a German father and a Spanish mother, and he was the grandson of both the

Holy Roman emperor Maximilian I and the Spanish king Ferdinand V. He held lands in present-day Spain, France, Italy, Germany, and Austria—along with the unimaginable riches of the recently acquired lands in the New World. By 1519 Charles V—simultaneously Charles I of Spain—ruled the largest empire the world has ever known.

For most of his life, Charles traveled from one of his possessions to another, fighting battles, arranging peace treaties, and attempting to unify his empire by personal control and compromise. His attention was often divided, and he found himself caught between two powerful foes—especially the French to the west and the Ottoman Turks in the east—who drained both his personal energies and his imperial resources.

Within the Holy Roman Empire, the princes of the German principalities often took advantage of his prolonged absences and his preoccupation with the French and the Turks. Their ability to gain political power at the emperor's expense increased after Martin Luther's revolt and the beginning of the Protestant Reformation (see Chapter 13). Charles also weakened his own position by his contradictory policies. At times he angered the disaffected German princes by meddling in their affairs and condemning Lutheran doctrines, and at other times he angered the popes by making concessions to the Protestants.

Exhausted and disillusioned by his inability to prevail in Europe, Charles abdicated in 1556 and retired to a monastery. His brother Ferdinand took control of the German-Austrian inheritance and was soon elected Holy Roman emperor. His son Philip assumed control of the Spanish Hapsburg holdings, including Spain, the New World territories, and the Netherlands. Thus ended Charles's vision of a united Europe and Christendom, which had turned into a nightmare of endless meetings, gory battles, and false hopes of peace and unity.

ECONOMIC EXPANSION AND SOCIAL DEVELOPMENTS

By the end of the fifteenth century, Europe had nearly recovered from the impact of the plague; the sixteenth century continued to be a time of growing population and increasing prosperity. The center of commerce shifted from the Mediterranean to the Atlantic coast, making cities like London and Antwerp financial and merchandising centers. Skilled craftspeople turned out quality products, and enterprising merchants distributed these finished goods across much of northwestern Europe. The daring sailing expeditions and discoveries of the late fifteenth and early sixteenth centuries provided new raw materials from America.

Figure 12.3 TITIAN. *Charles V with a Dog.* Ca. 1533. Oil on canvas, 6′3″ × 3′8″. Prado, Madrid. *Titian's full-length, standing portrait of Charles V was painted when the Hapsburg emperor was at the height of his power. By rendering the "ruler of the world" in contrapposto, his fingers casually holding the collar of his dog, Titian endows the emperor with a natural grace. The lighting that illuminates Charles from the dark background and the breathless hush that seems to envelop the man and dog are trademarks of Titian's style.*

Innovative manufacturing methods spurred economic growth and expanded worldwide markets.

Although the data are scattered and often unreliable, evidence indicates that the population of Europe increased from about 45 million in 1400 to 69 million in 1500 and to about 89 million by 1600. There was a major population shift from rural to urban areas, and the number of cities with populations over 100,000 grew from five to eight between 1500 and 1600. Rome, for example, grew from about 50,000 in 1526—the year before the sack—to 100,000 by the end of the century.

Timeline 12.1   ITALIAN CULTURAL STYLES BETWEEN 1494 AND 1564

1494		1520					1564
	High Renaissance		Early Mannerism				
French invasion of Italy	1508–1512 Michelangelo's Sistine Chapel ceiling frescoes	1519 Death of Leonardo da Vinci 1520 Death of Raphael	1532 Publication of Machiavelli's *Prince*	1536–1541 Michelangelo's *Last Judgment* fresco	1550 Palladio's Villa Rotonda		1564 Death of Michel-angelo

Prosperity brought a higher standard of living to most of the urban middle class, but throughout much of the century prices rose faster than wages. Those who were not profiting from increased economic growth, such as poor peasants or impoverished nobility living on unproductive farms, suffered the most. In areas of Europe hardest hit by inflation or agricultural and commercial stagnation, economic crises often became intertwined with social and religious matters that intensified long-standing regional and local differences.

Yet the boom offered economic opportunities to some. Many merchants made fortunes and provided employment for others. These merchants and the bankers who offered loans were also accumulating capital, which they then invested in other types of commercial activity. The campaigns of Charles V were financed by wealthy bankers operating in a well-organized money market. The amassing of surplus capital and its reinvestment ushered in the opening phase of commercial capitalism that laid the foundation for Europe's future economic expansion.

During the first half of the sixteenth century, the abundance of raw materials and the vast market potential of the New World had just begun to affect Europe's economy. South American gold and silver played an important role in the upward price spiral. After 1650 New World agricultural products, such as tobacco, cotton, and cocoa, were used in new manufactured goods and profoundly altered consumer habits.

In the late 1500s, a major economic change had occurred that would make it possible to bring the natural resources of the New World to Europe. Some Europeans, taking advantage of the institution of slavery and the existing slave trade in western Africa, mercilessly exploited the local Africans by buying them and shipping them to European colonies in the New World. The Africans were forced to work in the gold and silver mines of Central and South America and on the cotton and sugarcane plantations in the West Indies, where they became a major factor in the production of these new forms of wealth.

FROM HIGH RENAISSANCE TO EARLY MANNERISM

The characteristics of High Renaissance style were largely derived from the visual arts. Led by painters, sculptors, and architects who worshiped ancient Classical ideals, notably those of late-fifth-century B.C. Greece, the High Renaissance was filled with images of repose, harmony, and heroism. Under the spell of Classicism and the values of simplicity and restraint, artists sought to conquer unruly physical reality by subjecting it to the principle of a seemingly effortless order.

Although the visual arts dominated the High Renaissance, literary figures also contributed to this era. From Classicism, the High Renaissance authors appropriated two of their chief aesthetic aims, secularism and idealism. Like their ancient predecessors, historians showed that contemporary events arose from human causes rather than from divine action—unmistakable evidence of a mounting secular spirit. Actually, secularism more deeply affected the writing of history than it did the arts and architecture, where church patronage and religious subjects still held sway. A rising secular consciousness can also be seen in the popular handbooks on manners that offered advice on how to become a perfect gentleman or lady. Although they have no counterpart in ancient literature, these books nevertheless have the Classical quality of treating their subject in idealized terms.

What distinguished the High Renaissance preoccupation with the Classical past from the Early Renaissance's renewed interest in ancient matters was largely a shift in creative sensibility. The Early Renaissance artists, in the course of growing away from the Late Gothic style, had invented new ways of recapturing the harmonious spirit of ancient art and architecture. The geniuses of the next generation, benefiting from the experiments of the Early Renaissance, succeeded in creating masterpieces of disciplined form and idealized beauty. The High Renaissance masters' superb confidence allowed them to produce works that were

Figure 12.4 *Pope Clement VII Besieged in Castel Sant' Angelo.* 1554. Engraving, 6⅙ × 9". Kunsthalle, Hamburg. *This engraving shows the imperial army of Charles V besieging Castel Sant' Angelo, one of the pope's palaces, during the sack of Rome in 1527. The engraver's sympathies with the pope are revealed by the huge statues of St. Peter (with keys, on the right) and St. Paul (with sword, on the left), who look on disapprovingly. Pope Clement VII, imprisoned in his own fortress, peers down on the scene from a balcony at the center top.*

in harmony with themselves and the physical world—a hallmark of Classical art.

In spite of its brilliance, the High Renaissance existed for only a fleeting moment in the history of Western culture—from the French invasion of Italy in 1494 until the death of Raphael in 1520 (preceded by the death of Leonardo in 1519) (Timeline 12.1). In this era, the Renaissance popes spared no expense in their patronage of the arts and letters. After the disasters of the fourteenth century, the papacy seemed to have restored the church to the vitality that it had enjoyed in the High Middle Ages. In reality, however, the popes of the early sixteenth century presided over a shaky ecclesiastical foundation. To the north, in Germany, a theological storm was brewing that would eventually split Christendom and destroy the papacy's claim to rule over the Christian world. This religious crisis, coupled with increasing tendencies to exaggeration in High Renaissance art and with the sack of Rome in 1527, contributed to the development of Mannerism and its spread through Italy and later across western Europe (Figure 12.4).

Mannerist painters, sculptors, and architects moved away from two of the guiding principles of the High Renaissance: the imitation of nature and the devotion to Classical ideals. In contrast to the High Renaissance masters, Mannerist painters deliberately chose odd perspectives that called attention to the artists' technical effects and their individual points of view. Mannerist sculptors, rejecting idealism, turned and twisted the human figure into unusual and bizarre poses to express their own notions of beauty. Likewise, Mannerist architects toyed with the emotions and expectations of their audience by designing buildings that were intended to surprise. Behind the Mannerist aesthetic lay a questioning or even a denial of the inherent worth of human beings and a negative image of human nature, along with a sense of the growing instability of the world.

Literature

The leading writers of the High Renaissance in Italy drew their themes and values from the Greco-Roman classics. Their artistic vision sprang from the Classical virtue of *humanitas*—a term coined by Cicero in antiquity (see Chapter 5) that can be translated as "humanity," meaning the wisdom, humor, tolerance, and passion of the person of good sense. With some reservations, they also believed in Classicism's basic tenet that human nature is inherently rational and good. One of the finest expressions of Classicism in Renaissance literature was the poetry of the Venetian Gaspara Stampa, whose lyric verses, though devoted to obsessive sexual love, asserted the moral worth of the lover.

But even as High Renaissance literature was enjoying its brief reign, the Mannerist works of the Florentine author Niccolò Machiavelli began to appear, and at the heart of his thought is an anti-Classical spirit. Despite his education in Classicism and his strict rationalism, Machiavelli concluded that the human race was irremediably flawed. The contrast between the idealizing spirit of the High Renaissance and the anti-traditionalist views of Mannerism can be clearly seen by placing the work of the diplomat and courtier Baldassare Castiglione beside that of Machiavelli. Each wrote a book that can fairly be described as a manual of behavior—but there the resemblance ends.

Gaspara Stampa   Gaspara Stampa (about 1524–1554) embraced the classical tradition renewed by Petrarch in the 1300s; her work is thus typical of High Renaissance poetry. She adopted the Petrarchan sonnet as the preferred vehicle for her thoughts, and, like the earlier poet, she used her poetic gifts to investigate the byways of love. Rather than glorifying the distant beloved, however, she asserted the moral worth of the suffering lover, thus transforming the essentially male Petrarchan ideal into a female point of view. Stampa poured out her heart in her verses, confessing vulnerability and lamenting abandonment. She portrayed the abandoned one as superior to the unresponsive loved one—the same lesson taught by Socrates in one of Plato's dialogues (see Chapter 3).

That Gaspara Stampa became a poet at all is testimony to the changing mores of Renaissance Venice, a city fabled for its love of luxury and pleasure. Her autobiographical poetry grew out of her situation in Venice's marginal world of writers, musicians, and artists, including aristocrats and high officials of church and state, who were notably indifferent to Christian values. As a courtesan, or kept woman, she was a welcome member of this twilight world where sexuality was fused with art. Although she seems to have had several liaisons in her brief life, it was Count Collaltino di Collalto, a soldier, who won her heart. In time, Collaltino wearied of her, but Stampa transformed her hopeless love into some of the West's most touching poetry.

Castiglione   The reputation of Castiglione [kahs-teel-YOH-nay] (1478–1529) rests on *The Courtier,* one of the most influential and famous books of the High Renaissance. Intended for Italian court society, *The Courtier* was published in 1528 and translated into most Western languages by the end of the century. It quickly became the bible of courteous behavior for Eu-

Figure 12.5   RAPHAEL. *Baldassare Castiglione.* 1514. Oil on canvas, 32¼ × 26½″. Louvre. *Castiglione was memorialized in this handsome portrait by Raphael, one of the great portrait painters of the High Renaissance. Raphael's debt to Leonardo's portrait style, especially as represented by the* Mona Lisa, *is evident in the half-length, seated pose and the direct gaze of the subject. Elegantly groomed and completely at ease, Castiglione appears here as the age's ideal courtier.*

rope's upper classes and remained so over the next two hundred years. Even today, at the beginning of the twenty-first century, Castiglione's rules for civilized behavior are still not completely outmoded.

A Mantuan by birth, Castiglione (Figure 12.5) based his guide to manners on life at the north Italian court of Urbino, where, between 1504 and 1517, he was the beneficiary of the patronage of its resident duke, Guidobaldo da Montefeltro (see Figure 11.2). Impressed by the graceful conversations of his fellow courtiers and most especially taken with the charms of Urbino's duchess, Elisabetta, Castiglione was moved to memorialize his experiences in writing. *The Courtier* is composed as a dialogue, a literary form originated by Plato and favored by Cicero. Castiglione's dialogue is set in Urbino over a period of four evenings and peopled with actual individuals for whom he invents urbane and witty conversations that suit their known characters. Despite this realistic touch, his book's overall tone is definitely idealistic and hence expressive of High Renaissance style.

Castiglione's idealism shines forth most clearly in the sections in which the invited company try to define the perfect courtier, or gentleman. Under Duchess Elisabetta's eye, the guests cannot agree on which aspect of the ideal gentleman's training should take precedence: education in the arts and humanities or skill in horsemanship and swordplay. Some claim that a gentleman should be first a man of letters as well as proficient in music, drawing, and dance. In contrast, others believe that a courtier's profession is first to be ready for war, and hence athletics should play the central role. At any rate, both sides agree that the ideal courtier should be proficient in each of these areas. A sign that the Renaissance had raised the status of painting and sculpture was the group's expectation that a gentleman should be knowledgeable about both of these art forms.

The Courtier also describes the perfect court lady. In the minds of the dialogue participants, the ideal lady is a civilizing influence on men, who would otherwise be crude. To that end, the perfect lady should be a consummate hostess, charming, witty, graceful, physically attractive, and utterly feminine. She ought to be well versed in the same areas as a man, except for athletics and the mastery of arms. With these social attributes, the cultivated lady can then bring out the best in a courtier. But she must not seem his inferior, for she contributes to society in her own way.

Castiglione's book turned away from medieval values and led his followers into the modern world. First, he argued that social relations between the sexes ought to be governed by Platonic love—a spiritual passion that surpassed physical conquest—and thus he rejected medieval courtly love and its adulterous focus.

Second, he reasoned that women in society should be the educated equals of men, thereby sweeping away the barrier that had been erected when women were excluded from the medieval universities. In the short run, the impact of Castiglione's social rules was to keep women on a pedestal, as courtly love had done. But for the future, his advice allowed women to participate actively in every aspect of society and encouraged their education in much the same way as men's.

Machiavelli   In contrast to Castiglione's optimism, the Florentine Machiavelli [mak-ee-uh-VEL-ee] (1469–1527) had a negative view of human nature and made human weakness the central message of his writings. If *The Courtier* seems to be taking place in a highly refined never-never land where decorum and gentility are the primary interests, Machiavelli returns the reader to the solid ground of political reality. His Mannerist cynicism about his fellow human beings sprang from a wounded idealism, for life had taught him that his early optimism was wrong. His varied works, by means of their frank assessments of the human condition, were meant to restore sanity to a world that he thought had gone mad.

Except for Martin Luther, Machiavelli left a stronger imprint on Western culture than any other figure who lived between 1494 and 1564. His most enduring contribution was *The Prince*, which inaugurated a revolution in political thought. Rejecting the medieval tradition of framing political discussions in Christian terms, Machiavelli treated the state as a human invention that ought not necessarily conform to religious or moral rules. He began the modern search for a science of politics that has absorbed political thinkers and policy-makers ever since.

Machiavelli's career in sixteenth-century Italy, like that of many writers in antiquity, was split between a life of action and a life of the mind. Between 1498 and 1512, he served the newly reborn Florentine republic as a senior official and diplomat, learning statecraft firsthand. During these turbulent years, he was particularly impressed by the daring and unscrupulous Cesare Borgia, Pope Alexander VI's son. In 1512, after the fall of the Florentine republic to the resurgent Medici party, Machiavelli was imprisoned, tortured, and finally exiled to his family estate outside the city. There, as he recounts in one of his famous letters, he divided his time between idle games with the local farmers at a nearby inn and nightly communion with the best minds of antiquity in his study. From this background emerged in 1513 the small work known as *The Prince*, which circulated in manuscript until after his death. In 1532 it was finally published.

Machiavelli had several motives in writing this masterpiece. Despairing over Italy's dismemberment by

Figure 12.6 LEONARDO DA VINCI. *The Last Supper*. Restored. 1495–1498. Oil-tempera on wall, 13′10″ × 29′7½″. Refectory, Santa Maria delle Grazie, Milan. *Classical restraint is one of the defining characteristics of this High Renaissance masterpiece. Instead of overwhelming the viewer with distracting details, Leonardo reduces the objects to a minimum, from the austere room in which the meal is being celebrated to the simple articles on the dining table. The viewer's gaze is thereby held on the unfolding human drama rather than on secondary aspects of the scene.*

the French and the Spanish kings, he hoped the book would inspire an indigenous leader to unify the peninsula and drive out the foreigners. Enlightened by his personal experience in Florence's affairs, he wanted to capture in writing the truth of the politics to which he had been a witness. And, of equal importance, by dedicating *The Prince* to the restored Medici ruler, he hoped to regain employment in the Florentine state. Like other writers in this age, Machiavelli could not live by his wits but had to rely on secular or religious patronage.

Machiavelli's work failed to gain its immediate objectives: The Medici despot brushed it aside, and Italy remained fragmented until 1870. But as a work that exposed the ruthlessness needed to succeed in practical politics, *The Prince* was an instant, though controversial, success. The book was denounced by religious leaders for its amoral treatment of political power and read secretly by secular rulers for its sage advice. In the prevailing climate of opinion in the sixteenth century, which was still under the sway of Christian ideals, the name "Machiavelli" became synonymous with dishonesty and treachery, and the word **Machiavellianism** was coined to describe the amoral notion that "the end justifies any means."

From the modern perspective, this negative valuation of Machiavelli is both too simplistic and too harsh. Above all else he was a clear-eyed patriot who was anguished by the tragedy unfolding in Italy. *The Prince*

describes the power politics that the new sovereign states of France and Spain were pursuing in Italian affairs. Machiavelli realized that the only way to rid Italy of foreigners was to adopt the methods of its successful foes. Seeing his countrymen as cowardly and greedy, he had no illusions that a popular uprising would spring up and drive out Italy's oppressors. Only a strong-willed monarch, not bound by a finicky moral code, could bring Italy back from political chaos.

The controversial heart of Machiavelli's political treatise was the section that advised the ruler on the best way to govern. He counseled the prince to practice conscious duplicity, since that was the only way to maintain power and to ensure peace—the two basic goals of any state. By appearing virtuous and upright while at the same time acting as the situation demanded, the prince could achieve these fundamental ends. Machiavelli's startling advice reflected both his involvement in Italian affairs and his own view of human nature.

Painting

In the arts, the period between 1494 and 1564 was preeminently an age of painting, though several sculptors and architects created major works in their respective fields. The Classical values of idealism, balance, and restraint were translated by High Renaissance painters into harmonious colors, naturally posed figures with serene faces, realistic space and perspectives, and perfectly proportioned human bodies. After 1520 Mannerist tendencies became more and more evident, reflected in abnormal subjects, contorted figures with emotionally expressive faces, and garish colors.

Leonardo da Vinci   The inauguration of the High Renaissance in painting is usually dated from Leonardo's *The Last Supper*, which was completed between 1495 and 1498 (Figure 12.6). Painted for the Dominican friars of the church of Santa Maria delle Grazie in Milan, *The Last Supper* heralded the lucidity and harmony that were the essence of High Renaissance style. In executing the fresco, Leonardo unfortunately made use of a flawed technique, and the painting began to flake during his lifetime. Over the centuries, the work has been touched up frequently and restored seven times, with the most recent restoration completed in 1999. Nevertheless, enough of his noble intention is evident to ensure the reputation of *The Last Supper* as one of the best-known and most beloved paintings of Western art.

Leonardo's design for *The Last Supper* is highly idealized—a guiding principle of the High Renaissance. The fresco depicts the moment when Jesus says that one of the twelve disciples at the table will betray him. Ignoring the tradition that integrated this symbolic meal into an actual refectory, Leonardo separated the scene from its surroundings so that the figures would seem to hover over the heads of the clergy as they ate in their dining room. Idealism is also evident in Leonardo's straightforward perspective. The artist makes Jesus the focal center by framing him in the middle window and locating the vanishing point behind his head. In addition, the arrangement of the banqueting party—Jesus is flanked by six followers on either side—gives the painting a balanced effect. This harmonious composition breaks with the medieval custom of putting the traitor Judas on the opposite side of the table from the others.

A final idealistic touch may be seen in the way that Leonardo hides the face of Judas, the third figure on Jesus' right, in shadow while illuminating the other figures in bright light. Judas, though no longer seated apart from the rest, can still be readily identified, sitting cloaked in shadows, reaching for the bread with his left hand and clutching a bag of silver—symbolic of his treason—in the other hand. For generations, admirers have found Leonardo's fresco so natural and inevitable that it has become the standard version of this Christian subject.

Leonardo's setting and placement of the figures in *The Last Supper* are idealized, but his depiction of the individual figures is meant to convey the psychological truth about each of them. Jesus is portrayed with eyes cast down and arms outstretched in a gesture of resignation, while on either side a tumultuous scene erupts. As the disciples react to Jesus' charge of treason, Leonardo reveals the inner truth about each one through bodily gestures and facial expressions: Beneath the visual tumult, however, the artistic rules of the High Renaissance are firmly in place. Since neither biblical sources nor sacred tradition offered an ordering principle, Leonardo used mathematics to guide his arrangement of the disciples. He divides them into four groups of three figures; each set in turn is composed of two older men and a younger one. In his conception, not only does each figure respond individually, but also each interacts with other group members.

Besides mastering a narrative subject like *The Last Supper*, Leonardo also created a new type of portrait when he painted a half-length view of the seated *Mona Lisa* (Figure 12.7). As the fame of this work spread, other painters (and later, photographers) adopted Leonardo's half-length model as a basic artistic format for portraits. This painting, perhaps the most famous portrait in Western art, was commissioned by a wealthy Florentine merchant. Avoiding the directness of *The Last Supper*, Leonardo hints at the sitter's demure nature through her shy smile and the charmingly awkward gesture of having the fingers of her right hand caress her left arm. In her face, celebrated in song and legend, he blends the likeness of a real person with an everlasting ideal to create a miraculous image. Further heightening the painting's eternal quality, the craggy background isolates the figure in space and time, in much the same way that the grotto functioned in Leonardo's *Virgin of the Rocks* (see Figure 11.22). Finally, he enhances the *Mona Lisa*'s mystery by enveloping the subject in the smoky atmosphere called *sfumato*—made possible by the oil medium—that softens her delicate features and the landscape in the background.

During the High Renaissance, Leonardo's great works contributed to the cult of genius—the high regard, even reverence, that the age accorded to a few select artists, poets, and intellectuals. *The Last Supper* earned him great fame while he was alive. The history of the *Mona Lisa* was more complicated, since it was unseen while he lived and found among his effects when he died in 1519. After his death, as the *Mona Lisa* became widely known, first as a possession of the king of France and later as a jewel in the Louvre collection, Leonardo was elevated to membership among the immortals of Western art.

Michelangelo   While Leonardo was working in Milan during most of the 1490s, Michelangelo Buonarroti [my-kuh-LAN-juh-lo bwo-nahr-ROH-tee] (1475–1564) was beginning a career that would propel him to the

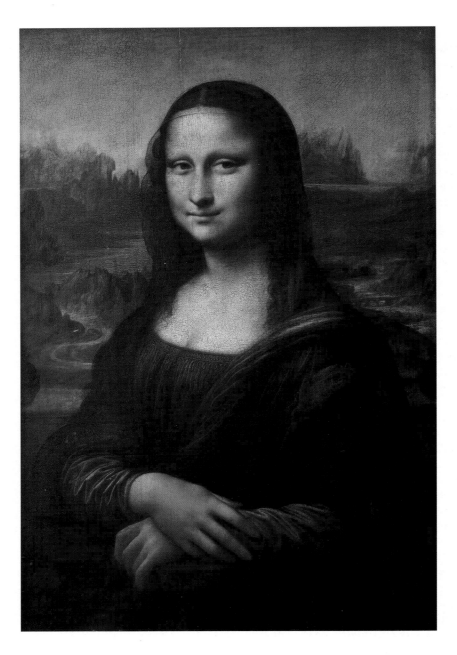

Figure 12.7 LEONARDO DA VINCI. *Mona Lisa.* 1503. Oil on panel, 30¼ × 21". Louvre. *Leonardo's* Mona Lisa, *a likeness of the wife of the merchant Giocondo, illustrates the new status of Italy's urban middle class. This class was beginning to take its social cues from the fashionable world of the courts, the milieu described by Castiglione. Leonardo treats his middle-class subject as a model court lady, imbuing her presence with calm seriousness and quiet dignity.*

forefront of first the Florentine and later the Roman Renaissance, making him the most formidable artist of the sixteenth century. Michelangelo's initial fame rested on his sculptural genius, which manifested itself at the age of thirteen when he was apprenticed to the Early Renaissance master Ghirlandaio and then, one year later, taken into the household of Lorenzo the Magnificent, the Medici ruler of Florence. In time, Michelangelo achieved greatness in painting and architecture as well as in sculpture, but he always remained a sculptor at heart.

Michelangelo's artistic credo was formed early, and he remained faithful to it over his long life. Sculpture, he believed, was the art form whereby human figures were liberated from the lifeless prison of their surrounding material. In this sense, he compared the sculptor's creativity with the activity of God—a notion that would have been judged blasphemous in prior Christian ages. Michelangelo himself, unlike the skeptical Leonardo, was a deeply pious man given to bouts of spiritual anxiety. His art constituted a form of divine worship.

Central to Michelangelo's artistic vision was his most celebrated image, the heroic nude male. Like the ancient Greek and Roman sculptors whose works he studied and admired, Michelangelo viewed the nude male form as a symbol of human dignity. In the High Renaissance, Michelangelo's nudes were based on Classical models, with robust bodies and serene faces. But in the 1530s, with the onset of Mannerism, the growing spiritual crisis in the church, and his own failing health, Michelangelo's depiction of the human figure changed. His later nudes had distorted body proportions and unusually expressive faces.

In 1508 Michelangelo was asked by Pope Julius II to decorate the Sistine Chapel ceiling. Michelangelo tried to avoid this commission, claiming that he was a sculptor and without expertise in frescoes, but the pope was unyielding in his insistence. The chapel had been built by Julius II's uncle, Pope Sixtus IV, in the late 1400s, and most of the walls had already been covered with frescoes. Michelangelo's frescoes were intended to bring the chapel's decorative plan closer to completion.

The challenge of painting the Sistine Chapel ceiling was enormous, for it was almost 70 feet from the floor, its sides were curved downward, necessitating numerous perspective changes, and its area covered some 5,800 square feet. Michelangelo overcame all these difficulties, teaching himself fresco technique and working for four years on scaffolding, to create one of the glories of the High Renaissance and unquestionably the greatest cycle of paintings in Western art (Figure 12.8).

Michelangelo, probably with the support of a papal adviser, designed a complex layout (Figure 12.9) for the ceiling frescoes that combined biblical narrative, theology, Neo-Platonist philosophy, and Classical allusions. In the ceiling's center, running from the altar to the rear of the chapel, he painted nine panels that illustrate the early history of the world, encompassing the creation of the universe, the fall of Adam and Eve, and episodes in the life of Noah. Framing each of these biblical scenes were nude youths, whose presence shows Michelangelo's belief that the male form is an expression of divine power.

On either side of the center panels, he depicted Hebrew prophets and pagan sibyls, or oracles—all foretelling the coming of Christ (Figure 12.10). The pagan sibyls represent the Neo-Platonist idea that God's word was revealed in the prophecies of pre-Christian seers. At the corners of the ceiling, he placed four Old Testament scenes of violence and death that had been allegorized as foreshadowing the coming of Christ. Michelangelo unified this complex of human and divine figures with an illusionistic architectural frame, and he used a plain background to make the figures stand out.

The most famous image from this vast work is a panel from the central section, *The Creation of Adam* (Figure 12.11). In the treatment of this episode from the book of Genesis, Michelangelo reduces the scene to a few details, in accordance with the High Renaissance love of simplicity. Adam, stretched out on a barely sketched bit of ground, seems to exist in some timeless space. Michelangelo depicts Adam as a pulsing, breathing human being. Such wondrous vitality in human flesh had not been seen in Western art since the vigorous nudes of ancient Greek art. In a bold move, Michelangelo ignored the Genesis story that told of God's molding Adam from dust. Instead, the artist paints Adam as half-awakened and reaching to God, who will implant a soul with his divine touch—an illustration of the Neo-Platonic idea of flesh yearning toward the spiritual.

By the 1530s, Michelangelo was painting in the Mannerist style, reflecting his disappointment with Florence's loss of freedom and his own spiritual torment. In this new style, he replaced his heroic vision with a fearful view of the world. A compelling example of this transformation is *The Last Judgment,* painted on the wall behind the Sistine Chapel's altar. This fresco conveys his own sense of sinfulness as well as humanity's future doom (Figure 12.12). Executed twenty-five years after the ceiling frescoes, *The Last Judgment,* with its images of justice and punishment, also reflects the crisis atmosphere of a Europe divided into militant Protestant and Catholic camps. In the center of the fresco, Michelangelo depicts Jesus as the divine and final judge, with right arm raised in a commanding gesture. At the bottom of the fresco, the open graves yield up the dead, and the saved and the damned (on Jesus' right and left, respectively) rise to meet their fate.

In this painting, Michelangelo abandons the architectural framework that had given order to the ceiling frescoes. Instead, the viewer is confronted with a chaotic surface on which a circle of bodies seems to swirl around the central image of Jesus. Michelangelo elongates the bodies and changes their proportions by reducing the size of the heads. There is no classical serenity here; each figure's countenance shows the anguish provoked by this dreaded moment. Faced with judgment, some gesture wildly while others look beseechingly to their Savior. In this Mannerist masterpiece, simplicity has been replaced by exuberant abundance, and order has given way to rich diversity.

Raphael   The youngest of the trio of great High Renaissance painters is Raphael [RAFF-ee-uhl] Santi (1483–1520). Lacking Leonardo's scientific spirit and Michelangelo's brooding genius, Raphael nevertheless

Figure 12.8 MICHELANGELO. Sistine Chapel Ceiling. (Restored.) 1508–1512. Full ceiling 45 × 128'. The Vatican. *Michelangelo's knowledge of architecture prompted him to paint illusionistic niches for the Hebrew prophets and the pagan sibyls on either side of the nine central panels. Neo-Platonism inspired his use of triangles, circles, and squares, for these geometric shapes were believed to hold the key to the mystery of the universe. These various framing devices enabled him to give visual order to the more than three hundred figures in his monumental scheme.*

Figure 12.9 Plan of Ceiling Frescoes, Sistine Chapel. 1508–1512. *The paintings on the Sistine Chapel ceiling may be grouped as follows: (1) the central section, which presents the history of the world from the creation (called "The Separation of Light from the Darkness") through the "Drunkenness of Noah"; (2) the gallery of portraits on both sides and at either end, which depict biblical prophets and pagan oracles; and (3) the four corner panels depicting Jewish heroes and heroines who overcame difficulties to help their people survive.*

Judith and Holofernes	Delphica	Josiah	Isaiah	Ezekias	Cumaea	Asa	Daniel	Jesse	Libyca	Moses and the Serpent of Brass
Zechariah	Drunkenness of Noah	The Flood	Sacrifice of Noah	Temptation and Expulsion	Creation of Eve	Creation of Adam	Separation of Land from Water	Creation of Sun, Moon, Plants	Separation of Light from Darkness	Jonah
David and Goliath	Joel	Zorobabel	Erythraea	Ozias	Ezekiel	Roboam	Persica	Salmon	Jeremiah	The Death of Haman

Figure 12.10 MICHELANGELO. *The Delphic Oracle* (Delphica). Detail of the Sistine Chapel ceiling. 1508–1512. The Vatican. *Michelangelo, despite his manifold gifts as painter, sculptor, architect, and poet, always thought of himself as a sculptor, and this is nowhere more evident than in his portrait of the Delphic Oracle from the Sistine Chapel ceiling frescoes. The oracle, or Delphica (her Latin name), is painted to resemble a sculpture, seated on an illusory throne and holding an open scroll, from whose reading she appears interrupted. Delphica's muscular body is a deviation from Classical sculptural ideals of feminine beauty and reflects, instead, Michelangelo's practice of using male models for female subjects. He was also fascinated by the anatomy of position, as in the effect on Delphica's body of her head turned to the left and of one arm upraised and the other at rest. In symbolic terms, Delphica, according to the ceiling's Neo-Platonic plan, represented the pagan Greek prophetess foretelling the coming of Jesus Christ.*

Figure 12.11 MICHELANGELO. *The Creation of Adam.* Detail (restored) of the Sistine Chapel ceiling. 1511. 9′5″ × 18′8″. The Vatican. *One of the most celebrated details of this fresco is the outstretched fingers of God and Adam that approach but do not touch. By means of this vivid symbol, Michelangelo suggests that a divine spark is about to pass from God into the body of Adam, electrifying it into the fullness of life. The image demonstrates the restraint characteristic of the High Renaissance style. The Vatican's ongoing restoration of the Sistine Chapel frescoes has revealed the brilliant colors of the original, apparent in this detail.*

Figure 12.12 MICHELANGELO. *The Last Judgment.* 1536–1541. 48 × 44'. Sistine Chapel, the Vatican. *This* Last Judgment *summarizes the anti-Classicism that was sweeping through the visual arts. Other painters studied this fresco for inspiration, borrowing its seemingly chaotic composition, its focus on large numbers of male nudes, and its use of bizarre perspective and odd postures as expressions of the Mannerist sensibility. This fresco was recently restored, its colors returned to the vivid primary colors of Michelangelo's original design and the draperies removed (they had been added during the Catholic Reformation).*

had such artistry that his graceful works expressed the ideals of this style better than did those of any other painter. Trained in Urbino, Raphael spent four years (from 1504 to 1508) in Florence, where he absorbed the local painting tradition, learning from the public works of both Leonardo and Michelangelo. Inspired by what he saw, Raphael developed his artistic ideal of well-ordered space in which human beauty and spatial harmony were given equal treatment.

Moving to Rome, Raphael had an abundance of patrons, especially the popes. At the heart of Raphael's success was his talent for blending the sacred and the secular, and in an age when a pope led troops into battle or went on hunting parties, this gift was appreciated and rewarded. Perhaps Raphael's most outstanding work in Rome was the cycle of paintings for the *stanze,* or rooms, of the Vatican apartment—one of the finest patronage plums of the High Renaissance. Commissioned by Julius .II, the *stanze* frescoes show the same harmonization of Christianity and Classicism that Michelangelo brought to the Sistine Chapel ceiling.

Raphael's plan for the four walls of the Stanza della Segnatura in the papal chambers had as its subjects philosophy, poetry, theology, and law. Of these, the most famous is the fresco devoted to philosophy called *The School of Athens* (Figure 12.13). In this work, Raphael depicts a sober discussion among a group of ancient philosophers drawn from all periods. Follow-

ing Leonardo's treatment of the disciples in *The Last Supper,* Raphael arranges the philosophers in groups, giving each scholar a characteristic gesture that reveals the essence of his thought. For example, Diogenes sprawls on the steps apart from the rest—a vivid symbol of the arch Cynic's contempt for his fellow man. In the right foreground, Euclid, the author of a standard text on geometry, illustrates the proof of one of his theorems. In his careful arrangement of this crowd scene, Raphael demonstrates that he is a master of ordered space.

The School of Athens has a majestic aura because of Raphael's adherence to Classical forms and ideas. The architectural setting, with its round arches, medallions, and coffered ceilings, is inspired by Classical architectural ruins and also perhaps by contemporary structures. Perfectly balanced, the scene is focused on Plato and Aristotle, who stand under the series of arches at the painting's center. Raphael reinforces their central position by placing the vanishing point just above and between their heads. The two thinkers' contrasting gestures symbolize the difference between their philosophies: Plato, on the left, points his finger skyward, suggesting the world of the Forms, or abstract thought, and Aristotle, on the right, motions toward the earth, indicating his more practical and empirical method. Raphael also uses these two thinkers as part of his ordering scheme to represent the division of philosophy into the arts and sciences. On Plato's side, the poetic

Figure 12.13 RAPHAEL. *The School of Athens.* 1510–1511. Fresco, 18 × 26′. Stanza della Segnatura, the Vatican. *Much of Raphael's success stemmed from the ease with which he assimilated the prevailing ideas of his age. For instance, the posture of the statue of Apollo in the wall niche on the left is probably derived from Michelangelo's* Dying Slave *(see Figure 12.1). For all his artistic borrowings, however, Raphael could be very generous, as indicated by the conspicuous way he highlights Michelangelo's presence in this fresco: The brooding genius sits alone in the foreground, lost in his thoughts and oblivious to the hubbub swirling about him.*

thinkers are gathered under the statue of Apollo, the Greek god of music and lyric verse; Aristotle's half includes the scientists under the statue of Athena, the Greek goddess of wisdom.

Of even greater fame than Raphael's narrative paintings are his portraits of the Virgin Mary. They set the standard for this form of portraiture with their exquisite sweetness and harmonious composition. The *Sistine Madonna* is probably the best known of this group (Figure 12.14). This painting shows Raphael at his best, borrowing from several sources yet creating his own convincing style. It is composed in the pyramid shape first popularized by Leonardo da Vinci (see Figure 11.22). The Virgin's head forms the apex of the pyramid, Pope Julius II (whose death the painting commemorates) stands bareheaded on her right, and St. Barbara, the patron saint of the arrival of death, on her left; the drape of the curtains underscores the pyramidal design. Raphael relieves the scene's somber mood by painting below the hovering figures two mischievous *putti,* or angels, who look upward, unimpressed with the scene-stealing baby Jesus. Raphael's assurance in handling these complex effects makes the *Sistine Madonna* a glowing masterpiece of the High Renaissance.

The Venetian School: Giorgione and Titian Venice maintained its autonomy during the High Renaissance both politically and culturally. Despite the artistic pull of the Roman and Florentine schools, the Venetian artists stayed true to their Byzantine-influenced tradition of sensual surfaces, rich colors, and theatrical lighting. The two greatest painters of the Venetian High Renaissance were Giorgione [jor-JO-na] (about 1477–1510), who was acknowledged to be Venice's premier artist at the end of his life, and Titian [TISH-uhn] (about 1488–1576), who in his later years was revered as Europe's supreme painter.

Little is known of Giorgione's life until the last years of his brief career. A student of Bellini, he won early fame, indicated by the rich private and public commissions he was awarded. Although only a few of his works survive, Giorgione's influence on the course of European art was substantial. His two major innova-

Figure 12.14 RAPHAEL. *Sistine Madonna.* 1513. Oil on canvas, 8′8½″ × 6′5″. Gemäldegalerie, Dresden. *Raphael's adherence to the rules of Classical art in the* Sistine Madonna *is nowhere more evident than in the painting's balanced composition. Bracketing the central image of the Virgin and child are a variety of pairings: At the top, two curtains are drawn open; toward the middle, two human figures kneel in prayer; and the open space between the draperies above is echoed by the two angels below. These artful pairings not only give visual variety to the simple scene but also outline and define the sacred space surrounding the Virgin and child.*

tions, the female nude and the landscape, contributed to the growing secularization of European painting. These developments helped to make Venetian art distinctive from that of Rome and Florence.

The Tempest (Figure 12.15) is probably his best-known work. Breaking free of Bellini's influence, Giorgione created a dramatic landscape, framed on the left by a soldier and on the right by a partly clothed mother nursing a child, which did not allude to mythology, the Bible, or allegorical stories. While Bellini's *St. Francis in Ecstasy* (see Figure 11.23) made the saint the focus of the painting, in *The Tempest* the framing figures are overshadowed by the menacing storm. Thus, Giorgione's landscape, freed of storytelling elements, becomes the subject and should be appreciated on its own terms.

Titian's paintings were prized not only for their easy grace and natural lighting—characteristics of the Venetian High Renaissance—but also for the masterful use of rich color to create dramatic effects (see Figure 12.3). Titian's adherence to the principles of High Renaissance style is evident in such narrative paintings as his *Presentation of the Virgin in the Temple,* a subject based on a legendary account of the life of Mary (Figure 12.16). Titian's careful arrangement of this complicated scene—with its landscape, classicizing architecture, and gathering of accessory figures—reflects his commitment to the principles of simplicity and naturalism. He conceived of the scene as a sweeping pageant, starting on the left with the pious procession and culminating with the young Mary, standing on the temple stairs in the middle right. Waiting to greet her at the head of the stairs are the high priest and other officials.

One deviation from Classical principles in this painting is the asymmetry of the closed architectural forms on the right set against the open landscape on the left. Instead of symmetry, Titian uses color as a unifying element. Cool colors, primarily blue, are prominent in the sky and the mountains on the left; warm

Figure 12.15 GIORGIONE. *The Tempest.* 1505. Oil on canvas, 31¼ × 28¾″. Galleria dell'Accademia, Venice. *Giorgione's mysterious painting evokes the period—called an "anxious hush"—that sometimes attends the prelude to a violent thunderstorm He creates this tense mood through atmospheric effects that suggest a gathering storm: billowing clouds; a flash of lightning and its watery reflection; and, in particular, the stark color contrasts between the harshly lighted buildings and the somber hues of earth, sky, and river. The mood is also heightened by the presence of two vulnerable figures, especially the nursing mother who gazes quizzically at the viewer, about to be engulfed by the storm. The painting has a typical Venetian feature in its carefully rendered textures—flesh, cloth, wood, stone, and foliage. Giorgione's painting blazed the path for later artists, chiefly in northern Europe, who took the landscape as a subject.*

Figure 12.16 TITIAN. *Presentation of the Virgin in the Temple.* 1534–1538. 11′ 4″ × 25′ 5″. Originally in the Scuola Grande di Santa Maria della Carità, now part of the Accademia di Belle Arte, Venice. *Titian's painting is filled with symbols conveying Christian ideas. The Virgin is bathed in an oval of light of which she is the source; light is a traditional symbol of God's presence. On the left, the tall, thin pyramid alludes to Mary's divine status; it is a Renaissance symbol of Holy Wisdom, an attribute of the Virgin. The large cumulus cloud in the distance refers to the Holy Spirit, and the begging woman at the rear of the procession symbolizes Charity, or Almsgiving. Most complex of all are the two images in front of the stairway: the old egg seller who appears oblivious to the momentous event taking place above her head, and, to the right of the door, an ancient bust. Scholars identify these two images, respectively, with Judaism and paganism, both of which were to be superseded by the coming of Christ.*

Figure 12.17 PARMIGIANINO. *Madonna with the Long Neck.* 1534–1540. Oil on panel, 7′ 1″ × 4′ 4″. Uffizi Gallery, Florence. *This Madonna by Parmigianino is one of the landmark works in the rise of the Mannerist style. Ignoring Classical ideals, Parmigianino exaggerates the Virgin's body proportions, especially the slender hands and long neck, and elongates the body of the sleeping Jesus. This anti-Classical portrait was greatly at odds with the prevailing High Renaissance image of the Madonna established by Raphael.*

Figure 12.18 MICHELANGELO. *Pietà.* 1498–1499. Marble, ht. 5′ 8½″. St. Peter's, the Vatican. *This* Pietà *is the only one of Michelangelo's sculptures to be signed. Initially, it was exhibited without a signature, but, according to a legend, when Michelangelo overheard spectators attributing the statue to a rival sculptor, he carved his signature into the marble strap that crosses Mary's chest.*

colors, mainly brown and pink, are the primary hues of the buildings and the vestments of the temple leaders on the right. Because he used subtle modulations of color to create harmony in his works, Titian became the leading "colorist"—as opposed to those more concerned with form—to future generations of painters.

The School of Parma: Parmigianino Parma, in northern Italy, was another center of High Renaissance art, but the city's best-known artist is a founder of Mannerism, Parmigianino [pahr-mee-jah-NEE-noh] (1503–1540). The *Madonna with the Long Neck* shows Parmigianino's delight in ambiguity, distortion, and dissonance and his love of eccentric composition (Figure 12.17). Mary is portrayed with sloping shoulders and long arms in the manner of Botticelli, and her sensuous figure is not quite hidden under diaphanous

draperies—a disturbing mix of sacred and profane love. A similar confusion exists in the depiction of the infant Christ: The bald baby Jesus appears more dead than alive, so that the subject invokes the Pietà image of the dead Christ stretched on his mother's lap along with the image of the Virgin and child. On the left, five figures stare in various directions. In the background, unfinished columns and an old man reading a scroll, perhaps an allusion to biblical prophecies of Jesus' birth, add to the feeling of multiple focuses and contradictory scales. Unlike the art of the High Renaissance, which offered readily understood subjects, this Mannerist painting, with its uneasy blend of religious piety and disguised sexuality, is enigmatic.

Sculpture

Michelangelo's art is as central to the High Renaissance style in sculpture as it is in painting. An early sculpture that helped to inaugurate this style was the *Pietà*, executed when he was twenty-one (Figure 12.18). The touching subject of the **Pietà**—Mary holding the body

Figure 12.19   MICHELANGELO. *David.* 1501–1504. Marble, ht. 14′ 3″. Accademia, Florence. *Michelangelo's colossal David—standing more than 14 feet tall—captures the balanced ideal of High Renaissance art. The "closed" right side with its tensed hanging arm echoes the right leg, which supports the figure's weight; in the same way, the "open" left side with its bent arm is the precise counterpart of the flexed left leg. Further tension arises from the contrast between David's steady stare and the readiness of the right fist, which holds the stone. Through these means, Michelangelo reinforces the image of a young man wavering between thought and action.*

PERSONAL PERSPECTIVE

GIORGIO VASARI
Lives of the Most Eminent Painters, Sculptors, and Architects

Vasari (1511–1574) actually studied painting under Michelangelo, but he is known today for his accounts of the lives of Renaissance artists, sculptors, and architects. In this excerpt, he describes how Michelangelo executed his most famous work, the David.

Some of his [Michelangelo's] friends wrote to him from Florence urging him to return there as it seemed very probable that he would be able to obtain the block of marble that was standing in the Office of Works. Piero Soderini, who about that time was elected Gonfalonier for life [head of the Florentine republic], had often talked of handing it over to Leonardo da Vinci, but he was then arranging to give it to Andrea Contucci of Monte Sansovino, an accomplished sculptor who was very keen to have it. Now, although it seemed impossible to carve from the block a complete figure (and only Michelangelo was bold enough to try this without adding fresh pieces) Buonarroti had felt the desire to work on it many years before; and he tried to obtain it when he came back to Florence. The marble was eighteen feet high, but unfortunately an artist called Simone da Fiesole had started to carve a giant figure, and had bungled the work so badly that he had hacked a hole between the legs and left the block completely botched and misshapen. So the wardens of Santa Maria del Fiore (who were in charge of the undertaking) threw the block aside and it stayed abandoned for many years and seemed likely to remain so indefinitely. However, Michelangelo measured it again and calculated whether he could carve a satisfactory figure from the block by accommodating its attitude to the shape of the stone. Then he made up his mind to ask for it. Soderini and the wardens decided that they would let him have it, as being something of little value, and telling themselves that since the stone was of no use to their building, either botched as it was or broken up, whatever Michelangelo made would be worthwhile. So Michelangelo made a wax model of the young David with a sling in his hand; this was intended as a symbol of liberty for the Palace, signifying that just as David had protected his people and governed them justly, so whoever ruled Florence should vigorously defend the city and govern it with justice. He began work on the statue in the Office of Works of Santa Maria del Fiore, erecting a partition of planks and trestles around the marble; and working on it continuously he brought it to perfect completion, without letting anyone see it. . . .

When he saw the David in place Piero Soderini was delighted; but while Michelangelo was retouching it he remarked that he thought the nose was too thick. Michelangelo, noticing that the Gonfalonier was standing beneath the Giant and that from where he was he could not see the figure properly, to satisfy him climbed on the scaffolding by the shoulders, seized hold of a chisel in his left hand, together with some of the marble dust lying on the planks, and as he tapped lightly with the chisel let the dust fall little by little, without altering anything. Then he looked down at the Gonfalonier, who had stopped to watch, and said:

"Now look at it."

"Ah, that's much better," replied Soderini. "Now you've really brought it to life."

And then Michelangelo climbed down, feeling sorry for those critics who talk nonsense in the hope of appearing well informed.

---

of the dead Christ—struck a responsive chord in Michelangelo, for he created several sculptural variations on the Pietà theme during his lifetime.

The first *Pietà*, executed in 1498–1499, about the same time as Leonardo's *Last Supper*, shows Michelangelo already at the height of his creative powers. He has captured completely a bewildering sense of loss in his quiet rendering of Mary's suffering. Everything about the sculpture reinforces the somber subject: the superb modeling of Jesus' dead body, with its heavy head and dangling legs; Mary's outstretched gown, which serves as a shroud; and Mary's body, burdened by the weight of her son. Like some ancient funeral monument, which the *Pietà* brings to mind, this sculpture of Mary and Jesus overwhelms the viewer with its sorrowful but serene mood.

In 1501, two years after finishing the *Pietà*, Michelangelo was given the commission by the city of Florence for the sculpture that is generally recognized as his supreme masterpiece, the *David* (Figure 12.19). Michelangelo was eager for this commission because it allowed him to test himself against other great sculptors who had tackled this subject, such as Donatello in the Early Renaissance (see Figure 11.11). Moreover, Michelangelo, a great Florentine patriot, identified David with the aggressive spirit of his native city.

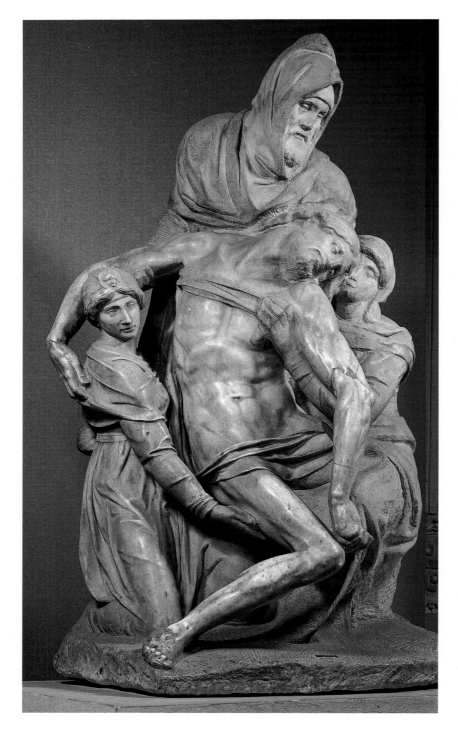

Figure 12.20 MICHELANGELO. *Pietà.* Before 1555. Marble, ht. 7′ 8″. Santa Maria del Fiore, Florence. *The rage that seemed to infuse Michelangelo's Mannerist vision in* The Last Judgment *appears purged in this Pietà—the work he was finishing when he died at the age of eighty-eight. Mannerist distortions are still present, particularly in the twisted body of the dead Christ and the implied downward motion of the entire ensemble. But the gentle faces suggest that serenity has been restored to Michelangelo's art.*

Michelangelo's *David* was instantly successful, and the republic of Florence adopted the statue as its civic symbol, placing the work in the open square before the Palazzo Vecchio, the town hall. Damage to the statue through weathering and local unrest caused the civic leaders eventually to house Michelangelo's most famous sculpture indoors, where it remains today.

Michelangelo's *David*, rather than imitating Donatello's partly clothed and somewhat effete version, portrays the young Jewish warrior as a nude, Classical hero. Taking a damaged and abandoned block of marble, Michelangelo carved the colossal *David* as a muscular adolescent with his weight gracefully balanced on the right leg, in Classical contrapposto. The *David* perfectly represents Michelangelo's conception of sculpture; imaging a human figure imprisoned inside marble, he simply used his chisel to set it free.

Michelangelo also made minor deviations from Classical principles in his rendition of David in the name of higher ideals, just as ancient artists had done. David's large hands, for example, are outside Classical proportions and suggest a youth who has yet to grow to his potential. And his furrowed brow violates the Classical ideal of serene faces but reflects his intense concentration.

Michelangelo's later sculpture is Mannerist in style, as are his later paintings. A second *Pietà* group—with Christ, Mary, Mary Magdalene, and Joseph of Arimathea—shows the change in his depiction of the human form (Figure 12.20). In this somber group, Michelangelo's anti-Classical spirit is paramount. Jesus' body is elongated and unnaturally twisted in death; the other figures, with great difficulty, struggle to support his dead weight. But rather than detracting from the sculpture's impact, the awkward body adds to the scene's emotional interest—an aim of Mannerist art, which did not trust the viewer to respond to more orderly images. Joseph, the rich man who, according to the Gospel, donated his own tomb to Jesus, has Michelangelo's face—a face that is more a death mask than a human countenance.

Architecture

The architectural heir to Alberti in the early sixteenth century was Donato Bramante [brah-MAHN-tay] (1444–1514), who became the moving force behind the High Renaissance in architecture. Trained as a painter,

Bramante rejected the reigning building style, called **scenographic,** in which buildings are composed of discrete, individual units. Instead, by concentrating on space and volume, Bramante created an architecture that was unified in all its components and that followed the rules of the Classical orders.

The clearest surviving expression of Bramante's architectural genius is the Tempietto, or little temple, in Rome (Figure 12.21). This small structure was designed both as a church, seating ten worshipers, and as a building marking the site of the martyrdom of St. Peter. Copied from the circular temples of ancient Rome, this small domed building became the prototype of the central plan church popularized in the High Renaissance and later.

Bramante's design for the Tempietto sprang from ancient Classical principles. Foremost was his belief that architecture should appeal to human reason and that a building should present a severe appearance and not seek to please through specially planned effects. Further, he thought that a building should be unified like a piece of sculpture and that ornamentation should be restricted to a few architectural details.

In accordance with this artistic credo, the Tempietto functions like a work of sculpture; it is raised on a pedestal with steps leading up to its colonnaded porch. In the absence of sculptural decorations, the temple's

Figure 12.21 BRAMANTE. Tempietto. After 1502. Marble, ht. 46'; diameter of colonnade 29'. San Pietro in Montorio, Rome. *Bramante's Tempietto is the earliest surviving High Renaissance building and an exquisite example of this style. Fashioned from pure Classical forms, the building is almost devoid of decoration except for architectural features, and the separate parts—dome, cylindrical drum, and base—are brought into a harmonious whole. The only significant missing feature (since High Renaissance buildings were always planned in relation to their enveloping space) is the never-finished courtyard.*

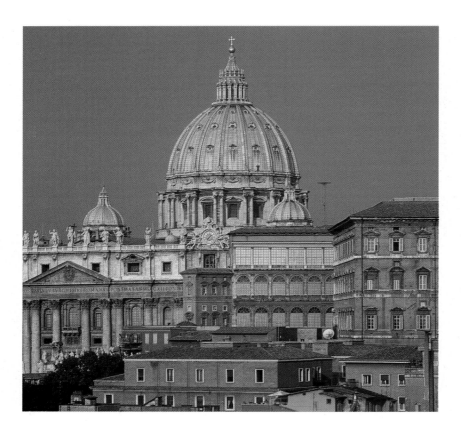

Figure 12.22 MICHELANGELO. Dome of St. Peter's. View from the southwest. 1546–1564. (Completed by Giacomo della Porta, 1590.) Ht. of dome 452'. Rome. *Its harmonious design and its reliance on Classical forms made Michelangelo's dome an object of universal admiration when it was completed in 1590, after his death. From then to the present day, other architects have used his dome as a model, hoping to reproduce its Classical spirit.*

exterior is accented with architectural details: the columns; the **balustrade,** or rail with supporting posts; and the dome with barely visible ribs. The proportions of its various features, such as the ratio of column widths to column heights, were based on ancient mathematical formulas. Unfortunately for Bramante's final conception, the plan to integrate the small temple into a circular courtyard of a nearby church was never completed. Despite the absence of this crowning touch, the Tempietto is one of the jewels of the High Renaissance.

Bramante had been commissioned by Pope Julius II to rebuild St. Peter's Basilica, the world's most famous church, but he died before his plans could be carried out. The supervision of the rebuilding of St. Peter's fell to other architects; eventually Michelangelo, at the age of seventy-one, was given this vital task. From 1546 until his death in 1564, Michelangelo, among his other artistic tasks, was occupied with St. Peter's, especially with the construction of the dome. Over the years, other building projects had come his way, but nothing could compare with the significance of this one. Although the dome was completed after his death and slightly modified, it remains Michelangelo's outstanding architectural monument and a splendid climax to his career.

Michelangelo's sculptural approach to architecture was similar to that of Bramante. In an attempt to integrate the dome of St. Peter's with the rest of the existing structure, Michelangelo used double Corinthian columns as a unifying agent. Because the facade of St. Peter's was altered in the 1600s, Michelangelo's dome

is best observed from the southwest (Figure 12.22). Beginning at ground level, the Corinthian order provides the artistic cement that pulls the entire building together. Sometimes as columns, sometimes as pilasters, and sometimes as ribs, the double Corinthian units move up the walls, eventually up the dome's drum, and up the dome itself.

This plan for St. Peter's shows that Michelangelo the architect differed from Michelangelo the painter and sculptor. In painting and sculpture, he had by the 1530s become a Mannerist in his use of exaggeration and expressive effects. But in architecture, he stayed faithful to the High Renaissance and its ideal of harmonious design.

The preeminent architect of the Mannerist style was Andrea di Pietro (1508–1580), known as Palladio [pah-LAHD-yo], whose base of operations was Vicenza, in northern Italy. The name Palladio derives from Pallas, a name for Athena, the goddess of wisdom. Palladio's artistic creed was rooted in Classicism, but his forte was the richly inventive way in which he could arrange the Classical elements of a building to guarantee surprise. He played with the effects of light and shadow, adding feature on top of feature, to create buildings that possess infinite variety in the midst of a certain decorative solemnity.

Palladio's most influential domestic design was the Villa Capra, more commonly called the Villa Rotonda because of its central circular area and covering dome (Figure 12.23). Inspired by ancient Roman farmhouses, the Villa Rotonda is a sixteenth-century country house

Figure 12.23 PALLADIO. Villa Rotonda (Villa Capra). Begun 1550. (Completed by Vincenzo Scamozzi.) Ht. of dome 70′, villa 80′ square. Vicenza. *Despite its harmonious proportions and Classical features, the Villa Rotonda belongs to the Mannerist style. Unlike High Renaissance buildings, which were designed to be integrated with their settings, this boxlike country house stands in an antagonistic relationship to its surrounding garden space. Furthermore, the Mannerist principle of elongation is apparent in its four long stairways. But the Villa Rotonda's most striking Mannerist feature is the surprise inherent in a plan that includes four identical porches.*

built of brick and faced with stucco and located on a rise overlooking Vicenza. A dome provides a central axis from which four symmetrical wings radiate. Each of the four wings in turn opens to the outdoors through an Ionic-style porch raised on a pedestal. The porticoes, or covered porches supported by columns, then lead to the ground level through deeply recessed stairways. Statues stand on the corners and peak of each of the four pediments, and others flank the four stairways.

Palladio's Mannerist spirit can be seen at work in the design of this building. Although the coldly formal porches are Classical in appearance, no Greek or Roman temple would have had four such identical porches, one on each side of the building (Figure 12.24). Palladio's design incorporates the unexpected and the contradictory within an apparently Classical structure.

Besides designing buildings, Palladio also wrote about architecture in his treatise *Quattro libri dell' architettura,* or *The Four Books of Architecture.* Through its

Figure 12.24 PALLADIO. Floor Plan of the Villa Rotonda. *Palladio designed the Villa Rotonda to further the social ambitions of its wealthy Venetian owner, so he made its most prominent interior feature a central circular area, or rotunda. Surmounted by a dome, this area was ideal for concerts, parties, and other entertainments. Palladio surrounded the rotunda with four identically shaped sets of rooms on two levels, where the family lived and guests were housed. Passageways led to the four porches, where villa residents could obtain relief from the summer's heat and enjoy diverting views of the surrounding countryside.*

English translation, this work gained wide currency and led to the vogue of Palladianism in the English-speaking world. English aristocrats in the eighteenth century commissioned country houses built on Palladian principles, as did plantation owners in America's antebellum South.

Music

No radical break separates the music of the High Renaissance from that of the Early Renaissance. Josquin des Prez, the leading composer of the dominant Franco-Netherlandish school, had brought to a climax the Early Renaissance style of music while he was employed in Italy by the popes and the local aristocrats (see Chapter 11). Josquin's sixteenth-century pieces, which consist chiefly of religious Masses and motets along with secular *chansons,* or songs, simply heightened the ideal already present in his earlier works: a sweet sound produced by multiple voices, usually two to six, singing *a cappella* and expressing the feelings described in the text. Despite his interest in music's emotional power, Josquin continued to subordinate the song to the words—thus reflecting the needs of the church, the foremost patron of the age. This balancing act between the music and the words, resulting in a clearly sung text, was also evidence of the Classical restraint of his High Renaissance style. A striking feature of this style was the rich multichoral effect produced when the singing group was subdivided into different combinations of voices.

Experimentation with choral effects was carried into the next generation by Adrian Willaert [VIL-art] (about 1490–1562), a member of the Netherlandish school and a disciple of Josquin's. After the death of his mentor, Willaert was probably Europe's most influential composer. He made his mark on musical history from his post as chapel master of the cathedral of St. Mark's in Venice, and he is considered the founder of the Venetian school of music. Taking advantage of St. Mark's two organs and the Venetian practice of blending instruments with voices, he wrote music for two choirs as well. By a variety of musical mechanisms, such as alternating and combining voices, contrasting soft and loud, and arranging echo effects, Willaert created beautiful and expressive sounds that were the ancestor of the splendid church concertos of the Baroque era. A benefit of Willaert's innovations was that the organ was released from its dependence on vocal music.

Except for the stylistic perfection achieved by Josquin and Willaert, the musical scene during this period witnessed only minor changes from that of the Early Renaissance. Instrumental music still played a secondary role to the human voice, though Josquin and Willaert composed a few pieces for specific instruments, either transposing melodies that originally had been intended for singers or adapting music forms from dance tunes.

The development that had the most promise for the future was the invention of families of instruments, ranging from the low bass to the high treble, which blended to make a pleasant sound (Figure 12.25). In most cases, these families, called **consorts,** consisted of either recorders or viols. The consorts represented the principle of the mixed instrumental ensemble, and from this beginning would emerge the orchestra. Recorders and viols could also be blended to make an agreeable sound; when human voices were added to the mixture, the conditions were ripe for opera.

Figure 12.25 HANS BURGKMAIR. *Maximilian with His Musicians.* Illustration from *Der Weisskunig.* Sixteenth century. Woodcut. Courtesy of the Metropolitan Museum of Art. Gift of William Loring Andrews, 1888. (88.1 fol. 142b). *This woodcut depicts the Holy Roman emperor Maximilian surrounded by his court musicians. Among the instruments being played are an organ, a flute, a harp, and a harpsichord-type instrument. On the tabletop at the right are a viol, recorders, and a cromorne (a curved instrument with a double reed), and piled together in the right foreground are a lute, drums, a kettledrum, and an ancestor of the slide trombone. Rounding out this musical scene is the quartet of singers in the upper left.*

The Legacy of the High Renaissance and Early Mannerism

From a contemporary perspective, the seventy-year period during which the High Renaissance and Early Mannerism flourished is the Golden Age of the West in certain artistic and humanistic areas. In the visual arts—painting, sculpture, and architecture—standards were set and indelible images created that have not been surpassed. In political theory, this age produced the Mannerist thinker Machiavelli, who is the founder of modern political thought.

Beyond those achievements, two other important steps were being taken on the road to the modern world. On a political level, the beginnings of the modern secular state may be seen in the changes taking place in France, Spain, and England. What was innovative, even revolutionary, for these countries in the early sixteenth century has become second nature to the states of the twenty-first century, both in the Western world and beyond. On a social level, a new code of behavior appeared in the Italian courts and was in time adopted throughout Europe. Not only did the rules of courtesy finally penetrate into the European aristocracy and alter their behavior, but also they eventually trickled down to the middle classes. By our day, the behavior of Castiglione's courtier and lady, though in diluted form, has become the model for all Western people with any shred of social ambition.

Another new idea was beginning to develop now as well. The Classical and the medieval worlds had praised what was corporate and public, in conformity with traditional, universal values. But in the 1500s a few artists and humanists, along with their patrons, began to revere what was individual and private. The supreme example of free expression and of the "cult of genius" in the High Renaissance was Leonardo da Vinci, whose encoded notebooks were meant for his personal use and not for general publication. Early Mannerism carried individual expression to extremes by finding merit in personal eccentricities and unrestrained behavior. That patrons supported the new works of these artists and humanists demonstrates the rise of the belief that free expression is both a social and a private good. Both the High Renaissance and Early Mannerism encouraged the daring idea of individualism and thereby introduced what has become a defining theme of Western culture.

KEY CULTURAL TERMS

High Renaissance	scenographic
Mannerism	balustrade
Machiavellianism	consort
Pietà	

SUGGESTIONS FOR FURTHER READING

PRIMARY SOURCES

CASTIGLIONE, B. *The Book of the Courtier*. Translated by G. Bull. New York: Penguin, 1967. A flowing translation; includes a helpful introduction and descriptions of characters who participate in the conversations recorded by Castiglione; first published in 1528.

MACHIAVELLI, N. *The Prince*. Translated by G. Bull. New York: Penguin, 1971. The introduction covers Machiavelli's life and other writings to set the stage for this important political work; written in 1513.

SUGGESTIONS FOR LISTENING

WILLAERT, ADRIAN (about 1490–1562). Willaert is particularly noted for his motets, such as *Sub tuum praesidium*, which reflect the Renaissance humanist ideal of setting the words precisely to the music. His *Musica nova*, published in 1559 and including motets, madrigals, and instrumental music, illustrates the complex polyphony and sensuous sounds that made him a widely imitated composer in the second half of the sixteenth century.

1500

1500

AD

Albertus Durerus Noricu
ipsum me proprijs sic effin
gebam coloribus ætatis
anno XXVIII.

13 NORTHERN HUMANISM, NORTHERN RENAISSANCE, RELIGIOUS REFORMATIONS, AND LATE MANNERISM 1500–1603

As the High Renaissance and Early Mannerism were unfolding in Italy (see Chapter 12), the rest of Europe was being transformed by three developments: a literary movement, two new artistic styles, and a religious crisis. The literary movement and the new artistic styles were partially inspired by the cultural changes under way in Italy. However, the religious crisis, in its early years, was unique to northern Europe; by midcentury, it had become intertwined with local and international politics. Northern (or Christian) humanism, as the literary movement was called, was inspired by both the Italian Renaissance, with its emphasis on Classical studies, and Late Medieval lay piety, with its focus on a simpler Christianity. Two distinct artistic styles now appeared in Europe: the Northern Renaissance, lasting from 1500 until about 1560, and Late Mannerism, enduring for the rest of the century. The course of these literary and artistic developments was, in turn, affected by the religious crisis that soon engulfed all of Europe (Timeline 13.1).

Germany became the epicenter of the spiritual earthquake called the **Reformation,** a movement that forever shattered the religious unity of the West. The Reformation, like the Renaissance, looked to the past for inspiration and ideas, but rather than focusing on the Classical world of Greece and Rome, the religious leaders of the Reformation looked to the early Christian church before it became hierarchical and bureaucratic. Almost immediately, these reformers met with unbending resistance from the contemporary church and its officials. From the confrontations between these hostile groups emerged the labels the two sides still wear today: the Protestants, who wanted a

◀ ALBRECHT DÜRER. *Self-Portrait.* 1500. Oil on panel, 26¼ × 19¼". Alte Pinakothek, Munich.

Timeline 13.1 THE SIXTEENTH CENTURY

1500				1545	1563			1600
The Reformation and Founding of the Protestant Order					Council of Trent	The Counter-Reformation		

| 1509 Erasmus's *The Praise of Folly* | 1517 Luther's Ninety-five Theses | 1521 Independent Lutheran churches founded | 1533 Church of England founded | 1540 Jesuit order founded | 1564 Death of Michelangelo | 1586 El Greco's *Burial of Count Orgaz* | 1592–1594 Tintoretto's *Last Supper* |
| 1513 Dürer's *Knight, Death, and the Devil* | | | | 1541 Independent Calvinist churches founded | 1566 Bruegel's *Peasant Wedding Dance* | 1590–1610 Shakespeare's plays performed | |

complete renovation of the church, and the Roman Catholics, who were largely satisfied with the church as it was.

The Catholics did not oppose all change, however. In the second half of the sixteenth century, they conducted the **Counter-Reformation,** purifying the church and setting it on the path that it followed until the 1960s. In contrast, the Protestants disagreed over basic Christian doctrines and soon split into separate sects.

In the 1560s, the Counter-Reformation began to have a strong impact on culture, especially in Spain and Italy. Late Mannerism in the arts, architecture, and music flourished in these areas, until the Baroque style rose at the end of the century. One outstanding exception to this late Mannerist trend was found in Spanish literature. Spanish writing, which had entered its Golden Age in about 1500, reached its zenith with the works of Cervantes.

NORTHERN HUMANISM

Northern humanism, also known as **Christian humanism,** shared some of the aesthetic values of the High Renaissance, such as idealism, rationalism, and a deep love for Classical literature. Unlike the humanist movement in Italy, however, the northern humanists were preoccupied with the condition of the church and the wider Christian world. For these northern thinkers, the study of Christian writings went hand in hand with research on the Greco-Roman classics, and their scholarship was meant to further the cause of ecclesiastical reform.

Like the lay pietists of the Late Middle Ages (see Chapter 10), from whom they drew inspiration, the northern humanists approached their faith in simple

terms. They taught that any Christian who had a pure and humble heart could pray directly to God. These scholars further strengthened the appeal of this simple creed by claiming that it was identical with Christ's scriptural message, which they were discovering in their vernacular translations of the New Testament.

The thinking of the Christian humanists, notably in Germany, was tinged with national feeling and hostility toward Italian interference in their local religious affairs. Their Christian humanism with its simple faith led them to believe that by imitating the early church— freed of corrupt Italian leaders—they could revitalize Christianity and restore it to its original purpose.

A notable French humanist was François Rabelais [RAB-uh-lay] (about 1494–1553), who wrote a five-part satire collectively titled *The Histories of Gargantua and Pantagruel.* In these works, Rabelais vigorously attacked the church's abuses and ridiculed the clergy and theologians. Beneath the satire, he affirmed the goodness of human nature and the ability of men and women to lead useful lives based on reason and common sense. However, his skepticism and secularism, as well as the ribald humor, obscene references, and grotesque escapades of his heroes, put Rabelais in a unique category, well outside the mainstream of northern humanism.

Another northern humanist outside the mainstream was Marguerite of Angoulême, queen of Navarre (1492–1549), sister of King Francis I. She was an important protector of Rabelais, Protestant reformers, and other free spirits. Most famously in literary history, Marguerite of Navarre—her more usual name— was associated with the *Heptameron* (from the Greek for "seven"), a collection of seventy frankly sexual tales in the style of Boccaccio's *Decameron* (see Chapter 10). Whether or not Marguerite actually wrote these tales is an unresolved topic of scholarly debate, al-

Figure 13.1 HANS HOLBEIN THE YOUNGER. *Erasmus of Rotterdam.* Ca. 1523–1524. Oil on panel, 16½ × 12½". Louvre. *This sensitive likeness of the great humanist was painted by one of the most successful Northern Renaissance portraitists, Hans Holbein. The artist conveys his subject's humanity and intellectual authority by depicting him engaged in writing one of his many treatises. The realistic detail, warm colors, and dramatic lighting are typical of Holbein's work.*

though it is generally agreed that the stories were written for the French court. Based on the evidence of the stories, the French nobility welcomed outspokenness in sexual matters (the themes of the tales are rape, seductions bordering on rape, incest, and trespasses of the sexual and marital codes of aristocratic life) and condoned Protestant-like religious views (the tale's villains are often members of monastic orders and are consistently portrayed as gluttons, parasites, and rapists). The social matrix that spawned the *Heptameron* was northern humanism, a world hostile to the dying ethos of medieval monasticism.

The outstanding figure among the northern humanists—and possibly among all humanists—is the Dutch scholar Desiderius Erasmus (Figure 13.1). Erasmus (about 1466–1536) was fully prepared for the great role that he played in the Christian humanist movement. He studied in the pietistic atmosphere of a school run by the Brethren of the Common Life, where he was introduced to the Greek and Roman classics. He later completed his education at the University of Paris. This training was supposed to lead to a church career, but Erasmus never wore clerical garb or lived as a priest, although he was ordained. On the contrary,

with the aid of patrons he patiently pursued a writing career, enjoying the comforts of a scholarly life. He also traveled widely throughout western Europe, eventually finding a second home in England among the intellectual circle gathered around Thomas More, England's lord chancellor and another well-known humanist.

As a humanist, Erasmus believed in education in the *humanitas* sense advocated by Cicero, emphasizing study of the Classics and honoring the dignity of the individual. As a Christian, he promoted the "philosophy of Christ" as expressed in the Sermon on the Mount and in Jesus' example of a humble and virtuous life. Erasmus earnestly felt that the church could reform itself and avoid division by adopting the moderate approach that he advanced.

Despite a prodigious output of books that include treatises, commentaries, collections of proverbs, a manual for rulers, and a definitive edition of the Greek New Testament, Erasmus's fame rests on his most popular work, *The Praise of Folly,* written in 1509. This lively book, filled with learned humor, captures the gentle grace and good sense of the Christian humanists. Even this work's Latin title, *Encomium Moriae,* reflects a lighthearted spirit, for it is a punning reference to the name of More—the English friend to whom the book is dedicated.

In this work, Erasmus pokes fun at the human race by making his mouthpiece a personified Folly—an imaginary creation who symbolizes human foolishness. In a series of sermons, Folly ridicules every social group, from scholars and lawyers to priests and cardinals. Erasmus's jolly satire, especially in its exposure of clerical hypocrisy, struck a responsive chord among educated people. But with the rapid growth of Protestantism, such cultivated criticism only got Erasmus into trouble. Roman Catholics felt betrayed by his mild barbs, and Protestants accused him of not going far enough. In the end, this mild reformer and gentle scholar sadly witnessed the breakup of his beloved church while being denounced by both sides.

For a time, Luther had hoped for the support of Erasmus in his reforming crusade. But that changed in 1524 when Erasmus asserted, contrary to Luther, that the human will was free; otherwise, according to Erasmus, the Bible would not have urged sinners to repent. Erasmus's argument so enraged Luther that he countered with a tract in which he declared that the human will was irrevocably flawed; in Luther's view, only God's free grace could save any man or woman from the fires of hell. So intemperate was Luther's reply that the two scholars never communicated again. Erasmus's calm voice went unheeded amid the wild rhetoric and religious mayhem that characterized this age.

THE NORTHERN RENAISSANCE

While Italy was experiencing the High Renaissance and Early Mannerism, northern Europe was also bursting with cultural vitality. The cultural scene was affected by the contemporaneous religious upheavals; late medieval trends, such as Gothic forms and mysticism; northern humanism; and Italy's High Renaissance and Mannerism. The result of these dissimilar tendencies was that the **Northern Renaissance,** the term used to describe the culture of sixteenth-century northern Europe, was a period marked by competing styles. By midcentury, however, the principles of Mannerism were encroaching on the ideals of Renaissance painting and literature.

Northern Renaissance Literature

The sixteenth century was truly an amazing period in literature, for the vernacular tongues now definitively showed that they were the equal of Latin as vehicles for literary expression. In the High Middle Ages, Dante led the way with his *Divine Comedy;* now, other authors writing in the vernacular found their voices. Montaigne, writing in French, and Shakespeare, writing in English, left such a rich legacy that, by common consent, each is revered as the outstanding writer of his respective tradition.

Michel de Montaigne   Like an ancient Roman senator, Michel de Montaigne [mee-SHEL duh mahn-TAYN] (1533–1592) balanced a public career with a life devoted to letters. While serving as a judge and a mayor, he worked on his lifelong project, which he called *Essays.* This collection of discursive meditations is essentially the autobiography of his mind and is thus representative of the individualistic spirit of the Renaissance. What emerges is a self-portrait of a man who is both intellectually curious and fascinated by his own mental processes and personality. He describes his contradictions, accidental as well as deliberate, though he writes that his loyalty is always to truth. What keeps the *Essays* from falling into sterile self-absorption is Montaigne's firm sense that in revealing himself he is speaking for others.

But the *Essays* are more than an early example of confessional literature. They also constitute, in the French tradition, the earliest work of *moralisme,* or moralism, and the beginning of modern skepticism. In terms of morality, Montaigne attached little importance to Christian ethics, since cruelty and barbarism in the name of religion were justified equally by Protestant and Catholic. His musings reflected France's chaotic condition during the religious wars, causing him to question the Renaissance's natural optimism. Montaigne searched for, without ever discovering, a moral code that was centered on a human world and that no one could deny. In his skeptical outlook, Montaigne rejected the Renaissance view of humanity as a microcosm of the universe. Indeed, he claimed that he saw nothing except vanity and insignificance in human beings and their reasoning. Montaigne, however, avoided total skepticism, for although he denied that humans could ever achieve perfect knowledge, he held that practical understanding was possible.

William Shakespeare   Montaigne wrote during a period when religious wars were disrupting France, but England at the same time was enjoying a relatively calm period of cultural exuberance, the Age of Elizabeth. Under Queen Elizabeth I, who reigned from 1558 to 1603, London rose to an eminence that rivaled that of Florence of the Early Renaissance. English playwrights rescued tragedy and comedy from the oblivion into which they had fallen with the collapse of Rome. As in ancient Greece, tragedy and comedy again became part of popular culture. A purely secular and commercial theater now emerged, with professional playwrights and actors, playhouses, and a ticket-buying public (Figures 13.2 and 13.3).

The revived popularity of the theater represented a dramatic reversal of a cultural outlook that had prevailed in the West since the time of Augustine in the fifth century (see Chapter 7). Christian scholars had condemned the stage for its wicked displays and seductive delights. On occasion, medieval culture had spawned morality plays and dramas with biblical themes, but these edifying works remained primitive in form with little care given to language, character, or plot. A play like the fifteenth-century *Everyman,* for example, was intended mainly to reinforce Christian values and only incidentally to entertain or to provoke thought. Under Elizabeth, many able dramatists began to appear, such as Thomas Kyd (about 1557–1595) and Christopher Marlowe (1564–1593). These playwrights revolutionized drama in a single generation. However, first honors must be given to William Shakespeare, the greatest dramatist in the English language.

Shakespeare (1564–1616) was born in Stratford-upon-Avon, a market-town, and educated in its grammar school. By 1590 his plays were being performed on the London stage, and his active public career continued until 1610, when he returned home to Stratford to enjoy country life. His early retirement reflected the success that he had achieved as an actor, a theater owner, and a playwright. But it was as the age's leading dramatist that he earned undying fame, mastering the three different genres of history, comedy, and tragedy. His thirty-seven dramas constitute his legacy

The Globe Playhouse 1599–1613

A Conjectural Reconstruction
by C. Walter Hodges

KEY

A — Main entrance
B — The Yard, where the 'groundlings' stood (for one penny admission)
CC — Entrances to lowest gallery (on payment of another penny)
D — Entrances to staircase and upper galleries
E — Corridor serving the different sections of the middle gallery
F — Middle gallery (The 'Twopenny Rooms')
G — 'Gentlemen's Rooms' or 'Lords' Rooms'
H — The stage
J — The hanging being put up round the stage (N.B. In some theatres this was boarded in)
K — The 'Hell' under the stage
L — The stage trap, leading down to the Hell
M — Stage doors, leading into the tiring-house
N — Curtained 'place behind the stage', sometimes opened for special scenes
O — Gallery above the stage, used as required sometimes by musicians, sometimes by spectators, and often as part of the play (e.g. *Romeo and Juliet*)
P — Back-stage area (the tiring-house)
Q — Tiring-house door
R — Dressing rooms
S — Wardrobe and storage
T — The hut housing the machine for lowering enthroned gods, etc., to the stage
U — The 'Heavens'
W — Hoisting the playhouse flag

Figure 13.2 Reconstruction of the Globe Playhouse, 1599–1613. *When the Globe Playhouse of London was razed in 1644 to make way for new buildings, one of the most significant monuments of Renaissance England disappeared: the theater where most of Shakespeare's plays were first performed. This cutaway drawing, made by C. W. Hodges, a leading expert on the theaters of the period, attempts to depict the Globe Playhouse as it appeared in Shakespeare's day. As shown in the drawing, the Globe was a sixteen-sided structure with the stage erected in an open courtyard bounded on three sides by three tiers of seats.*

Figure 13.3 The Reconstructed Globe Playhouse. 1996. London, England. *Spurred by the vision of the American actor Sam Wanamaker, an international effort resulted in the construction of a modern Globe Playhouse, near the site of the original theater of Shakespeare's time. This theater, which staged its first performances in August 1996, is true to Elizabethan design and construction methods, including wooden nails and thatched roof. Performances are staged in the daytime, when weather permits—just as they were four centuries ago.*

to the world. Just as tragedies ranked higher than comedies in ancient Greece, so have Shakespeare's tragedies enjoyed a reputation superior to that of his other writings. Of the eleven tragedies, many are regarded as masterpieces; *King Lear, Othello, Julius Caesar, Macbeth,* and *Romeo and Juliet* are constantly performed on the stage and often presented in films, in English as well as other languages. Perhaps the Shakespearean tragedy that stands above the rest, however, and that is reckoned by many as his supreme achievement is *Hamlet.*

Hamlet is a **revenge tragedy,** among the most popular dramatic forms in the Elizabethan theater. The revenge play had its own special rules, consisting chiefly of a murder that requires a relative of the victim, usually with the prompting of a ghost, to avenge the crime by the drama's end. The origin of this type of play, with its characteristic violence and suspense, has been obscured by time, although Seneca's Roman tragedies, which were known and studied in England, are almost certainly a source.

The basic plot, characters, and setting of *Hamlet* are drawn from a medieval chronicle of evil doings at the Danish court. Elizabethan theatergoers had seen an earlier dramatized version (now lost) before Shakespeare's play was performed in 1600–1601. Shakespeare thus took a well-known story but stamped it with his own genius and feeling for character. In its basic conception, *Hamlet* is a consummate expression of Mannerist principles. Shakespeare presents Hamlet from shifting perspectives, preferring ambiguity, rather than portraying him from a single vantage point in accordance with the Classical ideal. By turns, Hamlet veers from madman to scholar to prince to swordsman, so that a unified, coherent personality is never exposed to the audience. Because of Hamlet's elusive character, he has become the most frequently analyzed and performed of all Shakespeare's heroes.

Another aspect of this play reminiscent of the Mannerist aesthetic is the self-disgust that seems to rule Hamlet's character when he is alone with his thoughts. Whereas the High Renaissance reserved its finest praise for the basic dignity of the human being, Hamlet finds little to value in himself, in others, or in life. Instead, he offers a contradictory vision:

> It goes so heavily with my disposition that this goodly frame, the earth, seems to me a sterile promontory; this most excellent canopy, the air . . . this majestical roof fretted with golden fire, why, it appears no other thing to me but a foul and pestilent congregation of vapours. What a piece of work is a man, how noble in reason, how infinite in faculty; in form and moving how express and admirable, in action how like an angel, in apprehension how like a god! the beauty of the

world, the paragon of animals! And yet to me what is this quintessence of dust? Man delights not me. . . .
>
> (Act 2, Scene 2)

In its construction, the tragedy of *Hamlet* is typical of Shakespeare's plays. All his dramas were written for commercial theater troupes and were not intended especially for a reading public. Only after Shakespeare's death were his plays published and circulated to a general audience and thus regarded as "literature."

Northern Renaissance Painting

The Northern Renaissance emerged during an era of cultural crisis. In about 1500 the Late Gothic style of the Flemish school was starting to lose its appeal, except for one extraordinary artist, Hieronymus Bosch. At the same time, growing numbers of artists were attracted to the new Italian art, especially to Mannerism. In the 1520s, the influence of the Protestant Reformation also began to become apparent in the arts. Individual tastes and styles became important, and secular subjects were acceptable, in part because some of the more fervent Protestants looked on enjoyment of the visual arts as a form of idol worship. They even destroyed some paintings, statues, and stained glass that portrayed religious subjects. The combined influences of Mannerism and Protestantism produced three artists of unique stature who reflected the turbulent world of post-Lutheran Europe in quite different ways: Dürer, Grünewald, and Bruegel.

Albrecht Dürer Albrecht Dürer [AHL-brekt DYOU-ruhr] (1471–1528), the son of a goldsmith, pursued a career as an engraver and painter. After studying in Germany, he traveled widely in Italy, where he absorbed the lessons of Renaissance art. Between 1510 and 1519, he earned great fame for the works that he executed for the Holy Roman emperor, but he also discovered that his true artistic bent was for engraving, either on wood or on metal. His engravings, which were issued in multiple editions, enhanced his reputation, and as a result he received many commissions throughout Germany and the Netherlands. Near the end of his life, Dürer became a Lutheran, and some of his last paintings indicate his new faith.

Fully aware of himself and his place in the world, Dürer showed a Renaissance sensibility in introspective self-portraits, especially in the famous work in which he depicts himself as a Christ figure (Figure 13.4). In this stunning image—the intense stare suggests that it was painted while the artist was looking in the mirror—Dürer blends a dandified likeness of himself with a standard Flemish representation of Christ.

Figure 13.4 ALBRECHT DÜRER. *Self-Portrait.* 1500. Oil on panel, 26¼ × 19¼". Alte Pinakothek, Munich. *Reflecting the Renaissance's emphasis on the individual, Dürer was one of the first artists to make himself the subject of some of his paintings. In a series of self-portraits, starting at the age of thirteen, he examined his face and upper torso and rendered them in precise detail, recording his passing age and moods. This self-portrait is the last of the series and suggests that he has taken on the role of artist in much the manner that Jesus had taken on the role of Savior.*

Such an identification of his artistic self with Jesus' divine power would have been unthinkable before the Renaissance. Nevertheless, Dürer remained true to the spirit of the Middle Ages, for he was also following the tradition of mysticism in which he saw himself as striving to imitate the example of Christ.

Although Dürer's paintings brought him recognition and wealth in his day, his engravings constitute his greatest artistic legacy. At the time of Luther's revolt, Dürer engraved the scene called *Knight, Death, and the Devil* (Figure 13.5). This magnificent engraving shows a knight riding through a forest, ignoring both the taunts of Death, who holds up an hourglass to remind him of his mortality, and the fiendish Devil, who watches nearby. The knight is probably meant as a symbol of the Christian who has to live in the practical world.

Dürer's *Knight, Death, and the Devil* combines Late Gothic and Renaissance elements to make a disquieting scene. From the northern tradition are derived the exquisite details, the grotesque demon, and the varied landscape in the background. From Renaissance sources comes the horse, which Dürer copied from models seen during his Italian tour.

Figure 13.5 ALBRECHT DÜRER. *Knight, Death, and the Devil.* 1513. Engraving, approx. 9⅝ × 7⁷⁄₁₂". The Fogg Art Museum, Harvard University. Gift of William Gray from the Collection of Francis Calley Gray. *Dürer's plan for this work probably derived from a manual by Erasmus that advised a Christian prince on the best way to rule. In his version, Dürer portrays the Christian layman who has put on the armor of faith and rides steadfastly, oblivious to the various pitfalls that lie in his path. The knight is sometimes identified with Erasmus, whom Dürer venerated.*

Figure 13.6 MATTHIAS GRÜNEWALD. *The Crucifixion,* from the *Isenheim Altarpiece.* 1515. Oil on panel, 9′9½″ × 10′9″. Musée d'Unterlinden, Colmar, France. *Jesus' suffering and death were a central theme in north European piety, particularly after the plague of the fourteenth century. Northern artists typically rendered Christ's death in vivid and gory detail. Grünewald's* Crucifixion *comes out of this tradition; Christ's broken body symbolizes both his sacrificial death and the mortality of all human beings.*

Matthias Grünewald A second major German artist in this period is Matthias Grünewald [muh-THI-uhs GREW-nuh-vahlt] (about 1460–1528), who was less influenced by Italian art and more northern in his techniques than Dürer. His paintings represent a continuation of the Late Gothic style rather than a northern development of Renaissance tendencies.

Grünewald's supreme achievement is the *Isenheim Altarpiece,* painted for the church of St. Anthony in Isenheim, Germany. The altarpiece includes nine painted panels that can be displayed in three different positions, depending on the church calendar. When the *Isenheim Altarpiece* is closed, the large central panel depicts the Crucifixion (Figure 13.6). By crowding the five figures and the symbolic lamb into the foreground and making Christ's body larger than the rest, Grü-

newald followed the Late Gothic style. This style is similarly apparent in every detail of Christ's tortured, twisted body: the gaping mouth, the exposed teeth, the slumped head, and the torso raked by thorns. And Grünewald's Late Gothic emotionalism is evident in his treatment of the secondary figures in this crucifixion panel. On the right, John the Baptist points toward Jesus, stressing the meaning of his sacrificial death. John the Baptist's calmness contrasts with the grief of the figures on the left, including Mary Magdalene, who kneels at Jesus' feet, and the apostle John, who supports a swooning Mary. The swaying bodies of these three figures reinforce the anguish on their faces. One Renaissance feature in this otherwise Gothic painting is the low horizon line, which shows Grünewald's knowledge of Italian perspective.

Figure 13.7   Hieronymus Bosch. *Garden of Earthly Delights.* Ca. 1510–1515. Oil on wood, center panel 86⅝ × 76¾"; each side panel 86⅝ × 38¼". Prado, Madrid. *Careful study of the minute details of this triptych has uncovered the major sources of Bosch's artistic inspiration—namely, medieval folklore, common proverbs, exotic learning, and sacred beliefs. For example, folklore inspired the ravens and owl (left panel), traditional emblems of nonbelievers and witchcraft, respectively; the Flemish proverb "Good fortune, like glass, is easily broken" is illustrated by the lovemaking couple under the glass globe; allusions to exotic learning may be seen in the egg shapes (all three panels), symbolic of the world and sex in the pseudoscience of alchemy; and Christian belief is evident throughout the triptych, but especially in the right panel, showing the punishment of sinners.*

Hieronymus Bosch   Hieronymus Bosch [BOSH] (about 1450–1516), whose personal life is a mystery, painted works that still puzzle modern experts. Treating common religious subjects in bizarre and fantastic ways, he earned a reputation even among his contemporaries for being enigmatic.

Much of Bosch's distinctive art may be explained by the changes under way in northern Europe during his day. In the late fifteenth century, political upheavals in Burgundy caused aristocratic patronage to decline, and, at the same time, a feeling of dread, born perhaps of the periodic ravages of the plague, stalked the land. In the early sixteenth century, serious religious trouble that would end with the revolt of Martin Luther was brewing. Influenced by the foregoing forces and also perhaps subjected to his own private demons, Bosch

created a body of art that defies strict classification in the stylistic sense.

In his paintings, Bosch seems torn between the declining Late Gothic style and the soon-to-be-born Mannerist style. His addiction to precise detail and his frequent use of sweeping landscapes are clear signs of the debt he owed Flemish art and, in particular, the age's illuminated manuscripts; but his tendency to endow his works with ambiguous, or even cynical, moral messages points to the works of later Dutch artists, such as Pieter Bruegel the Elder. Perhaps the best way to look at Bosch is as an artist whose originality was so pronounced that he stands outside any historical period.

Of Bosch's thirty or more paintings, the most well known and controversial is *The Garden of Earthly Delights,* a work in oil on three wood panels, called a **triptych** (Figure 13.7). When open, the triptych displays three separate but interrelated scenes, organized around the theme of the creation, fall, and damnation of the human race. Most confusingly, the center and right panels are crowded with tiny figures—mostly human, though some are grotesquely monstrous—performing a variety of peculiar actions. Although no scholarly consensus exists as to the ultimate meaning of this work, certain features can be identified that may help the viewer understand it.

The left panel of *The Garden of Earthly Delights* shows the Garden of Eden, with Adam and Eve in the foreground and the first plants and animals (including "natural" animals but also weird monsters) scattered around. Contrary to the story in the Bible, Jesus holds the newly created Eve's hand and introduces her to Adam. Many scholars interpret this panel as making Eve the source of original sin.

The center panel—the dramatic focus of the triptych—depicts the sins of the flesh in lurid and metaphorical detail. In the top horizontal band, the waters of the earth converge to make a fountain, an image that has been identified as a false symbol of human happiness. In the middle band, naked young women cavort in a pool while a parade of naked youths riding animals—partly realistic, partly fantastic—encircles them. In the lower band, more naked men and women engage in various sex acts or are involved with huge birds, fruits, flowers, or fish. The diverse images in this central panel symbolize Bosch's perspective on the human condition: perpetual enslavement to the sexual appetite unleashed by Adam and Eve's first sin. Also worthy of note is that this crowded scene includes many black males and females, an early instance of nonwhites in Western art.

The triptych's right panel is a repulsive portrait of Hell and the pains human beings must suffer for their sins. A horrific scene of fiery ruins and grisly instruments of torture, this panel proclaims Bosch's hopeless vision of the futility of life on earth. For the artist, human beings cause their own destruction through wicked desires. Nowhere in the entire work is there a hint of salvation.

A few scholars reject this gloomy view of Bosch's message by trying to link the triptych to the beliefs of the Adamites, an underground, heretical sect. If their interpretation is correct, then the central panel may be understood as the Adamites' unusual vision of Paradise. Most scholars reject this view, however, and hold instead that Bosch was a stern moralist, mocking the corrupt society of his day.

Pieter Bruegel the Elder   The life and work of Pieter Bruegel [BREW-gul or BROY-gul] the Elder (about 1525–1569) indicate the changes in northern European art in the mid–sixteenth century. The great German artists Dürer and Grünewald were now dead, and German art, which had dominated northern Europe in the early sixteenth century, was in decline. Protestant iconoclasm had taken its toll, and the demand for religious art had markedly diminished. Within this milieu, Bruegel chose a novel set of artistic subjects—landscapes, country life scenes, and folk narratives—and in the process became the first truly modern painter in northern Europe. Bruegel's subjects, rooted in the Flemish tradition, were often devoid of overt religious content and presented simply as secular art, although he also

Figure 13.8   Pieter Bruegel the Elder. *Wedding Dance.* 1566. Oil on panel, 47 × 62". Detroit Institute of Arts. *Bruegel has made a sensuous arrangement out of the dancers and bystanders at this country wedding. The line of dancers winds from the foreground back through the trees, where it reverses itself and returns to its original starting point. The sense of lively movement is reinforced by the vivid red colors in the hats and vests and by the stomping feet and flailing arms.*

painted a number of pictures on standard religious themes such as the adoration of the Magi.

Bruegel's most memorable paintings are his scenes of peasant life. The peasants are always depicted in natural settings, neither romanticized nor patronized. Rather, Bruegel represents the common folk as types, never as individuals, and often as expressions of the blind forces of nature. For some viewers, these scenes also convey a pessimism tinged with grudging admiration about human nature as reflected in the peasants' simple, lusty behavior.

A painting that illustrates Bruegel's attitude toward country folk is his lively *Wedding Dance* (Figure 13.8). The painting records the exuberant revels of the lusty men and the kerchief-wearing women. The bride and groom cannot be distinguished from the other dancers. Typical of Bruegel's style, there is a high horizon and a high point of view, so that we look at the scene from above. This effect, along with the crude faces of the peasants, underscores the impression that these are types and not individuals. The painting's composition reinforces the sense of peasant types in the way that the swirling figures in the foreground are repeated in the background in ever diminishing size.

A darker side of Bruegel is evident in his painting *The Parable of the Blind*, based on Jesus' saying in Matthew 15:14: "If the blind lead the blind, both shall fall into the ditch" (Figure 13.9). Bruegel offers a literal reading of this text to show the tragedy that befalls those without proper spiritual guidance. The blind men here are ridiculed not because they are peasants or because they are blind. Rather, they represent everyone;

Figure 13.9   Pieter Bruegel the Elder. *The Parable of the Blind.* 1568. Oil on canvas, 33⅞ × 60⅝". National Museum, Naples. *Finished in the year before he died, this painting shows Bruegel in full command of Renaissance art techniques. Using assured linear and atmospheric perspective, he tilts the picture plane to create a stage on which the parable unfolds and creates a realistic setting (probably Flemish), complete with village church and meadow. The arrangement of the peasants—comprising five who are stumbling along a diagonal line running from left to right and culminating in a sixth one, the fallen leader—makes this moralizing work a painting of high drama. This dramatic sense is heightened by the deep contrast between the peasants' tragic fate and the calm naturalism of the nearby village.*

their blindness is a metaphor for spiritual ignorance—precisely the moral of the biblical parable. Perhaps on a deeper level, Bruegel was thinking of the fanatical leaders of his day, both Protestant and Catholic, who were waging war in the name of their faith.

THE BREAKUP OF CHRISTENDOM: CAUSES OF THE RELIGIOUS REFORMATIONS

Although the reasons for the breakup of Europe's religious unity are complicated, two basic causes are clear: the radical reshaping of Western society and culture that began about 1350 and the timeless spiritual yearnings of human beings. After 1500 these two forces came together in Germany to make conditions ripe for religious revolution. What made change virtually inevitable was the combination of the historical trends occurring during the Late Middle Ages: the corruption and abuses inside the church, the rise of sovereign states, the decay of medieval thought, and the revival of humanism.

The church had been plagued with problems since the Avignon papacy and the Great Schism of the fourteenth century and the challenges to its time-honored practices posed by the growth of heretical groups like the Hussites (see Chapter 10). Without firm guidance from the popes, many clergy led less than exemplary lives, particularly those inside the monasteries. Lay writers, now unafraid of the church, delighted in describing clerical scandals, and the populace gossiped about their priests' latest sins. Everywhere anticlericalism seemed on the rise.

Perhaps the church could have reformed the clergy and stemmed the tide of a rising anticlericalism if the papacy had been morally and politically strong, but such was not the case. By 1500 the popes were deeply distracted by Italian politics and fully committed to worldly interests. The church also lost power to secular rulers, who were determined to bring all their subjects under state control. By 1500 the English and the French kings, to the envy of other European rulers, had made their national churches relatively free of papal control.

In Germany, however, where no unified nation-state had developed, the local secular leaders had no say about clerical appointments, were unable to control the ecclesiastical courts, or prevent the Church from collecting taxes—conditions that intensified anticlericalism and hatred of Rome. The German princes, who were already struggling to be free from the control of Charles V, made church reform a rallying cry and

Map 13.1   THE RELIGIOUS SITUATION IN EUROPE IN 1560

Figure 13.10 LUCAS CRANACH THE ELDER. *Martin Luther.* 1520. Copper engraving, 5⁷⁄₁₆ × 3¹³⁄₁₆″. Courtesy of the Metropolitan Museum of Art. Gift of Felix Warburg, 1920. (20.64.21). *This portrait of Martin Luther, with its vivid rendering of his steel jaw and piercing eyes, shows some of the qualities that made him such a force during the Reformation. The admiring likeness was done by the German artist Lucas Cranach, a supporter of the new faith and a close friend of Luther's. At the time of this engraving, the Reformation was barely under way; the thirty-seven-year-old Luther was still in communion with the church in Rome and a member of a monastic order.*

Figure 13.11 ALBRECHT DÜRER. *Elector Frederick the Wise.* 1524. Copper engraving, 7³⁄₈ × 4¾″. Print collection, Miriam and Ira D. Wallach Division of Art, Prints, and Photographs, The New York Public Library, Astor, Lenox, and Tilden Foundations. *Dürer's portrait captures the princely bearing of Frederick the Wise, the ruler of Electoral Saxony and Luther's great patron. Ironically, Frederick owned one of the largest collections of relics in Christendom. It has been estimated that the 17,443 artifacts in the elector's collection in 1518 could reduce the time in purgatory by 127,799 years and 116 days.*

turned against Rome as well as the Holy Roman emperor. As events unfolded, the popes were incapable of preventing these princes from converting their lands into independent states outside papal jurisdiction (Map 13.1).

The Protestant Order

Protestantism first appeared in Germany, where Martin Luther led the founding of a new religious sect in the 1520s. In the 1530s a second generation of Protestants acted on the opportunity created by Luther. John Calvin, a French scholar, formed an independent church in Geneva, Switzerland, and King Henry VIII removed the English church from Roman rule (see Timeline 13.1).

Luther's Revolt One of the church's more glaring abuses was the selling of indulgences—pardons that reduced the amount of penance that Christians had to perform to atone for their sins—a practice that dated from the High Middle Ages. In 1517, in response to the archbishop of Mainz's sale of indulgences to raise money, Martin Luther (1483–1546), a monk teaching at nearby Wittenberg University, published his famous Ninety-five Theses (Figure 13.10). These were questions and arguments about the legitimacy of indulgences, and they implicitly challenged the sacraments of confession and penance and the authority of the pope. Luther had simply hoped to arouse a debate in the university, but instead he ignited criticism against the church and placed himself in the vanguard of a reform movement.

The church's response to Luther was initially hesitant, but in 1520 Pope Leo X excommunicated him. When Luther burned the papal document of excommunication in public, the church branded him a heretic and an outlaw. Luther survived because he was under the protection of his patron, Elector Frederick the Wise of Saxony, who had led the German princes opposed to the Holy Roman emperor (Figure 13.11).

LUTHER'S BELIEFS Luther's attack on indulgences arose from the spiritual quest to understand sin and salvation that had led him to become a monk. Through long study of the scriptures, he reached the understanding that salvation comes not from good works but from God's unmerited love, or grace, or, as Luther phrased it, "justification by faith alone." According to Luther, salvation is achieved by faith in Jesus' sacrificial death; thus, buying indulgences is trying to buy

Figure 13.12 WORKSHOP OF LUCAS CRANACH. *Katherine von Bora. Ca 1526. Oil on panel, 7½ × 5". Wartburg-Stiftung, Germany. Katherine von Bora was one of a dozen nuns liberated from a convent near Wittenberg in the heady days of 1523. She joined the mixed collection who lived with Luther in the Black Cloisters, his old monastery given him by Frederick the Wise. Despite Luther's protests, she determined to become his wife, and she did. He treated her with great deference, calling her "My lord Kate," though he poked fun at her supposed greed for property. This small portrait was executed in the workshop of Lucas Cranach the Elder, who was also a witness to the marriage of Luther and Katherine von Bora.*

Luther's voluminous writings constitute the largest legacy of any German author. Among his vast output of tracts, essays, and letters, his German translation of the Bible has had the most enduring influence. He introduced a new era in biblical scholarship by basing his translation on the original languages of the scriptures, the technique that had been developed by the northern humanists, particularly Erasmus. He also set the path followed by subsequent Protestant reformers in choosing what books to include in the Bible: Rejecting the Apocrypha of the Jewish Septuagint, Luther relied on the canonical books of the Hebrew Bible, or Old Testament, and the New Testament. Although nineteen German Bibles were in print by 1518, Luther's version was the one that survived and left its stamp on the German language. His pithy style engaged the reader's emotions with realistic images and idiomatic speech.

SOCIAL AND POLITICAL IMPLICATIONS OF LUTHER'S REVOLT The Ninety-five Theses circulated widely throughout Germany, and in 1521 Lutheran churches sprang up in most German towns. Simultaneously, radical followers of Luther fomented new problems, causing riots, driving priests from their homes, closing monasteries, and destroying religious images. Luther rejected this violence and advocated moderation. He did accept the abolition of monasticism, however, dropping the monk's habit in 1523 and marrying Katherine von Bora, a former nun, in 1525 (Figure 13.12). When he and Katherine had children, they created a familial tradition for Lutheran clergy, unlike the celibate tradition of Catholic Europe. Lutheran women thus seemed to make gains with the closing of convents and the giving of new respectability to married life, but these steps proved illusory, since Luther affirmed male rule and female submission within the family.

Another area profoundly altered by Luther's beliefs was that of education. His supporters set up their own schools and universities, replacing Catholic founda-

salvation—a direct contradiction of the biblical truth Luther had experienced in his theological studies.

In his theology, which became known as **Lutheranism,** he tried to revive a Christianity based on biblical precedents and reminiscent of the early church. He believed that the sole source of religious authority was the Bible, not the pope or church councils, and that people could lead simple lives of piety and repentance without the need for priests to mediate with God. Luther also repudiated the mystical definition of the sacraments, the notion of purgatory, the adoration of the saints, and Masses for the dead; he retained only baptism and the Lord's Supper, as he called the Eucharist. Preaching in German became the heart of the liturgy, replacing the Latin Mass.

PERSONAL PERSPECTIVE

ALBRECHT DÜRER
On Luther

The German artist Dürer, writing in 1521, feared for Martin Luther's life when he heard rumors that the reformer had been taken prisoner by the Holy Roman emperor's soldiers. The rumors later proved false; Luther had been kidnapped for his own safety by his protector, Frederick the Wise.

On Friday before Whitsunday in the year 1521, came tidings to me at Antwerp that Martin Luther had been so treacherously taken prisoner; for he was escorted by Emperor Charles' herald with imperial safe-conduct and to him he was entrusted. But as soon as the herald had conveyed him to an unfriendly place near Eisenach he rode away, saying that he no longer needed him. Straightway there appeared ten horsemen and they treacherously carried off the pious man, betrayed into their hand, a man enlightened by the Holy Ghost, a follower of Christ and the true Christian faith. And whether he yet lives, or whether they have put him to death— which I know not—he has suffered this for the sake of Christian truth and because he rebuked the unchristian Papacy, which strives with its heavy load of human laws against the redemption of Christ; and be-cause we are so robbed and stripped of our blood and sweat, and that the same is so shamefully and scandalously eaten up by idle-going folk, while the poor and the sick therefore die of hunger. But this is above all the most grievous to me, that, maybe, God will suffer us to remain still longer under their false, blind doctrine, invented and drawn up by the men alone whom they call Fathers, by which also the precious Word of God is in many places wrongly expounded to us or not taught at all. . . .

May every man who reads Martin Luther's books see how clear and transparent is his doctrine, when he sets forth the Holy Gospel. Wherefore his books are to be held in great honor and not to be burnt; unless indeed his adversaries, who ever strive against the truth were cast also into the fire, together with all their opinions which would make gods out of men, provided, however, books of Luther's were printed anew again. Oh God, if Luther be dead, who will henceforth expound to us the Holy Gospel with such clearness? What, of God, might he not still have written for us in ten or twenty years? . . .

tions. Unlike church-run Catholic schools, the Lutheran schools were financed by taxes, so that teachers became state employees—a reflection of Luther's belief that church and state should work hand in hand. For Lutheran women, the changes in education created a dilemma. On the one hand, women were denied access to these schools, but, on the other hand, they were expected to know their Bibles, as both pious Lutherans and knowledgeable mothers capable of guiding their children's moral education.

Luther distanced himself from the anti-government political and social reforms espoused by some of his followers. In 1523 a brief Peasants' War erupted under the banner of Luther's faith, but Luther urged suppression of the workers by the nobility, clearly showing his preference for the status quo. His reliance on Saxony's rulers for protection set the model for his religion; in the Lutheran faith, the church acted as an arm of the state, and the clergy's salaries were paid from public funds. Luther's revolt did not embrace individual rights in the political or social arena; indeed, the Protestant princes were more powerful than their predecessors, since their powers were not limited by Rome.

The Reforms of John Calvin Among the second generation of Protestant reformers, the most influential was John Calvin (1509–1564) (Figure 13.13). After earning a law degree in Paris, he experienced a religious conversion and cast his lot with the Reformation. Coming under the suspicion of the French authorities, he fled to Basel, Switzerland, a Lutheran center, where he began to publish *The Institutes of the Christian Religion,* which, in its final form, became a theological document of immense importance.

In his theology, Calvin, like Luther, advocated beliefs and practices having biblical roots. He differed from Luther over the nature of God, church–state relations, and Christian morals. Calvin's religious thought, called **Calvinism,** rested on his concept of an awesome, even angry, God, which led him to make predestination (the belief that God predestines certain souls to salvation and others to damnation) central to his faith. Calvin also espoused a theocratic state in which the government was subordinate to the church. Within this state, he favored strict ethical demands, regulating everything from laughter in church to public shows of affection between the sexes. Because of such rules, which later became associated with the

Figure 13.13   ANONYMOUS. *John Calvin.* 1550s. Bibliothèque Publique et Universitaire de Geneva. *This anonymous portrait of Calvin shows the way that he probably wanted to be viewed rather than a natural likeness. Still, the angular features, the intense gaze, and the set mouth suggest that the reputation Calvin had for strict discipline was justified. The well-trimmed beard and somewhat extravagant fur collar, although typical of middle-class fashion of the era, create an ironic contradiction in this otherwise austere portrait.*

reform movement known as **Puritanism,** Calvinism acquired the reputation for being a joyless creed.

More important than the puritanical streak in Calvin's theology was the impact of his thought on political, social, and economic life. Calvinism encouraged thrift, industry, sobriety, and discipline—precisely the same traits that made for business success. Calvin's teachings spurred on the Christian capitalist in his accumulation of wealth, so that gradually there developed the idea that worldly success was tantamount to God's approval and that poverty was a sign of God's disfavor. In addition, of all the new sects, Calvinism was the most international, and reformed congregations spread across Europe, especially in Scotland and the Netherlands (see Map 13.1). The readiness of Calvin's followers to oppose tyranny with arms also made them dangerous everywhere.

The Reform of the English Church   A second major religious reformer in the 1530s was King Henry VIII (r. 1509–1547), who founded the Church of England (also

called the Anglican Church) largely out of political considerations. In 1529 Henry asked the pope to annul his marriage to Catherine of Aragon, who, though she gave birth to a daughter, had failed to produce a male heir. In Henry's eyes, Catherine's supposed failure was a divine punishment for his sin of having married his dead brother's widow—an incestuous union in the eyes of the church. In favorable times, the pope might have given Henry a dispensation, but the troops of Holy Roman Emperor Charles V, Catherine's nephew, had just sacked Rome and virtually imprisoned the pontiff. Charles also opposed any step that would nullify his aunt's marriage and make her daughter a bastard. In 1533 Henry pushed through Parliament the laws setting up the Church of England with himself as the head and granting him a divorce.

Figure 13.14   MARCUS GHEERAERTS THE YOUNGER. *Elizabeth I.* Late sixteenth century. Oil on panel, 7′11″ × 5′. National Portrait Gallery, London. *The so-called Ditchley portrait presented Queen Elizabeth in all her Renaissance finery. Following the Spanish fashion, the queen wears a neck ruff and yards of pearls, and she carries a fan. She stands atop a map of England, which she ruled for forty-five years with compassion and firmness, until her death in 1603.*

Although **Anglicanism** was founded by Henry VIII, the ground had been prepared locally by Christian humanists and English Lutherans. The work of both groups led to the so-called Reformation Parliament (1529–1535), which had begun to reform the English church even before Henry made the decisive break with Rome.

Religious turmoil followed Henry's death in 1547, and the fate of the English Reformation stayed in doubt until his daughter Elizabeth (r. 1558–1603) became queen and the head of the Anglican Church (Figure 13.14). In 1559 Elizabeth resolved the crisis, with the aid of Parliament, by steering a middle course between Catholicism and Calvinism, which had gained many English converts. Anglican beliefs were summarized in the Thirty-nine Articles, and people who wished to sit in Parliament, earn university degrees, or serve as military officers had to swear allegiance to them. Hence, Calvinists and Catholics were excluded by law from English public life and remained so for about 275 years.

The Counter-Reformation

Before Martin Luther took his stand in Germany, a Roman Catholic reform movement had begun quietly in isolated parts of Europe. Confronted with the surprising successes of the various Protestant groups, the Roman Catholic Church, as it was now called, struck back with a Counter-Reformation. By 1600 this superbly organized campaign had slowed Protestantism and won back many adherents. The Catholics held on to southern and most of central Europe, halting Protestantism's spread in Poland, France, and Switzerland and limiting the movement to northern Europe. The Counter-Reformation moved forward on three fronts: a revitalized papacy, new monastic orders, and an effective reforming council. Together, these forces confronted the Protestant threat, purified the church of abuses, and reorganized its structure.

The Reformed Papacy   With the reign of Paul III (pope 1534–1549), there appeared a series of reform-minded popes who reinvigorated the church. To counter the inroads made by Protestantism, Paul enlisted the support of the full church by convening a council representing Roman Catholic clergy from all over Europe and launched new monastic orders.

Paul and his successors reclaimed the moral leadership of the church and reorganized the papal bureaucracy so that discipline was now enforced throughout the ecclesiastical hierarchy. Sensing that Protestantism would not go away and recognizing the increasing availability of written material now that the printing

press had appeared, these popes tried to isolate the church from deviant ideas. A committee of churchmen drew up an Index of Forbidden Books, which listed writings that were off limits to Roman Catholic readers because they were considered prejudicial to faith or morals. The first Index included the works of Luther, Calvin, and other Protestants. In the long run, this tactic failed to suppress hated ideas, but the Index continued to be updated until the 1960s.

New Monastic Orders   The work of new monastic orders also contributed to the Counter-Reformation. Since the High Middle Ages, monastic reform had played only a small role in the life of the church. Suddenly in the sixteenth century, new monastic groups arose to fill a variety of needs, such as preparing men and women to minister directly to the masses and reclaiming lapsed believers to the faith.

Typical of monastic reform for women in Counter-Reformation Europe was the fate of the Company of St. Ursula, or the Ursulines, founded in 1535 in Brescia, Italy, by Angela Merici [ma-REE-chee] (about 1470–1540). The Ursulines were named after a legendary British princess who, with eleven thousand virgin companions, was martyred on the way to her wedding. Reflecting the same ideals as contemporary early Protestantism in stressing individual grace and keeping apart from clerical rule, the Ursulines were originally intended to be exclusively for laywomen, without any intrusion by male church officials. Merici's followers, divided into "daughters" and "matrons," were to live in their own homes, practice chastity without taking formal vows, serve the sick and the poor, and educate the young. In 1540, after Merici's death and under pressure from Protestantism, the Ursulines were reformed by church leaders, who cloistered the order and placed its members under male control. What happened to the Ursulines became the way of life for women in Catholicism: Laywomen were to be organized into formal structures under male supervision.

The most significant new order was the Society of Jesus, commonly known as the **Jesuits.** Recognized by Pope Paul III in 1540, the Jesuits had emerged by 1600 as the church's leading monastic order, with special blessings from the popes. The dedicated members helped to curb Protestantism in Europe, and their missionary efforts abroad represented the first steps in making Roman Catholicism a global faith. After a shaky beginning, their rise to power was quick, and their success was largely due to the order's founder, the Spaniard Ignatius Loyola (about 1493–1556) (Figure 13.15).

Loyola's life was imbued with more than a touch of medieval knight errantry. His first calling was as a professional warrior, defending his country from invaders.

Figure 13.15 ATTRIBUTED TO JUAN DE ROELAS. *St. Ignatius Loyola.* 1622. Oil on canvas, approx. 7′3″ × 5′6″. Museo Provincial de Bellas Artes, Seville, Spain. *This portrait, painted the year Loyola was canonized and nearly seventy-five years after his death, evokes the determination and strength of the founder of the Society of Jesus. In his right hand Ignatius holds the graphic symbol of Jesus' name, and under his left arm he carries a Bible. Such posthumous portraits were not intended to be exact likenesses but were designed to confirm the high status of the distinguished subject.*

When in 1521 a battle injury to his leg left Loyola crippled for life, he underwent a religious conversion that led him to become a "soldier" in the army of Christ. Eventually, he founded the Society of Jesus, which resembled a military company in its rigid hierarchy, close discipline, and absolute obedience to the founder.

The Jesuits were initially concerned with working among the unchurched and the poor, focusing especially on teaching their children. But that mission was modified in the 1540s. Guided by the Spaniard Francis Xavier (1506–1552), they established outposts in the Far East and converted thousands to the Christian faith. Other Jesuits had similar success in missions to North and South America.

The Jesuits' special vow of loyalty to the pope set them apart from other monastic orders. Because of this connection and their expertise in education, the Jesuits soon became the church's chief weapon against the Protestants. In their writings, the Jesuits answered the church's critics, setting forth their orthodox beliefs in a clear and straightforward manner.

The Council of Trent   The third force contributing to the Counter-Reformation was the reform established by the council conducted at Trent in northern Italy, meeting in three separate sessions between 1545 and 1563. Dominated by papal supporters, Italian delegates, and the Jesuits, the Council of Trent offered no sympathy to the Protestants and thus accepted the split in Christian Europe as an unfortunate fact of life. The council reaffirmed all the practices condemned by the Protestants, such as monasticism, indulgences, and holy relics, although mechanisms were set in motion to eliminate abuse of these practices. In addition, the council initiated some clerical reforms, notably in the realm of education and training.

The council's unyielding position toward the Protestants was based on its belief that both the Bible and church tradition—not the Bible alone as advocated by the Protestants—were the bases of authority and the word of God. To the council, the Vulgate (including the Apocrypha of the Jewish Septuagint) was the official and only Bible; all other versions were rejected. The council reaffirmed that salvation should be sought by faith *and* by good works, not by faith alone; it also reaffirmed the seven sacraments. The moral, doctrinal, and disciplinary results of the Council of Trent laid the foundations for present-day Roman Catholic policies and thought.

Warfare as a Response to Religious Dissent, 1520–1603

As religious dissent spread, the secular rulers watched with mounting concern. Until 1530 compromise between the Lutheran rebels and the dominant faith seemed possible, but with the constant growth of mutually hostile sects, secular rulers increasingly relied on warfare to deal with the crisis.

War between Charles V's armies and the Lutheran forces erupted on German lands in 1546, the year Luther died, and lasted until 1555, when the Religious Peace of Augsburg brought it to an end. This armistice granted toleration to the Lutheran states, but on strict terms. The ruler's religion became the official faith of each territory; members of religious minorities, whether Roman Catholic or Lutheran, could migrate and join their coreligionists in nearby lands. But because the rights of other minority sects, such as the Calvinists, were ignored, the Peace of Augsburg contained the seeds of future wars.

In 1556 Philip II (r. 1556–1598) inherited the Spanish crown from Charles V and became the head of the Roman Catholic cause. Besides Spain, Roman Catholic regimes now ruled Italy, Portugal, and Austria; Protestants reigned in Scandinavia. Elsewhere the religious rivals vied for supremacy. For the rest of the century, until 1603, Germany was at peace, but western Europe suffered religious violence.

Financed by gold and silver from Mexico and Peru, Philip dominated European politics. His well-prepared armies enabled him to control much of Europe. He expelled suspected Muslims from Spain and defeated the Turks in the Mediterranean; he invaded Portugal and joined that country to Spain. But his fortunes declined when he launched a bloody campaign against the United Provinces in the northern Netherlands. (Eventually, in 1609, the United Provinces became an independent Protestant state.) As the Dutch war was winding down, Philip turned his attention to Protestant England, a supporter of the Dutch revolt. In Philip's eyes, only England stood between him and a reunited Christendom; moreover, Spain and England were rivals for the precious metals of the New World. Philip's solution was to attempt an invasion of England. In 1588 his scheme ended in disaster when the Spanish Armada was defeated by English sea power and a violent storm.

Philip II's dream of a reunited Christendom had been impossible from the beginning. The Protestant world was too dedicated, the growth of national consciousness too powerful, and the rise of a system of sovereign states too far advanced for any one monarch to succeed in unifying Europe under a single banner or cause. When Philip died in 1598, Spain was declining and Europe was divided into independent states and several religions.

LATE MANNERISM

The strongest impact of the Counter-Reformation on the arts, architecture, and music began after the Council of Trent, in 1563. Spain and the Italian states, the areas least attracted to Protestantism, were greatly influenced by the council's decisions. The council decreed that the arts and music should be easily accessible to the uneducated. In sacred music, for example, the intelligibility of the words should take precedence over the melody, and in architecture the building should create a worshipful environment. The church council envisioned paintings and sculptures that were simple and direct as well as unobjectionable and decent in appearance. Guided by this principle, the

Counter-Reformation popes declared that some of the male nudes in Michelangelo's *Last Judgment* were obscene and ordered loincloths to be painted over them. General church policy now returned to the medieval ideal of an art and music whose sole aim was to serve and clarify the Christian faith.

Since the Roman Catholic Church after Trent wanted a simplified art that spoke to the masses, its artistic policy tended to clash with Mannerism, which embodied a self-conscious vision that was elitist and deliberately complex. Only with the rise of the Baroque after 1600 was there a style that could conform to the church's need for art with a mass appeal. In the meantime, the general effect of Trent on the last stage of Mannerism was to intensify its spiritual values.

Late Mannerism, which emerged across Europe after 1564, dominated Spanish painting, but it had little influence on Spanish literature. Under the influence of the Renaissance, Spanish literature flourished with the revival of the theater and the birth of new literary genres.

Spanish Painting

No Catholic artist expressed the spirit of the Counter-Reformation better than El Greco (1541–1614) in his Spanish paintings after 1576. These visionary works epitomize the spirit of Late Mannerism. El Greco's real name was Domenikos Theotokopoulos. A native of Crete, he had lived in Venice, where he adopted the colorful style of Venetian painting. Unsuccessful in Venice, he also failed to find rich patrons in Rome, though he learned from the works of Michelangelo and the Mannerists. He arrived in Toledo, Spain, about 1576, and there he found an appreciative public among the wealthy nobility. But much to El Greco's despair, he never became a favorite of the Spanish ruler, Philip II, who found the Greek painter's works too bizarre.

For his select audience of aristocrats and Roman Catholic clergy, however, El Greco could do no wrong. They believed that his paintings of saints, martyrs, and other religious figures caught the essence of Spanish emotionalism and religious zeal—the same qualities that had led Loyola to found the Jesuits. In effect, El Greco's extravagant images gave visible form to his patrons' spiritual yearnings. In his paintings, he rejected a naturalistic world with conventional perspective, especially when a divine dimension was present or implied; his spiritualized vision came to be distinguished by elongated bodies, sharp lines in the folds of cloth, and luminous colors.

El Greco's masterpiece is *The Burial of Count Orgaz,* painted to honor the founder of the church of Santo Tomé in Toledo (Figure 13.16). This painting was

Figure 13.16 EL GRECO. *The Burial of Count Orgaz.* 1586. Oil on canvas, 16′ × 11′10″. Church of Santo Tomé, Toledo, Spain. *A Manneristic invention in* The Burial of Count Orgaz *was the rich treatment of the robe of St. Stephen, the first Christian martyr and, in this painting, the beardless figure supporting the body of the dead count. Sewn onto the bottom of this robe is a picture of the stoning of St. Stephen, an episode narrated in the New Testament. By depicting one event inside another, El Greco created an illusionistic device—a typical notion of Mannerist painters, who were skeptical about conventional reality.*

Figure 13.17 EL GRECO. *Cardinal Guevara.* 1596–1600. Oil on canvas, 67¼ × 42½″. Courtesy of the Metropolitan Museum of Art. The H. O. Havemeyer Collection. Bequest of Mrs. H. O. Havemeyer, 1929. (29.100.5). *El Greco's painting of Cardinal Guevara illustrates his mastery of Mannerist portraiture. Disturbing details are visible everywhere. Guevara's head is almost too small for his large body, made even grander by the red cardinal's robe, and the divided background—half wooden panel, half rich tapestry—sets up a dissonant effect. Even the cardinal's chair contributes to the air of uneasiness, for its one visible leg seems barely to touch the floor.*

designed to fit into a special place beside the church's high altar. Its subject is the miraculous scene that, according to legend, occurred during the count's burial, when two saints, Augustine and Stephen, appeared and assisted with the last rites.

From this legend, El Greco fashioned an arresting painting. The large canvas is divided into two halves, with the lower section devoted to the count's actual burial and the upper section focused on the reception of his soul in heaven. Except for a few men who tilt their faces upward, the town dignitaries seem unaware of what is happening just above their heads. El Greco has devised two distinct styles to deal with these different planes of reality. The dignitaries below are rendered in realistic terms, showing fashions of El Greco's era, such as the neck ruffs, mustaches, and goatees. The heavenly spectacle is depicted in the ethereal manner that he increasingly used in his later works.

El Greco also painted several portraits of church officials; the best known is *Cardinal Guevara* (Figure 13.17). This painting portrays the Chief Inquisitor, dressed in his splendid red robes. El Greco has cap-

tured the personality of this austere and iron-willed churchman who vigorously pursued heretics and sentenced them to die in an *auto-da-fé,* Portuguese for "act of faith"—that is, a public ceremony in which heretics were executed, usually by being burned at the stake. El Greco's likeness suggests much about the inner man: Cardinal Guevara seems to have an uneasy conscience, as betrayed by the shifty expression of the eyes, the left hand clutching the chair arm, and the general sense that the subject is restraining himself. Through these means El Greco created another model for Mannerist portraiture.

Another Mannerist artist-in-exile working in Spain in the late sixteenth century was Sofonisba Anguissola [an-gwee-SOL-uh] (about 1532–1625), a northern Italian from Cremona who, along with El Greco, is credited with helping to introduce the Italian school of painting into Spanish culture (Figure 13.18). Praised and encouraged by the aging Michelangelo, Anguissola began her rise to international fame when King Philip II of Spain chose her to be his court painter from 1559 to 1579. She painted mainly portraits, as, for example, the

Figure 13.18 SOFONISBA ANGUISSOLA. *Bernardino Campi Painting Sofonisba Anguissola.* Ca. 1550. Oil on canvas, 43¹¹⁄₁₆ × 43⁵⁄₁₆". Pinacoteca Nazionale, Siena. *Unusual for her time, the aristocratic Sofonisba Anguissola pursued a painting career, and, even rarer, she studied painting apart from her parents' household, under the artist Bernardino Campi (1522–1591), living in his home as a paying guest. From him, she learned the Mannerist style, as in this double portrait of herself and her mentor, both presented in three-quarter length. Within the painting, she depicts her likeness on a canvas supported by an easel. Campi, standing before her likeness, holds a paintbrush in his right hand, which is steadied by a hand rest (a device used to prevent smudges). The sharp contrasts of light and dark and the characteristic "square-U" shape to the hands are typical of Anguissola's Mannerist style. By depicting Campi at work, she also broke new ground in the portrait genre, which hitherto had focused on subjects seated or standing, but always in static situations (see Figures 12.5 and 12.7).*

Figure 13.19 SOFONISBA ANGUISSOLA. (Formerly attributed to Alonzo Sánchez Coello.) *Portrait of Don Carlos.* Ca. 1560. Oil on canvas, 42¹⁵⁄₁₆ × 34³⁄₁₆". Prado, Madrid. *This painting of Prince Don Carlos shows typical features of the artist's personal style. Like most women of the period. Anguissola was skilled in the needle arts, and she reveals this knowledge in the painstaking detail she has lavished on the prince's court costume—her trademark, according to one scholar. She also had a signature way of rendering hands—in a "square-U" pattern, so that the index and little fingers are parallel and act as the raised portions of a "U" connected by an imaginary line—which may be seen in both of Don Carlos's hands.*

Portrait of Don Carlos (Figure 13.19). In this three-quarter-length likeness of Spain's crown prince, Anguissola shows her mastery of the Mannerist style, including the challenging gaze of the young subject and the painting's highly polished surface and dark olive background. Another Mannerist feature of this work is the nonrealistic scene, visible through the open window: an eagle flying and holding a column—a Hapsburg emblem—in its talons. The column functions as an allegory, referring to Don Carlos's position as heir to the Spanish throne and to the very real power of the Hapsburg family. Such enigmatic puzzles as this scene were beloved by the spirit of Mannerism.

Anguissola's international acclaim was due, in part, to her aristocratic breeding and her education in Renaissance learning, rare for women of the times. This background, coupled with rich artistic gifts, enabled her to overcome the prejudices and guild restrictions that had previously kept women from pursuing careers in the arts. Sofonisba Anguissola was the ablest of the women artists who began to emerge in sixteenth-century Europe.

Spanish Literature

Known in Spanish as *Siglo de Oro,* or Golden Century, the sixteenth century was the high point in Spain's literary history. The writings were characterized by direct observation of life, satiric treatment of earlier epics and ballads, religious zeal, and Spanish themes, values, and subject matter; they also reflected minor influence from Renaissance humanism. Plays and novels were the most popular forms of literary expression.

As in England, theater was now revived in Spain for the first time in centuries. Spanish playwrights began to write dramas, including tragedies and comedies, and invent new dramatic forms, such as allegorical religious plays. The dramatist Lope de Vega [BAY-gah] (1562–1635), author of 426 secular plays and 42 religious dramas, is generally credited with almost single-handedly founding the Spanish national theater.

The **chivalric novel,** a late medieval literary form that presented romantic stories of knights and their ladies, was now challenged by the more realistic **picaresque novel.** The picaresque novel (Spanish *picaro,* "rogue") recounted the comic misadventures of a roguish hero who lived by his wits, often at the expense of those above him in society. Although having the hero question the social order was a revolutionary step, the novels were immensely popular in Spain and across Europe. The first picaresque novel was the anonymous *Lazarillo de Tormes,* published in 1554, in which the poor hero, Lazaro, encounters several masters, each of whom is a shady character suffering from self-deception. In translation, *Lazarillo de Tormes* found new audiences across Europe and influenced the writing of novels in England, France, and Germany for about two hundred years.

The Spanish novel was raised to new heights by Miguel de Cervantes Saavedra [sir-VAN-tez] (1547–1616) in his masterpiece *Don Quixote* (Part I, 1605; part II, 1615). Poet, playwright, and novelist, Cervantes is the greatest figure in Spanish literature and one of the most respected writers in the world. In *Don Quixote* he satirized the chivalric novel, mocking its anachronistic ideals. Although the long, rambling structure was borrowed from the chivalric novel, *Don Quixote* is the prototype of the modern novel, with its psychological realism, or probing into the motives of the main characters. These characters, the hero, Don Quixote, and his servant, Sancho Panza, whose lives are intertwined, embody the major themes of the work. The tormented Don Quixote, driven half-mad by his unreachable quest, represents the hopeless visionary, while the plodding Sancho Panza, never taken in by his master's madness, stands for the hardheaded realist. At one level, the characters signify the dual nature of the Spanish soul, the idealistic aristocrat and the down-to-earth peasant. At a higher level, the characters personify a universal theme, that idealism and realism must go hand in hand.

Late Mannerist Painting in Italy: Tintoretto

With the death of Michelangelo in 1564, Venice displaced Rome as the dominant artistic center in Italy. From then until the end of the century, Venetian painters carried the banner of the Italian Renaissance, bringing Mannerism to a brilliant sunset. The leading exponent of Late Mannerism in Italy is Tintoretto [tin-tuh-RAY-toe] (1518–1594). This Venetian artist created a feverish, emotional style that reflected impetuosity in its execution. With his haste, Tintoretto was reacting against his famous Venetian predecessor Titian, who had been noted for extraordinary discipline. But in other respects, he followed Titian, adopting his love of color and his use of theatrical lighting. The special quality of Tintoretto's art, which he achieved in his earliest paintings, was to place his human figures in arrangements that suggest a sculptural frieze.

Tintoretto's rendition of the familiar biblical account of the Last Supper shows his feverish style (Figure 13.20). Unlike the serene, classically balanced scene that Leonardo had painted (see Figure 12.6), Tintoretto portrays an ethereal gathering, illuminated by eerie light and filled with swooping angels. The diagonal table divides the pictorial space into two halves; on the left is the spiritual world of Jesus and his disciples, and

Figure 13.20 TINTORETTO. *The Last Supper. 1592–1594. Oil on canvas, 12′ × 18′8″. San Giorgio Maggiore, Venice. Nothing better illustrates the distance between the High Renaissance and Mannerism than a comparison of Leonardo's* Last Supper *(Figure 12.6) with that of Tintoretto. Everything about Tintoretto's spiritualized scene contradicts the quiet Classicism of Leonardo's work. Leonardo's painting is meant to appeal to the viewer's reason; Tintoretto's shadowy scene is calculated to stir the feelings.*

on the right is the earthly realm of the servants. Tintoretto's depiction of these different levels of reality is reminiscent of a similar division in El Greco's *The Burial of Count Orgaz* (see Figure 13.16). Especially notable is Jesus' body, including the feet, which glows as if in a spotlight. *The Last Supper,* finished in Tintoretto's final year, is a fitting climax to Mannerist painting.

Music in Late-Sixteenth-Century Italy and England

Unlike painting, Italian music remained under the sway of High Renaissance ideals, keeping to the path pioneered by Josquin des Prez (see Chapter 12). Nevertheless, the Council of Trent, along with other forces, led to the decline of the High Renaissance style and created the conditions for the rise of the Baroque. For one thing, the council ruled that the Gregorian chant was preferable to polyphony for church liturgy and that the traditional chants should be simplified to ensure that the words could be easily understood. Most composers, considering the chants to be barbarous, continued to use polyphony but pruned its extravagant effects. The best of these composers and the chief representative of Counter-Reformation music was Giovanni Pierluigi da Palestrina [pal-uh-STREE-nuh] (about 1525–1594). His controlled style established the Roman Catholic ideal for the next few centuries—polyphonic masses sung by choirs and with clearly enunciated and expressive texts.

Nevertheless, the future of Italian music lay outside the church. Ironically, secular vocal music was also moving toward an ideal in which the words took precedence over the sound, but secular composers, unlike those in the church, rejected polyphony because it did not allow the text to be fully understood. The move to make the words primary in secular music was triggered by Renaissance humanists who were convinced that ancient music's power stemmed from the expressive way that the setting suited the clearly articulated words of the text. The most evident signs of this humanistic belief were in the works of the Florentine Camerata, a group of musical amateurs. Rejecting polyphony, the Florentine musicians composed pieces for a text with a single line of melody accompanied by simple chords and sung in a declamatory style.

The trend to expressive secular music in Italy was reflected most completely in the **madrigal,** a song for four or five voices composed with great care for the words of the poetic text. The novelty of this vocal music was that it vividly illustrated the meanings and emotions in the words, rather than the structure of the music. Madrigals were first written in the 1520s, but their heyday was the second half of the sixteenth century. Late in the century, they were imported to England and quickly became the height of fashion there. The success of madrigals in England had to do with the vogue there for Italianate things, as is evident from the settings and sources of Shakespeare's plays and the translation into English of Castiglione's *Book of the Courtier* during this period.

England's leading madrigal composer was Thomas Weelkes [WILKS] (about 1575–1623), whose works often made use of the technique called **word paintings,** or word illustrations, a musical illustration of the written text. For example, in the madrigal "As Vesta was from Latmos hill descending," Weelkes uses a descending scale for the word "descending," an ascending scale for the words "a maiden queen ascending," and a hill-shaped melodic phrase for the words "Latmos hill descending." Such clever fusing of music and lyrics appealed to listeners, many of whom, in the spirit of the Renaissance, were amateur musicians themselves.

Madrigals eventually achieved a European-wide popularity, but it ended with the Renaissance. Nevertheless, the technique of word painting continued to be a favorite of composers, down through Bach and Handel in the Baroque age (see Chapter 14).

The Legacy of Northern Humanism, Northern Renaissance, Religious Reformations, and Late Mannerism

The period from 1500 until 1520 in northern Europe witnessed important developments in painting and literature. The German painters Grünewald and Dürer and the Flemish painter Bosch brought the Late Gothic style to its final flower, though Dürer was also influenced by the methods of the Italian Renaissance. In the Netherlands, Erasmus launched Christian humanism, and, in France, Rabelais and Marguerite of Angoulême followed in this tradition. The movement was undermined by Luther's break with the Roman Catholic Church and was finally ended by the wars of religion.

The period from 1520 until 1603 brings to a close the third and final phase of the Renaissance. This eighty-three-year-period, framed by the deaths of Raphael and Queen Elizabeth I, saw the foundations of early modern Europe move firmly into place. A world culture and economy, in embryo, begins during this period. This momentous development was foreshadowed in the shift of Europe's commercial axis from the Mediterranean to the Atlantic, as well as in the start of Europe's exportation of peoples, technology, religions, and ideas to colonies in Asia, Africa, and the Americas.

Probably the most important material change during this era was the rise of a system of sovereign and mutually hostile states. No single state was able to assert its authority over the others; the pattern set by their struggles would govern Western affairs until the emergence of global politics in the twentieth century. The European state system also spelled the doom of a united Christendom.

The religious reformations further split Christian Europe, dividing it into Protestant and Catholic armed camps. As a result, religious wars afflicted this century and the next, fading away only by about 1700. On a local level, religious differences led to intolerance and persecution. Although Europe's religious boundaries today remain roughly the same as they were in 1600, it took over three hundred years for Protestants and Catholics to accept that they could live together in harmony.

The reformations also left different cultural legacies to their respective Christian denominations. From Protestantism came a glorification of the work ethic, Puritanism, and a justification for capitalism. At the heart of the Protestant revolution, despite its insistence on the doctrine of original sin, was the notion that human beings can commune directly with God without church mediation. Whereas Protestantism tended to view human beings as adrift in the universe, the Catholic Church tried to control the spiritual and moral lives of its members and to insulate them from the surrounding world. This policy eventually placed the church on a collision course with the forces of modernity, but it nevertheless was followed by most of the popes until after World War II.

In the aftermath of the religious crisis, the legacy of northern humanism—rational morals allied to a simple faith—went unheeded by Protestants and Catholics alike. Not until the eighteenth century and the rationalist program of the Enlightenment did Christian humanist ideas find a willing audience.

In the arts and humanities, however, the legacy was clear: This period left a rich and varied inheritance, including the work of Cervantes and the rest of Spain's Golden Age authors and the work of Shakespeare, the most gifted and influential individual writer in the history of Western civilization.

KEY CULTURAL TERMS

Reformation	Puritanism
Counter-Reformation	Anglicanism
Christian humanism	Jesuits
Northern Renaissance	Late Mannerism
revenge tragedy	chivalric novel
triptych	picaresque novel
Lutheranism	madrigal
Calvinism	word painting

SUGGESTIONS FOR FURTHER READING

PRIMARY SOURCES

CALVIN, J. *Institutes of the Christian Religion.* Translated by F. L. Battles. Philadelphia: Westminster Press, 1960. A translation of Calvin's theological masterpiece.

CERVANTES, M. DE. *Don Quijote [Quixote].* Translated by B. Raffel with volume edited by D. de Armas Wilson. New York: Norton, 1999. An up-to-date translation of the first modern novel with accompanying commentary; another excellent volume in the Norton Critical Edition series.

ERASMUS, D. *Praise of Folly.* Translated by B. Radice. New York: Penguin, 1971. A lively translation of Erasmus's satire that ridiculed the hypocrisy of the age, especially in the church; originally published in 1509.

LUTHER, M. *Three Treatises.* Translations by various authors. Philadelphia: Fortress Press, 1960. Good versions of the short works that helped to make Luther an outstanding and controversial public figure in his day.

MONTAIGNE, M. *Essays and Selected Writings.* Translated and edited by D. Frame. New York: St. Martin's Press, 1963. The *Essays* reveal Montaigne as one of the founders of French skepticism.

RABELAIS, F. *The Histories of Gargantua and Pantagruel.* Translated by J. M. Cohen. Franklin Center, Pa.: Franklin Library, 1982. An excellent modern version of this lusty masterpiece.

SHAKESPEARE. *Hamlet. Othello. King Lear. Romeo and Juliet. Antony and Cleopatra. Macbeth.* One of the best editions available of Shakespeare's tragedies is the New Folger Library, published by Washington Square Press. This series is inexpensive and profusely illustrated, and it offers extensive editorial notes.

SUGGESTIONS FOR LISTENING

PALESTRINA, GIOVANNI PIERLUIGI DA (about 1525–1594). A prolific composer of Masses, Palestrina is the major musical figure of the Counter-Reformation. Unlike the highly emotional style of Josquin, Palestrina's music is noted for its tightly controlled quality and its perfection of detail, as illustrated in such Masses as *Hodie Christus natus est, Assumpta est Maria,* and *Ave Maria.*

WEELKES, THOMAS (about 1575–1623). An English composer and organist, Weelkes is an important figure in Late Renaissance music. A composer of sacred vocal music and instrumental works for viols and harpsichord, he is best known for introducing the Italian madrigal to England and adapting it to the tastes of his compatriots. His madrigals are characterized by clever word paintings, as in "O, care, thou wilt despatch me" and "The Andalusian merchant" (both 1600).

AFRICA

HISTORY

East Africa *Coastal trading states.* Portuguese took control of gold trade. *Zimbabwe.* In decline, but a cult center for the Shona. *Zambezi Valley.* Butwa, the most prosperous state. Portuguese (ca. 1575) tried to control trade.

North Africa Egypt and the Maghreb conquered by Ottoman Empire (after 1517). *Morocco.* Sharifian Dynasty founded (1524); still rules today. Repelled Portuguese invaders (1578).

West Africa *Songhai Empire.* Greatest expanse under Askia Muhammad I (d. 1528). Fell to Moroccans (1591). *Yoruba culture.* Oyo Empire rose to power. Benin Kingdom grew powerful under Oba Esgi; became involved in the slave trade.

ART & MUSIC

West Africa *Yoruba culture.* Height of Benin bronzes.

ARCHITECTURE

West Africa *Songhai Empire.* Gao, the capital, became an Islamic city, with mosques, minarets, and the tomb of Emperor Askia Muhammad I.

RELIGION, PHILOSOPHY, LITERATURE

Islam, paramount in North Africa, made inroads into coastal and inland East and West Africa but failed to penetrate south of inland central Africa. Christianity was the state religion in Ethiopia; Christian missionaries in scattered areas on the tropical east and west coasts. Native religions and practices in rest of Africa.

AMERICAS

HISTORY

Throughout the Americas epidemics of European diseases, introduced by the explorers, decimated native populations.

South America *Inca culture.* Francisco Pizarro conquered Incas for Spain (1534). *Early Colonial period, 1534–1600.* Spanish founded Buenos Aires, Bogotá, Caracas. Pedro Álvares Cabral claimed Brazil for Portugal (1500). African slave trade began.

Mesoamerica *Aztec culture.* Hernán Cortés defeated Montezuma II. Tenochtitlán became Mexico City, capital of New Spain.

Native North America *Mississippian culture.* Calusas and Timucuas (Florida) resisted Spanish expeditions (1513–28). Hernán de Soto's expedition from Florida to Texas (1539–43). *Eastern woodlands.* Hurons traded furs and fish to French. *Southwest.* Francisco Coronado's expedition through Pueblo lands (1540–41).

ART & MUSIC

South America *Early Colonial period.* A hybrid style that fused Inca and Spanish Christian traditions.

Mesoamerica *Aztec culture.* Stone chacmools; feathered headdresses; and polychrome ceramics. Temple Stone, a throne for Montezuma II (1507). *Early Postconquest period, from 1519.* Wall painting; painted manuscripts (codices) of native history and religion, at the request of Franciscan friars.

Drinking Cup (Qero). Sixteenth century. Wood. Peru. University Museum of Archeology and Ethnology, Cambridge.

ARCHITECTURE

South America *Early Colonial period.* Inca's main temple in Cuzco—the Qorikancha, or "Golden House"—incorporated into a Christian church.

Mesoamerica *Aztec culture.* Tenochtitlán reached its final form (1487). *Early Postconquest period.* Spanish recycled stones from indigenous temples into civic buildings, churches, and homes. Monastic complexes for missionary friars and open-air chapels for converts.

RELIGION, PHILOSOPHY, LITERATURE

South America *Early Colonial period.* Founding of University of Lima (1551) and Central University of Quito (1594).

Mesoamerica *Early Postconquest period.* Indigenous scribes, sponsored by Franciscans, wrote histories, almanacs, and religious tracts. Aztec dictionary published (1555). *Florentine Codex: General History of the Things of New Spain* (ca. 1566–77, 1585), compiled by Father Bernardino de Sahagún.

Eagle in a Cactus (Symbol of Mexico), from frontispiece, Codex Mendoza. *Ca. 1550. Mexico. Bodleian Library, Oxford MS Arch. Selden A1.*

ASIA

China

Ming Dynasty. Weak rulers; peaceful period; Portuguese traders settled in Macao (1517); legal restrictions on foreigners and foreign trade (after 1570); breakdown in relations with Japan (1592).

India

Mogul Empire, began 1526. Delhi Sultanate conquered by Bābur, head of the Moguls, a Muslim dynasty from central Asia. Empire (zenith: Akbar, r. 1556–1605) included all of India, except for extreme south. Strong and effective centralized government. Portuguese made Goa headquarters of their Far Eastern trading empire.

Japan

Muromachi period, ended 1573. Civil war among feudal overlords. Portuguese traders arrived (1543). The samurai Oda Nobunaga overthrew the shōgun (1573). *Azuchi-Momoyama period, 1573–1603.* Period named for castle-towns of the two main warlords. The samurai Hideyoshi brought feudal lords under control (1591); restored internal peace and stability; invaded Korea (1592, 1597); thousands of Koreans massacred.

Ch'iu Ying. Saying Farewell at Hsün-yang. Detail of handscroll painting. First half sixteenth century. China. Nelson Gallery–Atkins Museum, Kansas City.

Ming Dynasty. Increased use of color in landscape scroll painting and five-color porcelains.

Deccan Plateau. Idealized version of the Persian miniature, with native Indian and Western features; practiced at Hindu and Muslim courts. *Mogul Empire.* During Akbar's reign, a realistic approach to the Persian miniature, combining European realism and native Indian tradition, as in the manuscript *Romance of Amir Hamza.* Hindustani music at its zenith.

Gardeners Beating the Giant Zamurrad Trapped in a Well, from Romance of Amir Hamza. 1567–82. Paint on cloth. India. Victoria and Albert Museum, London.

Azuchi-Momoyama period. Zen landscape painting at its height; screen painting by Kanō Eitoku at Azuchi castle; Kanō school colors-on-gold paintings; ink-wash murals by Hasegawa Tōhaku.

Ming Dynasty. Continued building of Forbidden City; developed small courtyard gardens (such as the Wang Shiyuan garden) and large parklike gardens.
The Wang Shiyuan Garden. Sixteenth century. Suzhou.

Mogul Dynasty. Tomb of Akbar's father, Humāyūn (1565), a blend of Persian and Indian features. New cities with public buildings and tombs. Fatehpur Sikri, a city planned by Emperor Akbar, based on Islamic and Hindu designs, only partially completed.

Panch Mahal (Palace of Five Stories). Begun 1571. Fatehpur Sikri, India.

Azuchi-Momoyama period. Two building styles: fortified stone castles with small windows and timbered roofs and the Shōin style with built-in desks and shelves, and rooms divided by sliding rice-paper screens (used by samurai as private retreats). Rustic teahouses influenced domestic architecture.

Ming Dynasty. Voyage to the West (1570), a classic comic novel; *The Peony Pavilion* (1598), with libretto by T'ang Hsien-tsu, a classic of K'un-ch'u opera; Tung Ch'i-ch'ang's *Talking of Painting,* a highly influential critique. Jesuit missionaries, headed by Matteo Ricci, arrived.

Delhi Sultanate. Under Sultan Sikander (1489–1517) poetry, music, and scholarship flourished. *Mogul Dynasty.* During Akbar's reign, Tul-sī-dās, Hindu author of poetic works on the god Rama; the *ghazal,* a type of Urdu lyric poetry. Akbar introduced religious toleration; the Sikh religion founded by the poet Nānak.

Muromachi period. Kabuki theater originated. Dance added to Nō plays. Jesuits active (after 1549). *Azuchi-Momoyama period.* Christians persecuted (1590s).

14 THE BAROQUE AGE
Glamour and Grandiosity
1600–1715

As the Roman Catholic Church pursued its goal of eradicating Protestantism, and as powerful sovereign secular states became established in Europe, a new age—the **Baroque**—dawned in the early seventeenth century. It was a period characterized by grandeur, opulence, and expanding horizons. Baroque art and architecture provided spectacular and compelling images with which the church could reassert its presence and dazzle and indoctrinate the faithful. The Baroque also offered secular rulers a magnificence that enhanced their political power. Art became a propagandistic tool in a way that the individualistic Mannerist art of the previous period—with its focus on the distorted and the eccentric—never was.

The term *baroque* was coined by eighteenth-century artists and scholars whose tastes were attuned to Classical ideals. To them, much seventeenth-century culture was imperfect, or "baroque," a term probably derived from the Portuguese word *barroco,* meaning an irregular pearl. Not until the mid–nineteenth century did the word acquire a positive meaning, and now "Baroque" is a label for the prevailing cultural style of the seventeenth century.

The Baroque period was an era of constant turmoil, and until midcentury, Europe was plagued by religious warfare, a legacy of the Reformation. The conflicts of the second half of the century had secular motivations: territorial expansion and the race for overseas empires. The seventeenth century was also a period of great scientific discoveries and intellectual change. Because the Scientific Revolution, as this intellectual movement is called, so keenly influenced the making of the modern world, it is covered separately in Chapter 15, along with related philosophical ideas. This chapter focuses

◀ VELÁZQUEZ. *Las Meninas (The Maids of Honor).* 1656. Oil on canvas, 10′5″ × 9′. Prado, Madrid.

Map 14.1   EUROPE IN 1714

on the art, literature, and music of the Baroque age and their historical, political, and social contexts.

ABSOLUTISM, MONARCHY, AND THE BALANCE OF POWER

Although the Baroque style in art originated in Rome and from there spread across the Continent, the Italian city-states and the popes were no longer at the center of European political life. By the time Europe had recovered from the first wave of religious wars in 1600, a new system of sovereign states had replaced the old dream of a united Christendom. By 1715 there was a balance of power in Europe among five great military states—England, France, Austria, Prussia, and Russia (Map 14.1). The rise of these states was due to a new breed of rulers fascinated with power. Known as *absolutists,* they wanted complete control over state affairs, unlike the medieval monarchs, who had to share authority with the church and the feudal nobles. Steeped in the works of Machiavelli, the new monarchs buttressed their claims to power with theories of divine right and natural law. France's greatest monarch, Louis XIV, was the most extreme in his claims, glorifying himself as the Sun King—a title derived from the late Roman emperors (Figure 14.1).

In their bid for absolute power, these monarchs founded new institutions and reformed old ones. For example, administrative bureaucracies, which had

Figure 14.1 Attributed to François de Troy. *Louis XIV and His Heirs.* Ca. 1710. Oil on canvas, 4′ 2¾″ × 5′ 3¾″. Wallace Collection, London. *Louis XIV's dynastic ambitions are reflected in this collective portrait of himself surrounded by his heirs. To his right stands his only legitimate son, the "Grand Dauphin," and the king's infant great-grandson, the duc de Bretagne, who is attended by a governess. To the king's left is his grandson, Louis, the duc de Bourgogne. Ironically, none of these heirs became king, because all of them died of illness within two years. In the painting, the Baroque love of grandeur is apparent in the opulent setting, the formal poses, and ornate dress. The king and the dauphin wear rich velvet suits and large, full-bottomed wigs, typical of seventeenth-century style. In contrast, the duc de Bourgogne represents the younger generation with his bright-colored suit and less formal wig. The wall painting within this portrait depicts the Greek sun god Helios, driving his chariot—a reference to Louis's claim to be the Sun King.*

existed since the High Middle Ages, were reformed to become the exclusive domain of university-trained officials drawn from the middle classes. These career bureaucrats began to displace the great lords who had previously dominated the kings' advisory councils. As a consequence, the authority of the feudal nobility began to diminish.

The absolute monarchs also established permanent diplomatic corps to assist in foreign policy. The great states of Europe set up diplomatic missions in the major capitals, staffed with trusted officials who served as their rulers' eyes and ears in foreign cities. Another new institution was the standing army funded from state revenues, led by noble officers, and manned by lower-class soldiers. New weapons—the flintlock rifle and the bayonet—and an improved breed of horse made these armies more efficient.

France: The Supreme Example of Absolutism

At the opening of the seventeenth century, France was ruled by Henry IV, the first of the Bourbon dynasty, who had converted from Calvinism to Catholicism to restore peace to his largely Roman Catholic state. Like the medieval kings, Henry shared authority with the feudal nobles, though he began to reward middle-class supporters with high office. Henry was a pragmatist; he felt no need to force his adopted faith on the Huguenots, as the French Calvinists were called, and al-

lowed them limited freedom of worship. The atmosphere changed when Henry was assassinated in 1610. Between then and 1715, France became the model absolutist state (Timeline 14.1).

Henry IV was succeeded by Louis XIII, but real authority passed to Cardinal Richelieu, who was the virtual ruler of France from 1624 until his death in 1642. Gifted with political acumen, Richelieu worked tirelessly to wrest power from the nobles. He was also a pragmatic statesman. For example, at home he restricted the freedom of the Protestant Huguenots, but abroad he allied himself with Swedish Protestants. His pragmatic policies were continued by his protégé and iron-fisted successor, Cardinal Mazarin, who served as regent for the young Louis XIV. Mazarin's rule moved France closer to absolutism, but it also coincided with the beginning of a golden age in France; for more than a century, French politics and culture dominated Europe, and French was the language of diplomacy.

When Mazarin died, Louis XIV, aged twenty-three, decided to rule France in his own right. Throughout his fifty-four-year reign, Louis made his private and public life the embodiment of the French state: "L'État c'est moi"—"I am the state"—is what he allegedly said about his concept of government. Determined that nothing should escape his grasp, Louis XIV canceled what freedom remained to the Huguenots, persecuting them until they converted to Roman Catholicism, fled into exile, or were killed. As king, he perfected the policies of his Bourbon predecessors, becoming the chief of a bureaucratic machine that regulated every phase of

Timeline 14.1 RULERS OF FRANCE AND ENGLAND DURING THE BAROQUE PERIOD

1589	1610	1643	1715
Henry IV, First Bourbon King	Louis XIII	Louis XIV	

FRANCE

1624 Authority passes to Cardinal Richelieu

1642 Death of Cardinal Richelieu

1661 Death of Cardinal Mazarin

1603	1625	1649	1660	1685	1689	1702	1714
James I, First Stuart King	Charles I	The Common-wealth	Charles II	James II	William III of Orange and Mary II	Anne	

Death of Elizabeth I

1688 Glorious Revolution

ENGLAND

French life, from economics to culture. His economic policy was called mercantilism, a system that rested on state control. Through his ministers, Louis regulated exports and imports, subsidized local industries, and set tariffs, customs duties, and quotas.

Louis waged a spectacular campaign of self-glorification, and in so doing he made France the center of European arts and letters. His palace at Versailles became the symbol of his regal style (Figure 14.2). He also encouraged the work of the emerging academies, particularly the French Academy, founded in 1635 by Cardinal Richelieu to purify the French language and honor the state's most distinguished living authors, and the Royal Academy of Painting and Sculpture, founded by Cardinal Mazarin in 1648 to recognize the country's best artists. These seventeenth-century French academies became the models for similar institutions in other Western states.

England: From Monarchy to Republic to Limited Monarchy

Like France, England turned toward absolutism at the beginning of the seventeenth century. Following the death of Elizabeth I, the new Stuart dynasty assumed the throne. King James I considered himself ruler by divine right, but certain aspects of English life held royal power in check. Specifically, the English nobles made common cause with the middle-class members of Parliament; England's Parliament met regularly and considered itself the king's partner rather than his enemy; and England's Calvinist minority, called Puritans, were not despised by the Anglican majority, many of whom shared their zeal. When England became embroiled in a constitutional crisis between Parliament and the headstrong Charles I, the successor of James I, Puritans and Anglicans joined forces in a civil war, toppling the monarchy and setting up a republic, called the Commonwealth, in 1649. But the Commonwealth soon lost its allure when its leader, the Puritan Oliver Cromwell, turned it into a military dictatorship.

Disappointed by the republic, the English restored monarchy in 1660, recalling Charles I's son from exile in France to become Charles II, an event known as the Restoration. The king's powers were now tempered by vague restrictions, but lack of clarity about the arrangement soon led to renewed conflicts between the crown and Parliament. In 1688 King James II, brother of Charles II, was expelled in a bloodless coup known as the Glorious Revolution, and his daughter and son-in-law, Mary II and William III of the Netherlands, became England's joint sovereigns. With their reign, England's constitutional crisis was finally resolved, for they understood that they could rule only if they recognized citizens' rights and Parliament's power over most financial matters. By 1715 England had become the classic example of limited monarchy under written laws. In the ensuing years, political philosophers cited England's experience as a successful example of the principle that government should rest on the consent of the people.

Warfare in the Baroque Period: Maintaining the Balance of Power

Warfare was crucial in establishing the configuration of the great powers because the most successful states were those in which the king could marshal his country's resources behind his military goals. But when one state began to stand out from the rest, the other states pursued policies designed to hold it in check—that is, to keep a balance of power. This system had several consequences. For one, it prevented any single state from controlling the rest. For another, it was a practical way to discourage the ambition of empires like that of the Ottoman Turks, because the great powers were willing to unite to stop Turkish expansion. Finally, this system relegated many countries, such as Spain and Poland, to secondary power status and spelled the end of a significant international role for city-states like Florence and Venice.

The Thirty Years' War, 1618–1648   The first half of the seventeenth century was mired in the destructive Thirty Years' War (actually a series of four wars), the last great European-wide struggle between the Protestants and the Roman Catholics. Besides the great powers of Austria, France, and Brandenburg (soon to be Prussia), states involved at one time or another included Denmark, Sweden, Spain, Venice, the United Provinces of the Netherlands, and Poland. Germany suffered the most because the war was fought largely on its soil, wiping out a generation of Germans and inaugurating more than a century of cultural decline.

The Treaty of Westphalia, which ended the war in 1648, nullified the religious objectives that had caused the war and also created the conditions for the rise of Brandenburg-Prussia to great power status. Germany itself remained divided; Calvinism was now tolerated, but true religious freedom did not appear, for the

Figure 14.2   Louis Le Vau and Jules Hardouin-Mansart. Palace of Versailles. 1661–1688. Versailles, France. *As the seat of government and the center of fashionable society, Versailles was the greatest symbol of this age of kings. Here, nobles competed for Louis XIV's favors and a royal post. He shrewdly rewarded them with menial positions and lofty titles and thus undermined their political influence. At the height of Louis's power, this complex of buildings could house ten thousand people—members of the royal court, hangers-on, and servants.*

PERSONAL PERSPECTIVE

Samuel Pepys
On the Great Fire of London, 1666

The English diarist Samuel Pepys described the Great Fire of London, a four-day-long conflagration in 1666 that destroyed much of the city, including the Cathedral of St. Paul's. Pepys, a minor official in the government, clearly had access to King Charles II. The fire was the most devastating event in the city's history prior to the German bombings of World War II.

[September 2] Jane [the Maid] called us up, about 3 in the morning, to tell us of a great fire they saw in the City. . . . I thought it far enough off, and so went to bed again and to sleep. About 7 rose again to dress myself. . . .

So I made myself ready presently, and walked to the Tower and there got up upon one of the high places, Sir J. Robinsons little son going up with me; and there I did see the houses at that end of the bridge all on fire, and an infinite great fire on this and the other side the end of the bridge—which, among other people, did trouble me for poor little Michell and our Sarah on the Bridge. So down, with my heart full of trouble, to the Lieutenant of the Tower, who tells me that it begun this morning in the King's bakers house in Pudding Lane, and that it hath burned down St Magnes Church and most part of Fish Streete already. So I down to the waterside and there got a boat and through the bridge, and there saw a lamentable fire. Poor Michells house, as far as the Old Swan, already burned that way and the fire running further, that in a very little time it got as far as the Stillyard while I was there. Everybody endeavour-

ing to remove their goods, and flinging into the river or bringing them into lighters that lay off. Poor people staying in their houses as long as till the very fire touched them, and then running into boats or clambering from one pair of stair by the waterside to another. And among other things, the poor pigeons I perceive were loath to leave their houses, but hovered about the windows and balconies till they were some of them burned, their wings, and fell down. . . .

I to Whitehall with a gentleman with me who desired to go off from the Tower to see the fire in my boat—to Whitehall, and there up to the King's closet in the chapel, where people came about me and I did give them an account dismayed them all; and word was carried in to the King, so I was called for and did tell the King and Duke of York what I saw, and that unless his Majesty did command houses to be pulled down, nothing could stop the fire. They seemed much troubled, and the King commanded me to go to my Lord Mayor from him and command him to spare no houses but to pull down before the fire every way. . . .

[I] walked through the City, the streets full of nothing but people and horses and carts loaden with goods, ready to run over one another, and removing goods from one burned house to another—they now removing out of Canning Street (which received goods in the morning) into Lumbard Streete and further; and among others, I now saw my little goldsmith Stokes receiving some friend's goods, whose house itself was burned the day after.

---

principle established at Augsburg in 1555 was retained: The religion of each state was to be dictated by its ruler (see Chapter 13). A divided Germany served the interests of Brandenburg-Prussia and its rulers. Commencing with the Treaty of Westphalia, these Calvinist leaders began to amass additional territories, becoming kings of Prussia in 1701 and finally emperors of a united Germany in 1871.

The Thirty Years' War also had major consequences for the emerging system of great powers. The peace conference was the first in which decisions were arranged through congresses of ambassadors. Both the war and the conference revealed Spain's impotence, showing that it had fallen from its peak in the 1500s. In contrast, Sweden and the Netherlands gained advantages that made them major powers for the rest of the century. The Hapsburg rulers were forced to accept

that Protestantism could not be turned back in their German lands; henceforth they concentrated on their Austrian holdings, ignoring the Holy Roman Empire, which now seemed a relic of the feudal age.

France profited the most from the Thirty Years' War. By shifting sides to support first Roman Catholics and then Protestants, the French rulers demonstrated a particularly shrewd understanding of power politics. Even after the religious wars were over, France continued to struggle against Roman Catholic Spain until 1659. Having taken control of France in 1661, Louis XIV launched a series of aggressive wars four years later against various coalitions of European states that lasted until 1713.

The Wars of Louis XIV, 1665–1713 Louis XIV used various means, including marriage and diplomacy, to assert French might on the Continent, but it was chiefly through warfare that he left his enduring mark. In his own mind, he fought for *la gloire* ("glory"), an elusive term that reflected his image as the Sun King but that in practice meant the expansion of France to imperial status.

Louis XIV fought the states of Europe in four separate wars and was finally defeated by a coalition that included virtually all of Europe's major and minor powers. Because of its wide-ranging nature, Louis's last struggle, the War of the Spanish Succession, is generally regarded as the first of the world wars—a new type of war. The Treaty of Utrecht, signed in 1713, not only settled this last war but also showed that the great power system was working.

The peace constructed at Utrecht was a reaffirmation of the balance of power principle. The victors set aside Louis's most extravagant acquisitions of land, but they granted those additions that still serve as France's borders today. Brandenburg-Prussia gained territory, and England emerged with the lion's share of the spoils, acquiring Gibraltar and the island of Minorca from Spain and areas of Canada from France. From this augmented base, England became the leader of world trade in the 1700s.

THE BAROQUE: VARIATIONS ON AN INTERNATIONAL STYLE

The Baroque mentality originated in a search for stability and order in a restless age. Encouraged by the Catholic Church, artists and writers sought to reveal the order they believed lay beneath the seeming chaos of life. In this, they shared certain aims with the artists of the High Renaissance. But although both styles were devoted to order, they differed in their concept of how harmony was best achieved. High Renaissance artists valued repose; a single, static perspective; and designs that were complete in themselves. Baroque artists, on the other hand, created dynamic, open-ended works that threaten to explode beyond their formal boundaries. These exuberant works are characterized by grand, sweeping gestures; flowing, expansive movement; and curving lines and oval and elliptical shapes. Reflecting the excitement of overseas explorations and of the new discoveries in astronomy, Baroque artists were fascinated with the concept of infinite space.

Despite religious differences among various regions of Europe, the Baroque style spread readily from its origin in Rome to the entire Continent and to England. Lines of communication—through trade, diplomacy, and marriage—facilitated its spread, as did the persistence of Latin as the common language of scholarly works and diplomatic exchanges. Travel was also a factor in the export of Baroque ideals to the rest of Europe. Many Protestant families in northern and western Europe sent their sons, and sometimes their daughters, on grand tours of the Continent to "complete their education." English travelers to Rome and other Catholic bastions included such faithful Protestants as poet John Milton and architect Christopher Wren.

Although the Baroque was an international style, it was reinterpreted in different regions, so that three distinct manifestations of the style emerged. The Florid Baroque, dominated by Roman Catholic religious ideals and motivations, was a product of the Counter-Reformation. This style developed in Italy and flourished there and in Spain and central Europe. The Classical Baroque, aristocratic and courtly, was a more subdued interpretation of Baroque ideals. This style was associated with French taste, which had been guided by the values of simplicity and harmony since the early 1500s, when Renaissance culture was first introduced into France. The French preference for the Classical fit well with the absolutist policies of Louis XIV, who promoted the adoption of strict rules in all aspects of cultural life as a way to reinforce his own obsession with order and control.

The third manifestation of this style was the Restrained Baroque, which arose in the middle-class United Provinces of the Netherlands and aristocratic England. Repelled equally by Catholicism and French absolutism, the artists and writers of the Restrained Baroque cultivated a style in keeping with their own Protestant values, a style simpler and less ornate than either the Florid or the Classical Baroque.

The Florid Baroque

The most important formative influence on the evolution of the Baroque style in the arts and architecture was the Council of Trent (see Chapter 13). In this series of sessions held between 1545 and 1563, church leaders had reaffirmed all the values and doctrines rejected by the Protestants and called for a new art that was geared to the teaching needs of the church and that set forth correct theological ideas easily understood by the masses. To achieve these goals, the popes of the late sixteenth century began to hold a tighter rein on artists and architects and to discourage the individualistic tendencies of the Mannerist style.

The seventeenth-century popes used their patronage powers to bring to life the **Florid Baroque** style. Once again, as in the Middle Ages, aesthetic values were subordinated to spiritual purposes. The popes enlisted architects, painters, and sculptors to glorify the Catholic message. Architects responded with grand building plans and elaborate decorative schemes that

Figure 14.3 CARLO MADERNO AND GIANLORENZO BERNINI. Plan of St. Peter's Basilica with Adjoining Piazza. 1607–1615 and 1665–1667. *This plan of St. Peter's Basilica shows the design of Maderno for the church (left), dating from 1607–1615, and the adjoining piazza and colonnade (right) by Bernini, dating from 1665–1667.*

symbolized the power and richness of the church. Painters and sculptors represented dramatic incidents and emotion-charged moments, particularly favoring the ecstatic visions of the saints and the suffering and death of Jesus. They portrayed these subjects with a powerful realism intended to convey the physical presence and immediacy of the church's holiest figures. In everything, vitality and theatrical effects were prized over such Classical elements as restraint and repose.

Architecture The church of St. Peter's in Rome became the age's preeminent expression of the Florid Baroque building style. First conceived in the early 1500s by Donato Bramante as a High Renaissance temple in the shape of a Greek cross, St. Peter's was now redesigned to conform to the ideals of the Council of Trent. Rejecting the Greek cross as a pagan symbol, Pope Paul V commissioned Carlo Maderno [mah-DAIR-noh] (1556–1629) to add a long nave, thereby giving the floor plan the shape of a Latin cross (Figure 14.3). Not only did the elongated nave satisfy the need to house the large crowds drawn to the mother church of Roman Catholicism, but also the enormous size of the building signified the church's power.

St. Peter's exterior was basically finished after Maderno designed and built the building's facade, but the popes wanted to integrate this huge church into its urban setting—a Classical ideal that was now adapted to Baroque taste. For this task, Pope Alexander VII commissioned Gianlorenzo Bernini [bayr-NEE-nee] (1598–1680). Bernini's solution was a masterstroke of Florid Baroque design in which he followed the principle of abolishing all straight lines. He tore down the buildings around St. Peter's and replaced them with a huge public square where the faithful could gather to see and hear the pope. Bernini then outlined this key-

hole-shaped space with a sweeping colonnade topped with statues of saints (Figure 14.4). For worshipers assembled in the square, the curved double colonnade stood as a symbol of the church's welcoming arms.

From its origin in Rome, the Florid Baroque style in architecture spread to Spain, Austria, and southern Germany. By 1650 this lush style had appeared in Spanish and Portuguese colonies in the Americas, and there it flourished until well into the nineteenth century.

Sculpture During the Baroque period, sculpture once again became a necessary complement to architecture, as it had been in medieval times. This change was hastened by the Council of Trent's advocacy of religious images to communicate the faith as well as the need to decorate the niches, recessed bays, and pedestals that were part of building facades in Florid Baroque architecture. The demand for sculpture called forth an army of talented artists, of whom the most outstanding was Bernini, one of the architects of St. Peter's.

Bernini brought the Florid Baroque to a dazzling climax in his sculptural works. His pieces, executed for such diverse projects as churches, fountains, and piazzas, or squares, often combined architecture with sculpture. His sculptural ideal was a dynamic composition that used undulating forms to delight the eye. His sensuous sculptures with their implicit movement were the perfect accompaniments to Florid Baroque structures with their highly decorated walls.

Bernini's most famous sculptures are those he made for the interior of St. Peter's—including altars, tombs, reliefs, statues, and liturgical furniture—during a fifty-year period, commencing in 1629. His masterpiece among these ornate works is the **baldacchino,** the canopy, mainly bronze and partly gilt, that covers the spot where the bones of St. Peter are believed to lie—

Figure 14.4 GIANLORENZO BERNINI. Piazza of St. Peter's. 1665–1667. The Vatican. *Bernini's plan for the piazza leading up to St. Peter's was instrumental in making exterior space a major concern of Baroque architects. The ancient Romans had integrated buildings into their urban settings, as had High Renaissance planners, but no architect had ever achieved such a natural blending of a monumental structure with its surroundings as Bernini did in this design.*

directly under Michelangelo's dome. Combining architectural and sculptural features, the baldacchino is supported by four huge columns whose convoluted surfaces are covered with climbing vines (Figure 14.5). Bernini crowned this colossal work with a magnificent display of four large angels at the corners, four groups of cherubs in the centers of the sides, and behind the angels four scrolled arches that rise to support a ball and cross at the top.

The baldacchino's twisting columns were modeled on the type that by tradition supported Solomon's Temple in Jerusalem and had been used in the old St. Peter's Basilica. Thus these columns symbolized the church's claim to be the true successor to the Jewish faith. So popular was Bernini's Solomonic canopy that in southern Germany it inspired many imitators and became the standard covering for altars for the next two centuries.

The sculpture that marks the highest expression of Bernini's art is *The Ecstasy of St. Teresa* (Figure 14.6). Using stone, metal, and glass, he portrays the divine moment when the saint receives the vision of the Holy Spirit—symbolized here by the arrow with which the angel pierces her heart. In his conception, Bernini imagines the pair floating on a cloud and bathed by light from a hidden source; the light rays seem to turn into golden rods that cascade onto the angel and the saint. The intensity of the saint's expression, the agita-

tion of the draperies, and the billowing clouds all contribute to the illusion that the pair are sensuously real. By depicting St. Teresa's supernatural experience in physical terms, Bernini intended to force the viewer to suspend disbelief and accept the religious truth of the scene.

Painting   In the Baroque period, painting once again became an essential part of church decoration. In pursuit of church ideals, the painters of this tradition tended to use rich color and unusual lighting effects to depict spectacular or dramatic moments. They represented nature and the human form realistically to make art intelligible and meaningful to the ordinary viewer.

The earliest great Florid Baroque painter was Michelangelo Merisi (1573–1610), better known as Caravaggio [kahr-ah-VAHD-jo]. Caravaggio rejected the antinaturalism of Mannerism in favor of a dramatic realism. His concern with realism led him to pick his models directly from the streets, and he refused to idealize his subjects. To make his works more dramatic and emotionally stirring, he experimented with light and the placement of figures. His paintings offer startling contrasts of light and dark—the technique known as chiaroscuro—and he banished landscape from his canvases, often focusing on human figures grouped tightly in the foreground.

Figure 14.5 GIANLORENZO BERNINI. The Baldacchino. 1624–1633. Ht., approx. 100'. St. Peter's, Rome. *This magnificent canopy reflects the grandiose ambitions of its patron, Pope Urban VIII, a member of the Barberini family. The Barberini crest was the source for the huge stylized bees displayed on the flaps of the bronze canopy. In his desire for worldly immortality, this pope shared a common outlook with the secular rulers of the Baroque age.*

A superb example of Caravaggio's work is *The Martyrdom of St. Matthew,* one of a series of works he painted on the life of this early Christian saint (Figure 14.7). His revolutionary use of chiaroscuro, whereby the light drenches the foreground figures and the darkness renders the background indistinct, makes the agony of the saint dramatically vivid. The tension in the scene is intensified by the thrusting limbs of the various figures.

Caravaggio had an enormous influence on other painters both in Italy and elsewhere, notably France, Spain, and the Netherlands. Perhaps the most original of Caravaggio's Italian disciples—known as Caravaggisti—was Artemisia Gentileschi [ahrt-uh-MEEZ-e-uh jain-teel-ESS-key] (1593–1653), his only female follower. Unlike most women artists of the early modern period, who limited their art to portraits, such as the late-sixteenth-century painter Sofonisba Anguissola (see Chapter 13), Gentileschi concentrated on bib-

lical and mythical subjects, as many male artists did. However, she did paint her own portrait in *Self Portrait as the Allegory of Painting.* Trained by her painter-father Orazio, himself a disciple of Caravaggio, Gentileschi adapted the flamboyant and dramatic style of Caravaggesque realism and made it her own. In almost thirty surviving paintings, she followed this style's preference for "night pictures," dark scenes whose blackness is illuminated by a single internal light source.

What distinguishes Artemisia Gentileschi's art from that of the rest of the Caravaggisti is its female assertiveness, a highly unusual quality in the Baroque period, when women artists were still making their way without guild support or access to nude modeling. Female assertiveness is expressed throughout her works in an androgynous (having female and male characteristics) ideal, as may be seen in *Judith and Her Maidservant with the Head of Holofernes* (Figure 14.8), which depicts a scene from an apocryphal book of the Old Testament, the Book of Judith. The painting's central figure—Judith—is decidedly female (as shown in the vulnerable throat and fleshy body) and yet exhibits masculine strength (as shown in the commanding gesture accentuated by the firmly grasped sword). Judith, often treated in Italian painting and sculpture in the Renaissance and Baroque eras, is a perfect subject for Gentileschi, since the biblical story describes a woman of destiny. In the story, Judith saves the Jewish people by beheading their enemy Holofernes having first seduced him. In the painting, Holofernes's bloody head, partly visible in the basket, starkly dramatizes the point that Judith is a forthright woman who plans and acts, just as men do. Gentileschi's Judith typifies a heroic female ideal who is endowed with the traits of that fuller humanity that by tradition had been allowed only to male figures. Through such dramatic works as this, Gentileschi helped to spread the Caravaggesque style in Italy.

About the same time that Caravaggio was creating his dramatic works, a new form caught the imagination of painters in the Florid Baroque tradition—the illusionistic ceiling fresco. In these paintings, artists constructed imaginary continuations of the architectural features already present in the room, expanding up through layers of carefully foreshortened, sculptured figures and culminating in patches of sky. Looking up as if at the heavens, the viewer is overawed by the superhuman spectacle that seems to begin just overhead.

The superb example of this **illusionism** is the nave ceiling of the church of Sant' Ignazio (St. Ignatius) in Rome, painted by Andrea Pozzo [POE-tzo] (1642–1709). In this fresco, entitled *Allegory of the Missionary Work of the Jesuits,* Pozzo reveals a firm mastery of the technique of architectural perspective (Figure 14.9). The great nave ceiling is painted to appear as if the viewer were looking up through an immense open colonnade. Figures stand and cling to the encircling architectural supports, and, in the center, an expansive vista opens to reveal Ignatius, the founder of the Jesuit order, being received by an open-armed Christ. The clusters of

Figure 14.6 GIANLORENZO BERNINI. *The Ecstasy of St. Teresa.* 1645–1652. Marble, glass, metal, life-size. Cornaro Chapel, Santa Maria della Vittoria, Rome. *Even though this sculpture captures an ecstatic vision, its portrayal reflects the naturalism that was central to the Baroque style. Bernini based this work on the saint's personal account, in which she described how an angel pierced her heart with a golden spear—a mystical moment the tableau faithfully reproduces. The sculpture's subject, St. Teresa of Avila (Spain) (1515–1582), founded the Carmelite order of nuns (1562); she recorded her mystic visions in works such as* Camino de perfección (The Road to Perfection).

Figure 14.7   CARAVAGGIO. *The Martyrdom of St. Matthew.* 1602. Oil on canvas, approx. 10′7¹⁄₁₆″ × 11′3″. Contarelli Chapel, San Luigi dei Francesi, Rome. *Caravaggio's paintings made monumentality an important feature of the Florid Baroque style. By presenting the human figures in close-up and giving full weight to their bodies, as in this painting, the artist made their presence an inescapable fact to the viewer. This approach gave his paintings a dramatic immediacy.*

columns on either side are labeled for the four continents—Europe, Asia, America, and Africa—symbolizing the missionary zeal of the Jesuits around the globe. Pozzo was motivated by spiritual concerns when he painted this supernatural vision. He believed that the illusion of infinite space could evoke feelings of spiritual exaltation and even religious rapture in the viewer. Illusionism, infinite space, and spectacular ef-

fects make this a masterpiece of the Florid Baroque. To see the dramatic differences between Baroque and High Renaissance ideals, compare this ceiling fresco with the ceiling of the Sistine Chapel by Michelangelo (see Figure 12.8).

Outside Italy, the principal centers of Florid Baroque painting were the studio of Velázquez in Spain and the workshop of Rubens in Flanders (present-day Belgium).

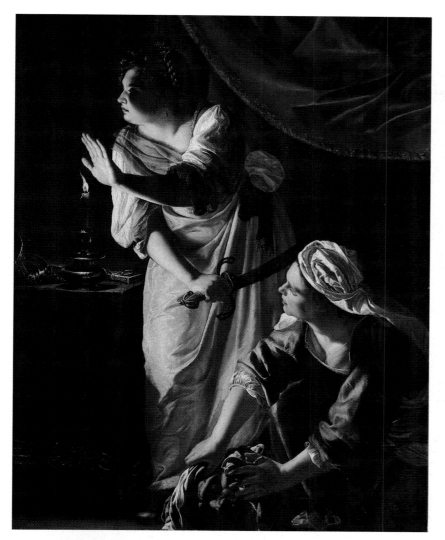

Figure 14.8 ARTEMISIA GENTILESCHI. *Judith and Her Maidservant with the Head of Holofernes.* Ca. 1625. Oil on canvas. Detroit Institute of Arts. *Gentileschi's style in this painting is strongly indebted to the style of Caravaggio: The natural background is painted black and thus virtually eliminated, the central figures are shown in tight close-up, and the action is frozen like a single frame in a film sequence. The aesthetic impact of this cinematic method is to draw viewers into the scene and to personalize the figures. The artist's interest in the personal psychology of her characters is part of the trend toward naturalism that characterized Baroque culture in general.*

Figure 14.9 ANDREA POZZO. *Allegory of the Missionary Work of the Jesuits.* Ca. 1621–1625. Ceiling fresco. Sant' Ignazio, Rome. *The meaning of Pozzo's fresco is based on* ignus, *Latin for "fire," a pun on the name of St. Ignatius (Loyola), the founder of the Jesuit order. In church tradition, the saint and the Jesuit mission are linked with the power of fire and light. At the fresco's center, Christ, holding the cross, emits rays of light from his wounded side, which pierce the figure of Ignatius (sitting on the cloud bank nearest Christ), who acts as a mirror; from him the light then radiates to the four corners, symbolic of the four continents. Thus, Ignatius and his missionary followers mediate Christ's saving light to the whole earth, as commanded by the scriptures.*

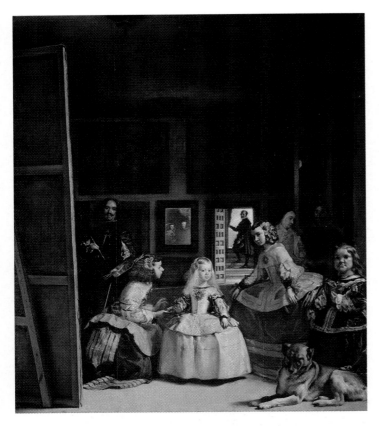

Figure 14.10 VELÁZQUEZ. *Las Meninas (The Maids of Honor)*. 1656. Oil on canvas, 10′ 5″ × 9′. Prado, Madrid. *Velázquez uses the mirror on the back wall, reflecting the Spanish king and queen, to enhance the dynamic feeling of the scene. This illusionistic device explodes the pictorial space by calling up presences within and outside the painting.*

Whereas Velázquez softened the Florid Baroque to his country's taste, Rubens fully embraced this sensual style to become its most representative painter.

The work of Diego Velázquez [vuh-LAS-kus] (1599–1660) owes much to the tradition of Caravaggio but without the intense drama of the Italian's painting. Velázquez also used chiaroscuro, but he avoided the extreme contrasts that made Caravaggio's paintings controversial. Velázquez's greatest work is *Las Meninas,* or *The Maids of Honor* (Figure 14.10). In his role as official artist to the Spanish court, Velázquez painted this group portrait of the Infanta, or princess, surrounded by her maids of honor (one of whom is a dwarf). What makes this painting so haunting is the artful play of soft light over the various figures. In the background, a man is illuminated by the light streaming through the open door, and even more abundant sunshine falls on the princess from the window on the right.

Velázquez also plays with space and illusion in this painting. On the left side, he depicts himself, standing before a huge canvas with brush and palette in hand. The artist gazes directly at the viewer—or is he greeting the king and queen, who have just entered the room and are reflected in the mirror on the rear wall?

The princess and two of her maids also look attentively out of the picture, but whether at the artist painting their portrait, at the royal couple, or at the viewer is left unclear. This fascination with illusion and with the effects of light and shade reveals Velázquez's links with Caravaggio and the art of the Florid Baroque.

In contrast to Velázquez's devotion to the ideal of grave beauty, the work of Peter Paul Rubens (1577–1640) is known for its ripe sensuality and for his portrayal of voluptuous female nudes. Rubens had already forged a sensuous style before he sojourned in Italy for eight years, but his encounters with Caravaggio's tradition impressed him deeply, causing him to intensify his use of explosive forms and chiaroscuro. From the Venetian painters, especially Titian, he derived his love and mastery of gorgeous color. In his mature works, he placed human figures in a shallow foreground, bathed them in golden light with dark contours, and painted their clothes and flesh in sensuous tones.

As the most sought-after artist of his day, Rubens was often given commissions by the kings of the great states, and he produced works for royalty, for the church, and for wealthy private patrons. As official painter to the French court before the ascendancy of Louis XIV, who preferred the Classical style, Rubens was commissioned to paint a cycle of works glamorizing the life of Queen Marie de' Medici, widow of Henry IV and powerful regent for her son, Louis XIII. One of the typical works from this series is *The Education of Marie de' Medici* (Figure 14.11). In this huge canvas, Rubens used Roman mythological figures to transform a mundane episode in the life of a queen into a splendid pageant of the French monarchy. All action is centered on the kneeling future queen. Minerva, the goddess of wisdom, offers instruction in reading and writing; Mercury, the god of eloquence, hovers overhead and offers his blessing; Apollo (or Orpheus, or Harmony) plays a stringed instrument, thereby inculcating a love of music; and the three Graces, attendants of the goddess Venus, encourage the perfection of feminine grace. A waterfall cascades in the background, a drapery billows above, and various images of Greco-Roman culture (a mask of tragedy and a musical instrument) are displayed in the foreground. Rubens's mastery of both spiritual and secular subjects and the turbulent drama of his works made him the finest artist of the Florid Baroque.

The Classical Baroque

Although the Baroque originated in Rome, the pronouncements of the church had little effect on the art and architecture of France. Here, the royal court was the guiding force in the artistic life of the nation. The

Figure 14.11 Peter Paul Rubens. *The Education of Marie de' Medici.* 1621–1625. Oil on canvas, 12′11″ × 9′8″. Louvre. *The Medici cycle, of which this work is a superb example, not only established the artist's European-wide reputation but also defined historical narrative—the combining of a historical event with mythological motifs—as one of the great themes of Baroque art. By 1715 the French Academy had created a ranked set of painting subjects, of which historical narrative occupied the highest level.*

rulers and the royal ministers provided rich commissions that helped to shape the **Classical Baroque,** giving this style a secular focus and identifying it with absolutism. A second powerful influence on the Baroque in France was the pervasiveness of the Classical values of simplicity and grave dignity. Accordingly, after Louis XIV became king, French artists and architects found the Florid Baroque alien and even offensive; their adaptation of the Baroque was more impersonal, controlled, and measured.

Architecture The palace of Versailles was the consummate architectural expression of the Classical Baroque. Versailles, a former hunting lodge, was transformed by Louis XIV into a magnificent royal residence that became the prototype of princely courts in the West. At Versailles, where all power was concentrated in the royal court, were collected the best architects, sculptors, painters, and landscape architects as well as the finest writers, composers, and musicians that France could produce. The duty of this talented assemblage was to use their gifts to surround Louis XIV with the splendor appropriate to the Sun King.

The redesign of Versailles gave Louis XIV the most splendid palace that has ever been seen in Europe. The chief architects of this revamped palace were Louis Le Vau [luh-VO] (1612–1670) and Jules Hardouin-Mansart [ar-DWAN mahn-SAR] (1646–1708), but the guiding spirit was the Sun King himself. When finished, the palace consisted of a huge central structure with two immense wings (see Figure 14.2). The architecture is basically in the style of the Renaissance, with rounded arches, Classical columns, and porticoes inspired by Roman temples, but the overall effect is a Baroque style that is dignified yet regal.

The most striking aspect of Versailles is its monumentality: The palace is part of an elaborate complex that includes a royal chapel and various support structures, all of which are set in an elaborate park over two miles long. The park, designed by André Le Nôtre [luh-NOH-truh] (1613–1700), is studded with a rich display of fountains, reflecting pools, geometric flower beds, manicured woods, exotic trees, statues, urns, and graveled walks—a gorgeous outdoor setting for royal receptions and entertainments (Figure 14.12).

Figure 14.12 André Le Nôtre, Landscape Architect, and Various Sculptors. Versailles Gardens. The Pool of Latona with adjacent parterres. 1660s. Versailles, France. *This fountain, composed of four concentric marble basins, is named for its crowning statue of Latona, the mother of the sun god Apollo, who was the inspiration for Louis XIV's reign. On either side of the fountain are parterres, or flower gardens with beds and paths arranged into patterns. Beyond the fountain stretches an avenue flanked by wooded areas that culminates in the grand canal, which extends the view into infinity. The rich profusion of this scene is a hallmark of Baroque design.*

Figure 14.13 CHARLES LEBRUN AND JULES HARDOUIN-MANSART. Hall of Mirrors, Versailles Palace. 1678–1684. Versailles, France. *Lebrun and Mansart designed this enormous hall to overlook the vast park at Versailles. Viewed through the floor-to-ceiling windows, which are placed along the width of the room, the majestic park becomes an extension of the interior space. The inside space in turn is enlarged by the tall mirrors that match the windows, echoing the outside view.*

The most famous room in Versailles Palace is the Hall of Mirrors, a central chamber with a tunnel-vaulted ceiling (Figure 14.13). The grandiose design of this hallway reflects its original function as the throne room of Louis XIV. Named for its most prominent feature, this long hall is decorated with Baroque profusion, including, in addition to the mirrors, wood parquetry floors of intricate design, multicolored marbles, ceiling paintings depicting military victories and other deeds of Louis XIV, and gilded statues at the base of the paintings. In modern times, major political events have taken place in the Hall of Mirrors: The Germans proclaimed their empire from here in 1871 after having vanquished the French, and the peace treaty that ended World War I was signed here in 1919.

Painting Classical values dominated Baroque painting in France even more completely than architecture. In pursuit of ancient Roman ideals, Classical Baroque artists painted mythological subjects, stressed idealized human bodies, and cultivated a quietly elegant style. The outstanding Classical Baroque artist was Nicolas Poussin [poo-SAN] (1594–1665). Ironically, except for two disappointing years in Paris, Poussin spent his professional life in Rome, the home of the Florid Baroque. Although he was inspired by Caravaggio's use of light and dark, the style that Poussin forged was uniquely his own, a detached, almost cold approach to his subject matter and a feeling for the unity of human beings with nature.

A beautiful example of Poussin's detached style is *Et in Arcadia Ego*, a painting in which the human fig-

Figure 14.14 NICOLAS POUSSIN. *Et in Arcadia Ego*. Ca. 1640. Oil on canvas, 34 × 48". Louvre. *In sacred art, painters expressed the theme of the inevitability of death in portraits of the sufferings of Jesus and the saints, and in secular art, in depictions of skeletons and death's heads, or images of human skulls. But Poussin, whose art was fired by Classical ideals and who was thus more reflective than others of his age, treated death in a much more detached way, as in this painting. Poussin's puzzled shepherds are a gentle reminder that the reality of death always comes as a surprise in the midst of everyday existence.*

ures are integrated into a quiet landscape (Figure 14.14). In ancient mythology, Arcadia was a land of pastures and flocks. In Poussin's painting, four shepherds, modeled on ancient statuary and clothed in Roman dress, are portrayed standing around a tomb, evidently absorbed in a discussion provoked by the Latin words carved into the tomb: *Et in Arcadia Ego,* that is, "I too once dwelled in Arcadia." One shepherd traces the letters with his finger, spelling out the words. The magnificent stillness, the mythological subject, and the gentle melancholy evoked by this reminder of death were central to Poussin's art and evidence of his Classical spirit. Typically Baroque are the use of chiaroscuro, which makes the exposed limbs and the faces of the shepherds stand out vividly from the shadowy middle ground, and the sensual tones and rich colors.

The Restrained Baroque

The Protestant culture of northern and western Europe created simpler works that humanized Baroque exuberance, appealed to democratic sentiments, and reflected common human experience. This style of art is called the **Restrained Baroque,** and it was founded by the painters and architects of the Netherlands and England.

Painting   The Calvinist Netherlands pointed the way in the arts in Protestant Europe until 1675. The Dutch Republic was ruled by a well-to-do middle class whose wealth was based largely on their dominant role in international shipping. Led by these sober-minded burghers, as the townspeople were called, the Netherlands was briefly one of Europe's great powers. During the middle of the century, the Dutch virtually controlled northern Europe, using their military and naval might to fight England, check French ascendancy, and destroy Spanish sea power. Amsterdam became one of Europe's largest cities, and an important school of painting flourished there. In about 1675 a series of military disasters ended the Netherlands' economic expansion, and the state's fortunes declined sharply. By this time, the great days of Dutch art were over.

During the heyday of the Dutch Republic, a school of painters arose whose works defined the Restrained Baroque. Attuned to the sober values of their religion and sympathetic to the civic ideals of the republic, these artists created a secular style that mirrored the pious outlook of the ruling middle class. An important development that helped to shape the course of Dutch painting was the rise of an art market. Venice had shown some tendencies in this direction in the 1500s, but in the Netherlands in the 1600s the first full-

Figure 14.15   REMBRANDT VAN RIJN. *The Blinding of Samson.* 1636. Oil on canvas, 7′9″ × 9′11″. Staedelsches Kunstinstitut, Frankfurt. *The influence of Caravaggio on Rembrandt, particularly in his early works, can be seen in this painting. It is evident in the passionate energy, the handling of contrasts of light and shade, and the modeling of the bodies and faces of ordinary people. Later in his life, Rembrandt's style became less dynamic and sensual.*

fledged art market made its debut. The impact of this market on the Dutch school was instantaneous and dramatic. Driven by a demand for home decoration, especially small works to hang on the wall, the market responded with specific subjects—still lifes, landscapes, portraits, and genre, or "slice-of-life," scenes. Paintings were sold by dealers as wares, and buyers speculated in art objects. The market dictated success or failure; some painters pursued other careers as a hedge against financial ruin.

The greatest artist of the Dutch school and probably one of the two or three greatest painters of Western art was Rembrandt van Rijn (1606–1669). His early genius lay in his subtle and dramatic use of lighting and his forceful expressiveness—both qualities that reflected the distant influence of Caravaggio. He also was supremely gifted in his ability to portray the range of moods and emotions he found in humanity, as expressed through the ordinary people he used as models.

A splendid illustration of Rembrandt's early style is *The Blinding of Samson,* a work inspired by the biblical story of seduction and betrayal (Figure 14.15). In the biblical account, Samson was a powerful warrior whose hair—the source of his strength—was cut off by the beautiful Delilah; she then betrayed him to his enemies, who were able to capture and blind him. This painting, with its lush colors and dramatic detail, reflects the Baroque vogue for sensuality and violent episode. Much of the scene is rendered in near dark-

Figure 14.16   REMBRANDT VAN RIJN. *The Night Watch (The Militia Company of Captain Frans Banning Cocq).* 1642. Oil on canvas, 12′2″ × 14′7″. Rijksmuseum, Amsterdam. *Because of its murky appearance, this painting acquired its nickname,* The Night Watch, *in the nineteenth century. But a cleaning of the painting's deteriorated surface showed that it was actually set in daylight. Restored to its original conception, this work now reveals Rembrandt's spectacular use of light and dark.*

ness, but Rembrandt uses subtle lighting to focus attention on the central action and to stir the viewer's emotions. Light falls through the tent opening revealing soldiers wrestling with Samson, the Jewish hero. One figure bends over the struggling Samson, putting out his eye, while the figure with the pike stands guard. Behind the soldiers is Delilah, brandishing Samson's

shorn locks as she hastily exits the tent. Through works such as this, Rembrandt became one of the most successful painters working in Amsterdam.

The culmination of Rembrandt's early style is a painting entitled *The Militia Company of Captain Frans Banning Cocq* but commonly known as *The Night Watch* (Figure 14.16). The painting was commissioned by one

Figure 14.17 REMBRANDT VAN RIJN. *Self-Portrait.* 1669. Oil on canvas, 23¼ × 20″. Mauritshuis, The Hague. *In this last self-portrait, Rembrandt's eyes reveal the personal anguish of a man who has outlived wife, beloved mistress, and children. By this means, Rembrandt expresses one of the most popular themes of Baroque art, that of pathos—the quality that arouses feelings of pity and sorrow.*

of Amsterdam's municipal guard troops in a typical display of Dutch civic pride. Instead of painting a conventional group portrait, however, Rembrandt created a theatrical work filled with exuberant and dramatic gestures and highly charged chiaroscuro effects. He gave the composition added energy by depicting the guardsmen marching toward the viewer. The militia is led by Captain Cocq, the black-suited figure with the red sash and white ruff who marches with arm outstretched in the center foreground. On his left marches his attentive lieutenant, dressed in yellow, with his halberd in his hand. Behind them, the members of the surging crowd, engaged in various soldierly activities and looking in different directions with expressive faces, seem ready to burst forth from the space in which they are enclosed. Of Rembrandt's vast repertory, this painting is one of his most representative.

In the later work painted in the mid-1640s, Rembrandt's style became more personal and simpler. His paintings now expressed a stronger naturalism and an inner calm, a change that paralleled the rise of the quieter Classical Baroque. This final stage of his art is most beautifully and movingly rendered in his last self-portrait (Figure 14.17). During his career, he had often painted his own likeness, coolly revealing the effects of the aging process on his face. The last self-portrait is

most remarkable for the expressive eyes, which, though anguished, seem resigned to whatever happens next. Rembrandt's pursuit of truth—inspired by his own meditations—is revealed here with clarity and acceptance. Looking into this time-ravaged face, the viewer recognizes the universality of growing old and the inevitability of death.

Another great Dutch artist was Jan Vermeer [ver-MEER] (1632–1675), who specialized in domestic genre scenes. His works reveal a calm world where ordinary objects possess a timeless gravity. Color was important for establishing the domesticity and peacefulness of this closed-off world; Vermeer's favorites were yellow and blue. These serene works evoked the fabled cleanliness of Delft, the city where he lived and worked.

One of the most beautiful of his domestic scenes is *The Lacemaker* (Figure 14.18). Like most of his thirty-five extant paintings, *The Lacemaker* depicts an interior room where a single figure is encircled by everyday things. She is lit by a clear light falling on her from the side, another characteristic of Vermeer's paintings. The composition (the woman at the table and the rear wall parallel to the picture frame), the basic colors (yellow and blue), and the subject's absorption in her task typified Vermeer's works. *The Lacemaker* also has a moral message, for a woman engaged in household tasks symbolized the virtue of domesticity for Vermeer.

One of the few Dutch female artists was Judith Leyster (1609–1660), who, like her male colleagues, was a member of an artists' guild (in Haarlem) and painted for the art market. She opened her own studio, where she also instructed aspiring artists. Leyster's specialties were genre scenes, portraits, and still lifes. Her *Self-Portrait* (Figure 14.19), painted when she was about twenty, demonstrates early mastery of artistic technique. Leyster's skill at genre painting enabled her to experience modest success in her profession.

England also contributed to the creation of the Restrained Baroque, but conditions there led to a style markedly different from that of the Dutch school. Unlike the Netherlands, England had no art market, was dominated by an aristocracy, and, most important, had as yet no native-born painters of note. Painting in England was controlled by aristocratic patrons who preferred portraits to all other subjects and whose taste was courtly but restrained. The painter whose style suited these aristocratic demands was a Flemish artist, Anthony van Dyck [vahn-DIKE] (1599–1641). A pupil of Rubens, van Dyck eventually settled in England and became court painter to Charles I.

Van Dyck's elegant style captured the courtly qualities prized by his noble patrons. He depicted his subjects' splendid costumes in all their radiant glory, using vibrant colors to reproduce their textures. He invented

Figure 14.18 JAN VERMEER. *The Lacemaker.* Ca. 1664. Oil on canvas, 9⅝ × 8¼″. Louvre. *Unlike Rembrandt, Vermeer was not concerned with human personality as such. Rather, his aim was to create scenes that registered his deep pleasure in bourgeois order and comfort. In* The Lacemaker, *he gives his female subject generalized features, turning her into a social type, but renders her sewing in exquisite detail, giving it a monumental presence. The painting thus becomes a visual metaphor of a virtuous household.*

Figure 14.19 JUDITH LEYSTER. *Self-Portrait.* Ca. 1630. Oil on canvas, 29 × 25½″. National Gallery of Art, Washington, D.C. Gift of Mr. and Mrs. Robert Wood Bliss. Photo by Lorene Emerson. (1949.6.1). *Leyster's Self-Portrait shows her command of the painting tradition in which she was trained. The casual pose—a model turned in a chair with an arm resting on its back—was pioneered by the Dutch artist Franz Hals (see Figure 15.7), who may have been Leyster's teacher in Haarlem. Her smiling, open mouth represents a "speaking portrait," a frequent pose in this period, in which the subject seems to be wanting to make a statement. The merrymaking fiddler in the easel painting within the portrait was a popular genre subject among the Dutch art-buying public.*

Figure 14.20   ANTHONY VAN DYCK. *Lords John and Bernard Stuart.* Ca. 1639. Oil on canvas, 7'9⅓" × 4'9½". National Gallery, London. *Van Dyck has depicted these dandies in the carefully disheveled style preferred by the era's aristocrats. Their doublets (jackets) are of plain, muted colors and slashed on the chest and sleeves to allow a contrasting color to show. The deliberately casual look is especially prominent in the unbuttoned doublet worn by Lord John (left) and the cloak thrown over the shoulder of Lord Bernard (right). Both men wear the soft leather boots, partly rolled down the legs, that were now replacing the shoes of an earlier time.*

a repertory of poses for individual and group portraits that showed his subjects to their greatest advantage. But van Dyck did more than cater to the vanity of his titled patrons. With superb sensitivity, he portrayed their characters in their faces, showing such qualities as intelligence, self-doubt, and obstinacy. His psychological insights make his courtly portraits genuine works of art.

Van Dyck's fluent style is clearly shown in his double portrait of Lords John and Bernard Stuart, two of the dandies of the court of Charles I (Figure 14.20). This painting indicates the artist's mastery of the society portrait. The subjects' fashionable dress and haughty expressions establish their high social status. Van Dyck skillfully renders the play of light on the silk fabrics of their clothing. He creates an interesting design by placing their bodies opposite one another, but this positioning also offers psychological insight into their characters as the mirrorlike pose suggests that they are vain young men. Van Dyck's deftness at creating elegant likenesses set the standard for English portraiture and influenced French artists well into the eighteenth century.

Architecture   The architecture of the Restrained Baroque drew strongly on the Classical tradition. One of the most influential English architects of this period was Sir Christopher Wren (1632–1723), whose Baroque

Figure 14.21 CHRISTOPHER WREN. St. Paul's Cathedral. 1675–1710. London. *Wren was a true child of the Baroque age. An astronomy professor at Oxford University, he made discoveries that brought him to the attention of the age's greatest scientist, Isaac Newton. When opportunity called and Wren was given the royal commission to rebuild the churches of London, he approached this task with the same passionate love of geometry that had motivated his scientific researches. St. Paul's design united his sense of beauty with his mathematical bent.*

style had two sources. From the Classical Baroque of Versailles came his love of rich ornamentation, and from Bramante's High Renaissance style came his devotion to pure Classical forms, such as the dome and the Classical orders. Following these traditions, Wren created his own unique style, with spacious interiors and elaborately decorated facades.

Although Wren created many brilliant secular works, he is best known for his churches, which he built in the aftermath of the Great Fire of London in 1666. His masterpiece is St. Paul's cathedral in London (Figure 14.21). Intended as a Protestant rival to St. Peter's in Rome, St. Paul's has a longitudinal floor plan similar to St. Peter's but with Gothic features in the interior, including transept and choir and a dome reminiscent of Bramante's Tempietto (see Figure 12.21). The church has many Classical elements, such as the pairs of columns on two levels, the symmetrical towers and decorations, and the elaborate pediment. At the same time, its Baroque nature is revealed in the ornate facade punctuated by niches, the robust twin steeples with their shadowy recesses and staggered columns,

and the dramatic play of light across the face of the building. The most outstanding feature of St. Paul's is the magnificent dome, inspired by the one designed by Michelangelo for St. Peter's (see Figure 12.22), with its encircling colonnade. This elegant dome still dominates central London's skyline, a splendid reminder of Baroque glory.

Literature

The Council of Trent's decrees, which had such a powerful impact on artists and architects, were hardly felt by seventeenth-century writers. Nevertheless, a style of literary expression arose that is called Baroque and that became international in scope. The most enduring literary legacy of this period is drama. Baroque audiences delighted in works that blended different forms, and drama mixed literature, costume design, set painting, and theatrical spectacle. Tragedy, based on Roman models, was the supreme achievement of the Baroque stage, but comedies of all types, including satires, farces, and sexual comedies, were also important. After centuries of neglect, tragedy and comedy had been brilliantly revived in Elizabethan England, and their appearance in France was evidence of the continuing growth of secular consciousness. Another ancient literary genre that gained wide favor was the epic, a reflection of the love of power typical of the age. Finally, Baroque literature began to acknowledge the world outside Europe, as may be seen in the rise of writings with a non-Western dimension. These non-Western aspects included settings (for example, Mexico in the poetry of the Mexican nun Sor Juana Inés de la Cruz [1648–1695]), characters (for example, the Aztec ruler Montezuma, the hero of the play *The Indian Emperor* [1665], by John Dryden [1631–1700]), and themes (especially the comparison of Western and non-Western customs in travel literature, as in *A New Voyage Round the World* [1697], by William Dampier [1652–1715], and *Travels in Persia* [1686], by Jean Chardin [1643–1713]).

Despite the variety of their works, the Baroque writers had common characteristics, including a love of ornate language and a fascination with characterization, either of individuals or of types. Baroque authors often dealt with emotional extremes, such as gross sensuality versus pangs of conscience. With such emotionally charged themes, Baroque writers could and did employ dramatic rhetoric, slipping occasionally into empty bombast.

Baroque Literature in France Drama was France's greatest contribution to the literature of the Baroque period. Secular drama revived under the patronage of

Louis XIII in the 1630s and reached a climax during Louis XIV's reign. Strict control was exercised over the plays staged at the royal court, although comic playwrights were given more freedom, as long as they did not offend common decency or good taste.

The tragic playwrights were expected to obey the rules of literary composition identified by the French Academy and based on the theories of Aristotle (see Chapter 3). The ideal play must observe the unities of time, place, and action—that is, it must take place during a twenty-four-hour time span, have no scene changes, and have a single uncomplicated plot. Furthermore, the plays were supposed to use formal language and to focus on universal problems as reflected in dilemmas experienced by highborn men and women. Because of the playwrights' strict adherence to these rules, it is sometimes claimed that the dramas of this period are expressive of a Classical style. But the French preference for order, gravity, and severity was evidence of a Baroque sensibility—just as was the case in the French style of Baroque painting and architecture.

The two great French tragedians of the Baroque period are Pierre Corneille [kor-NAY] (1606–1684) and Jean Racine [ra-SEEN] (1639–1699). Corneille wrote tragedies in verse based on Spanish legends and Roman themes. Drawing on the Hellenistic philosophy of Stoicism, his dramas stressed the importance of duty, patriotism, and loyalty—ideals that appealed to his courtly audience. His finest work is *Le Cid,* based on a legendary figure of Spanish history and concerned with the hero's choice between personal feelings and honor.

In Racine, drama found a voice whose refined language and penetrating psychological insight have never been equaled in the French theater. Preoccupied with the moral struggle between the will and the emotions, Racine created intensely human characters in classically constructed plays. A subject that intrigued Racine was the doomed woman who was swept to her destruction by obsessive sexual passion. This Baroque theme was most perfectly expressed in his masterpiece, *Phèdre* (*Phaedra*), his version of the Greek tale of incestuous love first dramatized by Euripides in the fifth century B.C. Where Euripides makes fate a central reason for the heroine's, Phèdre's, downfall, Racine portrays the unfortunate woman as a victim of her passion for her stepson. Even though he explored other types of love in his plays, such as mother love and even political passion, it was in his study of sex as a powerful motive for action that Racine was most original.

The Baroque period in French drama also produced one of the comic geniuses of the Western theatre, Jean Baptiste Poquelin, better known as Molière [mole-YAIR] (1622–1673). Molière analyzed the foibles of French life in twelve penetrating satirical comedies that had the lasting impact of tragedy. He peopled his plays with social types—the idler, the miser, the pedant, the seducer, the hypochondriac, the medical quack, the would-be gentleman, the pretentiously cultured lady—exposing the follies of the entire society. To create his comedic effects, Molière used not only topical humor and social satire but all the trappings of farce, including pratfalls, mistaken identities, sight gags, puns, and slapstick.

Molière was appointed official entertainer to Louis XIV in 1658; even so, he made many enemies among those who felt they were the butt of his jokes. When he died, for example, the French clergy refused to give him an official burial because they believed some of his plays to be attacks on the church. The testament to Molière's enduring brilliance is that many of his comedies are still performed today, including *Tartuffe, The Miser, The Would-Be Gentleman,* and *The Misanthrope,* and they are still enormously entertaining.

Baroque Literature in England   The outstanding contribution in English to the literature of the Baroque period was provided by John Milton (1608–1674), a stern Puritan who held high office in Cromwell's Commonwealth. The deeply learned Milton had a grand moral vision that led him to see the universe as locked in a struggle between the forces of darkness and the forces of light. Only an epic was capable of expressing such a monumental conception.

His supreme literary accomplishment was to Christianize the epic in his long poem *Paradise Lost.* Inspired by Homer's and Vergil's ancient works, but also intended as a Protestant response to Dante's *Comedy,* Milton's poem became an immediate classic. His grandiose themes in *Paradise Lost* were the rebellion of the angels led by Lucifer, the fall of Adam and Eve in the Garden of Eden, and Christ's redemption of humanity.

An astonishing aspect of *Paradise Lost* is Milton's portrait of Lucifer, which some readers have seen as a Baroque glamorization of evil. Lucifer is characterized as a creature of titanic ambition and deceitful charm. Despite his powerful presence, however, this epic story has moral balance. At the end, Adam, the author of original sin, is saved instead of being condemned to Hell. Adam's redemption occurs when he accepts Jesus as Lord. Adam's choice reflected Milton's belief in free will and the necessity of taking responsibility for one's actions.

In addition to its grand theme, *Paradise Lost* is Baroque in other ways. The mixing of Christian legend and ancient epic, for example, is typical of Baroque taste. Milton's convoluted style is Baroque with its occasionally odd word order, Latinisms, and complex metaphors. Most of all, Milton's epic is Baroque in its lofty tone and exaggerated rhetoric—literary equivalents, perhaps, of Rubens or Rembrandt.

A secondary achievement of the literary Baroque in England was that literature began to reflect the West's overseas expansion, as in the publishing of travel books, memoirs, and letters describing real and fictional contacts with peoples and lands around the globe. Part of a European-wide trend, the growth of English literature with a non-European dimension expressed the Baroque theme of pushing against the boundaries of life and art. A pioneering work on this Baroque theme was the short prose story *Oroonoko* (1688) by Aphra Behn (1640–1689), an English writer who exploited her firsthand experiences as a resident of Surinam (modern Suriname) to provide a vivid, exotic setting. Situated in South America and told with a blend of realism and romance, *Oroonoko* condemns the culture of slavery through the story of the doomed love affair between a black slave-prince and a slave woman. The author portrays the black hero as untutored in Western ways yet polished and educated on

his own terms, and, above all, superior to the natural depravity of the European characters. This is an early version of the myth of the noble savage, the cultural archetype that reached its climax in the Romantic era (see Chapter 17). England's first professional woman writer, Behn also wrote about twenty comedies for the stage and a poem collection, but *Oroonoko* is her chief claim to renown.

Music

Unlike the Renaissance, when a single musical sound prevailed (see Chapter 12), the Baroque had no single musical ideal. Nonetheless, four trends during the Baroque period give its music distinctive qualities. First, the development of major and minor tonality, which had been prefigured in Josquin des Prez's music in the early 1500s, was a central feature of the works of this time, making it the first stage in the rise of modern music. Second, the mixing of genres, which has been noted in literature and the arts, also occurred in

Figure 14.22 JAN BRUEGEL. *Hearing.* Ca. 1620. Oil on canvas, approx. 2′ 3″ × 3′ 6″. Prado, Madrid. *One of a series of allegorical paintings representing the five senses, this work by Jan Bruegel depicts the sense of hearing. Set in a Renaissance interior framed by three rounded arches, it shows a variety of sources that make sounds pleasing to the human ear. Most prominent are the musical instruments, which collectively constitute an anthology of the instruments used in Baroque music.*

Baroque music. Third, the expressiveness that had entered music in the late 1500s now became even more exaggerated, being used to stress meanings and emotions in the musical texts that otherwise might not have been heard. And last, this was an age of **virtuosos,** master musicians, especially singers, who performed with great technical skill and vivid personal style, and of a growing variety of musical instruments (Figure 14.22). The musical form that drew these trends together was **opera,** making it the quintessential symbol of the age.

Opera originated in Italy in the late sixteenth century among a group of Florentine musicians and poets with aristocratic ties. The first great composer of opera was Claudio Monteverdi [mon-teh-VAIR-dee] (1567–1643), whose earliest opera, *Orfeo* (1607), was based on the legend of the ancient Greek poet-musician Orpheus. *Orfeo* united drama, dance, elaborate stage mechanisms, and painted scenery with music. Monteverdi wrote melodic arias, or songs, for the individual singers, and he increased the opera's dramatic appeal by concluding each of its five acts with a powerful chorus. His setting truly mirrored the text, using musical phrases to serve as aural symbols and thus to enhance the unfolding of events.

By the 1630s, opera began to shed its aristocratic origins and become a popular entertainment. This change did not affect opera's focus on ancient myths and histories about noble men and women, nor did it halt the trend to brilliant singing called *bel canto,* literally "beautiful song." However, to appeal to a wider audience, operatic composers added elements from Italy's popular comic theater, such as farcical scenes and stock characters, notably humorous servants. By the end of this age, the operatic form was stylized into a recipe, including improbable plots, inadequate motivations for the characters, and magical transformations—signs of its Baroque nature.

Opera became immensely popular in Europe, especially in Italy, where it remains so today. By 1750 opera houses had been built in many major cities; Venice led the way with more than a dozen establishments. The rise of opera in Italy during the 1600s, like the founding of a commercial theater in London in the 1500s, presaged the downfall of the aristocratic patronage system and the emergence of entertainments with mass appeal.

The winding down of the Thirty Years' War allowed Italian opera to be exported to the rest of Europe. Only in France were composers able to defy the overpowering Italian influence and create an independent type of opera. This development was made possible by the grandeur of Louis XIV's court and by French taste, which was more restrained than the opulent Italian. Nevertheless, French opera was founded by an Italian, Jean-Baptiste Lully [loo-LEE] (1632–1687), who later became a French citizen and Louis's court composer. Under Lully's direction, French opera developed its identifying features: dignified music, the full use of choruses, the inclusion of a ballet, and, most important, a French text. Lully's patron, the Sun King, sometimes performed in the opera's ballet sequences himself, dancing side by side with the composer. Lully's works, which dominated French music until 1750, ensured a powerful role for French music in the Western tradition.

Baroque music reached its climax after 1715 in Protestant northern Europe. Two German composers were responsible for this development—Bach in his homeland and Handel in England.

The greater of these late Baroque masters was Johann Sebastian Bach (1685–1750). A devout Lutheran who worked for German courts and municipalities far from the major cities, Bach created a body of sacred music that transcends all religious creeds and nationalities. Employing all the Baroque musical genres, his works are distinguished by their inventiveness and complete mastery of major and minor tonality. His most memorable achievements are the Passions, the musical settings of the liturgy to be performed on Good Friday—the most tragic day in the Christian calendar. Composed in about 1727, the *St. Matthew Passion* expresses the collective grief of the Christian community for the death of Jesus. Bach used a German text with arias and choruses, making the music bring out all the emotional implications of the words. Thus, the *St. Matthew Passion* is more dramatic than most operas and a sublime religious experience in itself.

Although Bach's religious music is his greatest legacy, he also left a body of secular music, including orchestral works and works for various instrumental groups. A musician's musician, Bach composed *The Well-Tempered Clavier* as an ordered set of studies in all the major and minor keys. The forty-eight preludes and fugues in this work set a heroic challenge for keyboard performers and are still an essential part of the piano repertoire today. (A **clavier** is an early keyboard instrument; a **fugue** is a composition in which a theme is introduced by one instrument and then repeated by each successively entering instrument until a complicated interweaving of themes, variations, imitations, and echoes results.) This work contributed to the standardization of the pitches of the notes of the musical scale and of the tuning of keyboard instruments.

Of Bach's secular works, the most popular today are probably the six *Brandenburg Concertos* (written for the duke of Brandenburg), whose tunefulness and rhythmic variety the composer rarely surpassed. The concertos were composed for the type of ensemble found in the German princely courts of the time—a group of string players of average ability along with a few woodwind and brass instruments, perhaps a total of twenty to twenty-five musicians. Bach's dominant idea in these concertos was to demonstrate the interplay between individual soloists and the larger group. As in most of his work, the composer wove different melodic lines and different harmonies together into elaborate, complex structures of tremendous variety, power, and scope.

The other great late Baroque master was George Frideric Handel (1685–1759), who was renowned for his Italian-style operas. More cosmopolitan than Bach, Handel eventually settled in London, where he composed thirty-six operatic works. His operas succeeded in their day because of the brilliant way in which the music allows the singers to show their virtuosity, but they are generally not to the taste of modern audiences and have not found a place in the standard operatic repertory. In contrast, his mastery of sacred music, particularly the **oratorio**—an opera-like form but without any stage action—which he perfected, has made his name immortal. Of the oratorios, *Messiah*, based on biblical texts and sung in English, holds first place. Its popularity stems from its Baroque qualities: the emotionally stirring choruses and the delightful embellishments the soloists are permitted in their arias. As a result, *Messiah* is probably the best-known work of sacred music in the English-speaking world.

The Legacy of the Baroque Age

The Baroque period left a potent legacy to the modern world in politics, economics, religion, and the arts. The system of great states governed by a balance of power dominated European affairs until 1945. From the Baroque period date the roles of France and England as Europe's trendsetters, both politically and culturally. The concept and practice of "world war" also dates from this period. The economic system known as mercantilism originated during the Baroque period and prevailed in Europe into the nineteenth century. The religious orientation of the European states became well established in the seventeenth century, along with the division of the vast majority of Westerners into Protestant and Catholic camps. In the Netherlands, artists operated in an open market, painting works for wealthy citizens, thus launching the trend toward today's commercial art world. The Baroque idea of spectacle is a thread that runs throughout the culture of this period and helps to explain not only the propagandistic aspects of politics and religion but also the theatrical elements in the arts and entertainment. Culturally, the Baroque is still with us, even though much about this style seems excessive to modern taste. Although Baroque operas are not often performed, the idea of opera originated in this age of spectacle. Other Baroque musical works, notably the majestic oratorios of Handel and the powerful compositions of Bach for church and court, are part of the regular concert repertoire in the West today. Some of the most admired and enduring artworks in Western history were created during this time, including Bernini's *Ecstasy of St. Teresa* and the paintings of Rembrandt. Many cities of Europe are still showcases of Baroque splendor. The church of St. Peter's in Rome, St. Paul's cathedral in London, and the palace and gardens at Versailles are but three of the living monuments of this period, reminding us of the grand religious and political ideals of a very different age.

KEY CULTURAL TERMS

Baroque	virtuoso
Florid Baroque style	opera
baldacchino	*bel canto*
illusionism	clavier
Classical Baroque style	fugue
Restrained Baroque style	oratorio

SUGGESTIONS FOR FURTHER READING

PRIMARY SOURCES

BEHN, A. *Oroonoko and Other Stories.* Edited and introduced by M. Duffy. London: Methuen, 1985. An edition of Behn's stories, with a useful introduction; these short works prepared the way for the novel genre, born after 1700. *Oroonoko* was first published in 1678.

CORNEILLE, P. *The Cid.* Translated by V. J. Cheng. Newark: University of Delaware Press, 1987. A version of Corneille's drama, recounting the story of a hero torn between honor and love; imitates the poetic form of the original, first staged in 1636.

MILTON, J. *Paradise Lost.* New York: Norton, 1975. Milton's Baroque epic about rebellion—Lucifer's revolt in heaven and Adam and Eve's defiance on earth; Scott Elledge provides a useful introduction and notes to the text, which was first published in 1667.

MOLIÈRE (POQUELIN, J. B.). *The Misanthrope.* Translated by R. Wilbur. London: Methuen, 1967. A good translation by a leading American poet. Useful English versions by various translators of Molière's other frequently performed comedies are also available, including *The Miser* (New York: Applause Theatre Book Publishers, 1987), *Tartuffe* (London: Faber and Faber, 1984), and *The Bourgeois Gentleman (The Would-Be Gentleman)* (New York: Applause Theatre Book Publishers, 1987).

RACINE, J. B. *Phaedra* [*Phèdre*]. Translated by R. Wilbur. New York: Harcourt Brace Jovanovich, 1986. A solid translation of this French tragic drama.

SUGGESTIONS FOR LISTENING

BACH, JOHANN SEBASTIAN (1685–1750). The greatest composer of the Baroque era, Bach is best known for his sacred music, which has tremendous emotional power. His church music for voices includes more than two hundred cantatas, or musical settings of biblical and choral texts, such as *Jesu der du meine Seele (Jesus, Thou Hast My Soul), Wachet Auf (Sleepers Awake),* and *O Haupt voll Blut und Wunden (O Sacred Head Now Wounded);* six motets, such as *Jesu meine Freude (Jesus, My Joy);* two Passions, or musical settings of biblical passages and commentaries on the Easter season (the *St. Matthew Passion* and the *St. John Passion*); and a Mass, the *Mass in B Minor.* He also composed instrumental church music, notably about 170 organ chorales required by the liturgy for the church year. Besides sacred music, Bach wrote secular music, including the *"Little" Fugue in G Minor,* the *Brandenburg Concertos,* and *The Well-Tempered Clavier* (1722; 1740), a collection of works for keyboard that consisted of one prelude and fugue for each of the twelve major and minor keys.

HANDEL, GEORGE FRIDERIC (1685–1759). The German-born Handel, who lived and worked mainly in England, made eighteenth-century England a center of Baroque music. Of the thirty-six Italian-style operas that he composed and produced in London, three of the best known are *Rinaldo* (1711), *Giulio Cesare* (1724), and *Serse* (1738). His oratorios—including *Messiah*—were performed in public theaters rather than churches and especially appealed to the rising middle classes. Handel also produced a body of instrumental music, of which the most significant are the two suites known as the *Fireworks Music* (1749) and the *Water Music* (about 1717) and six concertos for woodwinds and strings.

LULLY, JEAN-BAPTISTE (1632–1687). Lully's eleven operas helped to define the operatic genre in France, giving it an opening overture and a ballet movement. Of his operas, the best known are probably *Theseus* (1675) and *Amadis* (1684). Especially appealing to modern ears are the massed choruses and rhythmic dances of his operas.

MONTEVERDI, CLAUDIO (1567–1643). A prodigious composer of madrigals and sacred music, Monteverdi is best remembered as a pioneer of opera. He composed his operas in a highly expressive style that matched the spirit of the music to the meaning of words in the text, as in *Orfeo* (1607) and *The Coronation of Poppea* (1642).

AFRICA

AMERICAS

HISTORY

North Africa Part of Ottoman Empire. *Tunisia.* Ruled by beys (provincial governors) (after 1612).

Northeast Africa *Ethiopia.* Unrest after Catholic missionaries arrived. Europeans expelled (1648). Beset by Muslim states.

East Africa *Zambezi Valley.* Butwa expelled Portuguese (about 1700). Monomotapa collapsed (1666). *Zimbabwe:* Absorbed by Rozvi Empire (1693).

West Africa Small traditional kingdoms (e.g., Mossi and Ashanti) competed for trade routes; repulsed Islamic and European inroads. *Niger Bend.* Timbuktu, Gao, and Jennejero escaped Moroccan control (1618). *Yoruba culture.* Oyo Empire at height (after 1650). Benin prospered. *Dahomey Kingdom.* Founded (about 1645).

South Africa Dutch (Boers) founded coastal colony (1652).

Latin America *Caribbean.* French, English, and Dutch challenged Spanish rule. *Mexico and Central America.* Ruled by Spanish viceroy from Mexico City; native peoples continued to lose land to Spanish; slave trade grew. *South America.* Ruled by Spanish viceroy from Lima; Europeans settled along the coasts.

Brazil Slave-based economy flourished.

Native North America *Eastern woodlands.* English built Jamestown on Powhatan land (1607). French built Québec on site of old Iroquois village (1608). English built Plymouth on Wampanoag land (1620). Dutch obtained Manhattan Island from Shinnecocks (1626). Iroquois Wars between Dutch-allied tribes and French-allied tribes (1643–1701). *Southwest.* After Spanish introduced sheep, Navajo became sheepherding culture.

ART & MUSIC

East Africa *Zambezi Valley.* Kingdom of Butwa: royal control of weaving, ivory and stone carvings.

West Africa *Yoruba culture.* Benin bronze plaques and figures, some with Western influences; artistic tradition suddenly ended (1700).

European Soldier with Firearm. Sixteenth or seventeenth century. Bronze, ht. 25". Benin. Nigerian Museum, Lagos.

Latin America Catholic European styles prevailed, influenced by native and regional tastes. *Mexico.* Native sculptors (until the 1700s) ignored church rulings against Renaissance nudity and other "pagan" practices, so sculpture strongly reflected native points of view.

Native North America *Eastern woodlands.* European floral designs introduced into beadwork by students of Catholic nuns in Canada (ca. 1640).

ARCHITECTURE

East Africa *Zambezi Valley.* Kingdom of Butwa: stone palaces and fortresses.

Latin America Late Renaissance, Plateresque, and Baroque styles imported from Spain and Portugal; influenced by geography, local materials, and indigenous and (especially in Brazil) African tastes. Churches built over native cult sites. *Mexico.* Church of Santa Clara (1633). Cathedral of Puebla (dedicated 1649). *Peru.* Cuzco cathedral (facade carved 1651–54) and Jesuit church (1651–68) blended European Baroque style with native elements, such as Indian faces, native birds, and ears of corn.

Facade of Jesuit church. Detail. 1698. Arequipa, Peru.

RELIGION, PHILOSOPHY, LITERATURE

Northeast Africa *Ethiopia.* Coptic Church only unifying element in country (after 1667).

West Africa *Dahomey.* Ritual sacrifice of slaves on the death of a king.

Latin America Catholic public ceremonies, such as processions, pilgrimages, and mystery plays introduced. *Mexico.* Sister (Sor) Juana Inés de la Cruz, nun and poet, supported education for women.

Native North America *Eastern woodlands.* Jesuit missionaries from France (1612). *Southwest.* Spanish soldiers raided kivas and burned kachina masks in attempt to eradicate Pueblo religion (1661); rebellion led by Pueblo religious leaders drove Spanish out of New Mexico for 12 years (1680).

ASIA

China

Ming Dynasty, ended 1644. Decadence and decline. Tea trade with Europe began. Ch'ing Dynasty, began 1644. Country unified a second time under foreign rulers (Manchus from Manchuria). Kept the Confucian classics central to governmental service. Emperor K'ang-hsi extended empire, adding Taiwan (1683); raised culture to new heights.

India

Mogul Empire. Religious toleration and arts support ended with overthrow (1659) of Shāh Jahān by his son Aurangzeb, who imposed Muslim orthodoxy, ended art patronage, and expanded the empire. Civil war with Sikhs and Maratha Hindus. Sikhs became a military theocracy.

Bichtir. Shāh Jahān. Ca. 1632. Paint on paper. India. Victoria and Albert Museum, London.

Japan

Edo period, began 1603. Tokugawa shōgunate with capital Edo (modern Tokyo); founded by Tokugawa Ieyasu (1603). Centralized rule; rapid urbanization; a merchant aristocracy challenged the feudal order; foreigners expelled and country closed to world; dramatic rise in literacy; 250-year period of peace began.

Ming Dynasty. Colorful porcelains, burial ware, enamel on metalwork (cloisonné), and rich silks and rugs. Ch'ing Dynasty. Two painting schools: court artists, including the Four Wangs school (imitated historic styles, yet borrowed from Western realism); and "individualists" (commercial artists who freed themselves from traditional art). K'ang-hsi founded imperial ceramic factories; porcelains decorated with polychrome landscapes.

Mogul Empire. Miniature paintings, made in the imperial workshop (to 1659) and at various Hindu courts, such as Rajasthan; often depicted courtiers or the ruler.

Edo period. Rinpa school artists, such as Tawaraya Sōtatsu and Ōgata Kōrin. Calligraphy, lacquered boxes, and silk garments. Hishikawa Moronobu pioneered black-and-white ukiyo-e woodblock prints, depicting lively scenes of Edo life.

Ch'ing Dynasty. Rebuilding of structures in Forbidden City, Beijing, such as the Pao-ho-tien, a banquet hall built in official Chinese style but painted with bright colors reflecting Manchu taste.

Pao-ho-tien. Ca. 1700. Beijing. Wood with tile roof.

Mogul Empire. The Golden Age of Indian Muslim architecture: the Tāj Mahal, the Jami Masjid mosque, the Red Fort towns, the Peacock Throne, the Great Mosque at Lahore, and the Golden Temple of the Sikhs. The Tāj Mahal, perhaps the most famous building in India, was constructed by Shāh Jahān as a domed tomb for his favorite wife, Mumtāz Mahal ("Chosen One of the Palace").

Tāj Mahal. 1632–1654. White marble. Agra, India.

View of Shōin. Katsura Imperial Villa. 1620–24. Kyōto.

Edo period. Edo Castle; Nikko Pagoda; urban entertainment districts for merchants. Sukiya style, inspired by wooden rustic teahouses; used for lower-class housing. The Shōin style, developed in the Momoyama period for the samurai, influenced the simple style of the Katsura imperial villa complex (residences, gardens, and teahouse), built as a retreat for the royal family.

Ch'ing Dynasty. K'ang-hsi sponsored scholarship (a history of the Ming Dynasty; dictionaries and encyclopedias); welcomed Jesuits at court.

Mogul period. Adi Granth (1604), the Sikhs' sacred scriptures.

Edo period. Saikaku Ihara's Life of an Amorous Man, a classic novel; Matsuo Bashō revitalized haiku verse with the spirit of Zen Buddhism. Kabuki theater (catering to the merchant class) began; performed solely by male actors (by 1700). Massacre of Christians (about 37,000) (1637).

15 THE BAROQUE AGE II
Revolutions in Scientific and Political Thought
1600–1715

The Baroque age was more than a time of political upheaval and artistic spectacle. It was also the period when the Scientific Revolution took place. As centuries-old beliefs were challenged by discoveries in astronomy and physics, a whole new way of viewing the universe emerged. In England, a revolution in political philosophy was also occurring, leading to the notion that states ought to be governed by the people rather than by paternalistic rulers. These momentous changes added to the pervasive restlessness of the times.

The term *Scientific Revolution* applies chiefly to astronomy and physics, although major advances were also made in medical science, and changes occurred in chemistry, biology, and embryology. In addition, the Scientific Revolution gave rise to a type of literature that considered the impact of the new science on secular and religious thought. A few scholars composed literary works that redefined the place of human beings in the cosmos and the purpose of human life. The chief result was to bring to a climax the separation of philosophy from theology, a gap that had been widening since the 1300s (see Chapter 10). From this point, philosophy begins to address secular concerns, and theology is relegated to a minor cultural role.

The climax of this revolutionary age occurred between 1685 and 1715, a period that witnessed what one twentieth-century historian has called "the crisis of the European conscience." For a handful of scholars, the balance tipped from traditional ideas to modern views. These early modern scientists and philosophers countered faith with reason, dogma with skepticism, and divine intervention with natural law. They made mathematics their

◄ **Detail** Maria Sibylla Merian. *Insect Metamorphoses in Surinam*. 1705. Hand-colored engraving. (Reprinted in F. Schnack. *Das Kleine Buch der Tropenwander*. Leipzig: Insel-Verlag, 1935. Plate 11. 4¾ × 7".)

Timeline 15.1 **REVOLUTIONS IN SCIENTIFIC AND POLITICAL THOUGHT**

1543	1600		1700	1715
	The Scientific Revolution and Early Modern Political Philosophy			

1543	**1570–1600**	**1609**	**1625**	**1637**	**1651**	**1687**	**1690**
Copernicus's *Revolutions of the Heavenly Bodies*	Brahe's observations	Kepler's *On the Motion of Mars*	Grotius's *The Law of War and Peace*	Descartes's *Discourse on Method*	Hobbes's *Leviathan*	Newton's *Mathematical Principles*	Locke's *Two Treatises of Government* and *An Essay Concerning Human Understanding*

1610
Galileo
sights
four
moons
of Jupiter

1632
Galileo's
*Dialogues on the
Two Chief Systems
of the World*

Figure 15.1 PETER APIAN. Geocentric Diagram of the Universe, from the *Cosmographia*. 1539. The Bancroft Library, University of California, Berkeley. *This schematic diagram illustrates the geocentric universe in the pre-Copernican era. The unmoving earth is at the center and is surrounded by ten moving spheres, containing, in sequential order, the moon, Mercury, Venus, the sun, Mars, Jupiter, Saturn, the fixed stars, the aqueous or crystalline heaven, and the empty sphere called the primum mobile. The ninth sphere, the crystalline heaven, was added by medieval scholars to address a problem raised by the account of creation in Genesis. The tenth sphere, the primum mobile, was logically necessary in Aristotle's theory because it moved first and brought the other nine into motion. Beyond the tenth sphere was the Empyrean, home of the Unmoved Mover in philosophy or of God in theology.*

guiding star in the search for truth, accepting as true those things that could be proven mathematically and rejecting as untrue those that could not. Their new philosophy eventually concluded that the universe was like a great clock that operated according to universal laws. Although we today tend to discount this clockwork image, we still owe a debt to these thinkers, who set Western culture on its present course and brought modernity into being (Timeline 15.1).

THEORIES OF THE UNIVERSE BEFORE THE SCIENTIFIC REVOLUTION

The Scientific Revolution was both an outgrowth and a rejection of the Aristotelian cosmology that had held Western thinkers in thrall for two thousand years. The Aristotelian system, named for the fourth-century-B.C. philosopher, was developed by the ancient Greeks and transmitted to the West through Roman and Islamic culture and the medieval scholastic tradition. The fundamental principle of this cosmology is **geocentrism,** the theory that the universe is earth-centered. Around the earth revolved the five known planets (Mercury, Venus, Mars, Jupiter, and Saturn) and the sun and the moon, each held aloft by a crystalline sphere. The earth, which did not move, was not considered a planet. Nearest the earth was the moon, and there was a complete division between the supralunar world, the region beyond the moon, and the sublunar world, the region beneath the moon (Figure 15.1). In the supralunar world, the planets moved in circular orbits and were made of an incorruptible element, aether; in the sublunar world, change was constant, motion was rectilinear, and matter was composed of the four elements, earth, air, fire, and water.

This system had an absolute up and down: "Up" referred to the area beyond the spheres inhabited by the Unmoved Mover—Aristotle's philosophical term for the source of all celestial motion—and "down" referred to the center of the earth.

In the second century A.D., the Egyptian scholar Ptolemy updated Aristotle's geocentric theory with new astronomical data and improved mathematical calculations. During the golden age of Muslim culture (800–1000 A.D.), Arab intellectuals preserved this geocentric legacy, improving and refining it to reflect new planetary sightings. In the High Middle Ages (1000–1300), Western scholars recovered the Ptolemaic heritage—with its Muslim additions—and gave it a Christian interpretation: Medieval Christian scientists began to identify the Unmoved Mover as God and the space beyond the spheres as heaven. More important, the church became attached to the geocentric theory because it seemed to validate the doctrine of original sin: The corrupt earth inhabited by fallen mortals—corresponded to the sublunar world of decay and constant change.

At the University of Paris in the 1300s, a more self-assured and skeptical outlook arose among a few thinkers. Unconvinced by Aristotle's solution to the problem of motion (which was to attribute the forward motion of a projectile to air movement), the Parisian scholars offered an alternative explanation. They asserted that a projectile acquired "impetus," a propulsive quality that gradually diminished as the projectile moved through space. The theory of "impetus" commanded scholars' attention for centuries, leading them to consider a new range of scientific problems.

From the modern perspective, it matters little that the theory of "impetus" was untrue. It was a first step away from the Aristotelian tradition because it made Western scientists aware that the great Greek thinker was not always right. And scholars at Paris and other universities began to advocate applying mathematics to practical problems as well as directly observing nature—in other words, collecting data (**empiricism**) and framing hypotheses from observable facts (**inductive reasoning**).

Aristotle had also used empirical data and inductive logic, but his writings had become so revered that for generations scholars did not examine his methodology and were afraid to tamper with his conclusions. Indeed, his followers relied on **deductive reasoning;** that is, they only explored the ramifications of accepted truths. But with the new critical spirit that appeared in the Late Middle Ages, scholars began to look at the world with new eyes. In time, this spirit led to the greatest achievement of Baroque science, the Scientific Revolution that overturned the geocentric Ptolemaic system and established **heliocentrism,** the theory that the universe is centered on the sun.

Figure 15.2 MARIA SIBYLLA MERIAN. *Insect Metamorphoses in Surinam*. 1705. Hand-colored engraving. (Reprinted in F. Schnack. *Das Kleine Buch der Tropenwander*. Leipzig: Insel-Verlag, 1935. Plate 11. 4¾ × 7".) *A painter and a scientist, the German-born Maria Sibylla Merian (1647–1717) traveled to the South American Dutch colony of Surinam, where, for two years, she collected and raised insects and made notes and illustrations. Her illustration of the metamorphosis of a moth, from caterpillar through pupa (covered by a cocoon) to mature adult, along with a flowering branch of an orange tree, captures the exotic character of the New World, adds to the growing body of scientific knowledge, and reflects the high standards of seventeenth-century Dutch art.*

THE MAGICAL AND THE PRACTICAL IN THE SCIENTIFIC REVOLUTION

The Scientific Revolution is notable for the paradoxes and ironies that the movement gave rise to, some of which will be discussed in a later section of this chapter. A paradox that should be noted at the outset, however, is that this revolution in human thought, which ushered in modern science, was rooted in both magical beliefs and practical technological achievements. With one or two exceptions, the makers of the Scientific Revolution were motivated by two divergent and rather contradictory sets of beliefs. On the one hand, they followed the lead of late medieval science by collecting empirical data, reasoning inductively, and using mathematics to verify results (Figure 15.2). Significantly, the most startling changes occurred in those areas where mathematics was applied to long-existing intellectual problems, namely in astronomy, physics, and biology.

On the other hand, the makers of the Scientific Revolution were entranced by Neo-Platonism, the philosophy that revived the ancient Greek philosophy in the Early Renaissance (see Chapter 11). Like late medieval science, Neo-Platonism stressed the role of mathematics in problem solving, but Neo-Platonism also had a mystical streak—a legacy from Pythagoras—that led its devotees to seek harmony through numbers (see Chapter 2). Thinkers who followed Neo-Platonism believed that simplicity was superior to complexity in mathematical figuring because simplicity was the supreme sign that a solution was correct. This belief has become a guiding ideal of modern science, although other aspects of Neo-Platonism are rejected today, such as the attribution of mysterious powers to the sun. One effect of Neo-Platonism's occult side was to tighten the link between astronomy and astrology, a connection as old as Greek science. Most of those who made the revolution in science supported this linkage, and a few even cast horoscopes for wealthy clients.

As for the role of technology in the Scientific Revolution, many of its achievements would have been impossible without the telescope and the microscope, both of which were invented in about 1600 in the Netherlands. Without them, scholars would have simply remained "thinkers," as they had been since the time of the ancient Greeks. But with the telescope and the microscope, they could penetrate deep into hitherto inaccessible areas—outer space and the inner workings of the human body. Henceforward, scholars with a scientific bent allied themselves with the crafts tradition, becoming experimenters and empiricists.

Astronomy and Physics: From Copernicus to Newton

The intellectual shift from the earth-centered to the sun-centered universe was almost 150 years in the making and involved an international community of scholars. Heliocentrism, the new model of the world, was first broached in modern times by the Polish thinker Copernicus in 1543, and incontrovertible mathematical calculations to prove this view were published by the English scholar Newton in 1687. Between those dates, major steps in the revolution in science were taken by Tycho Brahe of Denmark, Johannes Kepler of Germany, and Galileo Galilei of Italy. Isaac Newton spoke the truth when he claimed that he "stood on the shoulders of giants" (see Timeline 15.1).

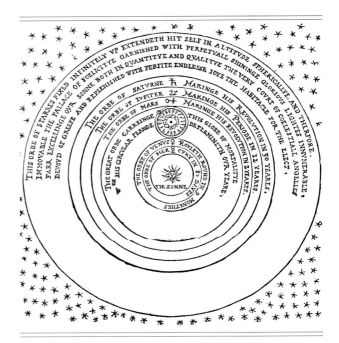

Figure 15.3 THOMAS DIGGES. The Sun-Centered Universe of Copernicus, from *A Perfit Description of the Celestiall Orbes*. 1576. The Huntington Library, San Marino, California. *This diagram drawn by the Englishman Thomas Digges agrees with the Copernican system except in one major way. Copernicus believed the universe was a finite, closed system, but Digges represents it as infinite, expressed in the stars scattered outside the orbit of fixed stars.*

Nicolas Copernicus When Nicolas Copernicus (1473–1543) published *Revolutions of the Heavenly Bodies* in 1543, he was reviving the discarded heliocentric theory of the third-century-B.C. Greek thinker Aristarchus. In this highly technical work, Copernicus launched a head-on assault against Ptolemaic geocentrism. The main issue between Copernican astronomy and the older worldview was not one of mathematical precision, for both were mathematically solid and thus equally able to predict planetary positions and solar and lunar eclipses. Rather, the basic question between the two systems was which one was simpler. Copernicus reasoned that a more convincing picture of the universe could be achieved by transposing the positions of the sun and the earth. Instead of the Ptolemaic notion of a finite world centered on a fixed earth, Copernicus envisioned a vastly expanded, but not infinite, universe with the planets orbiting the sun (Figure 15.3).

Recognizing the revolutionary nature of his hypothesis, Copernicus delayed printing his ideas until he was dying. In an attempt to mollify clerical critics, he dedicated his book to the pope, Paul III. Later the religious establishment concluded that heliocentrism was dangerous and contrary to scripture; they therefore condemned it as a false system. What disturbed them was that when the earth was removed from the center of the universe, the place of human beings in the divine order was also reduced. In effect, human beings were no longer the leading actors in a cosmic drama, staged for them alone.

Catholics and Protestants alike denounced the ideas of Copernicus. Lutheran and Calvinist authorities condemned his views as unbiblical, and in 1610 the pope placed *Revolutions of the Heavenly Bodies* on the Index, the list of forbidden books created during the Counter-Reformation. Eventually, the two religious groups came to a parting of the ways over Copernican ideas. For more than two hundred years, until 1822, the Roman Catholic Church, with all of its considerable power and influence, opposed the sun-centered theory, thus reversing a centuries-old tradition of being open to innovative scientific thought. However, in Protestantism—where authority was not centralized as it was in Roman Catholicism—some sects slowly accepted and adapted their beliefs to the new astronomy.

Johannes Kepler The reception of Copernican astronomy by the scientific community was neither immediate nor enthusiastic. For example, the great Danish astronomer Tycho Brahe [TEE-ko BRAH-hee] (1546–1601) adopted a modified Copernicanism, believing that the other planets moved around the sun but that the earth did not. Brahe nevertheless contributed to the ultimate triumph of heliocentrism through his copious observations of planetary movement. So accurate were his sightings (without the aid of a telescope) that they set a new standard for astronomical data (Figure 15.4).

Among Brahe's assistants was Johannes Kepler (1571–1630), a brilliant mathematician who dedicated his life to clarifying the theory of heliocentrism. When the Danish astronomer died, Kepler inherited his astronomical data. Inspired by Neo-Platonism to make sense of the regular and continuous sightings of Brahe, Kepler in 1609 published *On the Motion of Mars*, setting forth his solution to the problem of what kept the planets in their orbits. His findings were expressed in two scientific laws that were elegant in their simplicity. In the first planetary law, Kepler substituted the ellipse for the circle as the descriptive shape of planetary orbits. And his second planetary law, which was set forth in a precise mathematical formula, accounted for each planet's variable speed within its respective orbit by showing that nearness to the sun affected its behavior —the closer to the sun, the faster the speed, and the farther from the sun, the slower the speed. Together, these laws validated sun-centered astronomy.

Figure 15.4 *Tycho Brahe in his Observatory.* Engraving, from Brahe's *Astronomiae Instauratae Mechanica.* 1598. Joseph Regenstein Library, University of Chicago. *Tycho Brahe is shown in his observatory at Uraniborg, on the island of Ven, in Denmark. With right hand pointing upward, he instructs his assistants in the use of the wall quadrant, the semicircular instrument (below the table) he developed for measuring the position of stars. In the background, other assistants work on various astronomical instruments and perform chemical experiments. Behind Brahe are his royal patrons and a globe. The dog at his feet is an emblem of loyalty.*

Kepler continued to manipulate Brahe's undigested data, convinced that other mathematical laws could be derived from observations of the heavens. In 1619 he arrived at a third planetary law, which relates the movement of one planet to another. He showed that the squares of the length of time for each planet's orbit are in the same ratios as the cubes of their respective mean distances from the sun. Through this formula, he affirmed that the solar system itself was regular and organized by mathematically determined relationships. This was the first expression of the notion that the universe operates with clocklike regularity, an idea that became an article of faith by the end of the Baroque age. Kepler took great pride in this discovery, because it confirmed his Neo-Platonist belief that there is a hidden mathematical harmony in the universe.

Galileo Galilei While Kepler moved in the rarefied realm of theoretical, even mystical, science, one of his contemporaries was making major breakthroughs with experiments that relied on precise mathematics and careful logic. This patient experimenter was Galileo Galilei (1564–1642), whose most valuable contributions were his accurate celestial observations and his work in terrestrial mechanics, the study of the action of forces on matter. Inspired by news that Dutch lens grinders had made a device for viewing distant objects, in 1609 Galileo made his own telescope, which enabled him to see stars invisible to the naked eye.

With these sightings, Galileo demonstrated that the size of the universe was exponentially greater than that computed on Ptolemaic principles. Further, his observations of the moon's rough surface and the sun's shifting dark spots provided additional proofs against the ancient arguments that the heavenly bodies were perfectly formed and never changed. But his most telling discovery was that the planet Jupiter has moons, a fact that contradicted the Ptolemaic belief that all celestial bodies must move about a common center. Galileo's research affirmed that Jupiter's four satellites rotated around it in much the same way that the six planets orbited the sun. These telescope observations hastened the demise of geocentrism.

Similarly, Galileo's research in terrestrial mechanics proved conclusively that both Aristotle and his fourteenth-century critics in Paris were wrong about one of the central questions of earthly motion—that is, the behavior of projectiles. Aristotle had claimed that projectiles stayed in flight because of the pushing motion of the air, and the Parisian scholars had countered with the theory of "impetus." Through experimentation, Galileo showed that a mass that is moving will go on moving until some force acts to stop it—the earliest expression of the modern law of inertia.

Galileo was probably the first scientist to make a clock a basic means for measuring time in his experiments. Like his contemporary Kepler, he reported his findings in the form of simple mathematical laws. Galileo's work was later validated by Newton, who proved that the laws of mechanics on earth were the same as the laws of mechanics in the sky.

At the same time that Galileo was conducting the experiments that would make him a hero of modern science, he ran afoul of the religious authorities, who brought his career to a humiliating end. The church, as noted previously, had by now abandoned its relative openness to ideas and was moving to stifle dissent. In 1633 Galileo was arrested by the Inquisition, the church court created in the 1200s to find and punish heretics. The great astronomer was charged with false teachings for his published support of the idea that the earth moves, a notion central to Copernicanism but

Figure 15.5 GODFREY KNELLER. *Sir Isaac Newton*. 1702. Oil on canvas, 29¾ × 24½". National Portrait Gallery, London. *As the most celebrated intellectual of his generation, the middle-class Newton was given star treatment in this portrait by the reigning society painter in England. Decked out fashionably in an elaborate Baroque wig, Newton peers somewhat uncomfortably at the viewer. The likeness tends to support Newton's reputation for vanity and ostentation.*

untrue according to Aristotle and the church. Threatened with torture, Galileo recanted his views and was released. Despite living on for several years, he died a broken man. This episode abruptly ended Italy's role in the burgeoning revolution in science.

Isaac Newton Building on the research of the heirs to Copernicus, including Kepler's laws of planetary motion and Galileo's law of inertia, the English mathematician Isaac Newton (1642–1727) conceived a model of the universe that decisively overturned the Ptolemaic scheme and finished the revolution in astronomy begun by Copernicus. In Newton's world picture, there is uniform motion on earth and in the heavens. More significant, Newton presented a satisfactory explanation for what held the planets in their orbits. Newton's solution was the force of gravity, and this topic formed the heart of his theory of the universe (Figure 15.5).

In a precise mathematical formula, Newton computed the law of universal gravitation, the formula whereby every object in the world exerts an attraction to a greater or a lesser degree on all other objects. By this law, the sun held in its grip each of the six planets, and each in turn lightly influenced the sun and the other planets. The earth and its single moon as well as

Jupiter and its four satellites similarly interacted. In effect, because of gravity, the heavenly bodies formed a harmonious system in which each attracted the others.

Having described gravity and asserted its universal nature, Newton declined to speculate about what caused it to operate. For him, the universe behaved precisely as a machine, and his law was nothing but a description of its operation. Because Newton refused to speculate beyond what mathematics could prove, he has been called a "mind without metaphysics." Modern scientists have followed Newton's lead, preferring to ignore the *why* of things and to concentrate on the *how* and *what*.

Newton's views were set forth in his authoritative work *Mathematical Principles of Natural Philosophy*. Known more familiarly as the *Principia* (the first word of its Latin title), this book quickly gained an authority that made Newton the modern world's equivalent of Aristotle. By the eighteenth century, the English poet Alexander Pope could justifiably write:

Nature and Nature's Laws lay hid in Night;
God said, *Let Newton be!* and All was *Light*.

Even though Newton's work was the culmination of the revolution that brought modern science into being, he was not fully free of older attitudes. True, he believed that the discovery of scientific truth was simply a matter of using methodical principles. He made mathematics his guiding ideal and used patient and careful observation. But Newton cared little for his own scientific achievement, believing that his lasting monument would be his religious writings. A pious Christian, he devoted his last years to demonstrating that the prophecies in the Bible were coming true.

Newton also invented a form of calculus, a mathematical method of analysis that uses a symbolic notation. This breakthrough had huge potential for solving problems in physics and mechanics by providing a tool for computing quantities that had nonlinear variations. Simultaneously and independently of Newton, Gottfried Wilhelm von Leibniz [LIBE-nits] (1646–1716), a German thinker, invented a more useful version of calculus. By 1800 Leibniz's symbols had become the universally accepted language of calculus.

Medicine and Chemistry

At the same time that Western understanding of the universe at its outer limits was being radically altered, another breakthrough involved anatomical knowledge and the discovery of the true circulation of the human blood. Unlike developments in astronomy, this breakthrough in medical science happened largely without the aid of technology. Only during the last step in the solving of the mystery of the blood's circulation did early modern scientists use the newly invented microscope.

In 1600 anatomical knowledge was extremely limited, primarily because the church forbade the violation of corpses, a position based on the teaching that the body would be resurrected from the dead. Biological research had been limited to the dissection of animals, with generalizations then applied to the human body, leading to a great deal of misinformation and half-truths.

Besides, in biology as in astronomy and physics, the authority of ancient Greek thinkers reigned supreme —Aristotle since the fourth century B.C. and Galen since the second century A.D. Galen's vast researches covering nearly all aspects of ancient medicine were lost in the fall of Rome, but some works were preserved by Arab scholars and were translated from Arabic into Latin by Western scholars from the eleventh century onward. Though offering rival theories, Aristotle and Galen shared many false ideas, namely the notions that air ran directly from the lungs into the heart, that blood flowed from the veins to the outer part of the body, and that different types of blood coursed in the arteries and the veins.

The problem of the circulation of the blood was eventually resolved by scientists at the University of Padua in Italy, the most prominent of whom was Andreas Vesalius [vuh-SAY-lee-us] (1514–1564). His painstaking observations led him to deny Galen's theory that blood passed from one side of the heart to the other through the septum, an impermeable membrane (Figure 15.6).

The research of Vesalius and his successors set the stage for William Harvey (1578–1657), an English scientist who studied and taught at the University of Padua. In 1628 Harvey published his groundbreaking work, which produced the correct view of circulation, including the roles of the heart, the lungs, the arteries, and the veins. Mathematical calculation played a decisive role in this scientific triumph, just as it had in Newton's gravitation theory. Using arithmetic, Harvey proved that a constant quantity of blood continuously circulated throughout the body, thereby invalidating Galen's ebb-and-flow theory. However, Harvey lacked knowledge of the capillaries, the connectors between the arteries and the veins. In 1661 the Italian scientist Marcello Malpighi [mahl-PEE-gee] (1628–1694) identified these tiny vessels with the aid of the microscope, and with this critical piece of information an essentially correct, modern description of the blood's circulation was complete.

Chemistry did not become a separate discipline in the Baroque age, but the English physicist Robert Boyle (1627–1691) did establish the groundwork for

Figure 15.6 REMBRANDT VAN RIJN. *The Anatomy Lesson of Dr. Tulp.* 1632. Oil on canvas, 66¾ × 85¼". Mauritshuis, The Hague. *The pioneering work of Vesalius made the study of anatomy a central concern of medical science in the seventeenth century. In this painting, Rembrandt depicts Dr. Nicholas Tulp of Amsterdam as he demonstrates the dissection of the left arm. Rembrandt's use of Baroque effects, such as the dramatic light on the corpse, the contrast between Dr. Tulp's calm demeanor and the inquisitive faces of his pupils, and the flayed arm of the corpse, make this an arresting image.*

modern chemistry. A major aspect of Boyle's thought linked him to Newton, for both believed that the universe is a machine. Boyle believed that the workings of nature could be revealed only through experimental study—the inductive method. Boyle's zeal for experimentation led him to study the behavior of gases and to formulate the famous law that bears his name.

Boyle was also one of the first to distinguish chemistry from alchemy, a set of magical practices that had been allied with chemistry since the time of the ancient Greeks. In medieval Europe, alchemy had led scholars to search vainly for the "philosopher's stone" that would miraculously turn a base metal such as lead into gold. Rejecting alchemy's assumptions and methodology, Boyle sought to understand only those chemical reactions that happened naturally and could be analyzed in mathematical terms.

The Impact of Science on Philosophy

The Scientific Revolution had a profound influence on Western thought and also gave rise to a type of literature that reflected the impact of science on the wider culture. Three prominent contributors to this literature were the English jurist and statesman Francis Bacon and two brilliant French mathematicians, René Descartes and Blaise Pascal, whose speculative writings continued the French rationalist tradition begun by Montaigne in the 1500s (see Chapter 13).

Francis Bacon Francis Bacon (1561–1626) owes his fame to his ability to write lucid prose about science and its methodology. In a field that was dominated by scholars whose writings were accessible only to those

THE MAGICAL AND THE PRACTICAL IN THE SCIENTIFIC REVOLUTION

learned in mathematics, Bacon's clear prose informed a curious and educated public. In the process of clarifying the techniques and the aims of the new science, he became the spokesman for the "experimenters," those who believed that the future of science lay in discarding Aristotle. Condemning Aristotle for relying on deductive reasoning and unproven axioms, Bacon advocated the inductive method, the procedure that embraced the conducting of experiments, the drawing of conclusions, and the testing of results in other experiments. His claims were not new, but they were forcibly and memorably expressed; few scholars exhibited Bacon's optimism about the usefulness of science. He sincerely believed that the march of science inevitably led to mastery over the natural world, a view summarized in the famous phrase attributed to him, "knowledge is power."

René Descartes An outstanding critic of the belief that the experimental method was the correct path to knowledge was René Descartes [day-KAHRT] (1596–1650), a philosopher who urged a purely mathematical approach in science (Figure 15.7). Descartes's love of numbers came from a mystical side of his personality, as illustrated by his confession that a dream had inspired his belief that mathematics holds the key to nature. Descartes was the founder of analytic geometry, that branch of mathematics that describes geometric figures by the formulas of algebra, and the author of a widely influential philosophical treatise, *Discourse on Method*, published in 1637.

In the *Discourse on Method*, Descartes outlined four steps in his approach to knowledge: to accept nothing as true unless it is self-evident; to split problems into manageable parts; to solve problems starting with the simplest and moving to the most complex; and to review and reexamine the solutions. He used deductive logic in his method, making inferences only from general statements. But more important than his stress on deductive reasoning was his insistence on mathematical clarity. He refused to accept anything as true unless it had the persuasiveness of a proof in geometry.

Descartes's most influential gifts to Western philosophy were skepticism and a dualistic theory of knowledge. He rejected the authoritarian method of medieval scholasticism and began with universal doubt in order to determine what was absolutely certain in the universe. Step-by-step, he questioned the existence of God, of the world, and of his own body. But he soon established that he could not doubt the existence of his own doubting self. He reached this absolute conclusion in the oft-quoted phrase *"Cogito ergo sum"*—I think, therefore I am. Having first destroyed the age-old certainties, he then, through deduction, reestablished the existence of his own body, the world, and, finally, God.

Figure 15.7 FRANZ HALS. *René Descartes*. After 1649. Oil on canvas, 30¾ × 26¾". Louvre. *In this likeness, Frans Hals, the great Dutch portrait artist and contemporary of Rembrandt, has captured the complex personality of the great French philosopher and mathematician. Descartes's piercing gaze shows his skeptical spirit. His disdainful presence and rough features reveal his early background as a soldier. Hals apparently felt no need to flatter his sitter in this compelling portrait.*

Descartes's speculations were aimed at identifying clear and distinct ideas that were certain for everyone, but his efforts had a deeply ironic result. In the long run, his thought fostered the growing awareness among the educated elite that absolute truth was not possible. Many who read his *Discourse* were unimpressed by his rational arguments, but they nevertheless accepted his radical doubt, and some even became atheists. That his work contributed to the rise of atheism would have horrified Descartes, since, to his own way of thinking, he had proven the existence of God. He had used skepticism merely as a means of achieving certainty.

Descartes's other great legacy, dualism, made a division between the material world and the human soul or mind. According to him, mathematics permitted natural truths to be revealed to the human understanding. He thought, however, that the mind itself was beyond mathematical knowing and hence was not a fit subject for study. From this dichotomy arise two contrasting traditions, the scientists who reduce the natural world to order through mathematics and the thinkers who focus on human psychology. The second group—the psychologists—represent another ironic legacy, for through the study of such topics as depth psychology and alienation they want to prove that Descartes was wrong and that the human self is knowable in all of its irrationality.

Even though Descartes's speculations were aimed at achieving certainty, his focus on deductive logic has not withstood the test of time. This is because modern scientists think that inductive reasoning—building a model of truth on the facts—is more valid. But Descartes was proven correct in assigning to mathematics its paramount role in establishing precision and certainty in science. Today, those sciences that have the greatest degree of mathematical rigor have better reputations for accuracy and believability than those sciences whose formulations cannot be achieved mathematically.

Descartes made another contribution to the Scientific Revolution when he applied his method to terrestrial mechanics. It was he, rather than Galileo, who gave final expression to the law of inertia. He concluded that a projectile would continue to move in a straight line until it was interrupted by some force. With this language Descartes finally debunked the myth of circular motion, and his definition of the law of inertia became part of the scientific synthesis of Newton.

Blaise Pascal   Descartes's work was barely published before it elicited a strong reaction from Blaise Pascal [BLEHZ pas-KAHL] (1623–1662), an anguished thinker who made radical doubt the cornerstone of his beliefs. Like Descartes, Pascal left his mark in mathematics, notably in geometry and in the study of probability. Pascal was a Jansenist, a member of a Catholic sect that to some observers was Calvinistic because it stressed original sin and denied free will. Pascal's Jansenism permeates his masterpiece, the *Pensées*, or *Thoughts*, a meditative work of intense feeling published in 1670, eight years after his death.

In the *Pensées,* Pascal went beyond Descartes's skepticism, concluding that human beings can know neither the natural world nor themselves. Despite this seemingly universal doubt, Pascal still reasoned that there were different levels of truth. Regarding science, he thought that what he called the geometric spirit— that is, mathematics—could lead scholars to a limited knowledge of nature. Pascal's most controversial opinions, however, concerned human psychology. He felt that the passions enabled human beings to comprehend truths about God and religion directly. He

summed up this idea in his often quoted words, "The heart has reasons that reason does not know." In another passage, he justified his continued belief in God, not by intellectual proofs in the manner of Descartes, but by a wager—a notion he derived from his probability studies. Pascal claimed his faith in God rested on a bet: If God exists, then the bettor wins everything, but if God does not exist, then nothing is lost. Pascal's fervent belief in God in the face of debilitating doubt makes him a forerunner of modern Christian existentialism.

Ironies and Contradictions of the Scientific Revolution

Ironies abound in the seventeenth century's most characteristic development, the Scientific Revolution. To begin with, it must be remembered that only a handful of thinkers contributed to the scientific changes, that the vast majority of the populace remained unaware of their findings, and that they could not have understood them even if they had been informed of them. Furthermore, those who made the scientific discoveries were engaged primarily in solving practical problems rather than in trying to build a new model of the universe. They also believed that what they were doing was entirely within an orthodox Christian framework (although some were aware that religious leaders might think otherwise), and few foresaw that their efforts would eventually lead to a conflict between religion and science.

Another irony was that the scientific advancements were not always completely original creations but were rooted in late medieval rationalism and the Renaissance revival of Classical learning. Indeed, the new thinkers were often more concerned with working out minor inconsistencies in the calculations of medieval scholars than in overturning the accepted picture of the universe.

Not only did seventeenth-century science have roots in medieval science, but it was also influenced by superstitions and mystical beliefs. During the Scientific Revolution, even the greatest intellectuals still held firmly to nonrational medieval views. Brahe and Kepler, for example, supported their research by pursuing careers as court astrologers. Harvey imagined that the heart restored a "spiritous" quality to the blood during circulation. Newton and Boyle were both involved in secret experiments with alchemy. A mystical experience lay behind Descartes's mathematical zeal, and Neo-Platonism motivated the thought of Copernicus, Kepler, and Galileo. Many scholars were conventionally devout in their religious convictions, and Newton tried to correlate biblical prophecy with

PERSONAL PERSPECTIVE

Johannes Junius
Secret Letter to His Daughter

In June 1628, the fifty-five-year-old mayor of Bamberg, Germany, Johannes Junius, was accused of witchcraft—of renouncing God, worshiping the Devil, attending witches' Sabbaths, desecrating the Eucharist wafer, and committing other crimes. Under torture, he confessed. Before his execution, he managed to smuggle this letter to his daughter.

Innocent have I come into prison, innocent have I been tortured, innocent must I die. For whoever comes into the witch prison must become a witch or be tortured until he invents something out of his head—and God pity him—bethinks him of something. I will tell you how it has gone with me. When I was the first time put to the torture, Dr. Baum, Dr. Kotzendorffer, and two strange doctors were there. Then Dr. Baum asks me, "Kinsman, how come you here?" . . . I said, "I am no witch. I have a pure conscience in the matter; if there are a thousand witnesses, I am not anxious, but I'll gladly hear the witnesses." Now the Chancellor's son was set before me . . . and afterward Hopffens Elsse. She had seen me dance on Haupts-moor. . . . I answered: "I have never renounced God, and will never do it—God graciously keep me from it. I'll rather bear whatever I must." And then came also—God in highest Heaven have mercy—the executioner, and put the thumb-screws on me, both hands bound together, so that the blood ran out at the nails and everywhere, so that for four weeks I could not use my hands, as you can see from the writing. . . . Thereafter they first stripped me, bound my hands behind me, and drew me up in the torture. Then I thought heaven and earth were at an end; eight times did they draw me up and let me fall again, so that I suffered terrible agony. . . .

When at last the executioner led me back into the prison, he said to me: "Sir, I beg you, for God's sake confess something, whether it be true or not. Invent something, for you cannot endure the torture which you will be put to; and, even if you bear it all, yet you will not escape. . . . Not before that," he said, "will they let you go, as you may see by all their trials, for one is just like another." . . .

And so I begged, since I was in wretched plight, to be given one day for thought and a priest. The priest was refused me, but the time for thought was given. . . .

At last there came to me a new idea. I would not be anxious, but, since I had been given no priest with whom I could take counsel, I would myself think of something and say it.

. . . And so I made my confession, as follows; but it was all a lie.

---

history. Despite their medieval roots, these scholars did point European thought in a new direction. In the next century, a new generation of intellectuals constructed a set of beliefs based on the achievements of the Scientific Revolution and their implications for the improvement of humanity.

THE REVOLUTION IN POLITICAL THOUGHT

Political philosophy reflected the nature of the shifting political, economic, social, scientific, and religious institutions of the seventeenth century. The Thirty Years' War, the Wars of Louis XIV, and the English Civil War (see Chapter 14) forced political theorists to reconsider such basic themes as the nature of government, the relations between rulers and subjects, the rivalries among sovereign states, and the consequences of war on society and the individual.

Political writers, stimulated by the rise of the nation-state in the 1500s, addressed themselves in the 1600s to the fundamental questions of who holds the final sovereignty in a state and how power should be exercised. Realizing that new states were rapidly extinguishing the rights held by the feudal estates, these theorists tried to define the best form of government. They all supported their arguments with the same sources—the Bible, the concept of natural law, scientific discoveries, and their own views of human nature—but they came to widely differing conclusions.

Natural Law and Divine Right: Grotius and Bossuet

Hugo Grotius [GRO-she-us] (1583–1645) thought that natural law should govern the relations between states. He arrived at this belief chiefly because of his personal sufferings during the Thirty Years' War and the intolerance that he observed in religious disputes. A Dutch citizen but also an ambassador for Sweden, he saw at first hand the ambiguity of diplomatic relations between the great powers.

Drawing on the idea of natural law as set forth by the ancient Stoic thinkers, Grotius urged that the states follow a law that applied to all nations, was eternal and unchanging, and could be understood by human reason. Like the Stoics, Grotius was convinced that the natural law was founded on human reason and was not the gift of a loving God. He rejected original sin, believing instead that human beings were not motivated merely by selfish drives. He thought that because all mortals were rational, they wanted to improve themselves and to create a just and fair society. In his treatise *The Law of War and Peace,* he applied this rational view of human nature to his description of sovereign states. He concluded that nations, like individuals, should treat each other as they would expect to be treated. Today, the writings of Grotius are recognized as the starting point of international law.

Taking a contrary point of view to Grotius was Bishop Bossuet [bo-SWAY] (1627–1704), who defended the theory that kings rule by divine right. This French church leader echoed the opinions of James I of England, who maintained that God bestowed power on certain national monarchs. The French bishop avowed that absolutism, as ordained by God in past societies, was now manifested in the rule of Louis XIV, king of France. Louis, as God's chosen vessel on earth, had the power to intervene in the lives of his subjects, not because of natural law, but by divine right. According to this theory, for corrupt and sinful humans to rebel against the king was to go against God's plan. The bishop believed that the age's conflicts made autocratic rule a political necessity. Bossuet's belief in autocracy was shared by the Englishman Thomas Hobbes, although he explained absolute rule in different terms.

Absolutism and Liberalism: Hobbes and Locke   Thomas Hobbes (1588–1679) grew up in an England increasingly torn by religious, social, and political discord. A trained Classicist and a student of the new science, Hobbes came to believe that everything, including human beings and their social acts, could be explained by using mechanistic, natural laws to describe various states of motion or movement.

Hobbes's efforts to synthesize a universal philosophy founded on a geometric design and activated by some form of energy culminated in his best-known work, *The Leviathan,* published in 1651 (Figure 15.8). *The Leviathan* sets forth a theory of government based on the pessimistic view that individuals are driven by two basic forces, the fear of death and the quest for power. Hobbes imagined what life would be like if these two natural inclinations were allowed free rein and there were no supreme power to control them. Hobbes described human life under these circumstances as "solitary, poor, nasty, brutish, and short."

Hobbes thought that human beings, recognizing the awfulness of their situation, would decide to give up such an existence and form a civil society under the rule of one man. This first step in the evolution of government was achieved by means of a **social contract** drawn up between the ruler and his subjects. By the terms of this covenant, the subjects surrendered all their claims to sovereignty and bestowed absolute power on the ruler. The sovereign's commands were then to be carried out by all under him, including the religious and civic leaders. Armed with the sword, the sovereign would keep peace at home and protect the land from its enemies abroad.

Hobbes made no distinction between the ruler of a monarchy and the head of a commonwealth, for he was less concerned with the form of government than with the need to hold in check destructive human impulses. In the next generation, Hobbes's pessimistic philosophy provoked a reaction from John Locke, who repudiated absolutism and advocated a theory of government by the people.

Despite their contradictory messages, Hobbes and John Locke (1632–1704) had been subjected to similar influences. Both adapted ideas from the new science, witnessed the English Civil War, and sought safety on the Continent because of their political views. But Locke rejected Hobbes's gloomy view of humanity and his theory of absolutism; he taught instead that human nature was potentially good and that human beings were capable of governing themselves. The two thinkers originated opposing schools of modern political thought: From Hobbes stems the absolutist, authoritarian tradition, and from Locke descends the school of liberalism. Their works represent two of the most significant legacies of the Baroque age to the modern world.

Locke set forth his political theories in his *Two Treatises of Government,* which he published anonymously in 1690. In the *First Treatise* he refuted the divine right of kings, and in the *Second Treatise* he laid out the model for rule by the people. The latter work has become the classic expression of early **liberalism.** In it Locke described the origins, characteristics, and purpose of the ideal political system—a government limited by laws, subject to the will of its citizens, and existing to protect life and property.

Locke's treatise shared some of Hobbes's ideas, such as the view that human life is violent and disorderly in the state of nature, that human beings must form civil governments to protect themselves, and that a social contract is the necessary basis of civil society. But Locke believed that basic rights, including life and property, exist in the state of nature. He also believed that human beings possess reason, are fundamentally decent and law abiding, and are slow to want change.

Figure 15.8   Frontispiece of *The Leviathan*. 1651. The Bancroft Library, University of California, Berkeley. *The original illustration for Hobbes's* Leviathan *conveys the political message of this controversial work in symbolic terms. Towering over the landscape is the mythical ruler, whose body is a composite of all his subjects and in whose hands are the sword and the scepter, symbols of his absolute power. Below this awesome figure is a well-ordered and peaceful village and countryside—Hobbes's political dream come true.*

From these principles, he concluded that human beings would contract together to create a limited government that had no other purpose than the protection of the basic natural rights of life and property.

Locke rejected the idea that by making a social contract citizens surrender their sovereignty to a ruler. He argued instead that the people choose rulers who protect their rights in a fiduciary trust; that is, they expect their rulers to obey the social contract and govern equitably. If the rulers break the agreement, then the people have the right to revolt, overthrow the government, and reclaim their natural rights. Unlike Hobbes, Locke asserted that rulers possess only limited authority and that their control must be held in check by a balanced governmental system and a separation of powers. In later years, Locke's tract influenced American and French political thinkers and patriots who used its ideas to justify the right to revolt against a tyrant and to establish a government of checks and balances.

Locke was not only a political theorist but also the preeminent English philosopher of his day. He grappled with many of the same problems as Descartes, although his conclusions were radically different from the French thinker's. In his important philosophical work *An Essay Concerning Human Understanding,* published in 1690 (the same year he published *Two Treatises of Government*), Locke addressed the question, How is knowledge acquired? Descartes had proposed that the germs of ideas were inborn and that people were born knowing certain truths, such as mathematical principles and logical relationships; education required nothing more than the strenuous use of the intellect without concern for new information from the senses.

Locke repudiated these views and described the mind at birth as a *tabula rasa* (blank tablet) on which all human experiences were recorded. Locke maintained that all that human beings can know must first be received through their senses (a basically Aristotelian viewpoint) and then registered on their minds. The raw sensory data are manipulated by the mental faculties, such as comparing and contrasting, so that abstract concepts and generalizations are formed in the mind. As a result, reason and experience are united in human thought and together determine what is real for each person. Locke's explanation of the origin of ideas is the basis of modern empiricism—the theory that all knowledge is derived from or originates in human experience. His influence has been so great that many of his ideas seem to the modern reader to be just "common sense."

EUROPEAN EXPLORATION AND EXPANSION

The exploration begun in the late fifteenth century had led to a series of encounters with new peoples that slowly eroded the isolation and self-absorption of Europe. In the sixteenth century, the pace of exploration quickened, and the globe was circumnavigated—events that intensified rivalries among the European states, increased the Continent's economic power, and diffused European culture and customs around the world.

The greatest success of European expansion was achieved through a series of permanent settlements in North and South America and by the opening of new trade routes to the Far East (Map 15.1). Expansion and colonization affected Europe in numerous ways: the introduction of new foodstuffs and other products, the establishment of innovative business methods, the disruption of old economic and social patterns, the introduction of novel ways of looking at the world, and the adoption of new symbols and themes in the arts.

Whatever may have been the beneficial or harmful effects of these changes on European life, the negative impact on non-Europeans tended to outweigh the good that came with the introduction of Western culture. In Africa, the Europeans expanded the slave trade; in North, Central, and South America and the Caribbean, they annihilated many native tribes; and everywhere they forced trade agreements favorable to themselves on the local people.

The earliest leaders in the European penetration of the Western Hemisphere were Spain and Portugal. Since the 1500s, these two states had claimed South and Central America and the southern reaches of North America. Where possible, they mined the rich gold and silver veins, flooding Europe with the new wealth and gaining power and influence for themselves. But during the seventeenth century, the mines were nearing exhaustion, and the glory days were a thing of the past.

While Spain's and Portugal's ties with the New World languished during the Baroque age, England, France, and the Netherlands were accelerating theirs, especially with North America (Table 15.1). In 1607 English farmers settled along the Atlantic seaboard in Virginia, ready to exploit the land, and in 1620 English Puritans emigrated to New England in search of religious freedom. To the north, French explorers, missionaries, and fur traders founded Quebec in 1608 and then spread along the St. Lawrence River valley and southward into the Great Lakes region. At the same time, the French moved into the Caribbean basin, occupying many islands in the West Indies. After 1655 the English worked their way into the southern part of the Atlantic coast and the West Indies. These newly arrived colonists eventually either drove out the Spaniards or drastically reduced their influence. Meanwhile, the Dutch set up their own colonies in North America, on the banks of the Hudson River and in scattered areas of the mid-Atlantic region (Figure 15.9).

The English, French, and Dutch recognized the economic advantages of sending more explorers and families abroad and encouraged the founding of colonies. Relying chiefly on state or royal charters, they created large overseas settlements that soon led to a brisk trade in which raw products from the New World were exchanged for finished goods from the Old World. William Penn (1644–1718) founded Pennsylvania in 1681 on the basis of such a charter from England.

In the Far East, colonial developments relied less on charters than on joint-stock companies, a private enterprise technique exploited by both England and the Netherlands. The English East India Company and the Dutch East India Company were the means whereby England and the Netherlands, respectively,

Map 15.1   EXPANSION OF EUROPE, 1715

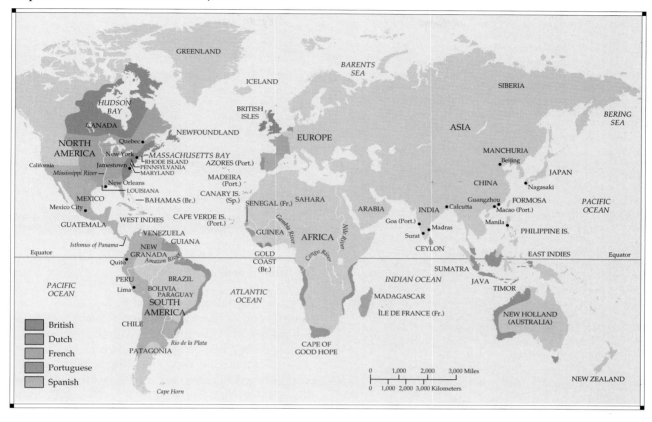

Table 15.1   SETTLEMENTS IN THE NEW WORLD DURING THE BAROQUE AGE

LOCATION	DATE OF FOUNDING	SETTLERS
Jamestown (Virginia)	1607	English
Quebec (Canada)	1608	French
Plymouth (Massachusetts)	1620	English
St. Kitts (West Indies)	1623	English
New Amsterdam (New York)	1624	Dutch
Barbados	1627	English
Brazil	1632–1654	Dutch
Curaçao (West Indies)	1634	Dutch
Martinique (West Indies)	1635	French
Saint Lucia (West Indies)	1635	French
Honduras (Belize)	1638	English
Saint Dominique (Haiti)	1644	French
Bahamas (West Indies)	1648	English
Jamaica (West Indies) (Captured from Spain)	1655	English

opened trade routes and secured markets in the Far East. The two companies made lucrative contracts with Indian princes and Japanese and Chinese state officials (Figure 15.10).

RESPONSES TO THE REVOLUTIONS IN THOUGHT

The scientific discoveries, the growth of skepticism, the new political theories, and the overseas explorations provoked a variety of responses among the artists, intellectuals, and educated public of the 1600s. In the aristocracy, for example, a new social type appeared—the **virtuoso,** a person who dabbled in the latest science and gave it respectability. A new type of literature also appeared, in which scientific concepts and discoveries were popularized for the consumption of an educated elite. Overall, the innovations and changes of the seventeenth century found ample creative expression in the attitudes and images of the period.

Figure 15.9 HARTGER. *New Amsterdam.* 1626. Engraving. Museum of the City of New York. The J. Clarence Davies Collection. *This engraving shows the early Dutch settlement of New Amsterdam. A windmill and numerous houses stand outside the Dutch fort. Dutch sailing vessels are anchored at the mouth of the East River, and Indians in canoes and Dutch sailors in a row-boat navigate the Hudson River (foreground). European views of the New World were influenced by this type of engraving. In 1664 English troops under the Duke of York captured New Amsterdam and subsequently changed its name to New York.*

Figure 15.10 *A Chinese Interpretation of Dutch Traders.* Porcelain. Ch'ing Dynasty, K'ang-hsi period, seventeenth century. Formerly owned by the Dutch East Indies Company. *As Europeans spread Western culture around the globe in the seventeenth century, they were sometimes confronted with images of themselves created by artists in older cultures, as in these Chinese representations of Dutch traders. These figures express a stereotype of a European man, dressed in the costume of the day (long coat, knee breeches, and hat) and with distinctive features (marked cheekbones, curly hair [wig?], and smiling face). Dating from the reign of China's Emperor K'ang-hsi (1661–1722), these porcelains were made as "curiosities" for the European market. They are enameled glaze porcelains, in which green, yellow, purple, and white enamels were applied to a prefired, or biscuit, body and then given a second firing.*

The Spread of Ideas

In the exciting dawn of the Scientific Revolution, some scientists and intellectuals realized that new scientific findings needed to be given the widest dissemination possible, since the information would be of inestimable value to others who were engaged in their own research. Their enthusiasm for this task led them to share ideas. At first, they exchanged information informally through personal contacts or by chance encounters in the universities. But by midcentury, the scientific society became the usual method for communicating new knowledge. The first one was in England, where King Charles II gave a charter to the Royal Society in 1662. Only a few years later, in 1666, Louis XIV supported the creation of the French Academy of Science (Figure 15.11), and in 1700 German scientists instituted the Berlin Academy of Science.

At the same time, many intellectually curious men and women, who wanted to learn more about the changes taking place in science and mathematics but who lacked specialized training, turned to writers who could demystify the new discoveries and explain them in popular language. One who responded to this interest was the French thinker Bernard de Fontenelle [fon-tuh-NELL] (1657–1757), the long-lived secretary of the Academy of Science. His *Conversations on the Plurality of Worlds* set the early standard for this type of popular literature. With learning and wit, Fontenelle created a dialogue between himself and an inquiring countess in which Newtonian physics and the new astronomy were explained in an informative and entertaining way. Through publicists like Fontenelle, the new theories and ideas became available to a general public and entered the broader culture.

Another French publicist, Pierre Bayle [BAYL] (1647–1706), launched the intellectual fashion for

Figure 15.11 J. GOYTON after a painting by S. Leclerc. *Louis XIV at the Academy of Science.* 1671. Engraving. Bibliothèque Nationale, Paris. *Science became fashionable during the Baroque age, and rulers provided funds to advance the new discoveries. Louis XIV, king of France, is shown here visiting the Royal Academy of Science, the premier organization of scientists in France. From this period dates the close alliance between science and government, a linkage based on mutual self-interest.*

arranging ideas in systematic form, as in dictionaries and encyclopedias. Bayle's great popularizing work was called the *Historical and Critical Dictionary,* and it was probably the most controversial book of the Baroque age. For this encyclopedic work, Bayle wrote articles on biblical heroes, Classical and medieval thinkers, and contemporary scholars, many of which challenged Christian beliefs. Each article was a little essay with a text and lengthy footnotes. He approached the work with the aim of setting forth rival and contradictory opinions on each topic; if the result proved to be offensive to the pious, he pointed out that he himself was only following the Bible and the teachings of the Christian faith. Many readers responded to the essays by becoming skeptical about the subjects, as Bayle clearly was. Others questioned Bayle's motives and accused him of atheism. The controversy over his works did not cease with his death. By 1750 his *Dictionary* had been reprinted many times and had spawned many imitations.

Bayle's *Dictionary* marked a new stage in the history of literature for two reasons. First, the work was sold to subscribers, which meant that royal, aristocratic, or ecclesiastical patronage was no longer necessary to publish a book. Second, the extravagant success of his venture showed that a literate public now existed that would buy books if they appealed to its interests. Both of these facts were understood very well by authors in the next generation, who freed writing from the patronage system and inaugurated the world of modern literature with its specialized audiences.

Impact on the Arts

The innovations in science and philosophy coincided with and fostered a changed consciousness not only in the educated public but also in artists and writers. New attitudes, values, and tastes reflecting these ideas are evident in the creative works of the Baroque period, many of which are discussed and illustrated in Chapter 14. Central among the new ideas was the belief that there is a hidden harmony in nature that may be expressed in mathematical laws. In the arts, this belief was expressed by order and wholeness beneath wild profusion, such as the geometric order that organizes the gardens and grounds of Versailles or the theme of redemption that unifies Milton's sprawling epic, *Paradise Lost*.

A second reflection of the Scientific Revolution, and particularly of the discoveries in astronomy, is the feeling of infinite space that pervades Baroque art. The love of curving lines, elliptical shapes, and flowing contours may be related to the new, expansive views of the planets and the universe. The ultimate expression of these interests and feelings, of course, is the illusionistic ceiling painting (see Figure 14.9).

A final effect of the Scientific Revolution was the elevation of analytic reasoning skills to a position of high esteem in the arts. Just as Newton's genius led him to grasp concepts and laws that had eluded others, so artists and humanists were inspired to use their powers of analysis to look below the surface of human life and search out its hidden truth. Racine's plays, for example, reveal acute insight into human psychology, as do the political philosophies of Hobbes and Locke; and Rembrandt's cycle of self-portraits shows his ability and his desire to reveal his innermost feelings. Baroque art and literature demonstrate that although the Scientific Revolution may have displaced men and women from the center of the universe, an optimistic view of the human predicament was still possible.

The Legacy of the Revolutions in Scientific and Political Thought

One historian of science claims that the Scientific Revolution "outshines everything since the rise of Christianity and reduces the Renaissance and Reformation to the rank of mere episodes . . . within the system of medieval Christendom." Although others hesitate to go that far in praise of this singular event, enough evidence exists to show that the revolution in science caused a dramatic shift in the way people viewed themselves and their world. The Newtonian system became the accepted view of the universe until the twentieth century. Likewise, the new methodology—collecting raw data, reasoning inductively to hypotheses, and verifying results with mathematics—remains the standard in modern science. Out of the gradual spread of this method of reasoning to other areas of thought have emerged the modern social sciences. Even certain disciplines in the humanities—such as linguistics, the study of language—use scientific methods to the extent that is possible.

At the same time that science held out the promise that it could unlock the secrets of nature, it was also contributing to a dramatic upsurge in skepticism. Since the end of the Baroque age, virtually everything in Western culture has been subjected to systematic doubt, including religious beliefs, artistic theories, and social mores. Although many causes besides science lie behind this trend to question all existing standards, the Scientific Revolution created a highly visible model and ready tools for universal doubt. In effect, because Aristotle's and other ancient thinkers' ideas were proven false, modern scholars were inclined to question all other beliefs received from the past. This trend has encouraged the intellectual restlessness that is perhaps the most prominent feature of modern life.

The legacies left by the innovations in Baroque political thought and the expansion of European culture cannot compare with the effects of the rise of modern science. Nevertheless, the changes in political theory and in the relations of Europe with the rest of the world did have strong consequences for modern life. In general, the new political theories gave rise to two rival heritages, the authoritarian tradition, which claims that a strong centralized government is the best way to ensure justice for all citizens, and the liberal tradition, which holds that the citizens are capable of ruling themselves. From this time forward, politics in the West has been organized around the conflicting claims of these two points of view. Until relatively recently, the symbol of this development was the division of the world between the supporters of the authoritarian Soviet Union and the supporters of the democratic United States.

The colonizing efforts in the New World during the 1600s served to extend the geographic limits of the West. As a result, Western ideas and technology may be found today even in the most far-flung reaches of the globe. A negative consequence of the opening of the New World was that slavery, an institution that had virtually died in Europe in the early Middle Ages, was reintroduced, with destructive consequences for the non-Western people who became enslaved. We in the modern age are reaping the bitter harvest of this development.

KEY CULTURAL TERMS

Scientific Revolution	heliocentrism
geocentrism	social contract
empiricism	liberalism
inductive reasoning	*tabula rasa*
deductive reasoning	virtuoso

SUGGESTIONS FOR FURTHER READING

PRIMARY SOURCES

BACON, F. *The Essays.* New York: Penguin, 1985. Judicious editing of Bacon's highly readable text, dating from 1625, which contributed significantly to the rise of modern scientific thinking.

BAYLE, P. *Historical and Critical Dictionary: Selections.* Translated by R. H. Popkin and C. Brush. Indianapolis: Bobbs-Merrill, 1965. Typical and controversial excerpts from one of the first modern dictionaries; a work originally published in 1697.

DESCARTES, R. *Discourse on Method.* Edited and translated by E. Anscombe and P. T. Geach. Indianapolis: Bobbs-Merrill, 1971. A lucid translation of one of the key tracts of modern philosophy; Descartes's arguments and evidence are relatively easy to understand. First published in 1637.

GALILEI, G. *Dialogue Concerning the Two Chief World Systems—Ptolemaic and Copernican.* Translated by S. Drake, foreword by A. Einstein. Berkeley: University of California Press, 1953. Written in a conversational style, this work—first published in 1632—aligned Galileo with the supporters of the Copernican system and led to his trial by the Roman Catholic authorities.

HOBBES, T. *The Leviathan.* Buffalo, N.Y.: Prometheus Books, 1988. A recent edition of Hobbes's most important work—first issued in 1651—advocating absolutist government without any restraint by the people; this work has inspired many modern forms of authoritarian rule.

LOCKE, J. *An Essay Concerning Human Understanding.* New York: Collier Books, 1965. A good edition, introduced by M. Cranston, of Locke's essay arguing that the mind is shaped by the environment, an assertion that made the progressive theories of the modern world possible; first published in 1690.

———. *Two Treatises of Government.* Cambridge: Cambridge University Press, 1967. An excellent edition with introduction and notes by the distinguished scholar P. Laslett; Locke's *Second Treatise,* making the case for the doctrine of government by consent of the governed, has become the bible of modern liberalism.

16 THE AGE OF REASON
1700–1789

The scientific discoveries and philosophic ideas that made the seventeenth century so intellectually exciting bore fruit in the eighteenth century, a period often referred to as the Age of Reason. The great revelations of the Scientific Revolution led thinkers in the 1700s to believe they were living in a time of illumination and enlightenment. Committed to scientific methodology, mathematical reasoning, and a healthy skepticism, they fervently believed their knowledge could lead to the improvement of both the individual and society.

The Age of Reason was marked by four different trends. The first was the growing concentration of political power in the great states, a process that had begun during the Baroque era. France was the most powerful state, followed by Great Britain (the new name of a unified England and Scotland), Prussia, Austria, Russia, and the Netherlands (Map 16.1). The second trend was the return of the aristocracy to prominence after a century or more of decline. In time, the ostentatious culture spawned by the resurgent aristocrats proved to be their swan song, as the French Revolution, at the end of the century, destroyed their bases of power (see Chapter 17). The third trend was the rise to political and cultural eminence of the middle class (Figure 16.1), who supported those progressive thinkers who advocated social equality, social justice, and a thorough revamping of society. The intellectual and cultural movement spawned by these thinkers is called the **Enlightenment,** which constitutes the fourth and most important trend that helped to reshape Western life in the 1700s.

At the same time that these political and social trends were occurring, a

◄ **Detail** JEAN-HONORÉ FRAGONARD. *The Lover Crowned*. 1771–1773. Oil on panel, 10′5⅛″ × 7′11¾″. The Frick Collection, New York.

French
Hohenzollerns
Hapsburgs
British
Russian
—— Boundary of the Holy Roman Empire

Figure 16.1   JEAN-BAPTISTE-SIMEON CHARDIN. *The Morning Toilette.* 1741. Oil on canvas, 19¼ × 15⅓″. Nationalmuseum, Stockholm. *Chardin's* The Morning Toilette *serves as a symbol of the middle class, whose rise to cultural prominence in the Age of Reason was a foretaste of their political power in the nineteenth century. The painting depicts a middle-class interior, as identified by the furniture, the toilet articles, and, most especially, the mother engaged in a task that a servant, in an aristocratic house, would have performed. More than a simple genre scene, the paint-ing also conveys a moral message that appealed to moralistic middle-class taste. In effect, Chardin warns of the vanity of women by showing the little girl, whose hair is being combed by her mother, turned so as to look at her reflection in the mirror.*

new style in art, architecture, and music was developing in France in reaction to the excesses of the Baroque. This style, known as Rococo, was more informal and graceful, less ponderous and oppressive than the Baroque. After about 1750, in reaction to both the Rococo and the Baroque, a very different style—the Neoclassical—developed. Unlike the Rococo, the Neoclassical style in art and architecture spread widely throughout Europe and the United States. In music, a refined and elegant Classical style developed, graced by the incomparable presence of Mozart, arguably the greatest musical genius who ever lived.

THE ENLIGHTENMENT

Eighteenth-century thinkers derived their ideals and goals from a variety of sources. Following the example of ancient Greece and Rome, they rejected superstition, sought truth through the use of reason, and viewed the world from a secular, human-centered perspective. Drawing on the Renaissance, they embraced humanism—the belief that a human being becomes a better person through the study and practice of literature, philosophy, music, and the arts. And from the seventeenth-century revolutions in science and philosophy, particularly the works of Newton, Bacon, Descartes, and Locke, they derived a reliance on rationalism, empiricism, skepticism, and the experimental method, along with a belief in human perfectibility through education and unlimited progress.

Despite the power of these ideas, they reached a relatively small percentage of Europe's population. The Enlightenment had its greatest effect in the cultural capitals of France and Great Britain—Paris, London, and Edinburgh. Many aristocrats read the works of Enlightenment writers, as did many members of the middle class, particularly educators, lawyers, journalists, and clergymen. Ultimately, enough literate and influential people were converted to the goals of the Enlightenment to have an effect on the revolutionary events that occurred later in the eighteenth century (Timeline 16.1).

The *Philosophes* and Their Program

The central figures of the Enlightenment were a small band of writers known as **philosophes,** the French word for "philosophers." Not philosophers in a formal sense, the *philosophes* were more likely to be popularizers who wanted to influence public opinion. They avoided the methods of academic scholars, such as engaging in philosophical debates or writing only for colleagues, and tried to reach large audiences through novels, essays, pamphlets, plays, poems, and histories. In this they were following the lead of Fontenelle, who had popularized the new astronomy in his *Conversations on the Plurality of Worlds* (see Chapter 15). When possible, they openly attacked what they deemed to be the evils of society and supported those rulers who favored change, the so-called enlightened despots. When the censors threatened, however, they disguised their radical messages or else published their criticisms in the Netherlands—the most liberal state in Europe at the time.

The Enlightenment was essentially a product of French cultural life, and Paris was its capital. The principal *philosophes* were Voltaire, Diderot, Montesquieu—all French—and by adoption the French-speaking Swiss writer Rousseau. But major *philosophes* appeared elsewhere in Europe, in Great Britain, and in Britain's North American colonies. The most influential of these voices were the English historian Edward Gibbon, the

Timeline 16.1   THE AGE OF REASON

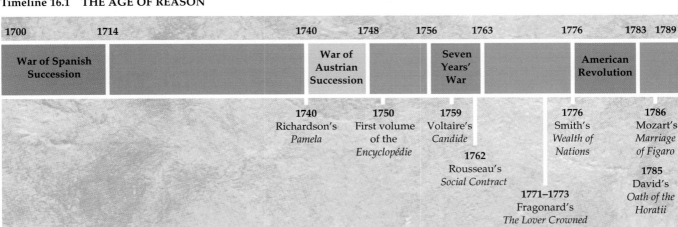

American writer Benjamin Franklin, and two Scottish thinkers, the economist Adam Smith and the philosopher David Hume.

The *philosophes,* though never in complete agreement and often diametrically opposed, shared certain assumptions. They had full confidence in reason; they were convinced that nature was orderly and fundamentally good and could be understood through the empirical method; they believed that change and progress would improve society, since human beings were perfectible. Faith in reason led them to reject religious doctrine, in particular Roman Catholic dogma; to denounce bigotry and intolerance; and to advocate freedom of religious choice. Maintaining that education liberated humanity from ignorance and superstition, the *philosophes* called for an expanded educational system independent of ecclesiastical control.

The *philosophes* thought that the political, economic, and religious institutions should be reformed to bring "the greatest happiness for the greatest numbers"—a phrase that expresses a key Enlightenment ideal and that, in the nineteenth century, became the battle cry of the English thinker and reformer Jeremy Bentham (see Chapter 18). These theorists anticipated a general overhaul of society, leading to universal peace and a golden age for humanity. In effect, they preached a secular gospel that happiness need not be delayed until after death but could be enjoyed here on earth.

Envisioning a rejuvenated society that guaranteed natural rights to its citizens, the *philosophes* were almost unanimous in thinking exclusively in terms of men and not of women. They still considered women their intellectual and physical inferiors and thus in need of male protection or guidance. Not until the next period were voices raised on behalf of women's rights and only then under the inspiration of the French Revolution.

One of those moved by the revolutionary winds blowing from France was the English writer Mary Wollstonecraft (1759–1797), who, in *A Vindication of the Rights of Woman* (1792), used Enlightenment ideals to urge the liberation of her own sex. Like Rousseau, Wollstonecraft was a democrat and opposed to hierarchy in all forms: in the aristocracy, the military, and the clergy to the extent that promotion was based on obsequiousness. Unlike Rousseau, she was dedicated to the rights of women, whom she repeatedly called "one-half of the human race." Rejecting the "Adam's rib" explanation of woman's inferiority as being simply a male fabrication, she claimed that women were as rational as men and thus should be treated the same. The heart of this latter-day *philosophe*'s argument was that women should abandon feminine artifice and cunning, especially the all-consuming need to be socially pleasing, and through education become equal partners with educated men. Starting in the nineteenth century, reformers gradually began to take up Wollstonecraft's challenge, particularly her call for female education and women's suffrage.

Deism

Newtonian science implied that God had set the universe in motion and then left it to run by its own natural laws. The *philosophes* accepted this metaphor of God as a clockmaker, and in place of traditional Christianity some thinkers now offered a version of Christianity called **Deism.** Deists focused on the worship of a Supreme Being, a God who created the universe and set the laws of nature in motion but who never again interfered in natural or human matters. Believing in this idea of a clockmaker God, the Deists rejected the efficacy of prayer and reduced the role of Jesus from that of savior to that of a good moral example.

Deism was espoused by only a relatively small percentage of Westerners, however, such as Benjamin Franklin in the British colony of Pennsylvania. Religions that ran counter to the Enlightenment's ideas—including the new sect of Methodists founded by John Wesley (1703–1791) in England—continued to attract most of the populace. Although it did not find wide acceptance, Deism's appeal marked another shift in religious attitudes and was added evidence of the growing secularization of European consciousness in the 1700s.

The *Encyclopédie*

The message of the *philosophes* was communicated by a variety of means: through pamphlets, essays, and books, through private and public discussions and debates, through the new journalistic press, and, especially in France, through the salon—the half-social, half-serious gatherings where the fashionable elite met to discuss ideas. But the principal work of the *philosophes* was the *Encyclopédie*—the monumental project that remains the summation of the Enlightenment. Two earlier works, Chambers's *Cyclopedia* in England (1728) and Bayle's *Dictionary* in France (1697) (see Chapter 15), paved the way for the *Encyclopédie.* Begun in 1750 and completed in 1772, the original work comprised seventeen text volumes and eleven books of plates and illustrations (Figure 16.2). More than 161 writers wrote articles for this educational venture, which was intended as a summary of existing knowledge in the arts, crafts, and sciences.

The editor of the *Encyclopédie* was Denis Diderot [DEED-uh-roh] (1713–1784), one of the giants of the

Figure 16.2 Illustration from the *Encyclopédie: Cotton Plantation in the French West Indies. 1751–1765. As principal editor of the* Encyclopédie, *Diderot adopted Francis Bacon's notion that all knowledge is useful. Thus, the articles and the illustrations for this reference work focused on practical data such as soapmaking, human anatomy, and military drill. In this drawing, for example, the readers could peruse the romanticized plantation scene to discover how raw cotton was prepared for shipment to European mills.*

Enlightenment. Diderot was constantly in trouble with the authorities because of the work's controversial essays, which he asserted were meant "to change the general way of thinking." Publication was halted in 1759 by the state censor but resumed secretly with the collusion of other government officials. Unlike most publications of the period, the project was funded by its readers, not by the crown or the church, and private circulating libraries rented the volumes to untold numbers of customers.

The Physiocrats

Under the broad umbrella of Enlightenment ideas, the *philosophes* were joined by a group of French writers concerned with economic matters—the **Physiocrats,** as they called themselves. (The term is a coined word, from Greek, meaning "rule of, or from, the earth.") The Physiocrats examined the general nature of the economy and, in particular, the strengths and weaknesses of mercantilism, the prevailing economic system, in which the state regulated trade and production for its own benefit. In their eyes, this state-run system had hindered the growth of the economies of the various European countries. Contrary to its goals, mercantilism had lowered the productivity of workers, especially farmers, and had led to labor unrest and riots.

Guided by Enlightenment doctrine that "natural laws" governed society, the Physiocrats assumed that similar "laws" applied to economic growth and decline. After a thorough analysis of the French economy, they concluded that certain fundamental economic principles did exist, such as the law of supply and demand, and that these laws operated best when free from governmental interference. Accordingly, they rec-

ommended the dismantling of mercantilism and the adoption of *laissez faire*, French for "to let alone"—in other words, an economy where the self-regulating laws of free trade were in effect. In addition, they argued that unrestricted enjoyment of private property was necessary for individual freedom. These French thinkers concluded that both the individual and the entire society automatically benefited when all people were allowed to serve their own self-interest instead of working for the good of the state.

At about the same time, the Scottish economist Adam Smith (1723–1790) was developing similar ideas. He reported his conclusions in *An Inquiry into the Nature and Causes of the Wealth of Nations* (1776), a book that became the bible of industrial capitalism for the next two centuries. In this work, Smith blamed mercantilism for the economic woes of his time, identified the central role played by labor in manufacturing, and called for open and competitive trade so that the "invisible hand" of a free-market economy could operate. Smith's ideas were quickly absorbed by budding entrepreneurs and had an immediate impact on the changes being generated by the Industrial Revolution (see Chapter 17).

THE GREAT POWERS DURING THE AGE OF REASON

In comparison with the seventeenth century, the period between 1715 and 1789 was relatively peaceful; national conflicts were few and brief. In addition, Europe experienced a slow but steady economic expansion that was supported by a continuing increase in population. The prosperity fueled the rise of the middle classes, especially in Great Britain and Holland. In

Figure 16.3 François de Cuvilliés. Hall of Mirrors, Amalienburg. 1734–1739. Munich. *Despite the growth of the middle class in the 1700s, the aristocracy still dictated styles in the arts. Inspired by the Hall of Mirrors at Versailles, this room in a hunting lodge built for the elector of Bavaria reflects the delicate Rococo sensibility that typified aristocratic European taste in the first half of the eighteenth century. Specific Rococo elements in this room are the ornate molding that separates the walls from the ceiling, the fanciful* rocaille *framing the windows and mirrors, and the oval shape of the room itself.*

France, however, the middle class made only modest gains, and in central and eastern Europe they were a small fraction of the population.

Society: Continuity and Change

A major consequence of the century's modest economic growth was the growing urbanization of society. Although most Europeans still followed traditional livelihoods on farms and in villages, cities and towns offered increasing opportunities for ambitious folk. The rural-to-urban shift originated in England, the home of the Industrial Revolution, and to a lesser extent in France. Only in the next century did it slowly spread to some parts of central and eastern Europe.

The traditional social hierarchy kept each class in its place. The aristocracy constituted only about 3 percent of the total population, but it possessed tremendous power and wealth (Figure 16.3). The upper middle class—encompassing rich merchants, bankers, and professionals—normally resided in the rapidly ex-

panding urban areas and influenced business and governmental affairs. In the broad middle class were the smaller merchants, shopkeepers, skilled artisans, and bureaucrats. Beneath the middle ranks were the lesser artisans and craftspeople, and below them, the metropolitan poor, who performed menial labor and were often unemployed.

In the countryside, the nobility and the prosperous farmers owned large sections of the land and controlled the rural populace. The small cultivators, tenant farmers, landless workers, and indentured contract laborers constituted a complex group whose legal, social, and personal rights varied widely across Europe. Next were the peasants, whose status ranged from freedom in western Europe to serfdom in Russia. (Serfs were bound to the land they worked, but they had customary rights, and strictly speaking they were not slaves.) These impoverished people often bore the brunt of the taxes and the contempt of the other classes.

With few exceptions, such as the upper-middle-class women who played influential roles in the salons, women remained subordinate to men. As mentioned earlier, the *philosophes*, who thoroughly critiqued society, failed to recognize women's contributions or champion their rights. Even Jean-Jacques Rousseau, who was often at odds with his fellow writers, agreed with the *philosophes* that women were inferior to men and should be submissive to them.

Another group who gained little from the Enlightenment were the African slaves in Europe's overseas colonies. During the eighteenth century, ships from England, France, and Holland carried about six million Africans to enslavement in the New World. Efforts to abolish the slave trade or even to improve the conditions of the slaves proved futile despite the moral disapproval of the *philosophes* and the pleas of English Christians.

Absolutism, Limited Monarchy, and Enlightened Despotism

The eighteenth century was the last great age of kings in the West. In most countries, the royal rulers followed traditional policies even in the face of criticism or opposition. Supported by inefficient bureaucracies and costly armies, they controlled the masses through heavy taxes and threats of brutality while holding in check the privileged groups. Although a few rulers attempted reforms, by the end of the century most of the monarchies were weakening as democratic sentiments continued to rise.

In France, the kings struggled to hold on to the power they inherited from Louis XIV. In Great Britain, the kings fought a losing battle against Parliament and the restrictions of constitutional monarchy. In Prussia and Austria, so-called enlightened despots experimented with reforms to strengthen their states, while in Russia the czars found new ways to expand absolutism. By midcentury, the Continent had undergone a series of brief wars that ended the several relatively peaceful decades Europe had enjoyed (see Timeline 16.1). For France and England, the Continental conflicts soon escalated into global commercial, territorial, and colonial rivalries that were resolved only with the outcome of the American Revolutionary War (1775–1783).

France: The Successors to the Sun King No French ruler was able to recapture the splendor of Louis XIV. Louis XV (r. 1715–1774), who succeeded to full political control at age thirteen and never acquired a strong will to rule, only compounded the problems of the French state. Those he chose as his subordinates were not always talented or loyal, and he permitted his mistresses, who were not trained in government, to influence his decisions about official matters. When Louis

XV, despairing over a military defeat, expressed his misgivings about the future of France to his royal favorite, Madame de Pompadour, she reportedly replied with the prophetic words, *"Après nous le déluge"* ("After us, the flood").

Life at Louis XV's court could not be sustained in the grand manner of the late Sun King, and the nobles began to leave Versailles for Paris. Whether at Versailles or elsewhere, educated aristocrats were becoming fascinated by Enlightenment ideas, and they and their wives read the *Encyclopédie* and studied the writings of the *philosophes*. Upper-class women played influential roles in presiding over salons, where the enlightened thinkers and their admirers gathered to dine and converse. Two of the most well known salons were conducted by Madame du Deffand [day-FAHN] (1679–1780) and Julie Lespinasse [les-pee-NAHS] (1732–1776). For a number of years, Madame du Deffand (Marie de Marquise du Deffand) claimed Voltaire as her most prominent literary celebrity, and his presence ensured that other *philosophes* would attend her gatherings. Julie de Lespinasse, serving first as companion to Madame du Deffand, broke away to found her own salon, where Jean d'Alembert, coeditor of Diderot's *Encyclopédie*, was a favored guest.

Even though the French elite debated the merits of reform and the more controversial topics raised by the *philosophes*, Louis XV clearly did not accept the movement's call for change. It is ironic that the country where the Enlightenment began failed to undertake any of its progressive reforms. Indeed, when changes were finally introduced under Louis XVI (r. 1774–1792), they were too little and too late.

Handicapped by the weak Louis XVI, France found its preeminent position in foreign affairs challenged by Great Britain, Austria, and Prussia. As a result of the Seven Years' War, which began in 1756, France suffered defeats in Europe and lost its holdings in North America and India. During the American Revolution, France sided with the colonists against Great Britain, its foe at home and overseas. France's aid to the Americans further diminished the government's financial resources and forced the nation deeper into debt.

France's kings also failed to solve the nation's domestic problems, the consequence of their own failures of leadership and that of the royal officials called *intendants*, who were supposed to coordinate the loose federation of provinces into a functioning French state. Meanwhile, the tax collectors failed to provide adequate revenues for the state because of the corrupt tax system. And, most important, the crown was faced with a resurgent aristocracy determined to recover the feudal privileges it had lost under Louis XIV. Rather than joining the king's efforts to reform the judicial system, the nobility blocked the crown at every step.

The middle class combined forces with some sympathetic aristocrats, transforming what had been a feudal issue into a struggle for freedom in the name of the people. In 1789, during the reign of Louis XVI, France started on a revolutionary course that united most of French society against the crown and that culminated in the French Revolution (1789–1799) (see Chapter 17).

Great Britain and the Hanoverian Kings To the *philosophes,* Great Britain was the ideal model of a nation. To them, Britain seemed more stable and prosperous than the states on the Continent, a success they attributed to the limited powers of the English monarchy imposed by Parliament during the Glorious Revolution of 1688. Britain's laws guaranteed to every Englishman certain political and social rights, such as free speech and fair and speedy trials. Britain's economy was strong as well. Prompted by enterprising merchants and progressive landowners, the nation was dominant in an expanding global market; at home, the standard of living was rising for the growing population.

After the death of Queen Anne in 1714, the English crown was inherited by George I, a great-grandson of James I and the Protestant ruler of the German principality of Hanover. The first two Hanoverian kings seemed more interested in events in Germany than in England, leading to a decline in their powers, and eventually the kings reigned in splendid isolation at the royal court. George I (r. 1714–1727) allowed Parliament to run the country. Under George II (r. 1727–1760), Britain was drawn into the Seven Years' War but emerged victorious, the dominant presence in world trade. From this pinnacle of international power, Great Britain occupied center stage until the outbreak of World War I in 1914.

Nevertheless, Great Britain faced serious domestic problems under George III (r. 1760–1820) because he sought to restore royal powers lost to Parliament by his predecessors. This internal struggle affected foreign policy when the king and Parliament offered differing proposals to control the economic development of the American colonies through export and import quotas, duties, and taxes. The differences between the two proposals hastened the onset of the American Revolution and probably contributed to Britain's eventual defeat.

Enlightened Despotism in Central and Eastern Europe
The system of European states underwent some modifications during the Age of Reason. Great Britain and France now dominated western Europe; the less populous countries of Holland and Sweden declined in power; Spain turned increasingly inward and all but disappeared from Continental affairs; and Italy, under Austrian and papal control, remained an economic backwater. Meanwhile, Prussia, Austria, and Russia jockeyed for control of central and eastern Europe. Under their absolutist rulers, these states pursued aggressive policies, seizing territories from one another and their weaker neighbors. Although these rulers portrayed themselves as enlightened despots, their regimes were generally characterized by oppressive and authoritarian policies.

By 1740 Prussia had a solid economic base, a hardworking bureaucracy, and an efficient army. Capitalizing on these advantages, Frederick II, known as Frederick the Great (r. 1740–1786), turned Prussia into a leading European power. A pragmatic diplomat, a skilled military tactician, and a student of the Enlightenment and French culture, Frederick was an enlightened despot of the type beloved by the *philosophes.* He even attempted (though failed) to reform his state's agrarian economy and social system in accordance with the rational principle that all individuals have the natural right to choose personally the best way to live.

Prussia's chief rival in central Europe was Austria. Throughout the 1700s, Austria's rulers struggled to govern a multiethnic population that included large numbers of Germans, Hungarians, Czechs, and Slovaks along with Poles, Italians, and various Slavic minorities. At the same time, the emperors tried, with mixed success, to assert Austria's role as a great power, both politically and culturally. Schönbrunn Palace in Vienna, for example, was built as a rival to France's Versailles (Figure 16.4). Two rulers stand out—the Hapsburg emperors Maria Theresa and Joseph, her son, whose combined reigns lasted from 1740 to 1790.

Unlike Frederick II of Prussia, Maria Theresa (r. 1740–1780) was not attracted to the ideas of the *philosophes.* More important was her Roman Catholic faith, which led her to portray herself to her subjects as their universal mother. She was perhaps the most beloved monarch in this age of kings. Maria Theresa's reforming zeal sprang not from philosophic principle but from a reaction against Austria's territorial losses during military defeats. She used all her royal prerogatives to overhaul the political and military machinery of the state. Along with universal military conscription, increased revenues, and more equitable distribution of taxes, she wanted a general reorganization of society that gave more uniform treatment to all citizens. Her efforts were not wasted, for her son Joseph II took up her uncompleted task and became the ultimate personification of enlightened despotism.

During his brief reign, from 1780 to 1790, Joseph II launched far-reaching changes to raise farm production and to provide more economic opportunities for the peasants. Convinced that his country's economic and social institutions had to be fully modernized if it was to survive, he abolished serfdom and passed decrees guaranteeing religious toleration and free speech. In the 1790s much of what he had accomplished was

Figure 16.4 JOHANN FERDINAND HETZENDORF VON HOHENBERG. Gloriette, or "The Temple of Fame." Schönbrunn Palace Gardens. 1768. Vienna. *The Gloriette, a triumphal arch flanked by colonnaded screens, is situated on the highest point within the vast gardens of Schönbrunn Palace. Designed by Johann Ferdinand Hetzendorf von Hohenberg (1732–1816), court architect to Empress Maria Theresa, it is the crowning touch of his beautification campaign for the palace grounds. It functioned as a theatrical backdrop for court rituals and receptions. Constructed partly from the ruins of a castle near the site, the Gloriette uses Classical features (colonnades, balustrades, and statuary and urns) though its style is Baroque (profuse decorative details and the reflecting pool).*

undone by his successors, who, fearing the excesses of the French Revolution, restored aristocratic and ecclesiastic control and privileges.

Russia was the newest member of the family of great powers, having achieved this stature during the reign of Peter the Great (r. 1682–1725). Abroad, Peter had made Russia's presence known, and at home he had begun to reform political, economic, and social institutions along Western lines. Most of his eighteenth-century successors were ineffective, if not incompetent, until Catherine the Great (r. 1762–1796) became empress. She pursued the unifying policies of Peter, but unlike him she was able to win the powerful support of the large landowners. A patron of the Enlightenment, Catherine sought the advice of a few *philosophes*, including Diderot. She also attempted to improve the low farm productivity and the nearly enslaved condition of the peasants, but the vastness of Russia's problems and the reactionary autocratic government defeated any genuine reforms.

CULTURAL TRENDS IN THE EIGHTEENTH CENTURY: FROM ROCOCO TO NEOCLASSICAL

Even though the eighteenth century was dominated by the Enlightenment, other cultural trends also held sway. The Rococo style in the arts mirrored the taste of the French nobility; the succeeding Neoclassical style was adopted and supported by the progressive writers, artists, intellectuals, and ambitious members of the middle class. Meanwhile, innovations in literature were pointing the way toward the modern world.

The Rococo Style in the Arts

Conceived on a more intimate scale than the Baroque and committed to frivolous subjects and themes, the **Rococo** style arose in France in the waning years of the Sun King's reign. With his death in 1715 and the succession of his five-year-old heir, Louis XV, the nobility were released both from Versailles and from the ponderous Baroque style. Paris once again became the capital of art, ideas, and fashion in the Western world. There, the Rococo style was created for the French elite almost single-handedly by the Flemish painter and decorator Jean-Antoine Watteau.

The Rococo gradually spread to most of Europe, but its acceptance was tied to religion and class. It was embraced by the aristocracy in Germany, Italy, and Austria; Roman Catholic nobles in Austria developed a version of Rococo that was second in importance only to that of France. The English, on the other hand, rejected the Rococo, possibly because its erotic undercurrent and sexual themes offended the Protestant middle-class sensibility. Consequently, Rococo style is a purely Continental phenomenon; there is no English Rococo.

Rococo Painting Jean-Antoine Watteau [wah-TOE] (1684–1721) specialized in paintings that depict *fêtes galantes,* or aristocratic entertainments. In these works, Watteau portrays the intimate world of the aristocracy, dressed in sumptuous clothing, grouped in parks and gardens, and often accompanied by costumed actors, another of Watteau's favorite subjects. He filled these bucolic settings with air and lightness and grace —all of which were a contrast to the occasionally

Figure 16.5 Jean-Antoine Watteau. *Departure from Cythera.* 1717. Oil on canvas, 4′3″ × 6′4½″. Louvre. *Watteau's aristocratic lovers, savoring a last few moments of pleasure, represent the idealized image that the eighteenth-century elite wanted to present to the world. No hint of the age's problems is allowed to disturb this idyllic scene. From the court costumes to the hovering cupids, this painting transforms reality into a stage set—the ideal of Rococo art.*

heavy-handed Baroque. Mythological allusions made Watteau's works depictions of Classical themes rather than merely scenes of aristocratic life.

In 1717 Watteau became the first Rococo painter to be elected to membership in the Royal Academy of Painting and Sculpture in Paris. As required by the terms of election, he submitted as his diploma piece *Departure from Cythera* (Figure 16.5). The setting is Cythera, the legendary island of Venus, whose bust on the right is garlanded with her devotees' roses. Forming a wavering line, the lovers express hesitation as they make their farewells: The couple under the statue are lost in reverie as a clothed cupid tugs at the woman's skirt; beside this group a suitor assists his lady to her feet; and next to them a gentleman accompanies his companion to the waiting boat as she longingly gazes backward. This melancholy scene, signified by the setting sun and the departing lovers, represents Watteau's homage to the brevity of human passion.

In *Departure from Cythera,* many of the new values of the Rococo style can be seen. Where the Baroque favored tumultuous scenes depicting the passions and ecstasies of the saints, the Rococo focused on smaller, gentler moments, usually involving love of one variety or another, whether erotic, romantic, or sentimental. Where the Baroque used intense colors to convey feelings of power and grandeur, the Rococo used soft pastels to evoke nostalgia and melancholy. The monumentality and sweeping movement of Baroque art were brought down to a human scale in the Rococo, making it more suited to interiors, furniture, and architectural details than to architecture itself. *Departure from Cythera* shows the Rococo to be a refined, sensual style, perfect for providing a charming backdrop to the private social life of the eighteenth-century aristocracy.

In one of his last works, *The Sign for Gersaint's Shop,* Watteau removed all mythological and idyllic references (Figure 16.6). His subject, a shop where paintings are sold (François-Edmé Gersaint [1696–1750] was one of the outstanding art dealers of the eighteenth century), indicates the importance of the new commercial art market that was soon to replace the aristocratic patronage system. Within the store's interior, elegantly dressed customers browse, flirt, and study the shopkeeper's wares. The sexual motifs in the pictures on the walls and in the oval canvas on the right reinforce the sensuous atmosphere of this painting. But Watteau also makes this Parisian scene dignified by giving

Figure 16.6 JEAN-ANTOINE WATTEAU. *The Sign for Gersaint's Shop.* Ca. 1720. Oil on canvas, 5′11⅝″ × 10′1⅛″. Schloss Charlottenburg, Berlin. *This painting of a shop interior illustrates the social dynamics of the emerging art market in the eighteenth century. The aristocratic customers act as if they own the place, turning it into a genteel lounge. The shop employees, on the other hand, have clearly inferior social roles; one brings forward a heavy painting for inspection, another holds a miniature work up to view, and a third stands downcast at the left. Through such details, Watteau reveals the social gulf between classes that was implicit in the Rococo style.*

equal focus to the human figures and the role each plays in the overall composition.

Watteau's painting is a telling metaphor of the end of an age and the beginning of another. This meaning can be interpreted in the crating of the portrait of Louis XIV (on the left), a punning metaphor for the demise of the old political order and the style of Louis XIV. Art collecting in the age of Louis XIV had been restricted largely to kings, princes, and nobles, but in the Rococo period, many new collectors came from the world of the upper bourgeoisie and shopped in commercial galleries like Gersaint's shop.

Watteau's paintings convey a dreamy eroticism, but those of François Boucher [boo-SHAY] (1703–1770) are characterized by unabashed sexuality. Boucher was the supreme exponent of the graceful Louis XV style, becoming official painter to the French crown in 1765. His voluptuous nudes, which were made more titillating by their realistic portrayal without Classical trappings, appealed to the king and to the decadent court nobility. Boucher's *Nude on a Sofa* is probably a study of one of Louis XV's mistresses (Figure 16.7). The casually suggestive pose, the rumpled bedclothes, and the delicate pastel shades are all designed to charm and to seduce. Boucher's art, though masterful, epito-

mizes the lax morals of French noble life that were becoming increasingly offensive even to other Rococo artists.

A different focus is evident in the Rococo portraits of Elisabeth-Louise Vigée-Lebrun [vee-ZHAY-luh-BRUHN] (1755–1842), who became the leading society painter of the later eighteenth century and one of the relatively few women to gain independent fame as an artist. In 1787 she painted a famous family portrait of Louis XVI's queen, Marie Antoinette, whom she served as court painter (Figure 16.8). With this work, Vigée-Lebrun solidified her status as the equal of the best court portraitists of the century. Elements of the Rococo style can be seen in this elegant portrait of the queen and her children in the dainty colors, the graceful gestures, and the feeling of domestic intimacy. The queen's role as mother is the focus as she sits with the baby Duke of Normandy in her lap, the small Madame Royale at her side, and the little Dauphin pointing at the empty cradle. Vigée-Lebrun's depiction of Marie Antoinette dressed as a lady of fashion instead of in the traditional trappings of royalty reflects the queen's well-known fondness for simplicity. Stifled by the formality of court life, the queen promoted a more relaxed social code at Le Hameau, a rustic hideaway

Figure 16.7 FRANÇOIS BOUCHER. *Nude on a Sofa.* 1752. Oil on canvas, 23⅜ × 25⅜". Alte Pinakothek, Munich. *The trend toward the secularization of consciousness that had been building since the Late Middle Ages reached a high point in this nude by Boucher. Boucher's frank enjoyment of sensual pleasure and his desire to convey that feeling to the viewer represented a new stage in the relationship between artists and the public. By portraying his subject without any justification except eroticism, Boucher embodied a new artistic sensibility.*

Figure 16.8 ELISABETH-LOUISE VIGÉE-LEBRUN. *Marie Antoinette and Her Children.* 1787. Oil on canvas, 9'¼" × 7'⅝". Musée National du Château de Versailles. *Like the greatest court painters, Vigée-Lebrun is able to provide psychological insight into her highborn subjects while flattering them. Here, Marie Antoinette, though surrounded by adoring children, seems uncomfortable in a maternal role. Instead, with her head held in an imperious manner and her face a beautiful mask, she looks every inch the lady of fashion, which she indeed was. Vigée-Lebrun has muted this psychological insight by providing rich distractions for the viewer's eye, such as the shiny surfaces of the queen's attire (satin gown, pearls, and hat) and the elegant room (carpet, chest, and tasseled cushion).*

she had built for herself at Versailles, where all rules of court etiquette were set aside.

The last great French Rococo painter, Jean-Honoré Fragonard [frag-uh-NAHR] (1732–1806), revived Watteau's graceful, debonair themes, as in *The Lover Crowned* (Figure 16.9). A young woman crowns her kneeling lover with a wreath of flowers, while an artist in the lower right corner sketches the enraptured pair. The man's red suit and the woman's yellow dress cause them to stand out dramatically from the setting in which they are placed. The terrace setting is rich in sensual, if not erotic, details, including rose blossoms, boxed orange trees, two guitars, and sheet music. The statue of a sleeping cupid, mounted on a pedestal, presides over this erotic episode.

What is fresh in Fragonard's art and prefigures Romanticism is his finely detailed treatment of the natural background, which, although resembling the idealized backgrounds of Watteau, has a vivid, luxuriant life of its own. In Fragonard's painting, nature seems almost to threaten the couple's romantic idyll. Despite his interest in landscape, however, Fragonard remained faithful to the Rococo style even after it fell out of fashion. His paintings continued to focus on the playful themes of flirtation and pursuit in a frivolous, timeless world.

Rococo Interiors The decorative refinement and graceful detail of the Rococo style made it well suited to interior design. A major Rococo design element was *rocaille:* fanciful stucco ornaments in the shape of ribbons, leaves, stems, flowers, interlaces, arabesques, and elongated, curving lines applied to walls and ceilings. The effect of *rocaille* was to make solid surfaces look more like fleeting illusions (see Figure 16.3). Mirrors further deceived the senses, and chandeliers provided jewel-like lighting; all elements worked together to create a glittering, luxurious setting for an ultra-refined society.

Germain Boffrand [bo-FRAHN] (1667–1754), France's royal architect, helped to establish Rococo's popularity with his "Salon de la Princesse" in the Hôtel de Soubise in Paris (Figure 16.10). Exploiting the room's oval shape, Boffrand eliminated the shadows and omitted Classical details such as pilasters and columns, which had been elements of decoration since the Renaissance. The floor-to-ceiling windows admit light freely, and the strategically placed mirrors reinforce the airy feeling. Instead of using a large overhead fresco, Boffrand divided the ceiling into many panel pictures. The characteristically nervous Rococo line—seen in the intricate designs of the gold edging—integrates the interior into a harmonious whole. The overall effect of airiness, radiance, and grace is worthy of a Watteau setting of aristocratic revelry.

Figure 16.9 JEAN-HONORÉ FRAGONARD. *The Lover Crowned.* 1771–1773. Oil on panel, 10′5⅛″ × 7′11¾″. The Frick Collection, New York. *This painting was one of a series of four panels known as* The Progress of Love, *commissioned by Madame du Barry, Louis XV's mistress and rival to Madame de Pompadour. Intended to adorn a pavilion nicknamed the "sanctuary of pleasure" at her palace, the panels were rejected by Madame du Barry, for reasons unknown, before they were installed. Like the other panels in this series,* The Lover Crowned *is a symbolic allegory. In effect, the couple's love has been consummated, as symbolized by the floral wreath and the sleeping cupid. All that remains is for the artist, a reference to Fragonard himself, to transform the lover's passion into a work of art.*

German decoration followed the French lead. The Residenz, a palace commissioned by the prince-bishop of the German city of Würzburg, is an example of Baroque architecture with Rococo interiors. Designed chiefly by Balthasar Neumann [NOI-mahn] (1687–1753), the building's glory is the main reception room, called the Kaisersaal, or Emperor's Room (Figure 16.11). The ceiling frescoes are by Giovanni Battista Tiepolo [tee-AY-puh-loh] (1696–1770), an Italian-born Rococo master. His paintings combine the theatricality of the Italian Florid Baroque and the love of light and color characteristic of Rubens and the Flemish school. But Tiepolo's frescoes are only one facet of the riotous splendor of this room, which abounds in crystal chandeliers, gilt ornamentation, marble statues, Corinthian

Figure 16.10 GERMAIN BOFFRAND. Salon de la Princesse, Hôtel de Soubise. Ca. 1735–1740. Paris. *The Salon de la Princesse was a reception room designed for the apartment of the Princess de Soubise. The graceful undulations of Boffrand's design represent the exquisite style of the Louis XV era. A typical Rococo design element is the blurring of the line between the walls and the ceiling.*

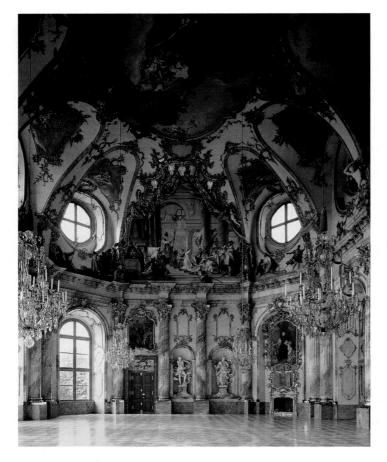

Figure 16.11 BALTHASAR NEUMANN AND OTHERS. Kaisersaal, the Residenz. View toward the south wall. 1719–1744. Würzburg, Germany. *In this magnificent room, the ceiling fresco by Tiepolo is gorgeously framed with multicolored marble curtains pulled back by stucco angels. Other sumptuous details include ornate framed paintings, cartouches, and mirrors; gilded Corinthian capitals and arabesques; and crystal chandeliers suspended low over a polychrome marble floor.*

capitals and arabesques, gold-edged mirrors, and cartouches, or scroll-like frames. In rooms such as this, the age's painters and decorators catered to their patrons' wildest dreams of grandeur.

The English Response   In Great Britain, where the Rococo was condemned as tasteless and corrupt, the painter William Hogarth (1697–1764) won fame as a social satirist, working in a style quite different from that of his French contemporaries. Even though his mocking works appealed to all social groups, the Protestant middle class most enthusiastically welcomed his biting satires. In the paintings, which sometimes ridicule idle aristocrats and always take a moralistic view of life, his bourgeois admirers discovered the same values that caused them to embrace the English novel. Taking advantage of his popularity, Hogarth made engravings of his paintings, printing multiple copies—the first major artist to take this step to reach a new clientele.

Figure 16.12 WILLIAM HOGARTH. *The Countess' Levée,* or *Morning Party,* from *Marriage à la Mode.* 1743–1745. Oil on canvas, 27 × 35″. Reproduced by courtesy of the Trustees, The National Gallery, London. *Hogarth's painterly techniques—learned in France—have transformed a potentially banal topic into a glittering social satire. On the left, a pig-snouted singer is used to ridicule the popular* castrati—*men who were emasculated as youths to preserve their boyish tenor voices. Hovering over the* castrato *is a flutist—his coarse features demonstrating the artist's loathing for this social type. Other rich details, such as the tea-sipping dandy in hair curlers and the female guest who is gesticulating wildly, confirm Hogarth's contempt for the entire gathering.*

Among the most popular of Hogarth's moral works was the series of paintings that depict the course of a loveless marriage between a profligate nobleman and the daughter of a wealthy middle-class businessman. Entitled *Marriage à la Mode,* this series comprises six scenes that show in exquisite detail the bitter consequences of an arranged marriage by following the husband and the wife to their untimely deaths. By the fourth episode, called *The Countess' Levée,* or *Morning Party,* Hogarth portrays the wife plotting a rendezvous with a potential lover (Figure 16.12). In this scene, which was typical of the age's aristocratic entertainments, the hostess is having her hair curled while the would-be suitor lounges on a sofa, charming her with conversation. Nearby, guests, servants, and musicians play their supporting roles in this sad tale. Hogarth, never willing to let the viewers draw their own conclusions, provides the moral lesson. In the right foreground, a black child-servant points to a small horned creature—a symbol of the cuckold, or the deceived husband—thus alluding to the wife's planned infidelity. Even the paintings on the walls echo Hogarth's theme of sexual abandon.

The Challenge of Neoclassicism

Soon after the middle of the eighteenth century, the Rococo began to be supplanted by a new style, known as **Neoclassical.** With its backward glance to the restrained style of antiquity, the Neoclassical had its origins both in a rejection of the Rococo and in a fascination with the new archeological discoveries made at mid-century. Excavations of Pompeii and Herculaneum—Roman cities buried by Mt. Vesuvius in A.D. 79 and only recently rediscovered—had greatly heightened the curiosity of educated Europeans about the ancient

world. At the same time, scholars began to publish books that showed Greek art to be the original source of ancient Classicism. The English authorities James Stuart and Nicholas Revett pointed out the differences between Greek and Roman art in *The Antiquities of Athens,* published in 1762. In 1764 the German Johann Joachim Winckelmann (1717–1768) distinguished Greek sculpture from the Roman in his *History of Art*—a study that led to the founding of the academic discipline of art history. The importance of Neoclassicism is indicated by the decision made in 1775 by the Paris Salon—the biennial exhibition that introduced the latest paintings to the public—to rebuff works with Rococo subjects and to encourage those with Classical themes.

Neoclassical Painting   In 1775, the first year of Louis XVI's reign and the same year the Salon began to promote Neoclassicism, the king appointed Joseph-Marie Vien to head the *Académie de France* in Rome, a leading art school. A strict disciplinarian, Vien returned the study of art to the basics by instructing his students to focus on perspective, anatomy, and life drawing, efforts that resulted in the purified style of Jacques-Louis David [dah-VEED] (1748–1825), the principal exponent of the Neoclassical style.

David's response to a commission from Louis XVI for a historical painting was the *Oath of the Horatii,* a work that electrified the Salon of 1785 (Figure 16.13). Taking a page from the history of the early Roman republic, this painting depicts the Horatii brothers vowing to protect the state, even though their stand means killing a sister who loves one of Rome's enemies. The patriotic subject with its tension between civic duty and family loyalty appealed to the *philosophes,* who preferred Neoclassicism, with its implicitly revolutionary morality, to the Rococo, with its frivolous themes.

Figure 16.13 JACQUES-LOUIS DAVID. *The Oath of the Horatii*. 1784. Oil on canvas, 10′10″ × 14′. Louvre. *David achieved a Classical effect in his works by arranging the figures so they could be read from left to right as in a sculptural frieze and by giving them the idealized bodies of Classical art. He further enhanced the sense that his central figures had been sculptured instead of painted by omitting distracting details. The resulting stark images contrast sharply with Rococo paintings and their luxuriant backgrounds (see Figures 16.5 and 16.9).*

Figure 16.15 ROBERT ADAM. Kenwood House. Exterior, the north front. 1764. London. *Adam's restrained style in the late eighteenth century represented a strong reinfusion of Classical principles into the English tradition. His style, with its reliance on the Classical orders and principles of balance and proportion, appealed to all classes but especially to the sober-minded middle class.*

David's *Oath of the Horatii* established the techniques and ideals that soon became typical of Neoclassical painting. His inspirational model was the seventeenth-century French artist Poussin, with his Classical themes and assured mastery of linear perspective. Rejecting the weightless, floating images of Rococo painting, David portrayed his figures as frozen sculptures, painted in strong colors. The Classical ideals of balance, simplicity, and restraint served as a basis for many of David's artistic choices.

David showed his mastery of these techniques and ideals in *The Death of Socrates*, which was exhibited in the Salon of 1787 (Figure 16.14). Like Jesus in scenes of the Last Supper, Socrates is portrayed shortly before his death, encircled by those men who will later spread his message. Just as in the *Oath of the Horatii*, David's arrangement of the figures reflected the Classical ideal of balance. Surrounded by grieving followers, the white-haired Socrates reaches for the cup of poison and gestures toward his heavenly goal—serene in his willingness to die for intellectual freedom.

◀ **Figure 16.14** JACQUES-LOUIS DAVID. *The Death of Socrates.* 1787. Oil on canvas, 4′11″ × 6′6″. Metropolitan Museum of Art. Wolfe Fund, 1931. *Neoclassicism usually relied on ancient literature and traditions for inspiration, as in this painting by David. The scene is based on Plato's dialogue* Phaedo, *though David has chosen to depict Plato present (at the foot of the bed), unlike in the literary account. Two of the domestic details, the lamp and the bed, are modeled on artifacts uncovered at Pompeii. The shackles and cuffs under the bed refer to the fact that Socrates was in chains just before drinking the hemlock.*

Neoclassical Architecture No other painter could compare with David, but the Scotsman Robert Adam (1728–1792) developed a Neoclassical style in interior decor that was the reigning favorite from 1760 until 1800. Classicism had dominated British architecture since the 1600s, and Adam reinvigorated this tradition with forms and motifs gathered during his archeological investigations. Kenwood House in London shows his application of Roman design to the exterior of a domestic dwelling, combining Ionic columns, a running frieze, and a triangular pediment to form a graceful portico, or porch, in the manner of a Roman temple (Figure 16.15). In the library, Adam mixed Classical elements with the pastel colors of the Rococo to produce an eclectic harmony (Figure 16.16). To continue this theme, he borrowed from Roman buildings with his barrel-vaulted ceiling and adjoining apse.

French architects too began to embrace the Neoclassical style in the late 1700s. The leader of this movement was Jacques Germain Soufflot [soo-FLOH] (1713–1780), who designed buildings based on Roman temples. Soufflot's severe Neoclassicism is characterized by its reliance on architectural detail rather than on sculptural decoration. Avoiding Adam's occasional

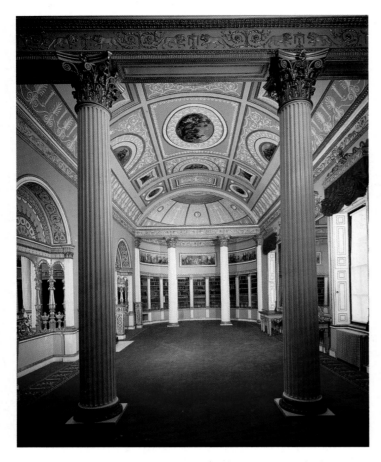

Figure 16.16 ROBERT ADAM. Library, Kenwood House. Begun in 1767. London. *Adam designed the library of Kenwood House with several basic elements of Classical architecture: columns, pilasters, and apses. By and large, he followed the Renaissance dictum of letting the architectural elements determine the chamber's decorative details. Nonetheless, he achieved a dazzling effect by his daring addition of mirrors and color.*

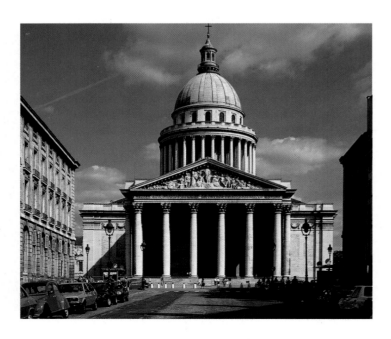

intermingling of Rococo and Classical effects, Soufflot preferred pure Roman forms. The most perfect expression of Soufflot's style is the Pantheon in Paris. Soufflot's Classical ideal is mirrored in the Pantheon's basic plan, with its enormous portico supported by huge Corinthian columns (Figure 16.17). Except for the statues in the pediment, the building's surface is almost devoid of sculptural detail. The only other decoration on the stark exterior is a frieze of stone garlands around the upper walls. For the dome, Soufflot found his inspiration not in Rome but in London—a sign that English architecture had come of age: The Pantheon's spectacular dome, with its surrounding Corinthian colonnade, is based on the dome of St. Paul's cathedral (see Figure 14.21).

Political Philosophy

Modern political theory continued to evolve after its founding in the seventeenth century. Absolutism, the reigning form of government in the eighteenth century, still had many staunch defenders. Voltaire, convinced that the people lacked political wisdom, advocated enlightened despotism. But the other leading *philosophes* of the Age of Reason rejected absolutism and supported alternative forms of government.

The Enlightenment's chief political theorists were Baron de Montesquieu and Jean-Jacques Rousseau, whose contrasting social origins probably to some extent account for their radically different definitions of the ideal state. Montesquieu, a titled Frenchman and a provincial judge, believed that rule by an enlightened aristocracy would ensure justice and tranquility. Rousseau, an impoverished citizen of the Swiss city-state of Geneva, advocated a kind of pure democracy. Rousseau's ideas about who should control the state were more far-reaching and revolutionary than Montesquieu's.

Montesquieu [mahnt-us-KYOO] (1689–1755) most persuasively expressed his political ideas in *The Spirit of the Laws* (1748), a work that compares systems of government in an effort to establish underlying principles. He concludes that climate, geography, religion, and education, among other factors, account for the world's different types of laws as well as governmen-

Figure 16.17 JACQUES GERMAIN SOUFFLOT. The Pantheon. 1755–1792. Paris. *By 1789 advanced thinkers in France had begun to appropriate Classical images for their movement, with David's Neoclassical paintings leading the way. When the revolution began, its leaders determined to build a suitable monument to house the remains of those* philosophes *whose works had furthered the cause of reform. Hence, it was natural that the revolutionary government turn Soufflot's Classical church—with its portico modeled from Roman styles—into a patriotic shrine.*

tal systems. Despite his misunderstanding of the roles of climate and geography, Montesquieu's analytical approach identified influences on governments that had not been considered before. One enduring idea in *The Spirit of the Laws* is that a separation of governmental powers provides an effective defense against despotic rule. Montesquieu was an admirer of England's parliamentary democracy and of the work of the English political philosopher John Locke, whose influence is evident here. American patriots adopted this principle of the separation of powers in the 1780s when they framed the Constitution, dividing the federal government's power into executive, legislative, and judicial branches.

In contrast to the conservative Montesquieu, Jean-Jacques Rousseau [roo-SOH] (1712–1778) framed his political theories within a more libertarian tradition. Rousseau set forth his model of the ideal state in *The Social Contract*, published in 1762. He agreed with John Locke that human beings are free and equal in nature, but he defined the "state of nature" as a paradoxical condition in which individuals can follow any whim and hence possess no moral purpose. On the other hand, the state, which is founded on a social contract (an agreement among people), gives its citizens basic civil rights (freedom, equality, and property) and a moral purpose—precisely the things that they lack in nature. That morality arises within the civil state is a function of the "General Will," his term for what is best for the entire community. If each citizen is granted the right to vote, and if each citizen votes on the laws in accord with the General Will, then the laws will embody what is best for the whole society. Thus, in Rousseau's thinking, citizens who obey the laws become moral beings. (It should be noted that who defines and implements the General Will and how it affects individual freedom remain ambiguous in *The Social Contract*.)

In contrast to Locke's form of democracy, where a representative group such as a legislature acts in the name of the people, Rousseau's asserted that the people themselves collectively personify the state through the General Will. Rousseau's ideal state, therefore, has to be relatively small, so that all citizens can know and recognize one another. His model for the ideal state was based on his experience as a citizen of the tiny Genevan republic. Nevertheless, Rousseau has had an incalculable influence on thinkers and politicians concerned about much larger states. Indeed, his impact in the nineteenth century extended far beyond democratic circles. Nationalistic philosophers such as G. W. F. Hegel borrowed Rousseau's theory of the all-encompassing state, and radical theorists such as Karl Marx adopted his doctrine of the General Will (see Chapters 17 and 18).

Literature

Western literature in the Age of Reason was dominated by French authors and the French language, which now replaced Latin as the international language of scholarship, diplomacy, and commerce. French writers made common cause with the progressive *philosophes*, sharing their faith in a glorious future. They wrote for the growing middle-class audience that was replacing the aristocratic patrons. Since these authors were under the constant threat of state censorship, they were often forced to disguise their more barbed social criticisms or to sugarcoat their beliefs. Those restrictions did not, however, deter them from their mission to liberate the consciousness of their readers and usher in an enlightened society.

French Writers: The Development of New Forms   The two political philosophers discussed earlier—Montesquieu and Rousseau—were also prominent figures in French literature. Early in his career, Montesquieu had written *Persian Letters*, a cleverly devised, wide-ranging critique of French institutions and customs in the guise of letters purporting to be written by and to Persian travelers during a trip to Paris. Through the eyes of the "Persians," Montesquieu ridiculed the despotism of the French crown, the idleness of the aristocracy, and the intolerance of the Roman Catholic Church. His device of the detached observer of Western life was a safeguard against censorship, as was the decision to print *Persian Letters* in the Netherlands. Montesquieu's publication inspired a new type of literature, a genre in which a "foreign" traveler voices the author's social criticisms.

Rousseau foreshadowed the Romantic sensibility of the next century with his intensely personal autobiography, *The Confessions*. Published after his death, this work was the frankest self-revelation that had yet been seen in print. It narrated Rousseau's lifelong follies and difficulties, including sexual problems, religious vacillation, a mismatched marriage, and his decision to place his five offspring in an orphanage as soon as each was born. Not only did he reveal his personal secrets, but he also tried to justify his failings, pleading with his audience that he not be judged too harshly. The revelations shocked many readers, but others praised him for his emotional truthfulness and were willing to overlook his rather self-serving treatment of a number of the facts of his own life. After Rousseau's candid admissions, the genre of autobiography was never the same again.

The third great French writer of the eighteenth century was François-Marie Arouet, better known by his pen name, Voltaire (1694–1778)—the outspoken leader of the Age of Reason and the *philosophe* who best

Figure 16.18 JEAN-ANTOINE HOUDON. *Voltaire.* 1780. Life-size. Bibliothèque Nationale, Paris. *Houdon's Neoclassical portrait in plaster of Voltaire shows the sculptor's determination to portray his subject as an ancient Roman. Houdon seated Voltaire in an armchair copied from ancient models and draped him in an ample robe that suggested Roman dress (but was actually based on the robe worn by the great* philosophe *to keep out the cold). He endowed his sculpture with a vivid sense of life, as may be seen in the fine details and the expressive face.*

personifies the Enlightenment (Figure 16.18). A restless genius, Voltaire earned success in many forms, including dramas, essays, poems, histories, treatises, novels, a philosophical dictionary, letters, and the first work of history—the *Essay on Customs*—to survey civilization from a world perspective.

Of Voltaire's voluminous writings, only one work is still widely read today: the novel *Candide,* published in 1759. The most popular novel of the Age of Reason, *Candide* exhibits Voltaire's urbane style, his shrewd mixture of philosophy and wit, and his ability to jolt the reader with an unexpected word or detail. Beneath its frivolous surface, this work has the serious purpose of ridiculing the fashionable optimism of eighteenth-century thinkers who, Voltaire believed, denied the existence of evil and insisted that the world was essentially good.

At one time an optimist himself, Voltaire altered his beliefs about evil after the 1755 Lisbon earthquake, a calamity that figures prominently in *Candide.* This comic adventure tale recounts the coming of age of the aptly named Candide, who is introduced to optimism by Dr. Pangloss, a caricature of a German professor. The naive hero suffers many misfortunes—war, poverty, religious bigotry, trial by the Inquisition, shipwreck—and through them all holds fast to Pangloss's

teaching that "this is the best of all possible worlds." But finally, faced with mounting incidents of pain and injustice, Candide renounces optimism. The story ends with the hero's newly acquired wisdom for combating the evils of boredom, vice, and want: "We must cultivate our garden."

Neoclassicism in English Literature In England, the presence of a Protestant middle class, which was growing larger and increasingly literate, created a demand for a literature that was decorous, conservative, and basically moralistic and religious in tone, even if that religion were little more than deference to nature and nature's God. The poetry of Alexander Pope and the monumental historical work of Edward Gibbon are typical of this style of literature, which is referred to as Neoclassical.

Alexander Pope (1688–1744) is the most representative voice of the English Neoclassical style. His poems celebrate the order and decorum that were prized by the middle classes—the social group from which he sprang. He became his age's leading spokesman for humane values such as reason, Classical learning, good sense and good taste, and hatred of hypocrisy and ostentation. His verses, marked by their satirical tone and sophisticated wit, made Pope the supreme inspiration of the Age of Reason until the Romantics, led by William Wordsworth in the 1790s, turned away from the Neoclassical ideal.

Pope wrote many kinds of poetry—pastorals, elegies, and satires, among others—but the work closest to the spirit of the Age of Reason is his *Essay on Man,* a didactic work combining philosophy and verse, published in 1733–1734. Issued in four sections and composed in rhymed couplets, this poem brings together one of the age's central ideas, optimism, with some notions inherited from antiquity. In the first section of this poem, Pope argues that God in his infinite power has created the best possible world—not a perfect universe—and that God's design rests on the concept of the great chain of being: Reaching from God to microscopic creatures, this chain links all living things together. Human beings occupy the chain's midpoint, where the human and animal species meet. Because of this position, two different natures fight in the human breast: "Created half to rise, and half to fall; / Great lord of all things, yet a prey to all."

Since humanity's place is unchanging, human reason is limited, and God does not make mistakes, humans should not question the divine plan. Pope concludes that "whatever is, is right." From this fatalistic principle it follows that what humans perceive as evil is simply misunderstood good. This qualified optimism was satirized by Voltaire in *Candide* through the character of Dr. Pangloss.

Having established a fatalistic outlook in the first

PERSONAL PERSPECTIVE

Lady Mary Wortley Montagu
Letter to Wortley, Avignon, 25 March 1744

Lady Montagu (1689–1762) was one of the great letter writers in the Western tradition. A free spirit and a keen observer, she lived apart from her husband, Lord Edward Wortley Montagu, for about twenty years, four of which were spent in Avignon, France. In this letter to her husband, Lady Mary explains how she was able to save a group of French Protestant Huguenots from being galley slaves.

I take this opportunity of informing you in what manner I came acquainted with the secret I hinted at in my letter of the 5th of Feb. The Society of Freemasons at Nîmes presented the Duke of Richelieu, governor of Languedoc, with a magnificent entertainment. It is but one day's post from hence, and the Duchess of Crillon with some other ladies of this town resolved to be at it, and almost by force carried me with them, which I am tempted to believe an act of Providence, considering my great reluctance and the service it proved to be to unhappy, innocent people.

The greatest part of the town of Nîmes are secret Protestants, which are still severely punished according to the edicts of Louis XIV whenever they are detected in any public worship. A few days before we came they had assembled; their minister and about a dozen of his congregation were seized and imprisoned. I knew nothing of this, but I had not been in the town two hours when I was visited by two of the most consider-able of the Huguenots, who came to beg of me with tears to speak in their favour to the Duke of Richelieu, saying none of the Catholics would do it and the Protestants durst not, and that God had sent me for their protection, [that] the Duke of Richelieu was too well bred to refuse to listen to a lady, and I was of a rank and nation to have liberty to say what I pleased. They moved my compassion so much I resolved to use my endeavours to serve them, though I had little hope of succeeding.

I would not therefore dress myself for the supper, but went in a domino to the ball, a mask giving opportunity of talking in a freer manner than I could have done without it. I was at no trouble in engaging his conversation. The ladies having told him I was there, he immediately advanced towards me, and I found from a different motive he had a great desire to be acquainted with me, having heard a great deal of me. After abundance of compliments of that sort, I made my request for the liberty of the poor Protestants. He with great freedom told me that he was so little a bigot, he pitied them as much as I did, but his orders from Court were to send them to the galleys. However, to show how much he desired my good opinion he was returning and would solicit their freedom (which he has since obtained).

---

section of *Essay on Man*, Pope became more optimistic in the remaining sections. Although God's ways may be unknowable, he reasoned that some truths may still be learned by human beings: "The proper study of mankind is man." From this belief he concluded that a paradise could be created on Earth if human beings would think and act rationally—an attitude dear to the hearts of the *philosophes*.

Edward Gibbon's (1737–1794) *History of the Decline and Fall of the Roman Empire* appeared in six volumes between 1776 and 1788. Gibbon's recognition was instant and universal; he was hailed across Europe both for the breadth of his historical knowledge and the brilliance of his style. His subject, the history of Rome, appealed to the age's Classical interests, and his skepticism, notably regarding the Christian faith, echoed the sentiments of the *philosophes*. Although Gibbon's authority as a scholar was eclipsed in the next century because of the progress of historical science, his work remains one of the Enlightenment's genuine literary masterpieces.

Gibbon's massive work reflects both the ancient historical tradition and the ideals of the Enlightenment. Following the ancient historians, he wrote with secular detachment and offered reasons for historical change based on human motives and natural causes. From the Enlightenment, he determined that history should be philosophy teaching through example. These influences come together in his history when he attributes Rome's decay to an unpatriotic and subversive Christian faith along with the Germanic invasions. In effect, Gibbon's history praises secular civilization and covertly warns against the perils of religious enthusiasm.

The Rise of the Novel Despite the contributions of Pope and Gibbon to Western letters, the most important literary development in England during the Age of Reason was the rise of the modern novel. The hallmark of the early English novel was its realism. In the spirit of the Scientific Revolution, the new authors broke with the past and began to study the world with fresh eyes. Previous writers had based their plots on historical events or fables, but now individual experience became the keystone of the writer's art, and authors turned away from traditional plots in favor of an accurate representation of real-life events.

The English novel was realistic in several ways. It focused on individual persons rather than universal types and on particular circumstances rather than settings determined by literary custom. Furthermore, its plots followed the development of characters over the course of minutely observed time. The sense of realism was complete when the author adopted a narrative voice that contributed to the air of authenticity.

The novel captured the wholehearted attention of the reading public, many of them women. The works of Samuel Richardson and Henry Fielding especially appealed to these new readers. The writings of these two Englishmen helped to define the modern novel and at the same time set the standards for later fiction. For centuries, tragedy, with its plots about aristocratic heroes and heroines, had been regarded as the highest literary form. But since the age of Richardson and Fielding, the novel, with its focus on ordinary people, has been and remains the dominant literary genre.

The novels of Samuel Richardson (1689–1761) focus on love between the sexes. For more than a thousand pages in *Pamela, or Virtue Rewarded* (1740) and almost two thousand pages in *Clarissa Harlowe* (1747–1748), he tells the contrasting stories of two young women whose virtue is sorely tested by repeated seduction attempts. Pamela, a resourceful and somewhat calculating maidservant, eventually finds happiness in marriage to her prosperous would-be seducer. Clarissa, from a higher social class but of weaker mettle, runs off with her seducer and dies of shame.

In contrast to Richardson's sentimental domestic dramas, the novels of Henry Fielding (1707–1754) depict a robust world of comedy and adventure. His best work is *The History of Tom Jones, a Foundling* (1749), a comic masterpiece that has been called the finest English novel. Tom, the hero, is a high-spirited young man who makes little effort to resist the temptations that come his way. His wealthy guardian rejects him for his immoral behavior, but Tom is shown to be good-hearted and honest and thus worthy of the good fortune that befalls him at the novel's end when he has learned the virtues of moderation. The novel contains a great deal of amusing satire, aimed particularly at the upper classes.

Music

The standard in music in the early part of the eighteenth century was set by the French, as it was in art and decoration. Rococo music, like Rococo art, represented a reaction against the Baroque. Instead of the complex, formal structure of Baroque music, eighteenth-century French composers strove for a light and charming sound with graceful melodies over simple harmonies. Known as the *style galant* (gallant style), this music was particularly fashionable during the reign of Louis XV.

The perfect instrument for Rococo music was the harpsichord, a keyboard instrument whose strings are plucked, giving it a delicate, refined sound. At the same time, improved instruments, such as brasses and woodwinds, were joining the musical family (Figure 16.19), and the violin was perfected by Antonio Stradivari. The earliest piano was invented in the first decade of the eighteenth century by Bartolommeo Cristofori, who installed a mechanism in a harpsichord that would strike the strings with hammers rather than pluck them. With this new instrument, a player could vary the loudness of the sound depending on the force exerted on the keys, something impossible to do on the harpsichord—thus the name **pianoforte,** from the Italian for "soft" and "loud."

The two outstanding composers of Rococo music were the Frenchmen François Couperin and Jean-Philippe Rameau. Couperin [koop-uh-RAN] (1668–1733) set the tone in court society for the early part of the eighteenth century. His finest works were written for the harpsichord; many contain dance pieces and are noted for their rhythmic virtuosity. His highly ornamented compositions are the perfect musical counterpart of Watteau's painting.

Rameau [rah-MOH] (1683–1764) shared Couperin's fascination with the harpsichord and small-scale works, but his major achievement was as a composer of dramatic operas. Following in the footsteps of the French-Italian operatic composer Jean-Baptiste Lully, he made a ballet sequence with a large corps of dancers a central feature of his operatic works. The best of his operas was *Hippolyte and Aricie* (1733), based on the French playwright Racine's tragedy *Phèdre*. Rameau heightened the tension of the gripping plot through his expressive music, underscoring the sexual tension between the doomed heroine and her stepson.

Like Rococo art, Rococo music was supplanted in the second half of the eighteenth century by the new **Classical** style, in which more serious expression seemed possible. An important characteristic of Classical music was its emphasis on form and structure. The most versatile and widely used form to emerge was the **sonata form,** in which a musical piece is written in three main sections, known as the exposition, the development, and the recapitulation. In the first, melodies and themes are stated; in the second, the same material is expanded and changed in various ways; and in the third, the themes are stated again but with

Figure 16.19 Illustration from the *Encyclopédie: A Brazier's Workshop.* 1751–1765. *This engraving shows the interior of a workshop where braziers (metalsmiths) are making copper musical instruments. Depicted in the figure are the various steps in the manufacture of a hunting horn. A workman first hammers a piece of copper around a form attached to the wall, turning the copper into a tube (fig. 1); a flared mouth is then soldered onto the tube at a forge (fig. 2); next, the tube is filled with molten lead to make it more malleable (fig. 3); and finally, the tube is curved upon itself like a snail (fig. 4). Two finished hunting horns can be seen on the wall. Such illustrations served to demystify the crafts by making practical knowledge readily accessible to educated readers.*

richer harmonies and more complex associations for the listener.

The sonata form was also used as the basis for whole compositions, including the **symphony** (a composition for orchestra), the **concerto** (a piece for a solo instrument and orchestra), and the **sonata** (a work for a small group of instruments). Such pieces often had three movements varying in **key, tempo,** and **mood.** The first was usually the longest and had a quick tempo. The second was slow and reflective, and the third was as quick as the first if not quicker. If there were four movements, the third was either a minuet, based on a French dance, or a **scherzo,** a lively Italian form. The sonata form provided general principles of composition that governed each movement and yet allowed composers to express their own ideas. Classical music retained the Rococo love of elegant melodic lines and clear, simple harmonies, but by using the sonata form, composers were able to add length and depth to their works.

Franz Joseph Haydn [HIDE-'n] (1732–1809) was the first master of the Classical style. Haydn spent almost thirty years as music director at the palace of a Hungarian noble family, where his status was that of a skilled servant of the reigning prince. At his death, however, he was both comfortably off and famous throughout Europe. He is largely responsible for the development of the sonata form, and his 104 symphonies helped to define the standard, four-movement symphony. Despite their formal regularity, the symphonies show Haydn's inventiveness and sense of freedom as he experiments with a large and imaginative variety of moods and structures.

Similarly, Haydn's more than seventy string quartets, each composed for first and second violins, viola, and cello, became the accepted norm for this type of chamber music. His supreme innovation was to allow each instrument to show its independence from the rest. Although the first violin has the most prominent role, the musical effect of a Haydn quartet is of four persons conversing.

However prodigious Haydn's efforts, they are overshadowed by the greatest exponent of the Classical style, Wolfgang Amadeus Mozart (1756–1791). From the age of six, he wrote music, alternating composing with performing. His travels around Europe as a child prodigy exposed him to the musical currents of his day, which he eagerly adapted into his own works. For nine years of his adult life, he was a court musician in the service of the archbishop of Salzburg, a post that caused him great anguish because of its low social position. Unlike Haydn, he would not accept the conventional position of musicians as liveried (uniformed) servants of wealthy patrons. The last decade of his life was spent as a freelance musician in Vienna, where he died in extreme poverty. Despite his brief and tragic life, Mozart left a huge body of music that later generations have pronounced sublime.

Mozart's gift was not for creating new musical forms; Mozart already had at hand the sonata, the opera, the symphony, and the quartet. Rather, his inimitable talent was for composing music with a seemingly effortless line of melody, growing naturally from the opening bars until the finale. His disciplined and harmonious works embody the spirit of the Enlightenment.

The transparency of Mozart's composing technique allowed him to give a unique stamp to every type of music that he touched, and he composed in every genre available to him. In vocal music, he composed religious works (such as Masses, oratorios, and an unfinished Requiem Mass) and dramatic works (for example, operas and a ballet). In instrumental music, he wrote orchestral and ensemble music, including symphonies, serenades, divertimentos, marches, minuets, and German dances; concertos for piano, violin, horn, flute, trumpet, and clarinet; chamber music for strings and winds; violin sonatas; and keyboard sonatas.

The fullest expression of Mozart's genius was reached in his operas, especially his comic operas, where he gave free rein to the playful side of his temperament, blending broad humor with dramatic characterization. His masterpiece in this genre is probably *The Marriage of Figaro*, based on a play by the French *philosophe* Pierre Beaumarchais [boh-mahr-SHAY] (1732–1799). Since its first performance in 1786, *Figaro*'s knockabout humor and rich musical texture have made it one of the most popular works in the entire operatic repertory. Beneath the farcical scenes and the enchanting melodies, however, lies a serious theme: By allowing the servant, Figaro, to outwit his arrogant master, Mozart joined the growing ranks of those who criticized the privileged classes and attacked the injustices of their times. In Mozart's other music, his personal presence was always obscured. But in *Figaro*, the disgruntled servant-musician who chafes at his hard lot speaks with Mozart's authentic voice.

The Legacy of the Age of Reason

After the Enlightenment, Western civilization was never the same. By the end of the period, the prevailing form of government—absolutism—was on the defensive, facing condemnation from all sides. Supporters of absolutism argued for enlightened despotism, aristocratic critics advocated a division of centralized rule into rival branches, and democrats wanted to abolish monarchy and give the power to the people. Under these assaults, absolutist governments began to crumble.

Another development in the eighteenth century with long-term consequences was the emergence of the middle classes as a potent force for change. By and large, the Enlightenment reflected their political, social, and economic agenda, though their advocates claimed to speak for all people regardless of background. The rise of the middle classes also opened the door to popular forms of culture, such as the novel. Today, this democratizing tendency continues and is one of the hallmarks of modern civilization.

Many of the ideas and principles of the Enlightenment are now articles of faith in the Western heritage. From it come the beliefs that governments should rest on the consent of the people, that the least amount of state interference in the lives of citizens is best, and that all people are created equal. More fundamentally, from the Enlightenment come the views that human nature is good and that happiness is the proper goal of human life.

Although the Enlightenment pointed the way to the future, we must not be misled by the modern-sounding language of the times. The *philosophes* wrote endlessly in support of free speech and religious toleration, and yet censorship and bigotry remained the normal condition of existence for most Europeans. Despite their brave words, most of these enlightened thinkers did not move from ideas to action, believing that ideas would triumph because of their inner logic and inherent justice. Moreover, they thought that the ruling classes would surrender their privileges once reason had shown them the error of their ways. The Enlightenment was the last era in which such simplistic beliefs held sway. The world in 1789 stood poised on the brink of an era in which ideas became politicized through action, war, and social agitation. In the postrevolutionary world, the radical power of ideas would be understood by all.

KEY CULTURAL TERMS

Enlightenment	Classical style (in music)
philosophes	sonata form
Deism	symphony
Physiocrats	concerto
Rococo style	sonata
fête galante	key
rocaille	tempo
Neoclassical style	mood
style galant	scherzo
pianoforte	

SUGGESTIONS FOR FURTHER READING

PRIMARY SOURCES

DIDEROT, D. *The Encyclopedia: Selections.* Edited and translated by S. J. Gendzier. New York: Harper & Row, 1967. Well-chosen selections from the most influential work of the Enlightenment; originally published between 1750 and 1772.

FIELDING, H. *The History of Tom Jones, a Foundling.* Middletown, Conn.: Wesleyan University Press, 1975. A recent edition of this rollicking novel about an orphan who through personal charm, good looks, and honesty survives misadventures and is finally restored to his rightful inheritance; first issued in 1749.

GIBBON, E. *The History of the Decline and Fall of the Roman Empire.* Abridged by M. Hadas. New York: Putnam, 1962. One of the landmarks of the Enlightenment, Gibbon's history attributes the fall of Rome to the rise of Christianity; published between 1776 and 1788.

HARDT, U. H. *A Critical Edition of Mary Wollstonecraft's "A Vindication of the Rights of Woman, with Strictures on Political and Moral Subjects."* Troy, N.Y.: Whitston, 1982. An authoritative text of one of the books that helped launch the modern feminist movement.

MONTESQUIEU, BARON DE. *The Persian Letters.* Translated by G. R. Healy. Indianapolis: Bobbs-Merrill, 1964. An excellent English version of this epistolary novel that satirizes European customs through the eyes of imaginary Persian travelers; the original dates from 1721.

———. *The Spirit of the Laws.* Translated and edited by A. M. Cohler, B. C. Miller, and H. S. Stone. New York: Cambridge University Press, 1989. A good recent English version of this groundbreaking work that claims people's choices are influenced by such matters as climate, geography, and religion.

POPE, A. *An Essay on Man.* Edited by M. Mack. London: Methuen, 1964. A poetic statement of the ideals of the Enlightenment by the leading English poet of the age.

RICHARDSON, S. *Pamela.* London: Dent, 1962. An edition of one of the earliest novels in the English language, recounting the tale of a servant girl whose fine moral sense enables her to prevail over adversity and rise to the top of aristocratic society.

ROUSSEAU, J.-J. *Basic Political Writings.* Translated and edited by D. A. Cress. Indianapolis: Hackett, 1987. Includes selections from *First Discourse* (1750), *The Social Contract* (1762), *Emile* (1762), and other writings.

———. *Confessions.* Translated by J. M. Cohen. New York: Penguin, 1954. A highly original book, the first in the tradition of confessional autobiographies; bridges the Enlightenment and the Romantic period.

SMITH, A. *The Wealth of Nations: Representative Selections.* Indianapolis: Bobbs-Merrill, 1961. The basic writings that set forth the theory of free-market economics; first published in 1776.

VOLTAIRE. *Candide.* Translated by L. Bair. New York: Bantam Books, 1981. The most popular novel of the eighteenth century; first published in 1759.

SUGGESTIONS FOR LISTENING

COUPERIN, FRANÇOIS (1668–1733). The harpsichord, with its delicate and lively sounds, was the symbol of Rococo music; Couperin's more than two hundred harpsichord works, composed usually in highly stylized and stately dance rhythms, helped to define the Rococo musical style. Typical works are *La visionaire (The Dreamer)* and *La misterieuse (The Mysterious One),* both from 1730.

HAYDN, FRANZ JOSEPH (1732–1809). Over a long and laborious career, Haydn honed his approach to music, moving from late Baroque forms until he established the sonata form of composition as the basic ingredient of the Classical musical style. Of the string quartets, those in Opus 17 and 20, composed respectively in 1771 and 1772, show his pure Classical style; the quartets he wrote in the 1790s (Opus 76 and 77) illustrate his later style, bursting with rhythmic vitality and harmonic innovation. Good examples of his more than one hundred symphonies are Symphony No. 45 (*Farewell*) (1772), Symphony No. 85 (*La reine,* or *The Queen*) (1785), Symphony No. 94 (*Surprise*), and Symphony No. 103 (*Drum Roll*) (1795). Besides instrumental music, Haydn composed religious works, notably the oratorios for orchestra and massed chorus, *The Creation* (1798) and *The Seasons* (1801)—inspired by Handel's *Messiah.*

MOZART, WOLFGANG AMADEUS (1756–1791). The most gifted composer of the period, Mozart helped to define the Classical style in virtually all forms of musical expression, including the symphony, the piano sonata, the concerto for piano and orchestra, the string quartet, and the comic opera. Mozart's religious music includes Masses, motets, and settings of sacred songs, such as *Solemn Vespers of the Confessor* (1780), with its serene "Laudate Dominum" section, as well as the *Epistle Sonatas* for organ and orchestra, composed between 1767 and 1780 as part of the Mass. Among his best-loved compositions are his last two symphonies, Nos. 40 and 41, composed in 1788; the six concertos for piano and orchestra written in 1784; the six string quartets in Opus 10 (1785), dedicated to Haydn; the opera *Don Giovanni* (1787) in Italian, combining comic and dramatic elements; and the comic operas *The Marriage of Figaro* (1786) and *Cosi fan Tutte (They All Do It This Way)* (1790) in Italian and *The Magic Flute* (1791) in German.

RAMEAU, JEAN-PHILIPPE (1683–1764). Rameau's musical fame rests largely on his operas, which combine late Baroque forms with Rococo elegance and grace. His best-known operas include *Hippolyte et Aricie* (1733), *Les Indes galantes (The Gallant Indies)* (1735), and *Castor et Pollux* (1737).

AFRICA

AMERICAS

HISTORY

Central Africa *Kongo Kingdom.* Slave trade, civil war, collapse. *Luba Kingdom.* Strong state (modern Democratic Republic of Congo) with satellite kingdoms.

East Africa *Zambezi Valley.* Butwa, the most prosperous kingdom.

North Africa Part of Ottoman Empire; Muslim way of life clashed with Western-style reforms. *Algeria and Tunisia.* Piracy flourished. *Egypt.* Napoleon invaded (1798).

South Africa Warfare between Boers and Xhosa.

West Africa *Niger Bend.* Berber tribal confederations raided cities and farms and controlled trade routes. *Dahomey Empire.* Expansive state based on slave trade; subjugated by Oyo Empire (1730). *Ghana.* Asante tribal confederacy founded (1701); trade, including gold and slaves.

Caribbean Spread of sugarcane plantations; African slaves replaced native workers.

Latin America *Mexico.* Roads linked capital with sea. Rapid urbanization. *Viceroyalty of La Plata (modern Argentina, Uruguay, Paraguay, Bolivia).* Potosí, economic hub of South America. *Viceroyalty of Peru.* Inca insurrection, led by Tupac Amarú (1780). *Brazil.* Economy based on coffee and wild rubber surpassed Portugal's. Diamond and gold mining began. Slave trade grew.

Native North America *Plains.* Sioux began hunting buffalo with Spanish horses from Southwest. *Eastern Woodlands.* French and Indian War; some tribes allied with French, others with British. Revolutionary War (1775–1781); some tribes sided with British, others with colonists. From 1783, forced to cede land to U.S. government. Settlers took over hunting grounds of Shawnee, Delaware, and Cherokee.

ART & MUSIC

Central Africa *Kongo Kingdom. Mintindi* stone figures (of kings?), seated with legs crossed. *Luba Kingdoms.* Wooden bow stands and women's heads.

West Africa *Ghana.* Asante Kingdom: golden objects, including royal stools, staffs, chains, and swords; *kente* cloth woven from cotton. *Yoruba culture.* Benin Kingdom: sculpted bronze heads, mounted on tall staffs around graves and altars.

Asante Golden Stool. Ghana.

Latin America Baroque style imported from Europe. *Mexico:* Florid sculptures at the Cathedral of Mexico City; local styles with native influences in small towns. *Viceroyalty of La Plata. Mestizo* (male and female) sculptors and painters at Cuzco and Potosí. *Brazil.* Many African-Portuguese artists, especially the sculptor and architect Antônio Francisco Lisboa, "Aleijadinho." Yoruban influence on music, religion, and the arts.

Antônio Francisco Lisboa. Daniel. 1757–1777. Soapstone. Courtyard, Church of Bom Jesus de Matozinhos, Congonhas do Campo, Minas Gerais, Brazil.

ARCHITECTURE

East Africa *Zambezi Valley.* Butwa: ceremonial and high prestige buildings made of stone.

North Africa *Egypt.* Ottoman style dominated, but Egyptian taste expressed in woodcarving and other crafts.

Latin America *Mexico.* Richly decorated churches: polychrome plasterwork, glazed tilework, pilasters based on inverted pyramid, and elaborately carved facades. Indigenous influences in interior towns and cities. *Brazil.* Mulatto influences, especially inland. Neoclassicism introduced (after 1780). *Viceroyalty of Peru.* Fusion of indigenous tradition with European Baroque, especially in the interior.

Church of Santiago. 1700s. Pomata, Peru.

RELIGION, PHILOSOPHY, LITERATURE

West Africa *Niger Bend.* Kunta tribe of Berbers: Sidi Mukhtar, spiritual leader of the Muslim Sufi sect, author, and educator. His schools opened the door to Islam for "outsider" black people.

Caribbean *Cuba, Trinidad, and Haiti.* Yoruban slaves influenced religious beliefs, music, and myth.

Latin America *Viceroyalty of La Plata.* First Argentine university, at Córdoba.

Native North America *California.* 21 Spanish missions founded by Father Junipero Serra (1769–1780); Chumash, Costanoan, and other Indians became laborers on mission lands.

ASIA

China

Ch'ing Dynasty. Height of power under Emperor Ch'ien-lung: greatest territorial extent (Outer Mongolia, Tibet, and Taiwan); farming, trade, and manufacturing grew; population more than doubled in 70 years; exodus of Chinese traders across Far East; foreign merchants restricted (1757).

India

Mogul Dynasty. Disintegration of empire into petty states, including two major Muslim kingdoms (Bengal and Deccan), two major Hindu dynasties (Rajputs and Marathas), and a Sikh kingdom (Punjab). British defeat French for trading rights and territories. Britain's East India Company became leading power (1757).

Japan

Edo period. Peace reigned under a despotic shōgunate; feudal order continued to be undermined by merchant class; extremes of wealth. Isolated from the world, except for Chinese contacts and medical texts imported from West. Shōgun's court became extravagant and inefficient. Edo's population of about 1 million (1800) made it one of the world's largest cities.

Ch'ing Dynasty. Ch'ien-lung supported the arts and patronized Jesuit painters and architects; Jesuit influence (expressed through rich ornamentation or nontraditional forms) in landscapes, portraits, and the applied arts, including embroidery, cloisonné, and jade carving. Commercial art market flourished; colored printmaking introduced; brisk art export trade to Europe.

Mogul Dynasty. Provincial schools, devoted to miniature painting, flourished, especially in northwestern Hindu courts, such as Kangra and Jaipur.

Tōshūsai Sharaku. Segawa Tomisaburō II as Yadorigi, Ōgishi Kurando's Wife. 1794. *Polychrome woodblock print on paper, 5 × 9½". Tokyo National Museum.*

Edo period. Traditional and innovative schools of painting, including Literati, Western, and Maruyama (mixing Western realism and traditional style, founded by Okyo). *Ukiyo-e* prints matured with the introduction of color by Harunobu (1770s); *ukiyo-e* artists specialized in popular subjects, such as beautiful women (Kitagawa) and Kabuki actors (Sharaku).

Ch'ing Dynasty. Jesuit architects designed Yuan-ming-yuan, a complex of parks, fountains, water works, and pavilions, including the Summer Palace, Peking. Altar of Heaven restored.

Mogul Dynasty. Capital of Sikh Kingdom founded at Lahore.

Edo period. Edo struck by fire (1772); rebuilt.

Rikugi-en, "Garden of the Six Principles of Poetry." Completed 1702. Tokyo.

Ch'ing Dynasty. The classic novel *The Dream of the Red Chamber.* Tai Chen, a scientist, scholar, and philosopher. Renewed interest in textual criticism. Emperor, court, and merchants patronized writers and scholars. Jesuits translated literary and philosophical works, which were transmitted to the West; fostered studies of astronomy, cartography, and mathematics.

Mogul Dynasty. Religious separatism, as Hindus, Muslims, and Sikhs formed their own states.

Edo period. Taniguchi Buson, painter and poet, master of *haiku;* Akinari Ueda's *Tales of the Rainy Moon,* supernatural stories. *Bunraku* (puppet theater) founded; many plays by Chikamatsu Monzaemon; appealed to merchant class. Shōguns encouraged Confucianism as an ethical framework for government.

Du 13. Juillet, 1793.
Marie anne Charlotte
Corday au citoyen
Marat.
il suffit que je sois
bien Malheureuse
pour avoir Droit
a votre bienveillance.

À MARAT,
DAVID.

17 REVOLUTION, REACTION, AND CULTURAL RESPONSE

1760–1830

The Age of Reason was a time of radical talk and little action, but by the end of the eighteenth century, three revolutions had changed the Western world forever—and today the period between 1760 and 1830 is considered a historical watershed. The Industrial Revolution created an industrialism that replaced agriculture as the soundest basis for the economic well-being of a state. The American Revolution demonstrated that government by the people was a workable alternative to monarchy. And the French Revolution forced sweeping changes in the distribution of political power in Europe.

These changes were not welcomed by all, and many groups tried to prevent the spread of revolutionary political ideas. However, the middle class, known as the *bourgeoisie,* benefited the most from these revolutions. The emboldened middle class asserted itself as the new standard-bearer of culture, first embracing Neoclassicism and then shifting favor to the powerful new spirit and style of the age—Romanticism.

THE INDUSTRIAL REVOLUTION

Even before the Industrial Revolution, agricultural innovations in England made industrialization possible. The shift toward enclosure, whereby common lands were fenced off by their wealthy owner and consolidated into one large estate, brought hardship to smaller farmers but resulted in increased farm productivity. Improvements in farming techniques increased crop yields and farm income. Better technology also led to improved tools and farm implements, such as the iron plow and the reaper.

◄ **Detail** JACQUES-LOUIS DAVID. *Death of Marat.* 1793. Oil on canvas, 65 × 50½". Musées Royaux des Beaux-Arts, Brussels.

Figure 17.1 MICHAEL ANGELO ROOKER. *The Cast Iron Bridge at Coalbrookdale.* 1782. Approx. 15½ × 24½". Aberdeen Art Gallery, Aberdeen, Scotland. *The earliest iron bridges, made from the superior grade of iron that was being produced in the new factories, were molded and cast to look like wooden bridges. The first iron bridge, located at Coalbrookdale, became a favorite subject for many artists. Architects did not begin to use iron in building construction until the early 1800s.*

Industrialization in England

By the mid–eighteenth century, changes at home and abroad had created conditions that steered England toward industrialization. A population increase provided both a labor force and a consumer market. Money to invest was available because of surplus capital generated by sound fiscal practices. Several decades of peace had created an atmosphere conducive to economic growth, and the government's policies promoted further expansion. Free of internal tariffs or duties, goods moved easily throughout Britain, and Britain's acquisition of colonies gave merchants access to raw materials and new overseas markets.

Three economic changes were necessary before these conditions could combine to produce industrialism: the substitution of machines for manual labor; the replacement of animal and human power with new sources of energy such as water and steam (the steam engine, patented by James Watt in 1769, transformed the generation of power); and the introduction of new and large amounts of raw materials, such as iron ore and coal. By 1800 these changes had taken place (Figure 17.1).

The changes in the cotton cloth industry dramatically illustrate the impact of the Industrial Revolution. Local woolen producers, threatened by competition from cotton, persuaded Parliament to prohibit the importation of inexpensive cotton goods from India; but still the demand grew. The English industry tried to meet the demand for cotton through the putting-out system—a method of hand manufacture in which workers wove the fabric in their homes—but this medieval technique proved hopelessly outdated. As a result, industrialists developed the factory system to speed manufacturing; flying shuttles and power looms were located under one roof, and this building was sit-

uated near a swiftly flowing stream that supplied the water for the steam engines that drove the massive equipment.

The laborers had to adjust their entire lives to the demands of the factory system. No longer could most rural workers stay at home and weave at their own pace. Towns near the factories rapidly expanded, and new ones sprang up in the countryside next to the mills. In both cases, employees were crowded into miserable living quarters, with little regard given for the basic amenities of human existence.

With the factories came the "working class." A realigned class system—with the capitalists and the workers at either extreme—transformed the social order, created new indicators of wealth and success, and established different patterns of class behavior. The earlier cooperation between the gentry and small farmers was replaced by increasingly strained relations between the factory owners and the working class.

Classical Economics: The Rationale for Industrialization

Although industrialization did not produce a school of philosophy, it did generate serious thinking about the newly emerging economic system. Much of this thought could be interpreted as a rationale for industrialization and a justification for profit-seeking. The French Physiocrats and the Scotsman Adam Smith both advocated the abolition of mercantilism—the economy at the service of the state—and its replacement with a laissez-faire system—the economy at the service of the individual entrepreneur. In England, Smith's ideas attracted a band of thinkers who became known as the Classical economists and included Thomas Malthus and David Ricardo.

Smith's key contribution to Classical economics was his advocacy of a free-market system based on private property that would automatically regulate prices and profits to the benefit of all. He focused his *Wealth of Nations* (1776) on agriculture and commerce, while only glancing at manufacturing. As manufacturing gained power in the English economy, however, businessmen read into his work a rationale for their activities. Smith argued that entrepreneurs acting mutually in enlightened self-interest would not only raise the standard of living for all but also get rich—if the government left them alone. Such an argument was welcome news to businessmen, factory owners, and other capitalists.

Thomas Malthus (1766–1834) and David Ricardo (1772–1823) also lent support to the changes wrought by the Industrial Revolution. In his *Essay on the Principle of Population* (1788), Malthus forecast a world burdened with misery that would worsen if the human population continued to increase. Since the population grew at a geometric rate and the food supply advanced at an arithmetical rate, the number of human beings would soon far exceed the amount of food, leading Malthus to conclude that famines, plagues, and wars were necessary to limit the world's population. His gloomy prediction persuaded most of the middle classes that laborers were victims of their own thoughtless habits, including unrestrained sexuality, and could not be helped.

In *Principles of Political Economy and Taxation* (1821), David Ricardo maintained that wages for laborers would always hover around the subsistence level and that workers would never be able to improve their standard of living beyond that level—his "iron law of wages." Tying Malthus's conclusion to his own, he argued that the working class was inevitably mired in poverty. Thus, the theories of the Classical economists provided the rationales for the business classes as they sought arguments to justify the methods of industrialization and the degradation it brought to workers.

POLITICAL REVOLUTIONS, 1760–1815

During the approximately fifty years between the Treaty of Paris (1763) and the Battle of Waterloo (1815), Europe saw monarchies fall and old societies swept away. By 1830 Europe was divided into a conservative eastern Europe and a progressive western Europe that included the former colonies in the New World. This twofold division persisted well into the twentieth century (Timeline 17.1).

The American Revolution

Although Great Britain was leading the way to industrialization, it was also suffering from an outmoded tax structure and from debts contracted in the Seven Years' War. The royal ministers tried numerous schemes and taxes to make the American colonists share in the burden of empire. The colonists, calling the British government's new taxes on sugar, stamps, and tea unconstitutional, claimed immunity from imperial taxation because, they asserted, they were not represented in the British Parliament.

Protests and violence succeeded in nullifying the parliamentary taxes and uniting the colonies in a common cause. In 1774 the colonists convened a Continental Congress in Philadelphia, which spoke for the American people against the "foreign power" of Great Britain. In April 1775 conflict between British troops and colonists in Massachusetts triggered a war. The congress in Philadelphia proclaimed the American goals in the Declaration of Independence, signed on July 4, 1776: government by consent of the governed

Timeline 17.1 REVOLUTION, REACTION, AND CULTURAL RESPONSE

	1776	1783	1789	1799	1815	1830
Industrial Revolution in England	**American Revolution**			**French Revolution**	**Napoleon and the French Empire**	**Restored Bourbon Monarchy in France**	

| 1769 Watt's steam engine | 1776 Smith's *Wealth of Nations* | | | 1793 David's *Death of Marat* | 1803 Beethoven's Third Symphony | 1808 Goethe's *Faust* (Part 1) | 1818 Géricault's *Raft of the "Medusa"* | 1830 Berlioz's *Symphonie fantastique* |

| | 1774 Goethe's *The Sorrows of Young Werther* | | | 1798 Wordsworth and Coleridge's *Lyrical Ballads* | 1813 Austen's *Pride and Prejudice* | 1821 Constable's *Hay Wain* |

Table 17.1 SHIFTS IN THE FRENCH GOVERNMENT, 1789–1830	
July 1789–September 1792	Limited constitutional kingdom; the Assembly
September 1792–August 1795	First Republic; Reign of Terror (1793–1794)
August 1795–November 1799	Directory
November 1799–May 1804	Consulate
May 1804–June 1815	First Empire
June 1815–July 1830	Restored Bourbon Monarchy

and the rights to life, liberty, and the pursuit of happiness. The American Revolution lasted until 1783 and resulted in victory and independence for the colonies.

To realize their democratic goals, the Americans developed two new ideas: the constitutional convention and a written constitution. Wary of centralized power, the framers of the United States Constitution met in Philadelphia in 1787 and created three coordinate branches of government—legislative, judiciary, and executive—with specified powers delegated to each. (The idea of a balance of powers is derived from the works of both the English political theorist John Locke and the French *philosophe* Montesquieu.) The central government could assess and collect its own taxes, regulate commerce, and make and enforce laws. The framers also limited the government's role in everyday life by accepting the superior claims of human rights.

The founders failed to extend rights to slaves, whose existence was barely noted, and women were not given the right to vote. Still, the Constitution made America the most democratic society of its day and the first successful democracy since Athens in the fifth century B.C. As an exemplary democracy, America offered hope to the oppressed, and the successful struggle for independence provided a model for future revolution.

The French Revolution

Despite the importance of the American Revolution, the revolution in France overshadowed it. Because of its dramatic break with the past and its lasting worldwide effects, the French Revolution is a key event of modern times.

When Louis XVI took the throne in 1774, the French crown was confronted with a challenge from two sides: the aristocrats, who were resurgent after the death of Louis XIV, and the emerging bourgeoisie, who were clamoring for power. The affluent bourgeoisie aligned themselves with the nobles in supporting laissez-faire economics, but they joined the king in calling for an end to the feudal privileges of the aristocracy.

The peasant farmers endured burdensome taxes and continued to be subjected to feudal claims. In urban France, the lower middle class, consisting of small shopkeepers, salaried workers, and semiskilled artisans, had little opportunity to escape their bleak existence. Below them existed wage earners, menial workers, and the marginal groups who drifted in and out of the criminal world. Oppressed by high taxes and harboring ill-disguised hatred for the classes above them, the lower orders schemed to stay one jump ahead of the tax collector.

In the 1780s, France began to develop a huge national debt, fueled by its support of America in its revolution. In 1789 Louis XVI finally agreed to convene the Estates-General, a representative body similar to the English Parliament, which had last met in the early 1600s. When this body gathered, the middle-class representatives shunted aside the nobles and the church leaders and formed themselves into the National Constituent Assembly. The Assembly then proceeded to end royal despotism and to turn France into a limited, constitutional kingdom similar to England (Table 17.1).

This first phase of the revolution lasted from 1789 until September 1792. Dominated by the well-to-do middle classes, the Assembly embraced laissez faire, restricted the vote to property owners, overhauled the legal system, and introduced representative government. Especially impressive was this body's approval of *The Declaration of the Rights of Man and Citizen* (1789), a document that guaranteed both natural and civil rights and that has served as the basis of subsequent French regimes. In framing the constitution of 1791, the Assembly attempted to embody the slogans of the revolution—liberty, equality, and fraternity—but class hatred made fraternity more an ideal than a reality. This stage of the revolution failed, however, because Louis XVI proved to be untrustworthy and forces inside France were pressing its leaders for increasingly radical reforms. In 1792 the constitution of 1791 was suspended along with the monarchy.

The revolution entered its second and most violent phase, which lasted from September 1792 to August

Figure 17.2 LOUIS-LEOPOLD BOILLY. *Simon Chenard as a Sans-culotte.* 1792. Oil on canvas, 13⅙ × 8⅝". Musée Carnavalet, Paris. *As French workers came into their own during the second phase of the revolution, their clothing became fashionable. The men dressed in short jackets and baggy trousers, rather than in the aristocratic costume of waistcoats and breeches, or culottes, with silk stockings. Because of the long trousers, these workers were known as sans-culottes (without breeches). The artist Boilly, a supporter of the revolution, sought to glorify the sans-culottes in this portrait of a typical worker—actually his friend, the actor Simon Chenard. Clad in worker's attire, including wooden shoes, and holding the tricolor (the red and white and blue banner of the revolution), Chenard strikes a heroic pose, as if ready to defend his newly won rights. Boilly has placed Chenard in the foreground so that he towers over the landscape, just as the newly enfranchised workers dominated the political scene.*

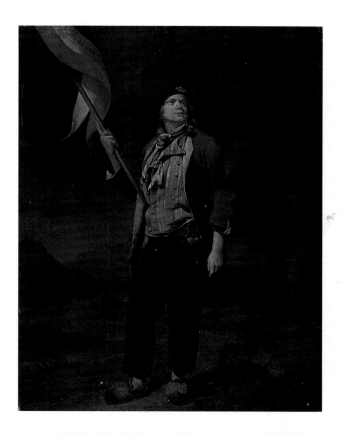

1795. This phase was dominated by leaders from the lower bourgeois and working classes, who executed the king, founded the French Republic, and briefly replaced Christianity with a state religion organized on rational ideals (Figure 17.2). Full voting rights were given to all males, including blacks and Jews, state education was opened to all, conquered people were allowed to vote on their future, and the slave trade was abolished (Figure 17.3). Women, however, were denied the vote and citizenship, but they acquired certain rights, as in marriage contracts.

Such far-reaching reforms alarmed many, and soon the fledgling Republic faced civil war at home and invasions from abroad, which in turn set off more domestic political and financial crises. These events led to the year-long Reign of Terror (1793–1794), the controversial policy whereby all suspected enemies of the revolution were executed. Its excesses overshadowed many of the Republic's accomplishments and discredited the idea of revolution among many of its early supporters. In August 1795 a more moderate republic, known as the Directory, was instituted, in which power was shared between two legislative houses and five directors.

The Directory lasted only four years. Although this government favored the commercial middle classes, it remained revolutionary. Its leaders faced nearly insurmountable problems, such as growing counterrevolution, the collapse of the currency, and a breakdown in

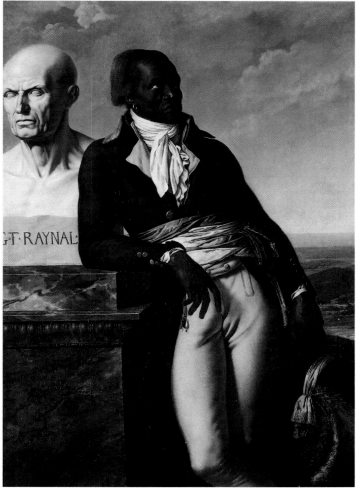

Figure 17.3 ANNE LOUIS GIRODET. *Jean-Baptiste Bellay, Deputy from Santo Domingo.* 1797. Oil on canvas, 63 × 45". Musée National du Château de Versailles, France. *The French Revolution fomented a slave uprising in the colony of Santo Domingo in 1791. Led by Toussaint L'Ouverture [TOO-san LOO-ver-tchur] (1743–1803), the revolt created the black republic of Haiti, which chose three delegates to the constitutional assembly called the Convention in Paris in 1794. In this portrait, Jean-Baptiste Bellay [buh-LAY]—one of Haiti's deputies—leans against a bust of Abbé Raynal [re-NAHL], the* philosophe *whose writings inspired L'Ouverture's struggle.*

Figure 17.4 Jean-Auguste-Dominique Ingres. *Napoleon I.* 1806. Oil on canvas, 8′6″ × 5′4″. Musée de l'Armée, Paris. *In this painting, Napoleon is depicted on a throne in the style of an ancient ruler, but with references that link him to the French monarchy. Wearing a wreath, a Greek symbol of victory, the emperor sits in serene isolation, dressed in a rich ceremonial robe trimmed with ermine. In his right hand he holds a long rod topped by a gold fleur-de-lis, the French lily that had served as France's national symbol since the High Middle Ages. His left hand holds a second rod, the ivory hand of justice, an image adopted by France's kings in 1314 and revived by Napoleon at his coronation in 1804. As a political statement, this portrait helped to establish Napoleon's authority and image. As a work of art, the painting temporarily undermined Ingres's self-confidence, because it was poorly received by the Parisian art establishment, including his mentor David. Today Ingres's* Napoleon I *is regarded as one of the outstanding portraits of the emperor.*

law and order. The directors appealed to the military for aid against their enemies, and in November 1799 General Napoleon Bonaparte staged a coup d'état that abolished the Directory and established the Consulate.

With the rise of Napoleon (1769–1821), events had come full circle, in effect returning France to a monarchy. Napoleon was a dictator and military genius who embodied the enlightened despotism of his century and at the same time anticipated modern totalitarianism. Above all, he was heir to the French Revolution.

Although the cost of Napoleonic rule between 1799 and 1815 was the loss of political liberty for the French, in exchange France received internal peace and a consolidation of most of the revolution's policies. Napoleon kept careers open to talent, suppressed aristocratic privilege, rewarded wealthy property owners, and refashioned public education. He welcomed home revolutionaries who had emigrated—provided they were loyal to his regime. He restored relations with the papacy, though his efforts failed to achieve religious harmony. He also ended the civil war that had raged for more than a decade, and he stabilized the economy.

Napoleon's most enduring legacy was the law code he helped draft. Intended for universal application, the Napoleonic Code introduced rational legal principles and legitimized the idea of the lay state. The code rested on reforms of the revolutionary era, such as the abolition of serfdom, the guilds, and feudal property. Despite its reactionary ideas of paternal rule and the subservience of women—thus reversing the small gains made by women in the revolutionary era—the code remains the basis of civil law in both France and its former colonies.

Napoleon's military conquests and diplomatic successes soon eclipsed his domestic achievements. A brilliant field general before he seized power, Napoleon launched a series of victorious wars once he became emperor in 1804 (Figure 17.4). When not winning battles, he managed to make the coalitions allied against him fall apart by exploiting his foes' basic distrust of one another. In particular, he worked to keep Great Britain out of Continental affairs while he crushed Prussia and Austria, who then sued for peace. Simultaneously, he annexed land for France and established satellite kingdoms ruled by members of his family or by his generals. As the self-proclaimed heir of the Age of Reason and the French Revolution, Napoleon reorganized his newly conquered territories along the lines of France. At first, many local reformers welcomed the French, but they soon learned the high costs of occupation and began to resist their "liberators" (Map 17.1).

Napoleon's empire upset the European balance of power at a basic level, so that ultimately the other nations united to defeat him once he was proven vulner-

Map 17.1   EUROPE AT THE HEIGHT OF NAPOLEON'S POWER, 1810–1811

able in battle by the failure of his invasion of Russia in 1812. An alliance of Great Britain and the European states defeated Napoleon in June 1815 at Waterloo (in modern Belgium). Exiled to an island in the South Atlantic, Napoleon died there in 1821, but his spirit hovered over France and Europe for much of the nineteenth century.

REACTION, 1815–1830

After 1815 the victorious nations tried to restore Europe to its prerevolutionary status, but the forces of change had already altered the future of Western—and world—history. As heirs of the Enlightenment notion that they were citizens of the world, the French largely ignored the traditions of the peoples whom they had conquered, believing that the principles of their revolutionary society represented what was best

for humanity. Ultimately, however, the French were not as successful as they had hoped in exporting their revolution. The European states and Great Britain shared a conservative agenda that aimed to suppress the advance of liberal ideas. At the Congress of Vienna in 1815, the victors stripped France of most of its conquests, restored the balance of power, halted or reduced reform programs, and inaugurated a period of reaction.

Despite this redesign of the map, many Napoleonic reforms remained in force until 1830 and beyond. Even in France, where the allies restored the Bourbons, Louis XVIII (r. 1815–1824) issued a charter that guaranteed a constitutional regime resembling the limited monarchy of 1791. Most western European states now had governments elected by their citizens and civil law based on the Napoleonic Code. In contrast, Prussia, Russia, and Austria remained basically untouched by democracy and representative government.

The fate of reform in Europe between 1815 and 1830 varied from modest changes in England to repression in Russia. In the immediate postwar period in Great Britain, the government resisted attempts to reform Parliament or to institute free trade, but in the 1820s, Britain began to modernize itself. France regressed toward absolutism as the restored Bourbon monarchy chipped away at the revolutionary heritage. By 1830 resistance to the crown was mounting, and in the July Revolution the people revolted and replaced the Bourbon monarchy with Louis Philippe, the Duke of Orléans (r. 1830–1848). Constitutional government now put the middle class in power.

In central Europe, Austria kept liberal sentiments under tight control at home and within the region. Prussia, which had made important liberal reforms in the Napoleonic era, now seemed more interested in efficiency than in modernizing the state. Russia became increasingly reactionary and repressive. Until the 1860s, Russia's autocratic regime and Austria's domination of central Europe widened the gulf between eastern and western Europe.

REVOLUTIONS IN ART AND IDEAS: FROM NEOCLASSICISM TO ROMANTICISM

The makers of the French Revolution had at hand an artistic style that was perfectly suited to their purposes—the Neoclassical. In contrast to the frivolous Rococo, this style was high-minded, ethical, and serious. Neoclassical artists and architects followed the ancient Greco-Roman ideals of balance, simplicity, and restraint, principles that were thought to embody the underlying order of the universe. Truth was seen as eternal, unchanging, the same for one and all. Art and literature created according to Classical principles were believed to be both morally uplifting and aesthetically satisfying.

In England, Classicism lingered on in the novels of Jane Austen. Untouched by the revolutions that dominated this age, Austen created fictional works that took England's deep countryside for their setting and dealt with the lives of the less wealthy gentry, an essentially middle-class world that appealed to her audience.

Advanced thinkers in France made the Neoclassical paintings of David a symbol of the new rational order they wanted to introduce into the world. The revolution intensified devotion to Classical ideals, and David became its official artist. Later, when the revolution lost its way and France began to see itself as a new Rome, Napoleon made David his court painter. After 1800 David transformed Neoclassicism into an imperial style that lingered on in France and on the Conti-

nent long after the French emperor was exiled from Europe in 1815.

Even earlier, starting about 1770, a new movement was emerging across Europe, one that was to have lasting effects on the Western consciousness. **Romanticism** was a whole way of thinking that came to dominate European arts and letters in the nineteenth century. Rejecting Neoclassicism as cold and artificial, the Romantics glorified unruly nature, uncontrolled feeling, and the mysteries of the human soul. They claimed that their ideals were more in tune with human nature than the order, reason, and harmony of Classicism. Certain ideas and elements of Romanticism have permeated our Western way of thinking and become articles of faith in the modern world.

Figure 17.5 JACQUES-LOUIS DAVID. *Death of Marat.* 1793. Oil on canvas, 65 × 50½″. Musées Royaux des Beaux-Arts, Brussels. *David's presentation of figures in the nude in his Neoclassical history paintings was often denounced by literal-minded critics as unrealistic, but David defended this choice as consistent with "the customs of antiquity." The critics were silenced by David's depiction of the Marat murder scene, since in this case the nudity was true to life. In this painting, David's Classical principles and the demands of realistic portrayal combined to produce a timeless image.*

Neoclassicism in Literature After 1789

During her brief life, Jane Austen (1775–1817) wrote six novels that together rank as the finest body of fiction produced in this period. Austen approached novel writing in a Classical spirit, portraying her characters as inhabiting a serene environment reminiscent of the quiet domestic scenes of the seventeenth-century Dutch painter Vermeer (see Chapter 14). Calling herself a miniaturist, she concentrated her author's eye on a vanishing world where the smallest important unit was the family and the most significant problems involved the adjustment of social relationships.

In the hands of a lesser writer, such a literary program might have failed by being too narrow, but Austen transcended her limited framework. She did this through clear writing, ironic understatement, and, above all, beautifully realized descriptions of the manners and little rituals of provincial life: the balls attended, the letters and conversations, the visits to relatives, and the unexpected social breakdowns, such as an elopement, a betrayed confidence, or a broken engagement. She was especially sensitive to the constraints her society imposed on women, depicting with great wit a world in which women were given little access to formal education, confined to the domestic sphere, kept economically dependent on men, and socialized to be weak and sentimental. The best known of Austen's novels is *Pride and Prejudice* (1813), a gently satirical work whose plot revolves around the problems that arise when the Bennets—a shabby genteel family—try to find suitable husbands for five daughters.

Neoclassical Painting and Architecture After 1789

Jacques-Louis David founded Neoclassicism in painting in the 1780s and remained its consummate exponent until his death in 1825. As official artist of the French Revolution, he rendered contemporary events in the ancient manner. David's most successful painting from this period was his study of the revolution's famous martyr, Jean Paul Marat [muh-RAH], who was assassinated while seated in his bath (Figure 17.5). Himself an ardent supporter of the revolution, David meticulously planned this work to give universal meaning to a specific moment in French history. The setting is historically accurate because Marat suffered from a skin disorder and often conducted official business while seated in the bathtub. Once having established the scene, David suppresses every detail that does not contribute to the general impression of tragedy. As a result, the few details take on a highly charged quality. The figure of Marat resembles a piece of Classical sculpture against the stark background. His torso is twisted so that the bleeding wound and the peaceful face are fully visible. The pen and the inkwell remind the viewer that Marat was killed while serving the revolution. In effect, David has portrayed Marat as a secular saint.

Barely escaping the revolution's most violent phase, David survived to become court painter to Napoleon, and modifications in the cause of political propaganda now appeared in his art. Napoleon, to enhance his image as a new Augustus, encouraged David to make his painting reflect the pomp and grandeur of the Napoleonic court. *The Coronation of Napoleon and Josephine* is typical of David's imperial paintings (Figure 17.6). This pictorial record of the investiture

Figure 17.6 JACQUES-LOUIS DAVID. *The Coronation of Napoleon and Josephine.* 1805–1808. Oil on canvas, 20′ × 30′ 6½″. Louvre. *Napoleon orchestrated his own coronation and then guided David in painting it. For instance, Napoleon's mother did not attend, probably because of her disapproval of her son's grandiose ambitions, but Napoleon insisted that David depict her seated prominently at the center of the festivities. David also shows the pope's hand raised in benediction, contrary to the report of eyewitnesses who described him sitting with both hands resting on his knees.*

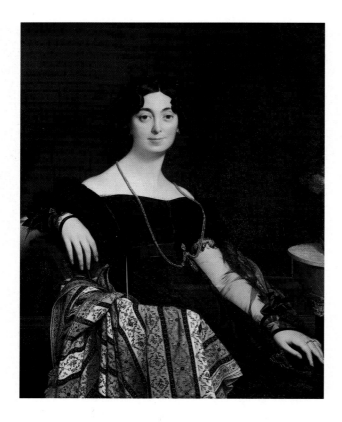

Figure 17.7   JEAN-AUGUSTE-DOMINIQUE INGRES. *Madame Jacques Louis Leblanc.* 1823. Oil on canvas, 47 × 36½″. Metropolitan Museum of Art. Wolfe Fund, 1918. *Ingres was the last great painter of portraits in a field that was to be taken over by the camera after 1840. Claiming that drawing was superior to painting, he was able to render intense, idealized but realistic likenesses, as evidenced in Madame Leblanc's portrait, which he painted in Florence during his years in Italy. Ingres conveys physical presence by placing his subject in the immediate foreground, by highlighting her physical features and the color of her flesh—in Ingres's words, making one side of the portrait light and the other dark—and by depicting the gleaming surfaces of her clothing and jewelry.*

Figure 17.8   THOMAS JEFFERSON. Monticello. 1770–1784; remodeled 1796–1806. Charlottesville, Virginia. *The Palladio-inspired architecture of Monticello reflected Jefferson's ethical vision. Its portico in the plain style of a Roman temple mirrored his admiration for the Roman republic and its ideals of simplicity and order. Its overall devotion to mathematical principles and unobtrusive details were expressions of his commitment to disciplined living. Though built for one of America's elite, Monticello was conceived as a visual rebuke to the luxurious palaces of Europe's aristocrats.*

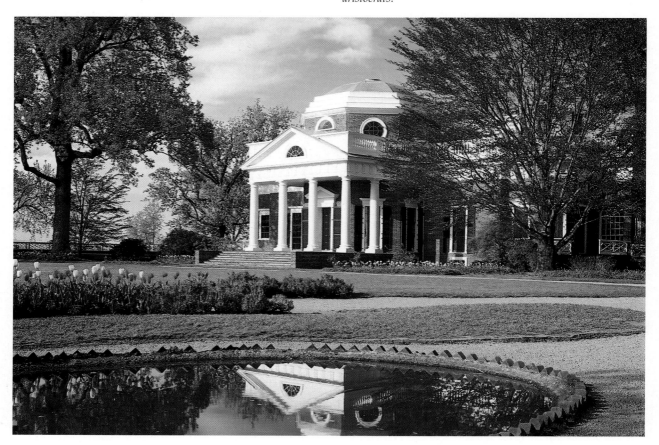

conveys the opulent splendor and theatrical ceremony that Napoleon craved as a way of validating his empire in the eyes of Europe's older monarchs, who regarded him as an upstart. Napoleon's family members, who had been made kings, princes, princesses, and so on, are depicted in elaborate court dress. In addition, David's treatment of the coronation reveals the modern conception of political power. Instead of being crowned by the pope, Napoleon placed the crown on his own head. This painting shows Napoleon preparing to crown his empress, who is kneeling. Virtually ignored in this splendid moment for the Bonaparte family is the pope, who is seated at the right.

The only Neoclassical painter comparable to David is his pupil Jean-Auguste-Dominique Ingres [ANG-gruh] (1780–1867). Ingres inherited the mantle of Neoclassicism from David, but he lacked his teacher's moral enthusiasm. As a result, Ingres's Classicism is almost cold-blooded and stark in its simple images. The finest expressions of Ingres's art are his portraits. With clean lines drawn with a sure and steady hand, he created almost photographic images of his subjects. Of Ingres's numerous portraits, one of the most exquisite is that of Madame Leblanc [luh-BLAH(N)], a member of the new social order of Napoleonic France (Figure 17.7). Ingres's portrait may not probe deeply into the subject's psychology, but he does convey the sitter's high social position, stressing her poise and alluding to her wealth through the rich details of the marble-topped table and the dangling watch and chain. In his own way, Ingres gives this member of the new bourgeois aristocracy the same glamorous treatment that had been accorded prerevolutionary nobles in Rococo portraits.

After 1789 the Neoclassical style in architecture spread to the European colonies, notably to the former British territories in North America. In the United States, the middle-class founders of the new republic made Neoclassicism synonymous with their own time, which is known as the Federal Period. They graced their capital, Washington, with the Classical architecture that symbolized devotion to republican and democratic sentiments.

The most profound influence on America's Classical heritage was exercised by Thomas Jefferson (1743–1826), the coauthor of the Declaration of Independence and the third president of the United States. Jefferson was also a master architect. Like other architects in this era, he was deeply indebted to the principles of the Italian Andrea Palladio (1508–1580), whose book on architecture he had read. Palladio's Villa Rotonda near Vicenza served as the model for Jefferson's home at Monticello near Charlottesville, Virginia (Figure 17.8). Like the Villa Rotonda (see Figure 12.23), Monticello is a country dwelling arranged around a domed central

Figure 17.9 THOMAS JEFFERSON. State Capitol of Virginia. 1785–1796. Richmond, Virginia. *Jefferson described the Maison Carrée, the model for this statehouse, as "the most perfect and precious remain of antiquity in existence." Political considerations also influenced Jefferson's choice, for he identified this Roman temple as a symbol of Roman republican values. Like Monticello, Jefferson's statehouse design was an outgrowth of his ethical vision.*

area, though it features only two symmetrical connecting wings. Executed in brick with wooden trim, Monticello has inspired so many imitations that it has come to symbolize the American dream of gracious living.

Just as Jefferson's plan for his personal residence influenced American domestic architecture, his design for Virginia's state capitol in Richmond has deeply influenced public architecture (Figure 17.9). From his plan for the Virginia statehouse arose the tradition of building public structures in the form of ancient temples. His model for the capitol was the Maison Carrée (see Figure 5.13), a Roman temple dating from the first century A.D. Though small by today's standards for public buildings, Jefferson's statehouse has a strong presence and is a marvel of refined elegance and simple charm. The most pleasing part of his original design is the central building, with its perfectly proportioned features—columns, pediment, and windows. Even though two smaller wings were added later, they enhance rather than detract from Jefferson's symmetrical and harmonious plan.

Romanticism: Its Spirit and Expression

In contrast to Neoclassicism, Romanticism stood for everything that was unbounded and untamed. The Romantics' patron saint was Rousseau, whose emotionalism and love of nature had made him out of step with his own time. Like Rousseau, the Romantics

Figure 17.10   PHILIP JACQUES DE LOUTHERBOURG. *Coalbrookdale by Night*. 1801. Oil on canvas, 26¾ × 42″. Science and Society Picture Library, London. *At first glance, this painting seems to portray the world engulfed in a flaming inferno. Only gradually does the meaning of the scene—a depiction of one of England's new industrialized towns—emerge. As a terrifying symbol of industrialism, the painting helps to explain what Romantic art was rebelling against.*

preferred to be guided by emotion and intuition. Following these guides, they conjured up an image of the world that was deeply personal and alive with hidden meanings. Nature itself became God for many Romantics, who spiritualized nature so that divinity was expressed through bucolic scenes as well as terrifying natural forces. To characterize the latter face of nature they invented the term *Sublime* to convey the awesome and majestic power of earthquakes, floods, and storms.

The Romantic reverence for nature stemmed partly from a desire to escape from the effects of the Industrial Revolution, which was altering the countryside for the worse (Figure 17.10). Not surprisingly, England, the first home of industrialization, became the center of a movement that exalted the Middle Ages, creating a world of natural sentiment that existed only in imagination. The Romantics' rejection of the industrial world had many other consequences, including a preoccupation with the exotic East and the domains of the imagination, dreams, drugs, and nonrational mental states.

Another formative force in Romanticism was the French Revolution. Many early Romantics willingly saw in this awesome upheaval Europe's future. The revolutionary watchwords "liberty," "rights of man," "the individual," and "equality" became the basis of a moral and humanitarian viewpoint that could be applied beyond the orbit of the French Revolution. When Greece declared its independence from the feeble Ottoman Empire and fought for its freedom in the 1820s, for example, many Europeans, influenced by revolutionary principles, declared their solidarity with the rebels. Among them was the English Romantic poet Lord Byron, who died in Greece while aiding in the cause of Greek independence.

The French Revolution also sparked a strong negative reaction among some Romantics, who criticized its seemingly random violence. They likewise deplored Napoleonic imperialism, which squeezed the life out of other cultures by conquering them and then imposing French customs. These conservative Romantics renounced the French Revolution's stress on abstract ideas and natural rights and focused their attention on history and the rights and traditions native to each country. They especially disagreed with the revolution's international spirit and advocated instead a nationalistic point of view.

At first, Romantic nationalism was little more than a rejection of foreign influences and a reverence for those unique aspects of culture that are created by the common people—folk dancing, folk sayings, folk tales, folk music, and folk customs. This benign nationalism later developed into an aggressive attitude that insisted on the moral superiority of one people over all others and expressed unrelenting hostility toward outsiders. In its extreme form, militant nationalism encouraged the expulsion of "alien" groups who were not recognized as members of the national heritage. Aggressive nationalism lasted almost a century, from 1848 to 1945, climaxing in Nazi Germany, and still remains a potent force today.

The Romantics also generated a cult of nonconformity and held in great esteem outlaws, gypsies, and those who lived outside middle-class society. This hostility toward middle-class life has an ironic twist because those who professed it generally came from this class and sought its patronage. The unruly presence of Romanticism coincided with the rise to political dominance of the middle class. Out of the love-hate relationship between Romantics and the middle class emerged another familiar emblem of modern life, the anti-bourgeois bourgeois—that is, middle-class people who scorn their own social origins. From the dawn of the Romantic period until the present day, modern culture has been filled with middle-class rebels in revolt against their class.

France played a central role in Romanticism because of its culturally strategic position, and England also produced major figures in Romanticism, particularly in poetry and painting. Notwithstanding these achievements, the heart of Romanticism was German-speaking Europe. The French writer Madame de Staël (1766–1817) helped popularize German culture and writers with her book *On Germany* (1810). So great was the German cultural response that Romanticism is often called a German invention.

The Romantic Movement in Literature

Romanticism in literature was foreshadowed in the German literary movement known as **Sturm und Drang,** or Storm and Stress. This movement flourished briefly in the 1770s and early 1780s, arising as a revolt against Classical restraint and drawing inspiration from Rousseau's emotionalism. On a positive level, this literary movement idealized peasant life and the unconventional, liberated mind. The Sturm und Drang writers attacked organized religion because of its hypocrisy and followed Rousseau in finding God in nature. These middle-class authors objected to the formality and tedium of eighteenth-century life and letters and valued free expression in language, dress, behavior, and love. By the mid–1780s, the movement had settled down, drained of its rebelliousness. The most influential members became fully integrated into the German literary scene.

The Sturm und Drang movement's outstanding writer was Johann Wolfgang von Goethe [GUHR-tuh] (1749–1832), the greatest of German writers. In 1774, while still in his twenties, Goethe acquired a European-wide reputation with *The Sorrows of Young Werther,* a novel in which the young hero commits suicide because of disappointment in love. So successful was this novel that it led to Wertherism, the social phenomenon in which young men imitated the hero's emotionalism, sometimes even to the point of killing themselves. Werther is a complex character: passionate and excitable, given to inappropriate outbursts, moved by the innocence of children, attracted to social misfits, and overwhelmed by God's presence in nature. He embodies many characteristics of Romanticism.

With the publication in England in 1798 of *Lyrical Ballads* by William Wordsworth (1770–1850) and Samuel Taylor Coleridge (1772–1834), a turning point in the history of literary style was reached, and Romanticism truly began. Rejecting what they considered to be the artificiality of the Neoclassicists, the two poets turned to more natural types of verse, Coleridge to ballad forms and Wordsworth to simple lyrics of plain folks, voiced in the common language of the "middle and lower classes of society." Henceforth many Romantic writers, both in poetry and in prose, sought to reproduce the language of customary speech—a literary revolution that was the equivalent of the coming of democracy.

The task Wordsworth assigned himself in *Lyrical Ballads* was to compose verses about the pleasures of everyday existence. He responded to this challenge with poems filled with deep feeling, which were mainly about finding wisdom in simple things. A famous poem from this collection entitled "Lines Composed a Few Miles Above Tintern Abbey" shows Wordsworth's pantheism, or the belief that God lives in nature. In it, speaking to his sister Dorothy, he recalls the strong emotions he felt in his early life when he "bounded o'er the mountains, by the sides / of the deep rivers, and the lonely streams, / wherever nature led." Now he describes himself as subdued but still "a worshipper of Nature." Wordsworth's nature is a world of overgrown hedgerows, meadows, orchards, and peasant cottages. The beauty of the ordinary became Wordsworth's lifelong preoccupation; he is regarded as the English language's most stirring poet of nature.

Soon after the appearance of the *Lyrical Ballads,* Goethe published his verse play *Faust* (Part I, 1808). Goethe's Werther had been a social rebel, the prototype of the anti-bourgeois bourgeois. But his Faust was a universal rebel, unwilling to let any moral scruple stand in the way of his spiritual quest for the meaning of life. Faust's two distinguishing marks are his relentless pursuit of knowledge and his all-consuming restlessness. Having exhausted book learning, Faust hopes that experience will satisfy his spiritual hunger, and thus he turns to the Devil (Mephistopheles), who proposes to give Faust all the exciting experiences that have so far been lacking in his life. If Faust finds any moment satisfying, then his immortal soul is forever condemned to hell. Under such conditions Faust signs the compact, in his blood, with Mephistopheles.

Mephistopheles helps Faust recover his youth and involves him in a series of adventures that include drunkenness, sexual excess, seduction, and murder. His mistress kills their illegitimate child and perishes in despair. *Faust,* Part I, concludes with Faust more dissatisfied than when he began and no nearer to his goal. Goethe later added Part II (1832) to his drama, in which God redeems Faust because of his willingness to sacrifice his life for others, but lacking the emotional intensity of the first part, this second half failed to reach a large audience.

Goethe's *Faust,* Part I, however, proved irresistible. His drama became the most often performed German-language play in the world. It inspired numerous paintings and several works of music. The word **Faustian** came into usage to characterize one who is willing to sacrifice spiritual values for knowledge, experience, or mastery.

Another powerful voice in Romantic literature was the English poet George Gordon, Lord Byron (1788–1824). Better known on the Continent than his compatriots Wordsworth and Coleridge, Byron was called by Goethe the "herald of world literature." The personality of Byron has fascinated successive generations of Western artists and thinkers. At a time when the middle classes were ruled by a restrictive code of respectability, he created a model for rebellious youth with his flowing hair, open shirt collar, and love of ungovernable forces (Figure 17.11). His greatest Romantic creation was probably himself—the "Byronic hero," who was moody, passionate, absorbed in exploring and expressing his innermost self.

Yet the English treated Byron as a pariah and drove him into exile for his unconventional life. Perhaps in retaliation, Byron, in his most admired poem, *Don Juan* (1819–1824), presented the notorious seducer as a virtuous hero—a literary device intended to expose the hypocrisy of society. Like Goethe's *Faust*, Byron's *Don Juan* was a study in moral duality and reflected the author's fascination with subterranean drives in human nature.

Byron was the best known of the trio of Romantic poets whose enduring lyrical works helped to define the period from 1810 to 1824 as England's great Age of Poetry. The other two poets were Byron's friend Percy Bysshe Shelley (1792–1822), famed for poetry that was often charged with radical politics, and John Keats (1795–1820), who drew on a tragic personal history to create works of quiet beauty and stoic calm. That all three writers led tragically shortened lives—Byron dying at age thirty-six, Shelley at twenty-nine, and Keats at twenty-five—contributed in later years to their Romantic image as doomed poets.

English Romanticism also produced two of the most pervasive figures of Western culture—Frankenstein and his manufactured monster. Made familiar through countless films and cartoons, these two fictional characters first appeared in the novel *Frankenstein* (1818) by Mary Wollstonecraft Shelley (1797–1851). Shelley was well connected to two of the most unconventional literary families of the day; she was the daughter of Mary Wollstonecraft, a founder of modern feminism (see Chapter 16), and she was the wife of the poet Percy Bysshe Shelley. In Shelley's novel, Dr. Frankenstein, having thoughtlessly constructed a humanlike being with no prospect for personal happiness, is eventually hunted down and killed by his own despairing creature. Part of the Romantic reaction against Enlightenment rationalism, which began with Rousseau (see Chapter 16), Shelley's novel presented Frankenstein as a man driven by excessive and obsessive intellectual curiosity and the monster as a tragic symbol of science out of control. Written in the optimistic dawn of the industrialized age, when humanity seemed on the verge of taming the natural world, Shelley's *Frankenstein* is one of the earliest warnings that scientific research divorced from morality is an open invitation to personal and social disaster.

Figure 17.11 RICHARD WESTALL. *George Gordon, Lord Byron.* 1813. Oil on canvas, 36 × 28". National Portrait Gallery, London. *Westall's portrait of Lord Byron captures the brooding and dark good looks that made him the exemplar of the Romantic hero. Gazing intently into the distance while resting his chin on his hand, Byron seems lost in thought. His isolation is heightened by the overall darkness except for his face, hand, and shirt collar. It was this image of Byron—a person coiled tight as a spring— that caused one female admirer to describe him as "mad, bad, and dangerous to know."*

Romantic Painting

Romanticism in painting appeared first in England, manifesting itself as part of a cult of nature with two distinct aspects, the pastoral and the Sublime. Painters of pastoral scenes specialized in landscapes in which peasant life was equated with the divine order of things, thus forging a moral link between human beings and the natural environment. The painter John Constable was the chief exponent of the pastoral. In contrast, painters of Sublime subjects focused on devastating natural or human-made calamities, reflecting a world order beyond mortal control or understanding. The leading exponent of the Sublime was the painter J. M. W. Turner.

Like the Dutch masters of the 1600s, John Constable (1776–1837) preferred to paint simple country landscapes. But more important than the Dutch influence on his art was the Romantic "cult of nature." Constable's landscapes, like Wordsworth's poetry, reflected the sense of God's universal presence in nature. Wordsworth claimed that nature aroused feelings which "connect the landscape with the quiet of the sky." In his canvases, Constable tried to awaken the viewer to the divinity in nature by focusing on ordinary scenes such as one might see on a country walk. Constable had an almost holy vision that was true to nature without using what he called tricks or crass emotional appeals.

Constable's landscapes often convey a feeling of having been painted right on the spot. In actuality, he liked to sketch on a site and then transform his impressions into a finished painting that preserved the feeling of immediacy. This two-step method resulted in a style that was both solid and sensitive to the natural world. Constable's innocent and sincere style was meant to convey the feeling that his vision sprang from a mystical communion with nature, rather than being an artificial scene conceived in an artist's studio.

Although Constable's art was not fully appreciated by his contemporaries, a few works won ac- claim and helped to redefine the way that the public looked at nature. Of these the most famous is *The Hay Wain* (Figure 17.12). Over the years, this painting has been reproduced so often that it is sometimes dismissed as "calendar art," but when it first appeared, it excited admiration at home and in Paris. The freshness of the simple images attracted viewers to the beauty of the scene. *The Hay Wain* added many features of everyday rural life to the repertoire of Romantic motifs, including a thatch-roofed cottage, a gently flowing stream, a dog running along a river bank, cows grazing in the background, and overhead the ever-changing English sky.

The sky, for Constable, served as the unique source of light. In 1821–1822, he conducted a program that he called "skying," capturing on canvas the cloud-filled English sky as it moved from sunshine to rain and back again (Figure 17.13). Dissatisfied with earlier artists who used artificial means to represent nature,

Figure 17.12   JOHN CONSTABLE. *The Hay Wain.* 1821. Oil on canvas, 51¼ × 73″. Reproduced by courtesy of the Trustees, The National Gallery, London. *Although the pastoral subject was alien to them at the time, French Romantic painters recognized in Constable a kindred spirit when* The Hay Wain *was exhibited at the Paris Salon of 1824. The scene's informality, the strong colors, and the natural lighting converted them, and a later French school of landscape painters was influenced by Constable.*

Figure 17.13 JOHN CONSTABLE. *Cloud Study.* 1821. Oil on paper on panel, 8⅜ × 11½". Yale Center for British Art, New Haven. Paul Mellon Collection. *As Constable made his cloud paintings, he kept precise records of the weather conditions. For example, in this Cloud Study, he recorded the date and time, September 21, 1821, between 2 and 3 P.M. and noted: "strong Wind at west, bright light coming through the Clouds which are laying one on the other." Thus, these paintings combine the scientist's meticulous eye with the artist's sensitive response to nature.*

Figure 17.14 JOSEPH MALLORD WILLIAM TURNER. *Snowstorm: Hannibal and His Army Crossing the Alps.* 1810–1812. Oil on canvas, 4′9½″ × 7′9½″. Tate Gallery. *Hannibal and his troops, stretching from left to right in the bottom third of the painting, are almost invisible; above them and dominating the scene is a raging snowstorm, through which may be glimpsed a ghostly sun. This painting, based on a Gothic novel of the time, was less about the ancient struggle between the Carthaginian general Hannibal and Rome than about the French general Napoleon and England in the 1800s; thus, this work implicitly reflects the period's political climate—a rare occurrence in Turner's art.*

Figure 17.15 Joseph Mallord William Turner. *The Bay of Baiae, with Apollo and the Sibyl.* 1823. Oil on canvas, 57¼ × 94". Tate Gallery. *Turner has deftly focused the viewer's eye on the painting's center by means of a circular arrangement of objects (boats, ruins, and rocks) and the use of shadows and light. Within this space, Turner places Apollo making overtures to the Sibyl, a tactic whose outcome is symbolized by the rabbit and the snake. The rabbit (center) represents love, referring to Apollo's pursuit of the Sibyl, and the snake (lower right) alludes to lurking evil, perhaps a reference to the Sibyl's fate for spurning Apollo. The god curses her so that she will grow old but never die— just as the ruins at the Bay of Baiae are reminders of Rome's former glory.*

Constable worked as a naturalist to record the truth in nature. Constable's cloud studies echoed Romantic poets, like Goethe and Wordsworth, who identified clouds as a symbol of various themes, such as loneliness and the fleeting quality of life. In his attempt to portray the out-of-doors in its lively colors and ever-changing light, Constable was an important influence on the nineteenth-century Impressionists.

As for the Sublime, Joseph Mallord William Turner (1775–1851) created a new type of subject, "the sublime catastrophe," in which he specialized from 1800 until about 1830. He was the most original artist of his age, prefiguring the Impressionists with his virtuosic use of color and anticipating modern abstract painting in his depictions of wild nature. An example of Turner's sublime catastrophes is *Snowstorm: Hannibal and His Army Crossing the Alps* (Figure 17.14). Although inspired by an episode from Roman history, this painting is more about the fury of nature than it is about the Carthaginian general Hannibal. The actual subject is the snowstorm, whose sweeping savagery threatens to annihilate everything, including soldiers and horses. No artist before Turner had handled paint in the way that he does here. He turns the sky, which occupies at least three-fourths of the canvas, into an abstract composition, a series of interpenetrating planes of differently colored light.

Turner also dealt with another aspect of the Sublime theme, the notion that all human endeavor is doomed, in *The Bay of Baiae, with Apollo and the Sibyl* (Figure 17.15). Inspired by his first visit to Italy, he portrays Classical motifs in a Romantic landscape. In ancient Rome, the imperial court built splendid villas and baths at the Bay of Baiae (near Naples), which by

Turner's time stood in ruins. The painter, using artistic license, rearranged the actual scene to make this vista much more appealing. By placing Apollo and the Sibyl in the foreground, Turner alludes to a Greek myth associated with the nearby port of Cumae, the home of the Cumaean Sibyl.

About the time the Sublime developed in England, it also was launched in Germany by Caspar David Friedrich (1774–1840), a painter who specialized in brooding landscapes, usually with a few human figures to give them a spiritual scale. A lifelong resident of Pomerania on northern Europe's Baltic coast, he drew artistic inspiration from his homeland's deserted beaches, dense forests, and chalky cliffs. What sets his landscapes apart from those of earlier artists on the same subject is his desire to turn natural scenes into glimpses of the divine mystery. Avoiding traditional Christian subjects, Friedrich invented his own symbols for conveying God's presence in the world.

In *Monk by the Sea* (Figure 17.16), the setting is the stark Baltic seacoast, where a hooded figure stands on the dunes before a great wall of sky. This figure— the "monk" of the title—forms the only vertical line in an otherwise horizontal painting. Below is the angry sea, but the sky is calm except for a bank of clouds lit by the moon or perhaps the coming dawn. By showing the monk from the back—he rarely painted faces— Friedrich encourages the viewer to see what the monk sees and to feel what he feels. Perhaps, filled with optimism, he awaits a new day. Or perhaps, despairing, he watches the descent of night. Or perhaps he feels insignificant when confronted with the limitless sky and sea. Infrared photographs have revealed that Friedrich originally included two ships struggling against the

Figure 17.16 CASPAR DAVID FRIEDRICH. *Monk by the Sea.* 1808–1810. Oil on canvas, 43¼ × 67½". Stiftung Preussischer Kulturbesitz, Schloss Charlottenburg, Berlin. *This painting is revolutionary in form and content. In form, it violates Classical perspective by using a low horizon line to create a sky of limitless space; it also rejects traditional design by reducing figures and setting to a minimum level. In content, the meaning is left deliberately ambiguous. These simplifications make the painting a nearly abstract image, and thus it points the way to Modernist art (see Chapter 19).*

waves in the painting. Ships are often present in Friedrich's works, symbolic of a divine messenger to the human realm. By painting them out, Friedrich removed an optimistic note that may have guided the viewer's interpretation. Nevertheless, the finished painting represents twin Romantic themes and favorites of Friedrich's—love of solitude and fascination with the infinite.

In Spain, Romanticism flourished in the anti-Classical paintings of Francisco Goya (1746–1828), a major figure in Spanish culture. Reflecting a nightmarish vision of the world, his art ranges from Rococo fantasies to sensual portraits to grim studies of human folly to spiritual evil and finally to scenes of utter hopelessness. Various reasons have been suggested for Goya's descent into despair, but certainly his dashed hopes for the regeneration of Spain's political and social order were central to his advancing pessimism, as was his slow decline into deafness.

In the 1790s, Goya was serving as court painter to King Charles IV, and signs of the artist's political disaffection can be detected in his revealing portrait of the royal family (Figure 17.17). He depicts the queen (center) as a vain, foolish woman and the king (right, front) as a royal simpleton. History has judged Goya's interpretations to be accurate, for this was a corrupt and stupid court. Perhaps the lace-covered gowns, the glittering medals, and the general elegance of the ensemble allowed him to get away with such unflattering portraits and survive within this dangerous environment.

In 1797 Goya published a collection of etchings that set forth his savage indictment of the age's social evils and established him as an outstanding humanitarian artist. The title of this series was *Caprichos,* or *Caprices,* a Romantic genre that allowed artists to express their personal feelings on any subject. One of the eighty *caprichos, The Sleep of Reason* was intended as the series' frontispiece and is the key to Goya's artistic purpose (Figure 17.18). The inscription on the desk reads, "The sleep of reason brings forth monsters," a statement that conveys the need for eternal vigilance against cruelty and superstition. The nocturnal creatures—bats, owls, and cats—symbolize the dark forces that continually threaten rationality.

Napoleon's conquest of Spain and the subsequent Spanish war of liberation form the background to Goya's masterpiece, *The Execution of the Third of May, 1808* (Figure 17.19). This protest against French imperialism is one of the world's most compelling depictions of the horrors of war. It shows Spanish captives being executed by a French firing squad. The French troops are a faceless line of disciplined automatons, and the Spanish soldiers a band of ill-assorted irregulars. The Spanish patriots are arranged in three groups: Those covered with blood and lying on the ground are already dead, those facing the firing squad will be dead in an instant, and those marching forward with faces covered are scheduled for the next round. The emotional center of this otherwise somber-hued painting is the white-shirted man bathed in brilliant light. With his arms outstretched, he becomes a Christ figure, symbolizing Goya's compassion for all victims who die for a "good cause."

Romantic painting arrived in France in 1819 with the appearance of *The Raft of the "Medusa,"* a work by Théodore Géricault [zhay-rih-KOH] (1791–1824) that was based on an actual incident (Figure 17.20). The *Medusa*, a sailing ship, had foundered in the South Atlantic, and it was believed that all aboard were lost. Then, after almost two months, a handful of survivors were rescued from a makeshift raft. From their story came shocking details of mutiny, crimes by officers, murder, cannibalism, and a government cover-up.

Géricault was attracted to this incident in which a few men outwitted death against all odds. Focusing on the precise moment of their rescue, he depicts these ordinary humans as noble heroes nearly overwhelmed by the terrible forces of nature. The nude and partially clad bodies in the foreground convey a powerful sense of dignity and suffering. From here, the figures surge upward toward the black youth who is hoisted aloft and waving a flag at the unseen rescue ship. Géricault wanted his painting to convey a political statement

Figure 17.17 Francisco Goya. *The Family of Charles IV.* 1800. Oil on canvas, 9′2″ × 11′. Prado, Madrid. *Following a well-established Spanish tradition, Goya has painted himself into the canvas on the left, from which vantage point in the shadows he observes the royal family. Velázquez had followed this tradition 150 years earlier (see Figure 14.10), which this painting echoes. Goya portrayed the ravaged face of the king's sister on the left as a reminder of the fleeting nature of human beauty.*

Figure 17.18 Francisco Goya. *The Sleep of Reason.* 1797. Etching and aquatint, approx. 8½ × 6″. Courtesy, Museum of Fine Arts, Boston. Bequest of William P. Babcock. *Goya's artistic technique in the* Caprichos *series is aquatint, a process that uses acid on a metal plate to create subtle shades of light and dark. The absence of color in the resulting engravings heightens the moral message of these works.*

◀ **Figure 17.19** FRANCISCO GOYA. *The Execution of the Third of May, 1808*. 1814–1815. Oil on canvas, 8′9″ × 13′4″. Prado, Madrid. *A comparison of this painting by Goya with David's portrait of the assassinated Marat (see Figure 17.5) shows the difference in tone between Romantic and Neoclassical art. David makes Marat's death a heroic sacrifice despite its tragic circumstances. In contrast, Goya's passionate portrayal of the Spanish martyrs shows that there is nothing heroic about their deaths; their cause may be just, but the manner of their death is pitiless and squalid.*

about the government and to be as realistic as possible—he interviewed survivors and had a replica of the raft constructed—but at the same time, he imbued it with expression and pathos. The result was a highly emotional work that embodied the spirit of Romanticism.

Géricault's *Raft of the "Medusa"* also illustrates Romanticism's connection to liberal political ideas. The devastated humanity on the raft underscored the breakdown in civilization that the entire *Medusa* incident came to represent. The painting itself became a rallying point for the critics of the restored Bourbon monarchy, who saw in the portrayal of a crew cast adrift a metaphor for the French nation.

Many of Géricault's ideas were taken up by Eugène Delacroix [del-uh-KWAH] (1798–1863), who became the leader of a school of Romantic painting that was in open rivalry with Ingres and the Neoclassicists. Like Géricault, Delacroix was a humanitarian who drew artistic inspiration from his violent times. In the 1820s, he identified with the Greeks in their war of independence against the Turks, expressing his support in the allegorical painting *Greece Expiring on the Ruins of Missolonghi* (Figure 17.21). Lord Byron had died at Missolonghi while trying to bring warring Greek factions together, an event the painting commemorates. Delacroix portrays Greece as a grieving woman kneeling on a group of blasted stones from which a dead hand protrudes. Behind her stands a turbaned Turk, the symbol of Greece's oppressors.

Delacroix's *Liberty Leading the People* was also inspired by a political incident, the July Revolution of 1830, which resulted in the establishment of a consti-

◀ **Figure 17.20** THÉODORE GÉRICAULT. *The Raft of the "Medusa."* 1818. Oil on canvas, 16′1″ × 23′6″. Louvre. *Other artists, including Turner and Friedrich, painted shipwrecks and their victims, but Géricault's enormous canvas is probably the best known. He so vividly caught his subjects' desperation and hope that his work received instant praise, regardless of the controversies surrounding the subject and its relationships to social and political issues. With his usual thorough preparation, Géricault made over fifty studies of the incident, rearranging the figures on the raft until he had created a pyramidal structure, moving from the lower left corner to the center and upper right.*

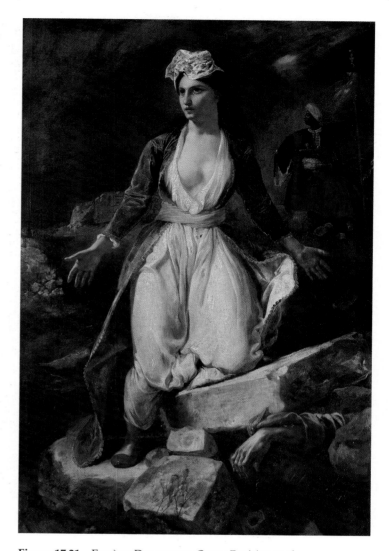

Figure 17.21 EUGÈNE DELACROIX. *Greece Expiring on the Ruins of Missolonghi*. 1826. Oil on canvas, 6′11½″ × 4′8¼″. Musée des Beaux-Arts, Bordeaux. *Delacroix's representation of Greece as a woman was part of the Romantic convention of using female figures as national symbols. This trend climaxed in the writings of the French historian Jules Michelet, who concluded in 1846 that "France is a woman herself."*

tutional government (Figure 17.22). The painting combines realism and allegory, depicting revolutionaries on the barricades led by an idealized, bare-breasted goddess of Liberty. Surrounding Liberty are three central figures who symbolize the various classes that constitute "the People": The man in the tall hat represents the middle classes, the chief beneficiaries of the revolution; the kneeling figure in the cap stands for the working-class rebels; and the boy brandishing the twin pistols is an image of the street urchin, among the lowest social groups.

The focal point of the painting is the tricolor, the revolutionary flag adopted in the revolution of 1789,

Figure 17.22   Eugène Delacroix. *Liberty Leading the People.* 1831. Oil on canvas,
8′6″ × 10′8″. Louvre. *Delacroix's canvas bears some meaningful resemblances to Géri-*
cault's Raft of the "Medusa." *Each painting takes a contemporary event as its subject*
and transforms it into a symbol of France. Moreover, Delacroix's placement of two dead
male figures, one partially nude and the other clothed, echoes similar figures in Géricault's
work. Delacroix's portrayal of the people triumphant thus seems to be an optimistic
response to Géricault's image of France adrift.

outlawed from 1815 until 1830 and now restored as
France's unifying symbol. The flag's red, white, and
blue determine the harmony of color in the rest of this
painting. Completed soon after the 1830 revolution,
this work was purchased by the new king as a fitting
tribute to the struggle that brought him to power. It
was quickly hidden away, however, for the bourgeois
establishment found the revolutionary heritage an em-
barrassment. Only later, with the creation of the Second Republic in 1848, did the French public see the
painting.

Despite paying homage to radical forces, Delacroix
was no true revolutionary. Even before painting *Liberty
Leading the People,* Delacroix had been turning toward

a more sensual art, an art that relied on gorgeous colors, as in *The Death of Sardanapalus* (Figure 17.23). Taking an anecdote from ancient history that had been
dramatized by Lord Byron, he converted it into an image of Romantic destruction. In Delacroix's version,
the doomed tyrant Sardanapalus, preparing to commit
suicide, gazes unemotionally on the chaos caused by
his order to kill everything—harem women, horses,
and dogs—that he has ever loved. Much of the success
of this haunting image depends on dramatic juxtapositions: passivity and passion, love and death, black
and white, male and female. In paintings like this,
Delacroix embodied the Romantic fascination with exotic, sensual, and violent subjects.

Figure 17.23   Eugène Delacroix. *The Death of Sardanapalus.* 1828. Oil on canvas, 12′ 10¼″ × 16′ ¼″. Louvre. *Delacroix's opulent painting caused a scandal when it was exhibited in the Paris Salon of 1827, but it also raised Delacroix to a position of leadership in the Romantic school. Its subject reflected the interest in the exotic Orient, which was a strong feature of French Romanticism. The subject allowed Delacroix's genius to run wild, imbuing the scene with confusion and surging colors.*

German Idealism

In philosophy, the Romantic spirit led to idealism, a system of thought that flourished mainly in Germany and that espoused a spiritual view of life. From Kant through Hegel, the Germans constructed idealism as a philosophic alternative to conventional religion. In the 1790s, Immanuel Kant [KAHNT] (1724–1804) began the revolution in thought when he distinguished the world of phenomena ("appearances") from the world of noumena ("things-in-themselves," or spirit). In Kantian terms, the phenomenal world may be understood by science, but the noumenal world may be studied, if at all, only by intuitive means.

Kant's followers, nonetheless, tried the impossible when they began to map out the spiritual realm. Johann Gottlieb Fichte [FICK-tuh] (1762–1814) found reality in the World Spirit, a force having consciousness and seeking self-awareness. Friedrich Wilhelm Joseph von Schelling [SHEL-ing] (1775–1854) equated nature with the Absolute, his name for ultimate reality. He also was the first to espouse the romantic belief in the religion of art by claiming that artists reveal divine truths in inspired works. Schelling's teaching on art influenced the English poet Coleridge and through him English Romanticism in general.

The climax of idealism came with Georg Wilhelm Friedrich Hegel [HAY-guhl] (1770–1831), who explained

Figure 17.24 Ferdinand Georg Waldmüller. *Ludwig van Beethoven*. 1823. Oil on canvas, approx. 28⅓ × 22⅝″. Archiv Breitkopf and Härtel, Leipzig, Germany. Original destroyed in World War II. *Beethoven in his later years was the embodiment of the Romantic genius, disheveled, singing to himself as he strolled Vienna's streets, mocked by street urchins; once, he was even arrested by the police as a tramp. In this 1823 portrait, Waldmüller suggests Beethoven's unkempt appearance, but through the strong expression, fixed jaw, and broad forehead he also conveys the great composer's fierce determination and intelligence.*

human history as the record of the World Spirit seeking to know its true nature. Self-knowledge for the World Spirit arose only through a dialectical struggle. In the first stage, the Spirit developed a thesis that in turn produced an antithesis; in the second stage, a conflict ensued between these two ideas that led to a synthesis, or a new thesis, which in turn gradually provoked new strife—a third stage, and so on ad infinitum. Hegel's theory of history ignored individuals because humans in the mass became tools of the World Spirit in its quest for freedom. In this view, wars, riots, and revolts were merely evidence of spiritual growth. For this reason, Hegel characterized Napoleon and his wars as embodiments of the World Spirit.

Hegelianism had a tremendous impact on later Western thought. Revolutionaries like Karl Marx borrowed his dialectical approach to history. Conservatives, especially in Germany, used Hegel's thought as a justification for a strong centralized state, and nationalists everywhere drew inspiration from his thought. Other thinkers rejected his denial of human responsibility and founded existentialist philosophies that glorified the individual.

The Birth of Romantic Music

As the middle class gained political power between 1789 and 1830, they converted the musical scene into a marketplace; that is, laissez-faire economics and music became intertwined. Replacing elite forms of patronage, programs that the bourgeoisie now attended required admission fees and paid performers. Salaries and the demand for performances freed musicians from the patronage system. With their newly won independence, they became eccentric and individualistic—attitudes that were encouraged by the Romantic cult of the artist. Music grew more accessible as democracy progressed, and new industrial techniques and production allowed more people to own inexpensive musical instruments.

The most gifted composer of this period, and one of the greatest musical geniuses of all time, was Ludwig van Beethoven [BAY-toe-vuhn] (1770–1827), a German who spent most of his life in Vienna. He personified the new breed of musician, supporting himself through concerts, lessons, and the sales of his music (Figure 17.24). His works represent both the culmination of Classical music and the introduction of Romantic music. Working with the standard Classical forms—the sonata, the symphony, and the string quartet—he created longer works, doubling and even tripling their length. He also wrote music that was increasingly expressive and that showed more warmth and variety of feeling. He made several other significant musical innovations, including the use of choral voices within the symphonic form and the introduction of **program music**—that is, music that portrays a particular setting or tells a story.

Beethoven's career may be divided into three phases, but his extreme individualism left his unique stamp on everything that he composed. In the first phase, from the 1790s until 1803, he was under the shadow of Haydn, with whom he studied in Vienna. His First Symphony (1800) may be termed a Classical work, but in it he reveals a new spirit by lengthening the first and third movements and making the middle movement more lively than usual.

In the second phase, from 1803 until 1816, Beethoven's genius gave birth to Romantic music. He began to find his own voice, enriching and deepening the older forms. The Third Symphony (1803), which Beethoven called the *Eroica* ("Heroic"), is the most characteristic work from this second stage. The composer originally dedicated this symphony to Napoleon, whom he admired as a champion of democracy. But when the French ruler declared himself emperor in 1804, Beethoven angrily tore up the page and dedicated it instead "to the memory of a great man." In the Third Symphony, Beethoven substantially expands the

PERSONAL PERSPECTIVE

Hector Berlioz
This Harmonious Revolution

Berlioz was an eyewitness to the 1830 Revolution in Paris, as well as a participant in the events of the day. In his memoirs, he recorded the frenzy and jubilation of the crowds rebelling against the Bourbon monarchy.

It was in the year 1830. I was just finishing my cantata when the Revolution broke out.

A number of families had taken shelter in the Palais de l'Institut, and it looked strangely transformed—with long-barreled muskets protruding from the barred doors, and its façade riddled with bullets, the air filled with the shrieks of women, and, in the lulls between the discharges of musketry, the shrill twitter of the swallows. I hurriedly dashed off the last pages of my cantata to the tune of the dry thud of the bullets as they struck close to my windows or on the walls of my room; and on the 24th I was free to loaf about Paris with the "*sacred rabble*," and my pistol in my pocket, till the next day.

I shall never forget the aspect of Paris during those memorable days—the wild bravado of the street Arabs, the enthusiasm of the men, the frenzy of the women, the mournful resignation of the Swiss and Royal Guards, the curious pride which the workmen exhibited in not pillaging Paris though they were masters of the situation, the astounding stories told by young fellows of their exploits, in which the real bravery of the deed was lost in the sense of the ridiculous aroused by the manner in which it was told; as, for instance, when they described the storming of the cavalry barracks of the Rue de Babylone—in which considerable loss had been incurred—with a gaiety worthy of Alexander's veterans, as "the capture of Babylon"—an abbreviation forced on them by the length of the real name. With what pompous prolongation of the "o" the name of "Babylon" was pronounced! . . . Oh Parisians, what buffoons you are! Great, if you will, but still buffoons! . . .

No words can give any idea of the music, the songs and the hoarse voices which rang through the streets!

And yet it was only a few days after this harmonious revolution that I received a most extraordinary musical impression, or shock. I was crossing the Palais Royal when I heard a tune which I seemed to recognize, issuing from among a crowd of people. As I drew nearer I perceived that ten or twelve young fellows were singing a war song of my own, the words of which, translated from one of Moore's *Irish Melodies*, happened exactly to suit the situation.

---

musical material beyond the limits characteristic of earlier symphonies, making it longer and more complex. The music is grand, serious, and dignified, a truly heroic work.

In the third phase, from 1816 until 1827, Beethoven's music became freer and more contemplative, reaching its culmination in the Ninth Symphony (1822–1824), the last of his large-scale works. In the last movement of this work, Beethoven included a choral finale in which he set to music the poem "Ode to Joy" by the German Romantic poet Friedrich von Schiller [SHIL-uhr] (1759–1805). Despite a life of personal adversities that included deafness from the age of thirty, Beethoven affirmed in this piece his faith in both humanity and God—"Millions, be you embraced! For the universe, this kiss!" The magnificent music and the idealistic text have led to the virtual canonization of this inspirational work.

Across these three phases, Beethoven was a prolific composer in all musical genres; many of these works are unrivaled in their expressiveness and originality. Besides the nine symphonies, he wrote two Masses, two ballets, one opera (*Fidelio*), sixteen string quartets, thirty-two piano sonatas (most notably the *Pathétique* and *Moonlight* sonatas), five concertos for piano, one concerto for violin, and numerous chamber and choral compositions.

Vienna contributed another outstanding composer in Franz Schubert [SHOO-bert] (1797–1828), who was famous for the beauty of his melodies and the simple grace of his songs. He lived a rather bohemian life, supporting himself, like Beethoven, by giving lessons and concerts. But unlike Beethoven, Schubert wrote mainly for the living rooms of Vienna rather than for the concert hall and is most famous for perfecting the **art song,** called in German **lied** (plural, *lieder*). The emergence of this musical form in the Romantic period was tied to the revival of lyric poetry. Schubert composed the music for over six hundred *lieder*, with texts by Goethe ("Gretchen at the Spinning Wheel"), Shakespeare ("Who Is Sylvia?"), and other poets. His efforts raised the song to the level of great art.

A final composer of significance in this first period of Romanticism was the Frenchman Hector Berlioz

[BAIR-lee-ohz] (1803–1869). His most famous work is the *Symphonie fantastique (Fantastic Symphony)* (1830), a superb example of program music. Subtitled "Episode of an Artist's Life," this symphonic work illustrates musically a story that Berlioz described in accompanying written notes. In the tale, which takes the form of an opium dream, an artist-hero hopelessly adores an unfaithful woman and eventually dies for her. Relatively conventional in form, the symphony is most original in its use of a recurring musical theme, called an *idée fixe,* or "fixed idea," that becomes an image of the hero's beloved. Because every section contains the *idée fixe* in a modified form, it unifies the symphony in an innovative way. The success of Berlioz's symphony helped to strengthen the fashion for program music in the Romantic period.

The Legacy of the Age of Revolution and Reaction

During this period of revolution and reaction, the West turned away from the past, with its monarchical forms of government, its hierarchical society dominated by aristocratic landowners, its glacial rate of change, and its patronage system ruled by social, ecclesiastical, and political elites. Three events in particular—the Industrial Revolution and the American and the French Revolutions—have left an indelible stamp on the modern world. The Industrial Revolution, which continues today, has gradually made humanity master of the earth and its resources, while at the same time accelerating the pace of life and creating the two leading modern social groups, the middle class and the working class. The Industrial Revolution also spawned Classical economics, the school of economists who justified the doctrine of laissez faire that is still held to be the best argument for capitalism and continuous industrial growth. This same doctrine altered the patronage system, subjecting the creative works of modern artists, writers, musicians, and humanists to the law of the marketplace.

The American Revolution produced the first successful modern democracy, one that today stands as a beacon of hope for those oppressed by authoritarian regimes. The French Revolution contributed the idea of an all-encompassing upheaval that would sweep away the past and create a new secular order characterized by social justice and fairness. Although viewed with skepticism by some, for multitudes of others the notion of such a revolution became a sustaining belief. From the French Revolution also arose the idea that race and religion should not be used to exclude people from the right to vote—a reflection of its emphasis on the "brotherhood of man." Another outgrowth of the French Revolution is the Napoleonic Code, the law code that is used in the French-speaking world today.

Both the French and the American Revolutions contributed certain beliefs that have become basic statements of Western political life, such as the idea that constitutions should be written down and that basic human liberties should be identified. Indeed, the progressive expansion of natural and civil rights to embrace all of society is an outgrowth of these two revolutions.

Other enduring legacies of this late-eighteenth- and early-nineteenth-century period are the Neoclassical buildings in Washington, D.C., and in most of the state capitals of the United States, the body of music of the Romantic composers, and the paintings of the Neoclassical and early Romantic schools. An ambiguous legacy of this period has been nationalism, the belief in one's own country and its people. At its best, nationalism is a noble concept, for it encourages people to examine their roots and preserve their collective identity and heritage. At its worst, it has led to cutthroat behavior, dividing the people of a country against one another and leading to the disintegration of nations. Both forms of nationalism remain potent forces in the world today.

On a more personal level, this period saw the development of the Romantic view of life, an attitude that stresses informality, identification with the common people, the importance of feeling and imagination, and enjoyment of simple pleasures. Perhaps more than any other legacy of this period, the Romantic outlook has helped to shape the way that most Western men and women live in today's world.

KEY CULTURAL TERMS

Romanticism	program music
Sublime	art song *(lied)*
Sturm und Drang	*idée fixe*
Faustian	

SUGGESTIONS FOR FURTHER READING

PRIMARY SOURCES

AUSTEN, J. *Pride and Prejudice. Sense and Sensibility.* Introduction by D. Daiches. New York: Modern Library, 1950. Both novels deal with English provincial life. *Pride and Prejudice* (1813) focuses on the proud Mr. Darcy, who must be humbled before the "prejudiced" Elizabeth Bennet can take seriously his marriage proposal; *Sense and Sensibility* (1811) uses practical-mindedness ("sense") to expose the self-indulgence of the "picturesque" spirit ("sensibility"), an aspect of genteel taste in the late eighteenth century.

BYRON, G. G., Lord. *Don Juan.* Edited by T. G. Steffan, E. Steffan, and W. W. Pratt. New York: Penguin, 1973. One of Byron's most admired works, full of autobiographical references; dates from 1819–1824.

FICHTE, J. G. *Addresses to the German Nation.* Translated by R. F. Jones and G. H. Turnbull. Chicago: Open Court, 1923. The work that helped to launch German nationalism when first published in the early 1800s.

GOETHE, J. W. v. *Faust.* Part I. Translated by M. Greenberg. New Haven: Yale University Press, 1992. A good recent English version of Goethe's drama of a man prepared to sacrifice his soul for the sake of knowledge based on feeling; originally published in 1808.

————. *The Sorrows of Young Werther.* Translated by E. Mayer and L. Bogan. Foreword by W. H. Auden. New York: Vintage, 1990. The 1774 Romantic novel that brought Goethe his earliest European-wide fame, translated by modern poets.

HEGEL, G. W. F. *Reason in History.* Translated and with an introduction by R. S. Hartman. New York: Liberal Arts Press, 1953. The best source for Hegel's theory that history moves through a dialectical process; first published in 1837.

KANT, I. *Critique of Pure Reason.* Introduction and glossary by W. Schwarz. Aalen, Germany: Scientia, 1982. A good version of Kant's difficult work that tried to establish what human reason can know apart from experience; dates from 1781.

MALTHUS, T. *On Population.* Edited and with an introduction by G. Himmelfarb. New York: Random House, 1960. One of the more recent editions of the influential essay, first published in 1788, that identified the modern dilemma of keeping population growth in equilibrium with food production.

RICARDO, D. *On the Principles of Political Economy and Taxation.* New York: Penguin, 1971. Ricardo's "iron law of wages"—that wages tend to hover around the subsistence level—became a central tenet of nineteenth-century laissez-faire theory.

SCHELLING, F. W. J. v. *Ideas for a Philosophy of Nature.* Translated by E. E. Harris. New York: Cambridge University Press, 1988. An excellent translation of Schelling's 1799 work, which helped shape Romantic thinking by claiming to find God both in nature and in the human intellect.

SHELLEY, M. *Frankenstein.* With an introduction by D. Johnson. New York: Bantam Books, 1991. The original source of the Frankenstein legend, published in 1818 when Shelley was twenty-one years old; inspired by an evening of reading and discussing ghost stories.

WORDSWORTH, W. *Lyrical Ballads.* Edited by R. L. Braett and A. R. Jones. London: Routledge and Kegan Paul, 1988. A new edition of the original volume (1798) by Wordsworth and Coleridge that initiated the age of Romantic poetry in England; contains good introductory material.

SUGGESTIONS FOR LISTENING

BEETHOVEN, LUDWIG VAN (1770–1827). Composing mainly in Classical forms, notably the symphony and the string quartet, Beethoven moved from a Classical style in the manner of Haydn and Mozart to a Romantic style that was his own. The First Symphony (1800) shows his Classical approach; the Third Symphony, the *Eroica* (1803), inaugurated his Romantic style with its intense emotionalism and rich thematic variations. Of special note is the Ninth Symphony (1822–1826), a semimystical work whose final section blends full orchestra with a massed chorus. The emotional nature of the Violin Sonata No. 9 (*Kreutzer* Sonata) inspired the Russian writer Leo Tolstoy to use the piece as a catalyst for murder in his story "The Kreutzer Sonata." Beethoven's stylistic development can also be traced in his sixteen string quartets: The first six quartets, dating from 1800, reflect the grace of Haydn and Mozart, and the last five, Nos. 12 through 16 (1823–1826), are technically difficult to play, enormously long, and characterized by mood shifts from light to tragic and unusual harmonic juxtapositions. The familiar piano piece "Für Elise" is a fine example of the rondo form.

BERLIOZ, HECTOR (1803–1869). Berlioz was typically Romantic in going beyond the forms of Classicism and stressing the emotional possibilities of his music. For example, his *Requiem* (1837) is less a religious work than a dramatic symphony for orchestra and voices; its inspiration was the tradition of patriotic festivals originated during the French Revolution. Similarly, his opera *Damnation of Faust* (1846) is not an opera in a conventional sense but a series of episodes based on Goethe's play, a form that allowed the composer to focus on those scenes that seemed full of theatrical potential. Finally, the *Symphonie fantastique* (1830) is more than a symphony; it has been called "a musical drama without words"—the prototype of Romantic program music.

SCHUBERT, FRANZ (1797–1828). Though a prolific composer of symphonies, operas, and piano sonatas, Schubert is most famous for perfecting the art song, or *lied*. Two of his best-known songs, with texts by Goethe, are "Gretchen am Spinnrade" ("Gretchen at the Spinning Wheel," 1814) and "Erlkönig" ("The Erlking," 1815). One of Schubert's most celebrated chamber works, a quintet for piano and strings, is "Die Forelle" ("The Trout," 1821), in which the lively, fluid music suggests the energetic movements of a swimming fish.

18 THE TRIUMPH OF THE BOURGEOISIE
1830–1871

The French and American Revolutions offered the hope of political power to all disenfranchised groups, and the Industrial Revolution promised material gains to the impoverished. These expectations remained largely unfulfilled in Europe, however, as the nineteenth century unfolded. Benefits were reaped mainly by one group— the middle class, especially its wealthiest sector.

Left behind was a new group created by industrialization—the proletariat, or working class. These urban workers expressed their frustrations through political uprisings and social movements, and often the lower middle class joined them in demanding universal suffrage and a fairer distribution of power and wealth. Against the liberalism of the bourgeoisie some of the workers set forth the ideals of socialism. But reform was limited at best, and successive waves of revolutionary uprisings failed to win significant improvements.

These changes were echoed in the cultural realm. From its brief peak in the 1820s, Romanticism declined and finally faded away. Embraced by the middle class, it gained respectability and lost much of its creative fire. By midcentury, a new, realistic style was emerging that reflected changing political and social conditions. Realism focused on ordinary people and attempted to depict in objective terms "the heroism of everyday life." At the same time, industrialization continued to spread, and people's ideas about themselves and the world were being challenged by everything from the theories of Charles Darwin to the invention of the camera (Timeline 18.1).

◄ **Detail** GUSTAVE COURBET. *Interior of My Studio: A Real Allegory Summing Up Seven Years of My Life as an Artist*. 1855. Oil on canvas, 11'9¾" × 19'6⅝". Louvre.

Timeline 18.1 THE AGE OF THE BOURGEOISIE

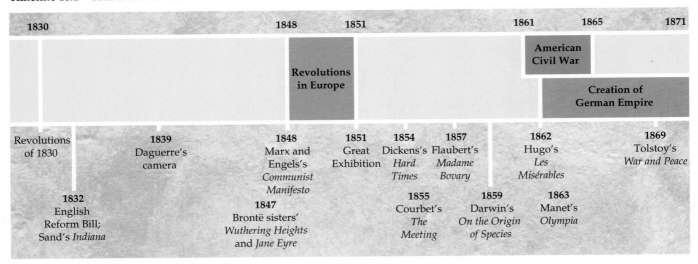

1830	1848	1851	1861	1865	1871

Revolutions in Europe

American Civil War

Creation of German Empire

Revolutions of 1830

1839 Daguerre's camera

1848 Marx and Engels's *Communist Manifesto*

1851 Great Exhibition

1854 Dickens's *Hard Times*

1857 Flaubert's *Madame Bovary*

1862 Hugo's *Les Misérables*

1869 Tolstoy's *War and Peace*

1832 English Reform Bill; Sand's *Indiana*

1847 Brontë sisters' *Wuthering Heights* and *Jane Eyre*

1855 Courbet's *The Meeting*

1859 Darwin's *On the Origin of Species*

1863 Manet's *Olympia*

Map 18.1 EUROPE AFTER THE CONGRESS OF VIENNA, 1815

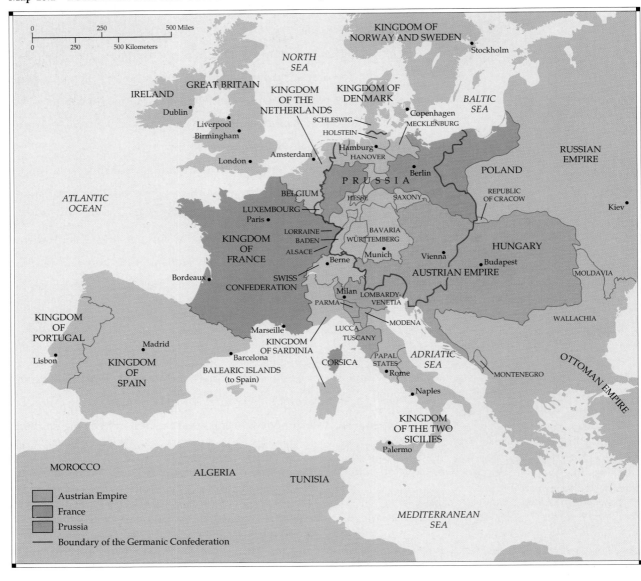

THE POLITICAL AND ECONOMIC SCENE: LIBERALISM AND NATIONALISM

The powerful forces of liberalism and nationalism drove many nineteenth-century events. The basic premise of liberalism was that the individual should be free from external control, a notion that resonated with the American and French Revolutions and the need of the bourgeoisie to liberate themselves from aristocratic society. The liberal political agenda included constitutionally guaranteed political and civil rights such as free speech, religious toleration, and voting rights for the propertied classes. Perhaps most important, liberalism embraced the laissez-faire economic ideals that allowed the wealthy middle class to maximize their profits in the business world. Liberalism was most successful in England, France, and Belgium; it failed to take root in Italy and central and eastern Europe, and Russia remained reactionary.

The other driving force of this era, nationalism, emphasized cooperation among all of a country's people who shared a common language and heritage. Overlooking class divisions, nationalists advocated humanitarian values, stressing the concept that all members of a nation are brothers and sisters. As nationalism spread, these concepts were often expanded to include liberal ideals, republican principles, and even democratic beliefs. Nationalism became a force in central, southern, and eastern Europe, where the states of what would become Germany and Italy were still little more than "geographic expressions" (Map 18.1). After 1848 nationalism became increasingly militant.

The Revolutions of 1830 and 1848

The repressive policies imposed by the Congress of Vienna in 1815 were challenged in 1830 by a series of uprisings, beginning with the July Revolution in France and the French overthrow of the Bourbon monarchy and the installation of Louis Philippe (r. 1830–1848), who pledged to uphold a liberal constitution (Figure 18.1). This regime increasingly became the tool of the rich middle class at the expense of the workers, however. Voting was limited to wealthy male property owners, and laws favored unregulated economic expansion. Having gained political dominance, the middle class intended to keep the benefits of the liberal agenda for themselves.

Liberal revolutions followed elsewhere, including in Belgium and areas of central and southern Europe, but they were unsuccessful. In central Europe, local conservatives backed by Austrian troops quickly crushed the liberal uprisings of 1830 and punished

Figure 18.1   FRANÇOIS RUDE. *The Departure of the Volunteers.* 1833–1836. Approx. 42 × 26'. Paris. *Under the "citizen king," Louis Philippe, bourgeois leaders were nervous about the revolutionary events that had brought them to power. Nevertheless, this group sculpture depicting the people on the march was hailed by all social ranks as an acceptable image of France's revolutionary past, including the revolution of 1830. Designed for the Arch of Triumph in Paris, the work came to be known affectionately as* La Marseillaise, *the name of the French national anthem.*

rebels, imposed martial law, reinstituted censorship, and took control of the school systems. Although liberals continued to hope for moderate reforms, conservatives made it difficult for them. Across central and eastern Europe, the one force emerging as a rallying point was nationalism, focusing as it did on ethnic identity and common cultural heritage.

In 1848 accumulated dissatisfactions and frustrations erupted in another series of uprisings across Europe (Table 18.1), starting with demonstrations and riots in February 1848 in Paris. The rebellions were propelled by liberal ideals and nationalistic goals, but their immediate causes were declining production, rising unemployment, and falling agricultural prices. By the spring of 1848, the path of revolution ran from Paris through Berlin to Vienna, and all along this route the bourgeoisie, intellectuals, workers, students, and nationalists toppled kings and ministers. Temporary

Table 18.1   MAJOR POLITICAL EVENTS OF THE 1815–1871 PERIOD

EVENT AND DATE	OUTCOME
Congress of Vienna, 1815	Inaugurates an era of repression
July Revolution in France, 1830	Ends the Bourbon dynasty and installs the bourgeois monarchy
First English Reform Bill, 1832	Extends voting rights to wealthy middle-class males
Revolution in France, 1848	Ends the bourgeois monarchy and installs the Second Republic, with Louis-Napoleon as president
Revolutions in Europe, 1848–1851	Their failure leads to an era dominated by realpolitik
Creation of Second French Empire, 1851	Louis-Napoleon becomes Napoleon III and leads empire until 1870
Kingdom of Italy, 1860	Sicily joins Piedmont
Creation of German Empire, 1862–1871	Engineered by Bismarck using a policy of "blood and iron"; unites German states around Prussia
American Civil War, 1861–1865	Preserves national union and abolishes slavery
Second English Reform Bill, 1867	Extends voting rights to working-class males
Franco-Prussian War, 1871	Destroys the Second French Empire, proclaims the German Empire, and leaves a legacy of French bitterness toward Germany

European Affairs in the Grip of Realpolitik

From 1850 to 1871, realpolitik guided the European states as conservative regimes turned to strong and efficient armies, short, fierce wars, and ambiguously written agreements to resolve the various problems that had surfaced in the 1848 revolts. Otto von Bismarck, the prime minister of Prussia and future architect of German unification, mocked the failure of the liberals' parliamentary reforms and asserted that his country's fate would be settled not with speeches but with "blood and iron." Nationalists in Austrian-occupied Italy learned that Italian unity could be achieved only by military force and clever diplomacy. The Russian czars, seldom supporters of any type of reform, became even more committed to the belief that if any change did come, it would begin at the top, not the bottom, of society.

Limited Reform in France and Great Britain   One of the most astute observers of the 1848 revolutions was Louis-Napoleon Bonaparte, nephew of the former French emperor. He became Emperor Napoleon III (r. 1852–1870) of the Second French Empire by appealing to both the bourgeoisie and the working class. A benign despot, he ruled over a sham representative government supported by a growing middle class made prosperous by the expanding industrial base. He also provided the poor with social services, and with an economic plan and subsidies, he enabled most urban workers and farmers to maintain a high standard of living.

In Great Britain, a liberal coalition of landed and business interests pushed a reform bill through the Parliament in 1832 over the protests of the conservatives. This new law redrew the political map of England to reflect the tremendous shift in population resulting from industrialization, and it enfranchised thousands of new male voters by lowering the property qualifications for voting, although millions of British citizens were still denied the vote. In 1867 a second reform bill extended voting rights to working-class males. With Queen Victoria (r. 1837–1901) on the throne and political forces balanced evenly between liberals and conservatives, Great Britain reached its apex of economic power and prestige (Figure 18.2).

Wars and Unification in Central Europe   Among the German-speaking states, the small principalities tended to discard liberalism and embrace militant nationalism. Their concerns were overshadowed, however, by the power struggle between Prussia and Austria for control of central Europe. William I became king of Prussia in 1861, and Bismarck was appointed his prime minister. Over the next few years, Bismarck built the Prussian

governments, led by liberals and reformers, drove out foreign troops and set up constitutional monarchies, republics, or democracies with universal male suffrage. A few governments—influenced by the new movement known as socialism—addressed economic problems by passing laws to stimulate productivity, improve working conditions, and aid the poor with relief or employment programs.

By the fall of 1848, the conservatives—the army, aristocrats, and church—had rallied to defeat the often disorganized revolutionaries, and by January 1849 many of the old rulers had reclaimed power. After 1848 the idealism of the liberals, social reformers, and nationalists gave way to an unsentimental vision of politics and diplomacy backed by pragmatic use of force. This perspective came to be known as realpolitik, a German term that means "practical politics," a tactful way of saying "power politics."

Figure 18.2   CHARLES BARRY AND A. W. N. PUGIN. The Houses of Parliament. 1836–1860. Big Ben (right) 320' high; Victoria Tower (left) 336' high; riverfront width 800'. London. *In contrast to the revolutionary tradition on the Continent, Great Britain struggled to respond to changing political and social realities through debate and reform. To many observers in England and abroad, Parliament symbolized the success of liberalism and the representative legislative system. The Gothic spires of the Houses of Parliament rose in the mid–nineteenth century after the old buildings burned. Along with the neighboring clock tower known as "Big Ben" (a name applied originally only to the bell), they still stand today as the most recognizable image of modern London.*

army into a fierce fighting machine, at the same time ignoring liberal protests and the Prussian assembly and its laws. Nationalism replaced liberalism as the rallying cry of the Prussians, and Bismarck used this shift to unite the Germans around the Prussian state at the expense of France and of Austria (see Map 18.1).

Bismarck achieved his goal by neutralizing potential enemies through deft diplomacy and, failing that, through force. By 1866 he had united the German states into the North German Confederation, a union that excluded Austria. In 1870 he engineered a diplomatic crisis that forced France to declare war on Prussia. Costly French defeats brought the Franco-Prussian War to an abrupt end later that year, toppled the Second Empire of Napoleon III, and resulted in France's humiliation in the treaty signed at Versailles in 1871, proclaiming the German Empire. The seeds of World War I were sown by this crucial turn of events (Map 18.2).

On the Italian peninsula, most of which was ruled by Austrian princes, liberalism and nationalism were also causes of disruption. In the 1830s, Italian liberals inspired by the revolutionary writings of Giuseppe Mazzini [maht-SEE-nee] (1805–1872) banded together to form Young Italy, a nationalistic movement, and the independent Italian state of Piedmont-Sardinia emerged as the hope of liberals. Piedmont was a constitutional monarchy that honored its subjects' civil and political rights. Its economy was well balanced between farming and trade, and under Prime Minister Count Camillo Benso di Cavour [kuh-VOOR]

(1810–1861), the standard of living was raised for many Piedmontese, especially middle-class merchants and manufacturers.

Between 1859 and 1871, Piedmont expelled most of the Austrians. As part of his grand strategy to unite Italy, Cavour, with the encouragement of Napoleon III of France, annexed parts of central and southern Italy. Further assistance came from the fiercely patriotic soldier Giuseppe Garibaldi [gahr-uh-BAHL-dee] (1807–1882), who, with his personal army of a thousand "Red Shirts," invaded and liberated the Kingdom of the Two Sicilies (see Map 18.1) from its Spanish Bourbon ruler. In 1860 Sicilians voted overwhelmingly to join Piedmont in a Kingdom of Italy, and soon thereafter the Italian mosaic fell into place. In 1866 Austria gave up Venetia, and in 1870 Rome fell to nationalist troops and became Italy's capital.

Civil War in the United States

Paralleling the turbulent unification of the modern states of Italy and Germany, the United States was also undergoing expansion and centralization, processes that carried within themselves the seeds of conflict. The economy was mixed and regionally divided. On one side stood the Northeast, the national leader in commerce, trade, and banking and the site of a growing factory system; on the other side was the South, dominated by huge cotton plantations cultivated by

Map 18.2   EUROPE IN 1871

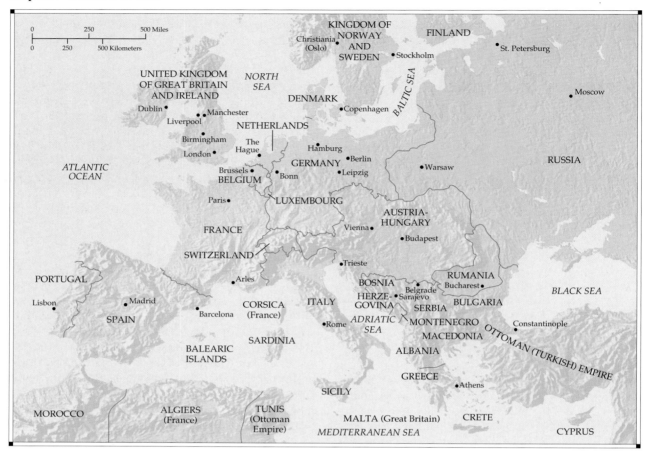

Figure 18.3 JOSEPH MALLORD WILLIAM TURNER. *The Slave Ship (Slavers Throwing Overboard the Dead and Dying, Typhoon Coming On).* Ca. 1840. Oil on canvas, 35¾ × 48¼". Courtesy, Museum of Fine Arts, Boston. Henry Lillie Pierce Fund. *Growing revulsion against slavery led Parliament to abolish it in the British colonies in the 1830s, but the slaves in the United States were not freed until 1863. Turner's terrifying image of natural calamity and human cruelty reflected the humanitarian values that had surfaced during the parliamentary and national debates about slavery. The ghoulish scene, painted in Turner's unique Romantic style, depicts the castaway bodies of the dead and dying, encircled by hungry fish, as they sink into the stormy sea.*

thousands of black slaves. The unsettled western lands formed a third region.

After 1830 the economic issues that divided the northern and southern states became intensified over the question of slavery (Figure 18.3). As settlers moved west, the debate over the spread of slavery into these new territories and states aggravated sectional interests. In 1861 the southern states seceded from the union, provoking a civil war.

Unlike Europe's contemporaneous wars, which were short and resulted in relatively few deaths, the American Civil War lasted four years and resulted in huge losses on both sides. The northern victory in 1865, engineered by President Abraham Lincoln (1861–1865), saved the union and guaranteed freedom for the slaves. But animosity between the North and the South continued to smolder during the war's aftermath, called Reconstruction (1865–1876), and relations remained strained, particularly over racial matters, for more than a century.

Figure 18.4 W. P. Frith. *The Railway Station.* Ca. 1862. Oil on canvas, 3′10″ × 8′5″. Royal Holloway College and Bedford New College, Surrey, England. *London was the hub of England's economy long before the Industrial Revolution, and with the coming of the railroads its position was enhanced. The massive new railway stations, often constructed of glass and iron, symbolized the changing business and leisure habits of life. In this painting of one of London's new rail stations, Frith's well-dressed middle-class citizens convey the excitement of travel as well as its novelty and uncertainty.*

The Spread of Industrialism

Underlying all the political upheavals of the nineteenth century was the growing industrialization of the Western world. After its eighteenth-century beginnings in England (see Chapter 17), industrialism started to take root in France in the 1830s, and a short time later Belgium entered the industrial age. For the next forty years, Belgium and France were the chief economic powers on the Continent, with factory and railway systems radiating from Paris and Brussels to Vienna and Milan by 1871. The expansion of rail lines meant that factories no longer needed to be near coal mines or clustered in urban areas. Inventions in communications, such as the telegraph, made it easier for industrialists to take advantage of distant resources and markets, and in 1866 engineers laid a transatlantic telegraph cable, linking Europe and America.

In the meantime, Great Britain passed into the second phase of the Industrial Revolution. It continued to build ships, to construct factories, and to lay rail lines; by 1850 all its major cities were linked (Figure 18.4). In England and on the Continent, the mining of new coal and iron deposits and the rise of imports in materials for textiles and other goods kept the machines of industry humming. British financiers, joined by Continental bankers, made loans to fledgling companies for new factories, warehouses, ships, and railways, thereby generating more wealth for capitalists who had surplus funds to invest.

Figure 18.5 JOSEPH NASH. Detail of *The Crystal Palace*. 1851. Color lithograph with watercolor, approx. 21½ × 29⅝". Victoria and Albert Museum, London. *This detail illustrates the splendor and pageantry surrounding the moment when Queen Victoria opened the Great Exhibition. After the fair closed, the Crystal Palace was disassembled and rebuilt in a suburb in south London, where it stood as an arts and entertainment center until it was destroyed by fire in 1936. Nevertheless, the "pre-fab" construction principles of the Crystal Palace foreshadowed modern building methods.*

As Europe's economy grew, two marvels of the industrial age—the Crystal Palace in London and the Suez Canal in Egypt—captured the world's imagination. The iron and glass Crystal Palace housed the Great Exhibition of 1851—in effect, the first world's fair. In a structure that used advanced architectural methods and building materials, the newest inventions and machine-made goods were displayed for everyone, rich and poor alike. Although other nations displayed products and inventions, Britain's exhibits were the most impressive and proved that it was the world's leading industrial and agricultural power (Figure 18.5).

The second marvel was the digging of the Suez Canal to link the Gulf of Suez and the Red Sea with the Mediterranean Sea. Funded by a French company and opened in 1869, the canal shortened the distance between Europe and India, thus enabling steamships to ferry passengers and goods around the globe more quickly and comfortably (Figure 18.6).

The Crystal Palace, the Suez Canal, and other wonders of the age were made possible by the labor of millions of workers—men, women, and children. On the Continent, the working and living conditions of this group were no better than the squalid circumstances found in Great Britain in the first stage of the Industrial Revolution. The social costs of industrialism, notably the rapid growth of cities that threw poor and ill-trained people into slums and ghettos, were part of its negative side. The slums became breeding grounds for class hatred and offered ready audiences for revolutionaries and socialists advocating revolt and social changes. The rebellions that flashed across the Continent in 1848 were caused partly by the mounting frustrations in these working-class areas.

Figure 18.6 ANONYMOUS. *Suez Canal Opening*. 1869. Colored engraving. British Library, London. *Just as Great Britain showed the world what it could achieve through industry and agriculture, so France demonstrated its technological and engineering genius in digging the Suez Canal. The Suez Canal Company, headed by the French entrepreneur Ferdinand de Lesseps [duh-lay-SEPS] (1805–1894), began its work in 1859 and completed the canal ten years later.*

Even a large segment of the middle class remained cut off from economic and political power. In the United States, all white males were granted suffrage in the 1820s, and in England voting rights were granted to working-class males in the Reform Act of 1867. The revolutions of 1830 and 1848 widened the franchise for French, Italian, German, and Austrian men, although important government posts were always reserved for aristocrats. Women still could not vote in 1871, nor could wage earners (except for British and American workers) and members of the lower middle class. Universal suffrage was not yet a reality.

NINETEENTH-CENTURY THOUGHT: PHILOSOPHY, RELIGION, AND SCIENCE

At the heart of the debate over liberalism was the question, Which is primary, the individual or the group? Liberalism glorified the value of free expression for each human being, and capitalists used liberal arguments to justify their economic policies. But the corollary of these policies seemed to be poverty, degradation, and injustice for workers, and new voices began to be raised in support of other approaches that promised antidotes to the injustices of industrial capitalism. Primary among these were a variety of socialisms, a form of political and social organization in which material goods are owned and distributed by the community or the government.

Liberalism Redefined

In the late eighteenth century, English philosopher and social theorist Jeremy Bentham (1748–1832) had developed a variant of liberalism known as **Utilitarianism.** Bentham made "utility" his supreme moral principle, meaning that what gave pleasure to both the individual and society was right and what gave pain was wrong. Utility for society was always identified with "the greatest happiness for the greatest number"—a view that reflected Bentham's commitment to democracy. Accepting liberalism's laissez-faire ideal, yet tempering it with the principle of utility, Bentham pushed for a renovation of the repressive and outmoded governments of his time, including reform of the legal system, prisons, and education.

After 1830 Bentham's ideas were eloquently reinterpreted by bourgeois liberalism's strongest defender, the English philosopher John Stuart Mill (1806–1873). Growing to maturity in the second phase of the industrial age, Mill became increasingly fearful that the masses and a powerful state would ultimately destroy individual rights and human dignity. In his essay *On Liberty* (1859), Mill argued that the continued existence of the "civilized community" required the fullest freedom of speech, discussion, and behavior that was possible among all citizens, as long as no person was physically harmed. Mill's essay represents the high point of English liberalism.

After having advocated laissez-faire economics in his 1848 edition of the *Principles of Political Economy,* in later editions Mill embraced a mild form of socialism. Condemning unbridled economic competition, he reasoned that though production was subject to economic laws, distribution was not, and thus humans should divide the benefits of industrialism along rational lines. Mill also campaigned for religious toleration and minority rights and became a staunch supporter of women's right to vote and own property. In many of his writings, Mill collaborated with Harriet Taylor, his wife.

Socialism

Liberalism provided support for bourgeois values, but **socialism** seemed to many to be the irresistible wave of the future. Socialism began as a reaction to industrialism and came to be its most severe critic, holding out a vision of what society might become if only certain fundamental reforms were made. Two main groups spoke for socialism in the 1800s: the utopian socialists and the Marxists. The utopians, who reached their peak before 1848, believed that the ills of industrial society could be overcome through cooperation between workers and capitalists. In contrast, the Marxists, who flourished after 1848, held the utopians in contempt as naive idealists and called for revolutions, violence, and the inevitable triumph of scientific socialism.

The principal utopian socialists—Robert Owen (1771–1858) (himself a wealthy industrialist), Comte de Saint-Simon [san-see-MOH(N)] (1760–1825), and Charles Fourier [FOOR-ee-ay] (1772–1837)—shared the belief that a more just society could be introduced using the discoveries about society made in communal associations that served as laboratories for their philosophical ideas. All three thinkers were concerned more about the consumption of the fruits of industrialism than they were about the creation of goods. To them, the workers were simply not receiving a fair share for their efforts and were being victimized by a ruthless, competitive system. To solve these problems, the utopian socialists proposed a number of alternatives, but their often impracticable schemes had little chance of succeeding in an age that was becoming more scientific and realistic.

The utopian socialists and their supporters quickly faded from view once Karl Marx (1818–1883) appeared on the scene. As a student at the University of Berlin, Marx studied Hegel's dialectical explanation of historical change, but as an atheist he rejected Hegel's emphasis on Spirit. Since Marx's radical politics made a teaching post untenable in reactionary Prussia, he became editor of a Cologne newspaper. When the police shut down the paper, Marx sought refuge abroad. From Brussels, he and Friedrich Engels (1820–1895), his lifelong friend and coauthor, were asked to develop a set of principles for a German worker's society. The resulting pamphlet, *The Communist Manifesto* (1848), became the bible of socialism. Both men played minor roles in the 1848 revolts, seeing in them the first steps of a proletarian revolution. Marx spent his last years in

PERSONAL PERSPECTIVE
The Industrial Revolution: Two Perspectives

CHARLOTTE BRONTË
On the Crystal Palace, 1851

Charlotte Brontë, while visiting the Great Exhibition, praised the benefits of the Industrial Revolution, including the new machines and tools and wealth from around the world. She was especially pleased by the orderly behavior of the crowds.

Yesterday I went for the second time to the Crystal Palace. We remained in it about three hours, and I must say I was more struck with it on this occasion than at my first visit. It is a wonderful place—vast, strange, new, and impossible to describe. Its grandeur does not consist in *one* thing, but in the unique assemblage of *all* things. Whatever human industry has created you find there, from the great compartments filled with railway engines and boilers, with mill machinery in full work, with splendid carriages of all kinds, with harness of every description, to the glass-covered and velvet-spread stands loaded with the most gorgeous work of the goldsmith and silversmith, and the carefully guarded caskets full of real diamonds and pearls worth hundreds of thousands of pounds. It may be called a bazaar or a fair, but it is such a bazaar or fair as Eastern genii might have created. It seems as if only magic could have gathered this mass of wealth from all the ends of the earth—as if none but supernatural hands could have arranged it thus, with such a blaze and contrast of colours and marvellous power of effect. The multitude filling the great aisles seems ruled and subdued by some invisible influence. Amongst the thirty thousand souls that peopled it the day I was there not one loud noise was to be heard, not one irregular movement seen; the living tide rolls on quietly, with a deep hum like the sea heard from the distance.

HIPPOLYTE TAINE
Derby Day Horse Races, 28 May 1861

Hippolyte Taine (1828–1893), a French philosopher, historian, and critic, was a spectator at the annual Derby Day Horse Races. He described the lively scene, including the landscape, the race course, and the spectators drawn from all levels of society. As a visitor to England, the world's most advanced industrial country, Taine was shocked by the miserable conditions of the lower classes in attendance.

Races at Epsom: it is the Derby Day, a day of jollification; Parliament does not sit; for three days all the talk has been about horses and their trainers. . . .

Epsom course is a large, green plain, slightly undulating; on one side are reared three public stands and several other smaller ones. In front, tents, hundreds of shops, temporary stables under canvas, and an incredible confusion of carriages, of horses, of horsemen, of private omnibuses; there are perhaps 200,000 human heads here. Nothing beautiful or even elegant; the carriages are ordinary vehicles, and toilettes are rare; one does not come here to exhibit them but to witness a spectacle: the spectacle is interesting only on account of its size. From the top of the Stand the enormous ant-

---

London, writing his major work, *Capital* (volume 1, 1867; volumes 2 and 3, completed by Engels, 1885–1894), and founding an international workers' association to implement his ideas.

Marx's approach to historical change differed radically from the utopian view. According to Marx, history moved in a dialectical pattern as the Hegelians had argued, but not in rhythm with abstract ideas or the World Spirit. Instead, Marx thought that material reality conditioned historical development; the various stages of history, which were propelled by class conflicts, unfolded as one economic group replaced another. For example, the middle class, which had emerged out of the collapse of the feudal system, rep-resented only a moment in history, destined dialectically to bring forth its own gravedigger, the proletariat, or the urban working class. Moreover, the institutions and ideas of a society constituted a superstructure erected on the foundation of economic reality; governments, law, the arts, and the humanities merely reflected the values of a particular ruling class.

Marx then forecasted a revolt by the proletariat, who would then install a classless society. Marx believed that the workers' revolution would be international in scope and that communist intellectuals would assist in bringing an end to bourgeois rule. Elaborating on his political, economic, and social theories, Marx's followers created Marxism and, inspired by his ideal society, heap swarms, and its din ascends. But beyond, on the right, a row of large trees, behind them the faint bluish undulations of the verdant country, make a magnificent frame to a mediocre picture. Some clouds as white as swans float in the sky, and their shadow sweeps over the grass; a light mist, charged with sunshine, flits in the distance, and the illuminated air, like a glory, envelops the plain, the heights, the vast area, and all the disorder of the human carnival.

It is a carnival, in fact; they have come to amuse themselves in a noisy fashion. Everywhere are gypsies, comic singers and dancers disguised as negroes, shooting galleries where bows and arrows or guns are used, charlatans who by dint of eloquence palm off watch chains, games of skittles and sticks, musicians of all sorts, and the most astonishing row of cabs, barouches, droskies, four-in-hands, with pies, cold meats, melons, fruits, wines, especially champagne. They unpack; they proceed to drink and eat; that restores the creature and excites him; coarse joy and open laughter are the result of a full stomach. In presence of this ready-made feast the aspect of the poor is pitiable to behold; they endeavour to sell you penny dolls, remembrances of the Derby; to induce you to play at Aunt Sally, to black your boots. Nearly all of them resemble wretched, hungry, beaten, mangy dogs, waiting for a bone, without hope of finding much on it. They arrived on foot during the night, and count upon dining off crumbs from the great feast. Many are lying on the ground, among the feet of the passers-by, and sleep open-mouthed, face upwards. Their countenances have an expression of stupidity and of painful hardness. The majority of them have bare feet, all are terribly dirty,

and most absurd-looking; the reason is that they wear gentlemen's old clothes, worn-out fashionable dresses, small bonnets, formerly worn by young ladies. The sight of these cast-off things, which have covered several bodies, becoming more shabby in passing from one to the other, always makes me uncomfortable. To wear these old clothes is degrading; in doing so the human being shows or avows that he is the off-scouring of society. Among us [the French] a peasant, a workman, a labourer, is a different man, not an inferior person; his blouse belongs to him, as my coat belongs to me—it has clothed no one but him. The employment of ragged clothes is more than a peculiarity; the poor resign themselves here to be the footstool of others.

One of these women, with an old shawl that appeared to have been dragged in the gutter, with battered head-gear, which had been a bonnet, made limp by the rain, with a poor, dirty, pale baby in her arms, came and prowled round our omnibus, picked up a castaway bottle, and drained the dregs. Her second girl, who could walk, also picked up and munched a rind of melon. We gave them a shilling and cakes. The humble smile of thankfulness they returned, it is impossible to describe. They had the look of saying, like Sterne's poor donkey, "Do not beat me, I beseech you—yet you may beat me if you wish." Their countenances were burned, tanned by the sun; the mother had a scar on her right cheek, as if she had been struck by a boot; both of them, the child in particular, were grown wild and stunted. The great social mill crushes and grinds here, beneath its steel gearing, the lowest human stratum.

organized to abolish the capitalist system, although their impact before 1871 was minimal.

From the first, socialism appealed especially to women, because it condemned existing social relations and called for universal emancipation. The ideal communal world would be free of every inequality, including sexual inequality. Utopian socialists were the most welcoming to supporters of female rights. For example, Fourier claimed that female freedom was the touchstone for measuring human liberation everywhere; Robert Owen espoused a new moral order in which sexual and class differences would be overcome in cooperative, loving communities; and Saint-Simon preached the moral superiority of women, though he preferred sexual complementarity to sexual equality.

Marx and Engels's views on women were ambiguous. They urged the full integration of women into the workforce as a condition of female emancipation, but insisted that freedom for male workers was key to radical social change. So, they encouraged women to curb their aspirations in the name of the greater good—that is, for an ideal Marxian workers' society.

Religion and the Challenge of Science

The growing interest in objective, rational analysis was not confined to investigations of the workings of society. In a development that alarmed some Christians, a group of Protestant scholars in Germany began to study the Bible not as a divinely inspired book incapable of error but simply as a set of human writings susceptible to varied interpretations. In Germany, this movement to treat the Bible like any other book was called **higher criticism.** Scholars began to try to identify the author or authors of each of the biblical books rather than rely on old accounts of their origins, to study each text to determine its sources rather than treat each book as a divine revelation, and, most important, to assess the accuracy of each account rather than accept it as God's final word. By 1871 orthodox Christians were engaged in intellectual battles with the higher critics, some of whom portrayed Jesus not as God's son but as a mythological figure or a human teacher.

While the higher critics chipped away at Christianity from within, science assaulted it from outside. Geologists first discredited the biblical story of creation, and then biologists questioned the divine origin of human beings. The challenge from geology was led by the Englishman Charles Lyell [LIE-uhl] (1797–1875), whose fossil research showed that the earth was much older than Christians claimed. By treating each of God's six days of creation as symbolic of thousands of years of divine activity, Protestant Christians were able to weather this particular intellectual storm. Not so easily overcome, however, was biology's threat to biblical authority.

Following the Bible, the church was clear in its explanation of humanity's origin: Adam and Eve were the first parents, having been created by God after he had fashioned the rest of the animate world. Paralleling this divine account was a secular argument for evolution. Based on Greek thought, but without solid proofs, it remained a theory and nothing more for centuries. In 1859, however, the theory of **evolution** gained dramatic support when the Englishman Charles Darwin (1809–1882) published *On the Origin of Species.* Marshaling data to prove that evolution was a principle of biological development rather than a mere hypothesis, Darwin showed that over the course of millennia modern plants and animals had evolved from simpler forms through a process of natural selection.

In 1871, in *Descent of Man,* Darwin applied his findings to human beings, portraying them as the outcome of millions of years of evolution. Outraged clergy attacked Darwin for his atheism, and equally zealous Darwinians heaped ridicule on the creationists for their credulity. Today, the theory of evolution is one of the cornerstones of biological science, despite some continuing criticism.

Other advances in science were helping to lay the groundwork for the modern world. In the 1850s, French scientist Louis Pasteur [pass-TUHR] (1822–1895) proposed the germ theory of disease, the notion that many diseases are caused by microorganisms. This seminal idea led him to important discoveries and proposals for change. Claiming that germs were responsible for the spread of disease, he campaigned for improved sanitation and sterilization and thus paved the way for antiseptic surgery. He demonstrated that food spoilage could be prevented by killing microorganisms through heating, a discovery that resulted in the "pasteurization" of milk. His studies of rabies and anthrax led him to the first use of vaccines against these diseases. As the founder of bacteriology and an important figure in the development of modern medicine, Pasteur is the embodiment of Francis Bacon's seventeenth-century assertion, "knowledge is power."

In chemistry, a fruitful way of thinking about atoms was finally formulated, moving beyond the simplistic notions that had been in vogue since fifth-century-B.C. Greece. In about 1808 the Englishman John Dalton (1766–1844) invented an effective atomic theory, and in 1869 the Russian Dmitri Mendeleev [men-duh-LAY-uhf] (1834–1907) worked out a periodic table of elements, based on atomic weights, a system that, with modifications, is still in use. By 1871 other chemists had moved from regarding molecules as clusters of atoms to conceiving of them as structured into stable patterns. Nevertheless, without means and equipment for studying the actual atoms, atomism remained merely a useful theory until the twentieth century.

Advances in chemistry also led to changes in anesthetics and surgery. In the 1840s, chemists introduced nitrous oxide, chloroform, and other compounds that could block pain in human beings. Use of these new painkillers in obstetrics increased after Queen Victoria was given chloroform to assist her in childbirth in 1853. These desensitizers revolutionized the treatment of many diseases and wounds and made modern surgery possible.

CULTURAL TRENDS: FROM ROMANTICISM TO REALISM

In its triumph, the middle class embraced both Neoclassical and Romantic styles in the arts. In Neoclassicism, the bourgeoisie found a devotion to order that appealed to their belief that the seemingly chaotic marketplace was actually regulated by economic laws. In Romanticism, they found escape from the sordid and ugly side of industrialism.

But both styles slowly grew routinized and pretentious under the patronage of the middle class, partly because of the inevitable loss of creative energy that sets in when any style becomes established and partly because of the conversion of the cultural arena into a marketplace. Because they lacked the deep learning that had guided many aristocratic patrons in the past, the new bourgeois audiences demanded art and literature that mirrored their less refined values. Catering to this need, artists and writers produced works that were spectacular, sentimental, and moralistic. Simply put, successful art did not offend respectable public taste.

Adding to this bourgeois influence was the growing ability of state institutions to control what was expressed in art and literature. The most powerful of these was France's Royal Academy of Painting and Sculpture, founded in 1648 for the purpose of honoring the nation's best painters. After 1830 its leaders became obsessed with rigid rules, thus creating what was called "official art." Those artists who could not obtain the academy's approval for exhibiting their works in the annual government-sponsored Salons, or art shows, were virtually condemned to poverty unless they had other means of financial support. Rejected artists soon identified the Royal Academy as a defender of the status quo and an enemy of innovation. No other Western state had a national academy with as much power as France's Royal Academy, although in other European countries similar bodies tried to regulate both art and literature.

In reaction to the empty, overblown qualities of official art, a new style began to appear in the 1840s. Known as **Realism,** this style focused on the everyday lives of the middle and lower classes (Figure 18.7). The Realists depicted ordinary people without idealizing or romanticizing them, although a moral point of view was always implied. Condemning Neoclassicism as cold and Romanticism as exaggerated, the Realists sought to convey what they saw around them in a serious, accurate, and unsentimental way. Merchants, housewives, workers, peasants, and even prostitutes replaced kings, aristocrats, goddesses, saints, and heroes as the subjects of paintings and novels.

Many forces contributed to the rise of Realism. In diplomacy, this was the era of Bismarck's realpolitik, the hard-nosed style that replaced more cautious and civilized negotiation. In science, Darwin demystified earthly existence by rejecting the biblical view of creation and concluding that the various species, including human beings, evolved from simpler organisms. The spread of democracy encouraged the Realists to take an interest in ordinary people, and the camera, invented in the 1830s, probably inspired the Realists in their goal of truthful accuracy. All these influences combined to make Realism a style intent on scientific objectivity in its depiction of the world as it is.

Literature

In literature, the Romantic style continued to dominate poetry, essays, and novels until midcentury, when it began to be displaced by Realism. The Romantic authors were concerned with the depth of their characters' emotions and had great faith in the power of the individual to transform his or her own life and the lives of others. The Realists, by contrast, tended to be deter-

Figure 18.7 ÉDOUARD MANET. *A Bar at the Folies-Bergère.* 1882. 3' 1½" × 4' 3". Courtauld Institute Galleries, London (Courtauld Collection). *The Folies-Bergère was the grandest of the glorified beer halls, or cafés-concerts, which sprang up in Paris after 1850, offering drinks and raucous stage entertainment. Catering initially to a lower middle class prospering from the booming economy, these cafés-concerts soon became classless settings in which all strata of society could anonymously rub elbows. In this painting, Manet captures the spectacle of the cafés-concerts: the ghastly white light, the crush of customers, the stoic barmaid, the trapeze artist whose green feet are just visible in the top left corner. Most of these details are shown in the mirror behind the barmaid. The painting presents a problem in the impossibly placed mirror; the barmaid appears to be looking at the viewer but is also standing before the top-hatted man (reflected in the mirror?).*

minists who preferred to let the facts speak for themselves. They rejected the bourgeois world as flawed by hypocrisy and materialism and denounced the machine age for its mechanization of human relationships. Realism in literature flourished between 1848 and 1871, chiefly in France, England, and Russia. A special contribution to Realistic literature was made by African American writers who found their voices during the slavery controversy preceding the Civil War.

The Height of French Romanticism   In France, the leading exponent of Romanticism was the poet, dramatist, and novelist Victor Hugo (1802–1885). His poetry established his fame, and the performance of his tragedy *Hernani* in February 1830 solidified his position as the leader of the Romantic movement. Enlivened with scenes of rousing action and by characters with limitless ambition, this play seemed with one stroke to sweep away the artificialities of Classicism. Its premiere created a huge scandal. When the bourgeois revolution erupted in July 1830, many French people believed that Hugo's *Hernani* had been a literary prophecy of the political upheaval.

Hugo became something of a national institution, noted as much for his humane values as for his writing. Because of his opposition to the regime of Napoleon III, he was exiled from France for eighteen years, beginning in 1851. While in exile, he published his most celebrated novel, the epic-length *Les Misérables (The Wretched)* (1862), which expresses his revulsion at the morally bankrupt society he believed France had become after Napoleon I.

The hero and moral center of the book is the pauper Jean Valjean, who is imprisoned for seventeen years for stealing a loaf of bread. He escapes and becomes a prosperous, respectable merchant, but the law is unrelenting in its pursuit of him, and he is forced into a life of hiding and subterfuge. Hugo makes Valjean a symbol of the rising masses' will to freedom, and his bourgeois readers were fascinated and horrified at the same time by Valjean's ultimate triumph.

Another popular Romantic literary figure was the French novelist and playwright George Sand (1804–1876), who was forced by need to become a writer. Amandine-Aurore-Lucie Dupin took the name George Sand in part to keep from embarrassing her own and her estranged husband's families and in part to assert herself in the male literary world; she was addressed by her friends as Madame George Sand.

Sand has been called "the first modern, liberated woman." She courted controversy as she engaged in highly public sexual liaisons with leading men of the times, including Romantic composer and pianist Frédéric Chopin. She often dressed as a typical bourgeois gentleman: coat and vest, cravat, trousers, steel-tipped boots, and top hat. Sand was the first Western woman to play an active part in a revolutionary government. In the Paris uprising of 1848, she sat on committees, delivered speeches and debated issues, and wrote in support of the short-lived radical socialist regime.

Because her father was descended from Polish royalty and her mother was the daughter of a Parisian birdseller, Sand found herself in a socially equivocal position in class-conscious France. Thus, she was predisposed to focus her writings on people without power, such as women, artists, and laborers. Her novels and plays, with their strong political undertones, illustrate Victor Hugo's claim that Romanticism was "liberalism in literature." For Sand, idealism simply meant another way to call for social reform.

Sand's first novel, *Indiana* (1832), is usually regarded as her best and is praised for its multifaceted characters and its accurate depiction of the constraints imposed on married women at that time. Indiana, the nineteen-year-old heroine, is unhappily married to an older man; she seeks true love apart from her spouse and in a relationship of equals. Unfortunately, because of her lover's treachery and society's inflexible marital code, she has to flee from France and scandal to Bourbon Island (modern Réunion), then a French colony in the Indian Ocean. There she finds a soul mate with whom she settles down in a Rousseau-like paradise. Critics read the work as an attack on France's Napoleonic Code, which placed wives under their husband's control (see Chapter 17). *Indiana* made Sand's reputation, and she followed it with about eighty more novels and twenty plays, a book of travel writings, and two volumes of children's stories.

Romanticism in the English Novel   In England, Romanticism found its most expressive voices in the novels of the Brontë sisters, Charlotte (1816–1855) and Emily (1818–1848). Reared in the Yorkshire countryside far from the mainstream of cultured life, they created two of the most beloved novels in the English language. Their circumscribed lives seemed to uphold the Romantic dictum that true artistic genius springs from the imagination alone.

Emily Brontë's *Wuthering Heights* (1847) creates a Romantic atmosphere through mysterious events, ghostly apparitions, and graveyard scenes, but it rises above the typical Gothic romance. The work is suffused with a mystical radiance that invests the characters and the natural world with spiritual meanings beyond the visible. A tale of love and redemption, the story focuses on a mismatched couple, the genteel Catherine and the outcast Heathcliff, who are nevertheless soul mates. In the uncouth, passionate Heathcliff, Brontë creates a Byronic hero who lives outside conventional morality. Her portrayal of him as a man made vengeful by cruel circumstances has led some to label this the first sociorevolutionary novel.

Charlotte Brontë published *Jane Eyre* in the same year *Wuthering Heights* appeared. A dark and melancholy novel, the work tells the story of a governess's love for her brooding and mysterious employer. Her hopes for happiness are crushed by the discovery that the cause of his despair is his deranged wife, kept hidden in the attic. Narrated in the first person, the novel reveals the heroine's deep longings and passions as well as her ultimate willingness to sacrifice her feelings for moral values. Recognized at the time as a revolutionary work that dispensed with the conventions of sentimental novels, *Jane Eyre* was attacked by critics but welcomed by the reading public, who made it a best-seller.

Romanticism in American Literature   Romanticism reached a milestone with the American literary and philosophical movement known as **Transcendentalism.** Flourishing in New England in the early and middle part of the nineteenth century, this movement was critical of formal religions and drew inspiration from the belief that divinity is accessible without the necessity of mediation. Unlike the God of traditional religion, the divine spirit (Transcendence) manifested itself in many forms, including the physical universe, all constructive practical activity, all great cultural achievements, and all types of spiritual expression. In their goal of seeking union with the world's underlying metaphysical order, the Transcendentalists followed in the steps of the German Idealists (see Chapter 17). Of the Transcendentalists, Henry David Thoreau (1817–1862) was probably the most influential. His most celebrated book, *Walden* (1854), the lyrical journal of the months he spent living in the rough on Walden Pond, is virtually the bible of today's environmental movement. Thoreau's *On the Duty of Civil Disobedience* (1849), an essay on the necessity of disobeying an unjust law, was one of the texts that inspired Martin Luther King, Jr.'s, protests of the 1950s and 1960s against America's segregated social system.

American poetry now became a major presence in Western literature with the writings of Emily Dickinson and Walt Whitman. Both poets worked within the Romantic style, drawing on intimate histories, in the manner of other Romantic poets. They also adopted offbeat techniques, including verse forms and punctuation, that have greatly influenced twentieth-century poets. Today, Dickinson and Whitman are regarded as two of the most innovative poets of nineteenth-century American literature. Dickinson, a virtual recluse in her day, published only seven poems during her lifetime. Since her death, her reputation has increased

dramatically, based on the almost 1,800 poems that make up the Dickinson canon. Whitman, vilified at first by the establishment, lived long enough to see himself become an American icon, the model of the good gray-haired poet. During his career, he effected a revolution in American poetry by creating a body of works based on his experience as an American, written in a specifically American language.

Realism in French and English Novels   Realism began in France in the 1830s with the novels of Honoré de Balzac [BAHL-zak] (1799–1850). Balzac foreshadowed the major traits of Realism in the nearly one hundred novels that make up the series he called *The Human Comedy.* Set in France in the Napoleonic era and the early industrial age, this voluminous series deals with the lives of over two thousand characters, both in Paris and in the provinces. Balzac condemns the hollowness of middle-class society, pointing out how industrialism has caused many people to value material things more than friendship and family, although there are virtuous and sympathetic characters as well.

France's outstanding Realist was Gustave Flaubert [floh-BAIR] (1821–1880), who advocated a novel free from conventional, accepted moral or philosophical views. His masterpiece is *Madame Bovary* (1857), which caused a scandal with its unvarnished tale of adultery. In contrast to Balzac's broad sweep, Flaubert focused on a single person, the unhappy and misguided Emma Bovary. In careful detail, he sets forth the inner turmoil of a frustrated middle-class woman trapped by her dull marriage and her social standing. By stressing objectivity and withholding judgment, Flaubert believed he was following the precepts of modern science. As a social critic, he portrays everyday life among the smug members of this small-town, bourgeois society. Notwithstanding the scandal it caused, *Madame Bovary* was an instant success and established the new style of Realism. For most readers, Emma Bovary became a poignant symbol of people whose unrealistic dreams and aspirations doom their lives to failure.

English novelists also wrote in the new Realist style. Like their French counterparts, they railed against the vulgarity, selfishness, and hypocrisy of the middle class, but unlike the French, who were interested in creating unique characters, they spoke out for social justice. England's most popular writer of Realist fiction was Charles Dickens (1812–1870), who favored stories dealing with the harsh realities of urban and industrial life. Writing to meet deadlines for serialized magazine stories, Dickens poured out a torrent of words over a long literary career that began when he was in his twenties.

In early works, such as *Oliver Twist* (1837–1839) and *David Copperfield* (1849–1850), Dickens was optimistic, holding out hope for his characters and, by implication, for society in general. But in later novels, such as *Bleak House* and *Hard Times,* both published between 1851 and 1854, he was pessimistic about social reform and the possibility of correcting the excesses of industrialism. Dickens's rich descriptions, convoluted plots with unexpected coincidences, and topical satire were much admired by Victorian readers, and his finely developed and very British characters, such as Mr. Pickwick, Oliver Twist, and Ebenezer Scrooge, have survived as a memorable gift to literature.

Realist fiction in England was also represented by important female writers. The two most successful were Elizabeth Gaskell (1810–1865) and Mary Ann Evans (1819–1880), better known by her pen name, George Eliot. Both wrote novels about the hardships imposed on the less fortunate by England's industrial economy. Gaskell's *North and South* (1855) underscores the widening gap between the rich, particularly in England's urban north, and the poor, concentrated in the rural south, within the context of the rise of the labor unions. Typically, her themes involve contrasts, contradictions, and conflicts, such as the helplessness of the individual in the face of impersonal forces and the simultaneous need to affirm the human spirit against the inequalities of the factory system. Similarly, in *Middlemarch* (1872) and other novels, George Eliot explores the ways human beings are trapped in social systems that shape and mold their lives, for good or ill. Eliot's outlook is less deterministic, however, stressing the possibility of individual fulfillment despite social constraints as well as the freedom to make moral choices.

The Russian Realists   During the Realist period, Russia for the first time produced writers whose works received international acclaim: Leo Tolstoy [TOHL-stoy] (1828–1910) and Feodor Dostoevsky [duhs-tuh-YEF-skee] (1821–1881). Like English and French Realists, these Russians depicted the grim face of early industrialism and dealt with social problems, notably the plight of the newly liberated serfs. Their realism is tempered by a typically Russian concern: Should Russia embrace Western values or follow its own traditions, relying on its Slavic and Oriental past? Significantly, Tolstoy and Dostoevsky transcend Western Realism by stressing religious and spiritual themes.

In his early works, Tolstoy wrote objectively, without moralizing. The novel Anna Karenina (1875–1877) describes the unhappy consequences of adultery in a sophisticated but unforgiving society. *War and Peace* (1865–1869), his greatest work, is a monumental survey of Russia during the Napoleonic era, portraying a huge cast of characters caught up in the surging tides of history. Although Tolstoy focuses on the upper class in this Russian epic, he places them in realistic situations without romanticizing them. In these early works, he was a determinist, convinced that human beings were at the mercy of forces beyond them. But in 1876, after he had a religious conversion to a simple form of Christianity that stressed pacifism, plain living, and radical social reform, he repudiated all art that lacked a moral vision, including his own. Tolstoy devoted the rest of his life to this plain faith, following what he believed to be Jesus' teachings and working for a Christian anarchist society.

Feodor Dostoevsky was a powerful innovator who introduced literary devices that have become standard in Western letters. For example, *Crime and Punishment* (1866), written long before Sigmund Freud developed psychoanalysis, analyzes the inner life of a severely disturbed personality. In *Notes from Underground* (1864), the unnamed narrator is the first depiction of a modern literary type, the anti-hero, the character who lacks the virtues conventionally associated with heroism but who is not a villain.

In *The Brothers Karamazov* (1879–1880), Dostoevsky reaches the height of his powers. Like Flaubert in *Madame Bovary*, Dostoevsky sets his story in a small town and builds the narrative around a single family. Each of the Karamazov brothers personifies certain traits of human behavior, though none is a one-dimensional figure. Using the novel to address one of life's most vexing questions—If God exists, why is there suffering and evil in the world?—Dostoevsky offers no easy solution. Indeed, he reaches the radical conclusion that the question is insoluble, that suffering is an essential part of earthly existence and without it human beings can have no moral life.

Realism Among African American Writers   In the 1840s, as public opinion in the United States became polarized over slavery, a new literary genre, the **slave narrative,** emerged. The narratives, whether composed by slaves or told by slaves to secretaries who wrote them down, were filled with gritty, harsh details of the unjust slave system; these stories in turn influenced Realist fiction and also fueled the fires of antislavery rhetoric. Many slave narratives were eventually published, but probably the most compelling was the *Narrative of the Life of Frederick Douglass* (1845), written by Douglass himself, which launched this literary tradition. Douglass's (1817–1895) narrative described a heroic struggle, starting from an early awareness of the burden of being a slave, continuing through successful efforts to educate himself, and concluding with a bolt to freedom and a new life as a spokesman for abolitionism. This eloquent narrative was one of the first great modern books in the West to be written by a person of color. Besides establishing a new genre, Douglass made a splendid addition to the old genre of autobiography and opened the door to a more inclusive world literature free from the racial segregation that had characterized the varied literatures of the world since the fall of Rome.

Another African American who contributed to the Realist tradition was Sojourner Truth (1795–1883). Given the slave name of Isabell ("Bell") Hardenberg at birth, she won her freedom and took a new name, symbolic of her vow to "sojourn" the American landscape and always speak the truth. Truth's voice, captured by her secretary, Olive Gilbert, is both colloquial and eloquent, teasing and sincere, homespun and filled with biblical knowledge. Her actual voice electrified listeners, causing Truth to be remembered as one of the most natural orators in the nineteenth-century United States. Sojourner Truth's "Ain't I a Woman?" speech, delivered in 1851 before the Women's Rights convention in Akron, Ohio, shows the simple eloquence that made her a legend in her own time.

Art and Architecture

Realism in art grew up alongside an exaggerated version of Romanticism that persisted well beyond midcentury. Even Neoclassicism was represented in the official art of France throughout this period. Both styles found favor with the wealthy bourgeoisie.

Neoclassicism and Romanticism After 1830   Jean-Auguste-Dominique Ingres, who had inherited the position of Neoclassical master painter from Jacques-Louis David, virtually controlled French academic art until his death in 1867. He understood the mentality of the Salon crowds, and his works catered to their tastes. What particularly pleased this audience—composed almost exclusively of the wealthy, educated middle class—were chaste nudes in mythological or exotic settings, as in *The Turkish Bath* (Figure 18.8). The women's tactile flesh and the abandoned poses, though superbly realized, are depicted in a cold, Classical style and lack the immediacy of Ingres's great portraits.

Eugène Delacroix, Ingres's chief rival, remained a significant force in French culture with almost comparable artistic power. Delacroix perfected a Romantic style filled with superb mastery of color and human feeling. One of his finest works from this period is *Hamlet and Horatio in the Graveyard,* based on Act 5, Scene 1, of Shakespeare's drama (Figure 18.9). In the painting, one of the gravediggers holds up a skull to Hamlet and Horatio. Delacroix, faithful to the Shakespearean text, captures the men's differing reactions: Hamlet, on the right, seems to recoil slightly, while Horatio appears more curious. In this and later paintings, Delacroix tried to work out the laws governing colors—especially the effects that they have on the

Figure 18.8 Jean-Auguste-Dominique Ingres. *The Turkish Bath.* Ca. 1852–1863. Oil on canvas, diameter 42½". Louvre. *Interest in oriental themes was a continuous thread in France's nineteenth-century bourgeois culture. In his rendering of a Turkish bath, Ingres used a harem setting in which to depict more than twenty nudes in various erotic and nonerotic poses. The nudes nevertheless are portrayed in typical Classical manner, suggesting studio models rather than sensual human beings.*

Figure 18.9 EUGÈNE DELACROIX. *Hamlet and Horatio in the Graveyard.* 1839. Oil on canvas, 32 × 26". Louvre. *Shakespeare's* Hamlet, *a tragedy of doomed love, became a touchstone for Romantic artists and poets. Delacroix, after having seen* Hamlet *performed in Paris, was so taken by the graveyard scene that he created at least three lithographs and two paintings of it. In this painting, he has reduced the scene to its bare essentials: The two gravediggers (foreground) confront Hamlet and Horatio (middle ground), while a cloud-filled sky takes up nearly half of the canvas. He makes the dark skull the focus of the painting by having all four figures gaze at it and placing it against the light sky. Dynamic tension is added by the diagonal line running from the upper right to the lower left side of the painting, a line made up of the descending hill and the gravedigger's upraised arm.*

viewer. The results in *Hamlet and Horatio in the Graveyard* are somber hues that reinforce the melancholy atmosphere. Later, the Impressionists based some of their color theories on Delacroix's experiments.

Like Romantic painting, nineteenth-century architecture tended to be romantically nostalgic, intrigued by times and places far removed from the industrial present. Particularly appealing were medieval times, which were considered exotic and even ethically superior to the present. Patriotism also contributed to the trend among Romantic architects to adapt medieval building styles, notably the Gothic, to nineteenth-century conditions, since the Middle Ages was when the national character of many states was being formed.

In London, when the old Houses of Parliament burned to the ground in 1834, a decision had to be made about the style of their replacement. Since English rights and liberties traditionally dated from the Magna Carta in 1215, during the Middle Ages, a par-

liamentary commission chose a Gothic style for the new building (see Figure 18.2). Designed by Charles Barry (1795–1860) and A. W. N. Pugin (1812–1852), the Houses of Parliament show a true understanding of the essential features of the Gothic style, using pointed arches and picturesque towers. Despite these features, this building is not genuinely Gothic, for it adheres to Classical principles in the regularity of its decorations and its emphasis on the horizontal.

The Rise of Realism in Art Dissatisfied with the emotional, exotic, and escapist tendencies of Romanticism, a new breed of painters wanted to depict the real-life events they saw around them. In 1848 the jury of the Salon, influenced by the democratic sentiments unleashed by the social revolutions during the year, allowed a new kind of painting to be shown. The artist most identified with this new style was Gustave Courbet [koor-BAY] (1819–1877), a painter renowned for his refusal to prettify his works in the name of an aesthetic theory. His provocative canvases outraged middle-class audiences and made him the guiding spirit of militant Realism. Until about 1900, most painters in one way or another followed in Courbet's footsteps. A man of the people, a largely self-taught painter, and a combative individual, Courbet began to attract notice in 1849 by painting common people engaged in their day-to-day activities. Above all, he strove for an art that reflected the conditions of ordinary life.

Courbet's art was not readily accepted under France's Second Empire. Salon juries rejected his pioneering works, such as *The Meeting*, or *"Bonjour Monsieur Courbet,"* a visual record of an encounter between the painter and his wealthy patron, Alfred Bruyas (1821–1877) of Montpellier (Figure 18.10). With an expansive gesture, the well-dressed Bruyas (center) greets Courbet (right), as a manservant (left) stands with head bowed. The painter's informal costume—with painting equipment and belongings strapped to his back—helped promote Courbet's image as a carefree artist serving the cause of Realism. With Bruyas's financial backing, Courbet installed this painting at the Realism Pavilion, next door to the official Salon of 1855. Critics ridiculed *The Meeting*, claiming it had no narrative, dramatic, or anecdotal subject, and accused Courbet of self-promotion and narcissism. Relishing the controversy, Courbet remained true to his vision and continued to make art from his own life—an ideal that influenced Manet and the Impressionists.

Another of Courbet's paintings rejected by the 1855 Salon jury and exhibited in the Realism Pavilion was his masterpiece, *Interior of My Studio* (Figure 18.11). An intensely personal painting that visually summarizes his approach to art until this time, this work uses realistic

Figure 18.10 GUSTAVE COURBET. *The Meeting,* or *"Bonjour Monsieur Courbet."* 1854. Oil on canvas, 50¾ × 58⅝″. Musée Fabre, Montpellier. *This painting is an allegory of the artistic and financial pact made between Courbet and his wealthy patron, Bruyas. Deeply attracted to Fourier's socialist ideas, both men thought they had found the* solution, *a Fourierist term, to the problem of uniting genius, capital, and work for the benefit of all. Recently published letters between the two show them involved in a mutual compact: for Bruyas, greater access to art circles and society, and for Courbet, the gaining of spiritual and economic freedom. Despite their partnership, the figural placement in the painting proclaims the preeminence of the artist: With his head tilted haughtily, the painter is privileged, placed nearest the viewer and isolated from the other two figures.*

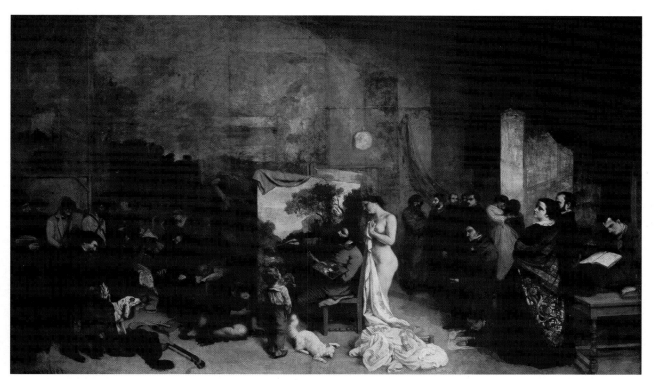

Figure 18.11 GUSTAVE COURBET. *Interior of My Studio: A Real Allegory Summing Up Seven Years of My Life as an Artist.* 1855. Oil on canvas, 11′9¾″ × 19′6⅝″. Louvre. *Romanticism and Realism are joined in this allegorical work. The subjects—the artist and artistic genius—were major preoccupations of the Romantic era, as was the use of allegory. But undeniably Realist is Courbet's mocking attitude toward academic art and society. This painting's fame rests on its deft three-part composition, its allegorical biography of the artist, and its painterly technique, which captures the sensuosity of different textures, such as the female model's skin, a lace shawl, and a dog's ruffled fur.*

Figure 18.12 HONORÉ DAUMIER. *The Freedom of the Press.* Caption: "Watch It!!" ["*Ne vous y Frottez Pas!!*"]. 1834. Lithograph, 16½ × 11½". British Museum, Department of Prints and Drawings, London. *Daumier's career as a caricaturist was made possible by technological advances associated with the industrial era. After drawing a cartoon, he reproduced it for the ever-expanding popular market using the lithographic process, the first application of industrial methods to art. In early lithography, the artist rendered an image on a flat stone surface and treated it so the nonimage areas would repel ink. Today's lithography makes use of zinc or aluminum surfaces instead of stone.*

contemporary figures to convey allegorical meaning. Its subtitle suggests Courbet's intent: *A Real Allegory Summing Up Seven Years of My Life as an Artist.* At the center of this canvas is the artist himself, in full light and painting a landscape while he is watched by a naked model and a small boy. The model and the fabric may be ironic references to the Salon's preference for nudes and still lifes. To the left of this central group, in shadow, are depicted those who have to work for a living, the usual subjects of Courbet's paintings, including peasants (the hunter and his dog) and a laborer. To the right, also in shadow, are grouped those for whom he paints, including his friends and mentors, each representing a specific idea. For example, the man reading a book is the poet Charles Baudelaire [bohd-LAIR], a personification of lyricism in art. As a total work, *Interior of My Studio* shows Courbet as the craftsman who mediates between the ordinary people pursuing everyday lives and the world of art and culture, bringing both to life in the process.

Although Courbet is considered the principal founder of the Realist style in art, he had a worthy predecessor in Honoré Daumier [DOH-m'yay] (1808–1879), a painter of realistic scenes before Realism emerged as a recognized style. Daumier chronicled the life of Paris with a dispassionate eye. In thousands of satirical lithographs, from which he earned his liv-

ing, and hundreds of paintings, he depicted its mean streets, corrupt law courts, squalid rented rooms, ignorant art connoisseurs, bored musicians, cowardly bourgeoisie, and countless other urban characters and scenes. His works not only conjure up Paris in the mid-century but also symbolize the city as a living hell where daily existence could be a form of punishment.

No one and nothing were safe from Daumier's gaze. For example, in *The Freedom of the Press*, he depicts a muscular printer, symbolic of free ideas, ready to fight oppressive regimes (Figure 18.12). On the right, Charles X, attended by two ministers, has been knocked down—a reference to the role of the press in the king's fall from power in the 1830 revolution. On the left, top-hatted Louis Philippe threatens the printer with an umbrella, egged on by two attendants. For such satire, Daumier was awarded a six-month prison term in 1832, but to his adoring audience he was a hero. Daumier often included printers in his political drawings until tighter censorship laws were passed in 1835.

One of Daumier's well-known paintings is entitled *The Third-Class Carriage* (Figure 18.13). In Paris, third-class coach was the cheapest sort of rail travel, and the resulting accommodations were cramped and plain. In Daumier's scene the foreground is dominated by three figures—a mother with her sleeping child, an old woman, and a sleeping boy. Behind them are crowded other peasants and middle-class businessmen, the lat-

Figure 18.13 HONORÉ DAUMIER. *The Third-Class Carriage.* Ca. 1862. Oil on canvas, 25¾ × 35½". Metropolitan Museum of Art. Bequest of Mrs. H. O. Havemeyer, 1929. *Close study of this oil painting reveals Daumier's genius for social observation: the mother's doting expression, the old woman's stoicism, and the melancholy profile of the top-hatted man in the shadows at the far left. None of the figures is individualized, however, for all represent social types. Despite the cramped quarters, Daumier stresses the isolation of individual travelers.*

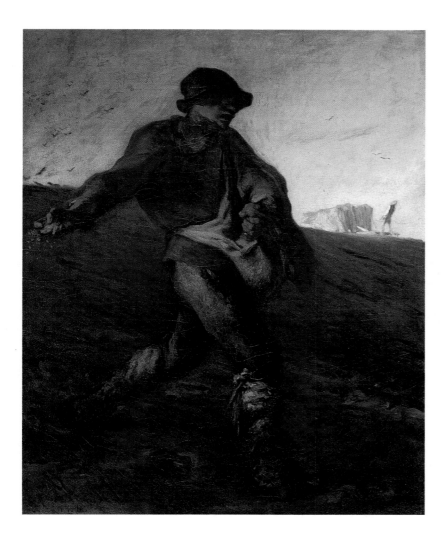

Figure 18.14 JEAN-FRANÇOIS MILLET. *The Sower.* 1850. Oil on canvas, 40 × 32½″. Courtesy, Museum of Fine Arts, Boston. Gift of Quincy Adams Shaw through Quincy A. Shaw, Jr., and Mrs. Marian Shaw Haughton. *Like Daumier's peasant travelers, Millet's farmhand is depicted as a social type rather than as an individual. But Millet's Realist vision of peasant life is less forgiving than that of Daumier. He portrays the sower as little more than an animal and places him in a dark, nearly monochromatic landscape. Whereas Daumier's caricatures had provoked laughter or anger, Millet's painting produced fear.*

ter recognizable by their tall hats. Although caricature is hinted at in this painting, it is a realistic portrayal of the growing democratization of society brought on by the railway.

In contrast to Daumier with his urban scenes, Jean-François Millet [mee-YAY] (1814–1875) painted the countryside near Barbizon, a village south of Paris where an artists' colony was located in the 1840s. Millet and the Barbizon school were influenced by the English Romantic Constable, whose painting *The Hay Wain* had been admired in the Paris Salon of 1824 (see Figure 17.12). Unlike Constable, who treated human beings only incidentally in his landscapes, Millet made the rural folk and their labors his primary subject.

One of Millet's early Barbizon paintings was *The Sower,* which he exhibited in the Salon of 1850 (Figure 18.14). This work depicts a youth casting seeds onto a freshly plowed field; dimly visible in the background are a flock of birds and two oxen with a plowman. Ordinarily, such a pastoral scene would have been a romantic idyll symbolizing the dignity of human work,

but in Millet's canvas the monotonous toil degrades the laborer. Millet forces attention on the solitary peasant, isolated from the world in a desolate landscape. The resulting image is that of a hulking presence, powerfully muscled and striding boldly across the canvas. Salon critics reacted by calling the picture "savage" and "violent."

In *The Gleaners,* Millet showed another type of farm worker, the women laborers whose daily bread depended on scavenging the grain left over from the harvest (Figure 18.15). These women were part of a depressed class that had fallen hopelessly behind in France's rush into industrialism. Millet's portrayal of stoop labor outraged some bourgeois critics, who called him a "socialist." But from today's perspective, this painting is a sympathetic and truthful record of a way of life that was fast disappearing.

However, Realist painters could focus on rural life and not be accused of socialism, as the career of Rosa Bonheur [boh-NURR] (1822–1899) reveals. Specializing in animal subjects, Bonheur enjoyed success with

Figure 18.15 JEAN-FRANÇOIS MILLET. *The Gleaners.* 1857. Oil on canvas, 33 × 44″. Louvre. *Millet's realistic scenes of peasants were inspired in part by the biblical quotation "In the sweat of thy face shalt thou eat bread" (Genesis 3:19). In* The Gleaners, *he expresses this idea with controlled beauty, depicting the women with simple dignity despite their hard lot. The painting's earth tones reinforce the somber nature of the subject.*

critics and public alike, starting with the Salon of 1841, when she was nineteen. In 1848 the Salon jury awarded Bonheur a Medal First Class for an animal scene. In 1853 *The Horse Fair* (Figure 18.16)—portraying spirited horses and their handlers at a horse market—made her an international celebrity, after a lithograph copy sold well in France, Britain, and the United States. What makes Bonheur's horses different from those painted by the Romantic Delacroix was her accuracy in depicting anatomy and movement—a reflection of her Realist faith in science. To prepare for this painting, Bonheur, dressed as a man, visited a horse market twice a week for two years to make sketches. Today, the work is considered her masterpiece, both for its impressive scale and for its knowledgeable portrayal of nineteenth-century country life.

If the Parisian art world was gratified by the paintings of Bonheur, it was outraged by the work of Édouard Manet [mah-NAY] (1832–1883), a painter whose style is difficult to classify. He contributed to the events that gradually discredited the Salon and the Academy, encouraging painters to express themselves as they pleased, and thus was a bridge between the Realists of the 1860s and the group that became known in the 1870s as the Impressionists. His notoriety arose in 1863 when Napoleon III authorized a Salon des Refusés (Salon of the Rejects) for the hundreds of artists excluded from the official exhibit. An audacious painting by Manet in this first of the counter-Salons made him the talk of Paris and the recognized leader of new painting.

In the official Salon of 1865, Manet exhibited *Olympia,* painted two years earlier, which also created a scandal (Figure 18.17). The painting presents a nude woman on a bed, a subject established by the painter Titian in the sixteenth century, but which Manet now modernized. Titian presented his nude as the goddess Venus in an idealized setting, but Manet rejected the trappings of mythology and depicted his nude realistically as a Parisian courtesan in her bedroom. The name Olympia was adopted by many Parisian prostitutes at the time, and Manet has portrayed her as being as imperious as a Greek goddess from Mount Olympus. Manet's Olympia is neither demure nor flirtatious; she gazes challengingly at the observer in a mixture of coldness and coyness. Her posture speaks of her boldness, as she sits propped up by pillows and dangles a shoe on her foot. She is attended by a black maid, whose deferential expression is in sharp contrast to Olympia's haughty demeanor. At her feet lies a black cat, an emblem of sexuality and gloom, perhaps inspired by a poem by his friend Baudelaire.

More important than these historical connections, however, are Manet's artistic theories and practices, which strained against the boundaries of Realism. Unlike the other Realists, whose moral or ideological feelings were reflected in the subjects they painted, Manet moved toward a dispassionate art in which the subject and the artist have no necessary connection. Manet's achievement was revolutionary, for he had discarded the intellectual themes of virtually all Western art: reliance on anecdote, the Bible, Christian saints, politics, nostalgia, Greece and Rome, the Middle Ages, and sentimental topics. With his work, he opened the door to an art that had no other purpose than to depict what the artist chose to paint—that is, "art for art's sake." In sum, Manet was the first truly modern painter.

Figure 18.16 ROSA BONHEUR. *The Horse Fair.* 1853. Oil on canvas, 8′ × 13′ 4″. Metropolitan Museum of Art. Gift of Cornelius Vanderbilt, 1867. *Artists specializing in animal scenes usually painted their subjects in loving detail but only sketched in the background—perhaps reflecting lack of landscape technique. In contrast, Bonheur fully renders the setting of* The Horse Fair, *including the feathery trees and dusty cobblestones. So precise is her design that the cupola in the distance has been identified as that of La Salpêtrière hospital in Paris—a landmark near a midcentury horse market. Such realism led to the work's favorable reception from Napoleon III, which in turn helped promote Bonheur as one of France's best painters. In 1864 Bonheur became the first woman to receive the Legion of Honor, France's highest award. However, the award was bestowed privately by the empress, for the emperor refused to give the medal to a woman in a public ceremony.*

Photography

One of the forces impelling painting toward a more realistic and detached style of expression was the invention of the camera. Two types of camera techniques were perfected in 1839. In France, Louis-Jacques-Mandé Daguerre [duh-GAIR] (1787–1851) discovered a chemical method for implanting images on silvered copper plates to produce photographs called daguerreotypes. In England, William Henry Fox Talbot (1800–1877) was pioneering the negative-positive process of photographic images, which he called "the pencil of nature." Not only did the camera undermine the reality of the painted image, but it also quickly created a new art form, photography. From the beginning,

Figure 18.17 ÉDOUARD MANET. *Olympia.* 1863. Oil on canvas, 51¼ × 74¾″. Musée d'Orsay, Paris. *Despite its references to traditional art,* Olympia *created a furor among the prudish and conservative public and critics. Parisian bourgeoisie expected to see nudes in the official Salon, but they were shocked by the appearance of a notorious prostitute, completely nude. The art critics, likewise, found the painting indecent and also condemned Manet's harsh, brilliant light, which tended to eliminate any details of the room's interior. Regardless of its initial negative reception,* Olympia *today is admired as a work that made a break with traditional art practices and opened the way for a modern art centered on the painter's own theories.*

Figure 18.18 Mathew Brady. *Abraham Lincoln.* 1860. Library of Congress. *Urged by his supporters in New York City, Lincoln hastily arranged to have Brady photograph him. Typical of the* carte-de-visite, *Lincoln is shown standing in a three-quarter-length frontal pose, a position influenced by the Western tradition of portrait painting. Dressed in the proper attire of the successful attorney that he was, Lincoln looks steadily at the viewer, while resting his left hand lightly on a stack of books. This photograph enhanced the Honest Abe image, with its dignity, seriousness, and air of calm resolve. On the left is the photographer's logo: Brady N.Y.*

many photographers began to experiment with the camera's artistic potential, though only recently has photography received wide acceptance as serious art.

Among these early photographers was the American Mathew Brady (about 1823–1896), whose reputation today is based mainly on his pictorial record of the American Civil War. Before the war, however, he operated a spacious Broadway studio and gallery in New York, and there, in February 1860, he photographed Abraham Lincoln of Illinois, who was campaigning to be the Republican nominee for president (Figure 18.18). This portrait introduced Lincoln to the East Coast public, who previously had thought the Midwesterner to be a coarse, backwoods politician. The original photograph achieved wide circulation when it was printed on a *carte-de-visite*, a 2½-inch print that was mounted on a calling card or collected as a personal memento. It was also reproduced in newspapers and lithographs. After Lincoln was elected president, he acknowledged to Brady that the photograph had been instrumental in securing his election.

Music

Originating shortly after 1800, Romantic music reigned supreme from 1830 until 1871. Romantic works grew longer and more expressive as composers forged styles reflecting their individual feelings. To achieve unique voices, Romantic composers adopted varied techniques such as shifting rhythms, complex musical structures, discordant passages, and minor keys. In addition, with the spread of nationalistic feelings across Europe, especially after 1850, composers began to incorporate folk songs, national anthems, and indigenous dance rhythms into their music. Nonetheless, throughout this era Romantic composers stayed true to the established forms of Classical music composition—the opera, the sonata, and the symphony.

Although a Baroque creation, opera rose to splendid heights under Romanticism. The bourgeois public, bedazzled by opera's spectacle and virtuoso singers, eagerly embraced this art form. Operatic composers sometimes wrote works specifically to show off the vocal talents of particular performers. So prolific were these musicians that they wrote over half of the operas performed today.

Romanticism had an important impact on opera. The orchestras for operas became larger, inspiring composers to write long, elaborate works requiring many performers. Composers also began to integrate the entire musical drama, creating orchestral music that accentuated the actions and thoughts of the characters onstage. Most important, the form of opera itself was transformed. At first, composers imitated the form that they had inherited, writing operas in which a series of independent musical numbers—that is, **arias** (melodious songs)—alternated with **recitatives** (text either declaimed in the rhythms of natural speech with slight musical variations or sung with fuller musical support). The Italian composer Verdi brought this type of opera to its peak, advancing beyond the mechanical aria-recitative alternation. But even as Verdi was being lionized for his operatic achievements, a new style of opera was arising in Germany in the works of Wagner, which were written not as independent musical sections but as continuous musical scenes.

Giuseppe Verdi [VAYR-dee] (1813–1901), Italy's greatest composer of opera, followed the practice of the time and borrowed many of his plots from the works of Romantic writers filled with passion and full-blooded emotionalism.

One of the operas that brought him international fame was *Rigoletto* (1851), based on a play by Victor Hugo. What makes it such a favorite with audiences are its strong characters, its beautiful melodies, and its dramatic unity—features that typify Verdi's mature works. A study in Romantic opposites, this work tells of a crippled court jester, Rigoletto, deformed physically but emotionally sensitive, coarse in public but a devoted parent in private. The jester's daughter, Gilda, is also a study in contrasts, torn between love for her father and attraction to a corrupt noble.

In *Rigoletto*, Verdi continues to alternate arias with sung recitatives, but overall his music for the orchestra skillfully underscores the events taking place onstage. In addition, he employs musical passages to illustrate the characters' psychology, using convoluted orchestral backgrounds to accompany Rigoletto's monologues, for example, or shifting from simple to showy musical settings to demonstrate Gilda's conflicted nature. Other operas followed, enhancing Verdi's mounting celebrity: *La Traviata* in 1853, based on a play written by the French Romantic writer Alexandre Dumas [doo-MAH] the younger, and *Aïda* in 1871, commissioned by Egypt's ruler and first performed in the Cairo opera house.

Romantic opera reached its climax in the works of Richard Wagner [VAHG-nuhr] (1813–1883), who sought a union of music and drama. A political revolutionary in his youth and a visionary thinker, Wagner was deeply impressed by the Romantic idea that the supreme expression of artistic genius occurred only when the arts were fused. To that end, he not only composed his own scores but also wrote the **librettos,** or texts, frequently conducted the music, and even planned the opera house in Bayreuth, Germany, where his later works were staged.

Wagner's major musical achievement was the monumental project entitled *The Ring of the Nibelung* (1853–1874), a cycle of four operas—or **music dramas,** as Wagner called them—that fulfilled his ideal of fusing music, verse, and staging. In these works, the distinction between arias and recitatives was nearly erased, giving a continuously flowing melodic line. This unified sound was marked by the appearance of recurring themes associated with particular characters, things, or ideas, known as **leitmotifs.** Based on a popular Romantic source—the medieval Norse myths—the *Ring* also reflected Wagner's belief that opera should be moral. The *Ring* cycle warns against overweening ambition, its plot relating a titanic struggle for world mastery in which both human beings and gods are destroyed because of their lust for power. Wagner may have been addressing this warning to the Faustian spirit that dominated capitalism in the industrial age—a message that went unheeded.

Another German, Johannes Brahms (1833–1897), dominated orchestral and chamber music after 1850 in much the same way that Wagner did opera. Unlike Wagner, Brahms was no musical innovator. A classical Romanticist, he took up the mantle vacated by Beethoven, and he admired the Baroque works of Bach. In Vienna, his adopted home, Brahms became the hero of the traditionalists who opposed the new music of Wagner. Neglecting the characteristic Romantic works of operas and program music, he won fame with his symphonies and chamber music. His characteristic sound is mellow, always harmonic, delighting equally in joy and melancholy.

Despite his conservative musicianship, Brahms's work incorporates many Romantic elements. Continuing the art-song tradition established by Schubert (see Chapter 17), he introduced folk melodies into his pieces. In his instrumental works, he often aimed for the expressiveness of the human voice, the "singing" style preferred in Romanticism. He was also indebted to the Romantic style for the length of his symphonies, the use of rhythmic variations in all his works, and, above all, the rich lyricism and songfulness of his music.

Despite the dominance of Classical musical forms, this period was the zenith of Romantic *lieder,* or art songs. The continuing popularity of *lieder* reflected bourgeois taste and power, since amateur performances of these songs were a staple of home entertainment for the well-to-do, especially in Germany and Austria. In the generation after Schubert, the best composer of *lieder* was the German Robert Schumann (1810–1856), a pianist who shifted to music journalism and composition when his right hand became crippled in 1832. Splendid fusions of words and music, his songs are essentially duets for voice and piano.

Schumann's *lieder* are often parts of song cycles held together with unifying themes. One of his best-known song cycles is *Dichterliebe (A Poet's Love)* (1840), set to verses by Heinrich Heine (1797–1856), Germany's preeminent lyric poet. This song cycle superbly illustrates the Romantic preoccupation with program music. For instance, the song "Im Wunderschönen Monat Mai" ("In the Marvelously Beautiful Month of May") conveys the longing of Heine's text through ascending lines of melody and an unresolved climax. The passion in this song cycle was inspired by Schumann's marriage to Clara Wieck (1819–1896), a piano virtuoso and composer in her own right.

The Legacy of the Bourgeois Age

We in the modern world still live in the shadow of the bourgeois age. The revolutions of 1830 and 1848 demonstrated that uprisings could bring about change but not always the desired results and that more drastic methods might be necessary in the future. These failed revolutions inspired the amoral concept of realpolitik, a guiding principle in much of today's politics. Realpolitik also contributed to the unification of Germany in 1871, which upset the balance of power on the Continent, unleashed German militarism, and led to France's smoldering resentment of Germany. The two world wars of the twentieth century had their seeds in these events.

With liberalism in the ascendant, the middle-class values of hard work, thrift, ambition, and respectability became paramount, as did the notion that the individual should take precedence over the group. However, the utopian socialists and the Marxian socialists, in criticizing liberalism and the industrial system, offered alternative solutions to social and economic problems. Their proposals foreshadowed approaches such as labor unions, mass political parties, and state planning.

The intellectual and artistic developments of this age had far-reaching repercussions. There is still interest in Marx's controversial analysis of history, despite the collapse of global communism; Darwin's theory of evolution, though intensely debated, is central to modern thought; Pasteur's contributions in immunology and microbiology have helped make the world a safer place; and higher criticism, by challenging the Hebrew Bible and the New Testament, has diminished the notion of religious revelation itself.

Romanticism, although under siege from other modes of thought after 1850, has not disappeared from the West, even today. Realism, its immediate successor, became the reigning style until 1900, partly because of the development of the camera and the art of photography. London's Crystal Palace inaugurated the high-tech tradition in art and architecture, and inventions and new techniques in printing and publishing laid the foundation for a mass market in the visual arts. Perhaps the most significant artistic development during this time was Manet's adoption of the credo "art for art's sake," which terminated the debate over the representational nature of art. Most artists in the post-1871 period followed Manet's bold move.

KEY CULTURAL TERMS

Utilitarianism	slave narrative
socialism	aria
higher criticism	recitative
evolution	libretto
Realism	music drama
Transcendentalism	leitmotif

SUGGESTIONS FOR FURTHER READING

PRIMARY SOURCES

BALZAC, H. DE. *Cousin Bette.* Translated by M. A. Crawford. New York: Penguin, 1972. A representative novel from the *Human Comedy* series, Balzac's monumental commentary on French bourgeois society in the post-Napoleonic era.

———. *Père Goriot.* Translated by J. M. Sedgwick. New York: Dodd, Mead, 1954. Another of the best known of Balzac's almost one hundred novels in the *Human Comedy* series.

BRONTË, C. *Jane Eyre.* Edited and with an introduction by M. Smith. London: Oxford University Press, 1973. A classic of Romanticism, this novel deals with a theme dear to the hearts of nineteenth-century women readers, the life and tribulations of a governess.

BRONTË, E. *Wuthering Heights.* Edited and with an introduction by I. Jack. New York: Oxford University Press, 1983. A classic of Romanticism, this novel recounts the doomed affair of the socially mismatched but passionate soul mates Heathcliff and Catherine.

DICKENS, C. *Hard Times.* London: Methuen, 1987. A depiction of life in the new industrialized cities, this grim tale of forced marriage and its consequences reveals what happens when practical, utilitarian thinking replaces human values.

———. *Oliver Twist.* London: Longman, 1984. Dickens's moving tale of the orphan Oliver and his experiences among London's poor in the sordid conditions of the 1830s.

DICKINSON, E. *Complete Poems of Emily Dickinson.* Edited by T. H. Johnson. Boston: Little Brown & Co., 1976. Excellent gathering of the complete corpus—all 1,775 works—of Dickinson's poetry, arranged in chronological order from awkward juvenilia to the morbid, hell-obsessed verses of her later years. Compiled by a respected Dickinson scholar.

DOSTOEVSKY, F. *The Brothers Karamazov*. Translated by D. Magarshack. New York: Penguin, 1982. In his novel, Dostoevsky deals with broad metaphysical and psychological themes, such as the right of human beings to reject the world made by God because it contains so much evil and suffering. These themes are dramatized through the actions and personalities of the brothers and their father.

————. *Crime and Punishment*. Translated by S. Monas. New York: New American Library, 1980. A masterpiece of psychological insight, this gripping tale of murder explores the themes of suffering, guilt, redemption, and the limits of individual freedom.

DOUGLASS, F. *Narrative of the Life of Frederick Douglass, an American Slave, Written by Himself*. Introduction by Henry Louis Gates. Bedford Books in American History. Bedford Press, 1993. A heartbreaking, but ultimately uplifting, autobiography of perhaps the most influential and celebrated African American of the nineteenth century. Originally published in 1845, this work launched the literary genre known as the slave narrative. A reprint of the 1960 Harvard University Press publication.

ELIOT, G. *Middlemarch*. New York: Penguin, 1965. This classic of Realist fiction explores the psychology and growth in self-understanding of the principal characters, Dorothea Brooke and Dr. Lydgate.

FLAUBERT, G. *Madame Bovary*. Translated by A. Russell. New York: Penguin, 1961. One of the first Realist novels, and possibly the finest, Flaubert's work details Emma Bovary's futile attempts to find happiness in a stifling bourgeois world.

GASKELL, E. C. *North and South*. New York: Dutton, 1975. A portrait of economic and social disparities in mid-nineteenth-century England.

GILBERT, O., AND TRUTH, S. *The Narrative of Sojourner Truth*. Dover Thrift Editions, 1997. This autobiography, as told to a secretary, recounts the amazing life story of the nineteenth-century African American woman who endured thirty years of slavery in upstate New York, after which she became a leading abolitionist and a fighter for various reforms including women's suffrage. Originally published in 1850.

HUGO, V. *Les Misérables*. Translated by L. Wraxall. New York: Heritage Press, 1938. A good English version of Hugo's epic-length novel of social injustice in early-nineteenth-century France.

MARX, K., AND ENGELS, F. *Basic Writings on Politics and Philosophy*. Edited by L. Feuer. Boston: Peter Smith, 1975. A representative selection of their prodigious writings, which challenged industrial capitalism in the mid–nineteenth century and provided the theoretical basis for socialism and communism.

MILL, J. S. *On Liberty*. New York: Norton, 1975. Mill's examination of the relationship between the individual and society.

————. *Utilitarianism*. Indianapolis: Hackett, 1978. A defense of the belief that the proper goal of government is to provide the greatest happiness for the greatest number.

SAND, G. *Indiana*. Translated by G. B. Ives. Chicago: Academy Chicago, 1977. Sand's first novel, with its Romantic themes and feminist message, established her as a writer of great promise.

TOLSTOY, L. *War and Peace*. Translated by L. and A. Maude. London: Oxford University Press, 1984. Tolstoy's epic novel traces the impact of the Napoleonic wars on the lives of his Russian characters and explores such themes as the role of individual human beings in the flow of history.

WHITMAN, W. *The Complete Poems*. Edited by F. Murphy. New York: Viking Press, 1990. The complete poems of arguably the best poet yet produced in the United States. An authoritative edition compiled by a longtime Whitman scholar.

SUGGESTIONS FOR LISTENING

BRAHMS, JOHANNES (1833–1897). Brahms's four symphonies (1876, 1877, 1883, and 1885) demonstrate the disciplined style and majestic lyricism that made him the leader of the anti-Wagner school. Brahms also excelled in chamber music, a genre usually ignored by Romantic composers. His chamber works show him to be a worthy successor to Beethoven, especially in the Piano Quartet in G minor, Op. 25 (late 1850s), the Clarinet Quintet in B minor, Op. 115 (1891), and three string quartets, composed between 1873 and 1876.

SCHUMANN, ROBERT (1810–1856). Continuing the art-song tradition perfected by Schubert, Schuman composed song cycles such as *Dichterliebe (A Poet's Love)* (1840) and *Frauenliebe und -leben (A Woman's Love and Life)* (1840), both filled with heartfelt passion and set to verses by Romantic poets. Schumann also had much success with his works for solo piano, including the delightful *Kinderszenen (Scenes from Childhood)* (1839), which he called "reminiscences of a grown-up for grown-ups." Unlike the *lieder* and piano music, Schumann's other works are often neglected today, such as his four symphonies (1841, 1845–1846, 1850, 1851); two choral offerings, *Das Paradies und die Peri (Paradise and the Peri)* (1843) and *Der Rose Pilgefahrt (The Pilgrimage of the Rose)* (1851); incidental music for the stage (Byron's *Manfred*); and assorted chamber works.

VERDI, GIUSEPPE (1813–1901). Primarily a composer of opera, Verdi worked exclusively in the Romantic tradition, bringing to perfection the style of opera that alternated arias and recitatives. His operatic subjects are based mainly on works by Romantic authors, such as *Il Corsaro (The Corsair)* (1848), adapted from Lord Byron, and *La Traviata (The Lost One)* (1853), adapted from Alexandre Dumas the younger. Shakespeare, whom the Romantics revered as a consummate genius, inspired the librettos for *Otello* (1887) and *Falstaff* (1893). Like the Romantics generally, Verdi had strong nationalistic feelings that he expressed in, for example, *Les Vêpres Siciliennes (The Sicilian Vespers)* (1855) and *La Battaglia di Legnano (The Battle of Legnano)* (1849).

WAGNER, RICHARD (1813–1883). Wagner created a new form, music drama, that fused all the arts—a development that reflected his theory that music should serve the theater. His early style may be heard in *Der Fliegende Holländer (The Flying Dutchman)* (1842), which alternates arias and recitatives in the traditional way. By 1850, in *Lohengrin*, he was moving toward a more comprehensive operatic style, using continuously flowing music and the technique of recurring themes, called leitmotifs. He reached his maturity with *Der Ring des Nibelungen (The Ring of the Nibelung)*, written between 1853 and 1874; in this cycle of four operas, he focuses on the orchestral web, with the arias being simply one factor in the constantly shifting sounds. His works composed after 1853 pushed the limits of Classical tonality and became the starting point for modern music.

AFRICA

AMERICAS

HISTORY

Algeria, Tunisia, Madagascar, Mali, Chad, Dahomey, and Senegal under French control. Egypt, Asante Kingdom, and most of Yorubaland under British control.

North Africa Tripoli and Algiers fought U.S.; slave trade and piracy suppressed. Suez Canal opened.

Northeast Africa *Ethiopia.* Defeated Italian invaders.

West Africa *Liberia.* Founded as haven for freed U.S. slaves. *Asante Kingdom.* Decline after end of slave trade (1807).

East Africa Cecil Rhodes's South Africa Company took over Nguni states, Matabeleland and Mashonaland.

South Africa British took Boer coastal lands; displaced Boers founded Transvaal and Orange Free State; gold and diamonds discovered. Boer War (1899–1902) between British and Boers. *Zululand.* Military regime under King Shaka overran Natal. Defeated by Britain (1879).

Latin America Successful wars of independence against Spain (1816–25). *Mexico.* After independence came civil wars, foreign wars (Texas and U.S.), and French occupation. *Argentina.* Large immigration from Spain and Italy. Made wealthy by export trade. *Peru.* Failed Inca uprising (1814). Lost war with Chile (1889). *Brazil.* Portugal's emperor ruled from Brazil (to 1821). Became independent as monarchy and republic. Slavery abolished (1888). *Cuba.* Spain defeated (1898); U.S. troops occupied island (1899).

Native North America *Eastern Woodlands.* Cherokee Trail of Tears, forced march from Georgia to Oklahoma. By 1880s, all eastern Indian nations had been moved west to reservations. *Plains.* Gold discovered on Indian lands. Battle of Little Bighorn. *Southwest.* Navajo forced onto reservation. Apache resistance to relocation, led by Geronimo.

ART & MUSIC

Central Africa *Kwele culture (Gabon).* Ritual masks in antelope and gorilla forms.

West Africa *Benin.* Carved ivory leopards with spots made from copper. *Dahomey. Bocios* (wood carvings or metal sculptures of human figures), meant to ward off evil.

Akati Ekple Kendo. Warrior Figure (bocio). 1858–1889. Benin. Iron, ht. 5' 5". Musée de l'Homme, Paris.

Latin America Painting and sculpture: academic art in European styles, including Romantic, Neoclassic, Realist, and Impressionist; and popular art drawing on New World themes, ideas, and attitudes. After 1850, artists increasingly worked with local themes. *Brazil.* Antônio Carlos Gomes, opera composer.

Native North America *Southwest.* Navajo renowned for intricately designed blankets; began silversmithing (1853).

José María Velasco. View of the Valley of Mexico from Hill of Santa Isabel. 1877. Oil on canvas, 63 × 90½". Mexico City, Museum of Modern Art.

ARCHITECTURE

East Africa *Swahili Language Areas.* Doors ornamented with a mixture of Islamic and African styles.

West Africa *Fulani Empire of Sokoto.* Caliph Muhammad Bello built capital city, Sokoto. *Yoruba culture.* Afro-Brazilian building style emerged after freed slaves returned from Brazil.

Latin America In urban and public architecture, Spanish Baroque, which patriots identified with tyranny, was replaced by French Neoclassicism, expressive of Enlightenment ideals and the newly independent states. Local traditions continued to be expressed in countryside.

Manuel Tolsá. Interior Courtyard, School of Mines, Mexico City. 1797–1813.

RELIGION, PHILOSOPHY, LITERATURE

South Africa M. K. Gandhi, the future leader of India, lived here (after 1893), becoming a successful lawyer and perfecting his technique of nonviolent resistance. Feminist Olive Schreiner's novel, *The Story of an African Farm* (1883).

West Africa *Fulani Empire of Sokoto.* Over 260 works on religion, law, politics, history, and poetry by Sheik Usman dan Fodio and his brother and his son. *Yoruba culture.* Samuel Crowther, first black African bishop (1864–90) of the Anglican Church, translated Bible into Yoruba. *History of the Yorubas* (1897), by Samuel Johnson, a Yoruba cleric.

Brazil Joaquim Machado de Assis's *Epitaph for a Small Winner* (1881), a classic novel.

Native North America By 1880s, traditional religious observances, such as Sun Dance and Ghost Dance, outlawed; Indian children forced to attend boarding schools, learn English, become Christian. *Eastern Woodlands.* Sequoyah invented Cherokee alphabet (1828); Cherokee-language newspaper (1828–35).

ASIA

China

Ch'ing Dynasty. Social conditions and state corruption worsened. Defeated by Britain in Opium War (1839–42); trade and port concessions extracted by Europeans. T'ai-p'ing revolt (1850–64) undermined regime. Officials and students studied in Japan and West. Boxer Rebellion (1900).

India

Mogul Dynasty, ended 1858. Country run by British East India Company. Indian Mutiny led to abolition of East India Company; power passed to the British state. *British Crown (Raj), began 1858.* British legal and bureaucratic systems introduced; industrialization began. Indian National Congress founded; began campaign for Indian self-rule (1885).

Japan

Edo period, ended 1867. Economic slowdown and threats of insurrection. U.S., followed by Europeans, forced opening of ports and trade concessions. Shōgunate abolished and Meiji Dynasty founded. *Meiji Restoration, began 1868.* Institution of Meiji Constitution (1889). Social, economic, and political reforms moved country toward becoming centralized and industrialized. Defeated China and awarded Taiwan (1895).

Ch'ing Dynasty. Scholarly painting, favored by imperial court, became stagnant. Schools of art drawing on Western models or on popular themes flourished in Guangzhou and Shanghai.

Ren Bonian, also known as Ren Yi. Young Woman at a Window with Plum Blossoms. *1884. Hanging scroll on paper. Liaoning Provincial Museum, Shenyang, China.*

Mogul Dynasty. Miniature painting, as practiced in provincial courts, ended. Sikh portrait painting declined. Western influence on the rise. *British Crown.* Rabindranath Tagore's musical settings of Bengali poems.

Edo period. Ukiyo-e prints were produced by Utagawa School and landscape artists Katsushika Hokusai and Andō Hiroshige. *Meiji Restoration.* Traditional, Western style, and hybrid schools of painting. Western textiles and art influenced by Japanese crafts and woodblock prints.

Hokusai. Mt. Fuji. *1823–1831. Woodblock print, 10 × 15".*

Ch'ing Dynasty. Hybrid style, mixing traditional and Western features. Western-style mercantile buildings, schools, and churches built in port cities. British troops burned Imperial Summer Palace.

Meiji Restoration. Western influence on urban buildings and public parks. Stone replaced wood for building.

Tatsuno Kingo. Bank of Japan (foreground). *Completed 1896. Tokyo.*

Ch'ing Dynasty. Shanghai's first illustrated magazine, the *Dianshi Studio Pictorial* (1884). Decreased government support of scholarship. Western science and religion made inroads. T'ai-p'ing rebels advocated an egalitarian and communal society, based on Chinese and Christian ideals.

British Crown. The Bengali poet Rabindranath Tagore wrote *Mānasi* (1890) and *Chitra* (1896).

Meiji Restoration. Literature influenced by Western Realism; many Western works translated into Japanese. Tsubouchi Shōyō's critical work *The Essence of the Novel* helped shape the Japanese novel; Futabatei Shimei's *The Drifting Cloud,* first modern Japanese novel; female poet and short story writer, Higuchi Ichiyō; Kawatake Mokuami, a prolific playwright (about 360 plays) for Kabuki theater. Bacteriologist Kiyoshi Shiga identified cause of endemic dysentery (1897).

19 THE AGE OF EARLY MODERNISM 1871–1914

Between 1871 and 1914, the European continent enjoyed an almost unprecedented period of tranquility, free of military conflict and considered by many to be the new age predicted by Enlightenment thinkers. But hindsight exposes this period as one of rampant nationalism, aggressive imperialism, and growing militarism, culminating in the outbreak of World War I in 1914. The prolonged, violent nature of that global struggle ended the optimism of prewar Europe.

At the same time, the phenomenon known as "modern life" was emerging, with people sharing in the benefits of strong nation-states and of the Second Industrial Revolution. In the cultural realm, **Modernism** was born; this movement rejected both the Greco-Roman and the Judeo-Christian legacies and tried to forge a new perspective that was true to modern secular experience. Modernism lasted about one hundred years, going through three distinct stages. During its first phase (1871–1914), which is treated in this chapter, artists, writers, and thinkers established the movement's principles through their creative and innovative works. The second phase, the zenith of Modernism (1914–1945), is the subject of Chapter 20; and the exhaustion and decline of the movement, the third phase (1945–1970), is covered in Chapter 21.

EUROPE'S RISE TO WORLD LEADERSHIP

The period between 1871 and 1914 was an age of accelerated and stressful change stimulated by imperialism, nationalism, and militarism. Acting as a catalyst was the middle class of central and western Europe (Figure 19.1).

◀ **Detail** Vincent van Gogh. *Self-Portrait with a Gray Hat.* 1887. Oil on canvas, 17¼ × 14¾". Vincent van Gogh Foundation/National Museum Vincent van Gogh, Amsterdam.

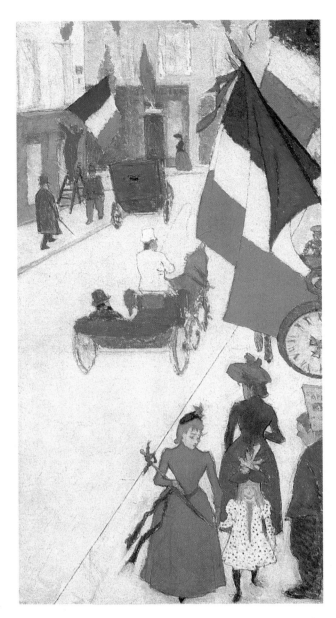

Figure 19.1 PIERRE BONNARD. *Paris, Rue de Parme on Bastille Day.* 1890. Oil on canvas, 31¼ × 15¾". National Gallery, Washington, D.C. *Bonnard's colorful depiction of Bastille Day, France's independence day, is a fitting symbol of nationalism and middle-class life. Middle-class men, women, and children, identified by their dress, leisurely stroll the street or ride in carriages. The tricolor flags lining the streets were patriotic reminders of France's revolutionary heritage.*

The Second Industrial Revolution and the Making of Modern Life

The Second Industrial Revolution differed from the first in several significant ways. First, Great Britain, the world's industrial leader since 1760, now faced strong competition from Germany and the United States. Second, science and research provided new and better industrial products and had a stronger influence than in the basically pragmatic first revolution. Finally, steam and water power were replaced by newer forms of industrial energy, such as oil and electricity. The internal combustion engine replaced the steam engine in ships and in the early 1900s gave rise to the automobile and the airplane.

Technology, the offspring of science, was also reshaping the world. The wireless superseded the telegraph, the telephone made its debut, and national and international postal services were instituted. Typewriters and tabulators transformed business practices. Rotary presses printed thousands of copies of daily newspapers for an increasingly literate public (Figure 19.2).

The Second Industrial Revolution affected almost every aspect of the economy. In transportation, more efficient engines meant lower transportation costs and cheaper products. Refrigeration permitted perishable foods to be transported great distances without spoiling. Advertising became both a significant source of revenue for publishers and a powerful force in the consumer economy. Increased wealth meant more leisure for more people, and new recreations appeared, such as seaside resorts, music halls, movies, and bicycles—all contributing to the phenomenon known as modern life.

Industrialized cities, with their promises of well-paying jobs, comfortable lives, and noisy entertainments, drew residents of small towns and farms, and by 1900 nearly 30 percent of the people in the West lived in cities (Figure 19.3). As cities grew in industrialized countries, the standard of living improved. Consumers benefited from a general decline in prices and from steady wages and salaries. The period from 1900 to the outbreak of World War I in 1914 was a golden age for the affluent and leisured middle classes.

While the middle and upper classes enjoyed unprecedented prosperity, misery mounted among urban workers despite the creation of state-funded social welfare programs. Urban slums grew more crowded, and living conditions worsened. The presence of squalor in the midst of plenty pricked the conscience of many citizens, who began to work for better housing and less dangerous working conditions for laborers. When these reform efforts proved inadequate, labor unions arose, along with their best weapon, the strike.

One reform did succeed spectacularly: the founding of secular public education. Reformers claimed that

Imperialism—the quest for colonies—began as a search for new markets and increased wealth. As Europe became a world power with a network of political and economic interests around the globe, rivalries among European states intensified, transforming most of them into armed camps. Combined with growing feelings of nationalism, imperialistic and militaristic impulses created an atmosphere that eventually led rival states to war.

Figure 19.2 MARY CASSATT. *Reading "Le Figaro."* 1878. Oil on canvas, 41 × 33". National Gallery, Washington, D.C. *Cassatt's woman reading a newspaper was a rare subject in the nineteenth century. Artists usually depicted women reading books, rather than newspapers, which were identified with the man's world outside the home. The woman is the artist's mother, Katherine Cassatt, who is reading* Le Figaro, *one of Paris's leading newspapers. Rich and well-educated, Mrs. Cassatt was a strong influence in her daughter's life and career. The formidable figure of the mother takes up much of the painting, and the mirror on the left reflects her and her surroundings. The artist has cropped the mirror, much in the style of a photograph, a popular technique among Early Modernist painters.*

Figure 19.3 CAMILLE PISSARRO. *The Great Bridge to Rouen.* 1896. Oil on canvas, 29 3/16 × 36½". Carnegie Museum of Art, Pittsburgh. Purchase. *Pissarro's painting captures the energy of Rouen and transforms this French river town into a symbol of the new industrial age. Contributing to the sense of vitality are the belching smokestack, the bridge crowded with hurrying people, and the dockworkers busy with their machinery. The fast pace is underscored by the Impressionist technique of "broken color," giving an immediacy to the scene.*

Figure 19.4 EYRE CROWE. *The Dinner Hour at Wigan.* 1874. Oil on canvas, 30 × 42¼". Manchester City Art Gallery, Manchester, England. *Social possibilities for English women expanded to some degree during this era. This painting depicts a factory scene in which the young female workers gain a brief respite from their tasks. A few talk together quietly, while others remain apart or finish a chore. They all seem dwarfed by the huge mill with the smokestacks in the background, a fitting symbol of industrial power.*

public schools, financed by taxes and supervised by state agencies, would prepare workers for jobs in industrialized society and create an informed and literate citizenry—two basic needs of modern life. An unanticipated result of the establishment of public school systems was that ties between children and their parents were loosened.

The status of women also changed dramatically. New employment opportunities opened for teachers, nurses, office workers, and sales clerks. Because some of these jobs required special skills, colleges and degree programs were developed to teach them to women. Many young women still turned to domestic service, but new household appliances reduced the need for servants. Female labor in factories was now regulated by state laws, but small shopkeepers continued to work long hours in family businesses (Figure 19.4).

Some women reformers, primarily from the middle class, advocated more freedom for women, continuing a tradition that had begun on a limited scale before 1871. These reformers launched successful campaigns to revise property and divorce laws, giving women greater control over their wealth and their lives. In several countries, they founded suffrage movements, using protests and marches to dramatize their situation. The word *feminism* entered the English vocabulary in 1895. Following a vigorous, occasionally violent, campaign, women won the right to vote in Great Britain in 1918 and in the United States in 1920.

Response to Industrialism: Politics and Crisis

At the dawn of Early Modernism, the assumptions of liberalism in industrialized countries were being challenged from many quarters. Except in Britain and the United States, liberals were under siege in national legislatures both by socialists—who wanted more central planning and more state services for the workers—and by conservatives—who feared the masses and supported militant nationalism as a way to unify their societies. After 1900 political parties representing workers and trade unionists, which were strong enough to push successfully for laws to correct some social problems of industrialism, further threatened the liberals' hold on power.

Events also seemed to discredit liberal theory. Theoretically, under free trade the population ought to decline or at least stabilize, and the economy ought to operate harmoniously, but neither happened. Population was surging and industrial capitalism was erratic, leading many to conclude that the so-called laws of liberal economics did not work.

Domestic Policies in the Heavily Industrialized West
Germany, France, Great Britain, and the United States all faced domestic problems during this period. Founded in 1871, the German Reich, or Empire, moved toward unity under the astute leadership of its first chancellor, Otto von Bismarck, and the new kaiser, or emperor, William I (r. 1871–1888), former King of Prussia (Figure 19.5). Despite the illusion of parliamentary rule, the tone of this imperial reich was conservative, militaristic, and nationalistic.

In France, the Third Republic was founded after the humiliating defeat of the Second Empire by Germany in 1871. Even though the government remained hopelessly divided between republicans and monarchists, it agreed on the need to correct the most glaring social injustices in an attempt to counteract the growing appeal of the workers' parties and socialism. The nation's liberal center gradually evaporated, creating bitter deadlocks between socialists and conservatives that no government could resolve.

Great Britain was more successful in solving its domestic problems during this period. Controlled by political parties that represented the upper and middle classes, the British government passed social legislation that improved the working and living conditions of many poor families and created opportunities for social mobility through a state secondary-school system. As in Germany and France, these reform efforts did not prevent workers from forming their own political party, the Labour party. Within a decade after World War I, it had gained enough support to elect a majority of Parliament and the prime minister.

PERSONAL PERSPECTIVE

LADY CONSTANCE LYTTON
From *Prisons and Prisoners*

Lady Constance Lytton was a leader of the women's suffrage movement in Great Britain. Arrested during a protest in Liverpool in 1910, she assumed the name and status of a working-class woman, Jane Warton, because she feared the police would release her due to her high social position. As Jane Warton, she went on a hunger strike and was force-fed by a doctor and wardresses (female guards), a horrifying tactic experienced by many suffragettes.

I was visited again by the Senior Medical Officer, who asked me how long I had been without food. I said I had eaten a buttered scone and a banana sent in by friends to the police station on Friday at about midnight. He said, "Oh, then, this is the fourth day; that is too long, I shall feed you, I must feed you at once," but he went out and nothing happened till about six o'clock in the evening, when he returned with, I think, five wardresses and the feeding apparatus. He urged me to take food voluntarily. I told him that was absolutely out of the question, that when our legislators ceased to resist enfranchising women then I should cease to resist taking food in prison. He did not examine my heart nor feel my pulse; he did not ask to do so, nor did I say anything which could possibly induce him to think I would refuse to be examined. I offered no resistance to being placed in position, but lay down voluntarily on the plank bed. Two of the wardresses took hold of my arms, one held my head and one my feet. One wardress helped to pour the food. The doctor leant on my knees as he stooped over my chest to get at my mouth. I shut my mouth and clenched my teeth. I had looked forward to this moment with so much anxiety lest my identity should be discovered beforehand, that I felt positively glad when the time had come. The sense of being overpowered by more force than I could possibly resist was complete, but I resisted nothing except with my mouth. The doctor offered me the choice of a wooden or steel gag; he explained elaborately, as he did on most subsequent occasions, that the steel gag would hurt and the wooden one not, and he urged me not to force him to use the steel gag. But I did not speak nor open my mouth, so

that after playing about for a moment or two with the wooden one he finally had recourse to the steel. He seemed annoyed at my resistance and he broke into a temper as he plied my teeth with the steel implement. He found that on either side at the back I had false teeth mounted on a bridge which did not take out. The superintending wardress asked if I had any false teeth, if so, that they must be taken out; I made no answer and the process went on. He dug his instrument down on to the sham tooth, it pressed fearfully on the gum. He said if I resisted so much with my teeth, he would have to feed me through the nose. The pain of it was intense and at last I must have given way for he got the gag between my teeth, when he proceeded to turn it much more than necessary until my jaws were fastened wide apart, far more than they could go naturally. Then he put down my throat a tube which seemed to me much too wide and was something like four feet in length. The irritation of the tube was excessive. I choked the moment it touched my throat until it had got down. Then the food was poured in quickly; it made me sick a few seconds after it was down and the action of the sickness made my body and legs double up, but the wardresses instantly pressed back my head and the doctor leant on my knees. The horror of it was more than I can describe. I was sick over the doctor and wardresses, and it seemed a long time before they took the tube out. As the doctor left he gave me a slap on the cheek, not violently, but, as it were, to express his contemptuous disapproval, and he seemed to take for granted that my distress was assumed. At first it seemed such an utterly contemptible thing to have done that I could only laugh in my mind. Then suddenly I saw Jane Warton lying before me, and it seemed as if I were outside of her. She was the most despised, ignorant and helpless prisoner that I had seen. When she had served her time and was out of the prison, no one would believe anything she said, and the doctor when he had fed her by force and tortured her body, struck her on the cheek to show how he despised her! That was Jane Warton, and I had come to help her.

Across the Atlantic, the United States began to challenge British industrial supremacy. America's rapidly expanding economy allowed big business to dominate politics at all levels until the reform movements of the early 1900s (Figure 19.6). These movements, spurred by America's democratic tradition, temporarily de-

railed the power of the large business conglomerations called trusts.

In the late nineteenth century, Europeans came to America in the largest migration of human population ever recorded. These immigrants—after painful adjustments, particularly in the crowded slums of the

Figure 19.5 ANTON VON WERNER. *The Proclamation of the King of Prussia as German Emperor at Versailles. 1877. Oil on canvas. This painting commemorates the moment when the German Empire was proclaimed and King William of Prussia became its first emperor. Von Werner uses reflections from the famed Hall of Mirrors at Versailles to make the stirring scene more theatrical, and added drama comes from the raised swords of the officers. The strong presence of the army was prophetic of the dominant role the military was destined to play in the German Empire.*

eastern cities—gradually entered the mainstream of American life. Largely from eastern and central Europe, they transformed the United States into a much richer ethnic society and made valuable contributions to the culture.

Domestic Policies in Central and Eastern Europe The less industrialized states of central, southern, and eastern Europe faced more difficult problems. As the fac-

tory system began to appear in the region, these countries had no well-developed political and economic policies for handling the problems that came with industrialization. Because some regional leaders were stronger than the prime ministers, the Italian government allowed the northern regions to become industrialized while the southern regions, including Sicily, remained in a semifeudal condition. As a result, the north, driven by an expanding middle class, moved far ahead of the agrarian south, where vast estates were worked by peasant labor.

In the Austro-Hungarian Empire, the government's biggest problem was ethnic unrest, a direct outgrowth of the denial of political freedom to Slavic minorities, notably the Czechs and the Slovaks. In 1867 the Austrian Germans had given political parity to the Hungarians, allowing them free rein within their land. But nothing was done to address the simmering discontent among the Slavs. Even while the region seethed with ethnic violence, its capital, Vienna, became a glittering symbol of Modernism. From *fin-de-siècle* ("end-of-the-century") Vienna came the cultural style called Expressionism and the psychology of Sigmund Freud.

Farther east, the Russian Empire slowly entered the industrial age, hampered by its vast size and its sluggish agrarian economy and its inefficient bureaucracy. Adding to Russia's woes were violent underground revolutionaries who despaired of any substantial reform in this autocratic society. In 1881 an anarchist assassinated the liberal Czar Alexander II, and his successors dismantled his reforms. Under them, Russia's economy worsened and the imperial ministers grew more

Figure 19.6 EDGAR DEGAS. *The Cotton Bureau in New Orleans.* 1873. Oil on canvas, 29⅛ × 36¼". Musée des Beaux-Arts, Pau, France. *By the third quarter of the nineteenth century, the United States was challenging English supremacy in world trade. The French painter Degas must have observed this scene—the interior of a cotton exchange in New Orleans—while visiting relatives in Louisiana. Whether consciously or not, Degas accurately depicted the social realities of this bourgeois work space: the capitalist idlers reading a newspaper, examining a cotton tuft, and lounging against a wall and, in contrast, the paid employees intent on their work.*

Map 19.1 IMPERIALISM IN AFRICA: COLONIAL STATES, 1914 515

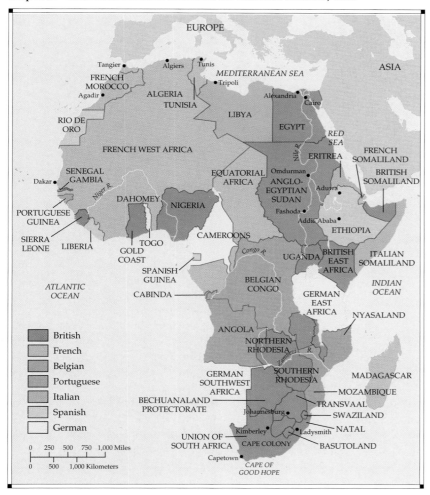

Source: Felix Gilbert, *The End of the European Era, 1890 to the Present.* New York: Norton, 1970, p. 23.

reactionary. In 1905 Japan defeated Russia in the brief Russo-Japanese War (1904–1905), setting off a short-lived revolution led by underpaid factory workers and starving peasants. By promising relief, Czar Nicholas II weathered the storm, but few of his pledges were fulfilled. Instead the state violently repressed dissent, and, as a result, the imperial court grew dangerously isolated.

Imperialism and International Relations

In 1871 most European nations believed that domestic issues were more important than colonial matters and that internal law and order was the first priority. By 1914 those beliefs had been reversed. Domestic politics were no longer primary, and national interests tended to be calculated by each state's role in the global economy and in foreign affairs.

The Scramble for Colonies Before 1875 the common wisdom was that a colony brought both benefits and problems to a modern state, but after that year Western thinking abruptly changed. Europe's industrial-ized states began to compete for colonies and for trade rights around the world. To maintain their high standard of living, they had to find new markets, under-developed areas in which to invest capital, and cheap sources of raw materials. Given these needs, the continent of Africa was an imperialist's dream. The European states claimed lands and shared the spoils of this product-rich continent. France and Britain got the best lands; Germany and Italy received the more barren, less commercially desirable areas (Map 19.1). In the Far East, imperialists competed for colonies in the South Pacific and China, making the Europeans rivals for land with the United States and Japan (the leading power in the Far East after military victories over China in 1895 and Russia in 1905) (Map 19.2).

Imperialism fomented many crises, particularly in Africa, but no major conflict occurred. In this mostly tranquil climate, people began to believe that peace depended on the secret alliances constructed by the major powers. The diplomatic pacts, reinforced by strong armies and navies, had originated after the Franco-Prussian War in 1871. By 1914 Europe was divided into two armed camps—France, Great Britain, and Russia

Map 19.2   IMPERIALISM IN ASIA: COLONIAL STATES, 1914

Source: Felix Gilbert, *The End of the European Era, 1890 to the Present.* New York: Norton, 1970, pp. 24–25.

Map 19.3   EUROPE ON THE EVE OF WORLD WAR I

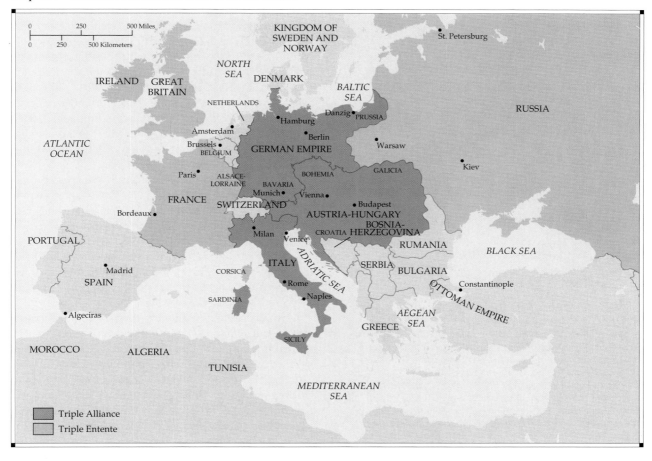

EARLY MODERNISM

(called the Triple Entente) against Germany, Austria-Hungary, and Italy (known as the Triple Alliance) (Map 19.3).

The Outbreak of World War I   In June 1914 an incident took place in Sarajevo for which diplomacy had no peaceful remedy: the assassination of the heir to the Austro-Hungarian throne, Archduke Francis Ferdinand. The Austrians were convinced that Serbia, a Balkan state and an ally of Russia, was behind the murder of the crown prince. They demanded a full apology and punishment of the guilty parties. Serbia's reply proved unsatisfactory and Austria declared war.

Austria's action set in motion the mobilization plans required by the alliance system. Frantic efforts to restore peace failed. By August 4, 1914, Russia, France, and Britain were fighting Germany and Austria-Hungary while Italy (a member of the Triple Alliance) watched from the sidelines. Modern life—symbolized by huge armies, military technology, and industrial might—had plunged Europe and, later, much of the world into the bloodiest war that civilization had yet witnessed.

As previously noted, at the dawn of the age of Modernism it was widely believed that the human race had turned a corner, that a golden era was about to begin. This sanguine outlook was fueled by the spread of self-government, new technology, and advances in science that held the promise of unlimited moral and material progress for humanity. As a result, there was everywhere a passion for novelty, a desire to cast off the dead hand of the past.

At the same time, however, a mood of uncertainty began to creep into the Modernist vocabulary and undercut the optimism. A few artists and thinkers, for whom rebellion was a primary response to the world, questioned traditional Western ethics, religion, customs, and other deeply held beliefs. They expressed their doubts in many ways, but chiefly through constant experimentation, through a desire to return to aesthetic fundamentals, and, especially among the painters, through a belief that the art process itself was more valuable than the completed work. As the pace of

Figure 19.7 UMBERTO BOCCIONI. *Unique Forms of Continuity in Space.* 1913. Bronze (cast 1931), 43⅞ × 34⅞ × 15¾" (111.2 × 88.5 × 40 cm). The Museum of Modern Art, New York. Acquired through the Lillie P. Bliss Bequest. Photograph © 1997 The Museum of Modern Art, New York. *"No more masterpieces!" With this battle cry, the Futurists—an Italian-based literary and artistic movement that typified Early Modernism's rejection of the past—set out to create a new concept of art. The Futurists called for the destruction of existing art forms and of museums and libraries. The streamlined sculptures of Umberto Boccioni are the most striking works of this school. In this striding bronze figure, Boccioni distorts form and space to create an airstreamed image of speed, the new modern icon.*

events accelerated in every area of life, a vigorous **avant-garde,** or vanguard of writers, artists, and intellectuals, pushed Western culture toward an elusive, uncertain future (Figure 19.7).

Philosophy and Psychology

Toward the end of the nineteenth century, new directions in philosophy and psychology reshaped these intellectual disciplines and fostered the shift to Modernism. These German-inspired ideas undercut cherished Western beliefs that dated from the Enlightenment— ideas about human rationality, universal moral order, and personal freedom. The creators of these seminal innovations were the philosopher Friedrich Nietzsche and the psychologists Sigmund Freud and Carl Jung.

Friedrich Nietzsche [NEE-chuh] (1844–1900) was a prophet of Modernism who was notorious for his corrosive thought. He saw beyond the optimism of his times and correctly predicted the general disasters, both moral and material, that would afflict Western

culture in the twentieth century. To him, the philosophies of the past were all false because they were built on nonexistent absolute principles. Denying moral certainty, Nietzsche asserted that he was the philosopher of the "perhaps," deliberately cultivating ambiguity. Nietzsche vehemently rejected middle-class and Judeo-Christian ideals, identifying them with "herd" or "slave" values. For the same reason, he heaped scorn on many of the "isms" of his day—liberalism, socialism, and Marxism—claiming that they appealed to humanity's lowest common denominator and were thus destroying Western civilization.

Nevertheless, there were affirmative, positive aspects to Nietzsche's thought. He believed in a new morality that glorified human life, creativity, and personal heroism. He forecast the appearance of a few *Übermenschen*, or supermen, who had the "will to power," the primeval urge to live beyond the herd and its debased values. He praised these supermen for living "beyond good and evil," for refusing to be bound by society's rules and mores.

Virtually unknown when he died, Nietzsche became one of the giants of twentieth-century thought. His radical thinking—notably in affirming that civilization itself is nothing more than a human invention—has touched nearly every phase of modern thought, including religion, philosophy, literary criticism, and psychology. An extreme individualist, he was contemptuous of the strong German state, though the Nazis in the 1930s used his writings to justify their theory of Aryan supremacy. His glorification of individualism was also a powerful stimulus to many artists, writers, and musicians.

Rather than making a blanket condemnation of much of human morality and behavior, Sigmund Freud [FROID] (1856–1939) offered an approach to human psychology that could be used for further explorations into the study of the self. Part of the highly influential group of intellectuals and artists who flourished in Vienna around 1900, Freud, a neurologist, invented a new way of thinking about human nature that profoundly affected Western society.

Freud's analysis of the human mind challenged the Enlightenment's belief that human beings are fully rational. Freud argued that the human personality is the product of an intense internal struggle between instinctual drives and social reality. According to Freud, each psyche, or self, is composed of an *id,* a *superego,* and an *ego.* The id is the source of primitive, instinctual drives and desires, notably sex and aggression. The superego corresponds to the will of society internalized as the conscience. The ego represents the conscious public face that emerges from the conflict between the inborn instincts and the conscience and acts as the balancing component that establishes inner resolutions. In

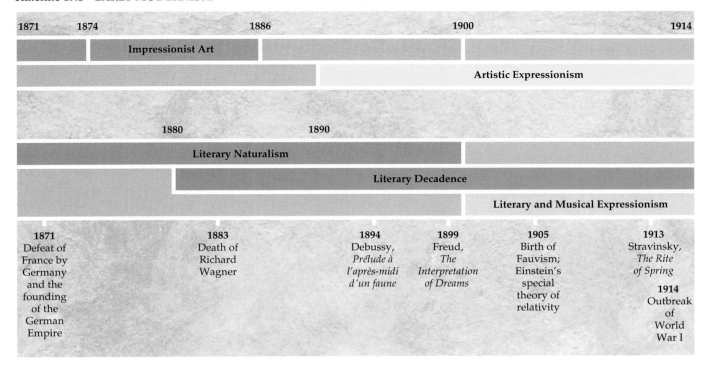

Freud's view, a true, lasting equilibrium among the three components of the psyche cannot be reached; the internal struggle is constant and inescapable. Those in whom the imbalance is pronounced suffer varying degrees of mental illness, ranging from mild neurosis to extreme psychosis. Even though Freud's theory tends toward determinism, he had hope for human freedom. For those who accepted their inescapable limitations, he believed that the truth about the human condition would liberate them from damaging habits of thought and enable them to function as morally free individuals.

Freud's greatest achievement was the founding of psychoanalysis, a type of therapy dedicated to the principle that once the roots of neurotic behavior are unraveled, a patient can lead a freer, healthier life. As part of treatment, he devised the "free association" method whereby his patients were asked to say, spontaneously and without inhibition, whatever came into their minds—memories, random observations, anything at all—and thus uncover traumas buried in their unconscious. He also studied his patients' dreams, which he thought were forms of wish fulfillment, a theory he set forth in *The Interpretation of Dreams* (1899). Freud's influence is pervasive today in Western culture, but recent research has called into question not only his conclusions but also his ethics.

A challenge was made to Freud's views by a former associate, the Swiss psychologist Carl Jung [YOONG] (1875–1961). Jung developed a theory of a universal, collective unconscious, shared by all humans, that exists in conjunction with each individual's own "personal" unconscious. Jung speculated that the secrets of the unconscious could be revealed by studying archetypes, ancient images that recur again and again in human experience and appear in dreams, myths, and folktales. His conception of archetypes opened a rich source of images and subjects for many Modernist artists and writers. Despite their differences, however, Freud and Jung agreed that the conscious mind is only a very small part of individual personality—a belief that is a cornerstone of Modernism.

Literature

Three overlapping and contradictory styles characterize the literature of Early Modernism: Naturalism, Decadence, and Expressionism. The first of these, **Naturalism,** was inspired by the methods of science and the insights of sociology to focus on such issues as working-class unrest and women's rights. Naturalistic writers strove for objectivity and tended to see modern industrial society in a harsh light. **Decadent** writers rejected material values, scorned science, and were in flight from bourgeois society, which they identified with respectability and mediocrity. **Expressionism** was built on the premise that bourgeois culture had robbed the traditional vocabulary of the arts of its capacity to express the truth and therefore new methods and forms of expression must be sought. To a greater or lesser degree, these three styles share a disdain for middle-class life and values (Timeline 19.1).

Naturalistic Literature   The founder and chief exponent of Naturalism was Émile Zola [ZOH-luh] (1840–1902), the French writer whose fame rests on the *Rougon-Macquart* series (1870–1893), twenty novels depicting the history of a single family under France's Second Empire. The novels treat socially provocative themes such as prostitution (*Nana,* 1880) and the horrifying conditions in the coal-mining industry (*Germinal,* 1884). They offer a richly detailed portrait of French society in the mid–nineteenth century and also illustrate Zola's belief in biological determinism. Whether the novels' characters became prostitutes or virtuous housewives, family men or drunken suicides, Zola traces their ultimate fates to inborn dispositions. Nevertheless, Zola was no rigid fatalist. His novels convincingly portray people fervently trying to control their destinies in an uncaring universe.

Another outstanding Naturalist was the Norwegian dramatist Henrik Ibsen (1828–1906). An important playwright, Ibsen helped to establish the **problem play** dealing with social issues such as the public welfare versus private interest. This type of play became the staple of the modern theater and Ibsen its most eloquent practitioner. Ibsen lived mainly in Germany and Italy, writing about the middle-class Norwegian world he had fled, treating with frankness such previously taboo themes as venereal disease, suicide, and the decay of Christian values.

In *A Doll's House* (1879), Ibsen portrays a contemporary marriage and questions the wife's subservient role. Perhaps because of its controversial ending—the wife leaves her husband, asserting that her duties to herself are more sacred than her duties to him—this play created a tremendous first impression. In Ibsen's play, Nora is treated by her husband, Torvald, as a charming child whose sole purpose is to amuse him. When Nora borrows money to save Torvald's life, she deceives him about it because she knows how "painful and humiliating" it would be for him to know he owed her anything. But his reaction when he discovers it—condemning her bitterly and then forgiving her like a father—makes her realize she is living with a stranger. Faced with such lack of understanding, she deserts both husband and family, closing the door on bourgeois "decency." Ibsen's play was an international success, and its liberated heroine became the symbol of the new woman of the late 1800s.

The preeminent Naturalistic writer from eastern Europe was the Russian Anton Chekhov [CHEK-ahf] (1860–1904), a physician turned playwright and short-story writer, who found his subject in the suffocating life of Russia's small towns. He peopled his gently ironic plays with men and women in anguish over their ordinary lives, although his most arresting characters are those who endure disappointment without overt complaint. It is this latter quality that has made Chekhov's comedies, as these bittersweet plays are called, such favorites of both actors and audiences.

The Three Sisters (1901), a play that dramatizes the uneventful lives of a landowning family confined to the drab provinces, is characteristic of Chekhov's work. The characters conceal their depression behind false gaiety and self-deceit. His heroines, the three sisters, are bored, restless, and frustrated, not quite resigned to their mediocre existence. They talk constantly of a trip to Moscow, a journey longed for but never made. Today, Chekhov's plays suggest the dying world of Russia's out-of-touch ruling class, who were about to be swept away by the Marxist revolution of 1917.

An important Naturalistic writer in the United States was Kate Chopin (born Catherine O'Flaherty, 1851–1904), a short-story writer and novelist whose fiction reflected the general trend in nineteenth-century American literature away from Romanticism and toward Realism and Naturalism. A prevalent theme in Chopin's writings was a romantic awakening, usually by a female character. The setting for it was sketched out in **local color,** or regional details, and her method of tracking the action was Naturalistic—that is, she based plot twists on biological and socioeconomic factors. A St. Louis native, Chopin focused her stories and novels on **Creole** and **Cajun** life in Louisiana, a world that caught her imagination during a twelve-year-long marriage to a Creole planter and merchant.

The Awakening (1899) was Kate Chopin's masterpiece and the novel that abruptly ended her literary career, as she was stunned into silence by a hostile public reaction. A tale of adulterous passion, this novel is an American *Madame Bovary* (see Chapter 18). The story of Edna Pontellier, the Kentucky-born wife of a Creole husband, *The Awakening* explores a woman's passionate nature and its relation to self, marriage, and society. Edna rejects conventional morality, social duty, and personal obligations to her husband and children. She establishes her own home, earns money with her painting, accepts one lover, and pursues another. Ultimately, however, Edna's bid for freedom fails. She drowns herself—brought down by tradition, prejudice, and other societal pressures. Chopin's ending has been criticized for its shift to commonplace morality, but the novel nevertheless is an early attempt to deal with the issue of woman's liberation. More than a simple Naturalist, Chopin is hailed today as a precursor of Post-Modernism (see Chapter 21) because of her keen interest in marginal people and feminist themes.

Decadence in Literature   The Decadent movement began in France with Joris-Karl Huysmans [wees-MAHNS] (1848–1907), a follower of Zola's, who in 1884 broke with the social-documentary style of Naturalism and wrote the perverse novel *À rebours (Against Nature).* Paris was astonished by this partly autobiographical work. In it, Huysmans presents an exotic hero, Des Esseintes, bristling with vivid eccentricity and neurotic feelings and yet filled with inexpressible spiritual yearnings. Des Esseintes, hating modern life for its vulgarity and materialism, creates a completely encapsulated, silent world where he cultivates affected pleasures. He collects plants whose very nature is to appear diseased. He stimulates his senses with unusual sounds, colors, and smells, orchestrating them to music so that he experiences a sensory overload. And, in a violent rejection of Classicism, he embraces the crude Latin works of late Rome.

In Great Britain, Oscar Wilde (1854–1900) was the center of the 1890s Decadent movement, with its generally relaxed view of morals and cynically amused approach to life (Figure 19.8). Like Huysmans, Wilde's own outrageous manner can scarcely be separated from his literary achievements. Dressed in velvet and carrying a lily as he sauntered down London's main streets, Wilde gained notoriety as an **aesthete**—one unusually sensitive to the beautiful in art, music, and literature—even before he achieved fame as a dramatist of witty comedies of manners, such as *The Importance of Being Earnest* (1895). Wilde's only novel, *The Picture of Dorian Gray* (1894), features a hero immersed in exotic pleasures and secret vices, his youth preserved while his portrait ages horribly.

Today's most widely admired Decadent writer, the Frenchman Marcel Proust [PROOST] (1871–1922), made his appearance at the end of this period. Starting in 1913 and concluding in 1927, Proust published a series of seven autobiographical novels collectively entitled *À la recherche du temps perdu (Remembrance of Things Past).* In this massive undertaking, he re-creates the world of upper bourgeois society that he had known as a young man but had deserted in 1903. Withdrawn into a cork-lined retreat reminiscent of Des Esseintes's silent hideaway in *À rebours,* Proust resurrected in the pages of his novels the aristocratic salons, the vulgar bourgeois world, and the riffraff of mistresses, prostitutes, and rich homosexuals. Today, Proust's novels may be read in contradictory ways, as the supreme expression of a life lived for art or as the exemplification of a life empty of spiritual meaning.

Expressionist Literature Expressionism, the third of these styles, was the only one that did not originate in France. Instead, it arose in Scandinavia in the works of the Swedish playwright August Strindberg and in central Europe in the fiction of Franz Kafka. Strindberg (1849–1912), having first achieved fame through Naturalistic drama, shifted to an Expressionist style in the 1890s. *The Dream Play* (first produced in 1907) is typical

Figure 19.8 Aubrey Beardsley. *The Dancer's Reward* from "Salomé." Pen Drawing, 9 × 6½". Fogg Art Museum, Harvard University. *The visual counterpart to Wilde's decadent style in literature was Art Nouveau, especially as practiced by Aubrey Beardsley. Typical of his work is this black-and-white illustration for Wilde's play-poem* Salomé, *based on the biblical story of the dancer. In this print, depicting the climactic scene, Salomé grabs a lock of the hair of the beheaded John the Baptist, whose death she has ordered. With her left finger, she touches the blood as if to confirm that it is real. The device in the left corner of three vertical lines and three arrow- or heart-shaped forms is a signature adopted by Beardsley in 1893. The floral motif—the carnations on Salomé's cloak and at her throat—allude to Oscar Wilde's fondness for wearing flowers. Blending organic shapes and flowing lines with perverse themes, Beardsley's artificial style reveals Art Nouveau's affinity with an underworld of depravity.*

of his Expressionist dramas in employing generic figures with symbolic, all-purpose names ("Daughter," "Father," and so on), shadowy plots, and absurd fancies. In *The Dream Play,* time and place become meaningless, as, for instance, when a lovesick soldier suddenly becomes old and shabby and his bouquet of flowers withers before the audience's eyes. Strindberg's innovative techniques were not meant to obscure his meaning but rather to initiate the public into new ways of seeing and understanding life.

The ultimate pioneer of Expressionism was Franz Kafka (1883–1924), whose strange, boldly symbolic stories question traditional concepts of reality. One of Kafka's most striking achievements is the short story *Metamorphosis* (1919), in which the hero awakens to

Figure 19.9 EDVARD MUNCH. *The Scream*. 1893. Oil on canvas, 36 × 29″. Nasjonalgalleriet, Oslo. *The Expressionists, whether writers, artists, or musicians, responded to the uncertainty of the modern world with images of despair, anxiety, and helplessness. The work of the Norwegian painter Edvard Munch provides a visual counterpart to the bleak and brooding plays of Strindberg and the terrifying stories of Kafka. Munch, whose paintings reflect a nightmarish vision of life as a tormented existence never being free from pain, once said, "I hear the scream in nature." The Scream is a visual metaphor of modern alienation. The skullheaded, sexless figure, with mouth opened and hands over ears, seems to be ignored by the couple walking away in the background. Typical of Expressionism, Munch depicts the world as unnatural, as evidenced by the painting's swirling patterns of lines and colors.*

discover that while asleep he has been transformed into a giant insect—a vivid image of an identity crisis and a gripping parable of what happens to a person who is suddenly perceived to be totally different from other people.

The Trial, a novel completed in 1914 and published in 1925, features a doomed main character with the generic name of Joseph K. An obscure minor government official, Joseph K. has his well-ordered world shattered when he is accused of a nameless crime. Unable to identify either his accusers or his misdeed and denied justice by the authorities, Joseph K. is eventually convicted by a mysterious court and executed by two bureaucrats in top hats. Kafka's faceless, powerless hero has become one of the most widely discussed figures of Modernism. In effect, Kafka has transformed his own alienation—as a German-speaking Jew from the Czech-speaking, Protestant section of predominantly Roman Catholic Austria—into a modern Everyman victimized by forces beyond human control (Figure 19.9).

The Advance of Science

Biology and chemistry, in particular, made rapid advances around the turn of the century. In biology, the Austrian monk Gregor Johann Mendel (1822–1884) had summarized his groundbreaking research in 1865, but his findings, the basis for the new science of genetics, were ignored until three researchers, working independently, rediscovered his reports in 1900. By applying mathematics to biological theory, Mendel proved the existence of dominant and recessive traits, and using the laws of probability, he worked out the pattern for offspring over the generations. Subsequent research showed that Mendelian laws applied to virtually all kinds of animals and plants.

In chemistry, the outstanding development was radiochemistry, the study of radioactive materials. The founder of this new discipline was Marie Sklodowska Curie (1867–1934), a Polish physicist and the first scientist to be awarded two Nobel prizes. Working with her French husband, Pierre Curie (1859–1906), Madame Curie identified two new radioactive elements, polonium and radium. The isolation of radium stimulated research in atomic physics. Another contributor to radiochemistry was the German physicist Wilhelm Conrad Roentgen [RENT-guhn] (1845–1923), whose 1895 discovery of X rays led to their use in diagnostic medicine.

The discoveries in genetics and radiochemistry boosted the optimism and faith in progress that characterized this period, but developments in physics had the opposite effect, adding to the undercurrent of uncertainty and doubt that also existed. Three brilliant scientists—Max Planck, Niels Bohr, and Albert Einstein—launched a revolution that led other scientists to discard the previously accepted belief that Newton's laws of motion were universal.

Max Planck (1858–1947) laid the foundation for modern physics in 1900 with research in quantum theory. His research called into question the wave theory of radiation, which dated from the 1700s. Working with hot objects, Planck observed that the radiative energy that emanated from a heat source did not issue in a smooth wave but in discrete bursts. He measured each burst of radiation and computed a mathematical formula for expressing the released energy, a unit that he called a *quantum*—a word meaning a specified amount, derived from the Latin *quanta*, or "how much." When Planck could not fit his quantum formula into traditional wave-theory physics, he realized the revolutionary nature of his discovery. Planck's quantum theory became a primary building block in the speculation of the second of the trio, Danish physicist Niels Bohr.

Bohr (1885–1962) was the prime mover in solving the mystery of the structure of the atom. When he began his research, the ancient Greek idea of the indivisible atom had already been laid to rest. Scientists in the early 1900s had proved that each atom is a neutral body containing a positive nucleus with negatively charged particles called electrons. And one researcher had speculated that electrons orbit a nucleus in much the same way that the planets move around the sun—suggesting a correspondence with Newtonian theory.

Until Bohr's theory of atomic structure was set forth in 1912, however, no one could explain how these miniature solar systems actually worked. Bohr's solution was based on bold assumptions: that an electron could revolve about a nucleus only in certain privileged orbits and that when it was in these orbits, it did not emit radiation. He concluded that an electron radiated only when it leaped from orbit to orbit. Using Planck's quantum theory, he called these leaps quantum jumps, referring to the amount of radiative energy released. Bohr's discovery had tremendous consequences, leading eventually to the development of nuclear energy for weaponry and electrical generation.

German-born Albert Einstein (1879–1955) also did important theoretical work in atomic physics, but his most significant research in the early twentieth century involved the relationship between time and space. Newton had maintained that there existed absolute rest and absolute velocity, absolute space and absolute time. Einstein asserted that the only absolute in the universe is the speed of light, which is the same for all observers. He concluded that all motion is relative and that concepts of absolute space and time are meaningless. If two systems move with relatively uniform motion toward each other, there exist two different spaces and two different times. He called this finding the special theory of relativity. This theory replaces Newtonian absolute space with a grid of light beams that in effect determines the meaning of space in each situation. Einstein's special theory was the first step in a reformulation of scientific concepts of space and time.

The Modernist Revolution in Art

After 1871 a revolution began in the arts and architecture whose aim was to replace Renaissance ideals with Modernist principles. Although there were many trends within this revolution, in painting and sculpture it generally meant a shift from an art that reflected the natural world to one rooted in the artist's inner vision, from an art based on representational or naturalistic images to one devoted to nonrepresentational or nonobjective forms, and from an art focused on content to one dedicated to the process of creation itself. By the time the revolution in painting and sculpture was complete, artists had given up realism and made **abstraction** their ideal. In architecture, the Modernist revolution was less radical, though architects slowly turned away from the forms of the Greco-Roman and Gothic styles and created functional buildings devoid of decoration.

Impressionism   The stylistic innovation in painting known as **Impressionism** began in the 1870s. In spite of owing much to Realism and even to Romanticism, this new style marked a genuine break with the realistic tradition that had dominated Western art since the fourteenth century. The Impressionists wanted to depict what they saw in nature, but they were inspired by the increasingly fast pace of modern life to portray transient moments. They concentrated on the play of light over objects, people, and nature, breaking up seemingly solid surfaces, stressing vivid contrasts between colors in sunlight and shade, and depicting reflected light in all its possibilities. Unlike earlier artists, they did not want to observe the world from indoors. They abandoned the studio, painting in the open air and recording spontaneous impressions of their subjects instead of making sketches outside and then moving indoors to complete the work from memory.

Some of the Impressionists' painting methods were influenced by technological advances. For example, the shift from the studio to the open air was made possible by the advent of cheap rail travel, which permitted easy access to the countryside or seashore, and by the discovery of chemical dyes and oils that allowed paint to be kept in tubes that the artists could carry with them.

Although Impressionism was a product of industrial society, it was at the same time indebted to the past. From Realism the Impressionist painters learned to find beauty in the everyday world. From the Barbizon painters (a group of French landscape painters active in the mid–nineteenth century) they took the practice of painting in the open air. From the Romantics they borrowed the techniques of "broken color"—splitting up complex colors into their basic hues—and of using subtle color shadings to create a shimmering surface effect.

Impressionism acquired its name not from supporters but from angry art lovers who felt threatened by the new painting. The term *Impressionism* was born in 1874, when a group of artists organized an exhibition of their paintings. Reaction from the public and the press was immediate, and derisive. Among the 165 paintings exhibited was *Impression: Sunrise*, by Claude

Figure 19.10 CLAUDE MONET.
Impression: Sunrise. 1872. Oil on canvas, 19½ × 25½". Musée Marmottan, Paris. *Monet's* Impression—Sunrise *illustrates the immediacy of Impressionism. From his window overlooking Le Havre harbor, he painted what he recorded in a letter to a friend: "sun in the mist and a few masts of boats sticking up in the foreground." The artist has transformed the substantial world of nature into fragmented daubs of broken color.*

Figure 19.11 CLAUDE MONET. *Water Lilies.* Ca. 1920. Oil on canvas, 16' × 5' 15⁄16". Carnegie Museum of Art, Pittsburgh. Acquired through the generosity of Mrs. Alan M. Scaife. *Knowledgeable about the art market and determined to escape a life of poverty, Monet produced nonthreatening works that appealed to conservative middle-class collectors. For these patrons, he painted natural scenes, such as water lilies, that evoked pleasant memories of simple rural values. Begun in 1899, the water lily series occupied him for the rest of his life. Setting up his easel in his splendid garden at Giverny and working at different times of the day, Monet captured the effect of changing sunlight on this beloved subject.*

Monet [moh-NAY] (1840–1926). Viewed through hostile eyes, Monet's painting of a rising sun over a misty, watery scene seemed messy, slapdash, and an affront to good taste (Figure 19.10). Borrowing Monet's title, art critics extended the term *Impressionism* to the entire exhibit. In response, Monet and his twenty-nine fellow artists in the exhibit adopted the name as a badge of their unity, despite individual differences. From then until 1886, Impressionism had all the zeal of a "church," as the painter Renoir put it. The Impressionists gave eight art shows. Monet was faithful to the Impressionist creed until his death, although many of the others moved on to new styles.

Monet wanted to re-create the optical sensations he experienced. Rejecting traditional content, he focused on light and atmosphere, simulating the visual effects of fog, haze, or mist over a landscape and, most especially, over water. That this approach succeeded so well shows the harmony between Monet's scientific eye and painterly hand. His studies of changing light and atmosphere, whether depicting haystacks, the Rouen cathedral, or water lilies (Figure 19.11), demonstrate Monet's lifelong devotion to Impressionism.

Unlike Monet, Auguste Renoir [REN-wahr] (1841–1919) did not remain faithful to the Impressionist movement. In the early 1880s, personal and aesthetic motives led him to move away from Impressionism and exhibit in the official Salon (when he could get his work accepted). In his modified style, he shifted from a soft-focus image to a concentration on form, a move that brought quick support from art critics and wealthy patrons.

Painted about the time of his break with Impressionism, *The Luncheon of the Boating Party* demonstrates Renoir's splendid mastery of form (Figure 19.12). Its subject is a carefree summer outing on a restaurant terrace on an island in the Seine, the company being composed of the painter's friends, including fellow artists, a journalist, the cafe owner, and an actress. *The Boating Party* shows that Renoir had not given up—nor would he ever—his Impressionist ties, for his stress in this work on the fleeting, pleasure-filled moment was basic to the style, as was his use of broken color in a natural background. Nevertheless, what remained central to Renoir's creed were the foreground figures, treated clearly and with substance.

In contrast to Monet and Renoir, whose careers bloomed in poverty, Berthe Morisot [mohr-ee-ZOH] (1841–1895) was a member of the upper middle class. Her wealth and artistic connections—Fragonard was

Figure 19.12 AUGUSTE RENOIR. *The Luncheon of the Boating Party.* 1881. Oil on canvas, 51 × 68″. The Phillips Collection, Washington, D.C. *Renoir's return to traditional values is reflected in this vivid painting. He uses the restaurant's terrace to establish conventional perspective, the left railing forming a diagonal line that runs into the distance. He balances the composition, weaving the young men and women into a harmonious ensemble, painting some standing and others sitting. He also employs colors effectively, using orange, blue, and black to offset the expanses of white in the tablecloth and the men's shirts and women's blouses.*

Figure 19.13 BERTHE MORISOT. *Laundresses Hanging Out the Wash.* 1875. Oil on canvas, 13 × 16″. National Gallery of Art, Washington, D.C. Collection of Mr. and Mrs. Paul Mellon. *Morisot's* Laundresses Hanging Out the Wash, *shown with the Impressionists in 1876, was praised by critics for its clarity of color and handling of light. It depicts, from a high vantage point, a group of commercial washerwomen hanging out laundry in a garden. Morisot was one of the few Impressionists to depict urban workers, because, in rapidly urbanizing France, artists nostalgically focused on farm laborers at their tasks. Typical of her art, she emphasizes the flatness of the picture plane, which is unlike the three-dimensionality of paintings such as Renoir's* The Luncheon of the Boating Party *(see Figure 19.12). Her vigorous brushwork, making the painting difficult to decipher, gives a feeling of immediacy—the aim of Impressionist art.*

her grandfather and Manet her brother-in-law—allowed her to apply herself to painting and play an important role in the founding of the Impressionist school. In her work, she focused on atmosphere and the play of light on the human form, although she never sacrificed her subjects to the cause of color alone. Her subjects were modern life, though limited to the confined world of domestic interiors and gardens (Figure 19.13).

A few Americans also made significant contributions to Impressionism. The most important of them was Mary Cassatt [kuh-SAT] (1845–1926), a young woman who joined the Impressionist circle while studying painting in Paris. Cassatt was from a prosperous, well-connected Philadelphia family, and it is largely through her social ties that Impressionist painting was introduced to America. She suggested to her wealthy friends that this art was worth collecting, and some of the most notable Impressionist works in American museums are there because of her influence.

Cassatt, however, was not devoted exclusively to Impressionism. Like other artists of this era, she was fascinated by Japanese prints from French collections that were on exhibit in Paris in 1890, and she was the first to imitate all aspects, including color, of the *ukiyo-e* [oo-key-yoh-AY] prints—the woodcuts that had developed in Japan in the 1600s—as in *The Bath,* or *The Tub* (about 1891; Figure 19.14). A mother and child was a typical subject in Cassatt's art.

Post-Impressionism

The rebellious, experimental spirit instilled by the Impressionists had freed art from the tyranny of a single style. Artists now moved in many directions, united only by a common desire to extend the boundaries of Impressionism. This ambition signified the triumph of the Modernist notion that art must constantly change in order to reflect new historical conditions—the opposite of the Classical ideal of eternal truths. Impressionism was succeeded by **Post-Impressionism** (1886–1900), whose four most important artists are Georges Seurat, Paul Cézanne, Paul Gauguin, and Vincent van Gogh.

Like the Impressionists, Georges Seurat [suh-RAH] (1859–1891) painted the ordinary pleasures of Parisian life in a sunlit atmosphere, but his way of doing so was formulaic and theoretical, markedly different from the approach of, say, Monet. After studying scientific color theory, Seurat developed a technique known as **Pointillism** (or Divisionism), which meant applying to the canvas thousands of tiny dots of pure color juxtaposed in such a way that, when viewed from the proper distance, they merged to form a natural, harmonious effect of color, light, and shade. His most famous Pointillist work is *A Sunday Afternoon on the Island of La Grande Jatte* (Figure 19.15), an affec-

Figure 19.14 MARY CASSATT. *The Bath.* Ca. 1891. Soft-ground etching with aquatint and drypoint on paper, 12⅜ × 8⅞″. National Museum of Women in the Arts, Washington, D.C. *This Cassatt print, in Japanese-inspired style, symbolizes the globalization of Western culture that was well under way in Early Modernism. The first of ten prints in a series, it is the only one that could be called a true imitation. It uses simple design, Japanese spatial pattern, flat areas of color, and a hint of Japanese facial features to create a Western version of a* ukiyo-e *print—except that it is made on a metal plate and not a woodblock. In the rest of this series, Cassatt adopted a more Western style, notably adding a complete background, such as wallpaper and windows. Her interest in Japanese prints coincided with Gauguin's experiments (see Figure 19.17) with Tahitian-inspired art; both are forerunners of Post-Modernism.*

tionate, good-humored look at Parisians enjoying themselves. The technique may be novel and "scientific," but the composition is Classical and serene, with carefully placed and balanced figures and repeated curved shapes, visible in the umbrellas, hats, and other objects. Seurat's style led to a minor school of painters, but his influence was overshadowed by that of Cézanne.

Paul Cézanne [say-ZAN] (1839–1906), a pivotal figure in Western art, was the prophet of abstraction in Post-Impressionism and a precursor of Cubism. With Édouard Manet, he is one of the founders of modern painting. He had exhibited with the original Impressionist group in 1874 but by 1878 had rejected the

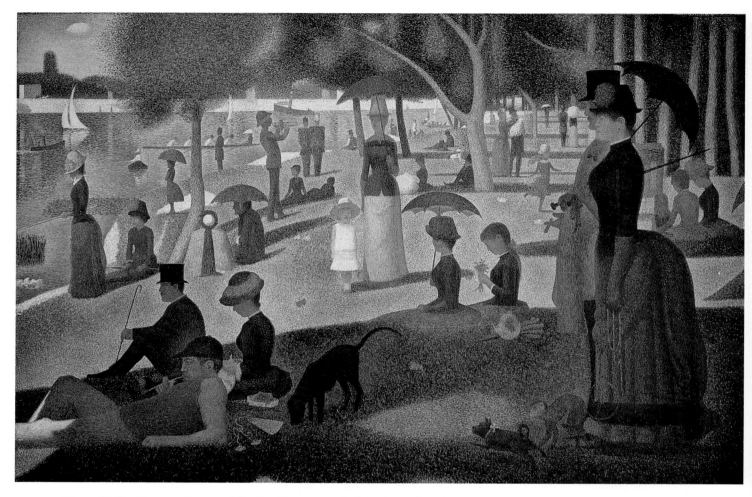

Figure 19.15 GEORGES SEURAT. *A Sunday Afternoon on the Island of La Grande Jatte.* 1884–1886. Oil on canvas, 6′9″ × 10′1″. Art Institute of Chicago. Helen Birch Bartlett Memorial Collection, 1926. *Unlike most Impressionists, Seurat worked slowly and methodically. In the case of* La Grande Jatte, *he spent years organizing the canvas and then painting the thousands of dots required by the Pointillist technique. Such painstaking attention to detail was necessary to achieve the harmonious effect his finished paintings demonstrate.*

movement because its depiction of nature lacked substance and weight. He sought a new way to portray nature so as to reveal its underlying solidity and order. After experimentation, Cézanne concluded that nature was composed of such geometric forms as cylinders, spheres, cubes, and cones. By trying to reveal this idea in his works, he opened up a new way of painting that has influenced art to the present day.

Cézanne's greatest works came after 1886, when he left Paris for his quiet home in Aix-en-Provence in southern France. Among his favorite subjects was the nearby mountain Mont Sainte-Victoire (Figure 19.16). Like many of his later works, *Mont Sainte-Victoire* points toward abstraction but never quite gives up representation. Amid the dense geometric forms in the picture's lower half, house shapes peek through daubs of green foliage, reminding the viewer that this is a realistic landscape. Later artists, such as Kandinsky and Malevich, took up Cézanne's challenge of telescoping the two-dimensional and the three-dimensional and

created the first truly abstract paintings, the most visible signs of twentieth-century art (see Chapter 20).

The Post-Impressionist Paul Gauguin [go-GAN] (1848–1903) began the movement known as **primitivism**—the term used to describe the West's fascination with non-Western culture as well as pre-Renaissance art. Gauguin's eccentric personal life also made him a legendary figure of Modernism. Rejecting the comforts of Parisian bourgeois life, he abandoned his career and his family and exiled himself to the French colony of Tahiti, living a decadent, bohemian existence.

Before moving to the South Pacific, Gauguin lived and painted among Breton peasants. He developed a personal style that favored flattened shapes and bright colors and avoided conventional perspective and modeling. He also became interested in non-Western, "primitive" religions, and many of his Tahitian works refer to indigenous beliefs and practices, as in *Manao Tupapau—The Spirit of the Dead Watching* (Figure 19.17). When exhibited in Paris, this painting created an up-

Figure 19.16 PAUL CÉZANNE. *Mont Sainte-Victoire*. 1904–1906. Oil on canvas, 28⅞ × 36¼". Philadelphia Museum of Art. George W. Elkins Collection. *Although Cézanne was the founder of the Post-Impressionist movement that culminated in abstraction, he had a conservative approach to art. He wanted to create paintings that had the solidity of the art in the museums, especially the works of the seventeenth-century painter Nicolas Poussin. Hence, Cézanne continued to rely on line and geometric arrangement as well as on color and light, simplifying his paintings into austere images of order and peaceful color. In this painting of Mont Sainte-Victoire—visible from his studio in Aix-en-Provence—Cézanne's closeness to abstract art may be seen. The distant mountain has a solid presence, but the houses, foliage, fields, and road disappear into a set of ambiguous forms and color planes. Cézanne's handling of the color planes, with their jagged edges and abrupt juxtapositions, inspired the Cubists to search for a new way to represent the world.*

Figure 19.17 PAUL GAUGUIN. *Manao Tupapau: The Spirit of the Dead Watching*. 1892. Oil on burlap mounted on canvas, 28½ × 36⅜". Albright-Knox Art Gallery, Buffalo. A. Conger Goodyear Collection, 1965. *Gauguin wrote of this painting that he wanted to convey the presence of* tupapau, *or the Spirit of the Dead, as envisioned by the young girl on the bed. He implies her fear through the mixture of the yellow, purple, and blue colors; by the sparks of light, or phosphorescences, which symbolize the spirits of the dead; and by the ghost depicted as an old woman in the left background. He felt it necessary "to make very simple paintings, with primitive, childlike themes" and to use "a minimum of literary means" in order for western Europeans to understand how Tahitians viewed life and death.*

roar, for Western audiences were not accustomed to seeing dark-skinned nudes in art, and certainly not presented reclining on a bed, a customary pose for female nudes since the Renaissance (see Figure 16.7). Furthermore, the seated ghost at the left was a direct challenge to a secular worldview. Today, Gauguin's role in art has been reevaluated. He is now honored for his introduction of other cultural traditions into Western art, which enriched its vocabulary, and for his expressive use of color.

With the Post-Impressionist Vincent van Gogh [van GO] (1853–1890), the tradition of Expressionism began to emerge in Western art, although he was not part of any of the various Expressionist schools of painters. "Expressionism" in his case meant that the work of art served as a vehicle for his private emotions to an unprecedented degree. Van Gogh sometimes allowed his moods to determine what colors to use and how to apply paint to canvas, a principle that led to a highly idiosyncratic style. Van Gogh's life was filled with

Figure 19.18   VINCENT VAN GOGH. *Self-Portrait with a Gray Hat.* 1887. Oil on canvas, 17¼ × 14¾″. Vincent van Gogh Foundation/National Museum Vincent van Gogh, Amsterdam. *Van Gogh's self-absorption is reflected in the thirty-six self-portraits he painted during his eleven-year artistic career. Anguished and prone to mental breakdown, he must have found a measure of reassurance in recording the subtle changes in his own countenance. A constant in all his likenesses is the haunted eyes, showing the inner torment from which he could never quite escape. The very execution of this work demonstrates van Gogh's passionate mood, as in the aggressive brushstrokes that congeal into a radiating pattern of energy lines covering the painting's surface.*

misfortune, and even his painting had little recognition in his lifetime. In his early years, he was rebuffed in his efforts to do missionary work among poverty-stricken Belgian coal miners. All his attempts at friendship ended in failure, including a celebrated episode in the south of France with the painter Gauguin. Throughout his life, overtures to women resulted in utter humiliation. In the end, he became mentally unstable and committed suicide.

From his personal pain he created a memorably expressive style, however. Rejecting the smooth look of traditional painting and stirred by the colorful canvases of the Impressionists, he sometimes applied raw pigments with his palette knife or fingers instead of with a brush. His slashing strokes and brilliant colors often mirrored his mental states, giving the viewer a glimpse into his volatile personality. For instance, his *Self-Portrait with a Gray Hat* is dominated by shades of blue, suggesting his profound melancholy (Figure 19.18). The anguish in his eyes is reinforced by the vortex of color framing the head and the deep facial lines.

The most memorable of van Gogh's paintings is *The Starry Night* (Figure 19.19). Executed in the last year of van Gogh's life, the painting depicts a tranquil village

under an agitated sky filled with pulsating stars, an unnatural crescent moon, and whirling rivers of light. Intensifying the strange imagery is the grove of cypress trees (left foreground), rendered in the shape of flames. The ensemble of convoluted shapes and bold colors expresses the artist's inner turmoil. In a sense, van Gogh's works constitute his psychological signature; his style is perhaps the most easily recognizable one in Western art.

Fauvism, Cubism, and Expressionism   The preeminence of Paris as the hub of Western culture was enhanced by the arrival of Henri Matisse and Pablo Picasso in about 1900. These innovative and prolific artists emerged as the leaders of the pre–World War I generation, later dominating the art world in the twentieth century in much the same way that Ingres and Delacroix had in the nineteenth century.

Henri Matisse [ma-TEES] (1869–1954) rose to fame in 1905 as a leader of **Fauvism.** The Fauves—French for "wild beasts," a name their detractors gave to them— were a group of loosely aligned painters who exhibited together. Matisse's work, like that of his colleagues, stemmed from the tradition of van Gogh, with color as its overriding concern. In *Open Window, Collioure,* Matisse paints a kaleidoscope of colors—pinks, mauves, bluish greens, bright reds, oranges, and purples—that do not derive from the direct observation of nature but from the artist's belief that color harmonies can control the composition (Figure 19.20). The colors are "arbitrary" in the sense that they bear little resemblance to what one would actually see from the window, but they are far from arbitrary in their relation to one another—which is what interests Matisse.

Pablo Picasso [pih-KAH-so] (1881–1973), a talented young Spanish painter, was attracted to Paris's avant-garde art community in about 1900. In 1907 he proved his genius with *Les Demoiselles d'Avignon (The Young Ladies of Avignon),* perhaps the most influential painting of the twentieth century (Figure 19.21). This revo-

Figure 19.19 VINCENT VAN GOGH. *The Starry Night.* 1889. Oil on canvas, 29 × 36¼" (73.7 × 92.1 cm). The Museum of Modern Art, New York. Acquired through the Lillie P. Bliss Bequest. Photograph © 1997 The Museum of Modern Art, New York. *Van Gogh's* The Starry Night *is a stunning symbol of the unstable world of Early Modernism. The whirling, luminous sky, formed with wild patches of color and tormented brushstrokes, reflects the psychic disturbance of the painter—an early example of Expressionist art. But van Gogh was more than an artist beset by personal demons; he wanted to follow Delacroix (see Chapters 17 and 18) and depict nature, using color and drawing, without slavishly copying reality. In van Gogh—as in his contemporary, the philosopher Nietzsche—psychic turmoil and artistic vision were virtually inseparable.*

Figure 19.20 HENRI MATISSE. *Open Window, Collioure.* 1905. Oil on canvas, 21¾ × 18⅛". Courtesy Mrs. John Hay Whitney, New York. *Like van Gogh, Matisse resisted quiet surface effects, preferring the look of paint applied in thick daubs and strips of varying length. His dazzling optical art was created by his use and placement of vibrant colors. In this painting, Matisse interprets the glorious view from his studio overlooking the Mediterranean.*

Figure 19.21 PABLO PICASSO. *Les Demoiselles d'Avignon. (The Young Ladies of Avignon.)* Paris (June–July 1907). Oil on canvas, 8′ × 7′ 8″ (243.9 × 233.7 cm). The Museum of Modern Art, New York. Acquired through the Lillie P. Bliss Bequest. Photograph © 1997 The Museum of Modern Art, New York. *This painting's title derives from Picasso's native Barcelona, where Avignon Street ran through the red-light district. First intended as a moral work warning of the dangers of venereal disease (the figures still show provocative poses), the painting evolved over the months, changing as Picasso's horizons expanded. That he left the painting unfinished—like a scientist's record of a failed laboratory experiment—illustrates a leading trait of Modernism, the belief that truth is best expressed in the artistic process itself.*

Figure 19.22 PABLO PICASSO. *Man with a Hat.* (Also known as *Portrait of Braque.*) Paris (after December 3, 1912). Pasted paper, charcoal and ink on paper, 24 × 19⅝″ (62.2 × 47.3 cm). The Museum of Modern Art, New York. Purchase. Photograph © 1997 The Museum of Modern Art, New York. *This image alludes to the close working relationship between Picasso and Braque. Whether the portrait is of Braque is debatable, especially since Picasso denied it. He claimed he worked without a model and added, "Braque and I [later] pretended it was his portrait." This anecdote forcibly stresses the point that Picasso and Braque, the founders of Cubism, were less interested in content than in creating a new visual reality through nontraditional means.*

Figure 19.23 WASSILY KANDINSKY. *Improvisation 33 for "Orient."* 1913. Oil on canvas, 34¾ × 39¼". Stedelijk Museum, Amsterdam. *Kandinsky's radical Expressionism rested on the Romantic idea that serious art can function as a substitute for religion; the artist serves as a sort of "priest" who, through mystical insight, can tap into the divine. In 1912 he published his aesthetic beliefs in the treatise* Concerning the Spiritual in Art, *which became a fundamental text for modern artists. Later abstract artists, such as Robert Rauschenberg (see Chapter 21), ridiculed this theory as pretentious and showed that a nonrepresentational art that has no meaning outside itself is possible.*

lutionary work moved painting close to abstraction—the realization of Cézanne's dream. An unfinished work, *Les Demoiselles* reflects the multiple influences operating on Picasso at the time—the primitivism of African masks, the geometric forms of Cézanne, and the ancient sculpture of pre-Roman Spain. Despite its radical methods, this painting still has a conventional composition: five figures with a still life in the foreground. Nevertheless, with this painting Picasso redirected objective art beyond abstraction and into the development of nonobjective painting—thus overturning a standard founded in the Renaissance.

Les Demoiselles was the prelude to **Cubism,** one of the early-twentieth-century styles leading Western art toward abstraction. With his French colleague Georges Braque [BRAHK] (1882–1963), Picasso developed Cubism. This style of painting, which went through different phases at the hands of different artists, basically fragments three-dimensional objects and reassembles them in a pattern that stresses their geometric structure and the relationships of these basic geometric forms. Braque and Picasso worked so closely together that their paintings could sometimes not be separately identified, even, it is said, by the artists themselves. An example of Picasso's Cubist style is *Man with a Hat* (also known as *Portrait of Braque*) (Figure 19.22). With Cubism, Picasso gave up Renaissance space completely, representing the subject from multiple angles simultaneously and shaping the figures into geometric de-

signs. He also added a new feature to Cubism when he applied bits and pieces of other objects to the canvas, a technique called **collage** (French for "pasting"). Collage nudged Cubism closer to pure abstraction; the flat plane of the painting's surface was now simply a two-dimensional showcase for objects.

Although Paris remained the capital of Western art, other cities were also the scene of aesthetic experiment. Oslo, Munich, Vienna, and Dresden became artistic meccas, especially for Expressionist painters who followed the path opened by van Gogh and the Fauves.

In Munich, for example, Expressionism led to the formation of an international school of artists known as Der Blaue Reiter (The Blue Rider), named after a painting of the same name. Rejecting the importance of artistic content and refusing to paint "safe" objects, this group of painters concentrated on basics such as color and line, which were meant to express inner feelings. Founded by the Russian exile Wassily Kandinsky [kan-DIN-skee] (1866–1944) in 1911, this school made the first breakthrough to abstract art—nonrepresentational or nonobjective paintings that defy any sense of reality or connection to nature and are, as the artist himself put it, "largely unconscious, spontaneous expressions of inner character, nonmaterial in nature." Kandinsky's "improvisations," as he labeled them, were free forms, possessing no objective content, consisting only of meandering lines and amorphous blobs of color (Figure 19.23). For all their seeming random-

Figure 19.24 AUGUSTE RODIN. *Eve.* 1881. Bronze, ht. 67".
Rodin Museum, Philadelphia Museum of Art. *This life-size
statue of Eve was originally conceived as half a pair, with Adam,
to flank* The Gates of Hell, *Rodin's masterpiece, loosely based on
Dante's* Inferno *(see Chapter 9). The figure of Eve owed much to
Michelangelo's expressive forms, particularly that of Eve in* The
Expulsion from the Garden of Eden *on the Sistine Chapel ceiling. Reflecting her dual roles as first mother and coauthor of original sin, Rodin's Eve is both voluptuous (beautiful face and cur-
vaceous form) and ashamed (face averted and, in gestures of
modesty, arms shielding breasts and right leg raised).*

ness, however, his paintings were planned to look that
way. He consciously worked out the placement of the
lines and the choices of color, leaving nothing to
chance. He also linked the fluidity of painting with the
lyricism of music, a connection suggested in this work
by the meandering lines.

New Directions in Sculpture and Architecture Few
sculptors of any consequence appeared in the 1871–
1914 period and only one genius: Auguste Rodin [roh-
DAN] (1840–1917). Rejecting the static Classicism of
the mid–nineteenth century, Rodin forged an eclectic
style that blended Romantic subject matter, Renaissance simplicity, and Gothic angularity with the radical changes under way in painting. In the sculpture *Eve*
(Figure 19.24), he created a rough Gothic effect using
modern means, torturing the surface, especially of the
stomach and the head. The result was both Impressionistic (the play of light on the scored surfaces) and
Expressionistic (the traces of Rodin's fingers on the
bronze medium, which so dramatically suggest the intensity of the artist's involvement).

Having lagged behind the other arts for most of the
century, architecture began to catch up in the 1880s.
The United States led the way, notably in the works of
the Chicago School. The skyscraper, perfected by
Chicago-based architects, became synonymous with
Modernism and modern life. Unlike Modernist painting and sculpture, the new architecture arose for practical reasons: dense populations and soaring real estate
values.

Using the aesthetic dictum that "form follows function," the Chicago School solved design problems
without relying on past techniques and traditions.
This dictum means that a building ought to be a workable organism where the pressure of daily existence is
channeled into a harmonious, functioning whole; in
practical terms, the pressure is called function, the re-
sultant building, form. The author of this dictum,
Louis Sullivan (1856–1924), produced a masterly example of the Chicago School's style in the Guaranty
Building in Buffalo, New York, a structure whose steel
frame is covered by a skin of stone and glass (Figure
19.25). Sullivan's imprint can be seen in the way he allows the building to speak for itself: The plan of the
exterior skin reflects the internal steel skeleton in the
thin, continuous piers between the windows that rise
from the base to the rounded arches at the top. The effect of this organization is to turn the building's exterior into a grid, a visual expression of the structural
frame underneath. Although Sullivan rejected the rich
ornamentation of the nineteenth-century Gothic as
well as the balanced decorations of Classicism, he
nevertheless devised his own decorative scheme,
which may be seen in the vertical and horizontal ele-

Figure 19.25 LOUIS SULLIVAN. Guaranty Building, Buffalo. 1895. © Wayne Andrews/Esto. *Purity became an identifying characteristic of Modernist style. It was apparent in Matisse's color experiments, in Picasso's abstract Cubist forms, and even in the Expressionist goal of unvarnished truth. In architecture, Louis Sullivan introduced the purity principal with his artistic credo that "form follows function."*

ments, for example, and the spaces (blocks) between the windows.

Sullivan defined the public building for the twentieth century, and his disciple Frank Lloyd Wright (1869–1959) did the same for domestic architecture in about 1910. In the Victorian era, architects had discovered that the middle-class demand for comfortable, spacious housing was an excellent source of income. This same class of patrons continued to demand well-built homes, and for them Wright created a new type of dwelling he called "organic," a term he coined to describe a building that was constructed of local woods and stone and therefore harmonized with the physical environment. Although unconventional in his own life, he was rather a romantic about his bourgeois patrons. To strengthen domestic values, he planned houses that encouraged the inhabitants to identify with the natural surroundings; his structures also broke down the typical reliance on fixed interior walls to encourage fluid family relationships and a free flow

of traffic. In time, Wright's style became standard for progressive architects throughout the United States, expressed in the exterior in strong horizontal lines, overhanging eaves, banks of windows, and a minimum of decorative detail (Figure 19.26).

Music: From Impressionism to Jazz

Richard Wagner died in 1883 (see Chapter 18), but in certain respects he is the commanding musical presence in Early Modernism. Most composers were either utilizing in their own way the harmonic advances he had made, working out the implications of those advances, or reacting to his influence by elaborately rejecting it. For example, a musical style influenced by Wagner was Impressionism, which was in part inspired by his shimmering, constantly alternating chords. The Impressionist composers did not stay under his tutelage, however. Where Wagner was philosophical and

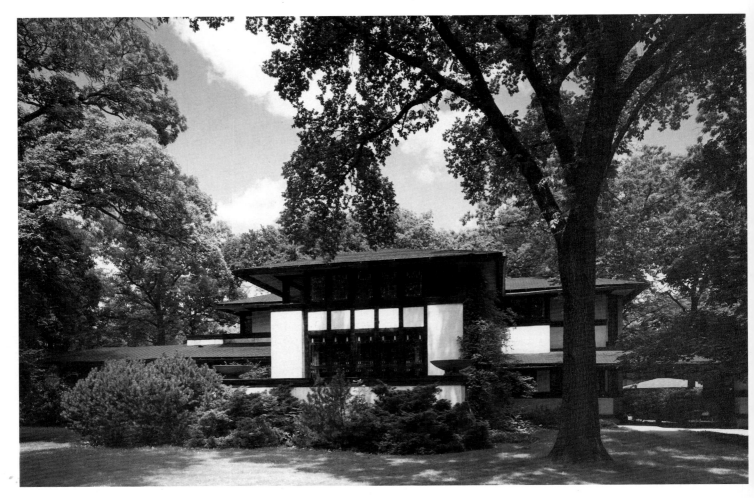

Figure 19.26 FRANK LLOYD WRIGHT. W. W. Willits House. 1902. Highland Park, Illinois. Copyright © Chicago Historical Society. *Between 1900 and 1910, Wright introduced his "prairie houses," named for the* Ladies Home Journal *article (1901) in which their designs first appeared. The Willits house, built in an affluent Chicago suburb, is a fine example of this Midwestern American style that became a model for domestic buildings all over the United States. Laid out in a cruciform shape, this dwelling has a central chimney core. The style's strong focus on horizontal lines, resulting in shifting planes of light across the facade, may be compared to the multiple perspectives of Cubism, the parallel development in painting.*

literary, seeking to fuse all the arts, the Impressionists explored sound for its own sake. Like Impressionist painters, Impressionist composers thought that all moments—no matter how real—were fleeting and fragmentary, and their musical compositions illustrated this principle. Their music, without conventional thematic development or dramatic buildup and release, often sounds veiled or amorphous when compared with the music of, for example, Haydn.

Claude Debussy [duh-byoo-SEE] (1862–1918), a French composer, founded the Impressionist style. He created constantly shifting colors and moods through such musical methods as gliding chords and chromatic scales derived from non-Western sources. Debussy's music represents the climax of the nineteenth-century interest in programmatic titles, large orchestras, rich chords, and relatively free rhythms and forms.

One of Debussy's programmatic works, *Prélude à l'après-midi d'un faune (Prelude to the Afternoon of a Faun)* (1894) is generally recognized as the first Impressionist orchestral masterpiece. This work is a sensuous confection of blurred sounds and elusive rhythms. To achieve its mood of reverie, Debussy used a meandering musical line played by a soulful solo flute, backed by muted strings and delicately voiced brasses and woodwinds.

Impressionist music produced a second major voice in France during this period: Maurice Ravel [ruh-VEL] (1875–1937), a composer loosely indebted to Debussy. Unlike Debussy, Ravel had a taste for the clear structure of Classical musical forms as well as established dance forms. Perhaps the most Impressionistic of Ravel's compositions is *Jeux d'eau (Fountains)* (1901), a programmatic work for piano marked by sounds evoking sparkling and splashing water. Even before the writing of *Jeux d'eau,* Ravel's Classical inclinations were evident in *Pavane pour une infante defunte (Pavane for a Dead Princess)* (1899), a work for piano with a melancholy quality; here, the music captured the stately rhythm of the Baroque **pavane,** an English court dance of Italian origin. Dance also inspired Ravel's *Valses nobles et sentimentales (Waltzes Noble and Sentimental)* (1911), a work for piano based on the waltzes of Schubert (see Chapter 17) and the Parisian ballrooms of the 1820s, and *La Valse (The Waltz)* (1920), an orchestral work that is a sardonic homage to the waltzes of nineteenth-century Vienna. Ravel's best-known work, *La Valse* is in actuality an embittered metaphor in which the increasingly discordant sounds of the music represent the forces that generated the catastrophe of World War I.

A trend in opposition to Wagner was Expressionism, which developed simultaneously with Expressionist art in Vienna. Drawing on the insights of Freudian psychology, musical Expressionism offered a distorted view of the world, focusing on anguish and pain. Its most striking feature was its embrace of **atonality,** a type of music without major or minor keys. To the listener, atonal music sounds discordant and even disturbing, because it offers no harmonious frame of reference. It is characterized by wide leaps from one tone to another, melody fragments, interrupted rhythms, and violent contrasts. Rejecting traditional forms, Expressionist composers made experimentation central to their musical vision.

The founder and leader of the Expressionist school was Arnold Schoenberg [SHUHN-burg] (1874–1951), who gave up a Wagnerian style in about 1907 and moved toward atonality. At first, Schoenberg employed traditional musical forms, as in the Second String Quartet (1908), although no string quartet had ever sounded like his dissonant creation. Scored without a designated key and filled with snatches of melody, this work offered the listener no recognizable frame of reference. Violinists were required on occasion to play the most extreme notes of which their instruments were capable.

Besides traditional forms, Schoenberg also established a favorite compositional method of Expressionism: setting a literary text to music and following its changes in character and feeling. An influential example of Expressionist music with text was *Pierrot lunaire (Moonstruck Pierrot)* (1912), based on poems by a Belgian writer and scored for chamber quintet and voice. Though Schoenberg downplayed the source text's importance, the music's violent shifts and prevailing discord clearly complement the alienated psychology and shocking language of the text. Instead of conventionally singing the text, the solo vocalist declaims or chants the text by combining speech and song.

Pierrot lunaire represents the extreme of Schoenberg's Expressionism before World War I. This work made him one of the two most highly respected composers of Early Modernism. Unwilling to rest on his laurels, he continued to experiment with innovative musical techniques (see Chapter 20).

The other outstanding twentieth-century musical genius active during this period was the Russian Igor Stravinsky [struh-VIN-skee] (1882–1971). Untouched by Wagnerism but attuned to the revolutionary events unfolding in the arts and in literature, Stravinsky acquired his reputation at about the same time as Schoenberg. In 1913 Stravinsky wrote the music for *The Rite of Spring,* a ballet produced by Sergei Diaghilev [dee-AHG-uh-lef] (1872–1929) for the Ballets Russes in Paris. Stravinsky's music and the ballet's choreography tapped into the theme of primitivism in art that was currently the rage in the French capital. Stravinsky's pounding rhythms evoke a pagan ritual, using abrupt meter changes, a hypnotic beat, and furious **syncopation,** the musical technique of accenting a weak beat when a strong beat is expected. The "savage" music coupled with the erotic dancing created a scandal that made Stravinsky the leading avant-garde composer in the world. Despite his innovative rhythms, Stravinsky was no relentless experimenter. After World War I, Stravinsky, though touched by Modernism's influences, became the head of a Classical school that was centered in France and opposed the more extreme theories being introduced by Schoenberg through his work in Vienna.

As Western music moved away from ancient and medieval sources, a new tradition, **jazz,** rooted in African American tradition, began to emerge in the United States. The word *jazz,* originally a slang term for sexual intercourse, reflects the music's origins in the New Orleans sexual underworld. Jazz combined West African and African-Caribbean rhythms with Western harmony, along with an improvisatory call-and-response style rooted both in African songs and in gospel songs of the urban Protestant revival in the 1850s. Jazz drew on two other African American musical forms as well—ragtime, which was chiefly instrumental, and the blues, which originated as a vocal art.

Ragtime flourished from 1890 to 1920. The word *ragtime* is derived from the phrase "ragged time," the original name for this type of syncopated music perfected by black pianist and composer Scott Joplin (1868–1917) and based on a blend of African American rhythms and Western harmony. The **blues** grew out of the rural African American tradition of work songs and spirituals and evokes the pain to be found in life, love, poverty, and hard work. Blues and jazz are both powerfully expressive musical forms, considered specifically American contributions to world music.

The Legacy of Early Modernism

From the unsettled period of 1871–1914 come many of the trends that made the twentieth century such an exciting—and dangerous—era. The legacy of militant nationalism gave birth to the two great world wars that devastated the century. Even today, nationalism remains a potent force, threatening to overturn state boundaries and governments. Imperialism, another legacy, had radically contradictory consequences. On the one hand, it exported Western peoples, values, and technology around the globe, bringing a higher standard of living and greater expectations for the future. On the other hand, it disturbed if not destroyed older ways of life and led to a series of wars as colonial peoples struggled to cast off the yoke of Western oppression. And militarism, a third legacy, made rivalry among states a perpetual source of anxiety and destruction.

On the cultural scene, the era of Early Modernism set the stage for the twentieth century. The rise of the masses led to a growing proletarization of culture. As a result, the middle classes were subjected to a cultural assault from urban workers in much the same way that aristocrats had been attacked and displaced by the middle classes. Technology fueled the rise of mass culture. A second legacy of this era was the avant-garde, whose leaders systematically tried to destroy the last vestiges of Judeo-Christian and Classical Greco-Roman traditions. In rejecting the Classical ideal of the search for eternal truths, artists followed the Impressionists' lead and continued to strive for change as a reflection of the new historical conditions that surrounded them. And finally, Early Modernism established the emotional and aesthetic climate of the century—its addiction to experimentalism, its love-hate relationship with uncertainty and restlessness, its obsession with abstraction, its belief in the hidden depths of the human personality, and its willingness to think the unthinkable.

KEY CULTURAL TERMS

Modernism
avant-garde
Naturalism
Decadence
Expressionism
problem play
local color
Creole
Cajun
aesthete
abstraction
Impressionism
ukiyo-e

Post-Impressionism
Pointillism
primitivism
Fauvism
Cubism
collage
pavane
atonality
syncopation
jazz
ragtime
blues

SUGGESTIONS FOR FURTHER READING

PRIMARY SOURCES

CHEKHOV, A. P. *Plays.* Translated and edited by E. K. Bristow. New York: Norton, 1977. Excellent versions of Chekhov's most memorable plays: *The Sea Gull, Uncle Vanya, The Three Sisters,* and *The Cherry Orchard.*

CHOPIN, K. *The Awakening.* Edited by M. Culley. New York: Norton, 1976. The story of a sensual woman's coming of age that shocked the American public, whose outrage then silenced its author; with notes, excerpts from contemporary reviews, and essays in criticism. The novel was first published in 1899.

FREUD, S. *Civilization and Its Discontents.* Translated and edited by J. Strachey. New York: Norton, 1962. Freud's ideas about history and civilization, based on his psychological findings and theories; Strachey is the editor of the Standard Edition of Freud's complete works.

———. *The Interpretation of Dreams.* Translated and edited by J. Strachey. New York: Basic Books, 1955. Freud's seminal work about the role of the unconscious in human psychology and his new theory of psychoanalysis; considered by many his most important work.

HUYSMANS, J.-K. *Against Nature.* Translated by R. Baldick. New York: Penguin, 1966. A superb English version of this curious work, first published in 1884.

IBSEN, H. *A Doll's House.* Translated by C. Hampton. New York: S. French, 1972. An excellent English version of Ibsen's most often performed play, the story of a woman's awakening to the facts of her oppressive marriage.

JUNG, C. G. *Basic Writings*. Edited with an introduction by V. S. de Laszlo. New York: Modern Library, 1959. A good selection of the most important works of the Swiss psychiatrist who explored the importance of myths and symbols in human psychology.

———. *Memories, Dreams, Reflections*. Edited by A. Jaffé. New York: Vintage, 1963. Jung's highly readable autobiography, in which he describes the origins of his theories.

KAFKA, F. *The Metamorphosis, The Penal Colony, and Other Stories*. Translated by W. and E. Muir. New York: Schocken Books, 1988. This volume contains the best of Kafka's brilliant short prose works, all concerned with anxiety and alienation in a hostile and incomprehensible world.

———. *The Trial*. Translated by W. and E. Muir. New York: Schocken Books, 1968. A definitive edition of Kafka's nightmare novel in which the lead character is tried and convicted of a crime whose nature he cannot discover.

NIETZSCHE, F. W. *The Portable Nietzsche*. Selected and translated by W. Kaufmann. New York: Penguin, 1976. A collection of the most important writings of the German philosopher, compiled by the American scholar who rescued Nietzsche from the charge of proto-Nazism into which his philosophy had fallen during the Nazi era.

PROUST, M. *Remembrance of Things Past*. Translated by C. K. Scott Moncrieff, T. Kilmartin, and A. Mayor. London: Chatto & Windus, 1981. Contains all seven volumes of Proust's monumental work, which portrays the early twentieth century as a transitional period with the old aristocracy in decline and the middle class on the rise.

WILDE, O. *The Picture of Dorian Gray*. New York: Oxford University Press, 1981. Wilde's only novel recounts the story of a man whose portrait ages and decays while he remains young and handsome despite a dissolute life; the most enduring work of the Decadent school of late-nineteenth-century English literature.

ZOLA, E. *Germinal*. Translated and with an introduction by L. Tancock. New York: Penguin, 1954. A Realist novel that exposes the sordid conditions in the French mining industry.

SUGGESTIONS FOR LISTENING

DEBUSSY, CLAUDE (1862–1918). Debussy's veiled, subtly shifting harmonies helped to found Impressionist music. Excellent examples of his style may be heard in the orchestral works *Prélude à l'après-midi d'un faune (Prelude to the Afternoon of a Faun)* (1894) and *Nocturnes* (1899); in the collections for piano called *Estampes (Prints)* (1913) and *Préludes* (1910–1913); and in the opera *Pelléas et Mélisande* (1902). Not all of his music was Impressionistic, however; for example, in the piano music called *Children's Corner* (1908), he blended Classical values with his typical harmonic structures.

JOPLIN, SCOTT (1868–1917). Typical of Joplin's ragtime compositions with a syncopated beat are *Maple Leaf Rag* (1899), *Sugar Cane Rag* (1908), and *Magnetic Rag* (1914). He also wrote a ragtime opera *Treemonisha* (1911), a failure in his lifetime but a modest success in recent revivals.

RAVEL, MAURICE (1875–1937). Working in the shadow of Debussy, Ravel was an Impressionist with Classical inclinations; where Debussy was rhapsodic, Ravel was restrained. The work for solo piano *Jeux d'eau (Fountains)* (1901) shows Ravel's Impressionist style to perfection. His Classicism is most evident in compositions indebted to dance forms, including two works for solo piano, *Pavane pour une infante defunte (Pavane for a Dead Princess)* (1899) and *Valses nobles et sentimentales (Waltzes Noble and Sentimental)* (1911), and two works for orchestra, *La Valse (The Waltz)* (1920) and *Bolèro* (1928).

SCHOENBERG, ARNOLD (1874–1951). By the end of this period, in 1914, Schoenberg was recognized as the leader of Expressionist music, particularly with the atonal work *Pierrot lunaire (Moonstruck Pierrot)* (1912), scored for chamber quintet and voice. In earlier works, he was less radical, as in the Second String Quartet (1908), which fused Classical forms and fragmentary melodies. Only after 1923 did Schoenberg make a breakthrough to serial composition, the type of music with which he is most identified (see Chapter 20).

STRAVINSKY, IGOR (1882–1971). Stravinsky, who along with Schoenberg dominated twentieth-century music, also began writing music during this period, principally as a composer of ballet scores based on Russian folk tales and traditions. These were *The Firebird* (1910), *Petrushka* (1911), and *Le Sacre du printemps (The Rite of Spring)* (1913). With *Le Sacre*, he established his originality as a composer, especially in his innovative rhythms and his handling of folk themes.

20 THE AGE OF THE MASSES AND THE ZENITH OF MODERNISM

1914–1945

The events of the first half of the twentieth century are seen quite differently today from the way they were seen at the time. Historians are beginning to view World War I (1914–1918) and World War II (1939–1945) not as two separate conflicts but as a single struggle divided by a twenty-year peace. They believe that the Great Depression of the 1930s was not a signal that the capitalist system did not work but was simply an episode of economic downturn. And they know that the making of the masses into a historically powerful force was the most significant event of this time. The rise of the masses heralded the onset of a new phase of culture in which ordinary men and women from the lower middle class and the working class challenged bourgeois dominance in much the same way that the bourgeoisie had earlier challenged and eventually overcome the aristocracy.

The needs of this public led to the birth of mass culture, resulting in fresh forms of popular expression. Mass culture triggered negative responses in most serious artists, writers, and musicians, who preferred the difficult and somewhat remote style of Modernism. The leaders of Modernism, partly because of the extreme popularity of mass culture, now fashioned works that grew more and more revolutionary in form, constantly testing the limits of the arts. The period between 1914 and 1945 thus saw both the rise of mass culture and the zenith of Modernism.

◄ **Detail** FRIDA KAHLO. *Self-Portrait Dedicated to Dr. Eloesser.* 1940. Oil on masonite, 22¼ × 15¾". Private collection, U.S.A.

Figure 20.1 PABLO PICASSO. *Guernica*. 1937. Oil on canvas, 11′ 5½″ × 25′ 5¾″. Prado, Madrid. *Picasso's* Guernica *is a vivid symbol of the violent twenty years between World War I and World War II. Depicting the bombing of the unarmed town of Guernica by Nazi planes during the Spanish Civil War, the painting transforms the local struggle into an international battle between totalitarianism and human freedom—the issue that also dominated the age's ideological debates.*

Figure 20.2 PAUL NASH. *"We Are Making a New World."* 1918. Oil on canvas, 28 × 36″. Imperial War Museum, London. *Paul Nash, one of Britain's official artists during World War I, made the reality of the war's destructive power evident to civilians at home. In his battle scenes, farmlands were turned into quagmires and forests into "no-man's lands." The artist's choice of the title for this painting mocks the politicians' promises that tomorrow will be better.*

THE COLLAPSE OF OLD CERTAINTIES AND THE SEARCH FOR NEW VALUES

Before World War I, liberal values guided most people's expectations. Between the outbreak of World War I and the ending of World War II, however, the values of liberalism were severely tested and in some cases overthrown. Wars, revolutions, and social upheavals often dominated both domestic and foreign affairs. To those who clung to liberal ideals, the world seemed to have gone mad (Figure 20.1). In Russia, Italy, Germany, and Spain, individual rights became secondary to the needs of society or simply to the wishes of the ruling totalitarian party. The doctrine of laissez faire also fell into discredit during the Depression of the 1930s, bringing capitalism itself into question and leading to the rise of state-controlled economies.

World War I and Its Aftermath

In 1914 came the war that nobody expected and that took an estimated ten million lives. On one side were the Central Powers—Germany, Austria-Hungary (members of the Triple Alliance), Turkey, and Bulgaria. The principal war aim of these countries was to assert the power of the central European region, which had been eclipsed by western Europe for almost two hundred years. Central Europe's new sense of importance was due to the unification of Germany in 1871, which had made the German Empire the most powerful industrial and military state on the Continent.

Opposed to the Central Powers were the Allied Powers: France, Russia, and Great Britain (members of the Triple Entente), joined in 1915 by Italy (a former member of the Triple Alliance). The Allies refused to allow the Central Powers to revise the balance of power and, in particular, were determined to keep Germany from gaining new lands. The two sides found themselves bogged down in siege warfare that led to huge losses on the battlefield and appalling hardships at home (Figure 20.2).

In the spring of 1917, the stalemate between the two sides was upset by two key events. First, the United States entered the war on the Allied side, promising fresh troops and supplies. Second, revolution broke out in Russia, interrupting its war effort and eventually causing the newly formed Communist regime to make peace with the Central Powers in 1918. The Germans launched a massive attack on the western front, but the Allies, supported by American troops, foiled the Germans and forced them to surrender in November 1918.

The peace that ended the war—the 1919 Treaty of Versailles—was based partly on a plan of the U.S. president, Woodrow Wilson (1913–1921). The goal of Wilson's plan was to keep Europe safe from war, and it called for the self-determination of nations, democratic governments, and the establishment of the League of Nations, an international agency to maintain the peace. Despite the optimism surrounding its signing, the Versailles Treaty sowed the seeds of discord in Germany that contributed to World War II (Map 20.1).

Map 20.1   EUROPE AFTER WORLD WAR I

Figure 20.3 DOROTHEA LANGE. *Migrant Mother, Nipomo, California. 1936. Library of Congress. Migrant workers were increasingly attracted to the vegetable fields of California during the Great Depression. Seasonal laborers, they harvested crops for very low wages under miserable working conditions and usually lived in crowded, unsanitary camps. This photograph shows a migrant mother, surrounded by three children, whose bleak future has been made worse by the failure of the pea crop. Dorothea Lange's poignant photographs, collected in* An American Exodus: A Record of Human Erosion *(1939), reflected her strong sense of social justice, her sympathy for the downtrodden, and her own life as the child of a broken home.*

Defeated German officials and officers would later rally nationalistic feelings by denouncing the treaty as a humiliation for their country.

Peace brought boom times to the economies of the victorious Allied Powers, however. Britain and France returned to business as usual. The United States reverted to its prewar isolationism, and between 1924 and 1929 it exhibited the best and the worst of free enterprise—unprecedented prosperity and rampant greed.

The Central Powers also rebuilt their economies in the 1920s. After a shaky start, Germany survived near bankruptcy to regain its status as the leading industrial state on the Continent. Under the Weimar Republic, Germany's first democratic parliamentary government, the country once again became a center for European culture, providing key leaders in avant-garde painting and literature. Conversely, Austria-Hungary was divided into separate nations, and its Slavic population dispersed among several states. Lacking a sound eco-

nomic base, the one-time empire never fully recovered from its defeat.

As the 1920s drew to a close, a warning signal sounded: the crash of the New York stock market in October 1929. After the crash, the buoyant atmosphere of the twenties lingered for only a few months. Then economic depression in the United States, a key player in the world's economy, pulled down Europe's financial house.

The Great Depression of the 1930s

The Depression wiped out prosperity and brought mass unemployment, street demonstrations, and near starvation for many people. In Europe and the United States, governments were forced to take extreme measures to restore their economies. Great Britain and France had to discard free trade and move toward government-controlled economies. Under President Franklin Delano Roosevelt (1933–1945) and his New Deal program, the United States followed a policy of state intervention to revitalize the economy (Figure 20.3). Roosevelt started public works projects, sponsored programs such as social security and unemployment insurance to benefit working people, and moved to regulate Wall Street and the banks. Depressed conditions hung on until World War II, however.

Germany suffered the most in Europe. Domestic problems, brought on in part by bank failures and rising unemployment, led to political crises that doomed the Weimar experiment in democracy and set the stage for the coming to power of the National Socialists, or Nazis, under Adolf Hitler.

While Europe suffered, Japan prospered. Since 1926 Japan had been ruled by Emperor Hirohito (r. 1926–1989), who was worshiped as a god, although actual power was wielded by military leaders and businessmen. In the 1930s, these groups pursued expansionist and militaristic policies, first taking over Manchuria and then making war on China. As the situation worsened in Europe in the late 1930s, Japan was able to take a free hand in Southeast Asia.

The Rise of Totalitarianism

With the peace treaty of 1919, democracy seemed triumphant. By 1939, a mere twenty years later, most of the new democracies—including Germany, Austria, Hungary, Italy, Spain, Bulgaria, and Rumania—had become totalitarian. Totalitarianism on such a huge scale is a twentieth-century phenomenon, but its roots reach back to the policies of Robespierre during the French Revolution. Totalitarian governments control every aspect of the lives and thoughts of their citizens. Art, literature, and the press exist only in the service of the state. "Truth" itself becomes a matter of what the state says it is. Between the wars, totalitarianism emerged in two forms: Russian communism and European fascism.

Russian Communism Russian communism was based on the writings of Karl Marx, whose theory was reinterpreted by the revolutionary leader V. I. Lenin (1917–1924). Lenin accepted Marx's basic premise that economic conditions determine the course of history and his conclusion that history leads inevitably to a communist society run by and for the workers. Unlike Marx, Lenin believed that radical reform could occur only when a small, elite group—rather than a mass movement—seized power in the name of the people.

In 1917 Russia was plagued by an incompetent ruler, an inefficient military staff, a weak economy, and rising social and political discord. Revolution broke out in February, and a small band of Marxist communists—the Bolsheviks—seized control of the government in October. Led by Lenin, the Bolsheviks began to restructure the economy and the political system. Under their plan, the state would control production and distribution, and soviets—or councils of workers, military personnel, and peasants—would restructure the social and economic order at the local level, as directed by the Communist party under Lenin.

After Lenin's death, Joseph Stalin (1928–1953) eventually emerged as the sole ruler of the Union of Soviet Socialist Republics, as the Russian Empire was now called, and he proceeded to impose his will over the state with a vengeance. Production was increased and modernization accomplished through state-owned farms, factories, and heavy industry. No political party other than the Communist party was permitted, however, and Stalin was ruthless in dealing with his opponents and critics. He had them either murdered or imprisoned in a vast network of forced-labor camps known as the Gulag in the wilderness of Siberia. The number of Stalin's victims is beyond imagining: More than ten million men, women, and children met unnatural deaths in the period of forced collectivization of agriculture, 1929–1936, and millions more were murdered during purges and in the Gulag.

European Fascism European fascism was based on the idea that the masses should participate directly in the state—not through a legislative or deliberative body such as a parliament, but through a fusion of the population into one "spirit." Fascism sought to bind the masses by appealing to nonrational sentiments about national destiny. Like communists, fascists believed that the individual was insignificant and the nation-state was the supreme embodiment of the destiny of its people.

In practice, fascism led to loss of personal freedom, as did communism, because its ideals of economic stability and social peace could be achieved only through dictatorship and tight control over the press, education, police, and the judicial system. Because of its idealistic nationalism, fascism was also hostile both to foreigners and to internal groups that did not share the majority's history, race, or politics. The movement's innate aggressiveness led to strong military establishments, which were used to conquer new lands in Europe and to win colonial empires. Fascism first appeared in Italy in the 1920s and then in Germany and Spain in the 1930s.

In Italy, a floundering economy and mounting national frustration led more and more people to follow the Fascists. Led by Benito Mussolini [moo-suh-LEE-nee] (1922–1945), the Fascists dreamed of a revitalized

Figure 20.4 Nuremberg Nazi Party Rally. 1933. *Under the skillful orchestration of their propaganda chief, Joseph Goebbels, the National Socialists staged massive demonstrations whose goal was to overpower the emotions of participants and observers alike. In this anonymous photograph, Nazi party members and private army units pass in review. In the 1930s, such demonstrations succeeded in uniting the German masses with the Nazi leader.*

Italy restored to its ancient glory. After seizing power in 1922, Mussolini achieved some success with his programs, and as the rest of Europe suffered through the Depression, his pragmatic policies gained admirers elsewhere.

Germany in the early 1930s was wracked by the Depression, unemployment, and political extremism, and in 1933 the German voters turned to the National Socialist (Nazi) party. Within three years, the Nazis had restored industrial productivity, eliminated unemployment, and gained the support of many business leaders and farmers. The success of the National Socialists depended ultimately on their *Führer*, or "leader," Adolf Hitler (1933–1945), a middle-class Austrian and veteran who had hammered together a strong mass movement built on anti-Semitism and anticommunism. He used his magnetic personality to attract devoted followers with promises to restore Germany to prewar glory. From the beginning, the Nazis' ruthless treatment of political enemies, of the Jews, and of any dissidents aroused fears, but most Europeans ignored these barbaric acts, preferring to focus on the regime's successes (Figure 20.4).

Spain's agrarian economy and traditional institutions began to be strained by industrial growth in the 1920s, and in the early 1930s a coalition of reformers overthrew the king and created a secular republic with a constitution guaranteeing civil rights. Conservative forces plotted to restore monarchical rule and the church's influence. In 1936 civil war broke out. General Francisco Franco (1939–1975) led the conservatives to victory in 1939, defeating an alliance of reformers. During hostilities, Hitler and Mussolini supplied Franco's fascist army with troops and equipment, and Stalin backed the losing faction. For the Germans and the Italians, Spain's civil war was a practice run for World War II. For example, the bombing of unarmed towns like Guernica (see Figure 20.1) foreshadowed the indiscriminate bombing and killing of civilians that characterized the later war.

World War II: Origins and Outcome

The origins of World War II lay in the Treaty of Versailles (which many Germans denounced as a "dictated peace" that brought the loss of territory in France and Poland), the Great Depression, and nationalism. After less than a year in office, Hitler launched a campaign to revise the Versailles Treaty and engaged in a propaganda crusade that focused on Germany's glorious past. His regime, he boasted, was the Third Reich, or empire, which would last for a thousand years—like the centuries-long Holy Roman Empire (1000–1806) rather than the short-lived German Empire (1871–1918). In 1936 he marched troops into the Rhineland, the industrial heartland of Germany, which had been demilitarized by the Versailles Treaty. When the world failed to respond to this challenge, Hitler concluded that Germany's former enemies were weak, and he initiated a plan to conquer Europe. In the next two years, Europe watched as Hitler took Austria and Czechoslovakia. World War II began on September 1, 1939, when Germany invaded Poland; France and Britain responded with declarations of war.

Within nine months, the Nazis occupied most of western Europe. By the fall of 1940, the British, under

PERSONAL PERSPECTIVE

ELIE WIESEL
From *Night*

In this excerpt from his autobiographical novel Night, *Wiesel describes the arrival of his family at Auschwitz, a Nazi death camp.*

The cherished objects we had brought with us thus far were left behind in the train, and with them, at last, our illusions.

Every two yards or so an SS man held his tommy gun trained on us. Hand in hand we followed the crowd.

An SS noncommissioned officer came to meet us, a truncheon in his hand. He gave the order:

"Men to the left! Women to the right!"

Eight words spoken quietly, indifferently, without emotion. Eight short, simple words. Yet that was the moment when I parted from my mother. I had not had time to think, but already I felt the pressure of my father's hand: we were alone. For a part of a second I glimpsed my mother and my sisters moving away to the right. Tzipora held Mother's hand. I saw them disappear into the distance; my mother was stroking my sister's fair hair, as though to protect her, while I walked on with my father and the other men. And I did not know that in that place, at that moment, I was part-

ing from my mother and Tzipora forever. I went on walking. My father held onto my hand.

Behind me, an old man fell to the ground. Near him was an SS man, putting his revolver back in its holster.

My hand shifted on my father's arm. I had one thought—not to lose him. Not to be left alone.

The SS officers gave the order:

"Form fives!"

Commotion. At all costs we must keep together.

"Here, kid, how old are you?"

It was one of the prisoners who asked me this. I could not see his face, but his voice was tense and weary.

"I'm not quite fifteen yet."

"No. Eighteen."

"But I'm not," I said. "Fifteen."

"Fool. Listen to what *I* say."

Then he questioned my father, who replied:

"Fifty."

The other grew more furious than ever.

"No, not fifty. Forty. Do you understand? Eighteen and forty."

He disappeared into the night shadows.

Figure 20.5 MARGARET BOURKE-WHITE. Russian Tank Driver. 1941. *Photojournalism, a popular form in which the photograph rather than the text dominates the story, reached new heights during World War II, particularly in illustrated magazines like* Life. *Margaret Bourke-White, one of the first women war journalists, was the only foreign correspondent–photographer present in the Soviet Union when the Germans invaded in June 1941. In this photograph, she shows a Russian tank driver peering through his window with the cannon jutting out over his head—a vivid image of the integration of human beings into mechanized warfare.*

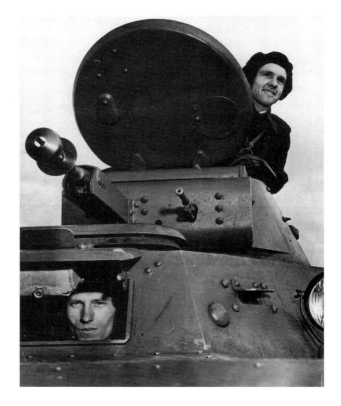

their wartime leader Winston Churchill, were bravely holding on, taking the brunt of the German air raids. Unable to defeat England by air, Hitler turned eastward and invaded the Soviet Union in 1941 (Figure 20.5). Shortly thereafter, the Soviet Union and Great Britain became allies against Nazi Germany. Then, on December 7, 1941, Japan attacked Pearl Harbor, an American military base in the Pacific, and a few days later Germany and Italy followed Japan in declaring war on the United States.

The war in Europe lasted until May 1945, when the combined armies of the Allied Powers—Britain, the Soviet Union, and the United States—forced Germany

Figure 20.6   Nazi Death Camp in Belsen, Germany. 1945. *When the Nazis came to power in Germany in 1933, they secretly began to imprison their political enemies in concentration camps, where they were tortured or executed. By 1942 the Nazis had extended this secret policy across Europe to include minority civilians, particularly Jews. Photographs such as this one revealed to the world the atrocities committed by the Nazi regime.*

to surrender. Italy had already negotiated an armistice with the Allies in September 1943 after anti-Fascists overthrew Mussolini and set up a republic. In the Pacific, where the Allies had captured key Japanese island strongholds, the war against Japan was brought to an abrupt end in August 1945, when the United States dropped atomic bombs on the Japanese cities of Hiroshima and Nagasaki. The more than 200,000 Japanese killed in these two raids climaxed the bloody six years of World War II, adding to its estimated thirty to fifty million deaths.

By 1945 the world had witnessed some of the most brutal examples of human behavior in history, but few were prepared for the shock of the Nazi death camps. Gradually it became known to the world that the Nazis had rounded up the Jews of Germany and eastern Europe and transported them in cattle cars to extermination camps, where they were killed in gas chambers. The Nazis referred to their plan to eliminate the Jewish people as the Final Solution, but the rest of the world called it the Holocaust. This genocidal policy involved the murder of six million Jews out of a population of nine million, along with millions of other people the Nazis deemed undesirable, such as gypsies and homosexuals (Figure 20.6).

In 1945, after six years of war, Germany and Japan lay in ruins. Italy escaped with less damage. France, partly occupied by the Germans for most of the war, was readmitted to the councils of the Allies. England, though victorious, emerged exhausted and in the shadow of her former allies, the United States and the Soviet Union. The old European order had passed away. The Soviet Union and the United States were now the two most powerful states in the world.

THE ZENITH OF MODERNISM

Modernism had originated in the latter part of the nineteenth century as a reflection of the fast-paced modern world whose foundations and boundaries seemed to be constantly shifting. The Modernist sensibility, with its underlying spirit of skepticism and experimentation, continued to guide artistic and literary expression in the twentieth century. But this style was limited in its appeal, and an ever-growing general public was isolated from avant-garde developments in art, music, and literature. When this wider audience was exposed to Modernist works, they often responded negatively to them, considering them incomprehensible, obscene, or decidedly provocative in some way. They turned instead to the increasingly available and affordable pleasures offered by **mass culture.**

Like Modernism, mass culture was a direct outgrowth of industrialized society. Its roots reached back to the late nineteenth century, when skilled workers began to enjoy a better standard of living than had previously been possible for members of the lower classes. This new generation of consumers demanded products and amusements that appealed to their tastes: inexpensive, energetic, and easily accessible.

In response to their desires, entrepreneurs using new technologies flooded the market with consumer goods and developed new entertainments. Unlike the folk culture or popular culture of earlier times, modern mass culture was also mass-produced culture. The untapped consumers' market led to the creation or expansion of new industries, in particular automobiles, household products, and domestic appliances. Most forms of mass culture—the radio, newspaper comic strips and cartoons, professional sports, picture magazines, recordings, movies, and musical comedies—had originated before World War I, but now, between the wars, they came into their own. The 1920s was the golden age of Broadway's musical comedies, and radio reached its peak in the years after 1935.

The spread of mass culture heightened the prestige of the United States as it became known as the source of the most vigorous and imaginative popular works. The outstanding symbol of America's dominance of popular culture is Walt Disney (1901–1966), the creator of the cartoon figures of Mickey Mouse (1928) and other characters. By 1945, mass culture was playing an ever-growing role in the public and the private lives of most citizens in the more advanced societies. A handful of creative people began to incorporate elements of mass culture into their works, using jazz in "serious" music or film in theatrical performances, for example, but in the main most artists, writers, and musicians stood apart from mass culture. Their isolation reflected an almost sacred commitment to the Modernist ideals of experimentation, newness, and deliberate difficulty. And some Modernists, especially among the visual artists, imbued these ideals with spiritual meaning.

Experimentation in Literature

Modernist writers between 1914 and 1945 maintained Early Modernism's dedication to experimentation, a stance that reflected their despair over the instability of their era. By challenging the traditional norms and methods of literature through their carefully composed experimental works, the Modernists were convinced that they could impose an order on the seeming randomness and meaninglessness of human existence.

The Novel   Depiction of the narrator's subjective consciousness was a principal concern of the Modernist novelists, who otherwise differed markedly from one another. The most distinctive method that arose from this concern was **stream-of-consciousness** writing, a method in which the narrative consists of the unedited thoughts of one of the characters, through whose mind readers experience the story. Stream-of-consciousness fiction differs from a story told in the first person—the grammatical "I"—by one of the characters (for example, Dickens's *David Copperfield*) in that it is an attempt to emulate the actual experience of thinking and feeling, even to the point of sounding fragmented, random, and arbitrary.

The Irish author James Joyce and the English writer Virginia Woolf were important innovators with the stream-of-consciousness technique. In his novel *Ulysses,* James Joyce (1882–1941) uses this device as a way of making the novel's characters speak directly to readers. For instance, no narrator's voice intrudes in the novel's final forty-five pages, which are the scattered thoughts of the character Molly Bloom as she sinks into sleep. This long monologue is a single run-on sentence without any punctuation except for a final period.

Despite the experimental style of *Ulysses,* Joyce aspired to more than technical virtuosity in this monumental work. He planned it as a modern version of the *Odyssey,* contrasting Homer's twenty-four books of heroic exploits with an ordinary day in the lives of three Dubliners. Joyce's sexual language, although natural to his characters, offended bourgeois morals. *Ulysses,* first published in France in 1922, became the era's test case for artistic freedom, not appearing in America or England until the 1930s.

Rejecting traditional narrative techniques, Virginia Woolf (1882–1941) experimented with innovative ways of exploring time, space, and reality. In her early novel *Jacob's Room* (1922), for example, she develops the title character through fragments of other people's comments about him. In *Mrs. Dalloway* (1925), she uses interior monologues to trace a woman's experiences over the course of a day in London. Like her contemporaries Joyce and Freud, Woolf was interested in examining the realities that lie below surface consciousness. Many consider *To the Lighthouse* (1927) Woolf's finest novel. In it she uses stream-of-consciousness to strip the story of a fixed point of view and capture the differing senses of reality experienced by the characters

Figure 20.7 PABLO PICASSO. *Gertrude Stein.* 1906. Oil on canvas, 39¼ × 32". Metropolitan Museum of Art. Bequest of Gertrude Stein, 1946. *Talented Americans were introduced to Paris by American writer and expatriate Gertrude Stein, who made her studio a gathering place for the Parisian avant-garde. There she entertained Matisse and Picasso, composer Igor Stravinsky, writers Ernest Hemingway and F. Scott Fitzgerald, and many other brilliant exponents of Modernism. Stein was shocked at first by the starkness and brooding presence of Picasso's portrait of her, but she came to regard it as an accurate likeness, saying, "For me it is I, and it is the only reproduction of me which is always I."*

—in much the same way that the Cubist painters aimed at representing multiple views. To that end, she focuses on the characters' inner selves, creating diverse effects through interior monologues. For instance, one character's narrow, matter-of-fact mentality differs from his wife's emotional, free-ranging consciousness. A distinguished literary critic and the author of well-known feminist works such as *A Room of One's Own,* Woolf gathered around her the avant-garde writers, artists, and intellectuals known as the Bloomsbury Group and founded, with her husband, Leonard, the Hogarth Press.

American writers also contributed experimental fiction to the Modernist revolution. By and large, these Americans made their first contacts with Europe during World War I and stayed on until the Great Depression drove them home (Figure 20.7). Ernest Hemingway (1899–1961) was the first of the Americans living abroad to emerge as a major literary star. His severely disciplined prose style relied heavily on dialogue, and he often omitted details of setting and background. His writing owed a debt to popular culture: From the era's hardboiled detective fiction he borrowed a terse, world-weary voice to narrate his works, as in his 1926 novel, *The Sun Also Rises.* In this novel, he portrays his fellow American exiles as a "lost generation" whose future was blighted by World War I—a Modernist message. In Hemingway's cynical vision, politics is of little importance; what matter most are drinking bouts with male friends and casual sex with beautiful women.

William Faulkner (1897–1962) was another American who became one of the giants of twentieth-century literature. The stream-of-consciousness technique is central to his 1929 masterpiece, *The Sound and the Fury.* With a story line repeated several times but from different perspectives, this novel is especially audacious in its opening section, which narrates events through the eyes of a mentally defective character. More important than his use of such Modernist devices was his lifelong identification with his home state of Mississippi, where, after a brief sojourn in Europe, he began to explore themes about extended families bound together by sexual secrets. Faulkner's universe became the fictional county of Yoknapatawpha, which he peopled with decaying gentry, ambitious poor whites, and exploited blacks. His artistic power lay in his ability not only to relate these characters to their region but also to turn them into universal symbols.

Although experimentalism was a highly visible aspect of Modernist fiction, not all Modernist writers were preoccupied with innovative methods. Other writers were identified with the Modernists because of their pessimistic viewpoints or their explosive themes. The Modernism of the British writer D. H. Lawrence (1885–1930), for example, was expressed in novels of sexual liberation. Frustrated by the coldness of sexual relations in bourgeois culture, Lawrence, the son of a miner, concluded that the machine age emasculated men. As an antidote, he preached a religion of erotic passion. He set forth his doctrine of sexual freedom most clearly in the 1928 novel *Lady Chatterley's Lover,* issued privately and quickly banned for its explicit language and scenes. Not until the 1960s, and only after bitter court battles, was this novel allowed to circulate freely. In the novel, the love-making episodes between Lady Chatterley, wed to an impotent aristocrat, and the lower-class gamekeeper Mellors were presented as models of sexual fulfillment with their mix of erotic candor and moral fervor.

Falling outside the Modernist classification is the English novelist and essayist George Orwell (1903–1950), who nevertheless was one of the major figures of the interwar period. Born Eric Blair to an established middle-class family, Orwell changed his name, rejected his background, lived and worked among the poor and downtrodden, and became a writer. He also became the conscience of his generation because he remained skeptical of all the political ideologies of his day. In the allegorical novel *Animal Farm* (1945), he satirized Stalinist Russia. In the anti-utopian novel *1984* (1948), he made totalitarianism the enemy, especially as practiced in the Soviet Union, but he also warned of the dangers of repression in capitalist society. What made Orwell remarkable in this age torn by ideological excess was his claim to be merely an ordinary, decent man. It is perhaps for this reason that today Orwell is claimed by socialists, liberals, and conservatives alike.

Poetry Modern poetry found its first great master in William Butler Yeats (1865–1939). His early poems are filled with Romantic mysticism, drawing on the myths of his native Ireland. By 1910 he had stripped his verses of Romantic allusions, and yet in his later works, he never gave up entirely his belief in the occult or the importance of myth. As Irish patriots grew more hostile to their country's continued submersion in the United Kingdom, climaxing in the Easter Rebellion of 1916, Yeats's poems took on a political cast. His best verses came in the 1920s, when his primary sources were Irish history and Greco-Roman myth. Perhaps his finest lyric is "Sailing to Byzantium," a poem that conjures up the Classical past to reaffirm ancient wisdom and redeem the tawdry industrialized world.

T. S. Eliot (1888–1965) was another founder of Modern poetry. Reared in St. Louis and educated at Harvard, Eliot moved to London in 1915, becoming an English citizen in 1927. He and Ezra Pound (1885–1972), another American exile, established a school of poetry that reflected the crisis of confidence that seized Europe's intellectuals after World War I. Like those of the late Roman poets, Eliot's verses relied heavily on literary references and quotations.

"The Waste Land," published in 1922, showed Eliot's difficult, eclectic style; in 403 irregular lines, he quotes from or imitates thirty-five authors, including Shakespeare and Dante, adapts snatches from popular songs, and uses phrases in six foreign languages. Form matches content because the "waste land" itself represents a sterile, godless region without a future, a symbol drawn from medieval legend but changed by Eliot into a symbol of the hollowness of modern life. In 1927 he moved beyond such atheistic pessimism, finding solace by being received into the Church of England—

a step he celebrated in the poem "Ash Wednesday," published in 1930.

The black American poet Langston Hughes (1902–1967) also belongs with the outstanding Modernists. Hughes drew inspiration from many sources, including Africa, Europe, and Mexico, but the ultimate power of his poetry came from the American experience: jazz, spirituals, and his anguish as a black man in a white world. Hughes's emergence, like that of many African American writers, occurred during a population shift that began in 1914 when thousands of blacks from the American South settled in northern cities like New York, Chicago, and Detroit in hopes of a better life (Figure 20.8).

At the same time that America's ethnographic map was being redrawn, a craze for Negro culture sprang up that was fueled by jazz and the avant-garde cult of primitivism. This craze sparked the Harlem Renaissance, a 1920s cultural revival in the predominantly black area of New York City called Harlem. Hughes was a major figure in this black literary movement. His earliest book of verses, *The Weary Blues* (1926), contains his most famous poem, "The Negro Speaks of Rivers." Dedicated to W. E. B. DuBois (1868–1963), the founder of the National Association for the Advancement of Colored People, Hughes's verse memorializes the deathless spirit of his race by linking black history to the rivers of the world.

Another outstanding figure of the Harlem Renaissance was Zora Neale Hurston (about 1901–1960), the most prolific African American woman writer of her generation. Poet, novelist, folklorist, essayist, Hurston made her literary task the exploration of what it means to be black and female in a white- and male-dominated society. An excellent example of her handling of this theme is the essay "How It Feels to Be Colored Me," published in 1928. In this short work, filled with self-mocking irony, she presents herself as torn between black and white culture and sometimes forced to choose between two then current stereotypes: the "happy Negro" who performs for white folks for money and sheer joy and the "exotic primitive," the educated black who, despite a veneer of learning, remains "uncivilized." Nevertheless, she rejects both stereotypes as caused by being born black in a white culture. In certain moments, she claims to transcend race though not gender: "I belong to no race nor time. I am the eternal feminine with its string of beads." Her ideal is of a future, free of racism, in which African Americans no longer have to struggle with culturally imposed identities.

Drama During the interwar years, drama moved in new directions in both Europe and America. An Expressionist in aesthetics and a Marxist in politics, the

Figure 20.8   JACOB LAWRENCE. *Migration Series, No. 58.* The original caption reads, "In the North the Negro had better educational facilities." 1940–1941. Tempera on gesso on composition board, 12 × 18". The Museum of Modern Art, New York. Gift of Mrs. David M. Levy. *Jacob Lawrence's* The Migration Series, *a cycle of paintings commissioned by* Fortune *magazine, depicted the mass flight of African Americans from the American South to the North in their quest for a better life. Lawrence (1917–2000) was a Harlem resident and the son of black migrants. These works are simplistic in format (standard small size and common color scheme); nevertheless, they reveal Lawrence's knowledge of High Modernism, especially in the flatness and angularity of the figures and the unusual perspective. The painting titled* No. 58 *evokes a sense of rhythm by having the number sequence repeated by the young girls' arm and leg movements and their swaying dresses. This series established Lawrence as a serious artist, and in 1941 he became the first African American included in the permanent collection of New York's Museum of Modern Art.*

German Bertolt Brecht [BREKT] (1898–1956) blended a discordant style learned from the Berlin streets with his hatred of bourgeois society into what he called **"epic theater."** Rebelling against traditional theater, which he thought merely reinforced class prejudices, he devised a radical theater centered on a technique called the "alienation effect," whose purpose was to make the bourgeois audience uncomfortable (Figure 20.9). Alienation effects could take any form, such as outlandish props, inappropriate accents, or ludicrous dialogue. By breaking the magic spell of the stage, Brecht's epic theater challenged the viewers' expectations and prepared them for his moral and political message. A victim of Nazi oppression, Brecht fled first to Scandinavia and then to America, where he lived for fifteen years before moving to East Berlin in 1952 to found a highly influential theater company.

A year before he officially embraced Marxism, Brecht teamed with the German-born composer Kurt Weill [WILE or VILE] (1900–1950) to create one of the best-known musicals in modern theater, *The Three-penny Opera* (1928). Loosely based on an eighteenth-century English opera, Brecht and Weill's Expressionist version was raucous, discordant, violent, and hostile to bourgeois values. The playwright, believing that bourgeois audiences wanted goodness to triumph over

Figure 20.9 GEORGE GROSZ. *Nude.* Ca. 1919. Watercolor, India ink, and collage, approx. 16½ × 11½". Thyssen-Bornemisza Foundation Collection, Madrid, Spain. © 1997 Estate of George Grosz/Licensed by VAGA, New York, NY. *The works of German artist George Grosz provide a visual counterpart to the dramas of Brecht. Grosz portrays bourgeois society as morally bankrupt, as in this painting of a brothel scene that shows a prostitute as a willing victim—note the prostitute's complicitous glance. Brecht makes the same point in the drama* Mother Courage *by presenting a businesswoman heroine interested only in making money even though it means sacrificing her sons in war. Grosz's* Life Model *reflected the influence of Dada art, which was imported into Berlin from Zurich in late 1918, at the end of World War I. Typical of Berlin Dadaists, Grosz added a political message to this subversive art, and he underscored his corrosive vision with a brutal, unsentimental collage technique, using photographic and painted images and overlapping planes of color.*

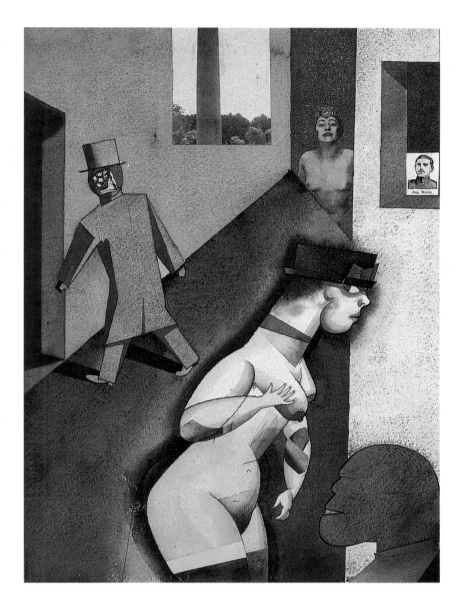

evil, made the hero a small-time hoodlum ("Mack the Knife") and then saved him at the last moment from a hanging that he richly deserved.

Besides such pathfinders as Brecht, this period also produced two major Modernist playwrights. The first of these was Jean Cocteau [kahk-TOE] (1889–1963), a French dramatist who helped to launch the French trend for modernizing the Greek classics. For example, Cocteau's *The Infernal Machine* (1934) updates Sophocles' *Oedipus.* In this modern retelling, the story is filled with Freudian overtones—Oedipus is portrayed as a "mother's boy"—and film clips are introduced for flashbacks. A second major Modernist was Eugene O'Neill (1888–1953), America's first dramatist to earn worldwide fame. Like Cocteau, O'Neill sometimes wrote new versions of Greek tragedies, as in

Mourning Becomes Electra (1931), which was modeled on Aeschylus's *Oresteia.* O'Neill's best plays are his tense family dramas in which generations battle one another, as in *Long Day's Journey into Night,* staged posthumously in 1956.

Philosophy and Science: The End of Certainty

During this period, the Idealist philosophy that had dominated Continental speculation since the early 1800s was replaced by two new schools of thought. First, in Austria and England Ludwig Wittgenstein developed ideas that helped establish the logical positivist school, which became known after World War II as the analytical school. Second, in Germany Martin

Heidegger founded the existentialist school. Both schools tried to create new philosophies that were in harmony with Modernist developments.

The Austrian Ludwig Wittgenstein [VIT-guhn-stine] (1889–1951) believed that the West was in a moral and intellectual decline that he attributed to faulty language, for which, he surmised, current philosophical methods were to blame. Wittgenstein asserted that traditional philosophical speculation was senseless because, of necessity, it relied on language that could not rise above simple truisms.

Wittgenstein's solution to this intellectual impasse was to dethrone philosophy and make it simply the servant of science. He set forth his conclusion in his *Tractatus Logico-Philosophicus* in 1922. In this treatise, he reasoned that, although language might be faulty, there were mathematical and scientific tools for comprehending the world. He proposed that thinkers give up the study of values and morals and assist scientists in a quest for truth. This conclusion led to **logical positivism,** a school of philosophy dedicated to defining terms and clarifying statements.

Wittgenstein later rejected the idea that language is a flawed instrument and substituted a theory of language as games, in the manner of children's play. Nevertheless, it was the point of view set forth in the *Tractatus* that made Wittgenstein so influential in the universities in England between 1930 and 1960 and in America after World War II.

While Wittgenstein was challenging philosophy's ancient role, Martin Heidegger [HI-deg-uhr] (1889–1976) was assaulting traditional philosophy from another angle by founding modern **existentialism.** The result of Heidegger's extensive criticism, however, was to restore philosophy to its central position as the definer of values for culture. Heidegger's major work, *Being and Time,* was published in 1927. The focal point of his thinking was the peculiar nature of human existence (the source of the term *existentialism*) as compared with other objects in the world. In his view, human existence leads to anxiety, a condition that arises because of the consciousness that there is a future that includes choices and death. He noted that most people try to avoid facing their inevitable fate by immersing themselves in trivial activities. For a few, however, Heidegger thought that the existential moment offered an opportunity in which they could seize the initiative and make themselves into authentic human beings. "Authenticity" became the ultimate human goal: to confront death and to strive for genuine creativity—a typical German philosophical attitude shared with Goethe and Nietzsche.

Heidegger is among the twentieth century's foremost philosophers, but his political activities have made him a controversial figure. He used his post as a German university professor to support the rise of Nazism in the 1930s. To hostile eyes, Heidegger's existential views—which acknowledged that individuals, powerless to reshape the world, could only accept it—seemed to support his political position. Indeed, some commentators have condemned existentialism for that reason.

Heidegger's best-known disciple, though one who rejected Nazism, was the French thinker Jean-Paul Sartre [SAHR-truh] (1905–1980). Sartre's major philosophical work, *Being and Nothingness* (1943), was heavily indebted to his mentor's concepts. From Heidegger came his definition of existentialism as an attitude characterized by concern for human freedom, personal responsibility, and individual choices. Sartre used these ideas to frame his guiding rule: Because human beings are condemned to freedom—that is, not free *not* to choose—they must take responsibility for their actions and live "without excuses." After 1945 Sartre rejected existentialism as overly individualistic and thereafter tended to support Marxist collectivist action.

In the sciences, physics remained the field of dynamic activity. The breakthroughs made before World War I were now corroborated by new research that compelled scientists to discard the Newtonian model of the universe as a simple machine. They replaced it with a complex, sense-defying structure based on the discoveries of Albert Einstein and Werner Heisenberg (Figure 20.10).

Einstein was the leading scientist in the West, comparable to Newton in the eighteenth century. His special relativity theory, dating from 1905, overturned the Newtonian concept of fixed dimensions of time and space (see Chapter 19). In Einstein's view, absolute space and time are meaningless categories, since they vary with the situation. In 1915 he expanded this earlier finding into a general theory of relativity, a universal law based on complex equations that apply throughout the cosmos.

The heart of the general theory is that space is curved as a result of the acceleration of objects (planets, stars, moons, meteors, and so on) as they move through undulating trajectories. The earth's orbit about the sun is caused not by a gravitational "force" but by the curvature of space-time around the sun. In 1919 a team of scientists observed the curvature of space in the vicinity of the sun and confirmed that space curves to the degree that Einstein's theory had forecast. Since then, his general theory has survived many tests of its validity and has opened new paths of theoretical speculation.

The other great breakthrough of modern physics was the establishment of quantum physics. Before 1914 the German physicist Max Planck had discovered the quantum nature of radiation in the subatomic

Figure 20.10 Alberto Giacometti. *Hands Holding the Void.* 1934. Plaster sculpture, original cast, ht. 61½". Yale University Art Gallery, New Haven, Connecticut. Anonymous gift. *The uncertainty of the modern world—as demonstrated by both physics and the economic and social realities of daily life—is poignantly symbolized in Giacometti's sculpture. His melancholy figure, clutching an invisible object, evokes the anguish humans suffered in no longer being able to expect answers from traditional sources, such as science and philosophy. Giacometti personally shared these fears as he created, in this Surrealistic work (inspired by his admiration for Egyptian sculpture), a semiseated female whose face is a mask. She seems to be, in the opinion of one critic, searching for what is truly human in a state of painful ignorance— the predicament of those in the modern world.*

realm (see Chapter 19). Ignoring the classical theory that energy is radiated continuously, he proved that energy is emitted in separate units that he called *quanta,* after the Latin for "how much" (as in *quantity*), and he symbolized these units by the letter *h*.

Working with Planck's *h* in 1927, which by now was accepted as a fundamental constant of nature, the German physicist Werner Heisenberg [HIZE-uhn-berg] (1901–1976) arrived at the uncertainty principle, a step that constituted a decisive break with classical physics. Heisenberg showed that a scientist could identify either an electronic particle's exact location or its path, but not both. This dilemma led to the conclusion that absolute certitude in subatomic science is impossible because scientists with their instruments inevitably interfere with the accuracy of their own work—the uncertainty principle. The incertitude involved in quantum theory caused Einstein to remark, "God does not play dice with the world." Nevertheless, quantum theory joined relativity theory as a founding principle of modern physics.

A practical result of the revolution in physics was the opening of the nuclear age in August 1945. The American physicist J. Robert Oppenheimer [AHP-uhn-hi-muhr] (1904–1967), having made basic contributions to quantum theory, was the logical choice to head the team that built the first atomic bomb. Oppenheimer's other role as a member of the panel that advised that the atomic bombs be dropped on Japan raised ethical questions that divided the scientific community then and continue to do so.

Art, Architecture, and Film

The art, architecture, and film of the interwar period were driven by the same forces that were transforming literature and philosophy. Modernism reached its zenith in painting and architecture, and the movies

Timeline 20.1   HIGH MODERNISM, 1914–1945

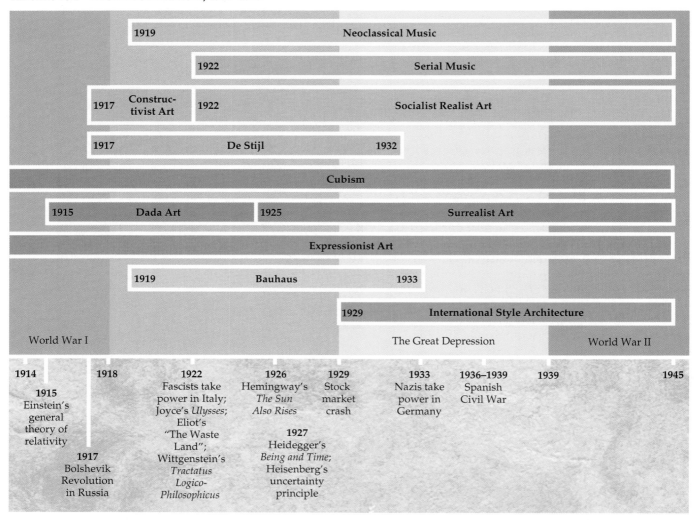

became established as the world's most popular form of mass culture (Timeline 20.1).

Painting   Painting dominated the visual arts in the interwar period. Painters launched new art movements every two or three years, although certain prevailing themes and interests could be discerned underneath the shifting styles: abstraction, primitivism and fantasy, and Expressionism. This era's most explosive art was produced within these stylistic categories. Picasso and Matisse, the two giants of twentieth-century art, continued to exercise their influence, yet they too worked within these three categories, all of which had arisen in the Post-Impressionist period.

ABSTRACTION   The history of modern painting has been rewritten in the past thirty years to accommodate the contributions of Soviet painters to abstract art. No one questions the primary role played by Picasso and

Braque in Cubist paintings before World War I, but Soviet painters, beginning in 1917, moved beyond Cubism and toward full abstraction, thus staking out claims as early founders of modern abstract art. The most influential of these Soviet artists was Kasimir Malevich [mahl-YAY-vich] (1878–1935).

Influenced by the Cubists and the Futurists—an Italian school of artists who depicted forms in surging, violent motion—Malevich was already working in an abstract style when World War I began in 1914. Four years later, he was painting completely nonobjective canvases. Believing that art should convey ethical and philosophical values, he created a style of painting devoted to purity, in which he made line, color, and shape the only purposes in his art. He called this style **Suprematism,** named for his belief that the feelings are "supreme" over every other element of life—"feelings," that is, expressed in a purely rational way.

Searching for a way to visualize emotions on canvas, Malevich adopted geometric shapes as nonobjective symbols, as in *Suprematist Painting* (Figure 20.11). In this painting, design has triumphed over representation. There are only geometric shapes of different sizes and varying lengths. The choice of the geometric shapes reflects their role as basic elements of composition with no relation to nature. The qualities shown in Malevich's painting—flatness, coolness, and severe rationality—remain central to one branch of abstract art today.

Malevich's Suprematism helped to shape **Constructivism,** the first art style launched by Lenin's regime in 1917 and the last modern art movement in Russia. Malevich's philosophical views, which were rooted in Christian mysticism, ran counter to the materialism of the Marxist government, however, and the flowering of abstraction in the Soviet Union was abruptly snuffed out in 1922. In that year, Lenin pronounced it a decadent form of bourgeois expression, and its leaders were imprisoned or exiled. In place of Constructivism, the Soviet leaders proclaimed the doctrine of **Socialist Realism,** which demanded the use of traditional techniques and styles and the glorification of the communist ideal. This type of realistic art also had greater appeal to the Soviet masses, who had been alienated by the abstract style of Constructivism.

A movement similar to Suprematism and Constructivism, called **de Stijl** (The Style), originated in the Netherlands during this period and lasted from 1917 to 1932. De Stijl artists shared the belief that art should have spiritual values and that if artists were to revamp society along rational lines, from town planning to eating utensils, a more harmonious vision of life would result.

The de Stijl movement was led by the painter Piet Mondrian [MAHN-dree-ahn] (1872–1944), who after 1919 worked successively in Paris, London, and New York. He developed an elaborate theory to give a metaphysical meaning to his abstract paintings. A member of the Theosophists—a mystical cult that flourished in about 1900—he adapted some of their beliefs to arrive at a grid format for his later paintings, notably using the Theosophists' stress on cosmic duality, in which the vertical represented the male and the horizontal the female. His paintings took the form of a rectangle divided by heavy black lines against a white background. Into this highly charged field he introduced rectangles of the primary colors—blue, yellow, and red—which in his mystic vision stood as symbols of the sky, the sun, and dynamic union, respectively. After 1932, Mondrian began to tire of black but it was only with the coming of World War II, when he emigrated to New York City, that he was able to completely eliminate black. However, he remained faithful to the grid and the primary colors (Figure 20.12).

Despite the pioneering work of Suprematism and the de Stijl school, Cubism remained the leading art movement of this period, and Pablo Picasso was still the reigning Cubist. Picasso's protean genius revealed itself in multiple styles after 1920, but he continually reverted to his Cubist roots, as in *The Three Musicians*

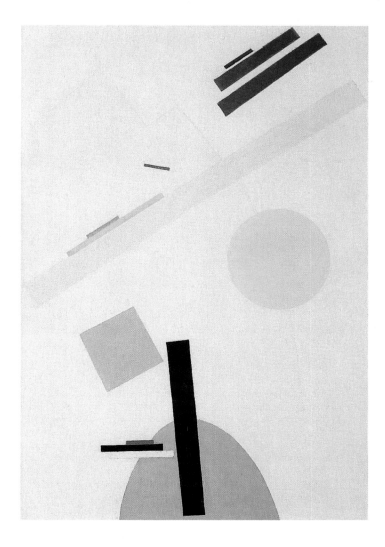

Figure 20.11 KASIMIR MALEVICH. *Suprematist Composition.* 1916–1917. Oil on canvas, 29 × 36¼″ (73.7 × 92.1 cm). The Museum of Modern Art, New York. Photograph © 1997 The Museum of Modern Art. *Malevich's geometric style reflected his belief that abstract images had a spiritual quality comparable to that of religious icons. Thus, if approached in the proper spirit, an abstract form could become a meditation device that could lead the viewer's thoughts beyond the physical realm. For Malevich, the physical realm was no longer of use, and painting was a search for visual metaphors (mainly geometric elements) that could evoke awareness of unconscious and conscious experiences in the individual. His belief was typical of thinking among the German and Russian avant-garde in the early 1900s.*

Figure 20.12 PIET MONDRIAN. *Broadway Boogie Woogie.* 1942–1943. Oil on canvas, 50 × 50". The Museum of Modern Art, New York. *Allied with those artists who identified abstract forms with spiritual values, Mondrian originated "the grid" as the ideal way to approach the canvas, allowing the verticals and horizontals to establish the painting area. In this painting, he pays homage to his new home and a dance craze of the era: The interaction of the colored lines evokes both the street map of Manhattan and the syncopated pattern of the Boogie Woogie. Mondrian's devotion to "the grid," along with his sparse use of color, gave rise to many of the dominant trends in art after World War II: two-dimensional images, geometric shapes, and "all over" paintings without a specific up or down.*

(Figure 20.13). Like the rest of his works, this painting is based on a realistic source, in this case a group of masked musicians playing their instruments. The forms appear flattened, as if they were shapes that had been cut out and then pasted to the pictorial surface—the ideal of flatness so prized by Modern painters.

The most famous work of Picasso's long career also dates from this period: the protest canvas *Guernica*, painted in a modified Cubist style. Picasso named this painting for an unarmed town that had been bombed by the Nazi air force (in the service of Franco) during the Spanish Civil War. Picasso used every element in the work to register his rage against this senseless destruction of human life (see Figure 20.1). The black, white, and gray tones conjure up newspaper images, suggesting the casual way that newspapers report daily disasters. An all-seeing eye looks down on a scene of horror made visible to the world through the modern media—as symbolized by the electric bulb that acts as a retina in the cosmic eye. Images of death

and destruction—the mother cradling a child's body, the stabbed horse, the enraged bull, the fallen man, and the screaming woman—are made even more terrifying by their angular forms. In retrospect, *Guernica* was a watershed painting both topically and stylistically. The blending of Cubism with social protest was new—as was Franco's type of unbridled warfare. *Guernica* forecast even more horrifying events to come.

The American painter Georgia O'Keeffe (1887–1986) refused to follow European painters down the path to pure abstraction. Instead, she pursued a distinctively American type of abstraction, using American subjects drawn from nature, which she pared to their pure form and color; at the same time, she kept representation of the natural world as a primary goal of her art. A native of Wisconsin, she found a spiritual home in the American Southwest—Texas and especially New Mexico—whose sun-drenched, stark landscapes inspired some of her most famous images. Sensitive to light, color, texture, and atmosphere, she registered in

Figure 20.13 PABLO PICASSO. *The Three Musicians.* 1921. Oil on canvas, 6'8" × 6'2". Philadelphia Museum of Art. The A. E. Gallatin Collection. *This Cubist painting captures the energy of a musical performance. Here and there among the flattened shapes can be seen hints of musical instruments being fingered by disembodied hands. Only a little imagination is needed to bring this masked trio to life. The brilliant colors coupled with the broken and resynthesized forms evoke the jagged rhythms the musicians must have been playing.*

her paintings the previously hidden beauties of this desert world, as in *Cow's Skull with Calico Roses* (Figure 20.14). As early as the Renaissance, painters had occasionally used death's heads as memento mori (reminders of death), but no artist before O'Keeffe had thought of presenting a cow's skull as an art subject. The already abstract form of the cow's skull, stripped bare of flesh, became even more abstract as she simplified it and presented it close up with two roses nearby. The result is an image of shocking beauty.

PRIMITIVISM AND FANTASY The Modernists' admiration for primitivism led to **Dada,** the most unusual art movement of the twentieth century. Named for a nonsense word chosen for its ridiculous sound, Dada flourished in Zurich and Paris between 1915 and 1925, chiefly as unruly pranks by disaffected artists who wanted to "hurl gobs of spit in the faces of the bourgeoisie." They staged exhibits in public lavatories, planned meetings in cemeteries, and arranged lectures where the speaker was drowned out by a bell. Slowly it became evident that these outrageous acts conveyed the message that World War I had made all values meaningless. These artists could no longer support the spiritual claims and traditional beliefs of Western humanism. The Dada group embraced anti-art as the only ethical position possible for an artist in the modern era.

The most influential exponent of Dada was the French artist Marcel Duchamp [doo-SHAHN] (1887–1968), who abandoned Cubism in about 1915. His best-known Dada piece is the "definitely incomplete" work called *The Bride Stripped Bare by Her Bachelors, Even,* a mixture of oil, wire, and lead foil on two glass panels made between 1915 and 1923, sometimes called *The Large Glass* (Figure 20.15). Although it is certainly enigmatic, and in the eyes of many viewers it looked like a giant swindle, much is clear about *The Large Glass.* It has an erotic theme, typical of Dada art. Duchamp makes this theme manifest in the sculpture by devoting the upper half to the bride (the amorphous shape floating on the left) and her "apartment" (the stretch of gauze with three holes) and populating the lower "chamber" with the bachelors (the nine objects to the left) and their sex organ (the contraption made of a water mill, grinder, and other bits of metal). Linking the bride with the bachelors are tiny capillaries, or thin tubes, filled with oil—symbolic of fertilization with sperm. Duchamp's point seems to be similar to that of the novelist D. H. Lawrence: Sex in the machine age has become boring and mechanized.

Dada led to **Surrealism,** an art movement that began in the 1920s. Unlike Dada, Surrealism was basically a pictorial art. Inspired by Freud's teaching that the human mind conceals hidden depths, the Surrealists wanted to create a vision of reality that also in-

Figure 20.14 GEORGIA O'KEEFFE. *Cow's Skull with Calico Roses.* 1932. Oil on canvas, 36⁵⁄₁₆ × 24⅛". Art Institute of Chicago. Gift of Georgia O'Keeffe. *The simplified forms—the skull and the rose—link this painting to the period's trend to abstraction, but their placement so as to suggest the image of a "face" devouring a rose implies a connection with another development of this period, Surrealism, a style that delighted in realistic images with double meanings (see Figure 20.16). Whether intentional or not, O'Keeffe's overlapping of stylistic boundaries was typical of the fluid artistic scene in the years between the two world wars.*

cluded the truths harbored in the unconscious. They portrayed dream imagery, fantasies, and hallucinations in a direct fashion that made their paintings more startling than Dada. Among the leading Surrealists were Salvador Dali and Paul Klee.

The Spanish painter Salvador Dali [DAH-lee] (1904–1989) concentrated on subjects that surfaced from his lively imagination and often contained thinly disguised sexual symbols. Probably his most famous work is the poetically named painting *The Persistence of Memory,* which depicts soft, melting watches in a desertlike setting (Figure 20.16). Sexual themes may be read in the limp images of watches—perhaps a reference to sexual impotence. Regardless of its meaning, the painting gives a strange twist to ordinary things, evoking the sense of a half-remembered dream—the goal of Surrealist art. Despite obvious painterly skills, Dali cultivated a controversial, even scandalous, personal image. His escapades earned him the public's ridicule, and the Surrealists even disowned him. From today's vantage point, however, Dali is admired for two reasons: for having created some of Modernism's most fantastic images and for being a link with the Pop artists of the 1960s.

The Swiss painter Paul Klee [KLAY] (1879–1940) may be grouped with the Surrealists, but he was too changeable to be restricted to a single style. He is best known for an innocent approach to art, which was triggered by his fondness for children's uninhibited scrawls. The childlike wonder portrayed in his whimsical works has made him a favorite with collectors and viewers. A professor from 1920 until 1930 at the Bauhaus, Germany's leading art institute between the wars, Klee created poetic images, rich in color and gentle wit, as in *Revolution of the Viaduct* (Figure 20.17). This painting depicts the breakup of a viaduct—a series of arches built to carry a road across a wide valley—when each arch, marching on thin "legs" and footlike bases, goes its own way. More than a cartoon, this whimsical work is Klee's allegorical response to Europe's growing fascist culture—an atypical gesture by this usually apolitical artist. Klee equates the viaduct with the neo-Roman buildings favored by the Nazis as an expression of a homogeneous community ideal. The viaduct's

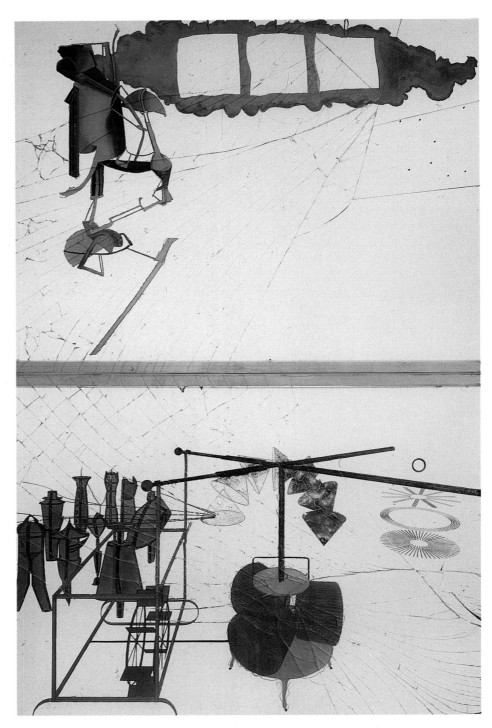

Figure 20.15   MARCEL DUCHAMP. *The Bride Stripped Bare by Her Bachelors, Even* (or, *The Large Glass*). 1915–1923. Oil and lead wire on glass, 9′ 1¼″ × 5′ 9⅛″. Philadelphia Museum of Art. Bequest of Katherine M. Dreier. *Shortly after this legendary assemblage was built, the glass shattered. Duchamp repaired the work, replacing the glass with heavier panes and installing a reinforced frame. But effects of the accident are still apparent. Duchamp claimed to be delighted by these chance additions to his original design. In making this claim, he was the forerunner of the Modernist idea that chance should play a guiding role in art. After World War II, many artists began to incorporate random effects into their works.*

Figure 20.16 SALVADOR DALI. *The Persistence of Memory (Persistance de la mémoire).* 1931. Oil on canvas, 9½ × 13″ (24.1 × 33 cm). The Museum of Modern Art, New York. Given anonymously. Photograph © 1997 The Museum of Modern Art. *Dali liked to paint images that were actually optical illusions. In this painting, the watch depicted on the right is draped over an amorphous shape that, on inspection, appears to be that of a man. Dali's use of such optical effects reflected his often-stated belief that life is irrational.*

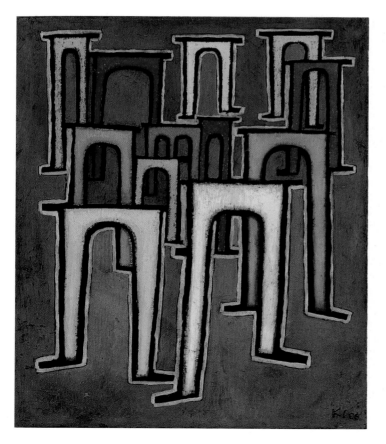

Figure 20.17 PAUL KLEE. *Revolution of the Viaduct.* 1937. Oil on canvas, 25⅝ × 19⅝″. Kunsthalle, Hamburg. *Klee painted this work in the aftermath of the* Degenerate Art *exhibition, which opened in Munich in July 1937. Mounted by the Nazis to showcase what they called subversive art—art that encouraged "political anarchy and cultural anarchy"—the show was a frontal assault on Modernism. Klee, living in Switzerland after having been fired from his German teaching post in 1933, was represented by seventeen works in this show, displayed under the topics "confusion" and "insanity." Klee's* Revolution of the Viaduct *was part of the response of the international Modernist art world to the Nazi challenge.*

breakup into individualized arches forecasts the downfall of Nazism. Klee thus espouses a quiet faith that fascist mass conformity may be undermined by the subversive acts of cultural revolutionaries—such as himself.

The Mexican painter Frida Kahlo [KAH-low] (1907–1954), famed for her unsettling self-portraits, might be classified with the Surrealists, though she is usually linked with the Mexican Muralists, the politically motivated artists who flourished between the two world wars and who painted mural (wall) cycles in public buildings to dramatize their socialist vision and solidarity with Mexico's native peoples. For most of her life, she was involved in a tempestuous mar-

riage to Diego Rivera (1886–1957), a leading Mexican Muralist, but she was much more than the wife of a famous painter. Kahlo was an important artist in her own right, creating works that reflected her physical and spiritual suffering (she had polio at age six and was in a serious accident at eighteen). Today, she is known as an artist who turned private anguish into art with universal resonance.

Kahlo's self-portrait (Figure 20.18) dates from a dark period in her life. Beset by marital and health problems and distraught over the assassination of her friend the Russian Marxist Leon Trotsky, who had been living in exile in Mexico, Kahlo was restored to health by the strict regimen of Dr. Eloesser of San Francisco.

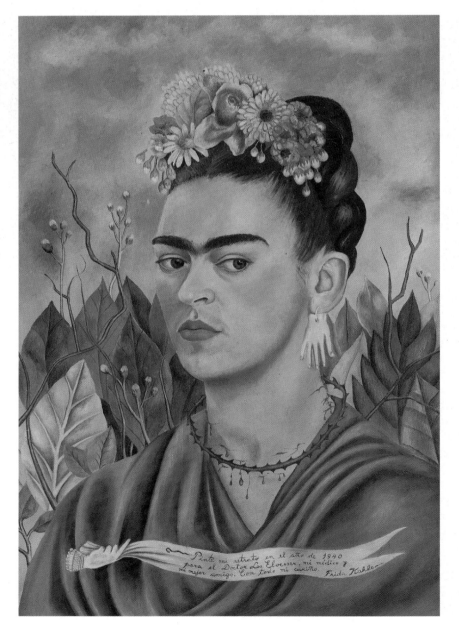

Figure 20.18 FRIDA KAHLO. *Self-Portrait Dedicated to Dr. Eloesser.* 1940. Oil on masonite, 22¼ × 15¾". Private collection, U.S.A. *Whereas Rennaissance artists occasionally portrayed themselves in Christ's image as the Suffering Savior (see Figure 13.4), Kahlo reveals a Modernist sensibility in this likeness, which draws on multicultural sources, including Christianity and her indigenous Mexican heritage. The necklace of thorns, which makes her neck bleed, refers both to Christ's crown of thorns worn during the Crucifixion and to the Aztec prophetic ritual that required self-mortification with maguey thorns. The earring in the form of a hand—a gift from Picasso—symbolizes the hand of fate, and the jungle of oversized leaves evokes an image of nature out of control. The sense of impending doom is relieved only by the colorful flowers in her hair.*

Figure 20.19 HENRI MATISSE. *Large Reclining Nude.* 1935. Oil on canvas, approx.
26 × 36⅕″. Baltimore Museum of Art. The Cone Collection. *Matisse's* Large Reclining
Nude *established the archetypal images—a still life and a model in an interior—that Matisse
painted for the rest of his life. It was also the first expression of his later style, which was
characterized by the human figure's being simply another element in an overall design.*

In gratitude, she dedicated this work to him, as indicated by the flying banner, which reads, in part, "to my doctor and my best friend, with all my love." Despite this upbeat motif, the portrait reflects Kahlo's obsession with death and suffering.

EXPRESSIONISM The chief Expressionist painters in this era were Henri Matisse, a founder of Fauvism before World War I (see Chapter 19), and Max Beckmann, the heir to German Expressionism. In the 1930s Matisse's art was distinguished by its decorative quality, a tendency since his Fauvist days. *Large Reclining Nude* shows his new style, which is characterized by a fresh approach to the human figure: enlarged, simplified,

though clearly recognizable (Figure 20.19). The nude figure is depicted completely flat, without modeling or shading, so that it looks as if it has been cut out and glued to the gridded surface. Matisse has also abandoned the highly saturated colors of Fauvism and replaced them with cooler tones—in this case a cotton-candy pink. Nevertheless, he stayed true to the leading Expressionist principle of distortion, as demonstrated by the nude figure's elongated body and dangling limbs.

Matisse was rebuked for concentrating on pretty subjects while the world slipped into anarchy. No such charge can be made against the German painter Max Beckmann (1884–1950), whose Expressionist paintings register horror at the era's turbulent events. *The Departure*

Figure 20.20   Max Beckmann. *The Departure*. 1932–1935. Oil on canvas, center panel 7′ × 3′9″, side panels 7′ × 3′3″. The Museum of Modern Art, New York. *In* The Departure, *Beckmann's Expressionism is revealed through the treatment of form and color. The flat, angular figures, arranged into awkward positions, and the unusual perspective reinforce the painting's disturbing theme. The dark hues of the side panel, appropriate for the violent images, contrast with the bright colors of the central panel and its message of salvation.*

is typical of his works, being concerned with both personal and spiritual issues (Figure 20.20). The structure of the painting—divided into three panels (a triptych) like a medieval altarpiece—suggests that it has religious meaning. It was the first of nine completed triptychs. Influenced by the mystical teachings of the German thinker Arthur Schopenhauer, East Asian philosophy, and the Jewish cabala (medieval writings), *The Departure* represents a yearning to be free of the horrors of earthly existence. In the side panels, Beckmann depicts images of cruelty, including bound human figures, one of whom is gagged, being subjected to torture—perhaps reflecting his fears of the rise of Nazism. In contrast, the central panel, in which a man, woman, and child are ferried across a lake by a hooded boatman, evokes the theme of deliverance. When the Nazis came to power in 1933, they declared Beckmann a degenerate artist, confiscated his works, and fired him from his academic post. In 1937, he sought refuge in Amsterdam, where he managed to survive World War II.

Figure 20.21   Le Corbusier. Savoye House. 1929–1931. ▶ Poissy, near Paris. *Le Corbusier wanted to make a break with previous styles of architecture and create a new style in tune with the machine age. His design for the Savoye House realizes this ambition completely through its severe geometrical form, its absence of decoration except for architectural details, and its sparkling white walls. When finished, the Savoye House had the streamlined look associated with industrial machinery, an achievement much admired in the 1930s.*

Architecture   In the 1920s and 1930s, architects continued their search for a pure style, free of decoration and totally functional. Their research resembled a mystical quest, stemming from the belief that new architecture could solve social problems by creating a new physical environment—a recurrent theme in European Modernism.

This visionary conception of architecture was best expressed in Germany's Bauhaus, an educational institution whose aim was to bring about social reform through a new visual environment, especially in the design of everyday objects. To that end, the school brought together artists, craftspeople, and architects. During its brief lifetime, which lasted from its founding in 1919 until 1933 when it was closed by the Nazis, the Bauhaus, under Walter Gropius [GROH-pee-uhs] (1883–1969), was the center of abstract art in Germany. The Bauhaus affected later culture in two ways. First, it developed a spartan type of interior decoration characterized by all-white rooms and wooden floors, streamlined furniture, and lighting supplied by banks of windows by day and recessed lamps at night. Second, it introduced the **International style** in architecture, which is sleek, geometrical, and devoid of ornament.

The International style's most distinguished representative in the period between the wars was the Swiss architect Charles-Edouard Jeanneret, better known as Le Corbusier [luh kor-boo-ZYAY] (1887–1965). Le Corbusier's artistic credo was expressed in the dictum "a house is a machine for living." In pursuit of this ideal, he pioneered building methods like prefabricated housing and reinforced concrete as ways to eliminate ordinary walls. His Savoye House became the prototype of private houses for the wealthy after World War II (Figure 20.21). The Savoye House was painted stark white and raised on columns; its ground floor had a curved wall; and its windows were slits. A painter before becoming an architect, Le Corbusier designed architecture that combined Cubism's abstractness (the raised box) with Constructivism's purity (whiteness).

Film   Motion pictures—the movies—were immediately popular when they were introduced early in the twentieth century, and by the mid–1920s they had become the most popular mass entertainment, drawing larger audiences than the theater, vaudeville, and the music halls. The American film director D. W. Griffith (1875–1948) showed in such pioneering works as *The Birth of a Nation* (1915) and *Intolerance* (1916) that it was possible to make movies that were serious, sustained works of art. His technical innovations, such as cross-cutting and the close-up, made more complex film narratives possible, but such attempts to develop the medium were rare. Although other directors quickly appropriated Griffith's techniques, few went beyond them, and the movies remained resolutely lowbrow. The present-day distinction between "movies" (the widest possible audience) and "film" (appealing to more educated, intellectual audiences) had not yet arisen.

One of the era's most inventive directors was the Russian Sergei Eisenstein [IZE-uhn-stine] (1898–1948), who introduced directorial techniques that had an enormous influence on the rise of art films. In *The Battleship Potemkin* (1925), he pioneered the montage technique, which consisted of highly elaborate editing patterns and rhythms. He developed the montage because he believed that the key element in films was the way the scenes were arranged, how they faded out and faded in, and how they looked in juxtaposition to one another. By focusing on the material of the film itself instead of highlighting the plot or the characters' psychology, Eisenstein showed his allegiance to the artistic aspect of moviemaking.

The United States (which eventually meant Hollywood, California) had dominated the motion picture industry since World War I, and the industry underwent important changes during the interwar years. Sound movies became technically feasible in the late 1920s, and in the early 1930s three-color cinematography processes were developed. Both these technical developments became basic to the movies throughout the world, but other experiments, such as wide-screen and three-dimensional photography, were less successful. Another important development in this period was the descent on Hollywood of many German filmmakers in flight from the Nazis. In the Hollywood of the 1930s, these exiles helped to create some of the outstanding achievements in world cinema.

A sign of the excellence of Hollywood movies in these years is Orson Welles's *Citizen Kane* (1941), often called America's best film. An American, Welles (1915–1985) had learned from the German exiles and borrowed their Expressionist methods, such as theatrical lighting and multiple narrative voices. Welles's own commanding presence in the lead role also contributed to making this an unforgettable movie. But one of the hallmarks of the movie—its dark look, which underscores the brooding theme of unbridled lust for power—was in actuality a money-saving device to disguise the absence of studio sets. Is *Citizen Kane* a "film" or a "movie"? It is a measure of Welles's success that it is triumphantly both: Its frequent showing both on television and in theaters attests to its popularity, yet its discussion and analysis in film journals and books points to its high prominence as a film.

Music: Atonality, Neoclassicism, and an American Idiom

During the 1920s and 1930s, Western music was fragmented into two rival camps as a result of developments that had begun in the period before World War I (see Chapter 19). On one side was the Austro-German school headed by Arnold Schoenberg, who had introduced atonality before 1914 and in the 1920s pioneered serial music. On the other side was the French school led by Igor Stravinsky, who had experimented with primitive rhythms and harsh dissonances in the early 1900s but after World War I adopted a stern Neoclassical style.

Having abandoned tonality in 1909, Schoenberg in the 1920s introduced **serial music,** a method of composing with a **twelve-tone scale**—twelve tones that are related not to a tonal center in a major or minor key but only to each other. Lacking harmonious structure, serial music sounded dissonant and random and tended to create anxiety in listeners. As a result, serial music appealed to cult rather than mass audiences. Lack of a huge responsive public did not halt Schoenberg's pursuit of atonality. His serial system culminated in *Variations for Orchestra* (1928), a composition that uses the Classical form of theme with variations. In 1933 he emigrated to America, where his devotion to atonality mellowed. Some of Schoenberg's later works mix twelve-tone writing with tonality.

Stravinsky, in exile from the Soviet Union after 1917, went to live in Paris, where he became the dominant figure of **Neoclassicism** in music, borrowing features from seventeenth- and eighteenth-century music (Figure 20.22). In his Neoclassical works, he abandoned many of the techniques that had become common to music since the Baroque period, such as Romantic emotionalism and programmatic composition as well as Impressionism's use of dense orchestral sounds. Austere and cool, his Neoclassical compositions used simple instrumental combinations and sounded harmonious. Stravinsky's works from this period made him the outstanding composer of the twentieth century.

Stravinsky originated Neoclassicism in 1919 with the ballet *Pulcinella* and brought the style to a close in 1951 with the opera *The Rake's Progress.* Between these two major works is one of his most admired compositions, the *Symphony of Psalms,* dating from 1930. *Pulcinella* and *The Rake's Progress* owe much to the music and comic operas of the Classical composers Pergolesi and Mozart, respectively, and the *Symphony of Psalms* follows a Baroque model in its small orchestra and musical structure. Despite borrowing forms and ideas, Stravinsky made them his own, introducing occasional dissonances and continuing to experiment with complex rhythmic patterns.

Figure 20.22 PABLO PICASSO. *Stravinsky.* 1920. Pencil on gray paper, 24⅜ × 19⅛". Musée Picasso, Paris. *Picasso's pencil sketch of Stravinsky is a perceptive character study. Long before Stravinsky became almost unapproachable, Picasso portrayed him as an aloof, self-absorbed young man. Stravinsky's cold demeanor is obvious in the tense posture, the harsh stare, and the clasped hands and crossed legs. Picasso's sketch also hints at Stravinsky's genius by exaggerating the size of his hands, perhaps to emphasize their role in the composer's creative life.*

American music, meanwhile, was discovering its own idiom. Charles Ives (1874–1954) focused on American melodies, including folk songs, hymns, marches, patriotic songs, ragtime tunes, and music of his beloved New England. Working without models, Ives experimented with tonality and rhythm in ways similar to those of the European avant-garde. Typical of his work is the *Concord Sonata* for piano (1909–1915). Another American composer, Aaron Copland (1900–1990), had achieved some success by imitating European styles, but in the 1930s he began to develop a distinctive American style. His ballet scores *Billy the Kid* (1938), *Rodeo* (1942), and *Appalachian Spring* (1944), commissioned by choreographers Agnes de Mille and Martha Graham, drew on hymns, ballads, folk tunes, and popular songs of the period. His delightful melodies, brilliant sound, jazzy experimentation, and upbeat rhythms ensured the popularity of these pieces.

A major American composer who cared less about developing a purely American idiom and more about exploring music's frontiers was George Antheil [an-TILE] (1900–1959). Living in Europe from 1922 to 1933, Antheil became part of the intellectual avant-garde who were intrigued by the machine-oriented culture of the Age of the Masses. In worshiping the machine, these artists and musicians followed in the steps of the Futurists, the Italian group who had raised "speed" to an artistic principle before World War I (see Figure 19.7). As part of the 1920s European scene, Antheil was led to incorporate industrial sounds—the music of the masses—into his compositions. Hence, his *Ballet mécanique (Mechanical Ballet)* (1924; revised 1952) included scoring for unusual "instruments" (electric bells, small wood propeller, large wood propeller, metal propeller, siren, and sixteen player pianos) as well as more traditional instruments (piano and three xylophones). Antheil claimed this as his goal in composing this iconoclastic work: "It is the rhythm of machinery, presented as beautifully as an artist knows how. . . . It is the life, the manufacturing, the industry of today."

During this period, jazz began to reach larger audiences, in part because of the development of the radio and the phonograph. Many jazz greats created their reputations in these years. The fame of the finest jazz composer, Duke Ellington (born Edward Kennedy Ellington, 1899–1974), dated from 1927 at Harlem's Cotton Club. Ellington's songs balanced superb orchestration with improvisation and ranged from popular melodies, such as "Sophisticated Lady" (1932), to major suites, such as *Such Sweet Thunder* (1957), based on Shakespeare. Jazz's premiere female vocalist, Billie Holiday (1915–1959), whose bittersweet style was marked by innovative phrasing, also appeared then.

Two jazz performers whose careers extended well beyond this period are Louis Armstrong (1901–1971) and Ella Fitzgerald (1918–1996). Armstrong, better known as "Satchmo," became a goodwill ambassador for the United States with his loud and relaxed New Orleans–style trumpet playing. Ella Fitzgerald, a vocalist noted for her bell-like voice and elegant phrasing, became the peerless interpreter of jazz standards as well as pop tunes. In the next period, jazz fragmented into a host of styles and was a vital ingredient in the explosive birth of rock and roll, the popular music form originating in the 1950s that has since dominated popular music.

The Legacy of the Age of the Masses and High Modernism

The Age of the Masses has transformed material civilization in the West in both good and bad ways. It has given us the most destructive wars of history, the greatest economic depression since the fourteenth century, the most absolute forms of government since the late Roman Empire, the first modern attempt to eliminate an entire people, and a weapon capable of destroying the planet. At the same time, it has brought a better standard of living to most people in the West and given millions of Westerners their first taste of democracy.

This age has also had a contradictory impact on cultural developments. On the one hand, it saw the growth of a worldwide mass culture, led by American ingenuity, which began to dominate public and private life for most people. On the other hand, it inspired a revolt by Modernist artists, writers, and musicians to create works free of mass culture's influence. Their creations were experimental, perplexing, and often committed to what they defined as spiritual values. A few Modernists refused to become mass culture's adversaries, and these moderating voices pointed toward a healthier relationship between mass culture and the elitist tradition after World War II.

Besides the polarization of mass and high culture, this period left other cultural legacies. Films became accepted as a serious art form, and they remain the greatest legacy of mass culture to the twentieth century. It was also during this period that America emerged as a significant cultural force in the West, partly because of the tide of intellectuals flowing from Europe, partly because of America's growing political, economic, and military power, and partly because of excellent native schools of writers, musicians, and artists. And finally, a questioning mood became the normative way of looking at the world, replacing the certainty of previous centuries.

The Modernists had pioneered a questioning spirit in about 1900, and in this period the revolution in physics seemed to reinforce it. Einstein's conclusion that space and time are interchangeable was echoed by artists, writers, and musicians who focused on form to define content in their work. And Heisenberg's uncertainty principle seemed to reverberate everywhere—from Wittgenstein's toying with language to the highly personal narrative voices that dominated the novel to the constantly shrinking set of basic beliefs that characterized the period's religious thought and, ultimately, to the widespread belief that Western civilization had lost its course.

KEY CULTURAL TERMS

mass culture
stream-of-consciousness
epic theater
logical positivism
existentialism
Suprematism
Constructivism
Socialist Realism

de Stijl
Dada
Surrealism
International style
serial music
twelve-tone scale
Neoclassicism

SUGGESTIONS FOR FURTHER READING

PRIMARY SOURCES

BRECHT, B. *The Threepenny Opera.* English version by D. Vesey and English lyrics by E. Bentley. New York: Limited Editions Club, 1982. An excellent adaptation of Brecht's biting drama about the underworld in Victorian England; Bentley's lyrics capture the slangy flavor of the German play first staged in 1928.

COCTEAU, J. *The Infernal Machine and Other Plays.* Norfolk, Conn.: New Directions, 1964. Cocteau fuses Classicism with experimental methods in his Modernist plays; he updates the Oedipus legend, for example, by introducing Freudian ideas and using film clips to present flashbacks.

ELIOT, T. S. *Collected Poems, 1909–1962.* New York: Harcourt, Brace & World, 1963. Eliot, a pillar of Modernism, portrayed his times as exhausted and abandoned by God.

FAULKNER, W. *The Sound and the Fury.* New York: Modern Library, 1946. The most admired novel from the Yoknapatawpha series, Faulkner's monumental study of post–Civil War Mississippi society.

HEIDEGGER, M. *Being and Time.* Translated by J. Macquarrie and E. Robinson. New York: Harper, 1962. First published in 1927, this work helped launch the existentialist movement by portraying the universe as a meaningless place and human existence as a never-ending quest for authenticity.

HEMINGWAY, E. *The Sun Also Rises.* New York: Scribner's, 1970. Hemingway's semiautobiographical first novel, set in France and Spain in 1925.

HUGHES, L. *Selected Poems of Langston Hughes.* London: Pluto, 1986. Poetry by one of the twentieth century's outstanding writers.

JOYCE, J. *Ulysses.* New York: Penguin, 1986. This classic of Modernism uses a tapestry of narrative styles to portray a day in the lives of three middle-class citizens of Dublin.

LAWRENCE, D. H. *Lady Chatterley's Lover.* New York: Modern Library, 1983. A controversial work that poses sex as a panacea for the ills of contemporary industrialized life.

O'NEILL, E. *Three Plays: Desire Under the Elms, Strange Interlude, Mourning Becomes Electra.* New York: Vintage, 1961. O'Neill's trilogy of plays based on Aeschylus's *Oresteia* and involving a contemporary New England family.

ORWELL, G. *Animal Farm; Burmese Days; A Clergyman's Daughter; Coming Up for Air; Keep the Aspidistra Flying; Nineteen Eighty-four.* New York: Octopus/Heinemann, 1980. This volume contains Orwell's most significant writings, most of which convey the author's hatred of tyranny and his skepticism about the future of humanity.

SARTRE, J.-P. *Being and Nothingness: An Essay in Phenomenological Ontology.* Translated and with an introduction by H. E. Barnes. Abridged. New York: Citadel Press, 1956. Sartre sets forth his existentialist philosophy, focusing on such key ideas as individual freedom and personal responsibility.

WALKER, A., ed. *I Love Myself When I Am Laughing . . . And Then Again When I Am Looking Mean and Impressive: A Zora Neale Hurston Reader.* Introduction by M. H. Washington. Old Westbury, N.Y.: The Feminist Press, 1979. A judicious collection of Hurston's writings, including excerpts from novels (*Their Eyes Were Watching God,* 1936) and autobiography (*Dust Tracks on a Road,* 1942); essays ("How It Feels to Be Colored Me," 1928, "Crazy for Democracy," 1945); and short stories ("The Gilded Six-bits," 1933); with an admiring "afterword" by the celebrated writer Alice Walker.

WITTGENSTEIN, L. *Tractatus Logico-philosophicus.* Translated by D. F. Pears and B. F. McGuiness, with an introduction by B. Russell. London: Routledge and Kegan Paul, 1974. An excellent English-language version of the treatise that led to logical positivism in philosophy.

WOOLF, V. *To the Lighthouse.* London: Hogarth Press, 1974. A typical Woolf novel in its stream-of-consciousness technique and its exquisitely detailed observations of contemporary thinking.

YEATS, W. B. *The Collected Poems of W. B. Yeats.* Edited by R. J. Finneran. New York: Collier Books, 1989. One of Modernism's leading voices, Yeats wrote poetry devoted to such themes as Celtic myth, the tragic violence of Irish history, and the mystical nature of human existence.

SUGGESTIONS FOR LISTENING

ANTHEIL, GEORGE (1900–1959). An American composer who worked in both experimental and traditional forms, Antheil lived in Europe in the 1920s and 1930s. His best-known experimental work is *Ballet mécanique (Mechanical Ballet)* (1924; revised 1952), scored for airplane propellers and other industrial noises. Recognizing that his mechanical aesthetic was at a dead end with this work, Antheil spent the rest of his career searching for a personal style: from Neoclassicism (1925–1927), as in the lyrical *Piano Concerto* (1926); to Americana experiments (1927–1942), as in the opera *Transatlantic* (1927–1928), a political farce about an American presidential election; to neoromanticism, as in Symphony No. 4 (1942) and Symphony No. 5 (1947–1948), which blend melodic and rhythmic experiments with Classical forms.

COPLAND, AARON (1900–1990). Copland's most popular works incorporate folk melodies and pay homage to the American way of life. Copland used cowboy songs in the ballet scores *Billy the Kid* (1938) and *Rodeo* (1942); he incorporated variations on the Shaker hymn "Simple Gifts" in *Appalachian Spring* (1944), originally a ballet score that was later rearranged as a suite for symphony orchestra. His faith in the future of democracy is expressed most fully in the short, often-performed work *Fanfare for the Common Man.*

ELLINGTON, EDWARD KENNEDY ("DUKE") (1899–1974). Ellington's jazz style blended careful orchestration with ample opportunity for improvisation. Many of his songs have become standards in the popular music repertory, such as *Creole Love Call* (1928), *Mood Indigo* (1934), *Don't Get Around Much Anymore* (1940), and *Sophisticated Lady* (1932). Less well known are his serious compositions, such as *Such Sweet Thunder* (1957) and *In the Beginning God* (1965), a religious work.

IVES, CHARLES (1874–1954). America's first great composer, Ives experimented with atonality, clashing rhythms, and dissonant harmony long before they became a standard part of twentieth-century music. He frequently drew on American themes, as in the *Concord Sonata* for piano (1909–1915) and the orchestral *Three Places in New England* (1903–1914, first performed in 1931), works that evoked the landscape of his native region. A good example of one of his atonal works is *The Unanswered Question* (1908), a small work for trumpet, four flutes, and strings.

SCHOENBERG, ARNOLD (1874–1951). During this period, Schoenberg, the leader of the school of atonality, originated serialism as a method of composing, as may be heard in *Variations for Orchestra* (1928), the unfinished opera *Moses and Aaron* (1932), and *Violin Concerto* (1936).

STRAVINSKY, IGOR (1882–1971). Schoenberg's rival Stravinsky became the leader of Neoclassicism in music with the ballet *Pulcinella* (1919) and continued this musical style in such works as the *Symphony of Psalms* (1930), the opera-oratorio *Oedipus Rex (Oedipus the King)* (1927), the *Symphony in C* (1940), and the opera *The Rake's Progress* (1951).

AFRICA

AMERICAS

HISTORY

North Africa Site of major WWII campaign. *Egypt.* British protectorate, then independent. *Libya.* Italian colony. *Morocco.* French, Spanish, and Moroccan zones.

Northeast Africa *Ethiopia.* Haile Selassie's reign began (1928). Conquered by Italy; liberated by Britain.

West Africa *French Equatorial Africa.* Modern Chad made French. *French West Africa.* French colony (modern Benin, Burkina Faso, Ivory Coast, Guinea, Senegal, Mauritania, Mali, and Niger). *Liberia.* Prosperity from rubber exports. *Nigeria.* Fulani Empire of Sokoto fell to British.

Central Africa *Congo Free State.* Annexed to Belgium.

East Africa *Tanganyika (with Zanzibar, modern Tanzania).* German, then British rule.

South Africa *Union of South Africa.* British and Dutch colonies united in self-governing state under British (1910).

Caribbean *Cuba.* Became independent with end of U.S. occupation (1902). Corrupt, brutal regimes followed; frequent U.S. intervention. *Jamaica.* Racial tension; weak economy.

Latin America *Mexico.* Revolution (1910–21). Natural resources, including oil, nationalized; church property appropriated by state; great estates broken up; education made secular. *Argentina.* Economic depression; military dominated politics. *Brazil.* Fascist under Getúlio Vargas. *Colombia.* Lost Panama after civil war. *Peru.* Prosperity under dictator Augusto Leguía (to 1930). Campaign for Indian rights (from 1920s).

Native North America Most Indians lived in poverty on 200 federal reservations. By end of WWII, uranium, oil, and other mineral resources found under many reservations in West.

ART & MUSIC

East Africa *Tanganyika.* Carved wooden canes and swagger sticks; figure heads on musical instruments and lids or stoppers on medicinal containers; ritual masks; and tomb figures.

South Africa *Union of South Africa.* Ndebele: beadwork (cloaks and long trains); mural art. Zulu: carved wooden ear plugs.

West Africa *Nigeria.* Carved wooden verandah and interior posts; palace doors; ritual vessels; shrine figures; headdresses and masks. Iron staffs with decorated ends. Decorated leather bags.
Olowe of Ise. Decorated column from the Palace of Ikere, Nigeria. 1910–1914. Wood and pigment. Art Institute of Chicago.

Caribbean *Cuba.* Wilfredo Lam, inspired by Picasso, Surrealism, and Afro-Cuban culture. *Haiti.* Primitivist school of art begun.

Latin America *Mexico.* Nationalist art and Symbolist-style painting (to 1920). Muralists including Diego Rivera, David Alfaro Siqueiros, and José Clemente Orozco produced public murals with political messages (1920–50). *Argentina.* Tango dance and music born in brothels and dance halls. *Brazil.* Cubist and Expressionist art with Brazilian themes (1920s). Nationalist art (1930s). *Peru.* Christ of the Andes sculpture, on Chile-Argentine border, commemorating peaceful settlement of border dispute.

Native North America Edward Curtis published 20 volumes of photographs of Native American peoples (1899–1924).

ARCHITECTURE

Latin America *Mexico.* Retail stores in major cities built in Art Nouveau style. Introduction of new materials (cast iron and reinforced concrete). *Brazil.* International style (to 1930s). Functional Modernism, marked by the sensuous curve (after 1936). *Peru.* Lima's Gran Hotel Bolívar (1924), the country's central meeting place.

Diego Rivera. The Arsenal, or Distribution of Arms. 1928. Mural, south wall, Courtyard of the Fiestas, Ministry of Public Education, Mexico City.

RELIGION, PHILOSOPHY, LITERATURE

South Africa Poet Nicolaas Petrus van Wyk Louw, perhaps the greatest figure in Afrikaans literature.

West Africa *Nigeria.* Daniel O. Fagunwa, Yoruba chief, first original writer in Yoruba, and popular novelist. *Senegal.* Poet and president of Senegal (1960–80) Léopold Senghor helped develop concept of Négritude, or blackness.

Caribbean *Jamaica.* Rise of Rastafarianism, a religious movement with political goals, especially returning black people to Africa (1904). *Martinique.* Poet Aimé Césaire helped develop concept of Négritude, or blackness.

Latin America *Mexico. Revista Moderna*, a journal read by artists and intellectuals. José Clemente Orozco's *Autobiography* (1945). *Nicaragua.* Poet Rubén Darío founded Spanish American Modernist literary movement. *Argentina.* Author Jorge Luis Borges, a founder of magic realism. *Chile.* Avant-garde poet and novelist Vicente Huidobro. Gabriela Mistral, first Latin American and first woman poet to be awarded Nobel Prize for literature (1945). *Peru.* César Vallejo, author of *Human Poems* (1939).

Native North America *Black Elk Speaks*, biography of Oglala Sioux holy man by John Neihardt (1932).

China

Ch'ing Dynasty, ended 1911. Last emperor abdicates (1911). *Republic of China, 1912–49.* Fragmented into regions controlled by rival warlords. Sun Yat-sen, the father of modern China, led the Kuomintang, or Nationalist Party, based on nationalism, democracy, and socialism. China mistreated at Versailles Conference; anti-Western feelings grew. Chiang Kai-shek set up Nationalist Government at Nanjing (1928). Japan invaded Manchuria (1931). Communists, led by Mao Zedong, made "Long March" into north China. War with Japan (1937–45).

India

British Crown (Raj), ended 1947. Amritsar riots against Britain. Indians allowed to sit in legislative councils (1919); Gandhi's nonviolent campaign for independence begun (1920). Britain separated India from Burma and Aden, and ruled India through 11 provinces, each with a governor. Vital to Allies in World War II.

Japan

Meiji Restoration, ended 1912. Emerged as a major Far East power, after defeating Russia (1905) and annexing Korea (1910). *Taishō period, 1912–26.* Forced trade concessions from China (1915). Less militant (1924–31). *Shōwa period, began 1926.* Turbulent reign of Emperor Hirohito. Resurgence of militarism and expansionism (1930s). Invasion of Manchuria (1931); war with China (1937–45); pact with Axis powers Germany and Italy (1940); war with U.S. and its allies (1941–45).

Republic of China. Kuomintang party pushed for official style blending traditional and Western art, but traditional painting, free of Western influence, was most popular.

Gao Jianfu. Flying in the Rain. Ca. 1920–1930. Art Museum of the Chinese Museum, Hong Kong (73.831).7

Fragmented art world; Western styles challenged traditional styles.

Yoshida Hiroshai. Sailboat, Morning. 1926. Polychrome woodblock print on paper, 20⅛ × 14⅛". Museum of Art, Atami, Shizuoka prefecture, Japan.

Meiji and Taishō periods. Quest for authentic Japanese painting (to 1921). Sculptors inspired by Western artists, mainly Rodin. Demise of *ukiyo-e* prints; new woodblock styles emerged. Hostile climate for innovation (after 1921). *Shōwa period.* Rival factions (1930s). Arts regulated during WWII.

Republic of China. Chung Shan Hospital, Shanghai, built in Chinese Revival style (1937).

British Crown. Sir Edwin L. Luytens, British architect, laid out the capital New Delhi and designed Viceroy House, which blended traditional Indian with European Classical forms.

Edwin L. Luytens. Viceroy House, East Front. 1931. Buff and rhubarb-red sandstone. New Delhi.

Taishō and Shōwa periods. Strong direct and indirect influence from the West, including Frank Lloyd Wright's Imperial Hotel (1923), Tokyo, and the Diet Building (1936), based on Western forms, designed by a committee of Japanese architects.

Ch'ing Dynasty. Lui E's novel, *The Travels of Lao Ts'an*, about the Boxer Rebellion. *Republic of China.* Writers and thinkers influenced by Western literature and thought, especially Marxism. Lu Hsün, a short story writer and translator of Western works. The author and philologist Lin Yu-t'ang wrote works of nonfiction (for example, *My Country and My People* [1936]) and novels and founded first satirical journal in China. Peking University established.

British Crown. British and Western styles of writing and learning flourished. Two trends in Hindi fiction: social realism and psychological profiles. Rabindranath Tagore awarded the Nobel Prize for literature (1913).

Meiji Restoration. Writing reflected Western and native themes. Mori Ōgai, a founder of modern Japanese literature. Shimazaki Tōson's *Broken Commandment*, a work of social realism (1906). *Taishō period.* Sōseki Natsume's novel *Kokoro* (1914), dealing with the crisis of Modernism. Akutagawa Ryūnosuke's "Rashōmon" short story (1915). *Shirakaba (White Birch)*, a journal that introduced Western styles. *Shōwa period.* Jun'ichirō Tanizaki's *Some Prefer Nettles* (1929), a novel of erotic despair.

21 THE AGE OF ANXIETY AND BEYOND
1945–

Fear of nuclear war had a pervasive effect on attitudes and events after 1945 and led to an enormous buildup of weapons by the United States and the Soviet Union. This arms buildup in turn contributed to uncontrolled military spending at the expense of domestic programs. For some, anxiety about nuclear war produced a sense of absurdity and a mood of despair. Against the backdrop of these realities, the cultural style known as Late Modernism captured the anguish experienced by many artists, writers, and intellectuals.

FROM A EUROPEAN TO A WORLD CIVILIZATION

The end of World War II brought the cold war, an era of international tensions and conflicting ideologies. World relations were governed by a bipolar balance of power between the United States and the Union of Soviet Socialist Republics (USSR). The American bloc included Western Europe, the British Commonwealth, and their former enemies, Japan, West Germany, and Italy. The Soviet bloc embraced virtually all of Eastern Europe and, after 1949, when the Communists took power, China.

The cold war escalated for two main reasons. First, the superpowers extended their confrontations to the Third World, rushing in to influence events as the West's colonial empires fell and were replaced by struggling independent states. Second, the development of ballistic missiles capable of hurtling nuclear weapons across intercontinental distances raised the possibility of sudden strikes and mass destruction without warning.

◀ **Detail** ANDY WARHOL. *Mao.* 1973. Acrylic and silkscreen on canvas, 14′6⅞″ × 11′4½″. Art Institute of Chicago. Mr. and Mrs. Frank G. Logan Purchase Prize and Wilson L. Mead Funds.

By the 1970s, other dramatic changes were intensifying the postwar period's growing mood of uncertainty, including an international population explosion that raised the specter of food shortages and famines, new technological breakthroughs that seemed to entail economic and employment crises, and environmental calamities that threatened the earth's ecosystem. These issues were being recognized as world problems and not simply Western dilemmas and thus contributed to the rise of a global culture.

The Era of the Superpowers, 1945–1970

Between 1945 and 1970, the West followed two patterns. For the American bloc, democracy was the rule, social welfare was slowly expanded, and the economies were booming. For the Soviet bloc, collectivist regimes prevailed, social welfare was comprehensive, and the economies either stagnated or grew slowly. The two systems emerged as seemingly inevitable consequences of World War II.

Postwar Recovery and the New World Order   The chief Allied powers—the United States, Great Britain, and the Soviet Union—began to plan for the postwar era before World War II ended. They agreed to occupy Germany and Japan, giving those nations representative forms of government and drastically curbing their military systems. They joined with forty-eight other countries in 1945 to found the United Nations, a peacekeeping and human rights organization dealing with international disputes (Figure 21.1). They also prepared for worldwide economic recovery by establishing a transnational monetary fund to help nations devastated by the war; however, the Soviet Union refused to participate in these economic arrangements.

When peace came in 1945, the Allies split Germany into four occupied zones. In 1949 Britain, France, and the United States united their zones into the Federal Republic of Germany (West Germany), and the USSR set up its zone as the German Democratic Republic (East Germany). By 1969 West Germany, led by moderates devoted to capitalism, had become Europe's chief industrial power, and East Germany, under a collectivist regime, lagged far behind.

In Japan, the American victors imposed a democratic constitution that kept the emperor as a figurehead; introduced a parliamentary system; gave the vote to women, workers, and farmers; and virtually eliminated the military. Between 1950 and 1973, under this renovated system, Japan's domestic product grew more than 10 percent a year on average, surpassing that of any other industrialized nation.

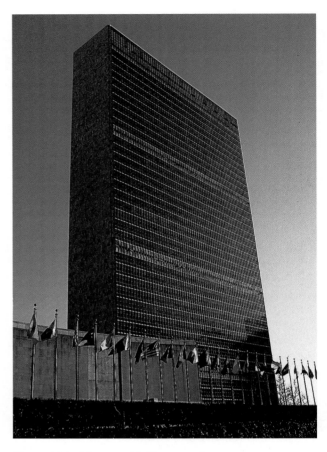

Figure 21.1   Wallace K. Harrison International Committee of Architects. United Nations Headquarters. Aerial view. 1949–1951. New York. *The decision to locate the United Nations headquarters in New York made that city the unofficial capital of the world, and the choice of a "glass box" skyscraper for the United Nations Secretariat helped to ensure that the International style would be the reigning style of architecture in the postwar period. Although this type of structure had been used in Europe before the war, the U.N. Secretariat was the first instance of it in New York.*

By the early 1950s, both Great Britain and France were enjoying moderate economic growth, although each was beset by continuing labor unrest. Left-wing governments in both countries nationalized major industries and founded national health-care systems, although conservatives periodically returned some businesses to private hands.

France and West Germany recognized that in the age of the superpowers the era of the small state was over and that it was necessary to join economic forces to gain economic stability. In 1957 they initiated a free-trade zone that also included Belgium, the Netherlands, Luxembourg, and Italy. Called the European Economic Community, or the Common Market, this organization became the driving force in Europe's prosperity over the next decade.

A large reason for the formation of the Common Market was that the USSR threatened to dominate Europe. After World War II, Soviet troops occupied neighboring countries in Eastern Europe, ostensibly to provide a military shield for the USSR. By 1948 the Soviets had converted these countries into Communist satellites, their industrial and agricultural systems tied to the Soviet economy. Thus, the USSR loomed more as a menace to than an ally of Western Europe.

The architect of the Soviet Union's rise to superpower status was Joseph Stalin, who was determined to keep the collectivist system free of the taint of capitalism and the Western idea of freedom. He demanded extreme sacrifices from Soviet citizenry to bring their war-shattered economy up to the level of the advanced industrialized countries. After Stalin's death in 1953, his successors were more moderate, but they continued the policies of censorship and repression.

The United States took up the torch of free-world leadership in 1945, claiming to have earned this status because of crucial contributions to Allied victory. It further believed that the war had been a moral crusade for human freedom, and thus it should protect the rights of people everywhere. On the basis of these beliefs, the United States justified an activist foreign policy, and between 1945 and 1970 it was probably the wealthiest and most powerful country that ever existed.

American domestic life was marked by a radical shift in mood from the 1950s to the 1960s. The 1950s was a decade of complacency and blandness. The 1960s, in contrast, was a turbulent decade around the world, of which the American experience was only a part. In the 1960s, millions of people protested against the Vietnam War, racism, and old ways of thinking. Hippies cultivated a bohemian lifestyle and contributed to the emergence of a counterculture that re-jected mainstream values and traditions.

Racial prejudice was the most pressing domestic problem in the United States because it was so embedded in the nation's history. In 1954 the Supreme Court declared segregation in public schools unconstitutional. The next year, Rosa Parks, a black Alabaman, refused to move to the back of a bus as required by state law and was jailed. The social protest that was sparked by the jailing of Parks marked a watershed in American race relations. Rejecting a historically passive role, black citizens began to use the tactics of civil disobedience in their crusade to win equal rights. Nevertheless, the civil rights movement did not begin on a national scale until the 1960s. After some stalling, the federal government instigated changes in education, living conditions, and voting rights. In 1968 the civil rights struggle temporarily lost direction and momentum when its leader, Martin Luther King, Jr., was assassi-nated, but new leaders arose in America's black community who have continued the struggle against racism.

The Cold War Hope for peace and cooperation among the victorious powers disappeared after 1945 as the USSR and the United States defined their respective spheres of influence. By 1949 an "iron curtain" had descended in Europe, dividing the West from the East (Map 21.1). In 1949 fear of a Soviet invasion led the Western democracies to form a military alliance called the North Atlantic Treaty Organization (NATO) with the United States as its leader. The Eastern bloc countered with the Warsaw Pact (1955), an alliance led by the Soviet Union. A race to stockpile weapons ensued, dividing the industrial world into armed camps. By 1955 a balance of terror seemed to have been reached because both the United States and the USSR possessed the atomic and hydrogen bombs. Nevertheless, the race for more weapons continued.

The East-West contest for power spread to other regions of the world. In 1949 Chinese Communists defeated the ruling Kuomintang party and commenced to build a socialist system under the leadership of Mao Zedong [MAU (D)ZE-DUHNG] (1949–1976) (Figure 21.2). The struggle between the superpowers shifted to the Far East, where a limited war emerged between North and South Korea, which had been divided after World War II into two independent states. In 1950 Soviet-dominated North Korea invaded South Korea to reunite the two states. Alarmed at this expansion of communism, the United States, under the auspices of the United Nations, sent troops in support of the South Koreans. Later in the year, China dispatched its soldiers to aid the North Koreans. After months of fighting, a stalemate resulted along the old borders, which were finally guaranteed in 1953 by an armistice. The Korean War ended in a draw, but it established one of the guiding principles of the nuclear age—that wars would not necessarily escalate into nuclear confrontations; they could be fought with conventional weapons rather than with nuclear arms.

Cold war tensions were heightened—and symbolized—by the Berlin Wall, which was built in 1961 by East Germany to prevent its citizens from going to West Berlin. Conceived as a way to save communism, this armed border only intensified divisions between Western and Eastern Europe. But the severest strain on the superpower system was the Vietnam War, which erupted in the early 1960s. Originating as a civil war, it became a cold war contest when the United States joined South Vietnam to repel the Communist troops invading from the north. For American soldiers, the war was doubly difficult to wage because it was fought

Map 21.1   EUROPE IN 1955

in unfamiliar jungle terrain against a guerrilla army and because it became so violently unpopular at home. Protests culminated in confrontations at universities in Ohio and Mississippi, leaving six students killed in clashes with public authorities (Figure 21.3).

The Vietnam War was a turning point in world affairs. The United States withdrew from South Vietnam in 1973, thereby allowing its conquest by North Vietnam in 1975. Certain conclusions were quickly drawn from this setback to American might. First, the country's superpower status was cast into doubt, and its leaders became reluctant to exercise military power. Second, the war illustrated a new principle of foreign relations—namely, that even superpowers could not defeat small states by means of conventional warfare. Taken together, these post–Vietnam era principles suggested that the international influence of the United States was in decline and opened the door to new forms of global cooperation in the 1970s.

Emergence of the Third World   After 1945 Europe's overseas territories began to struggle for freedom and self-government, and by 1964 most of the empires had been replaced by independent countries. In 1946 the United States let go of a former colony, the Philippines. In 1947 Great Britain agreed to divide India into a Hindu-dominated state—India—and a separate Muslim state—Pakistan. The Dutch gave up the East Indies, which in 1950 became Indonesia. France tried to retain Indochina but in 1954 was driven out, and the former colony was divided into North and South Vietnam.

In the Middle East, Arab states were freed by France and Britain, who had dominated them since 1919. After 1945 the region was in continual turmoil because its oil was needed by the industrialized states, its geopolitical position in the eastern Mediterranean attracted the superpowers, and Islamic fundamentalism led to militant Arab nationalism. But the founding of Israel as

Figure 21.2   ANDY WARHOL. *Mao.* 1973. Acrylic and silk-screen on canvas, 14′6⅞″ × 11′4½″. Art Institute of Chicago. Mr. and Mrs. Frank G. Logan Purchase Prize and Wilson L. Mead Funds. *A feature of totalitarian societies in this century has been the personality cult, the practice of giving a political leader heroic dimensions. In Communist China, the cult of Mao Zedong established Mao as a secular god. American Pop artist Andy Warhol turned Mao's official photograph into a pop culture icon, suggesting that there is no difference between propaganda in a totalitarian state and media stardom in a free society.*

a Jewish state in 1948, following World War II and the Holocaust, contributed the most to an unstable Middle East. Israel's founding resulted in the expulsion of more than a half million Arabs from Palestine, and the fate of these refugees has contributed to constant conflict in the region. Further instability has been caused by the decline of Iran and the rise of Iraq as an independent state.

In Africa, nearly all colonies became free, although through often painful and costly transitions. In the 1960s, France concluded a bloody war in Algeria, relinquishing it and most of its other colonies in West Africa. The British withdrew gradually from East Africa, leaving behind bureaucracies that could serve the new states. In southern Africa, Rhodesia became Zimbabwe in 1980, achieving independence from Great Britain and gaining black majority rule.

Toward a New Global Order, 1970 and Beyond

The year 1970 marked a turning point in history, not only for Western civilization but also for the world. The balance of political power began to shift from the bipolar, superpower model to a multipolar system that included Japan, China, and Western Europe. This global shift began when the superpowers moved toward détente, a French term meaning a waning of hostility. By the early 1970s, détente had produced several arms-limitation treaties between the USSR and the United States, creating a favorable climate for a reappraisal of cold war attitudes and a reduction of other global ideological battles. China, a previously closed

Figure 21.3   The National Guard at Kent State, Ohio. 1970. *This photograph bears a striking resemblance to Goya's* Execution of the Third of May, 1808 *(see Figure 17.19), a painting that protested the killing of Spanish civilians by French soldiers. In the tense days after the Kent State deaths, this photograph served a similar function in American society as many people began to think of the dead students as martyrs to the anti–Vietnam War cause.*

country, began to open slowly to interaction with the United States and other Western countries. In addition, the industrialized nations began to experience energy shortages that revealed their dependence on the oil-producing countries, which had formerly exerted little influence on world events.

National Issues and International Realignment   In the early 1970s, the standard of living declined for most citizens in Western Europe and the United States when the Organization of Petroleum Exporting Countries (OPEC), a cartel of the oil-rich states of the Middle East, raised prices. As a result, most Western nations went into a recession that resulted in rising unemployment and inflation. In the Soviet Union, it was becoming clear that the regimented system could no longer produce both arms and consumer goods.

The 1970s were a time of political drift in the United States in the wake of the Watergate scandal and President Nixon's resignation; in contrast, the 1980s brought dramatic changes both nationally and internationally. The government adopted laissez-faire economic policies and experienced an economic turnaround. The nation paid for this prosperity, however, with increased spending, a huge national debt, and a shift in foreign trade from creditor to debtor status. The gap between rich and poor also widened, leading to increasing polarization in American society.

Two events, both setbacks for détente, clouded the international scene: a Soviet invasion of Afghanistan in 1979 in support of local Communist leaders and the founding in 1980 of Solidarity in Poland, a labor movement that pushed for economic reform. The Polish government, supported by the USSR, ruthlessly suppressed the movement. Cold war sentiments revived, ongoing disarmament talks between the superpowers broke down, and an intensified arms race seemed imminent.

The international tension dissipated in 1985 with the appearance of Mikhail Gorbachev [GOR-bah-chof]

Figure 21.4   Fall of the Berlin Wall. 1989. *Given the Soviet Union's previous use of force in Eastern Europe, no one had predicted that the collapse of the Communist states would be so quick and bloodless. The most symbolic event of this extraordinary period has been the dismantling of the wall that separated East Berlin from West Berlin.*

(1985–1991) as the new moderate leader of the Soviet Union, whose economy was now in shambles. He introduced a new era of détente and helped guide the cold war to a peaceful close. His overtures to the United States resulted in limited arms reductions and opened communication between the two superpowers.

At home, Gorbachev made changes in the state bureaucracy and the Communist party that were designed to raise the standard of living. His plans—restructuring the economy's production and distribution system (*perestroika*) and allowing public criticism of the Communist party *(glasnost)*—dramatically altered the course of history in the USSR, Eastern Europe, and the world. Gorbachev's domestic reforms contributed to the breakup of the centralized structure of the USSR, as some member states declared their independence and others gained more local control. From the old Soviet system, following more than seventy years of communism, a desperately weakened Russia reemerged, shorn of its vast empire yet still managing to retain some ethnic republics through a commonwealth arrangement.

After 1989 Gorbachev's policies toward the satellite states led to the dissolution of the Communist bloc in Eastern Europe, symbolized by the actual destruction of the Berlin Wall (Figure 21.4). Newly independent, these former Communist states, including Russia itself, are struggling to maintain their social welfare programs and worker protection legislation and at the same time to move toward democratic government and a market economy. Within Russia, which is increasingly subject to ethnic and regional crises, Boris Yeltsin (1991–1999) tried to steer a course in uncharted political waters between the nationalists and Communists who want to restore their country's former imperial and economic systems and the reformers who want to expand the marketplace economy and ensure political freedom. With Vladimir Putin's (b. 1952) election as president, Russia's future remains uncertain.

Starting in about 1970, however, the threat of nuclear war began to subside and international tensions relaxed. In the arts, a more upbeat style, referred to as Post-Modernism, began to emerge. Characterized by a cautious optimism and an interest in reinterpreting past styles, Post-Modernism reflects a search for more positive responses to the world. Events in the late 1980s further altered and influenced the shape of the modern world. Political and economic changes in the former Soviet Union and Eastern Europe, a broadening of international influence beyond the traditional Western powers, and pressing worldwide environmental and economic issues have all contributed to the emergence of a global perspective. The growth of a global culture is reflected in Post-Modernism, which is

democratic and embraces diversity. The trend for the future seems to be toward a world civilization that recognizes common human concerns and honors the creative impulse in all people (Timeline 21.1), but the revival of militant nationalism and ethnic violence after 1990 threatens the realization of this goal.

The Post–Cold War World   In the 1990s, the multipolar system of international politics, which had been expected since the 1970s, did not emerge, leaving the United States as the world's lone superpower. The other countries who were to have been part of a multipolar arrangement have serious problems to deal with. Russia, beset by lawlessness and corruption, is too weakened to remain a superpower. Japan has yet to recover from the downturn its financial markets experienced in the early 1990s. The European Union, despite successfully launching the Euro as an alternative currency to the American dollar, has been unable to keep the peace at home in the Balkans, much less anywhere else in the world (Figure 21.5). China, though undergoing rapid economic growth in the private sector, has its hands full with democratic groups calling for a more open society.

As other nations have fallen by the wayside, the United States basks in its role as the lone superpower. It has achieved this position because its military arsenal and system of international alliances, dating from the cold war period, are still in place and, in part, because its tireless consumers have driven the global economic boom since the early 1980s. Contributing further to America's role as global leader is its unwillingness to work in full harmony with the United Nations. Believing the U.N. to be dominated by Third World interests, the United States often prefers to act alone or through coalitions of its own choosing or to work with established regional alliances.

An ironic consequence of the end of the cold war is the resurgence of late-nineteenth-century trends, especially nationalism and ethnic violence, which had been suppressed during the era of the superpowers. Nationalistic and ethnic interests today are often intertwined and occasionally involve religious issues. Worldwide flashpoints include, in Europe, the breakaway states of the former Soviet Union and Russia, the succession countries of the former Yugoslavia, and Turkey; in Asia, India and Pakistan, South and North Korea, China and Taiwan; in the Middle East, Iraq and its neighbors, Israel, the Palestinians, and the nearby Arab states; in Africa, Rwanda, the Sudan, the Republic of Congo, Nigeria, Sierra Leone, Algeria, and Somalia; and in Latin America, Mexico, Colombia, and Peru.

Throughout the 1990s, economic globalization has further developed because of the spread of free-market

Timeline 21.1   CULTURAL STYLES, 1945–PRESENT

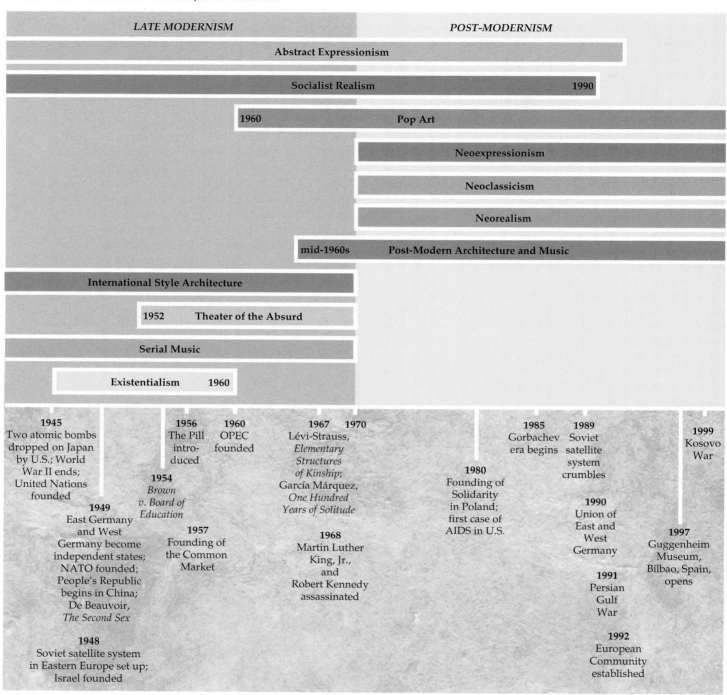

LATE MODERNISM   *POST-MODERNISM*

Abstract Expressionism

Socialist Realism   1990

1960   Pop Art

Neoexpressionism

Neoclassicism

Neorealism

mid-1960s   Post-Modern Architecture and Music

International Style Architecture

1952   Theater of the Absurd

Serial Music

Existentialism   1960

1945
Two atomic bombs
dropped on Japan
by U.S.; World
War II ends;
United Nations
founded

1949
East Germany
and West
Germany become
independent states;
NATO founded;
People's Republic
begins in China;
De Beauvoir,
The Second Sex

1948
Soviet satellite system
in Eastern Europe set up;
Israel founded

1956
The Pill
intro-
duced

1954
*Brown
v. Board of
Education*

1957
Founding of
the Common
Market

1960
OPEC
founded

1967   1970
Lévi-Strauss,
*Elementary
Structures
of Kinship*;
García Márquez,
*One Hundred
Years of Solitude*

1968
Martin Luther
King, Jr.,
and
Robert Kennedy
assassinated

1980
Founding of
Solidarity
in Poland;
first case of
AIDS in U.S.

1985
Gorbachev
era begins

1989
Soviet
satellite
system
crumbles

1990
Union of
East and
West
Germany

1991
Persian
Gulf
War

1992
European
Community
established

1999
Kosovo
War

1997
Guggenheim
Museum,
Bilbao, Spain,
opens

systems, but volatility in financial markets has led to social and political unrest and brought into question some of the assumptions of laissez-faire capitalism. In the decade's early years, the Pacific Rim countries, except for Japan, continued to enjoy an economic boom, but by 1998, the euphoria had disappeared (Figure 21.6). Paralleling globalization has been the rise of regional economic alliances, such as the formation of the European Union into a free trade zone and the creation of the North Atlantic Free Trade Association (NAFTA) among Canada, the United States, and Mexico. Other countries are exploring similar regional economic organizations. Fueling these trends are fast-paced technological innovations, such as the Internet

Figure 21.5 The Carinski Bridge in Mostar, Bosnia and Herzegovina. Reopened 1996. *The reopening of the Carinski Bridge in 1996 symbolized the hope for peace and reconciliation between Croatians and Muslims in Mostar. However, memories of ancient feuds linger among the various ethnic groups of the Balkan region. In 1999, to the south in Kosovo, the Yugoslav Serbs attempted to drive out the Kosovo Muslims until a coalition of United Nations and NATO forces halted this campaign. The Yugoslav troops were forced to withdraw and a joint U.N. and NATO peacekeeping team now occupies the territory, which remains unstable.*

and electronic commerce, which are revolutionizing the way the world conducts its business.

The emergence of the United States as the only superpower has enhanced its presence in Post-Modernism, which had a strong American component to begin with. Thus, the progress of Post-Modernism around the world leads to a paradoxical situation: American culture, especially popular culture, values, and technology, is eagerly adopted abroad, but with this adoption come voices denouncing America's cultural imperialism as well as its military strength.

THE END OF MODERNISM AND THE BIRTH OF POST-MODERNISM

In 1947 the British-American author W. H. Auden published a poem entitled "The Age of Anxiety," which expressed the melancholy spirit of his times. He described a period caught between a frantic quest for certainty and a recognition of the futility of that search. Responding to the unparalleled violence of World War II, Auden's anxious age was haunted by death and destruction, fueled by memories of the Holocaust in Europe and the two atomic bombs dropped on Japan. While relations between the Soviet Union and the United States deteriorated and World War III seemed inevitable, melancholy could and often did turn into despair. In this gloomy setting, Modernism entered its final phase.

Late Modernism, flourishing from 1945 until 1970, expressed the vision of a group of artists, writers, and thinkers who seemed almost overwhelmed by this despairing age. Existentialism—with its advice to forget the past and the future and to live passionately for the

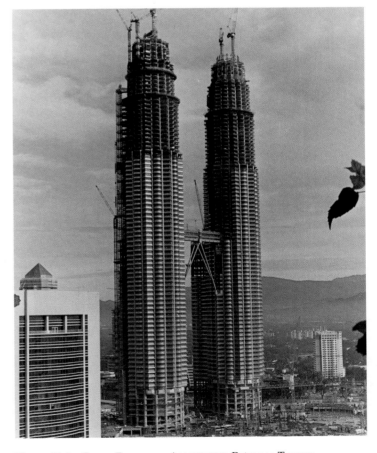

Figure 21.6 CESAR PELLI AND ASSOCIATES. Petronas Towers. Completed in 1996. 1483′. Kuala Lumpur, Malaysia. *The Petronas Towers are a fitting symbol of Post-Modernism. Designed by an American architectural firm, employing Islamic geometric principles and Western technology, the buildings will serve as the gateway to Kuala Lumpur's City Centre. The twin towers, claimed as the world's tallest, will stand as an image of Malaysia's rapidly expanding economic importance.*

Figure 21.7 NAM JUNE PAIK. *My Faust-Channel 5-Nationalism.* 1989–1991. Twenty-five Quasar 10-inch televisions, three Sony laser disc players, neogothic wood frame with base, 104 × 50 × 32". Private Collection, Seoul. *Designed by the Korean American artist Nam June Paik, this artwork is a playful commentary on war as a form of national religion. Housed in a neogothic frame, inspired by medieval altarpieces, the art is filled with military objects, such as bombs, jackboots, and helmets, as well as television screens and laser disc players. By covering the top and sides of the frame with flags from many of the world's nations, he suggests that all countries make sacred cults of their military establishments.*

present—appeared to be the only philosophy that made sense. Paradoxically, diminished faith in humanity kept the Modernists at their creative tasks and prevented them from falling into hopeless silence.

Like earlier Modernists, Late Modernists thought of themselves as an elite. They were committed to saving what they considered worth saving in Western culture while destroying all in the past that was irrelevant, ignoring mass culture, and borrowing insights from depth psychology and non-Western sources. Armed with a sense of mission, they stripped their works down to the most basic components, abandoning strict rationality and making randomness the rule. They threw subject matter out the window and pressed experimentation to the extreme, reducing painting to lines and colors, sculpture to textures and shapes, and music to random collections of sound. Like earlier Modernists, they then invested these works with spiritual or metaphysical meaning by claiming that abstract paintings and sculptures were meditation devices and that music that mixed noise and harmony echoed the natural world.

In the early 1970s, Late Modernism was challenged by a new movement that became known as **Post-Modernism.** Having grown to maturity after World War II and feeling that Late Modernism's anxiety was outdated, the Post-Modernists turned from existentialism to **structuralism,** a type of thinking that affirmed the universality of the human mind in all places and times. Unlike the Late Modernists, this new generation embraced mass culture and preferred a more playful approach to creativity (Figure 21.7). Because the United States is a microcosm of global society, its artists and scholars have played a key role in establishing the culture of Post-Modernism.

The Post-Modernists' cultural vision causes them to look in two directions at the same time—forward to an emerging global civilization that is many-voiced and democratic, and backward to the roots of the Western tradition. This vision embraces the works of women, minority group members, and representatives of the Third World at the same time that it reexamines both Classical and pre-Classical civilizations. Only time will tell if Post-Modernism is merely a period of fragmentation before regrouping or the beginning of a cultural revolution.

Philosophical, Political, and Social Thought

Existentialism, born between the two world wars, dominated Western thought from 1945 until the 1960s, when it was eclipsed by structuralism and other intellectual movements, notably feminism and black consciousness. Unlike existentialism, with its focus on freedom and choice, structuralism asserts that human freedom is limited. Structuralists maintain that innate mental patterns cause human beings to interact with nature and each other in consistent and recurring ways, regardless of the historical period or the social setting. It follows that civilization (as represented in governments, social relations, and language, for example) and ideas (such as freedom, health, and beauty) arise from deep-seated modes of thought instead of from the environment or progressive enlightenment. Structuralists reason that not only is all knowledge conditioned by the mind but also civilization itself reflects the mind's inborn nature. By defining and analyzing the substrata of culture, they attempt to garner some understanding of the elemental nature of the human mind.

The two leading structuralists are Noam Chomsky [CHAHM-skee] (b. 1928), an American linguist, and Claude Lévi-Strauss [lay-vee-STRAUS] (b. 1908), a French anthropologist. Chomsky's *Syntactic Structures* (1957) prompted a revolution in linguistics, the scientific study of languages. He argues that below the surface form of sentences (that is, the grammar) lies a deeper linguistic structure that is intuitively grasped by the mind and is common to all languages. Similarly, Lévi-Strauss made war on empirical thinking with his 1967 study, *The Elementary Structures of Kinship*. He claimed that beneath the varied relations among clans in different societies exist certain kinship archetypes with such common themes as the incest taboo and marriage patterns. Chomsky and Lévi-Strauss imply the existence of common universal structures running through all minds and all societies that can be expressed as a general code. This conclusion gives a strong psychoanalytic cast to structuralist thought, because it leads researchers to focus on the subconscious mind.

Following Chomsky and Lévi-Strauss, other scholars have studied subsurface patterns in such disciplines as history, child development, and literature. No thinker has yet unified the various structuralisms into a coherent theory of mind. It is an intriguing coincidence, however, that the trend of thought that points to a universally shared mind-set parallels the rise of a global culture under Post-Modernism.

The revival of feminist thought has been another significant development in philosophy since World War II. The French thinker and novelist Simone de Beauvoir [duh boh-VWAHR] (1908–1986) sparked this revival, following the dry spell that set in after many Western women won the right to vote in the 1920s. In her 1949 treatise *The Second Sex*, de Beauvoir argued that women are treated as "the Other," an anthropological term meaning that men accord women a different and lower existence than themselves. Drawing on personal anecdote and existentialist thought, she advised women who want independence to avoid marriage and, like men, create their own immortality (Figure 21.8).

De Beauvoir's message was heard around the world, but it was especially in the United States that women heeded her. America's best-known feminist in the 1960s was Betty Friedan (b. 1921). She awakened the dormant women's movement with *The Feminine Mystique* (1963), arguing that society conspired to idealize women and thus discourage them from competing with men. In 1966 she founded the National Organization for Women (NOW), a pressure group that has attracted millions of members. According to its founding manifesto, NOW supports "equal partnership with men" and is committed to "integrating women into the power, privileges, and responsibilities of the public arena." Friedan did not always agree with the more radical feminists of the 1970s, and in 1982 she showed that she was still a moderate in *The Second Stage,* a book that advocated men's liberation as a condition for women's equality.

Like feminism, the black consciousness movement has grown and flourished since 1945 (Figure 21.9). The earliest significant theorist of black identity was Frantz Fanon [fah-NOHN] (1925–1961), a psychiatrist from French Martinique who practiced medicine among the Arabs of Algeria. An eyewitness to French colonialism and oppression, Fanon became convinced that the West had doomed itself by abandoning its own moral ideals. By the late 1950s, Fanon had begun to justify black revolution against white society on the basis of existential choice and Marxism. In 1961 in *The Wretched of the Earth,* he issued an angry call to arms, urging nonwhites to build a separate culture. Some black leaders in America welcomed Fanon's message in the 1960s, as did Third World thinkers who turned their backs on Western ideologies in the 1970s.

America in the 1960s produced a radical black voice in Malcolm X (1925–1965), the pseudonym of Malcolm Little. A fiery personality, he made sharp ideological shifts, moving from advocacy of black separatism to a call for an interracial civil war and, after his conversion to orthodox Islam, to support of racial harmony. Assassinated allegedly by former colleagues, he remains today a prophetic voice for many African Americans who want a clearer sense of their history, culture, and accomplishments in a predominantly white society.

In the turbulent 1960s, Malcolm X's voice was overpowered by that of Martin Luther King, Jr. (1929–1968), a visionary who dreamed of a world free from racial discord. Probably the most famous black figure in Western history, King was an advocate of civil disobedience—based on Christian teachings, the writings of the New England philosopher and abolitionist

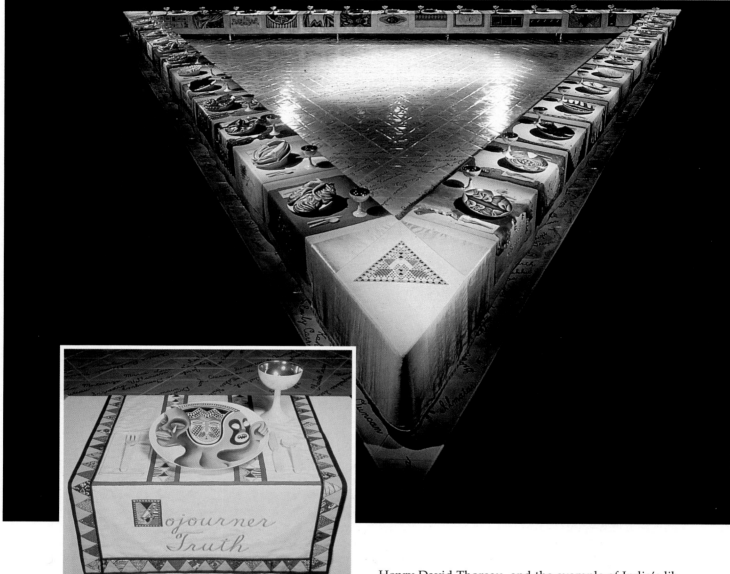

Figure 21.8 JUDY CHICAGO. *The Dinner Party.* 1979. Installation view. Multimedia, china painting on porcelain, needlework, 48 × 48 × 48' installed. © Judy Chicago. *The rebirth of feminism led some women artists to adopt explicit feminist themes in their art, as in the works of Judy Chicago (born Gerowitz, 1939). Chicago abandoned Abstract Expressionism in the late 1960s, at about the same time she changed her name, thereafter devoting her art to the feminist cause. The Dinner Party, her most ambitious project to date, is dedicated to leading historical and mythological women of Western civilization. In this work, she arranges a triangular-shaped dining table with thirty-nine places decorated in individual styles, honoring such famous women as Sappho and Sojourner Truth (inset; see also Chapter 18).*

Henry David Thoreau, and the example of India's liberator, Gandhi. An inspirational leader and a superb orator, King galvanized blacks, along with many whites, into the Southern Christian Leadership Conference, organized by ministers to end segregation in American life, notably in schools and universities. Though King was assassinated before his dream was fully realized, his vision of an integrated society lives on, and he left a cadre of able leaders.

Science and Technology

Although important theories were developed in biology and physics during the postwar period, the spectacular advances in applied science affected people more immediately. Ordinary life and manners have been irretrievably altered by an unending stream of inventions and discoveries, notably the birth control pill, communication satellites, and the computer. The invention of a safe birth control pill in 1956 triggered a sexual revolution that slowed down only in the 1980s with the advent of AIDS (acquired immune deficiency syndrome) and a dramatic rise in the incidence of other sexually transmissible diseases. The introduction of communication satellites, a by-product of the United States space program of the 1960s, has made a global

Figure 21.9 ROMARE BEARDEN. *The Prevalence of Ritual: Baptism.* 1964. Collage on board, 9 × 12". The Hirshhorn Museum and Sculpture Garden, Smithsonian Institution, Washington, D.C. © Romare Bearden Foundation/ licensed by VAGA, New York, NY. *Romare Bearden (1914–1988), the United States' most honored post–World War II black painter, blended Modernism with elements from his cultural heritage. In the 1960s, he developed a style reminiscent of Cubism that used collage and flattened, angular figures and that drew on his personal experiences, as in this collage of a baptismal scene—an allusion to the important role of churches in the black American tradition. Bearden places the person to be baptized in the center of the composition, a large hand over his head. The references to African masks suggest that this ritual unites an ancient way of life with the present.*

culture possible. Multinational corporations are linked by these satellites, and individuals all over the world watch televised events at the same time thanks to satellite communication.

Perhaps most important, the computer and the Internet have revolutionized life on every level, making previously unimaginable quantities of data immediately accessible, simplifying complex tasks, and transforming the traditional habits of personal and public life across the globe. Consumers, through e-commerce, purchase goods and services directly and, through e-trade, buy and sell stocks and bonds without brokers. Scholars, through IT (information technology), access journals, books, libraries, and databases to keep up with areas of expertise. Businesses, from websites, place orders, restock inventories, and sell to customers. Individuals can e-mail friends and family, keep up with current events, and pursue interests and hobbies. These developments have contributed to "cocooning," a mode of living in which people center their lives in their homes, surrounded by electronic devices, and venture out into the public domain for amusement and social contact less and less.

Breakthroughs in medicine also changed the nature of human life for millions. In the 1950s, polio was eradicated through vaccines developed by the American physicians Jonas Salk (1914–1995) and Albert Sabin (1906–1993). Innovative surgical methods, radiation treatment, and chemotherapy drastically reduced cancer mortality. Organ transplants and the use of artificial organs have prolonged life for many otherwise without hope. However, these practices have embroiled the medical profession in ethical controversy, including charges that only a few can afford these procedures and that they drain the health-care system. Likewise, new methods in human reproduction, such as test-tube fertilization and surrogate parenting, although helping a few, have raised moral dilemmas and led to court cases.

Advances in the biological sciences are revealing basic information about the origin of life. Since 1953, when Francis Crick (b. 1916) and James Watson (b. 1928) reported their discovery of the structure of deoxyribonucleic acid (DNA), the chemical substance ultimately responsible for determining individual hereditary characteristics, new findings have been made with regularity. In genetics, rival teams of researchers are moving rapidly to decode the human genome, composed of perhaps three billion units of DNA, arranged into twenty-three pairs of chromosomes. In biogenetics, scientists have cloned animal and plant products and organs, as well as their most spectacular achievement, whole sheep and mice. As in medicine, these breakthroughs are raising serious ethical questions, such as: What use will be made of the genome map? Should attempts be made to clone humans? Are genetically modified fruits and vegetables safe for human consumption? Despite attempts to resolve these questions within the scientific community, their final resolution will probably be determined within the legal system.

The Literature of Late Modernism: Fiction, Poetry, and Drama

France's leading postwar thinkers, Jean-Paul Sartre and Albert Camus, were among Late Modernism's outstanding voices. In a trio of novels called *Roads to Freedom,* published between 1945 and 1950, Sartre interwove Marxist collectivist beliefs with existentialism's focus on the individual. Although accepting the existentialist view that life is cruel and must be confronted, he portrayed his characters as cooperating for a new and better world, presumably one in which they would be able to live in harmony. Sartre also wrote a series of plays on current issues that are infrequently performed today. His most successful drama, and perhaps his most enduring literary work, was *No Exit* (1944), which shows how three characters turn their lives into living hells because of their unfortunate choices in desperate situations.

Like Sartre, the Algerian-born writer and thinker Albert Camus [kah-MOO] (1913–1960) wrote novels, plays, and philosophical works that mirrored his political thinking and personal values. His finest literary work was *The Fall* (1956), a novel published at the height of his reputation as one of the West's main moral voices. In 1957 he was awarded the Nobel Prize in literature, an honor that Sartre declined in 1964. Written as a single rambling monologue, *The Fall* portrays an anguished, self-doubting central character who accuses himself of moral fraud. When admirers recognized Camus himself in the narrator's voice, they were shocked because they were unwilling to accept this harsh self-judgment. Whether this self-mocking confession heralded Camus's move toward God—as some critics have maintained—can never be known, for an auto accident prematurely ended his life.

Existentialism's rejection of bourgeois values and its affirmation of identity through action appealed to black writers in the United States. As outsiders in a white-dominated society, these writers identified with the French thinkers' call to rebellion. The first black author to adopt an existential perspective was Richard Wright (1908–1960), whose outlook was shaped by his birth on a Mississippi plantation. His works, such as his novel *Native Son* (1940) and his autobiography, *Black Boy* (1945), were filled with too much rage at racism to be accepted by white literary critics in the 1940s. His later years were spent in Paris, where he further developed his interest in existentialism.

The most successful black American author of this time was James Baldwin (1924–1987), who began to write during a self-imposed exile in France (1948–1957), where he had fled from racial discrimination. In a series of novels and essays, he explored the consequences of growing up black in a predominantly white world. In his first novel, *Go Tell It on the Mountain* (1953), he drew on his Christian beliefs to mute his anger against the injustices that he believed blacks daily endured. This novel, which held out hope for an integrated society, established the literary theme that he pursued until Martin Luther King, Jr.'s, assassination caused his vision to darken. In later novels, such as *No Name in the Street* (1972), he regretfully accepted violence as the only path to racial justice for black Americans.

In postwar fiction, existentialism sometimes took second place to a realistic literary style that concentrated on exposing society's failings. Three major writers who blended existential despair with Realism's moral outrage were Norman Mailer (b. 1923), Doris Lessing (b. 1919), and Alexander Solzhenitsyn [sol-zhuh-NEET-suhn] (b. 1918). Their goal was to uncover the hypocrisy of their age.

Mailer, an American, drew on his experience as a soldier in World War II to capture the horror of modern war in his first and finest novel, *The Naked and the Dead* (1948). This work portrays a handful of enlisted men, a microcosm of America, as victims of their leaders' bad choices. He describes their officers as pursuing fantasies of glory, inspired by a notion that the world is godless and without lasting values. In the late 1960s, Mailer began to write journalism, eventually achieving so much fame that today his essays overshadow his novels. His best journalism is the book-length essay *The Armies of the Night* (1968), an account of the October 1967 peace march on Washington, D.C., in which he participated. This book won Mailer a Pulitzer Prize.

Doris Lessing, a white eastern African writer, used Realism to show the contradictions at work in her homeland, Rhodesia (modern Zimbabwe), between blacks and whites, British and Dutch, British and colonials, capitalists and Marxists, and, always, women and men. In the *Children of Violence* series (1950–1969), consisting of five novels, she presents the story of the rise of black freedom fighters and the diminishing of white control in what was then a British colony. This disintegrating world serves as a backdrop to the existential struggle for self-knowledge and independence by the main character, Martha Quest. In her best-known novel, *The Golden Notebook* (1962), Lessing addresses, among other issues, the socialization process that stifles women's creativity. Her concerns, however, are not just female identity but also the moral and intellectual fragmentation and confusion she sees in the modern world. In recent years, she has turned to science fiction to address these issues.

The Russian Solzhenitsyn writes realistic novels that praise the Russian people while damning Marxism, which he regards as a "Western heresy," opposed to Orthodox Christianity. His short novel *One Day in the Life of Ivan Denisovich* (1962) reflects his own rage at being unjustly imprisoned under Stalin. This novel, published during Khrushchev's de-Stalinization drive, offers an indelible image of the tedium, harassment, and cruelty of life in a forced labor camp. And yet Ivan Denisovich remains a Soviet John Doe, dedicated to Marxism, his work, and his comrades (Figure 21.10).

When Solzhenitsyn's later books, which were banned in the Soviet Union until its fading years, revealed his hatred for communism, he was deported, in 1974. Choosing exile in the United States, he settled in a Vermont hideaway from which he expressed moral disgust with the West for its atheistic materialism and softness toward the Soviet system. His values —Christian fundamentalism and Slavophilism, or advocacy of Russia's cultural supremacy—resemble those of Russia's great nineteenth-century preexistentialist novelist Dostoevsky. Believing that communism was finally dead, Solzhenitsyn returned to his homeland in 1994, but he has not become a moral force in post-Soviet Russia.

Many Late Modernist poets used a private language to such a degree that their verses were often unintelligible to ordinary people and thus did not have a wide audience. A few who used more conventional verse styles, however, earned a large readership. Of this latter group, the Welsh poet Dylan Thomas (1914–1953) was the most famous and remains so today. Thomas's poems mirror the obscurity favored by the Modernist critics, but what makes his works so memorable is their glorious sound. With their strong emotional content, jaunty rhythms, and melodious words, they are perfect to read aloud.

Better known than Thomas's poems, though, is his verse play *Under Milk Wood* (1954), arguably the best-loved poetic work of Late Modernism. Unlike the poems, this verse play is direct and imbued with simple emotions. Originally a play for radio, it presents a typical day in a Welsh village, a world he knew well, having grown up in such a place. His portrait of the colorful speech and intertwined lives of the eccentric villagers has moved millions of listeners, evoking for them bittersweet memories of their own youth.

A Late Modernist poet who was able to be experimental and yet win a large audience was the American writer Allen Ginsberg (1926–1997), the most significant poet produced by the Beat Generation of the 1950s. Like Dylan Thomas, he had an ear for colloquial speech, and his ability to construct new forms to convey iconoclastic views was unequaled by any other poet of his time. His most famous poem is "Howl" (1956), a work of homage to rebel youth and illicit drugs and sex. Overcoming censorship, this poem of Ginsberg's opposed capitalist, heterosexual, bourgeois society and became the anthem of the Beat Generation.

During Late Modernism, the most radical changes in literature took place in drama. Sharing existentialism's bleak vision and determined to find new ways to express that outlook, a group of dramatists called the **"theater of the absurd"** emerged. The absurdists shifted the focus of their plays away from the study of the characters' psychology to stress poetic language and abandoned realistic plots to concentrate on outrageous situations. A typical absurdist play mixed tragedy with comedy, as if the playwright thought that the pain of existence could be tolerated only if blended with humor.

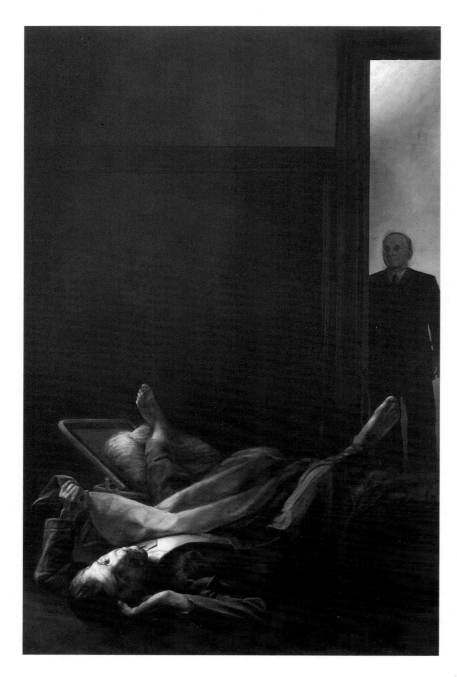

Figure 21.10 VITALY KOMAR AND ALEKSANDER MELAMID. *Stroke (About March 3, 1953).* 1982–1983. Oil on canvas, 6′ × 3′11″. Collection of Evander D. Schley. Courtesy Ronald Feldman Fine Arts, New York. Photo credit: D. James Dee. *The two Russian émigré painters Komar and Melamid—who work as a team—have devoted their artistic efforts to trying to understand the Russian Revolution and the reign of Stalin. In* Stroke, *they depict the lonely death of Stalin and the discovery of his body by a member of his inner circle. The artists subtly criticize both Stalin and the Soviet system in the way the official stares unmoved at the dead tyrant. Komar and Melamid show their Post-Modernist tendencies in their use of elements from earlier styles of art, such as the theatrical lighting and unusual perspective typical of Caravaggio.*

Samuel Beckett (1906–1989), an Irish writer who lived in Paris, was the best-known dramatist of absurdist theater. His *Waiting for Godot* (1952) is a play in which almost nothing "happens" in the conventional sense of that word. Combining elements of tragedy and farce, *Waiting for Godot* broke new ground with its repetitive structure (the second act is almost a replica of the first); its lack of scenery (the stage is bare except for a single tree); and its meager action (the characters engage in futile exchanges based on British music hall routines). What plot there is also reinforces the idea of futility, as the characters wait for the mysterious Godot, who never appears.

In later years, Beckett's works explored the dramatic possibilities of silence, as in the one-act drama *Not I* (1973). In this play, a voice—seen only as a mouth illuminated in a spotlight—tries to, but cannot, stop talking. Beckett's plays portrayed human consciousness as a curse; yet, at the same time, his works affirmed the human spirit's survival in the face of despair.

The Literature of Post-Modernism

Post-Modernist literature is notable for the inclusion of new literary voices in Latin America and in central and eastern Europe, marking a shift away from the dominance of the Paris–New York cultural axis and the rise of a more global culture. For the first time, Latin American authors attracted international acclaim. Most of these writers were distinguished by left-wing political opinions and devotion to a literary style called **"magic realism,"** which mixed realistic and supernatural elements. The ground had been prepared for the magic realists by the Argentinian author Jorge Luis Borges [BOR-hays] (1899–1986), whose brief, enigmatic stories stressed fantasy and linguistic experimentation.

The outstanding representative of the magic realist school is Gabriel García Márquez [gahr-SEE-uh MAHR-kays] (b. 1928) of Colombia, who received the 1982 Nobel Prize for literature—the first Latin American novelist to be so honored. His *One Hundred Years of Solitude* (1967) is among the most highly acclaimed novels of the postwar era. Inspired by William Faulkner's fictional county of Yoknapatawpha, Mississippi, García Márquez invented the town of Macondo as a symbol of his Colombian birthplace. Through the eyes of an omniscient narrator—probably an unnamed peasant—who sees Macondo as moving toward a predestined doom, he produced a hallucinatory novel that blends details from Latin American history with magical events, such as a character's ascent into heaven.

While Latin America's authors were enjoying international renown for the first time, the writers of central and eastern Europe—the other new center of Post-Modernism—were simply renewing an old tradition. From the early 1800s until Communist regimes were installed in this century, the finest writers of central and eastern Europe had often been honored in the West. The revival of the literature of this region was heralded by the 1950s cultural thaw initiated by Soviet leader Khrushchev, but this thaw proved premature, since controversial writers were either silenced or forced to seek refuge in the West.

Exile was the choice of the novelist Milan Kundera [KOON-deh-rah] (b. 1929) of Czechoslovakia, who moved to France after his first novel, *The Joke* (1969), put him in disfavor with Czech authorities. Kundera's style has affinities with magic realism, notably the blending of fantasy with national history, but unlike the Latin American authors, he uses fantasy to emphasize moral themes, never for its own sake. He is also more optimistic than the magic realists, hinting that the power of love can lead to a different and better life. Indeed, Kundera tends to identify sexual freedom with political freedom.

The equation of sexual and political freedom is certainly the message of Kundera's finest novel to date, *The Unbearable Lightness of Being* (1984). He made the center of this work two historic events—the coming of communism to Czechoslovakia in 1948 and its reimposition after the 1968 uprising. He describes the obsessive and ultimately destructive behavior of his main characters as they try to define their sexual natures in the repressive Czech state. Although his novel shows how insignificant human existence is in the face of political repression, he refuses to despair. That his characters struggle for sexual fulfillment, even when faced with overpowering odds, is his way of affirming the strength of human nature. Ultimately, Kundera endorsed the belief of humanism that the human spirit can be diminished but never broken.

A similar belief is apparent in the work of the American writer Alice Walker (b. 1944). In her poetry, essays, and fiction, she brings a positive tone to her exploration of the African American experience. Her novel *The Color Purple* (1982) is the story of a black woman abused by black men and victimized by white society. The literary device she uses to express this woman's anguish is an old one, a story told through an exchange of letters. What is unique is that in some letters the suffering woman simply pours out her heart to God—an unexpected but moving twist in the skeptical atmosphere of the postwar world. *The Color Purple* also drew on Walker's feminist consciousness, showing that the heroine's survival depended on her solidarity with other black women.

Toni Morrison, another American writer, is the first African American to win the Nobel Prize for literature. Awarded in 1993, the prize recognized her for a group of novels that explored the plight of black people in American society. Except for *The Song of Solomon* (1977), which has a male narrator, her novels focus on female characters who are victims of a racist society. For example, in her first novel, *The Bluest Eye* (1970), a young black girl, attracted by the standard of white beauty, yearns to have blue eyes. Morrison also shows how violence is a central part of the black experience, as, for instance, in *Sula* (1973), when a grandmother, wanting to support her family, deliberately injures herself in order to collect insurance money. Inspired by her sense of an African heritage, she draws on folklore, mythology, and sometimes the supernatural, as in *Beloved* (1987), where a ghost is the central character. Along with the racism and the violence, Morrison imbues her novels with spiritual longing, thus offering hope for a more just society in the future.

Maxine Hong Kingston (b. 1940) has enriched Post-Modernism by putting Chinese Americans into American literature through her autobiographical books, a novel, short stories, and articles. Her avowed aim as a writer has been to "claim America," meaning to show that the Chinese have the right to belong through their labor in building the country and supporting themselves. In staking out this claim, she was influenced by

PERSONAL PERSPECTIVE

TONI MORRISON AND BILL MOYERS
A Conversation, 1989

In a 1989 conversation with Bill Moyers, a journalist and former White House official, the African American writer Toni Morrison discussed the goals of her novels.

MOYERS: What do you think is the primary role of the novel? Is it to illuminate social reality, or is it to stretch our imagination?

MORRISON: The latter. It really is about stretching. But in that way you have to bear witness to what *is*. The fear of collapse, of meaninglessness, of disorder, of anarchy—there's a certain protection that art can provide in the guise, not even of truth, but just a kind of linguistic shape of a life or a group of lives. Through that encounter, when you brush up against that, if it's any good, or it touches you in some way, it does really rub off. It enhances. It makes one or two things possible in one's own life, personally. You see something. Somebody takes a cataract away from your eye, or somehow your ear gets unplugged. You feel larger, connected. Something of substance you have encountered connects with another experience.

Novelists can do that. Art can do it in a number of ways. But it certainly should stretch. I don't want to read a book that simply reinforces all my prejudices and ignorances and things I half-know. I want one that says, "Oh, I'd forgotten—but that is exactly the way it looks," or "Oh, that's what that feeling is."

MOYERS: That's what you've done for so many others. The paradox to me is that I grew up in a small Southern town in the 1930s and '40s and '50s—twenty-two thousand people, half black, half white. It wasn't until I read your novels and the novels of people writing, as you do, about the past that I really knew what the folks on the other side of the tracks were thinking and feeling and experiencing.

MORRISON: That's important if a book can do that.

MOYERS: If only a book could do it now, for people who are in our circle of the present. Why do we have to wait so long for reconciliation?

MORRISON: You were ready for the information. You were available to the book. Some people are not available to the book, to that information. I'm sure there are books that I am just not ready to hear. It's not that the novel batters you down and gets rid of barricades or opens doors. The person inside you has to be accessible. There has to be a little crack in there already, some curiosity. Some willingness, you know, to know about it. Some moment when you really don't have the blinders on. We know people who just zip their eyes shut, who are totally enclosed in the neurotic and frequently psychotic prison of racism. But if ever any chinks can be made from the inside or outside, then they become accessible to certain kinds of information.

MOYERS: Are you aware when you're writing that you're going to invade my imagination? That you're going to subvert my perception? Were you intentionally trying to do that?

MORRISON: Totally. I want the reader to feel, first of all, that he trusts me. I'm never going to do anything so bad that he can't handle it. But at the same time, I want him to see things he has never seen before. I want him to work with me in the book. I can rely on some things that I know you know. For instance, I know you don't believe in ghosts, none of us do, but—

MOYERS: I wouldn't go too far in that assumption.

MORRISON: Well, we were all children. We all knew that we did not sleep with our hands hanging outside the bed. To this day if you wake up and your hand is hanging out there you move it back in. So I can rely on readers to know those things. But I do want to penetrate the readerly subconsciousness so that the response is, on the one hand, an intellectual one to what I have problematized in the text, but at the same time very somatic, visceral, a physical response so that you really think you see it or you can smell it or you can hear it, without my overdoing it. Because it has to be yours.

the poet William Carlos Williams (1883–1963), a Modernist who envisioned an American culture distinct from Europe and fashioned from indigenous materials and forms. Not only does Kingston's writing celebrate Chinese strength and achievement, but it also serves to avenge wrongs—by calling exploitation, racism, and ignorance by their true names.

The daughter of Chinese immigrants whose language was Say Yup, a dialect of Cantonese, Kingston has used her own life as a paradigm of the Chinese American experience. Drawing on childhood stories told in the immigrant community, she wrote two works that summarize her Chinese heritage: *The Woman Warrior: Memoirs of a Girlhood Among Ghosts* (1976), dealing with matriarchal influence, and *China Men* (1980), telling of the patriarchal side.

Late Modernism and the Arts

In the postwar art world, leadership shifted from Paris to New York. The end of Parisian dominance had been predicted since the swift fall of France to the Nazis in 1940, and the economic and military superiority of the United States at the war's end ensured that America's largest city would be the new hub of Western culture. New York's cultural leaders were divided in 1945, however. On one side stood those who wanted to build on the native school of American art, which was realistic and provincial. On the other side was a group ready to take up the mantle of leadership of the West's avant-garde. The chief institutional ally of this latter group, which soon dominated the field, was the Museum of Modern Art (MOMA) in New York City, founded principally by the Rockefeller family in 1929.

In determining the direction of Modern art, the New York artists had to contend with the domination of painting by Picasso, whose restless experimentation seemed to define art's leading edge; the prevalence of psychological theories that encouraged artists to experiment with spontaneous gestures and to seek insights from primitive peoples and from religious experience; and the cardinal need for constant newness.

These had all been forces in Modernism since 1900, but as a result of World War II, the Holocaust, and the postwar arms race, the need to dispel illusions was greater and the level of despair higher.

Painting   Shortly after 1945, an energetic style of painting came to dominate Late Modernism and still plays a major role: **Abstract Expressionism,** sometimes called Action Painting. Like earlier Modernists, the Abstract Expressionists made spiritual claims for their work, saying their spontaneous methods liberated the human spirit. One of the founders of Abstract Expressionism was the American Jackson Pollock (1912–1956), who launched this style with his "drip paintings," created between 1947 and 1950. Influenced by Jungian therapy to experiment with spontaneous gestures, Pollock nailed his canvases to the floor of his studio and dripped loops of house paint onto them from buckets with holes punched in their bottoms (Figure 21.11). The drip canvases led to a new way of looking at art in terms of randomness, spontaneity, "alloverness," and stress on the actual physical process of painting. Pollock's tendency to move around the canvas during its execution also introduced the idea of the artist interacting with the artwork.

Figure 21.11   JACKSON POLLOCK. *Blue Poles.* 1952. Oil, enamel, and aluminum paint, 6'11" × 16'. Collection, Australian National Gallery, Canberra. *This painting is virtually unique among Pollock's drip canvases by having a recognizable image, the eight long, vertical, dark blue "poles." He achieved this effect by first swirling paint onto the canvas and then applying a stick covered in blue pigment onto its surface. His refusal to use traditional methods reflects his belief that rational approaches to art are flawed and his faith that subconscious feelings, when released, reveal hidden truths—an attitude typical of the Abstract Expressionists.*

Figure 21.12 MARK ROTHKO. *Ochre and Red on Red.* 1954. Oil on canvas, 7′8⅝″ × 5′3¾″. The Phillips Collection, Washington, D.C. *In his paintings, Rothko aims to create secular icons for a nonreligious age, a spiritual theory inherited from the Russian Constructivist tradition. Accordingly, he banishes all references to nature from his art and focuses on fields of color floating in space—timeless, universal images.*

Figure 21.13 HELEN FRANKENTHALER. *Jacob's Ladder.* 1957. ▶ Oil on unprimed canvas, 9′5⅜″ × 5′9⅞″ (287.9 × 177.5 cm). The Museum of Modern Art, New York. Gift of Hyman N. Glickstein. Photograph © 1997 Museum of Modern Art, New York. *Frankenthaler's staining method—pouring paint onto a canvas—illustrates the tension between spontaneity and control typical of Abstract Expressionism. On the one hand, this technique leads naturally to surprises because of the unpredictable flow of the paint. On the other hand, the artist exercises control over the process, from choosing the colors and thickness of the paint to manipulating the canvas during the staining. In effect, she becomes both a participant in and the creator of the final work of art.*

The first generation of Abstract Expressionists was attracted by the movement's energy, rawness, and seriousness. An outstanding recruit to the new art was Mark Rothko [RAHTH-koh] (1903–1970), a Russian émigré who painted in a style very different from Pollock's. A mystic, Rothko envisioned eliminating pigment and canvas and suspending clouds of shimmering colors in the air. After 1950 he settled for creating huge paintings that focused on no more than two or three fields of color (Figure 21.12).

By the mid-1950s, a new generation of Abstract Expressionists had emerged, the most important of whom were Helen Frankenthaler [FRANK-un-thahl-uhr] (b. 1928), Jasper Johns (b. 1930), and Robert Rauschenberg [RAU-shun-buhrg] (b. 1925). Following in Pollock's footsteps, Frankenthaler adopted a method of spilling pigment onto canvas from coffee cans. By guiding the paint's flowing trajectory, she stained the canvas into exquisite, amorphous shapes that, though completely flat, seem to suggest a third dimension (Figure 21.13).

Johns and Rauschenberg found Abstract Expressionism too confining and overly serious, however. Although he did not abandon Expressionism, Johns added ordinary objects to his works, as in *Target with Plaster Casts* (1955) (Figure 21.14). In this work, he paints a banal image below a row of wooden boxes enclosing molds of body parts. A basic feature of his art is the contrast between the precisely rendered human parts (above) and the painterly target (below). Johns's fascination with such tensions paved the way for the self-contradicting style of Post-Modernism. Similarly, Rauschenberg abandoned pure painting to become an **assemblage** artist, mixing found objects with junk and adding a dash of paint. In *Monogram,* he encircles a stuffed goat with a rubber tire and splashes the goat's head with color, thus turning ready-made objects into an abstract image (Figure 21.15).

Johns and Rauschenberg, with their playful attack on serious art, opened the door to the **Pop Art** movement. Rejecting the Modernist belief that spiritual values may be expressed in nonrealistic works, the Pop artists frankly admitted that they had no spiritual, metaphysical, or philosophic purpose—they simply created two-dimensional images. Even though a kind of Pop Art developed in London in the 1950s, it was not until a new generation of New York artists began to explore commercial images in the early 1960s that the movement took off.

The most highly visible Pop artist was Andy Warhol (1927–1987), a former commercial artist who was fascinated by the vulgarity and energy of popular culture. Warhol's deadpan treatment of mass culture icons became legendary, whether they were Campbell's Soup cans, Coca Cola bottles, or Marilyn Monroe (Figure 21.16). By treating these icons in series, much in the same way that advertisers blanket the media with multiple images, he conveyed the ideas of repetitiveness, banality, and boredom. An artist who courted fame, Warhol recognized America's obsession with celebrity in his often-quoted line, "In the future everyone will be famous for fifteen minutes."

Figure 21.14 JASPER JOHNS. *Target with Plaster Casts.* 1955. Encaustic on canvas with plaster cast objects, 51 × 44 × 3½". Courtesy Leo Castelli Gallery, New York. © Jasper Johns/ licensed by VAGA, New York, NY. *Johns is a key figure in the transitional generation of painters between the Abstract Expressionists and the Pop artists. He rebelled against the pure abstraction of the older movement, yet he shied away from embracing mass culture images as directly as did the younger school of painters. His* Target with Plaster Casts *is typical of his playful, witty style. In this work, he makes a visual play on words, juxtaposing a bull's-eye with plaster casts of body parts, each of which has been a "target"—that is, a subject for artists to represent throughout history.*

Figure 21.15 ROBERT RAUSCHENBERG. *Monogram.* 1959. Multimedia construction, 4 × 6 × 6'. Moderna Museet, KSK, Stockholm. © United Press, Inc./licensed by VAGA, New York, NY. *In his glorification of junk, Rauschenberg helped to open the door to Post-Modernism. In works such as* Monogram, *he showed that anything, no matter how forlorn, even a stuffed goat and a discarded automobile tire, could be used to make art. Such irreverence reflected a democratic vision in which no object is seen as having greater artistic merit than any other.*

Figure 21.16 ANDY WARHOL. *Marilyn Monroe.* 1962. Oil, acrylic, and silk-screen enamel on canvas, 20 × 16". *Warhol's portrait of Marilyn Monroe, America's most famous postwar sex symbol, was typical of his style, which placed little value on originality. Working from a photograph supplied by her Hollywood studio, he merely used his brushes and paint to exaggerate the image that studio hairdressers and cosmetologists had already created. His commercial approach to portraiture made him the most celebrated society artist of his generation.*

Sculpture Styles in sculpture were similar to those in painting. Abstract Expressionist painting had its equivalent in the works of several American sculptors, notably David Smith (1906–1965) and Louise Nevelson (1899–1988), a Russian émigrée. Smith's point of departure, however, differed from that of the painters in that he drew inspiration from the symbols of primitive cultures, as in *Cubi XIX,* a geometric work that, according to the artist, represents an altar with a sacrificial figure (Figure 21.17). If the viewer is unaware of this intended meaning, however, this stainless steel work has the inaccessible look of a Pollock drip canvas. In contrast, the wooden sculptures of Louise Nevelson are not about representation at all but are simple compositions fashioned from old furniture and wooden odds and ends (Figure 21.18). The use of found objects allowed Nevelson to realize the Abstract Expressionist's goal of spontaneous art devoid of references to the artist's life.

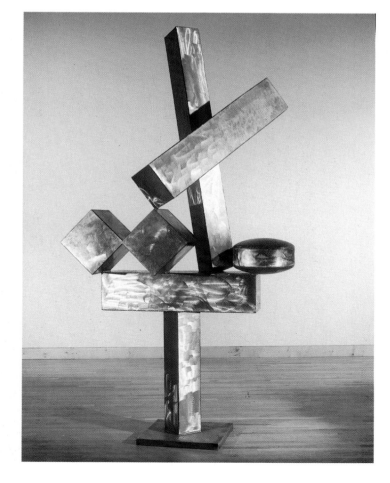

Figure 21.17 DAVID SMITH. *Cubi XIX.* 1964. Stainless steel, 9'5⅛" × 21¾" × 20¾". Tate Gallery. © Estate of David Smith/licensed by VAGA, New York, NY. *Smith's ability as a sculptor of enormous and rather destructive energies shines through in the monumental* Cubi *series, the last artworks he made before his accidental death. A machinist by training, Smith liked to work with industrial metals, welding and bending them into geometric units to meet his expressive needs. His desire to shape mechanical images into expressive forms related him to the Abstract Expressionist movement in painting.*

◀ **Figure 21.18**　Louise Nevelson. *Sky Cathedral.* 1958. Assemblage: wood construction, painted black, 11′¼″ × 10′¼″ × 1′6″ (343.9 × 305.4 × 45.7 cm). Museum of Modern Art, New York. Gift of Mr. and Mrs. Ben Mildwoff. Photograph © 1997 Museum of Modern Art, New York. *Though a Modernist, Nevelson anticipated Post-Modernism by combining genres, as in this free-standing wall that integrates architecture, sculpture, and painting. She divided the wall into a grid, stuffed found objects into the wall's compartments, and painted the finished work black.*

Pop Art was an influence in the works of George Segal (1924–2000). Segal's ghostly sculptures are plaster casts of live subjects, such as his dual portrait of Robert and Ethel Scull, leading patrons of the Pop Art movement (Figure 21.19). Segal himself rejects the Pop Art label—pointing out that his sculptures have expressionistic surfaces, like Rodin's works (see Chapter 19)—but his method reduces the body to a cartoon form and thus relates it to popular culture.

Architecture　In Late Modernist architecture, the most influential architect was the German-born Ludwig Mies van der Rohe [mees van duh ROH] (1886–1969). The last head of the Bauhaus, Germany's premier design school before World War II, Mies closed its doors in 1933 and moved to the United States in 1938. In the 1950s, he captured the world's attention with a glass skyscraper, New York's Seagram Building (Figure 21.20). Based on the artistic creed "less is more," this

Figure 21.19　George Segal. *Robert and Ethel Scull.* 1965. Plaster, canvas, wood, and cloth, 8 × 6 × 6′. Private collection. © George Segal/licensed by VAGA, New York, NY. Courtesy Sidney Janis Gallery, New York. Photograph © Geoffrey Clements. *Unlike his fellow Pop artists, Segal looks at the world through existential eyes. Where Warhol glamorized his celebrity subjects, Segal portrays his wealthy patrons, the Sculls, as beset by anxiety. He conveys their boredom and depression through fixed facial expressions and heavy limbs, while keeping their appearances generalized. His modeling technique, which requires subjects not to move until the plaster dries, reinforces the melancholy image.*

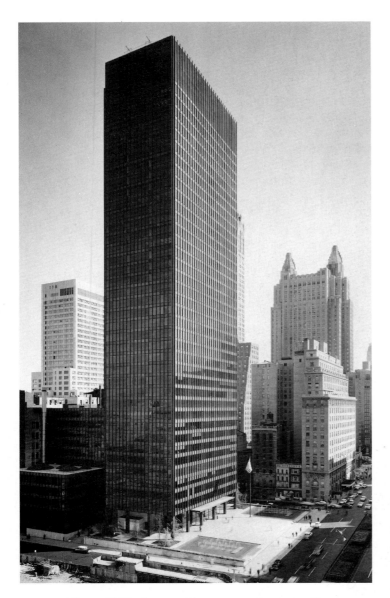

Figure 21.20 Ludwig Mies van der Rohe and Philip Johnson. Seagram Building. 1954–1958. New York City. *Ezra Stoller © Esto. Mies's decision to use bronze-tinted windows as virtually the only decorative feature of the Seagram Building's simple geometrical design had a profound impact on his contemporaries. Following his lead, other architects made the high-rise skeleton-frame building with tinted windows the most recognizable symbol of Late Modernism.*

building's design is simple, a bronze skeletal frame on which are hung tinted windows—the building's only decorative feature. The implementation of his ideals of simplicity and restraint also led him to geometrize the building, planning its structural relationships according to mathematical ratios. So successful was Mies van der Rohe's "glass box" building that skyscrapers built according to similar designs dominate the skylines of cities around the world.

Post-Modernism and the Arts

The arts had begun to change by about 1970, as artists and architects moved beyond Late Modernism, which seemed to have dissolved into weak minimalist schools. In Post-Modernism, the shock of the new gave way to the shock of the old. Seeking a way out of Late Modernism's chaotic pessimism and its focus on abstraction, Post-Modern artists were more optimistic and revived earlier styles, although always with added layers of meaning, nuance, or irony. Realism made a triumphant return to art, flourishing as **Neorealism,** a style based on photographic clarity of detail; as **Neoexpressionism,** a style that offers social criticism and focuses on nontraditional painting methods; and as **Neoclassicism** (not to be confused with the Neoclassicism of the late eighteenth century), which had been dormant since the early twentieth century and pronounced dead by the Late Modernists. Neoclassicism is the most striking style within Post-Modernism, in both painting and architecture, perhaps because it looks so fresh to modern eyes. In addition to these various forms of realism, Modernist abstraction remains a significant facet of Post-Modernism. In their openness to artistic possibilities and their refusal to adopt a uniform style, the Post-Modernists very much resemble the Post-Impressionists of the late nineteenth century.

Painting An outstanding Neorealist painter is the American Philip Pearlstein (b. 1924), who specializes in nonidealized nudes. Starting in the 1960s, he made his chief subject human bodies beyond their prime, perhaps as a way of reflecting the melancholy of the age. His nudes are rendered in stark close-up, the bodies at rest like hanging meat, and with cropped heads and limbs as in a photograph (Figure 21.21). His works seem to parody the "centerfold sexuality" that accompanied the sexual revolution brought on in part by the birth control pill.

Whereas Neorealism tends to neutrality or moral subtlety, Neoexpressionism uses realism to create paintings that are overtly socially critical. The outstanding Neoexpressionist and the most highly regarded painter among the Post-Modernists is the German artist Anselm Kiefer [KEE-fuhr] (b. 1945). Kiefer's works have blazed new trails with nontraditional painting materials, including dirt, tar, and copper threads. Existential anguish is alive in his works, which tend to focus on apocalyptic images of a blasted earth —a chilling reference to the threat of nuclear destruction (Figure 21.22). Post-Modern optimism may nevertheless be read in his borrowings from Mesopotamia and Egypt, which affirm the continuity of Western culture from its earliest stages to the present. In his use of personal references and historical allusions,

Figure 21.21 PHILIP PEARLSTEIN. *Female on Eames Chair, Male on Swivel Stool.* 1981. Watercolor, 60 × 40". Collection of Eleanor and Leonard Bellinson. Courtesy Donald Morris Gallery, Birmingham, Mich. *Pearlstein's refusal to glamorize his nude subjects is part of a democratizing tendency in Post-Modernism. Just as some Post-Modernist authors borrow freely from mass-circulation genres such as Sherlock Holmes and science fiction, so Pearlstein focuses attention on bodily features like sagging breasts and bulging veins that had been overlooked by realistic painters.*

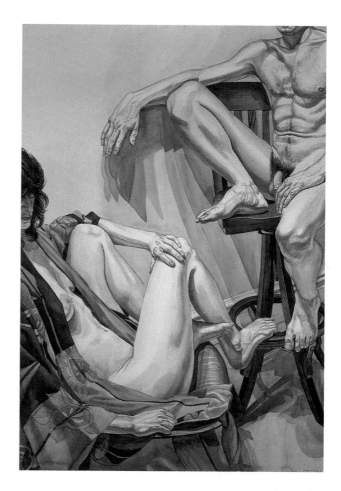

Figure 21.22 ANSELM KIEFER. *Osiris and Isis.* 1985–1987. Diptych, mixed media on canvas, 12'6" × 18'4½" × 6½". Courtesy Marian Goodman Gallery, New York. *Kiefer drew on an ancient Egyptian myth (see Figure 4.8) to give shape to his fears of modern technology. He represents Isis, the goddess who restored her husband-brother Osiris to life, as an electronic keyboard at the top of a pyramid. He adds actual copper wires to connect the circuit board to broken bits of ceramics, his symbol of Osiris's fragmented body. In Kiefer's Post-Modern imagination, technology has become a deity with the capacity to destroy or create.*

Figure 21.23 SUE COE. *Modern Man Followed by the Ghosts of His Meat*. 1990. Copyright © 1990 Sue Coe. Courtesy Galerie St. Etienne, New York. *This is one of the works in the protest booklet* **Meat: Animals and Industry** *by Sue Coe and her sister Mandy, inspired by visits to slaughterhouses and factory farms. This work is in the vein of an editorial cartoon inspired by a Dickens novel. Coe prefers to work with graphic arts ("handmade, mechanically reproduced images") because they engage the viewer more directly and allow the artist to reach a larger audience than do more traditional means.*

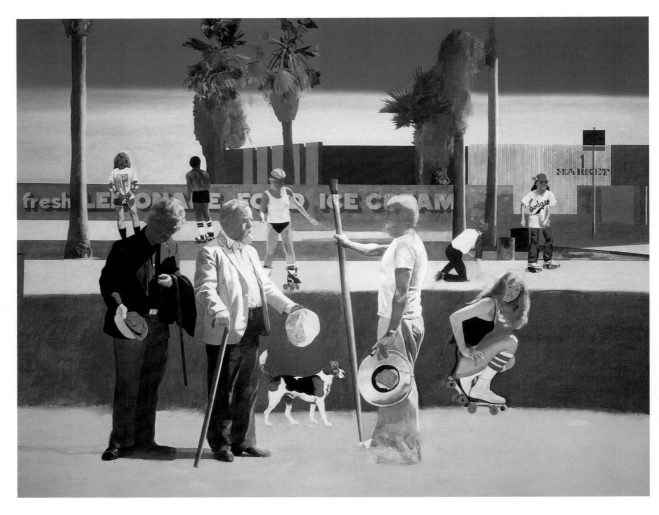

Kiefer is perhaps the contemporary artist closest to the German Expressionists of the early twentieth century.

The British painter Sue Coe (b. 1951), who now lives and works in America, is another important Neoexpressionist whose art serves social and political causes. Daughter of a working-class London family, she is a counterculturalist who came of age in the stormy 1960s. Committed to feminist and overtly political art, she does not espouse any specific ideology but simply confronts injustice wherever she sees it. She once described her creed in these words: "If you remove your armies from other people's countries, I won't paint war." In a broad sense, she wants her art to be a tool for change, to bear witness to the vices of capitalist and urban society, as in *Modern Man Followed by the Ghosts of His Meat* (Figure 21.23), one of the works in her indictment of the meat industry and its shocking treatment of animals. Although the message constantly threatens to overpower the art, Coe's paintings are meant to move viewers to share the artist's concerns and thus work for reform.

A painter who uses Neoclassicism to make subtle commentary on art history is Peter Blake (b. 1920). In *The Meeting,* or *"Have a Nice Day, Mr. Hockney,"* he depicts a meeting of three 1960s British Pop artists who in the 1980s joined the ranks of Post-Modernism (Figure 21.24). This new version of Courbet's *The Meeting,* or *"Bonjour Monsieur Courbet"* (see Figure 18.10), is both an ironic comment on contemporary Neoclassicism and a classical composition in itself. The three artists depicted here are, from left to right, Howard Hodgkin (b. 1932), Peter Blake, and David Hockney (b. 1937), the last-named grasping a huge paintbrush. Blake's *Meeting* abounds in ironic juxtapositions: age versus youth, Old World versus the New, the aesthetic life versus consumerism, work versus play, and timeless present versus fleeting moment. Blake's Post-Modernism fuses rival traditions, the eternal values of Classicism and the transience of Pop Art.

Modernist abstraction continues to have a powerful impact on Post-Modernism. The most brilliant current disciple of abstraction is Frank Stella (b. 1936), a painter who has produced an immense and varied body of work. A minimalist in the 1950s, painting black-striped canvases, he became a forerunner of Neoexpressionism in the 1970s, using gaudy color and decorative effects. He has remained true to abstract ideals, as in *Norisring,* one of the *Shard* series, which uses the scraps left over from other works (Figure 21.25). Fully abstract and nonrepresentational, this work is nevertheless Post-Modernist since it combines the genres of painting and sculpture—an ambition of many Post-Modernists.

Sculpture Like painters, Post-Modernist sculptors began to work with realistic forms. For example, serving as complements to the Neorealist paintings of Philip Pearlstein are the sculptures of the American John De Andrea (b. 1941). Typically, De Andrea uses

Figure 21.25 FRANK STELLA. *Norisring (XVI, 3X).* 1983. Mixed media on etched aluminum, 6'7" × 5'7" × 1'3". Collection of Ann and Robert Freedman. Courtesy Knoedler & Company, New York. *Largely because of his lively intelligence, Stella has stayed on the cutting edge of Post-Modernism. He has kept abstraction alive almost single-handedly at a time when realist styles are dominant. His 1960s innovation, the shaped canvas, allowed him to replace the rectilinear canvas with an abstract form. By the early 1980s, he had transformed the shaped canvas into a blend of sculpture and painting, as in the* Circuits *series.*

◄ **Figure 21.24** PETER BLAKE. *The Meeting,* or *"Have a Nice Day, Mr. Hockney."* 1981–1983. Oil on canvas, 39 × 49". Tate Gallery. *Blake brings Classicism up-to-date by applying its features and principles to a contemporary California setting. He fills the sun-drenched scene with double-coded references, including the pose of the girl in the right foreground (borrowed partly from a skating magazine and partly from Classical sculpture), the dog (an allusion to American youth culture and Alberti's Renaissance artistic theory), and the winged hat of the girl in the Dodgers shirt (a contemporary sports emblem and a symbol of the god Mercury). The result is a hybrid scene, marked by the ironic contrast between the grave and self-contained central figures and the "cool" teenagers in the background.*

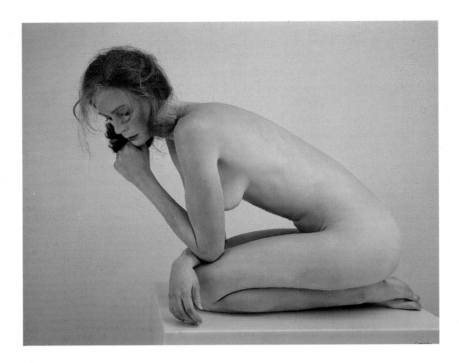

Figure 21.26 JOHN DE ANDREA. *Sphinx*. 1987. Polyvinyl, oil paint, life-size. Courtesy ACA Galleries, New York. *Unlike Pearlstein, who uses nudity to register his disgust, De Andrea designs his polyvinyl nudes to celebrate the glossy lives of the upper middle class. The bodies of his nude subjects convey what today's consumer culture urges everyone to be: healthy, sleek, athletic, and sexy.*

traditional poses, as in *Sphinx* (Figure 21.26). But De Andrea's human figures are fully contemporary, suggestive of young upwardly mobile professionals ("yuppies") who have taken off their clothes. Whether or not his works are satirical, he manages to capture in sculptural form the erotic quality considered so desirable by modern advertising, movies, and mass media.

The outstanding school of artists to emerge recently is the "Brit Pak," or, more seriously, the YBA, Young British Artists. Just as Labor prime minister Tony Blair has waged a campaign to nudge Great Britain from her stodgy past into a new era as "Cool Britannia," so has the YBA traded in the low-key style of older British art for an art that is attention-grabbing and often associated with scandal. Not surprising, the YBA's most recent show—which opened in London in 1997 and then traveled to the Continent, reaching New York in 1999—was entitled "Sensations." Probably the most praised artist among the YBA is the sculptor Rachel Whiteread (b. 1964). Unlike the works of many of this British school, Whiteread's sculptures are deeply serious and modest in execution. Inspired by American minimalist art of the 1960s and 1970s, her works usually represent simple ideas using familiar, everyday objects (Figure 21.27). She works in various mediums, including plaster, concrete, resin, and rubber.

Installation Art Enjoying a vogue today is **installation art,** a boundary-challenging type of art born in the 1960s that creates architectural tableaux, using objects drawn from and making references to artistic sources (such as music, painting, sculpture, and

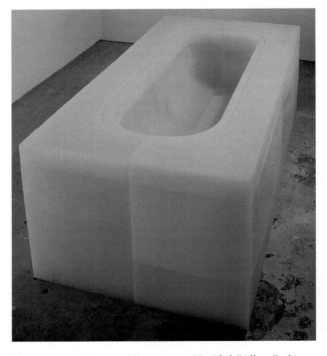

Figure 21.27 RACHEL WHITEREAD. *Untitled (Yellow Bath)*. 1996. Cast made of rubber and polystyrene. Luhring Augustine Gallery, New York. *Whiteread's wide-ranging eye has led her to sculpt many household objects, including mattresses, chairs and tables, bookshelves, and bathtubs. Her works are more than mere representations; she makes a cast of the spaces around an object, trying to capture traces of a human presence. In its new incarnation, Whiteread's bathtub has been compared to a sarcophagus. Such an interpretation is acceptable to the artist, as she is on record as comparing her casting technique to the making of a death mask. Indeed, there is a faint air of melancholy about Whiteread's sculptures, since they seem to affirm human mortality.*

Figure 21.28   ANN HAMILTON. View of *mantle*. Miami Art Museum. 1998. *Installation art has affinities with other innovative art forms, but it lacks the centrality of the videotaped image, as in video art, or a strong musical component, as in performance art. In* mantle, *there is a minor musical aspect: Radio receivers, placed amid the flowers, transmitted musical and other sounds during the event. Feminist in perspective, this installation may be interpreted as an ironical comment on the male-dominated art world, because, until recently, this world discouraged women from becoming artists and limited their artistic choices mainly to domestic chores, such as making clothes. In the photograph, Ann Hamilton is the woman sewing; volunteers and paid attendants performed this task when the artist was absent.*

theater) and the workaday world (such as everyday tasks, media images, and foodstuffs); the work may include a human presence. One of the most gifted installation artists is the American Ann Hamilton (b. 1956), who is known for her sensory works layered with meaning. The piece *mantle,* installed at the Miami Art Museum in 1998 (Figure 21.28), filled up a second-floor gallery and had as its human focus a woman performing a household task before an open window—a homage to Dutch genre art, which often pictured women in similar poses. The task the seated woman is performing—sewing sleeves onto the bodies of wool coats—gives rise to the piece's name (a "mantle" is, among other things, a sleeveless garment). Multiple wires dangle down the gallery's wall into a mound of 60,000 cut flowers displayed on a 48-foot-long table behind the woman. This mountainous display of slowly decaying flowers is a memento mori—a frequent theme of Renaissance art. Hamilton's growing reputation led to her choice as the American representative at the prestigious Venice Art Bienniale in 1999.

Video Art   Nam June Paik (b. 1932) is virtually the founder of video art and certainly the most influential artist working in this medium. **Video art** is made with a video monitor, or monitors, and may be produced using computerized programs or with handheld cameras; the work may be ephemeral or permanent. Working with videotapes since 1959, Paik has evolved from

an artist intent on being entertaining into one devoted to serious issues in his projects and, starting in the 1980s, embracing political ideas. A sophisticated work that represents his political beliefs is *My Faust (Stations): Religion* (1989–1991), which is part of a series of thirteen individual multimonitor installations (see Figure 21.7). Rich in allusions, this work refers to the thirteen channels available at the time for Manhattan television viewers and the word *stations* in the title, reinforced by the neogothic altarpieces, suggests Christianity's Stations of the Cross, the thirteen stages of Jesus' journey to his crucifixion. *Faust* was a symbol of both restlessness and relentless seeking of knowledge, even to the loss of the soul (see Chapter 17). Thus, Paik's *Faust* suggests humanity's pact with the devil for secular power and glory.

Architecture   The chief exponent of Post-Modern architecture is the American Robert Venturi (b. 1925), whose ideas are summarized in his book *Complexity and Contradiction in Architecture* (1966). Rejecting Modernist architecture, which he thinks inhuman because of its starkness, he attempts to create buildings that express the energy and ever-changing quality of contemporary life. Fascinated by mass culture, he is inspired by popular styles of architecture, such as Las Vegas casinos and motels in the form of Indian tepees—a kitsch style sometimes called "vernacular." A work that enshrines his love of the ordinary is his Guild

Figure 21.29 ROBERT VENTURI. Guild House. 1965.
Philadelphia. *Venturi's aesthetic aim is to transform the
ordinary into the extraordinary. He followed this democratic ideal
in Guild House, where he took a "dumb and ordinary" (his term)
concept and tried to give it a monumental look. His ironic intelligence and his perverse delight in mass culture have made him a
guiding spirit of Post-Modernism.*

Figure 21.30 RICHARD ROGERS AND
RENZO PIANO. The Georges Pompidou
Center for Art and Culture. 1971–1977.
Paris. *Designed in a gaudy industrial style
and erected in the heart of a quiet section
of Paris called Beaubourg, the Pompidou
Center was controversial from the start,
as it was planned to be. Its showy appearance sharply contrasted with the historic
styles of neighboring structures—a contrast that has become a guiding ideal of
Post-Modernist architects. The furor that
greeted the Pompidou Center on its opening has occurred in other places where
city governments have placed colorful
and brash high-tech temples amid their
more traditional buildings.*

House, a retirement home in a lower-middle-class section of Philadelphia (Figure 21.29). Faceless and seemingly artless, this building is indebted to popular culture for its aesthetic appeal; for instance, the wire sculpture on the roof looks like a television antenna, and the recessed entrance and the sign evoke memories of old-time movie houses. Venturi's playful assault on Modernism opened the door to the diversity of Post-Modernism.

One of the strains in Post-Modernism is **high tech,** a style that uses industrial techniques and whose roots stretch back to the Crystal Palace (see Figure 18.5) and the Eiffel Tower. Richard Rogers (b. 1933) of England and Renzo Piano (b. 1937) of Italy launched this revival with the Pompidou Center in Paris, which boldly displays its factory-made metal parts and transparent walls (Figure 21.30). Commissioned by France to restore Paris's cultural position over New York, the Pompidou Center has spawned many imitations as well as a style of interior decoration.

One of the most controversial buildings in Post-Modern architecture is the thirty-seven-story, pink granite headquarters building of American Telephone and Telegraph, executed in a Neoclassical style (Figure 21.31). Designed by Philip C. Johnson (b. 1906), an American disciple of Mies van der Rohe, this building was a slap in the face to the Modernist ideal because it used Classical forms. The AT&T Headquarters has a base, middle, and top, corresponding to the foot, shaft, and capital of a Greek column—the basic element of Greco-Roman building style. As a final blow to Modernist purity, Johnson topped his building with a split pediment crown, causing a hostile critic to compare it to an eighteenth-century Chippendale highboy. Notwithstanding the furor surrounding its creation, this building heralded the resurgence of Neoclassicism in the Post-Modernist age.

The Guggenheim Museum in the Basque city of Bilbao, Spain, designed by the American Frank Gehry (b. 1929), was recognized immediately as a classic when it opened in 1997. Hired by city officials to build the museum as part of a civic rejuvenation project, Gehry chose a building site on the Nervion River, a stream that has played a major role in the city's history. Gehry's design is in the form of a rose, or "metallic flower," with a rotunda at its center and the petals spiraling in waves of centrifugal force (Figure 21.32). Typical of Gehry's expressionist handling of flexible materials, strips of metal ripple and flare outward into the city. Within the Baroque interior are exhibition spaces, an auditorium, a restaurant, a café, retail space, and an atrium that functions as a town square. The choice of a rose, the symbol of the Virgin Mary, was appropriate for Catholic Spain. Gehry, by shifting this emblem from a church to a museum, transformed it into an ambiguous sign of the Post-Modern period.

Figure 21.31 PHILIP C. JOHNSON AND JOHN BURGEE. American Telephone and Telegraph Headquarters. 1979–1984. New York. © Peter Mauss/Esto. *Although Classical rules were followed in the planning of Johnson and Burgee's AT&T Headquarters, it was built using Modernist methods. Like Modernist structures, the building has a steel frame to which exterior panels are clipped. Despite its Modernist soul, the physical presence of this Post-Modernist building conveys the gravity and harmony customarily associated with Classical architecture.*

Figure 21.32 FRANK O. GEHRY. Guggenheim Museum. 1997. Bilbao, Spain. *Gehry is famed for pushing the boundaries of architecture, which has often been confined by set rules, because he, as a friend of painters and sculptors, sees himself as both an artist and an architect. Thus, the Bilbao Guggenheim has been labeled sculptural architecture, considered a work of art in itself. Gehry relied on a sophisticated computer program to achieve the building's dramatic curvature, and he chose metal titanium to sheath the exterior, thereby giving it a gleaming, wavy-in-a-stong-wind appearance.*

Late Modern and Post-Modern Music

The major musical styles that were dominant before World War II persisted in Late Modernism. New York was the world's musical capital, and styles were still polarized into tonal and atonal camps, led by Stravinsky and Schoenberg, respectively. After Schoenberg's death in 1951, however, Stravinsky abandoned tonality and adopted his rival's serial method. Stravinsky's conversion made twelve-tone serialism the most respected type of atonal music, though other approaches to atonality sprang up, notably in the United States. Under Late Modernism, this dissonant style became the musical equivalent of the spontaneous canvases painted by Pollock and the Abstract Expressionist school.

Despite embracing the dissonance and abstraction of serialism, Stravinsky filled his Late Modernist works with energy and feeling, the touchstones of his musical style. Two of his finest serial works are *Agon* (1957), a score for a ballet with no other plot than a competition among the dancers, and *Requiem Canticles* (1968), a religious service for the dead, marked by austere solemnity.

Dissonance also characterizes the music of Krzystof Penderecki [pahn-duhr-ETS-key] (b. 1933), a member of the "Polish School" who is anything but a doctrinaire Modernist. Committed to an older musical ideal, he believes that music, above all things, must speak to the human heart. Nevertheless, he has been a constant innovator, seeking especially to create new sounds through the unconventional use of stringed instruments and the human voice. Marked by Classical restraint, his compositions are clearly structured works permeated by fluctuating clouds of sounds, as in *Threnody for the Victims of Hiroshima* (1960), scored for fifty-two stringed instruments. (A "threnody" is a "song of lamentation.") Reflective of the melancholy mood of Late Modernism, this work conjures up the eerie minutes, in 1945 at Hiroshima, between the dropping of the atomic bomb and its detonation. Penderecki achieves unearthly effects through the use of **glissando** (the blending of one tone into the next in scalelike passages) in an extremely high register and by the string players' bowing their instruments in abnormal ways.

The most influential Late Modernist was John Cage (1912–1992), whose unusual, even playful, approach to music opened the door to Post-Modernism. Briefly Schoenberg's student, Cage gained most of his controversial notions—in particular, his goal of integrating noise into music—from the enigmatic teachings of Zen Buddhism. A work that demonstrates this goal is called *4'33"* (*Four Minutes and Thirty-three Seconds*). The title describes the time period that the performer is to sit immobile before a piano keyboard so that the concert hall sounds, in effect, become the music during the performer's silence. Cage's spirited experiments made him the darling of the avant-garde. Along with assemblage artists, choreographers, and sculptors, he helped to break down the divisions among the art forms—in anticipation of a Post-Modernist development.

In the 1960s, some innovative composers rejected atonality for its overintellectuality and its apparent devotion to harsh sounds. In place of atonality, they founded a Post-Modern style devoted to making music more emotionally appealing, though they remained committed to experimental methods. Among the most notable composers working within this style is the American Philip Glass (b. 1937), who has made it his mission to return exuberance to music. He has pursued this goal while working in a minimalist tradition, although he draws on varied sources, including classical Indian music, African drumming, and rock and roll. Much of Glass's music is written for **synthesizer,** a machine with a simple keyboard that can duplicate the sounds of up to twelve instruments simultaneously. He composes with simple tonal harmonies, pulsating rhythms, unadorned scales, and, above all, lilting arpeggios, the cascading sounds produced by playing the notes of a chord in rapid sequences. A Glass piece is instantly recognizable for its repetitiveness and obsessive quality.

A composer of chamber works, film scores, and dance pieces, Glass has gained the widest celebrity for his operas. His first opera, *Einstein on the Beach* (1976), produced in collaboration with the equally controversial American director Robert Wilson (b. 1941), was staged at New York's Metropolitan Opera, a rarity for a living composer in this century. In their kaleidoscopic work, Glass and Wilson redefined the operatic form, staging a production lasting four and one-half hours without intermission and with Glass's driving music set to Wilson's texts with no recognizable plot, no formal arias, and no massed choruses. So successful was this venture that Glass followed it with operas based on other remarkable figures, *Satyagraha* (1978), dealing with the life of Gandhi, India's liberator, and *Akhnaten* (1984), focusing on the Egyptian pharaoh who is sometimes called the first monotheist. Glass's interests took an even more multicultural turn in 1998 with the premiere and world tour of his multimedia opera *Monsters of Grace,* with a libretto based on the thirteenth-century mystical poetry of the Persian poet Jalal ad-Din ar-Rumi.

One of the best-known living composers is the American John Adams (b. 1947). Like many other composers of his generation, Adams is a minimalist, but he stands out for his resonant sounds and firm grasp of musical form. He has written for a wide range of media, including orchestra, opera, video, film, and dance, and he has composed both electronic and instrumental music. His operas, *Nixon in China* (1987), *The Death of Klinghoffer* (1991), and *I Was Looking at the Ceiling and Then I Saw the Sky* (1998), based on historical events, have been viewed by more audiences than any other operas in recent history. Two orchestral works, *The Chairman Dances,* adapted from *Nixon in China,* and *Shaker Loops* (1996), have been called "among the best known and most frequently performed of contemporary American music." Adams frequently conducts some of the world's most prestigious orchestras.

Figure 21.33 WILLIAM STRUHS. Laurie Anderson performing at the Spoleto Festival U.S.A., June 1999. *Laurie Anderson, second from left, whose works virtually define performance art, is pictured here in the midst of a performance of* Songs and Stories from "Moby Dick" *at the Spoleto Festival U.S.A., held in Charleston, South Carolina. Her nineteenth-century costume, the stovepipe top hat and frock coat, reflects the time period of Melville's famous novel. The setting of the performance, with its alienating effects created by electronic means, suggests the technological world that is the principal concern of her art. For example, on a background screen are projected, among other things, constantly shifting lines and words of Melville's text, letters of the alphabet, blown-up images of the performers, and dictionary definitions; similarly, in addition to instrumental music, there are songs, chanted passages, and spoken words, some of whose sounds are deliberately distorted by electronic means.*

Performance Art

Laurie Anderson (b. 1947) is a key artist in **performance art**—a democratic type of mixed media art born in the 1960s that ignores artistic boundaries, happily mixing high art (such as music, painting, and theater) and popular art (such as rock and roll, film, and fads) to create a unique, nonreproducible, artistic experience. Anderson's performance art consists of sing-and-tell story-songs about mundane events of daily life, which somehow take on unearthly significance. These monologues are often tinged with humor and are delivered in a singsong voice backed up by mixed media images, strange props, and varied electronic media, including electronic musical instruments, photo projec-

tion, manipulated video, and devices that alter the sound of her voice. Central to the performance is her stage persona, rather like Dorothy in *The Wizard of Oz*, in which she gazes with wide-eyed wonder on the modern technological world. A gifted violinist, she intends her music to play only a supporting role in her art, though her recordings—for example, *The Ugly One with the Jewels* (1995), based on a work called *Readings from the New Bible* (1992–1995)—have found eager listeners. In *Songs and Stories from "Moby Dick"* (1999), based on Herman Melville's nineteenth-century novel, she broke new ground by composing for male voices as well as her own (Figure 21.33). Anderson's ongoing popularity is a testament to her ability to stay ahead of the ever-shifting zeitgeist.

The American Cindy Sherman (b. 1954) also has created a body of performance art, but without music. Sherman first attracted notice in the 1970s with photographs of herself in elaborately staged poses, evocative of old movie scenes. Although these photographs focused on women as victims, their ambiguous nature made her controversial, especially to feminists. In the eighties, she made a series of History Portraits, in which she impersonated famous art subjects. In the nineties, she made photographs using pornographic subjects, mock fashion images, and fairy-tale characters (Figure 21.34). Sherman's art, with its staged and rather tacky quality, seeks to dethrone high art and bring it down to earth for today's audiences.

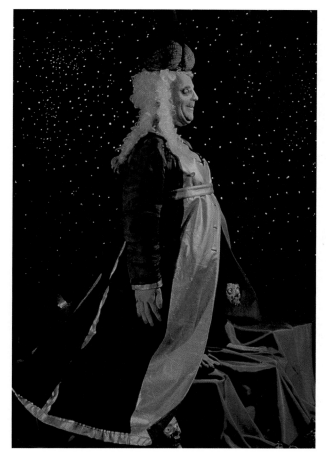

Figure 21.34 CINDY SHERMAN. *Untitled #298*. Photograph, 73 × 49½″. 1994. *In this photograph from the Fairy Tale Series, Sherman impersonates a medieval wizard, standing in profile against a star-filled "sky" and wearing a blonde wig and flowing robe whose inner lining is emblazoned with skulls. The props have been assembled by Sherman, based on some plan of her own, making this photograph a unique image. Works such as this bring into question the creating of art when there is no preexisting prototype. Interpretation of Sherman's art is difficult, as she is dismissive of what critics say, calling their analyses "a kind of side effect."*

Mass Culture

In the postwar era, American mass culture began to serve as the common denominator of an emerging world civilization. Because of its democratic and energetic qualities, sexual content, and commitment to free expression, this culture has attracted people around the globe. Scenes of American life—conveyed through television, movies, and advertising—have mesmerized millions, who imitate these images as far as they are able. The popularity of the clothing (jeans, T-shirt, and running shoes), the food (hamburgers, fries, and cola), and the music (rock and roll) of the American teenager has influenced behavior even in Eastern Europe, Russia, and the Third World.

The information boom has been the explosive force Americanizing the world and transforming it into a global village, with television providing the means of transformation. As the earth has shrunk, more elec-tronic gear—the videocassette recorder, the compact-disc player, the digital recorder, the camcorder, the computer—has reduced the individual's world even more, turning each home into a communications center. Further shrinkage is taking place with the coming of the global information highway, which includes the Internet and the World Wide Web.

The rise of a worldwide mass culture has produced an insatiable demand for popular entertainment. It has led to the replacement of old types of amusements with new forms, such as the rock concert and the rock video, along with the creation of innovative means of media coverage, including cable television with MTV and all-sports channels. This demand has given birth to extravagantly popular figures: Elvis Presley (1935–1977), America's first postwar music idol; Michael Jackson (b. 1958), superstar of the mid-1980s; Madonna (b. 1959), queen of popular songs in the early 1990s, and Ricky Martin (born Enrique Jose Martin Morales IV, in 1971), the reigning king of current pop music. Except for the Beatles, the British rock quartet that was the most popular rock group of the 1960s, few superstars are non-American. Only time will tell if Post-Modernist mass culture can produce a civilization that is truly pluralistic and global.

A SUMMING UP

We have entered a new millennium. Since 1945, the world has passed from a cold war "fought" between two superpowers and their allies into a period dominated by a single superpower. With the United States as the only superpower, its democratic institutions and free-market economy have become widely imitated by much of the world. However, the revival of militant nationalism and ethnic warfare in scattered areas on nearly every continent threatens the triumph of liberal democracy and laissez-faire capitalism.

After fifty years of breathtaking changes in the political, social, and economic realms, we can predict with a measure of confidence what the near future will bring. In our Post-Modern era, a new vision of the world may be seen, struggling to be born. It is global and democratic and embraces the contributions, tastes, and ideas of many groups of people—men and women of all races and of all countries. It is also open-ended, freely borrowing from high culture and mass culture. Nevertheless, the driving force for this emerging culture, at least in the foreseeable future, appears to be Western civilization, largely because of its immense capacity to adapt and bend and yet ultimately to survive—something Western artists, writers, and peoples have been doing since the first cities were founded in Sumer and Egypt five thousand years ago.

So much for the immediate future, but what of the millennium? When we consider our past, as we have in this book, one major lesson is clear: The long term in history is unpredictable. For example, five thousand years ago in 3000 B.C., who could have predicted that the fledgling Egyptian and Mesopotamian societies would become cradles of civilization, leaving enduring cultural forms before falling into decay? Or in 2000 B.C., who could have foreseen that a rejuvenated Egypt and Mesopotamia would eventually be undermined by Iron Age invaders? Or would it have been possible to guess in 1000 B.C., a time of disarray and decline in the eastern Mediterranean, that first Greece and later Rome would evolve into the civilizations that became the standard in the West? Or at the dawn of the Christian era, with the Roman Empire at its height, who would have dared forecast that Roman power would spread so widely but then collapse, to be succeeded by three separate and distinct civilizations—Islam, Byzantium, and the West? Or in A.D. 1000, who could have anticipated that the backward West would become the constantly revolutionizing industrial giant whose culture would dominate the world? Drawing a lesson from this quick survey, we readily admit that we cannot know what this millennium will bring. Perhaps all we can say is that, based on past history, civilization as we know it is likely to undergo fundamental change, for good or ill, due to the consequences of some currently unforeseen technological, political, religious, economic, or social innovation.

KEY CULTURAL TERMS

Late Modernism	Neoexpressionism
Post-Modernism	Neoclassicism
structuralism	installation art
theater of the absurd	video art
magic realism	high tech
Abstract Expressionism	glissando
assemblage art	synthesizer
Pop Art	performance art
Neorealism	

SUGGESTIONS FOR FURTHER READING

PRIMARY SOURCES

The Autobiography of Malcolm X. With the assistance of A. Haley. Secaucus, N.J.: Castle Books, 1967. In his own words, Malcolm X describes his rise from obscurity to become a powerful figure posing radical solutions to racial problems.

BALDWIN, J. *Go Tell It on the Mountain.* New York: Grossett and Dunlap, 1953. A novel representative of Baldwin's early optimism about reconciliation of the black and white races.

———. *No Name in the Street.* New York: Dial Press, 1972. A novel representative of Baldwin's bitterness after the murder of Martin Luther King, Jr.

BECKETT, S. *Waiting for Godot.* Edited and with an introduction by H. Bloom. New York: Chelsea House Publishers, 1987. The central image of Beckett's absurdist play—pointless waiting—has become a metaphor for the disappointed hopes of Late Modernism.

CAMUS, A. *The Fall.* Translated by J. O'Brien. New York: Knopf, 1957. Camus's most autobiographical novel, dealing with self-deceit and spiritual yearning.

CHOMSKY, N. *Syntactic Structures.* The Hague: Mouton, 1957. The work that revolutionized linguistics by claiming that there is a structure that lies hidden beneath the surface of language.

DE BEAUVOIR, S. *The Second Sex.* Translated and edited by H. M. Parshley. New York: Vintage, 1974. One of the books that helped launch the feminist revival by arguing that women must abandon "femininity" and create their own immortality just as men do.

FANON, F. *The Wretched of the Earth.* Translated by C. Farrington. New York: Grove Press, 1968. Fanon's groundbreaking study of racism and colonial liberation; a classic of modern revolutionary theory.

FRIEDAN, B. *The Feminine Mystique.* New York: Norton, 1963. The first acknowledgment of housewives' dissatisfaction with their role and desire for a career, this work was a milestone in the rebirth of feminism in the United States.

GARCÍA MÁRQUEZ, G. *One Hundred Years of Solitude.* New York: Cambridge University Press, 1990. A classic of Post-Modernism that mixes magical happenings with realistic events in the mythical Colombian town of Macondo.

GINSBERG, A. *Collected Poems, 1947–1980.* New York: Harper & Row, 1984. A Late Modernist, Ginsberg wrote poetry that reflected his openness to diversity and his passion for freedom.

KING, M. L., JR. *A Testament of Hope: The Essential Writings of Martin Luther King, Jr.* New York: Harper & Row, 1986. A good introduction to the thought of the most influential black American in history.

KINGSTON, M. H. *China Men.* New York: Knopf, 1980. Dealing with Kingston's patriarchal heritage, this autobiographical work complements *The Woman Warrior,* which focuses on matriarchal influences.

———. *The Woman Warrior: Memoirs of a Girlhood Among Ghosts.* New York: Knopf, 1976. A novel dealing with the confusion of growing up Chinese American in California; the "ghosts" of the subtitle refer to both the pale-faced Americans of the author's childhood and the spirits of Chinese ancestors and legendary female avengers brought to life by immigrant tales.

KUNDERA, M. *The Unbearable Lightness of Being.* Translated by M. H. Heim. New York: Harper & Row, 1984. A novel that explores the anguish of life under communism in Eastern Europe.

LESSING, D. *Children of Violence.* (Includes *Martha Quest, A Proper Marriage, A Ripple from the Storm, Landlocked.*) New York: Simon and Schuster, 1964–1966. *The Four-gated City.* New York: Knopf, 1969. Covering the period between the 1930s and 1960s, this series is Lessing's literary meditation on the transformation of her colonial homeland, Rhodesia, into the black state of Zimbabwe. Martha Quest, the focal point of this quintet of novels, is the author's surrogate witness to these turbulent events.

LÉVI-STRAUSS, C. *The Elementary Structures of Kinship.* Translated by J. H. Bell and others. Boston: Beacon Press, 1969. A classic of social anthropology, this work established that there are only a few basic patterns of kinship relationships in all societies.

MAILER, N. *The Naked and the Dead.* New York: Rinehart, 1948. Mailer's novel of World War II, his first and best work.

MORRISON, T. *Beloved.* New York: Plume, 1998. First published in 1987, *Beloved* widened Morrison's audience after it was made into a movie. Morrison transformed a true incident from pre–Civil War America into a haunting and complex story with the dimensions of a Greek tragedy.

SARTRE, J.-P. *The Age of Reason* and *The Reprieve.* Translated by E. Sutton. *Troubled Sleep.* Translated by G. Hopkins. New York: Knopf, 1947, 1947, and 1950. Sartre's trilogy of novels, called *The Roads to Freedom,* demonstrates existentialism in action.

———. *No Exit and Three Other Plays.* Translated by L. Abel and S. Gilbert. New York: Vintage, 1976. *No Exit* is Sartre's most famous drama, illustrating his idea that "hell is other people" because they strive to define us and see us as objects; also includes *Dirty Hands, The Respectful Prostitute,* and *The Flies.*

SOLZHENITSYN, A. *One Day in the Life of Ivan Denisovich.* Translated by R. Parker. New York: Dutton, 1963. Published with permission of the Soviet authorities, this novel revealed the existence of Stalin's slave labor camps.

THOMAS, D. *The Collected Poems of Dylan Thomas.* New York: New Directions, 1953. The finest lyric poet of the Late Modern period, Thomas wrote on such themes as sex, love, and death.

———. *Under Milk Wood, A Play for Voices.* New York: New Directions, 1954. A verse play set in a mythical Welsh village that comes to symbolize a lost world in an urbanized age.

WALKER, A. *The Color Purple.* New York: Harcourt Brace Jovanovich, 1982. An uplifting novel that describes the central black female character's rise from degradation to modest dignity. The heroine's awkward but poignantly moving letters reveal the difficulty and the ultimate heroism of her victory.

WRIGHT, R. *Black Boy: A Record of Childhood and Youth.* New York: Harper, 1945. Wright's description of his rise from sharecropper status to international renown.

———. *Native Son.* New York: Grossett and Dunlap, 1940. Wright's most celebrated novel, the powerful story of the violent consequences of racism in the life of a young black man.

SUGGESTIONS FOR LISTENING

ADAMS, JOHN (b. 1947). Adams, a minimalist, has emerged as one of the freshest composers working today. Noted for resonant sounds and strong mastery of form, his music embraces a wide array of media, including ochestra, as in *Harmonium* (1997), and especially opera, as in *Nixon in China* (1987), *The Death of Klinghoffer* (1991), and *I Was Looking at the Ceiling and Then I Saw the Sky* (1998).

ANDERSON, LAURIE (b. 1947). The premier performance artist of our time, Anderson has come a long way since 1973's *Duets on Ice,* when, dressed in a kilt and skating on ice, she played duets with herself on the violin (it had been altered to play a prerecorded solo) on Manhattan street corners, the duration of the piece dependent on the melting ice. More recent performances are memorialized through records such as *Mister Heartbreak* (1984); *Sharkey's Day* (1984), based on a Bauhaus work by Oskar Schlemmer; *Strange Angels* (1989), taken from the performance piece entitled *Empty Places; The Ugly One with the Jewels* (1995), generated by the performance called *Stories from the New Bible* (1992–1995); and *Songs and Stories from "Moby Dick"* (1999), based on Herman Melville's novel. Her most popular work to date—almost 900,000 copies sold—is *O Superman* (1980), a single record that was later incorporated into the epic-length *United States I–IV* (1983).

CAGE, JOHN (1912–1992). After the late 1950s, Cage's music came to be characterized by wholly random methods that he called *aleatory* (from the Latin *alea* for dice), as represented by *4'33"* (*Four Minutes and Thirty-three Seconds*) (1952), *Variations IV* (1963), and *Aria with Fonatana Mix* (1958).

GLASS, PHILIP (b. 1937). Glass's pulsating rhythms and cascading sounds have made him a popular and successful figure in Post-Modern music. He is best known for his operas, including *Einstein on the Beach* (1976), *Satyagraha* (1978), *Akhnaten* (1984), and *Monsters of Grace* (1998), and for his film scores, such as *Koyaanisqatsi* (1983), *Mishima* (1985), *Kundun* (1998), and the classic silent film *Dracula* (1999).

PENDERECKI, KRZYSTOF (b. 1933). Penderecki, an eclectic composer, draws inspiration from diverse sources, including Stravinsky and Classical and church music. Reflective of the turbulence of contemporary Poland, his music centers on themes of martyrdom, injustice, and persecution. The first work that made him an international musical star was *Threnody for the Victims of Hiroshima* (1960), a piece for orchestra that uses stringed instruments and human voices in unusual ways. Perhaps his masterpiece is the more traditional oratorio *Passion and Death of Our Lord Jesus Christ According to St. Luke,* more commonly called "The St. Luke Passion" (1966), which incorporates Gregorian chant, folk music, nonverbal choral sounds, and modified serialism. He also has had success with operas, as in the simultaneously dissonant and lyrical *Paradise Lost* (1978), based on Milton's epic poem (see Chapter 14).

STRAVINSKY, IGOR (1882–1971). After 1951 Stravinsky replaced his Neoclassical style with the technique of serial music, as in the song *In Memoriam Dylan Thomas* (1954), the ballet *Agon* (1954–1957), and the orchestral works *Movements* (1959) and *Orchestral Variations* (1964).

AFRICA

AMERICAS

HISTORY

North Africa *Morocco, Algeria, Tunisia, Libya, Egypt.* Became independent. *Egypt.* Suez Canal nationalized. Wars with Israel followed by peace negotiations.

Northeast Africa *Ethiopia.* Flourished under Emperor Haile Selassie (to 1977), followed by military coups, civil war, famine, secession of Eritrea.

West Africa *Nigeria.* Independent. Unstable rule.

Central Africa *Democratic Republic of Congo.* Independent (as Zaire).

East Africa *Tanzania.* Independent (as Tanganyika); union with Zanzibar formed Tanzania.

South Africa: *Zimbabwe.* Independent (as Rhodesia). Black majority to power; renamed Zimbabwe. *Republic of South Africa.* Apartheid segregated nonwhite majority (1948–1990). Black majority rule (1994).

Caribbean *Cuba.* Shift from right-wing to Marxist dictatorship, under Fidel Castro (1959). U.S.-Cuban missile crisis (1962). Loss of Soviet aid (1991); growing crisis.

Latin America *Mexico.* One-party governments. Joined Canada and U.S. in free-trade zone (1993). *Argentina.* Ruled by military juntas, starting with Juan Perón. Stability and prosperity under civilian president Carlos Menem. *Colombia.* Decade of political violence; followed by two-party government. Beset by guerrilla and drug wars. *Peru.* Military junta seized power; began to nationalize industries. Return to civilian government; fought Marxist rebels. *Brazil.* "Boom and bust" years, followed by military dictatorship, then civilian rule. Exploitation of Amazon basin.

Native North America Attempts in Congress to dismantle reservation system and Indian access to federal services (1948–62). Founding of American Indian Movement.

ART

Central Africa *Democratic Republic of Congo.* Kuba peoples: Textiles in patterns with natural motifs; carved wooden drinking vessels, masks, and royal thrones.

East Africa *Tanzania.* Carved wooden game boards. *Zimbabwe.* Art school teaching African painting and sculpture founded in Harare (1957).

Northwest Africa *Senegal.* School of the Beaux Arts founded in Dakar (1960s).

West Africa *Nigeria.* Nupe artists carved wooden doors, decorated with stylized figures and other designs. Art workshops *(mbari)* founded in Yoruba town of Oshogbo (1960s).

Latin America *Mexico. Ruptura* movement, inspired by Rufino Tamayo and led by José Luis Cuevas. *Argentina.* Neo-Expressionism and Post-Modernism. *Brazil and Chile.*

Conceptual, assemblage, and site-specific works. São Paulo Biennial International Art Exhibition founded. *Colombia.* On coast: folk art based on popular images. In interior: exaggerated figural style of painter and sculptor Fernando Botero and ironic style of Ramiro Arango.

Fernando Botero. Matador. 1986. Oil on canvas, 79⅕ × 47³/₅". Galerie Brusberg, Berlin.

ARCHITECTURE

Sub-Saharan Africa International and other European styles in African cities; traditional styles in towns and rural areas.

West Africa *Cameroon.* Rectangular forms used in forest, circular in grasslands. Palaces, regal tombs, and seats of secret societies built at bottom of slopes; less important buildings placed on higher ground.

State Throne Representing Chief Mene. Bamileke art. Musee de la Chefferie, Bansha. Cameroon.

Latin America *Mexico.* Thin-shell concrete design, in the Baroque spirit, pioneered by Spanish immigrant Félix Candela. University City complex, integrating visual and architectural design (1950s). *Brazil.* Brasilia, the futuristic capital city, built in the International Style of Le Corbusier; designed by Oscar Niemeyer. Use of thin-shelled, reinforced concrete.

Oscar Niemeyer. National Congress Building. 1958. Brasilia.

RELIGION, PHILOSOPHY, LITERATURE

North Africa Egyptian short story writer and novelist Naguib Mahfouz awarded Nobel Prize for literature (1988). Upsurge in Muslim fundamentalism threatens secular regimes (after 1990).

South Africa Archbishop Desmond Tutu, a leader of anti-apartheid movement, won Nobel Peace Prize (1984).

West Africa *Guinea.* Camara Laye, one of first sub-Saharan authors to win international acclaim. *Nigeria.* Igbo novelist Chinua Achebe, author of *Things Fall Apart* (1958); first major African writer to publish in English. Poet, playwright, and novelist Wole Soyinka awarded Nobel Prize for literature (1986). Novelist, poet, and sociologist Buchi Emecheta's *The Rape of Shavi* (1986).

Latin America Boom, Latin America's first major literary movement. Liberation theology, radical Catholic movement dedicated to helping the poor. *Mexico.* Poet Octavio Paz awarded Nobel Prize for literature (1990). *Argentina.* Julio Cortázar, author of *Hopscotch.* Manuel Puig, author of *Kiss of the Spider Woman. Chile.* Poet Pablo Neruda awarded Nobel Prize for literature (1971). *Colombia.* Gabriel García Márquez, author of *One Hundred Years of Solitude,* awarded Nobel Prize for literature (1982). *Peru.* Mario Vargas Llosa, author of *The War at the End of the World.* Gustavo Gutiérrez's *A Theology of Liberation,* the seminal text for liberation theology.

Native North America *House Made of Dawn,* by N. Scott Momaday (Kiowa), won Pulitzer Prize (1969). Other noted writers: Louise Erdrich, Vine Deloria, Simon Ortiz, Leslie Marmon Silko, Sherman Alexie.

China

Republic of China Civil war between Kuomintang and Communists before and after WWII.

People's Republic of China (PRC), 1949–present Nationalist forces retreated to Taiwan; Communists under Mao Zedong proclaimed People's Republic of China. Industry and agriculture nationalized. Cultural Revolution tore country apart (1966–69). Relations with U.S. restored, and relations with Soviet Union worsened (1971). Student demonstrations in Tiananmen Square (1989) and the rise of dissident voices. Relations with U.S. under stress (1990s).

India

British Crown. Self-rule (1947); mainly Muslim Pakistan and mainly Hindu India given independence. *Republic of India, 1947–present.* Stayed in British Commonwealth. Politics controlled by Congress Party and prime ministers drawn chiefly from Nehru family (to 1990). Pursued industrialization at home and neutrality in foreign affairs.

Pakistan Lost Bangladesh to Bengali separatists (1971); political instability.

Bangladesh Independent (1971). Political chaos, ethnic unrest, famine.

Japan

Shōwa period, ended 1989. Defeated (1945); occupied by U.S. troops (to 1952). New constitution (1947); monarchy based on English model with Shōwa emperor as figurehead; military dismantled; civil rights guaranteed. *Heisei period, 1989–present.* Economy prospered (to 1991). Ruled by single party (until 1993).

PRC Traditional landscape painting with political overtones. Hundred Flowers movement, a government program designed to open debate (1956–57). Cultural Revolution; artists executed and their works destroyed. Artistic controls loosened (1979); period of experimentation, especially with Western Expressionism.

Republic of India Art scene influenced by Western schools and "isms." Leading painters: Ram Kumar, Jyoti Bhatt, and Maqbool Fida Husain.

Maqbool Fida Husain. The Prancing Horse. *Oil on canvas, 25½ × 29½".*

Zhang Xiaogang. Painter with Mother as a Young Woman. *1993. Oil on canvas, 48 × 52". Collection of the Fukuoka Asian Art Museum, Japan.*

Shōwa period. Free expression returned with peace. Two schools: Nihonga, modified traditional painting, led by Kobayashi Kokei and Maeda Seison; Yoga, Western-style oil painting. Avant-garde artists, active in international circles, lacked audience at home.

PRC Massive building program in the wake of the Great Leap Forward, a drive to expand industry and agriculture (1958–60). Tiananmen Square complex, Beijing Great Hall of the People, surrounded by series of province halls.

Republic of India Indigenous vernacular buildings in villages and towns; hybrid style blending Indian and Western forms in large cities; and traditional styles for temple building. Designs by Western architects: the Swiss-French Le Corbusier in Chandigarh; the American Louis Kahn in Ahmadabad.

Shōwa period. Japanese architects, led by Tange Kenzo, developed a hybrid of Japanese and Western traditions, emphasizing simple lines, diffused lighting, and warm textures of Japanese style.

Tange Kenzo. Aerial view, Olympic Stadium. *1964. Reinforced steel, concrete. Tokyo.*

PRC *Quotations of Chairman Mao* (1966), an instant classic. Writers suppressed or driven to suicide during Cultural Revolution. Founding (1980s) of "Search for Roots," a cultural movement led by Zhang Yimou, director of the film *Raise the Red Lantern* (1991).

Republic of India Anantha Murthy's novel *Samskara* (1965) in the Kannada language. Popularity of English-language novels, led by the Hindu R. K. Narayan and the Muslim Salman Rushdie. Satyajit Ray's films, including *Pather Panchali* (1955).

Shōwa period. Mishima Yukio, author of *Confessions of a Mask* (1949) and director of *The Temple of the Golden Pavilion* (1959). Novelist Kawabata Yasunari won Nobel Prize for literature (1968). Film directors Akira Kurosawa (*Rashomon,* 1950; *Throne of Blood,* 1957); Juzo Itami (*A Taxing Woman,* 1988). *Heisei period.* Kenzaburo Oë, author of *A Personal Matter* (1964), won Nobel Prize for literature (1994).

APPENDIX
Writing for the Humanities: Research Papers and Essay Examinations

The most important part of a man's education is the ability to discuss poetry intelligently.

—PROTAGORAS, FIFTH CENTURY B.C.

I would have the ideal courtier accomplished in those studies that are called the humanities.

—CASTIGLIONE, SIXTEENTH CENTURY A.D.

The idea of "writing for the humanities" has a long history, extending back over twenty-five centuries to ancient Greece. There, in fifth-century-B.C. Athens, the Sophists invented what we today call a "liberal education." These philosophers, who could be termed the first humanists, taught literature, the arts, music, and philosophy, along with what we call political science, anthropology, psychology, and history, to young Athenians, particularly those who hoped to play a leading role in politics. Not only did the Sophists demand that their students master a specific body of knowledge, but they also took care to instruct them in putting the humanistic disciplines into practice. They believed that individuals who had honed their analytical skills in the study of the humanities would be able to make wise judgments in private and public matters and to contribute to the community's political affairs.

The Sophists' educational ideal—training for good citizenship—was later adopted by the Romans, who transmitted it to the medieval West, where it became a guiding principle of university education down to the present. Today, college humanities professors give writing assignments because of their belief in the liberal education ideal as well as because of their conviction that writing, despite the spread of mass media technology, remains an essential tool of private and public communication and the hallmark of the truly educated person.

AN INTEGRATIVE APPROACH TO WRITING ABOUT THE HUMANITIES

In your study of the humanities, you will probably be given writing assignments that reflect the integrative approach of *The Western Humanities* (see the Introduction). This means that your papers and examinations will not be limited to a single humanistic discipline. Instead, you will be expected to draw information from all the humanities as well as other disciplines that help illuminate the historical setting, such as political science, economics, and psychology. For example, if you were assigned a term paper on some aspect of nineteenth-century Europe, you would have to consider the civilization as a whole, both its material and its cultural developments, and at the same time bring into clearer focus such specific factors as the impact of the ruling middle class on stylistic changes in the arts and literature or the influence of the rise of nationalism on cultural developments. This integrative approach to writing reinforces the message of the textbook—that the humanities are best understood when studied holistically in their historical setting.

GENERAL RULES FOR WRITING

Typically, writing assignments for a college-level humanities course are out-of-class research or term papers and in-class essay examinations. Regardless of the writing format, keep in mind three general rules. First, think of writing as an exercise in persuasion. Assume the teacher is unfamiliar with the topic, and write to demonstrate your mastery of the material. Second, follow basic principles of good grammar and punctuation. Some teachers will penalize you for mistakes in grammar and punctuation. Even if that is not the case, instructors cannot help but be skeptical of your learning if your writing is riddled with errors. Third, accept criticism and learn from past mistakes. Few individuals are born with a gift for writing; most have to struggle to reach a writing level that is personally satisfying. Even many authors, including famous ones, still find the writing process itself deeply frustrating. Like swimming, writing cannot be learned by talking about it; it is a skill you acquire through experience. Writing well requires patience, practice, and the willingness to learn from mistakes.

RESEARCH AND TERM PAPERS

Learning to write well starts with good work habits. Establish a quiet and comfortable work space, such as a table at a library, a desk in a dormitory room, a computer station, or a desk in an empty classroom. A computer is necessary, as is access to references, such as dictionaries, biographical books and the Internet. Develop an orderly schedule of study; plan ahead so things are not left until the last minute. Balancing work and play is a prelude to writing well, since you need brief respites from intense study to rest and refresh your mind. If you arm yourself with good work habits, you will be ready to face the challenge of writing a research or term paper.

Steps in Writing a Paper

The first step in writing a research or term paper is to pick a topic. Choose a topic that is interdisciplinary, involving at least two humanistic fields of study, such as the arts and literature of a specific historical period. Make sure your topic is manageable, neither too narrowly nor too broadly focused for your paper's length. Above all, select a topic that sparks some intellectual interest in you. Otherwise, your finished paper, even if it is carefully researched, may turn out to be uninspired and pedestrian. If you cannot find something that appeals to you on a list of suggested topics, consult with your instructor about a new subject satisfactory to both of you. As part of choosing a topic, you should also decide what approach to use in your paper, such as analytical, impressionistic, overview, or other. These approaches are described in detail in the next section.

The next step is to establish a basic bibliography. Scan your school library's holdings, either through the card catalogue system or by computer, to identify books and articles relevant to your topic. Once you have accumulated a bibliography of perhaps twenty to thirty sources, check the library stacks for additional books with appropriate call numbers that you may have overlooked in your search thus far. Then survey all these sources, treating them as background reading. At this preparatory level, take some notes on file cards and draw up a fuller list of secondary and, if needed, primary sources, such as diaries or documents, from the bibliographies in the books you are examining. After completing this survey, you are ready to make an outline.

The outline—whether for a five-page paper or a major research project—is mandatory. The outline is a memory device that serves several functions: It forces you to stick to the main topics, keep an accurate perspective, incorporate relevant information, follow the framing narrative, and proceed in an orderly fashion from the opening to the conclusion. Rework your outline until it includes all relevant points and ideas. Think of it as the framework on which you raise your final piece of writing, molded into a coherent shape.

With the outline set, you are ready to make a first draft of your paper. One approach is to expand each section of the outline into a paragraph, incorporating your ideas, the facts, your examples, and your references into a narrative. Be sure to relate each paragraph to both the preceding and the succeeding paragraphs, keeping in mind the overall organization of the paper. Each paragraph should begin with a topic sentence, include examples and references to support the topic, and conclude with a summary sentence or an idea that leads into the next paragraph. Strive to remain invisible in the narrative except where a personal observation might be helpful, and try to write in the active rather than the passive voice. At times you will have to search for the word or phrase that best expresses your thought, perhaps with the help of a dictionary or a thesaurus.

The next step is to edit and re-edit your work until it sounds right. When you reread a first draft, it usually sounds like a first draft, tentative and filled with half-finished thoughts. A good test of your first draft is to read it aloud, either to yourself or to a fellow student. You will be more likely to notice gaps in logic, infelicitous words or phrases, and obvious errors in fact when you hear them out loud. At this point your good work habits will pay off, because you should now have time to polish and improve the text. Don't forget to proof the papers for misspelled words, typographical errors, and misstatements. Attention to literary style and correctness makes the difference between a satisfactory and an excellent paper.

Especially critical in writing a research paper is the citation of sources, or footnotes. Instructors have their varying policies about the use of footnotes, but the following rules apply in most situations. Short quotations (that is, a phrase or one or two sentences) may be cited in the text if the proper recognition is given. Sources for longer quotations (that is, three or more sentences) should be placed in a footnote. A full bibliography listing all books consulted, whether cited directly in the paper or not, should be included at the end of the paper. Regardless of the style you use, make sure the citation forms for footnotes are consistent throughout the paper. You should purchase a writing and style manual; often the instructor will tell you which one to buy. Two of the most frequently used manuals are the following:

Gibaldi, J. *MLA Handbook for Writers of Research Papers*. 5th ed. New York: Modern Language Association of America, 1999.

Turabian, K. Revised by J. Grossman and A. Bennett. *Student's Guide to Writing College Papers*. 6th ed. Chicago: University of Chicago Press, 1996.

Types of Term Papers Assigned in the Humanities

In your humanities course you may be assigned any one of various types of research or term papers, reflecting the breadth of the disciplines that are covered under the humanities rubric. The most common types are the impressionistic paper, the analytical paper, the historical overview, and the integrative paper. Each type requires a different approach, even though the basic writing techniques described above are valid for all.

The Impressionistic Paper   In this type of paper you offer a personal, though informed, reaction to some aspect of culture, such as the Gothic style or Post-Modernist art and architecture. Despite its focus on subjective feelings, the impressionistic paper nevertheless has to be documented with specific information, such as key historical events, biographical data, and details about particular works of art, literature, and music.

The Analytical Paper   Here, you compare and contrast two creative works. More strictly scholarly than an impressionistic paper, the analytical research paper usually requires that you study both the original works and the leading secondary sources that provide critical commentaries. Using this approach, you might examine two works within the same historical period, such as Aeschylus's tragedy *Agamemnon* and Sophocles' tragedy *Oedipus Rex;* or works across historical periods, such as Aeschylus's tragedy *Agamemnon* and Shakespeare's tragedy *Hamlet;* or works across genres, such as Aeschylus's tragedy *Agamemnon* and Verdi's opera *Rigoletto.*

The Historical Overview   In this type of paper you survey a specific time period to establish or explain a particular outcome, such as the prevailing worldview, or the leading cultural characteristics, or the impact of a particular social class. For example, if your topic were the role of aristocratic courts in the arts of the Italian Renaissance, you would have to survey fifteenth- and sixteenth-century Italian history and culture as well as the history of specific courts, such as that of the Medici in Florence and the Sforza in Milan.

The Integrative Paper   This type of paper offers a versatile approach, since it allows for a combination of many topics. For example, if you wanted to write on Freudian theory and its application to culture, you would have to research the principles of Freudian theory and discuss Freudian interpretations of specific examples of art and literature. Or, if your topic were the Classical ideal of restraint in the late eighteenth century, you would have to research the period's music, art, literature, economic theory, and political theory.

ESSAY EXAMINATIONS

Besides research papers, you will also have to write essay tests in most college-level humanities courses. The purpose of such tests is to allow you to demonstrate how well you comprehend the course lectures and readings. To succeed on essay tests, you must learn to take notes efficiently during class and while reading out-of-class assignments and to analyze the assigned material in study sessions.

The following steps will help you write better essays on examinations:

1. Before the exam, master the assigned material through sound and productive work habits. This means keeping up with daily assignments, rereading and studying lecture notes, and reviewing study materials over a four- to five-day period before the test.

2. During the exam, read the entire test carefully before beginning to write. This will ensure that you understand all the questions and allow you to set a time frame for completing each section of the exam. If you are unsure about the meaning of a question, do not hesitate to ask the instructor for a clarification.

3. If there are choices, answer those questions first that seem the easiest. This rule simply reflects common sense; it is always best to lead with your strength.

4. Briefly outline the answer to each question. The outline should include an introduction, a section for each part of the question, and a conclusion. If time permits, it is also helpful to include the major points you want to cover, specific examples or illustrations, and ideas for topic sentences and conclusions of paragraphs. The outline will help you stick to the main topics and finish the exam on time. It can also trigger more ideas while you are writing it.

5. Follow sound writing rules in composing each essay. Begin each paragraph with a topic sentence; then give examples from a wide range of sources in the humanities to support the opening statement; and conclude with a paragraph that pulls the main arguments together. Take nothing for granted. Be concise but specific. Unless they are asked for, keep your own opinions to a bare minimum.

6. Review the exam. Before turning in the exam to the monitor, review your test to correct errors, give added examples, and clarify arguments, where needed. Always allow time to proofread an essay exam.

If you score poorly on the first essay exam in a course, consult with the instructor about how to improve your performance. But remember that improvement is seldom instantaneous and good writing is achieved only after practice. Old habits die hard; the only way to do better on papers and essay exams is to keep on writing.

Glossary

Italicized words within definitions are defined in their own glossary entries.

abstract art Art that presents a subjective view of the world—the artist's emotions or ideas—or art that presents *line, color,* or shape for its own sake.

Abstract Expressionism Also known as Action Painting, a nonrepresentational artistic style that flourished after World War II and was typified by randomness, spontaneity, and an attempt by the artist to interact emotionally with the work as it was created.

abstraction In Modern art, nonrepresentational or nonobjective forms in sculpture and painting that emphasize shapes, *lines,* and *colors* independent of the natural world.

a cappella [ah kuh-PEL-uh] From the Italian, "in chapel style"; music sung without instrumental accompaniment.

aesthete One who pursues and is devoted to the beautiful in art, music, and literature.

aisles The side passages in a church on either side of the central *nave.*

Alexandrianism [al-ig-ZAN-dree-an-ism] A literary style developed in the *Hellenistic* period, typically formal, artificial, and imitative of earlier Greek writing.

ambulatory [AM-bue-la-tor-e] A passageway for walking found in many religious structures, such as outdoors in a cloister or indoors around the *apse* or the *choir* of a church.

Anglicanism The doctrines and practices of the Church of England, which was established in the early sixteenth century under Henry VIII.

anthropomorphism [an-thro-po-MOR-fizm] The attributing of humanlike characteristics and traits to nonhuman things or powers, such as a deity.

apocalypse [uh-PAHK-uh-lips] In Jewish and early Christian thought, the expectation and hope of the coming of God and his final judgment; also closely identified with the last book of the New Testament, Revelation, in which many events are foretold, often in highly symbolic and imaginative terms.

apse In architecture, a large projection, usually rounded or semicircular, found in a *basilica,* usually in the east end; in Christian *basilicas,* the altar stood in this space.

arabesque [air-uh-BESK] Literally, "Arabian-like"; decorative lines, patterns, and designs, often floral, in Islamic works of art.

arcade A series of arches supported by *piers* or columns, usually serving as a passageway along a street or between buildings.

Archaic style The style in Greek sculpture, dating from the seventh century to 480 B.C., that was characterized by heavy Egyptian influence; dominated by the *kouros* and *kore* sculptural forms.

architrave [AHR-kuh-trayv] The part of the *entablature* that rests on the *capital* or column in Classical *post-beam-triangle construction.*

aria [AH-ree-uh] In music, an elaborate *melody* sung as a solo or sometimes a duet, usually in an *opera* or an *oratorio,* with an orchestral accompaniment.

art song (lied) In music, a *lyric* song with *melody* performed by a singer and instrumental accompaniment usually provided by piano; made popular by Schubert in the nineteenth century.

ashlar [ASH-luhr] A massive hewn or squared stone used in constructing a fortress, palace, or large building.

assemblage art An art form in which the artist mixes and/or assembles "found objects," such as scraps of paper, cloth, or junk, into a three-dimensional work and then adds paint or other decorations to it.

ataraxia [at-uh-RAK-see-uh] Greek, "calmness"; in *Hellenistic* philosophy, the state of desiring nothing.

atonality [ay-toe-NAL-uh-tee] In music, the absence of a *key* note or tonal center and the use of the *tones* of the chromatic *scale* impartially.

atrium [AY-tree-uhm] In Roman architecture, an open courtyard at the front of a house; in Christian *Romanesque* churches, an open court, usually colonnaded, in front of the main doors of the structure.

attic The topmost section or crown of an arch.

audience The group or person for whom a work of art, architecture, literature, drama, film, or music is intended.

aulos In music, a reed woodwind instrument similar to the oboe, usually played in pairs by one player as the double aulos; used in Greek music.

autarky [AW-tar-kee] Greek, "self-sufficient"; in *Hellenistic* thought, the state of being isolated and free from the demands of society.

avant-garde [a-vahn-GARD] French, "advanced guard"; writers, artists, and intellectuals who push their works and ideas ahead of more traditional groups and movements.

baldacchino [ball-duh-KEE-no] An ornamental structure in the shape of a canopy, supported by four columns, built over a church altar, and usually decorated with statues and other ornaments.

balustrade In architecture, a rail and the row of posts that support it, as along the edge of a staircase or around a dome.

baptistery A small, often octagonal structure, separated from the main church, where baptisms were performed.

bard A tribal poet-singer who composes and recites works, often of the *epic poetry* genre.

Baroque [buh-ROKE] The prevailing seventeenth-century artistic and cultural style, characterized by an emphasis on grandeur, opulence, expansiveness, and complexity.

barrel vault A ceiling or *vault* made of sets of arches placed side by side and joined together.

basilica [buh-SILL-ih-kuh] A rectangular structure that included an *apse* at one or both ends; originally a Roman building used for public purposes, later taken over by the Christians for worship. The floor plan became the basis of nearly all early Christian churches.

bay A four-cornered unit of architectural space, often used to identify a section of the *nave* in a *Romanesque* or *Gothic* church.

bel canto [bell KAHN-toe] Italian, "beautiful singing"; a style of singing characteristic of seventeenth-century Italian *opera* stressing ease, purity, and evenness of tone along with precise vocal technique.

blank verse Unrhymed iambic pentameter (lines with five feet, or units, each consisting of an unaccented and an accented syllable).

blind arcade A decorative architectural design that gives the appearance of an open *arcade* or window but is filled in with some type of building material such as stone or brick.

blues A type of music that emerged around 1900 from the rural African American culture, was originally based on work songs and religious spirituals, and expressed feelings of loneliness and hopelessness.

Byzantine style [BIZ-uhn-teen] In painting, decoration, and architecture, a style blending Greco-Roman and oriental components into a highly stylized art form that glorified Christianity, notably in domed churches adorned with *mosaics* and polished marble; associated with the culture of the Eastern Roman Empire from about 500 until 1453.

Cajun A descendant of French pioneers, chiefly in Louisiana, who in 1755 chose to leave Acadia (modern Nova Scotia) rather than live under the British Crown.

calligraphy Penmanship or handwriting, usually done with flowing lines, used as a decoration or as an enhancement of a written work; found in Islamic and Christian writings.

Calvinism The theological beliefs and rituals set forth in and derived from John Calvin's writings, placing emphasis on the power of God and the weakness of human beings.

campanile From the Latin "campana," bell; a bell tower, especially one near but not attached to a church; an Italian invention.

canon A set of principles or rules that are accepted as true and authoritative for the various arts or fields of study; in architecture, it refers to the standards of proportion; in painting, the prescribed ways of painting certain objects; in sculpture, the ideal proportions of the human body; in literature, the authentic list of an author's works; in religion, the approved and authoritative writings that are accepted as divinely inspired, such as the *Scriptures* for Jews and Christians; and in religious and other contexts, certain prescribed rituals or official rules and laws. In music, a canon is a *composition* in which a *melody* sung by one voice is repeated exactly by successive voices as they enter.

canzone [kan-ZOH-nee] Latin, "chant"; a type of love poem popular in southern France during the twelfth and thirteenth centuries.

capital In architecture, the upper or crowning part of a column, on which the *entablature* rests.

cathedral The church of a bishop that houses a cathedra, or throne symbolizing the seat of power in his administrative district, known as a diocese.

cella [SELL-uh] The inner sanctum or walled room of a *Classical* temple where sacred statues were housed.

chanson [shahn-SAWN] French, "song"; a fourteenth- to sixteenth-century French song for one or more voices, often with instrumental accompaniment. Similar to a *madrigal*.

chanson de geste [shahn-SAWN duh zhest] A poem of brave deeds in the *epic* form developed in France during the eleventh century, usually to be sung.

character A person in a story or play; someone who acts out or is affected by the *plot*.

chiaroscuro [key-ahr-uh-SKOOR-oh] In painting, the use of dark and light contrast to create the effect of modeling of a figure or object.

chivalric code The rules of conduct, probably idealized, that governed the social roles and duties of aristocrats in the Middle Ages.

chivalric novel A late medieval literary form that presented romantic stories of knights and their ladies; the dominant literary form in Spain from the Late Middle Ages into the Renaissance.

choir In architecture, that part of a *Gothic* church in which the service was sung by singers or clergy, located in the east end beyond the *transept;* also, the group of trained singers who sat in the choir area.

chorus In Greek drama, a group of performers who sang and danced in both *tragedies* and *comedies,* often commenting on the action; in later times, a group of singers who performed with or without instrumental accompaniment.

Christian humanism An intellectual movement in sixteenth-century northern Europe that sought to use the ideals of the *Classical* world, the tools of ancient learning, and the morals of the Christian *Scriptures* to rid the church of worldliness and scandal.

chthonian deities [THOE-nee-uhn] In Greek religion, earth gods and goddesses who lived underground and were usually associated with peasants and their religious beliefs.

civilization The way humans live in a complex political, economic, and social structure, usually in an urban environment, with some development in technology, literature, and art.

Classic, or **Classical** Having the forms, values, or standards embodied in the art and literature of Greek and Roman *civilization;* in music, an eighteenth-century style characterized by simplicity, proportion, and an emphasis on structure.

Classical Baroque style A secular variation of the *Baroque* style that was identified with French kings and artists, was rooted in *Classical* ideals, and was used mainly to emphasize the power and grandeur of the monarchy.

Classicism A set of aesthetic principles found in Greek and Roman art and literature emphasizing the search for perfection or ideal forms.

clavier [French, KLAH-vyay; German, KLAH-veer] Any musical instrument having a keyboard, such as a piano, organ, or harpsichord; the term came into general usage with the popularity of Bach's set of studies entitled *The Well-Tempered Clavier.*

clerestory windows [KLEER-stor-ee] A row of windows set along the upper part of a wall, especially in a church.

collage [koh-LAHZH] From the French "coller," to glue, a type of art, introduced by Picasso, in which bits and pieces of materials such as paper or cloth are glued to a painted surface.

color Use of the hues found in nature to enhance or distort the sense of reality in a visual image.

comedy A literary genre characterized by a story with a complicated and amusing *plot* that ends with a happy and peaceful resolution of all conflicts.

comedy of manners A humorous play that focuses on the way people in a particular social group or class interact with one another, especially regarding fashions and manners.

composition The arrangement of constituent elements in an artistic work; in music, composition also refers to the process of creating the work.

concerto [kuhn-CHER-toe] In music, a composition for one or more soloists and *orchestra,* usually in a symphonic *form* with three contrasting movements.

consort A set of musical instruments in the same family, ranging from bass to soprano; also, a group of musicians who entertain by singing or playing instruments.

Constructivism A movement in nonobjective art, originating in the Soviet Union and flourishing from 1917 to 1922 and concerned with planes and volumes as expressed in modern industrial materials such as glass and plastic.

content The subject matter of an artistic work.

context The setting in which an artistic work arose, its own time and place. Context includes the political, economic, social, and cultural conditions of the time; it can also include the personal circumstances of the artist's life.

contrapposto [kon-truh-POH-stoh] In sculpture and painting, the placement of the human figure so the weight is more on one leg than the other and the shoulders and chest are turned in the opposite direction from the hips and legs.

convention An agreed-upon practice, device, technique, or form.

Corinthian The third Greek architectural order, in which temple columns are slender and *fluted,* sit on a base, and have *capitals* shaped like inverted bells and decorated with carvings representing the leaves of the acanthus bush; this style was popular in *Hellenistic* times and widely adopted by the Romans.

cornice In architecture, the crowning, projecting part of the *entablature.*

Counter-Reformation A late-sixteenth-century movement in the Catholic Church aimed at reestablishing its basic beliefs, reforming its organizational structure, and reasserting itself as the authoritative voice of Christianity.

covenant In Judaism and Christianity, a solemn and binding agreement or contract between God and his followers.

Creole An ambiguous term, sometimes referring to descendants of French and Spanish settlers of the southern United States, especially Louisiana; used by Kate Chopin in her short stories and novels in this sense. In other contexts, *Creole* can refer either to blacks born in the Western Hemisphere (as distinguished from blacks born in Africa) or to residents of the American Gulf States of mixed black, Spanish, and Portuguese ancestry.

cruciform [KROO-suh-form] Cross-shaped; used to describe the standard floor plan of a church.

Cubism A style of painting introduced by Picasso and Braque in which objects are broken up into fragments and patterns of geometric structures and depicted on the flat canvas as if from several points of view.

culture The sum of human endeavors, including the basic political, economic, and social institutions and the values, beliefs, and arts of those who share them.

cuneiform [kue-NEE-uh-form] Wedge-shaped characters used in writing on tablets found in Mesopotamia and other ancient *civilizations*.

Cynicism A *Hellenistic* philosophy that denounced society and its institutions as artificial and called on the individual to strive for *autarky*.

Dada [DAH-dah] An early-twentieth-century artistic movement, named after a nonsense word that was rooted in a love of play, encouraged deliberately irrational acts, and exhibited contempt for all traditions.

Decadence A late-nineteenth-century literary style concerned with morbid and artificial subjects and themes.

deductive reasoning The process of reasoning from the general to the particular—that is, beginning with an accepted premise or first statement and, by steps of logical reasoning or inference, reaching a conclusion that necessarily follows from the premise.

Deism [DEE-iz-uhm] A religion based on the idea that the universe was created by God and then left to run according to *natural laws,* without divine interference; formulated and practiced in the eighteenth century.

de Stijl [duh STILE] Dutch, "the style"; an artistic movement associated with a group of early-twentieth-century Dutch painters who used rectangular forms and primary colors in their works and who believed that art should have spiritual values and a social purpose.

devotio moderna [de-VO-tee-oh mo-DER-nuh] The "new devotion" of late medieval Christianity that emphasized piety and discipline as practiced by lay religious communities located primarily in northern Europe.

Diaspora [dye-AS-puhr-uh] From the Greek, "to scatter"; the dispersion of the Jews from their homeland in ancient Palestine, a process that began with the Babylonian Captivity in the sixth century B.C. and continued over the centuries.

Dionysia [DYE-uh-NYSH-ee-ah] Any of the religious festivals held in ancient Athens honoring Dionysus, the god of wine; especially the Great Dionysia, celebrated in late winter and early spring in which *tragedy* is thought to have originated.

Doric The simplest and oldest of the Greek architectural orders, in which temple columns have undecorated *capitals* and rest directly on the *stylobate*.

drypoint In art, the technique of incising an image, using a sharp, pointed instrument, onto a metal surface or block used for printing. Also, the print made from the technique.

Early Renaissance style A style inspired by *Classical* rather than *Gothic* models that arose among Florentine architects, sculptors, and painters in the late fourteenth and early fifteenth century.

empiricism The process of collecting data, making observations, carrying out experiments based on the collected data and observations, and reaching a conclusion.

engraving In art, the technique of carving, cutting, or etching an image with a sharp, pointed instrument onto a metal surface overlaid with wax, dipping the surface in acid, and then printing it. Also, the print made from the technique.

Enlightenment The eighteenth-century philosophical and cultural movement marked by the application of reason to human problems and affairs, a questioning of traditional beliefs and ideas, and an optimistic faith in unlimited progress for humanity, particularly through education.

entablature [en-TAB-luh-choor] In architecture, the part of the temple above the columns and below the roof, which, in *Classical* temples, included the *architrave,* the *frieze,* and the *pediment.*

entasis [EN-ta-sis] In architecture, convex curving or enlarging of the central part of a column to correct the optical illusion that the column is too thin.

epic A poem, novel, or film that recounts at length the life of a hero or the history of a people.

epic poetry Narrative poetry, usually told or written in an elevated style, that recounts the life of a hero.

epic theater A type of theater, invented by Brecht, in which major social issues are dramatized with outlandish props and jarring dialogue and effects, all designed to alienate middle-class audiences and force them to think seriously about the problems raised in the plays.

Epicureanism [ep-i-kyoo-REE-uh-niz-uhm] A *Hellenistic* philosophy, founded by Epicurus and later expounded by the Roman Lucretius, that made its highest goals the development of the mind and an existence free from the demands of everyday life.

eschatology [es-kuh-TAHL-uh-jee] The concern with final events or the end of the world, a belief popular in Jewish and early Christian communities and linked to the concept of the coming of a *Messiah.*

evangelists From the Greek *evangelion,* a term generally used for those who preach the Christian religion; more specifically, the four evangelists, Matthew, Mark, Luke, and John, who wrote about Jesus Christ soon after his death in the first four books of the New Testament.

evolution The theory, set forth in the nineteenth century by Charles Darwin, that plants and animals, including humans, evolved over millions of years from simpler forms through a process of natural selection.

existentialism [eg-zi-STEN-shuh-liz-uhm] A twentieth-century philosophy focusing on the precarious nature of human existence, with its uncertainty, anxiety, and ultimate death, as well as on individual freedom and responsibility and the possibilities for human creativity and authenticity.

Expressionism A late-nineteenth-century literary and artistic movement characterized by the expression of highly personal feelings rather than of objective reality.

fan vault A decorative pattern of *vault* ribs that arch out or radiate from a central point on the ceiling; popular in English *Perpendicular* architecture.

Faustian [FAU-stee-uhn] Resembling the character Faust in Goethe's most famous work, in being spiritually tormented, insatiable for knowledge and experience, or willing to pay any price, including personal and spiritual integrity, to gain a desired end.

Fauvism [FOH-viz-uhm] From the French "fauve," wild beast; an early-twentieth-century art movement led by Matisse and favoring exotic colors and disjointed shapes.

fête galante [fet gah-LAHNN] In *Rococo* painting, the *theme* or scene of aristocrats being entertained or simply enjoying their leisure and other worldly pleasures.

Flamboyant style [flam-BOY-uhnt] A Late French *Gothic* architectural style of elaborate decorations and ornamentation that produce a flamelike effect.

Florid Baroque style   A variation of the *Baroque* style specifically identified with the Catholic Church's patronage of the arts and used to glorify its beliefs.

fluting   Decorative vertical grooves carved in a column.

flying buttress   An external masonry support, found primarily in *Gothic* churches, that carries the thrust of the ceiling or *vault* away from the upper walls of the building to an external vertical column.

forms   In music, particular structures or arrangements of elements, such as *symphonies*, songs, concerts, and *operas*.

forum   In Rome and many Roman towns, the public place, located in the center of the town, where people gathered to socialize, transact business, and administer the government.

Fourth Century style   The sculptural style characteristic of the last phase of the *Hellenic* period, when new interpretations of beauty and movement were adopted.

fresco   A painting done on wet or dry plaster that becomes part of the plastered wall.

friars   Members of a thirteenth-century mendicant (begging) monastic order.

frieze [FREEZ]   A band of painted designs or sculptured figures placed on walls; also, the central portion of a temple's *entablature* just above the *architrave*.

fugue [fewg]   In music, a *composition* for several instruments in which a *theme* is introduced by one instrument and then repeated by each successively entering instrument so that a complicated interweaving of themes, variations, imitations, and echoes results; this compositional technique began in the fifteenth century and reached its zenith in the *Baroque* period in works by Bach.

gallery   In architecture, a long, narrow passageway or corridor, usually found in churches and located above the *aisles*, and often with openings that permit viewing from above into the *nave*.

gargoyle [GAHR-goil]   In architecture, a water spout in the form of a grotesque animal or human, carved from stone, placed on the edge of a roof.

genre [ZHON-ruh]   From the French, "a kind, a type, or a class"; a category of artistic, musical, or literary composition, characterized by a particular *style*, *form*, or *content*.

genre subject   In art, a scene or a person from everyday life, depicted realistically and without religious or symbolic significance.

geocentrism   The belief that the earth is the center of the universe and that the sun, planets, and stars revolve around it.

glissando [gle-SAHN-doe] (plural, **glissandi**)   In music, the blending of one *tone* into the next in scalelike passages that may be ascending or descending in character.

goliards [GOAL-yuhrds]   Medieval roaming poets or scholars who traveled about reciting poems on topics ranging from moral lessons to the pains of love.

Gospels   The first four books of the New Testament (Matthew, Mark, Luke, and John) that record the life and sayings of Jesus Christ; the word itself, from Old English, means good news or good tales.

Gothic style   A *style* of architecture, usually associated with churches, that originated in northern France and whose three phases—Early, High, and Late—lasted from the twelfth to the sixteenth century. Emerging from the *Romanesque* style, Gothic is identified by pointed arches, *ribbed vaults*, *stained-glass* windows, *flying buttresses*, and carvings on the exterior.

Greek cross   A cross in which all the arms are of equal length; the shape used as a floor plan in many Greek or Eastern Orthodox churches.

Gregorian chant   A style of *monophonic* church music sung in unison and without instrumental accompaniment and used in the *liturgy*; named for Pope Gregory I (590–604).

groined vault, or **cross vault**   A ceiling or *vault* created when two *barrel vaults*, set at right angles, intersect.

harmony   The simultaneous combination of two or more *tones*, producing a chord; generally, the chordal characteristics of a work and the way chords interact.

heliocentrism   The belief that the sun is the center of the universe and that the earth and the other planets revolve around it.

Hellenic [hell-LENN-ik]   Relating to the time period in Greek civilization from 480 to 323 B.C., when the most influential Greek artists, playwrights, and philosophers, such as Praxiteles, Sophocles, and Plato, created their greatest works; associated with the *Classical* style.

Hellenistic [hell-uh-NIS-tik]   Relating to the time period from about 323 to 31 B.C., when Greek and oriental or Middle Eastern cultures and institutions intermingled to create a heterogeneous and cosmopolitan *civilization*.

hieroglyphs [HI-uhr-uh-glifs]   Pictorial characters used in Egyptian writing, which is known as hieroglyphics.

High Classical style   The *style* in Greek sculpture associated with the ideal physical form and perfected during the zenith of the Athenian Empire, about 450–400 B.C.

higher criticism   A rational approach to Bible study, developed in German Protestant circles in the nineteenth century, that treated the biblical *Scriptures* as literature and subjected them to close scrutiny, testing their literary history, authorship, and meaning.

High Renaissance   The period from about 1495 to 1520, often associated with the patronage of the popes in Rome, when the most influential artists and writers of the *Renaissance*, including Michelangelo, Raphael, Leonardo da Vinci, and Machiavelli, were producing their greatest works.

high tech   In architecture, a *style* that uses obvious industrial design elements with exposed parts serving as decorations.

Homeric epithet   A recurring nickname, such as "Ox-eyed Hera," used in Homer's *Iliad* or *Odyssey*.

hubris [HYOO-bris]   In Greek thought, human pride or arrogance that leads an individual to challenge the gods, usually provoking divine retribution.

humanism   An attitude that is concerned with humanity, its achievements, and its potential; the study of the *humanities*; in the *Renaissance*, identified with *studia humanitatis*.

humanities   In the nineteenth century, the study of Greek and Roman languages and literature; later set off from the sciences and expanded to include the works of all Western peoples in the arts, literature, music, philosophy, and sometimes history and religion; in *Post-Modernism* extended to a global dimension.

hymn   From the Greek and Latin, "ode of praise of gods or heroes"; a song of praise or thanksgiving to God or the gods, performed both with and without instrumental accompaniment.

idealism   in Plato's philosophy, the theory that reality and ultimate truth are to be found not in the material world but in the spiritual realm.

idée fixe [ee-DAY FEEX]   *French, "fixed idea"; in music, a recurring musical *theme* that is associated with a person or a concept.

ideogram [ID-e-uh-gram]   A picture drawn to represent an idea or a concept.

idyll   A relatively short poem that focuses on events and themes of everyday life, such as family, love, and religion; popular in the *Hellenistic Age* and a standard form that has been periodically revived in Western literature throughout the centuries.

illuminated manuscript   A richly decorated book, painted with brilliant colors and gold leaf, usually of sacred writings; popular in the West in the Middle Ages.

illusionism   The use of painting techniques in *Florid Baroque* art to create the appearance that decorated areas are part of the surrounding architecture, usually employed in ceiling decorations.

impasto [ihm-PAHS-toe]   In painting, the application of thick layers of pigment.

Impressionism   In painting, a *style* introduced in the 1870s, marked by an attempt to catch spontaneous impressions, often involving the play of sunlight on ordinary events and scenes observed outdoors; in music, a style of *composition* designed to create a vague and dreamy mood through gliding melodies and shimmering tone colors.

impressionistic   In art, relating to the representation of a scene using the simplest details to create an illusion of reality by evoking subjective impressions rather than aiming for a totally realistic effect; characterized by images that are insubstantial and barely sketched in.

inductive reasoning   The process of reasoning from particulars to the general or from single parts to the whole and/or final conclusion.

installation art   A boundary-challenging type of art born in the 1960s that creates architectural tableaux, using objects drawn from and making references to artistic sources (such as music, painting, sculpture, and theater) and the workaday world (such as everyday tasks, media images, and foodstuffs) and that may include a human presence. Associated with the work of Ann Hamilton.

International style   In twentieth-century architecture, a *style* and method of construction that capitalized on modern materials, such as ferro-concrete, glass, and steel, and that produced the popular "glass box" skyscrapers and variously shaped private houses.

Ionic   The Greek architectural order, developed in Ionia, in which columns are slender, sit on a base, and have *capitals* decorated with scrolls.

Italo-Byzantine style [ih-TAL-o-BIZ-uhn-teen]   The *style* of Italian *Gothic* painting that reflected the influence of *Byzantine* paintings, *mosaics*, and icons.

jazz   A type of music, instrumental and vocal, originating in the African American community and rooted in African, African American, and Western musical forms and traditions.

Jesuits [JEZH-oo-its]   Members of the Society of Jesus, the best-organized and most effective monastic order founded during the *Counter-Reformation* to combat Protestantism and spread Roman Catholicism around the world.

key   In music, a tonal system consisting of seven *tones* in fixed relationship to a tonic, or keynote. Since the Renaissance, *key* has been the structural foundation of the bulk of Western music, down to the *Modernist* period.

keystone   The central stone at the top of an arch that locks the other stones in place.

koine [KOI-nay]   A colloquial Greek language spoken in the *Hellenistic* world that helped tie together that *civilization.*

kore [KOH-ray]   An *Archaic* Greek standing statue of a young draped female.

kouros [KOO-rus]   An *Archaic* Greek standing statue of a young naked male.

Late Gothic style   A *style* characterized in architecture by ornate decoration and tall cathedral windows and spires and in painting and sculpture by increased refinement of details and a trend toward naturalism; popular in the fourteenth and fifteenth centuries in central and western Europe.

Late Mannerism   The last stage of the *Mannerist* movement, characterized by exaggeration and distortion, especially in painting.

Late Modernism   The last stage of *Modernism,* characterized by an increasing sense of existential despair, an attraction to non-Western cultures, and extreme experimentalism.

lay   A short *lyric* or narrative poem meant to be sung to the accompaniment of an instrument such as a harp; based on Celtic legends but usually set in feudal times and focused on courtly love themes, especially adulterous passion. The oldest surviving lays are those of the twelfth-century poet Marie de France.

leitmotif [LITE-mo-teef]   In music, and especially in Wagner's *operas,* the use of recurring *themes* associated with particular characters, objects, or ideas.

liberalism   In political thought, a set of beliefs advocating certain personal, economic, and natural rights based on assumptions about the perfectibility and autonomy of human beings and the notion of progress, as first expressed in the writings of John Locke.

libretto [lih-BRET-oh]   In Italian, "little book"; the text or words of an *opera,* an *oratorio,* or a musical work of a similar dramatic nature involving a written text.

line   The mark—straight or curved, thick or thin, light or dark—made by the artist in a work of art.

Linear A   In Minoan civilization, a type of script still undeciphered that lasted from about 1800 to 1400 B.C.

Linear B   In Minoan civilization, an early form of Greek writing that flourished on Crete from about 1400 until about 1300 B.C. and lasted in a few scattered places on the Greek mainland until about 1150 B.C.; used to record commercial transactions.

liturgical drama   Religious dramas, popular between the twelfth and sixteenth centuries, based on biblical stories with musical accompaniment that were staged in the area in front of the church, performed at first in Latin but later in the *vernacular languages;* the mystery plays (*mystery* is derived from the Latin for "action") are the most famous type of liturgical drama.

liturgy   A rite or ritual, such as prayers or ceremonies, practiced by a religious group in public worship.

local color   In literature, the use of detail peculiar to a particular region and environment to add interest and authenticity to a narrative, including description of the locale, customs, speech, and music. Local color was an especially popular development in American literature in the late nineteenth century.

logical positivism   A school of modern philosophy that seeks truth by defining terms and clarifying statements and asserts that metaphysical theories are meaningless.

logos [LOWG-os]   In *Stoicism,* the name for the supreme being or for reason—the controlling principle of the universe—believed to be present both in nature and in each human being.

lute   In music, a wooden instrument, plucked or bowed, consisting of a sound box with an elaborately carved sound hole and a neck across which the (often twelve) strings pass. Introduced during the High Middle Ages, the lute enjoyed a height of popularity in Europe from the seventeenth to eighteenth century.

Lutheranism   The doctrine, liturgy, and institutional structure of the church founded in the sixteenth century by Martin Luther, who stressed the authority of the Bible, the faith of the individual, and the worshiper's direct communication with God as the bases of his new religion.

lyre   In music, a hand-held stringed instrument, with or without a sound box, used by ancient Egyptians, Assyrians, and Greeks. In Greek culture, the lyre was played to accompany song and recitation.

lyric   A short subjective poem that expresses intense personal emotion.

lyric poetry   In Greece, verses sung and accompanied by the *lyre;* today, intensely personal poetry.

Machiavellianism [mahk-ih-uh-VEL-ih-uhn-iz-uhm]   The view that politics should be separated from morals and dedicated to the achievement of desired ends through any means necessary ("the end justifies the means"); derived from the political writings of Machiavelli.

madrigal [MAD-rih-guhl]   A *polyphonic* song performed without accompaniment and based on a secular text, often a love *lyric;* especially popular in the sixteenth century.

maenad [MEE-nad]   A woman who worshiped Dionysus, often in a state of frenzy.

magic realism   A literary and artistic *style* identified with Latin American *Post-Modernism* that mixes realistic and supernatural elements to create imaginary or fantastic scenes.

Mannerism   A cultural movement between 1520 and 1600 that grew out of a rebellion against the *Renaissance* artistic norms of symmetry and balance; characterized in art by distortion and incongruity and in thought and literature by the belief that human nature is depraved.

Mass   In religion, the ritual celebrating the Eucharist, or Holy Communion, primarily in the Roman Catholic Church. The Mass has two parts, the Ordinary and the Proper; the former remains the same throughout the church year, whereas the latter changes for each date and service. The Mass Ordinary is composed of the Kyrie, Gloria, Credo, Sanctus, and Agnus Dei; the Mass Proper includes the Introit, Gradual, Alleluia or Tract, Sequence, Offertory, and Communion. In music, a musical setting of certain parts of the Mass, especially the Kyrie, Gloria, Credo, Sanctus, Benedictus, and Agnus Dei. The first complete Mass Ordinary was composed by Guillaume de Machaut [mah-SHOH] (about 1300–1377) in the fourteenth century.

mass culture   The tastes, values, and interests of the classes that dominate modern industrialized society, especially the consumer-oriented American middle class.

medallion   In Roman architecture, a circular decoration often found on triumphal arches enclosing a scene or portrait; in more general architectural use, a tablet or panel in a wall or window containing a figure or an ornament.

medium   The material from which an artwork is made.

melody   A succession of musical *tones* having a distinctive shape and rhythm.

Messiah   A Hebrew word meaning "the anointed one," or one chosen by God to be his representative on earth; in Judaism, a savior who will come bringing peace and justice; in Christianity, Jesus Christ (*Christ* is derived from a Greek word meaning "the anointed one").

metope [MET-uh-pee]   In architecture, a panel, often decorated, between two *triglyphs* on the *entablature* of a *Doric* Greek temple.

minaret   In Islamic architecture, a tall, slender tower with a pointed top, from which the daily calls to prayer are delivered; located near a *mosque.*

miniature   A small painting, usually of a religious nature, found in *illuminated manuscripts;* also, a small portrait.

minstrel   A professional entertainer of the twelfth to the seventeenth century; especially a secular musician; also called "jongleur."

Modernism   A late-nineteenth- and twentieth-century cultural, artistic, and literary movement that rejected much of the past and focused on the current, the secular, and the revolutionary in search of new forms of expression; the dominant style of the twentieth century until 1970.

modes   A series of musical *scales* devised by the Greeks and believed by them to create certain emotional or ethical effects on the listener.

monophony [muh-NOF-uh-nee]   A *style* of music in which there is only a single line of melody; the *Gregorian chants* are the most famous examples of monophonic music.

monotheism   From the Greek *monos,* single, alone, and the Greek *theos,* god; the belief that there is only one God.

mood   In music, the emotional impact of a *composition* on the feelings of a listener.

mosaic   An art form or decoration, usually on a wall or a floor, created by inlaying small pieces of glass, shell, or stone in cement or plaster to create pictures or patterns.

mosque   A Muslim place of worship, often distinguished by a dome-shaped central building placed in an open space surrounded by a wall.

motet   A multivoiced song with words of a sacred or secular text, usually sung without accompanying instruments; developed in the thirteenth century.

mural   A wall painting, usually quite large, used to decorate a private or public structure.

muse   In Greek religion, any one of the nine sister goddesses who preside over the creative arts and sciences.

music drama   An *opera* in which the action and music are continuous, not broken up into separate *arias* and *recitatives,* and the music is determined by its dramatic appropriateness, producing a work in which music, words, and staging are fused; the term was coined by Wagner.

narrator   The speaker whose voice we hear in a story or poem.

narthex   The porch or vestibule of a church, usually enclosed, through which worshipers walk before entering the *nave.*

Naturalism   In literature, a late-nineteenth-century movement inspired by the methods of science and the insights of sociology, concerned with an objective depiction of the ugly side of industrial society.

natural law   In *Stoicism* and later in other philosophies, a body of laws or principles that are believed to be derived from nature and binding on human society and that constitute a higher form of justice than civil or judicial law.

nave   The central longitudinal area of a church, extending from the entrance to the *apse* and flanked by *aisles.*

Neoclassical style   In the late eighteenth century, an artistic and literary movement that emerged as a reaction to the *Rococo* style and that sought inspiration from ancient *Classicism.* In the twentieth century, between 1919 and 1951, *Neoclassicism* in music was a style that rejected the emotionalism favored by Romantic composers as well as the dense orchestral sounds of the Impressionists; instead, it borrowed features from seventeenth- and eighteenth-century music and practiced the ideals of balance, clarity of texture, and nonprogrammatic works.

Neoclassicism   In the late third century B.C., an artistic movement in the disintegrating Hellenistic world that sought inspiration in the Athenian Golden Age of the fifth and fourth centuries B.C.; and, since 1970, *Neoclassicism* has been a highly visible submovement in *Post-Modernism,* particularly prominent in painting and architecture, that restates the principles of *Classical* art—balance, harmony, idealism.

Neoexpressionism   A submovement in *Post-Modernism,* associated primarily with painting, that offers social criticism and is concerned with the expression of the artist's feelings.

Neolithic   Literally, "new stone"; used to define the New Stone Age, when human *cultures* evolved into agrarian systems and settled communities; dating from about 10,000 or 8000 B.C. to about 3000 B.C.

Neo-Platonism   A philosophy based on Plato's ideas that was developed during the Roman period in an attempt to reconcile the dichotomy between Plato's concept of an eternal World of Ideas and the ever-changing physical world; in the fifteenth-century *Renaissance,* it served as a philosophical guide for Italian humanists who sought to reconcile late medieval Christian beliefs with *Classical* thinking.

Neorealism   A submovement in *Post-Modernism* that is based on a photographic sense of detail and harks back to many of the qualities of nineteenth-century *Realism.*

New Comedy   The style of comedy favored by *Hellenistic* playwrights, concentrating on gentle satirical themes—in particular, romantic *plots* with stock *characters* and predictable endings.

Nominalism [NAHM-uh-nuhl-iz-uhm] In medieval thought, the school that held that objects were separate unto themselves but could, for convenience, be treated in a collective sense because they shared certain characteristics; opposed to *Realism*.

Northern Renaissance The sixteenth-century cultural movement in northern Europe that was launched by the northward spread of Italian *Renaissance* art, culture, and ideals. The Northern Renaissance differed from the Italian Renaissance largely because of the persistence of the *Late Gothic style* and the unfolding of the *Reformation* after 1520.

octave In music, usually the eight-tone interval between a note and a second note of the same name, as in C to C.

oculus [AHK-yuh-lus] The circular opening at the top of a dome; derived from the Latin word for "eye."

Old Comedy The style of *comedy* established by Aristophanes in the fifth century B.C., distinguished by a strong element of political and social satire.

oligarchy From the Greek *oligos*, few; a state ruled by the few, especially by a small fraction of persons or families.

Olympian deities In Greek religion, sky gods and goddesses who lived on mountaintops and were worshiped mainly by the Greek aristocracy.

opera A drama or play set to music and consisting of vocal pieces with *orchestral* accompaniment; acting, scenery, and sometimes *choruses* and dancing are used to heighten the dramatic values of operas.

oratorio A choral work based on religious events or *scripture* employing singers, *choruses*, and *orchestra* but without scenery or staging and performed usually in a church or a concert hall.

orchestra In Greek theaters, the circular area where the *chorus* performed in front of the audience; in music, a group of instrumentalists, including string players, who play together.

organum [OR-guh-nuhm] In the ninth through the thirteenth centuries, a simple and early form of *polyphonic* music consisting of a main melody sung along with a *Gregorian chant*; by the thirteenth century it had developed into a complex multivoiced song.

Paleolithic Literally, "old stone"; used to define the Old Stone Age, when crude stones and tools were used; dating from about 2,000,000 B.C. to about 10,000 B.C.

pantheism The doctrine of or belief in multitudes of deities found in nature.

pantomime In Roman times, enormous dramatic productions featuring instrumental music and dances, favored by the masses; later, a type of dramatic or dancing performance in which the story is told with expressive or even exaggerated bodily and facial movements.

pastoral A type of *Hellenistic* poetry that idealized rural customs and farming, especially the simple life of shepherds, and deprecated urban living.

pavane [puh-VAHN] A sixteenth- and seventeenth-century English court dance of Italian origin; the dance is performed by couples to stately music. Ravel based *Pavane for a Dead Princess* (1899) on this *Baroque* dance form.

pediment In *Classical*-style architecture, the triangular-shaped area or gable at the end of the building formed by the sloping roof and the *cornice*.

pendentive [pen-DEN-tiv] In architecture, a triangular, concave-shaped section of *vaulting* between the rim of a dome and the pair of arches that support it; used in Byzantine and Islamic architecture.

performance art A democratic type of mixed media art born in the 1960s that ignores artistic boundaries, mixing high art (such as music, painting, and theater) and popular art (such as rock and roll, film, and fads), to create a unique, nonreproducible, artistic experience. Associated with the work of Laurie Anderson.

peristyle [PAIR-uh-stile] A colonnade around an open courtyard or a building.

Perpendicular style The highly decorative style of *Late Gothic* architecture that developed in England at the same time as the *Late Gothic* on the European continent.

perspective A technique or formula for creating the illusion or appearance of depth and distance on a two-dimensional surface. **Atmospheric perspective** is achieved in many ways: by diminishing color intensity, by omitting detail, and by blurring the lines of an object. **Linear perspective,** based on mathematical calculations, is achieved by having parallel lines or lines of projection appearing to converge at a single point, known as the *vanishing point*, on the horizon of the flat surface and by diminishing distant objects in size according to scale to make them appear to recede from the viewer.

philosophes [FEEL-uh-sawfs] A group of European thinkers and writers who popularized the ideas of the *Enlightenment* through essays, novels, plays, and other works, hoping to change the climate of opinion and bring about social and political reform.

phonogram A symbol used to represent a syllable, a word, or a sound.

Physiocrats [FIZ-ih-uh-kratz] A group of writers, primarily French, who dealt with economic issues during the *Enlightenment*, in particular calling for improved agricultural productivity and questioning the state's role in economic affairs.

pianoforte [pee-an-o-FOR-tay] A piano; derived from the Italian for "soft/loud," terms used to describe the two types of sound emitted by a stringed instrument whose wires are struck with felt-covered hammers operated from a keyboard.

picaresque novel From the Spanish term for "rogue." A type of literature, originating in sixteenth-century Spain, that recounted the comic misadventures of a roguish hero who lived by his wits, often at the expense of the high and mighty; influenced novel writing across Europe, especially in England, France, and Germany, until about 1800; the anonymous "Lazarillo de Tormes" (1554) was the first picaresque novel.

pictogram A carefully drawn, often stylized, picture that represents a particular object.

pier In architecture, a vertical masonry structure that may support a *vault*, an arch, or a roof; in *Gothic* churches, piers were often clustered together to form massive supports.

Pietà [pee-ay-TAH] A painting or sculpture depicting the mourning Virgin and the dead Christ.

pilaster [pih-LAS-tuhr] In architecture, a vertical, rectangular decorative device projecting from a wall that gives the appearance of a column with a base and a *capital*; sometimes called an applied column.

Platonism The collective beliefs and arguments presented in Plato's writings stressing especially that actual things are copies of ideas.

plot The action, or arrangement of incidents, in a story.

podium In architecture, a low wall serving as a foundation; a platform.

poetry Language that is concentrated and imaginative, marked by meter, rhythm, rhyme, and imagery.

Pointillism [PWANT-il-iz-uhm] Also known as Divisionism, a style of painting, perfected by Seurat, in which tiny dots of paint are applied to the canvas in such a way that when they are viewed from a distance they merge and blend to form recognizable objects with natural effects of color, light, and shade.

polyphony [puh-LIF-uh-nee] A style of musical *composition* in which two or more voices or melodic lines are woven together.

polytheism [PAHL-e-the-iz-uhm]   The doctrine of or belief in more than one deity.

Pop Art   An artistic *style* popular between 1960 and 1970 in which commonplace commercial objects drawn from *mass culture,* such as soup cans, fast foods, and comic strips, became the subjects of art.

portico   In architecture, a covered entrance to a building, usually with a separate roof supported by columns.

post-and-lintel construction   A basic architectural form in which upright posts, or columns, support a horizontal lintel, or beam.

post-beam-triangle construction   The generic name given to Greek architecture that includes the post, or column; the beam, or lintel; and the triangular-shaped area, or *pediment.*

Post-Impressionism   A late-nineteenth-century artistic movement that extended the boundaries of *Impressionism* in new directions to focus on structure, composition, fantasy, and subjective expression.

Post-Modernism   An artistic, cultural, and intellectual movement, originating in about 1970, that is more optimistic than *Modernism,* embraces an open-ended and democratic global civilization, freely adapts elements of high culture and *mass culture,* and manifests itself chiefly through revivals of earlier styles, giving rise to *Neoclassicism, Neoexpressionism,* and *Neorealism.*

Praxitelean curve [prak-sit-i-LEE-an]   The graceful line of the sculptured body in the *contrapposto* stance, perfected by the *Fourth Century style* sculptor Praxiteles.

primitivism   In painting, the "primitives" are those painters of the Netherlandish and Italian schools who flourished before 1500, thus all Netherlandish painters between the van Eycks and Dürer and all Italian painters between Giotto and Raphael; more generally, the term reflects modern artists' fascination with non-Western art forms, as in Gauguin's Tahitian-inspired paintings. In literature, primitivism has complex meanings; on the one hand, it refers to the notion of a golden age, a world of lost innocence, which appeared in both ancient pagan and Christian writings; on the other hand, it is a modern term used to denote two species of cultural relativism, which either finds people isolated from civilization to be superior to those living in civilized and urban settings, as in the cult of the Noble Savage (Rousseau), or respects native peoples and their cultures within their own settings, yet accepts that natives can be as cruel as Europeans (the view expressed by Montaigne).

problem play   A type of drama that focuses on a specific social problem; the Swedish playwright Ibsen was a pioneer of this *genre,* as in *A Doll's House* (1879), concerning women's independence.

program music   Instrumental music that depicts a narrative, portrays a *setting,* or suggests a sequence of events; often based on other sources, such as a poem or a play.

prose   The ordinary language used in speaking and writing.

Puritanism   The beliefs and practices of the Puritans, a small but influential religious group devoted to the teachings of John Calvin; they stressed strict rules of personal and public behavior and practiced their beliefs in England and the New World during the seventeenth century.

putti [POOH-tee]   Italian, plural of *putto;* in painting and sculpture, figures of babies, children, or sometimes angels.

ragtime   A type of instrumental music, popularized by African Americans in the late nineteenth and early twentieth centuries, with a strongly syncopated rhythm and a lively *melody.*

Rayonnant [ray-yo-NAHNN]   A decorative *style* in French architecture associated with the High *Gothic* period, in which walls were replaced by sheets of *stained glass* framed by elegant stone *traceries.*

Realism   In medieval philosophy, the school that asserted that objects contained common or universal qualities that were not always apparent to the human senses but that were more real or true than the objects' physical attributes; opposed to *Nominalism.* In art and literature, a mid- to late-nineteenth-century style that focused on the everyday lives of the middle and lower classes, portraying their world in a serious, accurate, and unsentimental way; opposed to *Romanticism.*

recitative [ress-uh-tuh-TEEV]   In music, a rhythmically free but often stylized declamation, midway between singing and ordinary speech, that serves as a transition between *arias* or as a narrative device in an *opera.*

Reformation   The sixteenth-century religious movement that looked back to the ideals of early Christianity, called for moral and structural changes in the church, and led ultimately to the founding of the various Protestant churches.

regalia   Plural in form, often used with a singular verb. The emblems and symbols of royalty, as the crown and scepter.

relief   In sculpture, figures or forms that are carved so they project from the flat surface of a stone or metal background. **High relief** projects sharply from the surface; **low relief,** or **bas relief,** is more shallow.

Renaissance [ren-uh-SAHNS]   From the French for "rebirth"; the artistic, cultural, and intellectual movement marked by a revival of *Classical* and *humanistic* values that began in Italy in the mid–fourteenth century and had spread across Europe by the mid–sixteenth century.

representational art   Art that presents a likeness of the world as it appears to the naked eye.

Restrained Baroque style   A variation of the *Baroque* style identified with Dutch and English architects and painters who wanted to reduce Baroque grandeur and exuberance to a more human scale.

revenge tragedy   A type of play popular in sixteenth-century England, probably rooted in Roman *tragedies* and concerned with the need for a family to seek revenge for the murder of a relative.

ribbed vault   A masonry roof with a framework of arches or ribs that reinforce and decorate the *vault* ceiling.

rocaille [roh-KYE]   In *Rococo* design, the stucco ornaments shaped like leaves, flowers, and ribbons that decorate walls and ceilings.

Rococo style [ruh-KOH-koh]   An artistic and cultural *style* that grew out of the *Baroque* style but that was more intimate and personal and that emphasized the frivolous and superficial side of aristocratic life.

romance   A story derived from legends associated with Troy or Celtic culture but often set in feudal times and centered on themes of licit and illicit love between noble lords and ladies.

Romanesque style [roh-muhn-ESK]   A *style* of architecture, usually associated with churches built in the eleventh and twelfth centuries, that was inspired by Roman architectural features, such as the *basilica,* and was thus Roman-like. Romanesque buildings were massive, with round arches and *barrel* or *groined vaulted* ceilings, and had less exterior decoration than *Gothic* churches.

Romanticism   An intellectual, artistic, and literary movement that began in the late eighteenth century as a reaction to *Neoclassicism* and that stressed the emotional, mysterious, and imaginative side of human behavior and the unruly side of nature.

rose window   A large circular window, made of *stained glass* and held together with lead and carved stones set in patterns, or *tracery,* and located over an entrance in a *Gothic* cathedral.

sacred music   Religious music, such as Gregorian chants, *masses,* and hymns.

sarcophagus [sahr-KAHF-uh-guhs]   From the Greek meaning "flesh-eating stone"; a marble or stone coffin or tomb, usually decorated with carvings, used first by Romans and later by Christians for burial of the dead.

satire   From the Latin, "medley"—a cooking term; a literary *genre* that originated in ancient Rome and that was characterized by two basic forms: (a) tolerant and amused observation of the human scene, modeled on Horace's style, and (b) bitter and sarcastic denunciation of all behavior and thought outside a civilized norm, modeled on Juvenal's style. In modern times, a literary work that holds up human vices and follies to ridicule or scorn.

satyr-play [SAT-uhr]   A comic play, often featuring sexual themes, performed at the Greek drama festivals along with the *tragedies*.

scale   A set pattern of tones (or notes) arranged from low to high.

scenographic [see-nuh-GRAF-ik]   In *Renaissance* architecture, a building style that envisioned buildings as composed of separate units; in the painting of stage scenery, the art of *perspective* representation.

scherzo [SKER-tso]   From the Italian for "joke"; a quick and lively instrumental *composition* or movement found in *sonatas* and *symphonies*.

scholasticism   In medieval times, the body or collection of knowledge that tried to harmonize Aristotle's writings with Christian doctrine; also, a way of thinking and establishing sets of arguments.

Scientific Revolution   The seventeenth-century intellectual movement, based originally on discoveries in astronomy and physics, that challenged and overturned medieval views about the order of the universe and the theories used to explain motion.

scripture   The sacred writings of any religion, as the Bible in Judaism and Christianity.

secular music   Nonreligious music, such as *symphonies*, songs, and dances.

serial music   A type of musical composition based on a *twelve-tone scale* arranged any way the composer chooses; the absence of a tonal center in serial music leads to *atonality*.

setting   In literature, the background against which the action takes place; in a representational artwork, the time and place depicted.

Severe style   The first sculptural style of the *Classical* period in Greece, which retained stylistic elements from the *Archaic* style.

sfumato [sfoo-MAH-toh]   In painting, the blending of one tone into another to blur the outline of a form and give the canvas a smokelike appearance; a technique perfected by Leonardo da Vinci.

shaft graves   Deep pit burial sites; the dead are usually placed at the bottom of the shafts.

skene [SKEE-nee]   A small building behind the *orchestra* in a Greek theater, used as a prop and as a storehouse for theatrical materials.

Skepticism   A *Hellenistic* philosophy that questioned whether anything could be known for certain, argued that all beliefs were relative, and concluded that *autarky* could be achieved only by recognizing that inquiry was fruitless.

slave narrative   A literary *genre*, either written by slaves or told by slaves to secretaries, which emerged prior to the American Civil War; the genre was launched by the *Narrative of the Life of Frederick Douglass, an American Slave* (1845); the harsh details of the inhumane and unjust slave system, as reported in these narratives, contributed to *Realist* literature.

social contract   In political thought, an agreement or contract between the people and their rulers defining the rights and duties of each so that a civil society might be created.

socialism   An economic and political system in which goods and property are owned collectively or by the state; the socialist movement began as a reaction to the excesses of the factory system in the nineteenth century and ultimately called for either reforming or abolishing industrial capitalism.

Socialist Realism   A Marxist artistic theory that calls for the use of literature, music, and the arts in the service of the ideals and goals of socialism and/or communism, with an emphasis in painting on the realistic portrayal of objects.

sonata [soh-NAH-tah]   In music, an instrumental *composition*, usually in three or four movements.

sonata form   A musical *form* or structure consisting of three (or sometimes four) sections that vary in *key*, *tempo*, and mood.

stained glass   An art form characterized by many small pieces of tinted glass bound together by strips of lead, usually to produce a pictorial scene of a religious theme; developed by *Romanesque* artists and a central feature of *Gothic* churches.

stele [STEE-lee]   A carved or inscribed vertical stone pillar or slab, often used for commemorative purposes.

Stoicism [STO-ih-sihz-uhm]   The most popular and influential *Hellenistic* philosophy, advocating a restrained way of life, a toleration for others, a resignation to disappointments, and a resolution to carry out one's responsibilities; Stoicism appealed to many Romans and had an impact on early Christian thought.

stream-of-consciousness   A writing technique used by some modern authors in which the narration consists of a *character's* continuous interior monologue of thoughts and feelings.

structuralism   In *Post-Modernism*, an approach to knowledge based on the belief that human behavior and institutions can be explained by reference to a few underlying structures that themselves are reflections of hidden patterns in the human mind.

studia humanitatis [STOO-dee-ah hu-man-ih-TAH-tis] **(humanistic studies)**   The Latin term given by *Renaissance* scholars to new intellectual pursuits that were based on recently discovered ancient texts, including moral philosophy, history, grammar, rhetoric, and poetry. This new learning stood in sharp contrast to medieval *scholasticism*.

Sturm und Drang [STOORM oont drahng]   German, "Storm and Stress"; a German literary movement of the 1770s that focused on themes of action, emotionalism, and the individual's revolt against the conventions of society.

style   The combination of distinctive elements of creative execution and expression, in terms of both form and *content*.

style galant [STEEL gah-LAHNN]   In *Rococo* music, a *style* of music developed by French composers and characterized by graceful and simple *melodies*.

stylobate [STY-luh-bate]   In Greek temples, the upper step of the base that forms a platform on which the columns stand.

Sublime [suh-BLIME]   In *Romanticism*, the term used to describe nature as a terrifying and awesome force full of violence and power.

Suprematism [suh-PREM-uh-tiz-uhm]   A variation of abstract art, originating in Russia in the early twentieth century, characterized by the use of geometric shapes as the basic elements of the composition.

Surrealism [suh-REE-uhl-iz-uhm]   An early-twentieth-century movement in art, literature, and theater, in which incongruous juxtapositions and fantastic images produce an irrational and dreamlike effect.

symbolic realism   In art, a *style* that is realistic and true to life but uses the portrayed object or person to represent or symbolize something else.

symphony   A long and complex *sonata*, usually written in three or four movements, for large *orchestras*; the first movement is traditionally fast, the second slow, and the third (and optional fourth) movement fast.

syncopation [sin-ko-PAY-shun]   In music, the technique of accenting the weak beat when a strong beat is expected.

syncretism [SIN-kruh-tiz-uhm]   The combining of different forms of religious beliefs or practices.

synthesizer [SIN-thuh-size-uhr]   An electronic apparatus with a keyboard capable of duplicating the sounds of many musical instruments, popular among *Post-Modernist* composers and musicians.

tabula rasa [TAB-yuh-luh RAH-zuh]   "Erased tablet," the Latin term John Locke used to describe the mind at birth, empty of inborn ideas and ready to receive sense impressions, which Locke believed were the sole source of knowledge.

technique   The systematic procedure whereby a particular creative task is performed.

tempo   In music, the relative speed at which a composition is to be played, indicated by a suggestive word or phrase or by a precise number such as a metronome marking. (A metronome is a finely calibrated device used to determine the exact tempo for a musical work.)

terza rima [TER-tsuh REE-muh]   A three-line stanza with an interlocking rhyme scheme (*aba bcb cdc ded,* and so on), used by Dante in his *Divine Comedy.*

texture   In a musical composition, the number and nature of voices or instruments employed and how the parts are combined.

theater of the absurd   A type of theater that has come to reflect the despair, anxieties, and absurdities of modern life and in which the characters seldom make sense, the plot is nearly nonexistent, bizarre and fantastic events occur onstage, and tragedy and comedy are mixed in unconventional ways; associated with *Late Modernism.*

theme   The dominant idea of a work; the message or emotion the artist intends to convey.

theocracy   From the Greek *theos,* god; a state governed by a god regarded as the ruling power or by priests or officials claiming divine sanction.

theology   The application of philosophy to the study of religious truth, focusing especially on the nature of the deity and the origin and teachings of an organized religious community.

tone   A musical sound of definite pitch; also, the quality of a sound.

tracery   Ornamental architectural work with lines that branch out to form designs, often found as stone carvings in *rose windows.*

tragedy   A serious and deeply moral drama, typically involving a noble protagonist brought down by excessive pride (hubris) and describing a conflict between seemingly irreconcilable values or forces; in Greece, tragedies were performed at the festivals associated with the worship of Dionysus.

transept   In church architecture, the crossing arm that bisects the *nave* near the *apse* and gives the characteristic *cruciform* shape to the floor plan.

triglyph [TRY-glif]   In Greek architecture, a three-grooved rectangular panel on the frieze of a *Doric* temple; triglyphs alternated with *metopes.*

triptych [TRIP-tik]   In painting, a set of three hinged or folding panels depicting a religious story, mainly used as an altarpiece.

trope [TROHP]   In *Gregorian chants,* a new phrase or melody inserted into an existing chant to make it more musically appealing; also called a turn; in literature, a figure of speech.

troubador [TROO-buh-door]   A composer and/or singer, usually an aristocrat, who performed secular love songs at the feudal courts in southern France.

twelve-tone scale   In music, a fixed *scale* or series in which there is an arbitrary arrangement of the twelve *tones* (counting every half-tone) of an *octave;* devised by Arnold Schoenberg.

tympanum [TIM-puh-num]   In medieval architecture, the arch over a doorway set above the lintel, usually decorated with carvings depicting biblical themes; in *Classical-*style architecture, the recessed face of a *pediment.*

ukiyo-e [oo-key-yoh-AY]   A type of colorful Japanese print, incised on woodblocks, that is characterized by simple design, plain backgrounds, and flat areas of color. Developed in seventeenth-century Japan; admired by late-nineteenth-century Parisian artists, who assimilated it to a Western style that is most notable in the prints of Mary Cassatt.

Utilitarianism [yoo-til-uh-TARE-e-uh-niz-uhm]   The doctrine set forth in the social theory of Jeremy Bentham in the nineteenth century that the final goal of society and humans is "the greatest good for the greatest number."

vanishing point   In linear *perspective,* the point on the horizon at which the receding parallel lines appear to converge and then vanish.

vault   A ceiling or roof made from a series of arches placed next to one another.

vernacular language [vuhr-NAK-yuh-luhr]   The language or dialect of a region, usually spoken by the general population as opposed to the wealthy or educated elite.

vernacular literature   Literature written in the language of the populace, such as English, French, or Italian, as opposed to the language of the educated elite, usually Latin.

via antiqua [VEE-uh ahn-TEE-kwah]   The "old way," the term used in late medieval thought by the opponents of St. Thomas Aquinas to describe his *via media,* which they considered outdated.

via media [VEE-uh MAY-dee-ah]   The "middle way" that St. Thomas Aquinas sought in reconciling Aristotle's works to Christian beliefs.

via moderna [VEE-uh moh-DEHR-nah]   The "new way," the term used in late medieval thought by those thinkers who opposed the school of Aquinas.

video art   A type of art made with a video monitor, or monitors; produced using either computerized programs or handheld cameras; can be ephemeral or permanent.

virtuoso [vehr-choo-O-so]   An aristocratic person who experimented in science, usually as an amateur, in the seventeenth century, giving science respectability and a wider audience; later, in music, a person with great technical skill.

voussoir [voo-SWAR]   A carved, wedge-shaped stone or block in an arch.

woodcut   In art, the technique of cutting or carving an image onto a wooden block used for printing; originated in the Late Middle Ages. Also, the print made from the technique.

word painting   In music, the illustration of an idea, a meaning, or a feeling associated with a word, as, for example, using a discordant *melody* when the word *pain* is sung. This technique is especially identified with the sixteenth-century *madrigal;* also called word illustration, or madrigalism.

ziggurat [ZIG-oo-rat]   A Mesopotamian stepped pyramid, usually built with external staircases and a shrine at the top; sometimes included a tower.

TEXT CREDITS

Chapter 1 Page 9, Samuel N. Kramer, "Sumerian Text of Father Rebuking Son," from *History Begins at Sumer*. Doubleday Anchor, 1959, pp. 12–16. Reprinted by permission of Mildred Kramer; page 19, Miriam Lichtheim, "Troubled Times" from "The Man Who Was Tired of Life" in *Ancient Egyptian Literature. Three Volumes.* Volume I, pp. 166–169. Copyright © 1973–1980 Regents of the University of California. Reprinted by permission. **Chapter 2** Page 45, Solon, "Political Verses: The Ten Ages of Man" from David Milroy, *Early Greek Lyric Poetry*, 1992, pp. 68–69. Reprinted by permission of the University of Michigan Press; Sappho, "He Seems to Be a God" from *7 Greeks*, translated by Guy Davenport. Copyright © 1995 by Guy Davenport. Reprinted by permission of New Directions Publishing Corporation. **Chapter 3** Page 71, Xenophon, "Secrets of a Successful Marriage," from *Oeconomicus: A Social and Historical Commentary*. Translated by S. B. Pomeroy, pp. 139–141, 143, 145. Copyright © 1994 Clarendon, a division of Oxford University Press. Reprinted by permission of the translator. **Chapter 4** Page 92, Theocritus, from *The Idylls of Theocritus: A Verse Translation*, translated by Thelma Sargent. Translation copyright © 1982 by Thelma Sargent. Reprinted by permission of W. W. Norton & Company, Inc. **Chapter 6** Page 151, Flavius Josephus, "The Destruction of the Temple at Jerusalem" from *The Jewish War* by Josephus. Translated by G. A. Williamson (Penguin Classics 1959). Copyright © 1959 G. A. Williamson. Reprinted by permission of Penguin Books, Ltd.; page 162, Perpetua, "Perpetua's Vision" from *The Acts of the Christian Martyrs*. Edited by Herbert Musurillo, 1972, pp. 109–111, 125–126, 129, 131. Reprinted by permission of Oxford University Press (Oxford, England). **Chapter 7** Page 174, Paulina, "Epitaph for Agorius Praetextatus" from Peter Dronke, *Women Writers of the Middle Ages*, 1984. Reprinted by permission of Cambridge University Press (New York). **Chapter 8** Page 208, Usamah, "The Curious Medicine of the Franks" from *Memoirs of Usamah*. Translated by Philip K. Hitti. Copyright © 1929 by Columbia University Press. Reprinted with permission of the publisher; Anna Comnena, "The Arrival of the First Crusade in Constantinople," from *The Alexiad of the Princess Anna Comnena*. Translated by Elizabeth A. S. Dawes. Reprinted by Routledge & Kegan Paul, London; page 209, Liudprand of Cremona, excerpt from "A Mission to the Byzantine Court" in *The Works of Liudprand of Cremona*. Translated by F. A. Wright, 1930. Reprinted by permission of Routledge (Hampshire, UK). **Chapter 9** Page 229, Hildegard of Bingen, "Scivias" from *Cry Out and Write*, by Edward Peter Nolan, 1994, p. 46. Reprinted by permission of the Continuum Publishing Group. **Chapter 11** Page 296, Laura Cereta, excerpt from "Defense of the Liberal Instruction of Women," January 13, 1488. From *Her Immaculate Hand: Selected Works by and about the Women Humanists of Quattrocento Italy*. Edited by Margaret King & Albert Rabil, 1992. Pegasus Press, #13. Reprinted by permission of MRTS, SUNY Binghamton, NY. **Chapter 12** Page 337, Georgio Vasari, "Michelangelo Sculpting David" from *Lives of the Artists Volume I*. Translated by George Bull (Penguin Classics, 1965, Revised Edition 1971). Copyright © 1965 George Bull. Reprinted by permission of Penguin Books, Ltd. **Chapter 20** Page 547, Elie Wiesel, excerpt from *Night*, translated by Stella Rodway. Copyright © 1960 by MacGibbon & Kee. Copyright renewed © 1988 by the Collins Publishing Group. Reprinted by permission of Hill and Wang, a division of Farrar, Straus and Giroux, LLC. **Chapter 21** Page 592, Bill Moyers, excerpts from "Bill Moyers: A World of Ideas II." Copyright © 1990 by Public Affairs Television, Inc. Used by permission of Doubleday, a division of Random House, Inc.

PHOTO AND ILLUSTRATION CREDITS

P. xxii, © Erich Lessing/Art Resource, NY; **p. xxiii,** The Museum of Modern Art, New York. Acquired through the Lillie P. Bliss Bequest. Photograph © 2000 The Museum of Modern Art, New York. © 2000 Estate of Pablo Picasso/Artists Rights Society (ARS), New York; **p. xxviii,** Georgia O'Keeffe, American, 1887–1986, *Cow's Skull with Calico Roses*, oil on canvas, 1932, 92.2 x 61.3 cm, Gift of Georgia O'Keeffe, 1947.712. Photograph © 2000 The Art Institute of Chicago, All Rights Reserved. © 2000 The Georgia O'Keeffe Foundation/Artists Rights Society (ARS), New York. **Chapter 1 CO-1,** © The British Museum; **1.1,** © The British Museum; **1.2,** © Jean-Marie Chauvet/Sygma; **1.3,** © Naturhistorisches Museum, Wien; **1.5,** © The British Museum; **1.6,** © Erich Lessing/Art Resource, NY; **1.7,** © The British Museum; **1.8,** © Hirmer Fotoarchiv, Munich; **1.9,** © Hirmer Fotoarchiv, Munich; **1.10,** © P & G Bowater/The Image Bank; **1.12,** Tim Schermerhorn; **1.13,** © Inge Morath/Magnum Photos, Inc.; **1.14,** © AKG London; **1.15,** Harvard University, Museum of Fine Arts Expedition. (11.1738). Courtesy Museum of Fine Arts, Boston. Reproduced with permission. © 2000 Museum of Fine Arts, Boston. All rights reserved. **1.16,** Courtesy The Metropolitan Museum of Art, Rogers Fund and contribution from Edward S. Harkness, 1929. (29.3.2); **1.17,** © Margarete Büsing/Bildarchiv Preussischer Kulturbesitz; **1.18,** © C. M. Dixon; **1.19,** © The British Museum; **1.20,** © The British Museum; **1.21,** © Boltin Picture Library; **1.22,** © The British Museum; **1.23,** Persepolis, Iran/© Bridgeman Art Library; **p. 28T,** © David Coulson/Robert Estall Photograph Library; **p. 28B,** © Robert & Linda Mitchell; **p. 29L,** British Museum, London, UK/© Bridgeman Art Library; **p. 29R,** © J. M. Kenoyer/Harappa. **Chapter 2 CO-2,** © George Grigoriou/Tony Stone Images; **2.1,** © C. M. Dixon; **2.2,** © Ronald Sheridan/Ancient Art & Architecture Collection; **2.3,** © Erich Lessing/Art Resource, NY; **2.4,** © Gordon Gahan/National Geographic Image Collection; **2.5,** © Hirmer Fotoarchiv, Munich; **2.6,** © Ira Block/National Geographic Image Collection; **2.7,** © Erich Lessing/Art Resource, NY; **2.8,** © George Grigoriou/Tony Stone Images; **2.9,** © The Granger Collection, New York; **2.10,** © Hirmer Fotoarchiv, Munich; **2.13,** © Vanni/Art Resource, NY; **2.14,** © Erich Lessing/Art Resource, NY; **2.15,** Courtesy The Metropolitan Museum of Art, Fletcher Fund, 1932. (32.11.1); **2.16,** © C. M. Dixon; **2.17,** © Hirmer Fotoarchiv, Munich; **2.18,** © C. M. Dixon; **2.19,** © Hirmer Fotoarchiv, Munich; **2.20,** © Hirmer Fotoarchiv, Munich. **Chapter 3 CO-3,** © Erich Lessing/Art Resource; **3.1,** Courtesy of the Arthur M. Sackler Museum, Harvard University Art Museums, Bequest of David M. Robinson. Photo by Michael Nedzweski; © President and Fellows of Harvard College, Harvard University; **3.2,** © Hirmer Fotoarchiv, Munich; **3.3,** © Hirmer Fotoarchiv, Munich; **3.4,** Courtesy Staatliche Museen, Berlin; **3.5,** © Hirmer Fotoarchiv, Munich; **3.6,** © Ara Guler/Magnum Photos, Inc.; **3.7,** © Erich Lessing/Art Resource, NY; **3.8,** © Ronald Sheridan/Ancient Art & Architecture Collection; **3.10,** © Kunsthistorisches Museum; **3.11,** © The British Museum; **3.12,** © The Granger Collection, New York; **3.13,** © C. M. Dixon; **3.14,** © Ronald Sheridan/Ancient Art & Architecture Collection; **3.15,** © Vanni/Art Resource; **3.16,** © René Burri/Magnum Photos, Inc.; **3.17,** © Hirmer Fotoarchiv, Munich; **3.18,** © Hirmer Fotoarchiv, Munich; **3.19,** © Photo RMN/Hervé Lewandowski; **3.20,** © Scala/Art Resource, NY; **3.21,** © Scala/Art Resource, NY; **3.22,** © Hirmer Fotoarchiv, Munich; **3.24,** © The British Museum; **3.25,** © Erich Lessing/Art Resource, NY; **3.26,** © Hirmer Fotoarchiv, Munich; **p. 84TL,** © R. Sheridan/Ancient Art & Architecture Collection; **p. 84TR,** © Corbis/Gianni Dagli Orti; **p. 84B,** © Dumbarton Oaks Research Library and Collections, Washington, DC; **p. 85T,** © Christie's Images, Ltd.; **p. 85B,** © Kyodo News International, Inc. **Chapter 4 CO-4,** © Louvre, Paris, France/Peter Willi/Bridgeman Art Library; **4.1,** Bibliothèque Nationale de France; **4.2,** © Bildarchiv Preussischer Kulturbesitz; **4.4,** © Photo RMN/Gérard Blot; **4.5,** Courtesy Yale University Art Gallery, Dura Europos Collection, Neg. #258; **4.6,** © Alinari/Art Resource, NY; **4.7,** Courtesy The Metropolitan Museum of Art, Rogers Fund, 1911. (11.90); **4.8,** © The British Museum; **4.9,** © C. M. Dixon; **4.10,** © Art Resource, NY; **4.11,** © Foto Marburg/Art Resource, NY; **4.12,** Pinacoteca Capitolina, Palazzo Conservatori, Rome, Italy/Index/© Bridgeman Art Library; **4.13,** Courtesy The Metropolitan Museum of Art, Rogers Fund, 1909. (09.39); **4.14,** © Erich Lessing/Art Resource, NY; **4.15,** Louvre, Paris, France/Peter Willi/Bridgeman Art Library; **4.16,** © Photo RMN/Hervé Lewandowski; **4.17,** © Nimatallah/Art Resource, NY; **4.18,** Courtesy Archivio Fotografico dei Musei Capitolini. Photo by Maria Teresa Natale; **4.19,** Vatican Museums and Galleries, Vatican City, Italy; © Index/Bridgeman Art Library. **Chapter 5 CO-5,** © Paul Chesley/Tony Stone Images; **5.1,** Scala/Art Resource, NY; **5.2,** © Alinari/Art Resource, NY; **5.3,** Scala/Art Resource, NY; **5.4,** Alinari/Art Resource, NY; **5.5,** Leonard von Matt, Buochs, Switzerland; **5.6,** © Hirmer Fotoarchiv, Munich; **5.7,** Fototeca Unione, Rome. American Academy in Rome; **5.8,** © Photo RMN-Jean/J. Schormans; **5.9,** © Ronald Sheridan/Ancient Art & Architecture Collection; **5.10,** © AKG London; **5.11,** © Scala/Art Resource, NY; **5.13,** © Giraudon/Art Resource, NY; **5.14,** © Scala/Art Resource, NY; **5.15,** © Paul Chesley/Tony Stone Images; **5.16,** © Steve Vidler/Tony Stone Images; **5.17,** Index/© Bridgeman Art Library; **5.18,** © Scala/Art Resource, NY; **5.19,** © Guido Rossi/The Image Bank; **5.20,** © Corbis/Bettmann; **5.21,** © Lionel Isy-Schwart/The Image Bank; **5.22,** © C. M. Dixon; **5.23,** Museum of Art, Rhode Island School of Design, Museum of Appropriation. Photograph by Del Bogart; **5.24,** © AKG London; **5.25,** © Nimatallah/Art Resource, NY; **5.26,** © Ronald Sheridan/Ancient Art & Architecture Collection; **5.27,** © Erich Lessing/Art Resource, NY; **5.28,** © Scala/Art Resource, NY; **5.29,** © Scala/Art Resource, NY; **5.30,** © R. Sheridan/Ancient Art & Architecture Collection; **5.31,** © Erich Lessing/Art Resource, NY; **p. 142T,** © Boltin Picture Library; **p. 142B,** © Staatliche Museen zu Berlin/Preussischer Kulturbesitz Museum für Völkerkunde; **p. 143T,** © Dinodia Picture Agency; **p. 143M,** © Robert Harding Picture Library, London; **p. 143B,** © Barnaby's Picture Library. **Chapter 6 CO-6,** National Museum, Damascus, Syria/Topham Picturepoint/Bridgeman Art Library; **6.1,** © Israel Museum, Jerusalem; **6.2,** Courtesy of the Oriental Institute of the University of Chicago; **6.3,** © The Jewish Museum, NY/Art Resource, NY; **6.4,** © Zev Radovan, Jerusalem; **6.5,** © Richard T. Nowitz; **6.6,** National Museum, Damascus, Syria/Topham Picturepoint Bridgeman Art Library; **6.7,** © Israel Museum, Jerusalem; **6.9,** Courtesy of Nancy L. Lapp; **6.10,** © Zev Radovan, Jerusalem; **6.11,** © Zev Radovan, Jerusalem; **6.12,** © Carl Purcell/Words & Pictures; **6.13,** © Phototheque André Held; **6.14,** © Phototheque André Held; **6.15,** © Hirmer Fotoarchiv, Munich; **6.16,** © Scala/Art Resource, NY; **6.17,** © Erich Lessing/PhotoEdit; **6.18,** © Hirmer Fotoarchiv, Munich. **Chapter 7 CO-7,** © Hirmer Fotoarchiv, Munich; **7.1,** © Hirmer Fotoarchiv, Munich; **7.2,** © Erich Lessing/Art Resource, NY; **7.3,** © Vanni/Art Resource, NY; **7.4,** © C. M. Dixon; **7.5,** © Scala/Art Resource, NY; **7.6,** © Phototheque André Held; **7.8,** © Foto Marburg/Art Resource, NY; **7.9,** © Scala/Art Resource, NY; **7.11,** © AKG London; **7.12,** © Erich Lessing/Art Resource, NY; **7.13,** © Scala/Art Resource, NY; **7.14,** © Arch. Phot. Paris; **7.15,** Courtesy Ministero per i beni Culturali e Ambientali, Istituto Centrale per il Catalogo e la Documentazione; **7.16,** © C. M. Dixon; **7.17,** © Deutsches Archäologisches Institut; **7.18,** © Alinari/Art Resource, NY; **7.19,** © Biblioteca Apostolica Vaticana, Minature 15 (Fol. 106); **7.20,** © Scala/Art Resource, NY; **7.21,** © Phototheque André Held; **7.22,** © Hirmer Fotoarchiv, Munich. **Chapter 8 CO-8,** © George Holton/Photo Researchers, Inc.; **8.1,** © C. M. Dixon; **8.2,** © AKG London; **8.3,** © Bridgeman/Art Resource, NY; **8.4,** © Kurgan-Lisnet/Liaison Agency, Inc.; **8.5,** © Ian Berry/Magnum Photos, Inc; **8.6,** © Scala/Art Resource, NY; **8.7,** © Scala/Art Resource, NY; **8.8,** © AKG London; **8.9,** © Colorphoto Hans Hinz; **8.10,** © Werner Foreman Archive/Art Resource, NY; **8.11,** Ampliaciones y Reproducciones MAS (Arxiu Mas), Barcelona; **8.12,** © The Granger Collection, New York; **8.13,** © George Holton/Photo Researchers, Inc.; **8.14,** © V&A Picture Library; **8.15,** Minbar from Kutubiyya Mosque, Marrakesh, Morocco. Islamic. Woodwork. 12th C., 1137–ca. 1145. H. 12 ft. 10 in.; W. 2 ft. 10-1/4 in.; D. 11 ft. 4-1/4 in. Three quarter view from right. Photography by Bruce White. Photograph © 1998, The Metropolitan Museum of Art; **8.16,** © Ronald Sheridan/Ancient Art & Architecture Collection; **8.18,** © Mark Romanelli/The Image Bank; **8.19,** Reproduced by the kind permission of the Trustees of the Chester Beatty Library, Dublin; **8.20,** © Erich Lessing/Art Resource, NY; **8.22,** Bibliothèque Nationale de France; **8.23,** © Foto Marburg/Art Resource, NY; **8.24,** Bibliothèque Nationale de France; **8.25,** © Instituto Poligrafico e Zecca dello Stato; **8.26,** Bayerische Staatsbibliothek; **p. 216T,** © Tony Morrison/South American Pictures; **p. 216B,** © Frank Willet; **p. 217T,** © The British Museum; **p. 216M,** © D. Donne Bryant/Art Resource, NY; **p. 217B,** © Adam Woolfitt/Woodfin Camp and Associates. **Chapter 9 CO-9,** © Giraudon/Art Resource, NY; **9.1,** © Erich Lessing/Art Resource, NY; **9.2,** © Caisse Nationale des Monuments Historiques et des Sites; **9.3,** Bibliothèque Nationale de France; **9.4,** © Giraudon/Art Resource, NY, with special authorization of the City of Bayeux; **9.5,** © Alinari/Art Resource, NY; **9.6,** © The Granger Collection, New York; **9.7,** © Scala/Art Resource, NY; **9.8,** © Catherine Karnow/Woodfin Camp and Associates; **9.9,** © Giraudon/Art Resource, NY; **9.10,** © Scala/Art Resource, NY; **9.11,** © Jean Bernard; **9.12,** From *Drawings of Great Buildings* by W. Blaser and O. Hannaford. Birkhauser Verlag, Basel; **9.13,** © Anthony Scibilia/Art Resource, NY; **9.14,** © Photographie Bulloz; **9.15,** © Caisse Nationale des Monuments Historiques et des Sites; **9.16,** © Hirmer Fotoarchiv, Munich; **9.17,** Courtesy the Master and Fellows of Corpus Christi College, Cambridge. © Corpus Christi College, Cambridge; **9.19,** © Hirmer Fotoarchiv, Munich; **9.20,** From *Gardner's Art Through the Ages*, 6/e by Horst de la Croix and Richard G. Tansey. © 1975 Harcourt Brace & Company. Reproduced by permission of the publisher; **9.21,** From *Drawings of Great Buildings* by W. Blaser and O. Hannaford. Birkhauser Verlag, Basel; **9.22,** © Hirmer Fotoarchiv, Munich; **9.23,** © Ronald Sheridan/Ancient Art & Architecture Collection; **9.24,** © Ronald Sheridan/Ancient Art & Architecture Collection; **9.26,** © Hirmer Fotoarchiv, Munich; **9.27,** © Jean Feuille/© C.N.M.H.S.; **9.28,** © Scala/Art Resource, NY; **9.29,** From *Drawings of Great Buildings* by W. Blaser and O. Hannaford. Birkhauser Verlag, Basel; **9.30,** © Hirmer Fotoarchiv, Munich; **9.31,** © Hirmer Fotoarchiv, Munich; **9.32,** Bibliothèque Nationale de France; **9.33,** Universitats Bibliothek, Munich; **p. 250TL,** © Frank Willet; **p. 250TR,** Courtesy Fundación Miguel Mujica Gallo, Museo Oro del Peru; **p. 250B,** © Werner Foreman Archive/Art Resource, NY; **p. 251T,** © Kyodo News International, Inc.; **p. 251M,** Private Collection; **p. 251B,** © Foto Wettstein & Kauf/Museum Rietberg, Zürich. **Chapter 10 CO-10,** © Photo RMN/J. G. Berizzi; **10.1,** Ampliaciones y Reproducciones MAS (Arxiu Mas), Barcelona; **10.2,** © Photo RMN; **10.3,** © Giraudon/Art Resource, NY; **10.4,** © Bibliothèque Royale Albert Ier, Bruxelles; **10.5,** © Scala/Art Resource, NY; **10.6,** Courtesy The Bancroft Library, University of California at Berkeley; **10.7,** © Foto Marburg/Art Resource, NY; **10.8,** © Scala/Art Resource, NY; **10.9,** © Scala/Art Resource, NY; **10.10,** © Scala/Art Resource, NY; **10.11,** © G. Tortoli/Ancient Art & Architecture Collection; **10.12,** © Scala/Art Resource, NY; **10.13,** © Scala/Art Resource, NY; **10.14,** © Art Resource, NY; **10.15,** © AKG London; **10.16,** © Bildarchiv Preussischer Kulturbesitz; **10.17,** © Scala/Art Resource, NY; **10.18,** © AKG London; **10.19,** © Alinari/Art Resource, NY; **10.20,** © Giraudon/Art Resource, NY; **10.21,** © Giraudon/Art Resource, NY; **10.22,** St. Bavo Cathedral, Ghent/© Giraudon/Art Resource, NY; **10.23,** © National Gallery, London; **10.24,** Photograph © Board of Trustees, National Gallery of Art, Washington, DC; **p. 286T,** © The British Museum; **p. 286M,** © N.J. Saunders/Art Resource, NY; **p. 286B,** Museo Nacional de Antropologia, Mexico City, Mexico; Sean Sprague/Mexicolore/© Bridgeman Art Library; **p. 287T,** © Mike Yamashita/Woodfin Camp and Associates; **p. 287B,** © Kim Newton/Woodfin Camp and Associates. **Chapter 11 CO-11,** © Scala/Art Resource, NY; **11.1,** © Erich Lessing/Art Resource, NY; **11.2,** © Scala/Art Resource, NY; **11.3,** © Erich Lessing/Art Resource, NY; **11.4,** © Scala/Art Resource, NY; **11.5,** © Scala/Art Resource, NY; **11.6,** © Scala/Art Resource, NY; **11.7,** From *Renaissance Architecture* by Peter Murray. © 1971 Electa International Publications. Drawing by Pepi Merisio; **11.8,** © Bill Chaitkin/Architectural Association, London; **11.9,** © Scala/Art Resource, NY; **11.10,** © Scala/Art Resource, NY; **11.11,** © Scala/Art Resource, NY; **11.12,** © Scala/Art Resource, NY; **11.13,** © Scala/Art Resource, NY; **11.14,** © Scala/Art Resource, NY; **11.15,** © Scala/Art Resource, NY; **11.16,** © Corbis/Karen Tweedy-Holmes; **11.17,** © AKG London; **11.18,** © Scala/Art Resource, NY; **11.19,** © Scala/Art Resource, NY; **11.20,** © Scala/Art Resource, NY; **11.21,** Galleria degli Uffizi Florence, Italy/Bridgeman Art Library, London; **11.22,** © Erich Lessing/Art Resource, NY; **11.23,** © The Frick Collection, New York. **Chapter 12 CO-12,** © Artothek; **12.1,** © Erich Lessing/Art Resource, NY; **12.2,** © AKG London; **12.3,** © Hans Hinz/Artothek; **12.4,** © Elke Walford, Hamburg; **12.5,** © Scala/Art Resource, NY; **12.6,** © Artothek; **12.7,** © AKG London; **12.8,** Courtesy of the Vatican Museum. Photo by A. Bracchetti and P. Zigrossi; **12.9,** From *Italian Renaissance Painting* by James Beck © 1981. Reprinted by permission of HarperCollins Publishers, NY; **12.10,** © Scala/Art Resource, NY; **12.11,** Courtesy of the Vatican Museum. Photo by A. Bracchetti and P. Zigrossi; **12.12,** Courtesy of the Vatican Museum. Photo by A. Bracchetti and P. Zigrossi; **12.13,** © Erich Lessing/Art Resource, NY; **12.14,** © Scala/Art Resource, NY; **12.15,** © Scala/Art Resource, NY; **12.16,** © Superstock; **12.17,** Galleria degli Uffizi Florence, Italy/© Bridgeman Art Library, London; **12.18,** © Alinari/Art Resource, NY; **12.19,** Galleria dell'Accademia, Florence/© Bridgeman Art Library, London; **12.20,** © Scala/Art Resource, NY; **12.21,** © SEF/Art Resource, NY; **12.22,** © Stephen Studd/Tony Stone Images; **12.23,** © Alinari/Art Resource, NY; **12.24,** From *Gardner's Art Through the Ages*, 6/e by Horst de la Croix and Richard G. Tansey. © 1975 Harcourt Brace and Company. Reproduced by permission of the publisher. **Chapter 13 CO-13,** © Blauel/Gnamm/Artothek; **13.1,** © Erich Lessing/Art Resource, NY; **13.2,** Conjectural Reconstruction of the Globe Playhouse by C. Walter Hodges. From *Introducing Shakespeare*, by G. B. Harrison, 3/e © G. B. Harrison

Page numbers in italics indicate pronunciation guides; page numbers in boldface indicate illustrations. For readers using the two-volume set of *The Western Humanities*, page numbers 1–344 (Chapters 1–12) refer to material in Volume I: *Beginnings through the Renaissance*, and page numbers 289–615 (Chapters 11–21) refer to material in Volume II: *The Renaissance to the Present*.